Andrew Rudge D-Book
Eleventh Edition

D-Book

*How to answer legal questions, draft legal opinions and pass
Paper D of the European Qualifying Examination*

written and edited by

Andrew Rudge

Eleventh Edition

Carl Heymanns Verlag 2023

Citation: Rudge, D-Book, 11th edition, para 35

Bibliographic information published by the Deutsche Nationalbibliothek
the Deutsche Nationalbibliothek lists this publication in the Deutsche Nationalbibliografie; detailed bibliographic data are available in the internet at http://dnb.d-nb.de

ISBN 978-3-452-30238-0

www.wolterskluwer.de

© 2023 Wolters Kluwer Deutschland GmbH, Wolters-Kluwer-Straße 1, 50354 Hürth, Germany.

Cover: Martina Busch, Grafik-Design, Homburg Kirrberg, Germany

Typesetting: Datagroup-Int SRL, Timisoara, Romania

Printed by Sowa Sp. z o.o., Piaseczno, Poland

Printed on non-acid and aging resistant paper.

In memory of Mark Thomas who is much missed.

Foreword

Since its first edition in 2005, the C-Book from Bill Chandler and Hugo Meinders has figured first and foremost among the books used by candidates to prepare themselves for Paper C of the EQE. There appears to be nothing like it and this is the reason why it continues to be the general reference text used in the CEIPI courses in Strasbourg for this paper. I am very pleased to see now the emergence of a corresponding D-Book that will undoubtedly find its place next to the C-Book on the personal bookshelf of all candidates preparing for the EQE.

It is with great pleasure that I contribute this foreword to the D-Book. I would like to acknowledge the creativity, the energic initiative and the work of the author Andrew Rudge. The result is of a very high level and goes beyond a textbook purely for examination preparation.

I am sure that the use of this new text, combined with attendance at one or more of the specifically designed CEIPI EQE courses and extensive study before the examination can bring only good results! The high quality of the D-Book reflects the high quality of tutoring on the CEIPI preparation courses that makes them among the best and most frequented in Europe.

I would like to express my thanks to the author for his commitment and long-time loyalty to CEIPI.

Strasbourg, September 2013

– Thierry Debled,
Director of the International Section of
CEIPI

Preface

This book has been prepared with the intention of offering advice and support for candidates preparing for the legal papers of the European Qualifying Exam and Pre-examination. It is split into three parts. Part A offers general advice on how the legal papers should be approached and should be used in conjunction with attempts at past papers in order to develop strategy and tactics before sitting the exam itself. It cannot be stressed too much that attempting a number of past papers is an essential preparation for the EQE, not least in order to become confident in the use of time. A certain number of key legal principles are also explained in Part A. However, an understanding of these principles is only a starting point. Candidates must undertake several years of private study in order to develop a broad and deep understanding of all the relevant legal texts before sitting the exams. Attendance at seminars, particularly those organised by CEIPI (Centre d'Études Internationales de la Propriété Intellectuelle) is also recommended. Parts B and C set out the relevant law under the EPC and PCT, respectively, that needs to be assimilated. Subject matter in these sections has been set out in a logical sequence that mirrors the stages of the patent examination and granting process an applicant encounters in real life. With all the relevant legal materials relevant to each topic brought together, and ordered systematically, it should be easier for even newcomers to patent law to locate important legal basis quickly. In Part B, the articles and rules cited are those of EPC2000 unless specified otherwise. In Part C, the articles and rules cited are those of the PCT unless specified otherwise. The chapters in parts B and C have been aligned to the maximum possible extent, allowing the reader to readily compare and contrast the counterpart stages of the EPC and PCT procedures. Every effort has been made to ensure these materials are complete, accurate and up to date as of the date of publication but experience suggests that omissions and errors will inevitably persist. Readers who have suggestions for amendment are warmly invited to e-mail the author (andrew.rudge@hotmail.co.uk).

Walmer, June 2023   *Andrew Rudge*

About the author

Andrew Rudge is British and lives in Kent, UK. He studied Natural Sciences at Cambridge University, UK, before completing a PhD in synthetic Organic Chemistry at the same institution. Having worked for several years as a medicinal chemist in industry, he trained to be a patent attorney, qualifying as a European Patent Attorney and Chartered Patent Attorney (UK) in 2004. Since then he has tutored occasionally on the 2-year basic CEIPI course in London, and yearly on the CEIPI Paper D Seminar and CEIPI Pre-examination seminar in Strasbourg.

Contents

Detailed Contents

Chapter 2: Paper D Part II - Legal Opinion

Chapter 3: Pre-examination - Legal Questions

PART B - THE EPC

Chapter 4: The EPC and EPO

Chapter 5: The Invention

Chapter 6: The Application

Chapter 8: Examination on Filing

Chapter 9: The Search Report and Opinion

Chapter 10: Publication of the Application and Search Report

Chapter 15: Opposition Proceedings

Chapter 21: Amendment and Correction

Chapter 22: Inventorship, Ownership and Suspension of Proceedings

Chapter 25: Miscellaneous Common Provisions

Chapter 26: Information Made Available by the EPO

Chapter 27: Special Agreements under the EPC

Chapter 28: Rules Relating to Fees

PART C - THE PCT

Chapter 29: Institutional Aspects and Definitions

Chapter 30: The Application

Chapter 34: Supplementary International Searches

Chapter 35: Amendment of the Application under Article 19

Chapter 36: Publication of the Application and the Search Report

Chapter 37: Communications to National and Regional offices

Chapter 38: Entry into the National~Regional Phase

Chapter 39: International Preliminary Examination

Abbreviations used

AdminInst	Administrative Instructions under the Patent Co-operation Treaty
AppGuide	The PCT Applicant's Guide
Art.	Article
EPC	Convention on the Grant of European Patents (European Patent Convention) of 05 October 1973 as revised by the Act revising Article 63 EPC of 17 December 1991 and the Act revising the EPC of 29 November 2000 (and its Regulations).
EPC2000	Convention on the Grant of European Patents (European Patent Convention) of 05 October 1973 as revised by the Act revising Article 63 EPC of 17 December 1991 and the Act revising the EPC of 29 November 2000 (and its Regulations).
EPC1973	Convention on the Grant of European Patents (European Patent Convention) of 05 October 1973 as revised by the Act revising Article 63 EPC of 17 December 1991 (and its Regulations).
EQE	European Qualifying Examination
EPO	European Patent Office
Guidelines	Guidelines for Examination in the European Patent Office or, where expressly indicated, Guidelines for Search and Examination at the EPO as PCT Authority (November 2017 versions)
ICEQE	Instructions to candidates concerning the conduct of the European Qualifying Examination
IPREQE	Implementing Provisions to the Regulation on the European Qualifying Examination
NatLaw	National Law relating to the EPC (EPO Brochure)
OJ	Official Journal of the EPO
PC	Paris Convention for the Protection of Industrial Property of 20 March 1883, as revised and amended.
PCT	Patent Cooperation Treaty of 19 June 1970, as amended and modified (and its Regulations).
PLT	Patent Law Treaty (of 01 June 2000)
r	Rule
REQEPR	Regulation on the European Qualifying Examination for professional representatives
PLT	Patent Law Treaty
PonC	Protocol on Centralisation
PonR	Protocol on Recognition
RPBA	Rules of Procedure of the Boards of Appeal
RPEBA	Rules of Procedure of the Enlarged Board of Appeal
RRF	Rules Relating to Fees
SoF	Schedule of Fees
WIPO	Website of the World Intellectual Property Organization

PART A - STRATEGY

Chapter 1: Paper D Part I - Legal Questions

1.1 General comments

In the first part of paper D of the EQE (from 2013 onwards), the candidate must answer 1
a series of short questions relating to aspects of substantive and procedural law under the
EPC and PCT (Part I: Legal Questions; Art. 1(4) REQEPR, r.26(1) IPREQE). These
short questions correspond to the kind of questions posed in the D1 paper of the EQE
up to and including 2012 and the overall length, content and style of the questions have
not changed at all in the new format – the only significant change is that the number of
questions has decreased in order to take into account the reduced time allocated to the
exam as a whole. The number of marks allocated to this part of paper D will vary between
40 % and 60 % of the marks allocated to paper D as a whole (notice from the Examination
Board dated 13 March 2019).

The balance between EPC and PCT questions varies from year to year but generally 2
about two thirds of the marks are allocated to questions relating to the EPC and one third
of the marks are allocated to questions relating to the PCT.

In order to secure full marks in these short questions, the candidate needs to identify 3
the legal provisions that are relevant and apply these provisions to the facts of the question
in order to identify the appropriate consequences and outcomes. Both the citation of the
legal basis and the reasoning relating to its application are necessary in order to secure any
marks: a simple yes/no answer will not generally score any marks on its own.

The extent of the legal knowledge that can be tested in Paper D, and indeed in the EQE 4
as a whole, is set out in the examination syllabus (Art. 13 REQEPR and r.22(1) IPREQE).
A thorough knowledge of the EPC and PCT is required. In terms of the EPC, the candidates must be particularly familiar with Arts. 1 to 25 and 52 to 153 of EPC2000 and the
corresponding Implementing Regulations. A knowledge of those important provisions
of EPC1973 which continue to apply, e.g. Art. 54(4) and r.23a EPC1973, and transitional
rules relating to them is also necessary. Furthermore, where recent changes to the regulations have taken place since the introduction of EPC2000, candidates are also expected to
know the transitional provisions that determine the coming into force of the changes and
the situations under which the previous rule may continue to apply.

Knowledge of the Protocols on Centralisation and Recognition (particularly the latter), 5
the Rules Relating to Fees, important case law, the ancillary regulations (notices from
the EPO and decisions of the President, including arrangements for debiting deposit ac-
counts), the national law book and the Guidelines for Examination is also required. The
relevant Guidelines include both Guidelines for Examination in the EPO and Guidelines
for Search and Examination at the EPO as PCT Authority. The most important case law
is that cited in the Guidelines together with the decisions of the Enlarged Board of Appeal. Students also need to be familiar with the content of the latest edition white Case
Law book (Case Law of the Board of Appeal of the European Patent Office), the annual
updates published in special editions of the Official Journal between new editions and any
case law published in the Official Journal in the year before the exam up until 31 October
(r.2 IPREQE).

In terms of the PCT, candidates must be particularly familiar with Arts. 1 to 49 and the 6
corresponding implementing regulations. Knowledge of the main provisions of the Paris
Convention (Articles 1 to 5*quater* and 11), which is directly applied under the PCT, is also
required. The syllabus further extends to a knowledge of the most significant provisions
of Japanese and US patent law.

The legal texts to be used in the exam are those that are in force on 31 October of the 7
year prior to the exam (r.2 and 22(1) IPREQE). Any changes, e.g. amendments to the
EPC regulations, coming into force between that date and the date of the exam are to be
ignored. It is a basic but important point that candidates should use these up-to-date texts
in preparation for the exam and in the exam itself! Sadly, the reports of the Examination
Committee suggest that this is not always the case.

8 Although this is an open-book exam (Point I.4, ICEQE, Decision of the Examination Board dated 24.10.2011), time is short and the opportunity to search for answers is severely limited. To ensure success, the candidate must be thoroughly familiar with the materials described above and know instantly where to locate the relevant information.

9 Apart from the guides to the EPC and PCT included in this publication (see below) and the sources they reference (EPC, PCT, Guidelines for Examination in the European Patent Office, ancillary regulations, case law), all of which you should be familiar with and have with you, several other reference works are useful in the exam. These include the PCT Applicant's Guide and a list of countries that are members of the EPC, PCT, Paris Convention and WTO (available from the WIPO website). In particular, an up to date copy of the PCT Applicant's Guide is virtually essential if you are to be able to answer fully many of the questions set on the PCT. It is also useful to have a pre-marked EPO calendar showing closed days for the year of the exam and the previous year and a copy of the EPO publication relating to aspects of national law.

1.2 How to tackle the questions

1.2.1 Time management – understanding the question

10 Paper D in the eEQE format is six hours long. The legal questions are split into two independent parts with three questions in each part. A well-planned and disciplined approach to time-management is absolutely essential for success. The planning must involve the allocation of an amount of time to be spent on each question that is commensurate with the number of marks available, allowing some time at the end, if possible, for checking. Discipline must be shown in adhering to this schedule properly so that a disproportionate amount of time is not spent answering questions for which only a few marks are available. It is important that the whole paper is answered.

11 The number of marks allocated to each short question is clearly marked on the examination paper so it is possible to calculate how many minutes are available for each question. If some time is to be reserved for a final check of the written answer, as is highly advisable, then about 3 minutes per mark should be allocated. So, for example, a typical question for which 6 marks have been allocated should be answered in a maximum of 18 minutes. Candidates should make a note of the time available for each question and not exceed it. It is better to leave a question half-answered and move on to the next question rather than risk running out of time at the end and not answering part of the paper. This is because it is easier to accumulate the first 50 % of the marks for any given question than the second 50 % and hence better to have partially answered all of the questions rather than fully answered half of the questions.

12 The other important aspect of time management is the allocation of the time available to a particular question between analysis and writing. There is a temptation to start writing the answer as soon as possible in order to make good progress and be able to complete the paper on time. However, the truth is that once the question has been properly analysed and the answer deduced, it does not take much time to draft a clear and concise answer. If, on the other hand, an attempt is made to start writing the answer during the analysis phase it is likely that much crossing-out and rewriting will be necessary, which will waste precious moments and lead to a poorly laid-out and sometimes illegible script. It is therefore important not to panic and to resist the temptation to start writing immediately when some aspect of the question has been appreciated. Take a few minutes to properly understand the question from beginning to end and what is being asked, identify the relevant legal provisions and analyse their effects on the facts of the question and identify the consequences. Then write the answer.

13 Many marks are lost in the legal paper by candidates answering a different question from that which is being asked or simply writing everything they know, in a general sense, about the legal provisions relevant to the question. This point is made again and again in the reports published by the Examination Committee. See, for instance, the 2010 report: "As always, reading the questions carefully is crucial for formulating a correct and complete response". Taking the time to understand the question as a preliminary step is therefore essential for success. It is very important to clearly establish the limits of the question: it is obviously important not to underestimate the scope of the question and overlook issues that need to be addressed but it is equally important, in view of time pressure, not

to overestimate the scope of the question and address issues for which no marks are available. One aspect of importance here is accepting the facts of the question as given (r.20(3) IPREQE) – do not waste time by speculating what different consequences could have arisen if the facts of the question had been slightly different, even if it is tempting to do so because it leads to an interesting scenario about which you are well informed. Stick to the question the Examiners have asked and do not consider alternatives. The Examination Committee have commented as follows: "We do not give any marks at all for an essay, however, brilliant, on an unasked topic" (Examiners' report, 1997). If you really don't know the answer to the question that has been posed it is actually better to write nothing and reserve extra time for answering the other questions than to write something irrelevant about a related topic. One aspect of sticking to the facts of the question is ignoring any special knowledge you may have relating to the technology with which the question is concerned – don't try and be too clever! It is important to give the examiners the answer they are expecting and not to waste time demonstrating the depth of your knowledge in a way which is irrelevant to that answer.

1.2.2 Finding the answer

Although the EQE is an open-book exam (Point I.4 ICEQE, Decision of the Examination Board dated 24.10.2011), a candidate's ability to use the wealth of literature that may be assembled is seriously compromised by the lack of available time. If a candidate knows what legal provision is pertinent to a question and has a good idea of where to find it within a set of well indexed materials then he or she will certainly have enough time to consult it and confirm its exact wording. There is not enough time, however, for extensive legal research. It is therefore imperative that candidates are not only very familiar with the law itself but also have materials that allow rapid identification of the combination of article, rule, Board of Appeal decision, decision of the President, section of the Guidelines and/or provision of national law that contributes to its full elucidation. **14**

Each candidate has his or her own favourite way of accumulating such materials. Many make their own cross-referenced, annotated and supplemented versions of the EPC, others rely on printed publications such as this one. Either approach is fine but the key to success in either case is to choose such materials early on and work with them consistently over a period of time during periods of private study, revision courses and attempts at past papers so that on the day of the exam itself they are very familiar and easy to use. Remember that only printed materials are allowed – no electronic devices may be brought into the examination (Point I.9(a) ICEQE). **15**

The guides to the EPC and PCT included in this publication have been arranged in a logical order to try and facilitate rapid access to specific information, even for a relative newcomer to European and PCT law. The order follows the sequence in which an applicant for a patent will encounter the stages of the European and PCT procedure. Thus, common sections relate to where to file an application, what to file, formalities examination, search, publication, national phase consequences and common provisions. Both guides also have unique sections: for instance, the EPC guide has sections relating to patentability, grant/refusal, opposition and appeal while the PCT guide has sections relating to Art. 19 amendment, supplementary international search, international preliminary examination and national/regional phase entry. These guides do not pretend to be completely comprehensive or completely accurate but they do bring together in a systematic and comprehensible fashion most of the relevant legal provisions relating to particular events in the procedures relevant to European and Euro-PCT applications and it is hoped they will be of use in preparing for and taking the legal papers of the EQE. **16**

The guide to the EPC is to be used in conjunction with the Guidelines for Examination in the European Patent Office, referenced in the text as 'Guidelines', the national law book, referenced in the text as 'NatLaw' and the latest anthology of ancillary regulations (decisions and notices published in the OJEPO) that are designated with the code 'OJ' in the text. Students should also use the white case law book in order to obtain greater knowledge of the case law – the guides only cite the most important cases directly. The guide to the PCT should be used in conjunction with the Paris Convention, referenced in the text as 'PC' and the Applicant's Guide which is designated as 'AppGuide' in the text. All articles and rules in the EPC relating to aspects of PCT procedure (e.g. regional phase **17** entry) have been consolidated in the PCT section. Particular attention should be paid to the Guidelines and Applicant's Guide since in recent years there has been a greater tendency for the legal paper to contain questions whose full answer can only be appreciated with reference to these texts – they are essential documents to have available in the exam itself.

18   Whatever materials are selected for the exam, it is of obvious importance that they are properly updated up until 31 October of the preceding year (IPREQE r.2). It seems from the comments published by the Examining Committee yearly that this basic point is ignored in a surprisingly large number of cases: some candidates are applying old, superseded versions of regulations, President's decisions or case law and losing marks unnecessarily.

1.2.3   Writing the answer

19   The answer should be short, focussed and legible (r.26(2) IPREQE). It should include a brief summary of what the relevant law says, an explanation of how this law applies to the facts of the question and an explanation of the consequences. If a specific question is posed, e.g. requiring a yes/no answer, then it is obviously important to make sure this question is addressed at some point. Considerable stress has already been placed on the importance of understanding exactly what the question is asking: it is therefore sensible to re-read the question once more before answering it to make sure that the answer is as focussed as possible.

20   If your answer is well structured and easily legible then it will be much easier to award marks. This is succinctly expressed in the Examiner's Report for the 1993 paper: "Scripts that cannot be read cannot be marked" (see also Point III.22(a) ICEQE). Be sure to use simple, grammatically correct language and not to use any abbreviations whose meaning may be obscure to others. Whilst errors of grammar or style should not be penalised when marking (r.3 IPREQE), examiners must obviously be able to understand the answer to award marks. Producing a legible and comprehensible examination script is obviously even more important if it needs to be translated prior to marking (r.5 IPREQE).

21   The summary of the law must cite all relevant legal basis. This is very important since an answer that does not cite adequate legal basis will receive very few marks or no marks at all, even if the answer is otherwise correct. This is particularly the case when the answer to the question is essentially a simple "Yes" or "No". This principle was expressed by the Examining Committee in 2008 in the following words: "As usual, it is essential that candidates give a complete and detailed legal basis including the appropriate article and rules". However, the converse is also true: an answer which cites the correct legal basis but does not explain the effect of these provisions on the facts of the question or come to a conclusion regarding the consequences will also score few marks if any. Legal basis supports the answer but does not replace it. As the Examining Committee said in 2010: "The mere citation of a legal basis cannot constitute an answer to a question and will not earn enough marks to pass the paper". It is imperative to give the appropriate answer **and** explain why it is the correct answer **and** justify that reasoning by referring to the relevant legal basis in order to pass.

22   Different kinds of legal basis can be categorised in a hierarchy with articles at the top and internal administrative instructions at the bottom and the answer should cite basis starting from the top of the hierarchy and extending down as far as necessary in order to fully support the law being summarised. If the relevant law is all set out in an article, therefore, the citation of this article is sufficient. This is, however, very rare since important aspects of the law will usually be set out in a rule or an aspect of national law which implements the article or in a rule of procedure of the Boards of Appeal. This is the next tier of the hierarchy. Under EPC2000 it is very often the case that a relevant article says very little of interest and one of its implementing regulations fills in the important details. The article should nevertheless be cited. For instance, the answer to a question which asks whether a set of documents sent to the EPO can be awarded a filing date should cite Art. 80 EPC even though the relevant criteria are actually laid out in r.40 EPC. Similarly, a discussion of the r.53 requirements for filing priority documents should cite Art. 88(1) EPC and any discussion of the opportunities to amend an application under r.137 should

also cite Art. 123(1) EPC. In brief: the mention of an implementing regulation should always be accompanied by a citation of the article it implements.

The articles and rules of the EPC are subject to amendment, the former primarily by a revision conference and the latter by the Administrative Council. It may therefore be necessary in some cases to make it clear which version of the article or rule is being applied (e.g. EPC2000 or EPC1973). Furthermore, such changes are often accompanied by transitional provisions and a relevant decision of the Administrative Council that explains which version of the law applies to a particular patent application may need to be cited.

Where a rule forms part of the relevant law, it may not itself tell the complete story. Many rules allow the President of the EPO to decide the details of how they are to be applied in practice. This is the case, for instance, with r.53, mentioned above, which indicates that a certified copy of a priority document does not have to be filed if it is already available to the EPO but leaves the President to decide the conditions under which it is deemed to be so available. Such decisions of the President of the EPO form the third tier of the hierarchy.

An article and/or rule may be also be incomplete basis since either may have been interpreted by a decision of a Board of Appeal or a decision or opinion of the Enlarged Board of Appeal. Case law represents the fourth tier of the hierarchy. Decisions of the Enlarged Board of Appeal, in particular, can often establish an interpretation of an article or rule which is not at all apparent from the wording of that provision itself. For instance, G1/86 establishes that an opponent may sometimes be entitled to a re-establishment of rights even though Art. 122(1) only refers to an applicant or a proprietor.

Occasionally, how the law is to be applied may still remain obscure even when all these sources have been considered. For instance, Art. 54(3) and Art. 89 EPC together provide that on publication a European patent application becomes prior art, for novelty purposes, as of its priority date. What happens if the priority claim is lost or withdrawn after publication? Does the prior art effect under Art. 54(3) revert to the filing date or remain effective as of the priority date? There is no implementing regulation or case law that gives us an answer to this question. In such cases we must consider any administrative instructions that the President of the EPO has promulgated according to Art. 10(2)(a) EPC that indicate how the EPO will actually proceed in these circumstances, most notably the Guidelines for Examination in the EPO. In this particular case, Guidelines G-IV, 5.1.1 tells us that the EPO will consider that the prior art remains effective as of the priority date. Such administrative instructions are the lowest tier in the hierarchy and the Guidelines only need to be cited if the relevant law cannot be fully established from sources in a higher tier.

For international applications in the international phase the articles of the PCT form the top tier of the legal hierarchy (supplemented by the Paris Convention in respect of priority), the implementing regulations the second tier and the general part of the Applicants Guide relating to general procedural questions the third tier. These sources may need to be supplemented with national law such as the reservations made by countries when the implementing regulations have been amended and the aspects of procedure relating to the interface of the PCT with national law on national/regional phase entry (which can be found in the specific sections of the Applicants Guide). Decisions of the Administrative Council establish the rights and responsibilities of the EPO as an international authority and may also need to be cited. In some cases, e.g. aspects of regional phase entry before the EPO, it may be necessary to cite both PCT and EPC provisions in order to provide comprehensive legal basis for the answer. In these cases, particularly, it is necessary to specify whether the article or rule being cited belongs to the EPC or PCT. In the case of a Euro-PCT application, remember to apply the PCT in the international phase and not the EPC! It seems from the Examiners' comments that this is a relatively common mistake.

In all cases it is necessary to cite the most relevant legal basis, starting at the top of the hierarchy and working down as far as necessary for the law to be completely clarified. It is not sufficient, for example, to just cite the Guidelines where an article and rule are relevant, even if these provisions are themselves cited in the relevant section of the Guidelines. Nor is it sufficient to quote case law where an article and rule are relevant. Sometimes, case law actually becomes incorporated into the regulations themselves and no longer needs to be cited at all. For instance, the question of whether new grounds can be introduced into opposition proceedings by the opposition division was answered under EPC1973 by decision G10/91 but under EPC2000 the principle established by this decision has been introduced into the Implementing Regulations as r.81(1) EPC.

29   In order to obtain all the available marks, it is also necessary that the legal basis is cited as specifically as it can be. For instance, if only one subsection of an article or rule is actually relevant to an answer then this subsection alone should be cited. In explaining why an amendment submitted before completion of the search report will not be taken into account, for example, more marks will be obtained by citing Art. 123(1) and r.137(1) EPC that by citing Art. 123 and r.137. This is particularly the case with the PCT regulations which are subdivided in a labyrinthine manner.

30   Having noted what the relevant law says and cited basis for it, it is necessary to apply that law to the factual situation presented by the question and come to the necessary conclusions that the question demands as an answer. There are no marks for just repeating the facts of the question. Rather, you must show how the facts and the law come together to lead to certain consequences, for instance how the requirement for 'all due care' under Art. 122 EPC combined with the fact that the applicant has deliberately decided not to respond to a communication pursuant to Art. 90(4) and r.55 EPC (invitation to correct when filing date cannot be awarded) means that re-establishment cannot be applied and the application will not be dealt with as a European patent application. The applicant must be advised to re-file the application.

31   Candidates are expected to come to a conclusion in answering a question and not present a series of possible conclusions or outcomes. If there is a genuine ambiguity in the question then it may be necessary to explain what the two different interpretations are and provide answers for each of them. In all other cases, a definitive conclusion needs to be reached. For example, if the client has missed a deadline and lost rights as a consequence it will be necessary to specify whether further processing or re-establishment is an appropriate remedy. To suggest pursuing both remedies or to cite them as alternatives will not lead to the award of any marks. As the Examination Committee said in 2007: "Candidates are expected to give a consistent answer to a question. When contradictory alternatives are given, no marks are awarded."

32   When the question requires that a client be advised in some way it is often difficult to know how comprehensive to make that advice, which different theoretical scenarios should be covered and how far into the future the advice should extend. There is no hard and fast rule here – unfortunately only the Examination Committee know the content of the marking schedule. The length of the answer and the number of points to be made should in some way correlate with the number of marks that are indicated to be available for the question and only experience in tackling past papers can help candidates develop a sense of good judgement that will correctly guide them in answering the question appropriately. Certainly, for example, if the conclusion reached is that an application is deemed withdrawn or refused, it would be sensible to indicate any ways in which legal rights can be saved.

1.3 Calculating time limits

33   In the legal paper it is a matter of fundamental importance to be able to calculate time limits properly. The answer to many questions depends on the accurate determination of the point at which rights have been lost and the periods during which various remedies are available.

1.3.1 Calculating time limits under the EPC

34   A time limit has three important components: (1) a starting point; (2) a duration; and (3) an end. It is therefore necessary first to identify the starting point (which might be the notification of a communication or decision from the EPO, the filing/priority date of an application, the mention of the publication of a document or the expiry of another time limit) and then to add the duration in weeks, months or years (almost always months) in order to identify the end point. In some cases this end point is then adjusted to take into account delays in the delivery of a document. Finally, if the end of the period falls on a day on which the EPO is shut for business then the end point needs to be adjusted accordingly.

For many time limits under the EPC the starting point is the notification of a communication or decision, by postal services (r.126) or electronically (r.127). Examples include the two month time limit for correcting a formal deficiency in an application according to Art. 90(4) and r.58 EPC, the 2–6 month time limit for correcting a substantive deficiency in an application according to Art. 94(3) and r.71(1) EPC, the two month time limit for requesting further processing according to Art. 121(1) and r.135(1) EPC and the two month time limit for filing an appeal according to Art. 108 EPC. In all these cases, from 01 November 2023 onwards, notification is deemed to occur on the date that the relevant document bears. Before 01 November 2023, notification was deemed to occur on the 10th day following the date of the relevant document, unless it actually reached the addressee at a later date, in which case that later date was the date of notification (Art. 120(b) and r.126(2) or r.127(2) EPC). In contrast to the corresponding regulation under the PCT, r.126(2) and r.127(2) EPC specify that the EPO bears the burden of proof in establishing the date of notification. Having established the date of notification, the duration of the time limit can be added in order to calculate the end point. This is usually a number of months that is added in accordance with Art. 120(b) and r.131(4) EPC. If notification is on 07 June, therefore, a two month time limit will expire on 07 August and if notification is on 31 May, a four month time limit will expire on 30 September. From 01 November 2023 onwards, the period must be extended, in certain cases, to compensate for delays in the delivery of the document. If the document is delivered more than seven days from the date it bears, the period is extended by the number of days by which that seven day period was exceeded. So, for example, if the document is delivered 11 days after the date it bears, the period is extended by 4 days in compensation. If the date of expiry of the period falls on a day on which one of the filing offices of the EPO is shut then the period is extended until the first day on which all the EPO filing offices are open, regardless of whether the filing office actually used was open on the last day of the period or not (Art. 120(b) and r.134(1) EPC). The EPO filing offices are Munich, the Hague and Berlin (r.35(1) EPC). Closed days include weekends and public holidays and the EPO publishes a list of such days annually. A period expiring on Good Friday, for example, will automatically be extended under r.134(1) EPC until the following Tuesday. 35

Time limits determined by the EPO (as opposed to time limits specified in the articles and rules of the EPC) can be extended on request under Art. 120(b) and r.132 EPC if the request is presented before expiry of the time limit. If such an extension is obtained, the time limit needs to be recalculated. It is important to understand that the extension is not a new period to be added to the end of the time limit as previously calculated but an extension of the original period. The whole time limit therefore requires recalculation by adding the new number of months (e.g. six instead of four) to the previously calculated notification date and then correcting for closed days under r.134(1) EPC at the end. Note that the extension of a time limit set by a Board of Appeal is assessed according to Art. 120(b) and Art. 12(7) RPBA and will only be granted if good reasons are presented. The extension of time limits before first instance departments is governed by the principles set out in Guidelines E-VIII, 1.6 and these vary as between the Examining Division and the Opposition Division. Before the Examining Division, a first extension will usually be granted automatically if the period set does not exceed six months as a result and no reasons need to be provided. Requests for extension of time limits in Opposition Proceedings, on the other hand, must also always be reasoned and will only be granted in exceptional cases. 36

A request for re-establishment of rights must be filed, at the latest, within two months of removal of the cause of non-compliance with the period that has not been observed vis-à-vis the EPO. Frequently, the cause of non-compliance is removed by receipt of a communication from the EPO pursuant to r.112(1) EPC noting a loss of rights. It is important to remember in these circumstances that the two month time limit runs from the actual date of removal of the cause of non-compliance, i.e. the date of receipt of the communication and not from the deemed notification of the communication. Thus, if a communication pursuant to r.112(1) EPC is received following the non-observance of a time limit and the time limit is subject to further processing, the two month period of r.135(1) is calculated from notification of the communication, whereas if the time limit is subject to re-establishment, then the two month period of r.136(1) EPC is calculated from the date of receipt of the communication. 37

38   According to the procedure before the EPO, one important document, the application itself, may be filed with the patent office of a Contracting State rather than with the EPO directly (Art. 75(1)(b) EPC). All national offices other than the Dutch office and the Belgian Office allow this (see NatLaw, Table II). If the application claims the priority of an earlier application then the 12 month time limit of Art. 87 EPC must be complied with. The starting point of this time limit is the filing date accorded to the earlier application and the 12 months is added according to Art. 120(b) and r.131(4) EPC – for example, for a first filing on 29 February in a leap year the priority "year" will expire on 28 February the year after! If the last day of the 12 month period is a day on which one of the filing offices of the EPO is not open for business then the priority period is extended until the first day on which they are all open under r.134(1) EPC, regardless of which EPO filing office is actually used. Equally, according to r.134(3) EPC, if the last day of the 12 month period is a day on which one of the national offices is not open for business, then the priority period is extended until the first day on which that office is open for business if the application is actually filed at that national office

39   The priority period is subject to re-establishment under Art. 122 EPC and the time limit for filing such a request for re-establishment is limited to two months from expiry of the priority period (r.136(1) EPC). This is an example of a time limit whose starting point is the expiry of a second time limit, a so-called aggregate time limit. When calculating an aggregate time limit, the second, earlier time limit is first extended under r.134(1) EPC in order to take into account days on which one of the filing offices of the EPO is shut for business and, where appropriate, this extended expiry date becomes the starting point for the second period which, if it itself expires on a day on which one of the filing offices of the EPO is shut for business, is also extended under r.134(1) EPC. Other examples of aggregate time limits include the two month grace period for paying extension fees late with a surcharge as laid down in the extension agreements (which runs from the expiry of the normal period for paying extension/designation fees according to r.39(1) EPC) and the six month grace period for paying a renewal fee late with a surcharge for a Euro-PCT application when the first renewal fee has fallen due during the international phase (which runs from the expiry of the 31 month period of r.159(1) EPC). Very occasionally, a doubly aggregate time limit may arise, for example if the one year time limit of r.136 (re-establishment) is to be calculated from the end of the six month period of r.51(2) (late payment of renewal fee) which is itself to be calculated from the end of the 31 month time of r.159(1) (regional phase entry) in the case of a first renewal fee falling due in the international phase.

40   On the subject of renewal fees, it is important to understand that some time limits are calculated according to special rules laid down in the case law. For a direct European filing, the first renewal fee falls due at the end of the month containing the second anniversary of the filing date according to Art. 86(1) and r.51(1) EPC. Even though this is a due date rather than a time limit, the case law has provided that if the due date falls on a day on which one of the filing offices of the EPO is shut, it may validly be paid on the next day on which all of the filing offices are open, by analogy to r.134(1) EPC (J4/91). The same case law has also provided that the six-month period for late payment with surcharge laid down in r.51(2) EPC (within six months of the due date) is to be considered to end on the last day of the sixth month following the month in which the anniversary falls due. If this last day of the sixth month is a day on which one of the filing offices of the EPO is closed for business then r.134(1) applies directly in this case to extend the deadline until the first day of the subsequent month when all the filing offices are open.

41   Referring back to the first paragraph of this section, it is important to understand what constitutes a time limit and what doesn't. Chapter V of the implementing regulations to the EPC (r.131–r.136) only applies to time limits and hence whether further processing or re-establishment applies, whether the late filing of a document can be excused under r.133 and whether days on which the EPO is closed are taken into account crucially depends on whether a time limit is concerned or not. One example is the due date for paying a renewal fee as mentioned above. According to r.51(1), a renewal fee "shall be due" on a certain day. This is not a time limit since there is no defined starting point and term from which an ending can be calculated, there is just a condition that must be met (fee must be paid by a certain date). Although, if the EPO is shut on the due date, the renewal fee can be paid on the next day the EPO is open, this is not an extension under r.134(1) but a period of

grace defined by the case law (J4/91) by analogy with r.134(1). Since there is no time limit, r.134(1) does not apply.

Another example of a condition to be met that does not concern a time limit is the requirement under Art. 54(1) EPC that to be new an invention must not form part of the state of the art. If, therefore, an invention is disclosed in some manner on a day on which the EPO is closed for business (e.g. a Sunday), it is not possible to file a European patent application (without priority claim) on the next day on which the EPO is open for business and obtain a patent. The state of the art determination is not extended under r.134(1) until the next day on which the EPO is open since no time limit is defined, just a condition. If an invention is disclosed on a Sunday then a European patent application for that invention must be filed on that Sunday or earlier in order for the claimed subject matter to be novel. This situation is to be contrasted with situation discussed above where the invention has already been the subject of an earlier filing and the priority period needs to be met. The priority period is indeed a time limit having a starting point (filing date of earlier application), a term (12 months) and an ending which can be calculated (and extended under r.134(1) EPC). Also on the subject of novelty, the fact that a disclosure does not form part of the state of the art, in certain circumstances, if it occurred no earlier than six months preceding the filing date of a European patent application is also a condition to be met – the six months in this case is not a time limit. This is apparent from the wording of the provision. Therefore, if a disclosure in breach of confidence is made on Monday 7th January 2013, a European patent application must be filed at the latest on Sunday 7th July 2013 in order to benefit from Art. 55(1)(a) EPC. European patent applications can be filed by hand, by fax or electronically on days on which the EPO is shut. Further situations that concern a condition to be met rather than a time limit are the requirement for a document received late under r.133(1) EPC to be received no later than three months after expiry of the relevant period and the requirement under r.36(1) EPC for a parent application to be pending when a divisional is filed. 42

1.3.2 Calculating time limits under the PCT

Time limits under the PCT are calculated in a similar manner to time limits under the EPC. The relevant provisions are Art. 47(1) and r.80 PCT. For all time limits which run from the date of notification of a communication, the starting point of the time limit is the date stamped on the relevant communication itself. The only exception to this principle is where the applicant can prove that the communication was actually mailed later than the date which it bears, in which case the starting point for the time limit is the actual date of mailing (r.80.6 PCT). The duration of the time limit, in years, months or days, is then added according to r.80.1–80.3 PCT in the same way as under the EPC. The end of the time limit may then be adjusted in order to take into account postal delays under r.80.6 PCT. If the notification was received more than seven days following the date it bears then the end of the time limit is extended by a number of days equal to x-7, where x is the number of days between the date of the notification and the date of receipt. For instance, if a notification bears the date of 04 June and is received by the applicant on 15 June an extra 4 days are added to the end of the time limit – but only if the applicant can provide satisfactory evidence that the notification was actually received on 15 June. Unlike the corresponding law under r.126(2) and r.127(2) EPC, it is the applicant that bears the burden of proof in establishing a date of receipt under r.80.6 PCT. If the time limit so calculated (as extended under r.80.6 or not) falls on a day on which the PCT authority with which a reply must be filed is closed for business then the time limit is further extended to the next day on which that PCT authority is open (r.80.5 PCT) in the same way as an EPC time limit is extended under r.134(1) EPC. 43

Many time limits under the PCT do not have the date of a notification as their starting point but run instead from the "priority date" of the application (e.g. the time limit for requesting a supplementary international search (r.45*bis*.1(a) PCT), the time limit for requesting Art. 19 amendments (r.46.1 PCT), time limit for national and regional phase entry (Art. 22(1) PCT), the time limit for requesting international preliminary examination (r.54*bis*.1(a) PCT), the time limit for requesting rectification of a mistake (r.91.2 PCT), the time limit for withdrawing the application (r.90*bis*.1(a) PCT) and the time limit for recording a change of applicant (r.92*bis*.1(b) PCT)). The term "priority date" has a special 44 meaning under the PCT (Art. 2(xi)) and refers to the filing date of the application where no priority is claimed or, if one or more priority dates is/are claimed, the earliest priority date. If a priority claim is withdrawn under r.90*bis*.3 PCT then the "priority date" is re-calculated for any time limit which has not yet expired (r.90*bis*.3(d) PCT).

1.4 Preserving the rights of an applicant, proprietor or opponent that have apparently been lost under the EPC

45   In Paper D of the EQE, things are always going wrong, sometimes in dramatic circumstances. In the 2008 D2 paper, for example, a patent department file room was gutted by fire during a candle-lit party and back-up files were compromised by water damage. It will be no surprise to learn that several due dates were missed as a consequence! Thus, in both the short and long questions, the candidate is often given the task of recommending appropriate remedial action to claw back rights that the client has apparently lost. In such a situation, the following remedies should be considered.

1.4.1 Was notification sent to the correct address?

46   Where a representative has been appointed, notification must be sent to the representative and not the applicant (r.130(1) EPC). Where the EPO has notified the wrong person then notification only takes effect when the correct person has been notified (T703/92). If the EPO has properly been informed of a change of representative, subsequent communications are not notified until they are delivered to the newly appointed representative. Since many time limits start from some kind of notification, it may be that the time limit has not actually even started yet.

1.4.2 Can the time limit be extended?

47   Time limits determined by the EPO (as opposed to time limits specified in the articles and rules of the EPC) can be extended on request under Art. 120(b) and r.132 EPC if the request is presented before expiry of the time limit. Such extension is usually granted automatically by an Examining Division provided that the period does not thereby exceed six months and no reasons are necessary. If the total period as extended would exceed six months, an extension will generally only be given if convincing reasons are provided to show that a reply in the period previously laid down will not be possible (Guidelines E-VIII, 1.6). An Opposition Division will only grant an extension in exceptional and duly substantiated cases, regardless of the length of the time limit. Any request for the extension of a time limit set by a Board of Appeal must also be reasoned, regardless of the length of the time limit (Art. 120(b) and RPBA Art. 12(7)).

48   Time limits specified in the Articles and Rules of the EPC are also extended where there is a general dislocation in the delivery or transmission of mail in a Contracting State (r.134(2) EPC).

1.4.3 Is a grace period available?

49   Specific grace periods exist under EPC2000 if the normal period for paying claims fees has been missed (r. 45(2) EPC) or the due date for paying a renewal fee has been missed (r.51(2) EPC). A grace period also applies under the Extension Agreements when an extension fee is not paid in due time.

1.4.4 Can further processing be applied?

50   Under EPC2000, further processing is the standard remedy when a loss of rights has occurred through failure to meet a time limit vis-à-vis the EPO in pre-grant proceedings. Whether the time limit is set by the EPO or in the EPC and its Regulations is not relevant. Nor is further processing restricted to any particular kind of loss of rights. It is, however, unavailable in post-grant proceedings and it is ruled out in the case of a large number of specific time limits listed in Art. 121 and r.135 EPC, generally those where another remedy is possible, those where greater legal certainty for third parties is important and those where the EPO needs to prepare for publication of the application. Further processing is

available within two months of notification of a loss of rights and within this period a fee must be paid and the omitted act performed. A request for further processing is deemed to have been made when the appropriate fee is paid. Where automatic direct debiting is being used, and the fee will be taken automatically by the EPO, further processing is requested by simply performing the omitted act.

1.4.5 Can re-establishment be applied?

Re-establishment (which was known as restitutio in integrum under EPC1973) is availa-   51
ble to the applicant pre-grant and the proprietor during post-grant proceedings (Art. 122). It is also available to an opponent who has validly filed a notice of appeal but missed the time limit for filing the grounds of appeal (G1/86). Under EPC2000, it is potentially available when any time limit vis-à-vis the EPO has been missed, resulting in a loss of rights, with two important exceptions. Firstly, it is not available in respect of the time limit for requesting re-establishment (Art. 122(4) EPC). Secondly, it is not available for any time limit to which further processing applies under Art. 121 since further processing is now the remedy of choice (r.136(3)). However, it is available in the case of those time limits for which further processing is ruled out according to Art. 121 and r.135 EPC and it is also available in respect of the time limit for requesting further processing itself. For example, it is possible to request re-establishment in respect of the priority period (though only in the two months following the expiry of that period). With re-establishment, there is a necessity to show that the relevant loss of rights occurred despite all due care having been taken, the application for re-establishment must be filed within two months of the removal of the cause of non-compliance and within 12 months of the expiry of the missed time limit (two months where the priority period or the period for filing a petition for review is concerned), and a fee must be paid.

1.4.6 Can proceedings be interrupted?

Proceedings can be interrupted in the event of the death or legal incapacity or bankruptcy   52
of the applicant or proprietor or his representative (r.142(1) EPC). Proceedings are automatically interrupted by such an event and the EPO is obliged to recognise this when informed. Periods which are running at the date of interruption are suspended at that point and run again, in full or in part (depending on the period in question) from the date of resumption set by the EPO.

1.4.7 Can the good faith principle be invoked?

Under certain circumstances (see G2/97) the EPO is under an obligation to warn the   53
applicant, proprietor or opponent of any loss of rights if such a warning can be expected in all good faith. Equally, the applicant, proprietor or opponent must not suffer a disadvantage as a result of having relied on erroneous information received from the EPO (e.g. J2/87) or on a misleading communication (e.g. J3/87).

1.4.8 Can an appeal be filed?

Any party adversely affected by a decision of the Receiving Section, an Examining Divi-   54
sion, an Opposition Division or the Legal Division (but not a Search Division) may file an appeal (Art. 106, 107 EPC).

   In the appeal proceedings, the decision can be challenged and, if convincing arguments   55
are brought forward, the original decision will be set aside. Furthermore, if the decision was to refuse a European patent application then a divisional application may still be filed until the expiry of the appeal period (G1/09) and, if an appeal is actually filed, the suspensive effect of the appeal means that the filing of a divisional application is possible for as long as the appeal is pending (J23/13). Note that filing an appeal against a decision to grant a patent, on the other hand, does not give the proprietor the chance to file a divisional application unless the appeal is actually allowed (J28/03).

   When an application is deemed withdrawn, the loss of rights notified according to   56
r.112(1) EPC cannot be directly challenged by the filing of an appeal since the noting of a loss of rights is not the same as the taking of a decision. A decision on the matter can be

requested under r.112(2) and, if the EPO is of the opinion that the application did indeed become deemed withdrawn, it will take a decision confirming the original finding. This decision can be appealed and its effect is suspended by the appeal in the usual way. However, as with a decision to grant, no divisional application is possible unless the appeal is allowed since, in this case, the application remains deemed withdrawn by virtue of the original finding (J18/08).

57   An appeal is possible not just following a refusal relating to a substantive matter in grant proceedings but also in response to a refusal under Art. 90(5) EPC when a formal matter is not corrected (e.g. no designation of the inventor is provided or a representative is not appointed). In this case the grounds for appeal are satisfied by the completion of the omitted act (J18/08).

1.4.9   Is conversion of a European patent application possible?

58   If a European patent is no longer obtainable (e.g. following a decision of a Board of Appeal confirming the refusal of an application by the Examining Division where no grounds for filing a petition for review exist or following deemed withdrawal of a patent application where no other remedy any longer exists) consider whether any national rights could be salvaged through conversion (Art. 135 EPC). The possibilities available vary from country to country – for details see Table VII in the EPO publication National Law relating to the EPC. For instance, Portugal allows conversion where a European patent application is deemed withdrawn because no translation pursuant to Art. 14(2) EPC was provided and Poland allows conversion where a European patent application is withdrawn or refused.

1.4.10   Can the failure to pay a fee on time be excused?

59   Under certain circumstances, where an effort to pay a necessary fee was made before the expiry of the relevant deadline but the money was not received by the EPO until after the deadline, the late payment can be excused (RRFArt. 7(3)–(4)).

1.4.11   Can the late arrival of a document sent by postal services in good time be excused?

60   If a document which arrives late at the EPO was delivered to a recognised postal service provider, five days or more before expiry of the relevant time limit, it may, in certain circumstances, be deemed to have been received in due time provided that it arrives within three months of the expiry of the time limit (r.133 EPC). To qualify, registered mail or equivalent must be used and any posting from outside Europe must be by airmail. Accepted postal service providers are designated operators within the meaning of Art. 1 of the Universal Postal Convention and Chronopost, DHL, Federal Express, flexpress, TNT, Skynet, UPS and Transworld.

61   This rule even applies to the filing of a priority-claiming European patent application if the application is accorded a filing date after the expiry of the priority period. If the relevant conditions are met, the priority period will be deemed to have been met (note that the actual filing date is unaffected). For a non priority-claiming application, of course, there is no time limit to be met and hence the rule does not apply. This is true even if the applicant had intended the application to be filed before some planned public disclosure of the invention and the application arrived after that date.

62   Furthermore, where a party can provide evidence that on any of the ten days preceding the expiry of a time limit the delivery or transmission of mail was disclocated due to an exceptional occurrence such as a natural disaster, war, civil disorder or general breakdown in any means of electronic communication in the locality where a party or his representative resides or has his place of business, late receipt of a document is excused if the mailing or transmission is effected at the latest on the fifth day after the end of the disclocation (r.134(5)).

1.4.12   Can a new application be filed?

63   Sometimes, the rights in an application are lost and there is no legal remedy. In these circumstances, the only possible way forward is to begin again by filing a new application. This is particularly useful where a priority period is still pending or where a priority

period can be re-established (only within two months of its expiry) since the effective date of claims entitled to the priority date will not change in these circumstances despite the loss of the original filing date. Even if a priority claim can no longer be used, if the lost application has not published then a new application may be just as effective in the event that no intervening prior art exists between the original filing date and the new filing date. Alternatively, if the lost application was a first filing and was at least awarded a filing date, it will be possible to file a new application claiming its priority without losing any substantive rights – indeed, this is the recommended course of action in any case in order to maximise patent term.

1.5   Preserving the rights of an applicant that have apparently been lost under the PCT

1.5.1   Can the time limit be extended?

Time limits set under the PCT are not generally subject to extension but in certain cases   64
the possibility of extension is specifically provided for. For example, the two month time limit for correcting a formal deficiency before the receiving Office may be extended at any time before a decision is taken (r.26.2 PCT) and the time limit set by an International Preliminary Examining Authority for filing a response to a written opinion may be extended at any time before it expires (r.66.2(e) PCT).

1.5.2   Is a grace period available?

Grace periods are available to the applicant in respect of paying the transmittal fee, inter-   65
national filing fee and search fee (r.16*bis* PCT), paying the supplementary search handling fee and supplementary search fee (r.45*bis*.4(b) and (c)) and paying the fees due for international preliminary examination (r.58*bis* PCT). A surcharge is payable. In some of these cases late payments with surcharge are accepted anyway if received before the relevant international authority declares a loss of rights.

1.5.3   Can the late arrival of a document posted in good time be excused?

In certain circumstances a missed time limit can be excused due to a loss or delay in the   66
postal system or when a document is sent by certain delivery services (r.82.1 PCT analogous to r.133 EPC). Amongst other requirements, the letter must have been sent by the applicant five days or more prior to the expiration of the time limit.

A delay in meeting a time limit can also be excused where evidence is provided that the   67
time limit was not met due to war, revolution, civil disorder, strike, a natural calamity, a general unavailability of electronic communications services or other like reason in the locality where the party concerned resides or has his place of business or is staying and the relevant action was taken as soon as reasonably possible (r.82*quater* PCT).

1.5.4   Can a loss of rights be excused by a national/regional office?

If a receiving Office refuses to accord an international application a filing date or declares   68
that an international application is considered withdrawn (e.g. if a formal defect is not remedied under Art. 14(1)(b) PCT, if a fee is not paid under Art. 14(3)(a) PCT or if a decision to award a filing date is reversed under Art. 14(4)) PCT) or if the International Bureau finds that an international application is considered withdrawn under Art. 12(3) PCT (record copy not received in time) there is no remedy available to the applicant by which the international application can be reinstated and the international phase of the application resumed.

Instead, the applicant must enter the national and regional phases that are of inter-   69
est and try and rescue the different parts of the international application separately. The applicant can request the International Bureau to send a copy of the application file to relevant offices within two months from notification of the loss of rights (Art. 25(1) and r.51.1 PCT). Within the same time limit the applicant must enter the relevant national and regional phases by paying the national fee and furnishing a translation if required (Art. 25(2)(a) and r.51.3 PCT). Each of the national and regional offices concerned must

then consider whether the loss of rights in the international phase was justified or whether it was in fact the result of an error or omission on the part of the responsible international authority. In the latter case, processing of the international application will be continued as far as that office is concerned and the loss of rights ignored (Art. 25(2)(a) PCT).

70   Where, on the other hand, the loss of rights is not considered to be the result of an error or omission on the part of an international authority, the office concerned is only obliged to process the application further if the loss of rights resulted from the applicant missing a time limit and the delay in meeting the time limit would have been excused under provisions of national law in corresponding circumstances (Art. 24(2) and Art. 48(2)(a) PCT). These provisions of national law include re-establishment e.g. Art. 122 EPC, and further processing, e.g. Art. 121 EPC (r.82*bis*.2 PCT). If, therefore, the corresponding loss of rights in the case of a European patent application would have been excusable under Art. 121 EPC or Art. 122 EPC then the appropriate remedy must be applied and the EPO as a designated office is required to continue to process the Euro-PCT application, setting the loss of rights in the international phase aside. It can be difficult in these circumstances to calculate the time limit (e.g. the further processing time limit) that applies since time limits are calculated differently under the EPC and PCT and it is not clear which applies – it would obviously be sensible to rely on the shorter of the two. It may also be noted that in the case that the international application is considered withdrawn though failure to pay a fee, the applicant will need to complete the omitted act by paying fees due to the receiving Office under the PCT to the EPO as designated office!

Mistakes in respect of the filing date and lost priority claims can also be rectified in the national/regional phase (r.82*ter* PCT).

1.5.5   *Can the application be re-instated where the national phase is not entered on time?*

71   Whatever remedies are provided under national/regional law when an applicant fails to perform the necessary acts under Art. 22 PCT to enter the national/regional phase, the PCT obliges national/regional offices to reinstate the applicant's rights in certain circumstances (r.49.6(a) PCT). Note that this remedy only applies to the acts listed in Art. 22 PCT – notably payment of a national fee and the filing of a translation. It does not therefore, apply to other acts which may be necessary on regional phase entry such as payment of an examination fee or supplementary search fee.

1.6 Enlarged Board Decisions

72   Decisions of the Enlarged Board of Appeal of the EPO are of fundamental importance, as discussed above. For ease of reference, headnotes and brief comments (where useful) have been compiled in this section.

G5/83 – Second medical indication/EISAI (see also G1/83 and G 6/83)

73   Headnote (1): "A European patent with claims directed to the use may not be granted for the use of a substance or composition for the treatment of the human or animal body by therapy."

74   Headnote (2): "A European patent may be granted with claims directed to the use of a substance or composition for the manufacture of a medicament for a specified new and inventive therapeutic application."

75   The Enlarged Board felt that there was no substantive difference, for the purposes of the EPC, between a use claim and a method claim and thus that a claim to the use of a substance or composition for treatment lacked industrial applicability under Art. 52(4) (now Art. 53(c) EPC2000) EPC in the same way as a method of treatment claim. However, it was decided that since, under Art. 54(5) EPC1973 (now Art. 54(4) EPC2000), a use-limited product claim was novel by virtue of the use feature, so a use-limited process claim (i.e. use of a substance/composition for the manufacture of a medicament for treatment of a disease) could be seen to be novel by virtue of the use feature. Swiss-style second medical use claims are therefore allowable and their novelty is recognised even if the process for manufacturing a medicament was already known. Note that the Swiss-style second medical use claim has now been superseded by the use-limited compound claim format

allowed by Art. 54(5) EPC2000 and is no longer accepted for first filings later than 28 January 2011 (G2/08).

G1/84 – *Opposition by proprietor/MOBIL OIL*

This decision, which allowed self-opposition, was overruled by G9/93.   76

G1/86 – *Re-establishment of rights of opponent/VOEST ALPINE*

Headnote: "Article 122 EPC is not to be interpreted as being applicable only to the applicant and patent proprietor. An appellant as opponent may have his rights re-established under Article 122 EPC if he has failed to observe the time limit for filing the statement of grounds of appeal."   77

An opponent may not apply for re-establishment under Art. 122 EPC for missing the   78
time limit for filing an appeal since the proprietor is seen to need some legal certainty as to whether an opposition decision is to be contested and the travaux preparatoires address this point. This is also in conformity with national laws. However, since the appeal procedure is essentially judicial and judicial procedures demand that parties be accorded equal rights, it was seen as appropriate that once an appeal was pending (notice of appeal filed and appeal fee paid) the opponent should also be able to take advantage of Art. 122 EPC in subsequent proceedings. This is a good example of an Enlarged Board decision establishing a purposive interpretation of the EPC very different from the simple meaning of the words used.

G1/88 – *Opponent's silence/HOECHST*

Headnote: "The fact that an opponent has failed, within the time allowed, to make any   79
observations on the text in which it is intended to maintain the European patent after being invited to do so under r.58(4) EPC does not render his appeal inadmissible." Note that r.58(4) EPC1973 is equivalent to r.82(1) EPC2000.

It had become practice that, in the event the opponent made no comment when invited   80
to do so pursuant to r.58(4) EPC1973 (now r.82(1) EPC2000), his silence was interpreted as tacit approval of the decision of the Opposition Division from which it was inferred that he was not "adversely effected" by the decision and could not appeal. The practice was reversed by this decision. Rule 58(4) EPC1973 was seen not as a mandatory procedure but one option for obtaining the proprietor's approval of the text (Art. 113(2)) and giving the opponent a chance to comment (Art. 113(1)). These objectives can also be achieved, for instance, at oral proceedings. The right to comment on the proposed text under r.58(4) EPC1973 was therefore seen as supplementary to the right to appeal the decision to uphold the patent in amended form.

G2/88 – *Friction reducing additive/MOBIL OIL III*

Headnote (1): "A change of category of granted claims in opposition proceedings is not   81
open to objection under Art. 123(3) EPC, if it does not result in extension of the protection conferred by the claims as a whole, when they are interpreted in accordance with Art. 69 EPC and its protocol. In this context, the national laws of the Contracting States relating to infringement should not be considered."

Headnote (2): "An amendment of granted claims directed to a compound and to a com-   82
position including such compound, so that the amended claims are directed to the use of that compound in a composition for a particular purpose is not open to objection under Art. 123(3) EPC."

Headnote (3): "A claim to the use of a known compound for a particular purpose,   83
which is based on a technical effect which is described in the patent, should be interpreted as including that technical effect as a functional technical feature, and is accordingly not open to objection under Art. 54(1) EPC provided that such technical feature has not previously been made available to the public."

Regarding Art. 123(3) EPC, the Enlarged Board reasoned that the extent of protection   84
conferred by the claims is to be decided under the EPC whereas the rights conferred (infringing acts, etc.) are a matter for national law. Here, the compound/composition claims conferred absolute protection in respect of all uses and hence the change to a use claim

necessarily narrowed the extent of protection. The new use was the use of a known compound, used in the same way to achieve a different purpose (reducing friction – previous purpose was rust inhibition). The Enlarged Board reasoned that the claim should be construed to include the functional feature of attaining the new technical effect. This technical feature was inherent in the prior art but not made available, by inevitable result or description. Second non-medical use claims are therefore allowable, even if the new use was inherent (but secret) in a prior art use.

G4/88 – Transfer of opposition/MAN

85   Headnote: "An opposition pending before the EPO may be transferred or assigned to a third party as part of the opponent's business assets together with the assets in the interests of which the opposition was filed."

86   The Enlarged Board considered that an opposition could not be transferred or assigned per se. However, since an opposition gives the opponent legal rights as a party to the proceedings and constitutes as inseparable part of that party's business assets it may be transferred with those assets if they are sold. See also G2/04 in which this question was considered again.

G5/88 – Administrative agreement/MEDTRONIC (consolidated with G7/88 and G8/88)

87   Headnote (1): "The capacity of the President of the EPO to represent the European Patent Organisation by virtue of Art. 5(3) EPC is one of his functions but is not one of his powers. The extent of the President's power is governed by the EPC, but not by Art. 5(3) EPC".

88   Headnote (2): "To the extent that the Administrative Agreement dated 29.6.1981 between the President of the EPO and the President of the German Patent Office contains terms regulating the treatment of documents intended for the EPO and received by the German Patent Office in Berlin, the President of the EPO did not himself have the power to enter into such an agreement on behalf of the EPO, at any time before the opening of the Filing Office for the EPO in Berlin on 1.7.1989."

89   Headnote (3): "In application of the principle of good faith and the protection of the legitimate expectations of users of the EPO, if a person has at any time since publication of the agreement in the OJ and before 1.7.1989, filed documents intended for the EPO at the German Patent Office in Berlin (otherwise than by hand), the EPO was then bound to treat such documents as if it had received them on the date of receipt at the German Patent Office in Berlin."

90   This decision reviewed the legality of an agreement between the EPO and the German Patent Office whereby documents intended for the EPO but mistakenly sent to the GPO would be considered received on behalf of the EPO and keep their date. The Enlarged Board took the view that Art. 10(2)(a), which gives the President the power to, "take all necessary steps … to ensure the functioning of the EPO" entitled him to set up the agreement in respect of the Munich Office but not the Berlin Office since in Berlin there was no EPO filing Office at the time and no risk of confusion. In fact, Berlin was inserted into the agreement by the German Patent Office for political reasons. When the EPO filing Office in Berlin came into being, however, the whole agreement was justified. In any case, those people who had relied on the unjustified part of the agreement should not be retrospectively penalised in order to protect their legitimate expectations. The agreement has since been terminated.

G6/88 – Plant growth regulating agent/BAYER

91   Headnote: "A claim to the use of a known compound for a particular purpose, which is based on a technical effect which is described in the patent, should be interpreted as including that technical effect as a functional technical feature, and is accordingly not open to objection under Article 54(1) EPC provided that such technical feature has not previously been made available to the public."

92   The decision given by the Enlarged Board in this case was essentially the same as the decision in G2/88 and the headnotes therefore correspond. In this case the known use was the use of a compound for influencing plant growth whereas the new use was the use of

the same compound, applied in the same way, for controlling fungi. A second non-medical use claim in these circumstance was seen as allowable in principle.

G1/89 – Polysuccinate esters

Headnote: "The agreement between the EPO and WIPO dated 7.10.87, including the   93
obligation under its Article 2 for the EPO to be guided by the PCT guidelines for international search, is binding on the EPO when acting as an International Searching Authority and upon the Boards of Appeal of the EPO when deciding on protests against the charging of additional search fees under the provisions of Article 17(3)(a) PCT. Consequently, as foreseen in these guidelines, an international application may, under Article 17(3)(a) PCT, be considered not to comply with the requirement of unity of invention, not only 'a priori' but also 'a posteriori', i.e. after taking prior art into consideration. However, such consideration has only the procedural effect of initiating the special procedure laid down in Article 17 and Rule 40 PCT and is, therefore, not a 'substantive examination' in the normal sense of the term."

Note that under EPC2000 a protest is no longer reviewed by a Board of Appeal.

G2/89 – Non-unity a posteriori

Headnote: "The EPO in its function as an International Searching Authority may, pursu-   94
ant to Article 17(3)(a) PCT, request a further search fee where the international application is considered to lack unity 'a posteriori'."

G3/89 – Correction under Rule 88, second sentence, EPC [NB. now r.139 EPC2000]

Headnote (1): "The parts of a European patent application or of a European patent relat-   95
ing to the disclosure (the description, claims and drawings) may be corrected under r.88, second sentence, EPC (r.139 EPC2000) only within the limits of what a skilled person would derive directly and unambiguously, using common general knowledge, and seen objectively and relative to the date of filing, from the whole of these documents as filed. Such a correction is of a strictly declaratory nature and thus does not infringe the prohibition of extension under Art. 123(2) EPC."

Headnote (2): "Evidence of what was common general knowledge on the date of fil-   96
ing may be furnished in connection with an admissible request for correction in any suitable form."

The Enlarged Board considered that Art. 123(2) EPC applies equally to amendments   97
which are and which are not corrections. Further, the requirements of r.139 EPC imply that the skilled person is able to recognise that certain information in the disclosure is incorrect as well as what the correct version should be. Hence, the correction is declaratory in the sense of the corrected version merely expressing what the skilled person would already understand. The only relevant evidence is that contained in documents shedding light on the common general knowledge of the skilled man at the filing date. These proceedings were joined with G11/91.

G1/90 – Revocation of the patent

Headnote: "The revocation of a patent under Art. 102(4) and (5) EPC requires a deci-   98
sion." [NB. Art. 102(4) and (5) EPC 1973 now corresponds to r.82(3) EPC2000.]

There was confusion as to whether, in the event of Art. 102(4) or (5) EPC1973 being   99
activated (patent revoked following a decision in opposition proceedings to maintain the patent in amended form and necessary fees or translations not filed in time (now r.82(3) EPC2000)), there was a deemed revocation of the patent leading to a loss of rights communication under r.112(1) or whether the Opposition Division needed to take a decision. The Enlarged Board considered that whereas grant proceedings can be terminated by a loss of rights or a decision, the EPC provides for opposition proceedings being terminated only by a decision and that this literal interpretation of the EPC was in accord with the travaux preparatoire, procedural convenience and legal certainty.

G2/90 – Responsibility of the Legal Board of Appeal/KOLBENSCHMIDT

100   Headnote (1): "Under Art. 21(3)(c) EPC, the Legal Board of Appeal is competent only to hear appeals against decisions taken by an Examining Division consisting of fewer than four members when the decision does not concern the refusal of a European patent application or the grant of a European patent. In all other cases, i.e. those covered by Art. 21(3)(a), 3(b) and (4) EPC, the Technical Board of Appeal is competent."

101   Headnote (2): "The provisions relating to competence in Art. 21(3) and (4) EPC are not affected by r.9(3) EPC." [NB. now r.11(3) EPC2000.]

102   The Enlarged Board decided that since only duties involving no legal difficulties could be entrusted to a formalities Officer under r.11(3) EPC, an appeal from such a decision should rightly be entrusted to the Technical Board of Appeal and no special considerations applied to change the normal operation of Art. 21(3) and (4) concerning which appeals are allocated to which Board.

G1/91 – Unity/SIEMENS

103   Headnote: "Unity of invention (Art. 82 EPC) does not come under the requirements which a European patent and the invention to which it relates must meet under Art. 102(3) EPC (NB. now Art. 101(3) EPC2000) when the patent is maintained in amended form. It is consequently irrelevant in opposition proceedings that the European patent as granted or as amended does not meet the requirement of unity."

      Hence, unity of invention is only of concern in pre-grant proceedings.

G2/91 – Appeal fees/KROHNE

104   Headnote (1): "A person who is entitled to appeal but does no do so and instead confines himself to being a party to the appeal proceedings under Art. 107 second sentence has no independent right to continue the proceedings if the appellant withdraws the appeal."

105   Headnote (2): "Appeal fees cannot be reimbursed simply because several parties to proceedings before the EPO have validly filed an appeal against the same decision."

106   Only the appellant or appellants can decide the fate of the appeal. Other parties to the proceedings have no such right. When all appeals have been withdrawn then the appeal proceedings are automatically terminated. This also applies to an intervener in opposition appeal proceedings who becomes a party as of right in the appeal – he has no independent right to continue with his intervention if the appeal or appeals are withdrawn (G3/04).

G3/91 – Re-establishment of rights/FABRITIUS II

107   Headnote: "Article 122(5) EPC1973 is applicable both to the time limits provided for in Articles 78(2) and 79(2) EPC1973 and to those provided for in Rule 104b(1)(b) and (c) EPC1973 in conjunction with Articles 157(2)(b) and 158(2) EPC1973."

108   This decision confirmed that Art. 122(5) EPC1973, restricting the application of restitutio in integrum, applied to the Art. 78(2) EPC1973 time limit (for paying the search and filing fees) and the Art. 79(2) EPC1973 time limit (for paying the designation fees), including the grace periods under r.85a EPC1973. By analogy, it was decided that Art. 122(5) EPC1973 also applied to the corresponding time limits for Euro-PCT applications entering the regional phase. In these circumstances the national basic fee equated to the filing fee. Note that Art. 122(5) EPC1973 has been deleted in EPC2000 and this decision no longer has any relevance.

G4/91 – Intervention/DOLEZYCH II

109   Headnote (1): "It is a prerequisite for intervention in opposition proceedings by an assumed infringer pursuant to Article 105 EPC that there are opposition proceedings in existence at the point in time when a notice of intervention is filed."

110   Headnote (2): "A decision by an Opposition Division which decides upon the issues raised by the opposition is a final decision in the sense that thereafter the Opposition Division has no power to change its decision."

111   Headnote (3): "Proceedings before an Opposition Division are terminated upon issue of such a final decision, regardless of when such decision takes legal effect."

Headnote (4): "In a case where, after issue of a final decision by an Opposition Divi-   112
sion, no appeal is filed by a party to the proceedings before the Opposition Division, a
notice of intervention which is filed during the two-month period for appeal provided by
Art. 108 EPC has no legal effect."

The Enlarged Board decided that an intervention can only be filed if opposition pro-   113
ceedings are in existence. This is not so where a decision of the Opposition Division has
been issued, such a decision being final in the sense that the Opposition Division has
no power to change it. Such a decision therefore terminates the opposition proceedings
regardless of the fact that it finally takes legal effect only after the period for appeal has
expired. For intervention in appeal proceedings, see G1/94 and G3/04.

G5/91 – Appealable decision/DISCOVISION

Headnote (1): "Although Art. 24 EPC applies only to members of the Boards of Appeal   114
and of the Enlarged Board of Appeal, the requirement of impartiality applies in principle
also to employees of the departments of first instance of the EPO taking part in decision
making activities affecting the rights of any party."

Headnote (2): "There is no legal basis under the EPC for any separate appeal against   115
an order of a director of a department of the first instance such as an Opposition Division rejecting an objection to a member of the division on the ground of suspected
partiality. However, the composition of the Opposition Division may be challenged on
such a ground of appeal against the final decision of the division or against an interlocutory decision under Article 106(3) EPC allowing separate appeal." [NB. now Art. 106(2)
EPC2000.]

The Enlarged Board concluded that the decision of an Examining Division or an Oppo-   116
sition Division may be appealed on the basis of suspected partiality. Article 125 provides
the legal basis. The Director of the department concerned decides on any request for a
change in composition – there is no automatic separate appeal from the decision (unless
it is deliberately taken as an interlocutory decision) but it may always be challenged as
part of an appeal following a final decision. If upheld on appeal, a substantial procedural
violation has occurred and the decision at first instance is void.

G6/91 – Fee reduction/ASULAB

Headnote (1): "The persons referred to in Art. 14(2) EPC (NB. Now Art. 14(4) EPC2000)   117
are entitled to the fee reduction under r.6(3) EPC if they file the essential item of the first
act in filing, examination or appeal proceedings in an official language of the state concerned other than English, French or German, and supply the necessary translation no
earlier than simultaneously."

Headnote (2): "The essential item of the first act in appeal proceedings is the notice of   118
appeal, so to secure entitlement to the reduction in the appeal fee it suffices that said document be filed in a Contracting State official language which is not an official language of
the EPO and translated into one of the latter languages, even if subsequent items such as
the statement of grounds of appeal are filed only in an EPO official language."

Note that the reduction of the appeal fee under r.6(3) was abolished for appeals filed on   119
or after 01 April 2014 but continued to apply to the filing fee and the examination fee. A
reduction of the appeal fee was then reintroduced as of 01 April 2018 by amendment of
RRF Art. 2(1)(11) for certain entities regardless of their residence or nationality and the
language in which the appeal is filed.

G7/91 – Withdrawal of appeal/BASF (consolidated with G8/91)

Headnote: "In so far as the substantive issues settled by the contested decision at first in-   120
stance are concerned, a Board of Appeal may not continue opposition appeal proceedings
after the sole appellant, who was the opponent in the first instance, has withdrawn his
appeal."

This is to be contrasted with proceedings before the Opposition Division, where under   121
r.84(2) EPC the examination of an opposition can be continued even if the opposition is
withdrawn, and is a reflection of the fact that Board of Appeal proceedings are judicial in
nature rather than administrative. The reasoning of the Enlarged Board was based on the

principle of party disposition whereby a court cannot continue proceedings if the procedural act giving rise to the proceedings has been retracted. See also G2/91.

G8/91 – *Withdrawal of appeal/BELL (consolidated with G7/91)*

122   Headnote: "In so far as the substantive issues settled by the contested decision at first instance are concerned, appeal proceedings are terminated, in ex parte and inter partes proceedings alike, when the sole appellant withdraws the appeal."

G9/91 – *Power to examine/ROHM AND HAAS*

123   Headnote: "The power of an Opposition Division or a Board of Appeal to examine and decide on the maintenance of a European patent under Arts. 101 and 102 EPC (NB. Now Art. 101 EPC2000) depends upon the extent to which the patent is opposed in the notice of opposition pursuant to r.55(c) EPC (NB. Now r.76(2)(c) EPC2000). However, subject-matters of claims depending on an independent claim, which falls in opposition or appeal proceedings, may be examined as to their patentability even if they have not been explicitly opposed, provided their validity is prima facie in doubt on the basis of already available information."

124   Rule 76(2)(c) was interpreted by the Enlarged Board as governing the legal and factual framework within which substantive examination of an opposition must in principle be conducted. Therefore, if the extent of the opposition is only partial (i.e. not all the independent claims are opposed) the Opposition Division has no competence to examine those claims which are not subject to any "opposition" at all. In contrast, where an independent claim is opposed, the Opposition Division may also examine any claims dependent on the opposed independent claim provided that their validity is prima facie in doubt on the basis of the available information.

G10/91 – *Examination of oppositions/appeals*

125   Headnote (1): "An Opposition Division or a Board of Appeal is not obliged to consider all the grounds for opposition referred to in Art. 100 EPC, going beyond the grounds covered by the statement under r.55(c) EPC (NB. Now r.76(2)(c) EPC2000)."

126   Headnote (2): "In principle, the Opposition Division shall examine only such grounds for opposition which have been properly submitted and substantiated in accordance with Art. 99(1) in conjunction with r.55(c) EPC (NB. Now r.76(2)(c) EPC2000). Exceptionally, the Opposition Division may in application of Art. 114(1) EPC consider other grounds for opposition which, prima facie, in whole or in part would seem to prejudice the maintenance of the European patent."

127   Headnote (3): "Fresh grounds for opposition may be considered in appeal proceedings only with the approval of the patentee."

128   The principle of G10/91, Headnote (2), has now been incorporated directly in the implementing regulations (r.81(1) EPC). Although the words "exceptionally" and "prima facie" in headnote (2) have been left out of r.81(1), this would seem to make little difference in practice.

G11/91 – *Glu-Gln/CELTRIX*

129   See above under G3/89. The headnotes and reasoning are identical.

G12/91 – *Final decision/NOVATOME II*

130   Headnote: "The decision-making process following written proceedings is completed on the date the decision to be notified is handed over to the EPO postal service by the decision-taking department's formalities section."

131   On this date the Examining or Opposition Division no longer have the power to change their minds. It corresponds to the moment in oral proceedings where debate is closed and the parties may no longer submit anything further. Further amendments or comments will therefore not be taken into account after this date.

G1/92 – Availability to the public

Headnote (1): "The chemical composition of a product is state of the art when the product as such is available to the public and can be analysed and reproduced by the skilled person, irrespective of whether or not particular reasons can be identified for analysing the composition."   132

Headnote (2): "The same principle applies mutatis mutandis to any other product."   133

Availability of a product to the public thus frequently makes available its composition and structure but not any properties that depend on further action being taken (e.g. a particular use).

G2/92 – Non-payment of further search fees

Headnote: "An applicant who fails to pay the further search fees for a non-unitary application when requested to do so by the Search Division under r.46(1) EPC (NB. Now r.64(1) EPC2000) cannot pursue that application for the subject matter in respect of which no search fees have been paid. Such an applicant must file a divisional application in respect of such subject matter if he wishes to seek protection for it."   134

The Enlarged Board felt that only one examination fee is payable and so only one invention may be examined and that this invention must have been one searched by the Search Division. The applicant who pays the extra fees may not only argue for unity subsequently before the Examining Division but may also select which of the inventions is examined if unsuccessful in this argument. These fees are not lost since the search fees payable on any divisional application which must be filed are reduced to the extent the first search can be used.   135

G3/92 – Unlawful applicant/LATCHWAYS

Headnote: "When it has been adjudged by a final decision of a national court that a person other than the applicant is entitled to the grant of a European patent, and that person, in compliance with the specific requirements of Art. 61(1) EPC, files a new European patent application in respect of the same invention under Art. 61(1)(b) EPC, it is not a pre-condition for the application to be accepted that the earlier original usurping application is still pending before the EPO at the time the new application is filed."   136

This case split the Enlarged Board of Appeal. The majority decided, as stated in the headnote, that the potential risk to legal certainty in respect of parties commencing commercial activities on the basis that the application was dead were outweighed by the damaging consequences of parties stealing an invention and withdrawing their application shortly after publication (they felt that national courts could take into account particular circumstances of this kind with regard to third parties). Nothing in the language of the EPC was seen to prevent this interpretation and, in particular, the provision governing divisional applications, that a pending parent application must be in existence, was seen not to apply. The Board felt that exercise of the remedies provided by Art. 61(1)(a) and (c) did require a pending application.   137

G4/92 – Basis of decisions

Headnote (1): "A decision against a party who has been duly summoned but who fails to appear at oral proceedings may not be based on facts put forward for the first time during those oral proceedings."   138

Headnote (2): "Similarly, new evidence may not be considered unless it has been previously notified and it merely supports the assertions of the party who submits it, whereas new arguments may in principle be used to support the reasons for the decision."   139

As the reasons make clear, this decision only applies to inter partes proceedings. Furthermore, according to T706/00 it no longer applies to the Boards of Appeal whose rules of procedure were later amended to specifically state that a decision in oral proceedings does not have to be delayed by virtue of the non-attendance of a party (RPBA Art. 15(3)). The decision should still apply, however, to an opposition division which, if it introduces a new document in oral proceedings, should continue the proceedings in writing for a non-attending proprietor to be able to comment before a decision based on that document is taken. The submission of new claims by the proprietor in the absence of the   140 opponent is not a new "fact" within the meaning of G4/92 according to Guidelines E-II, 8.3.3.2 and nor is the examination of claims for formal deficiencies in the absence of the proprietor a new "fact" of this kind.

G5/92 – *Re-establishment/HOUPT (consolidated with G6/92)*

141   Headnote: "The time limit under Art. 94(2) EPC (NB. Now r.70(1) EPC2000) is excluded from restitutio in integrum by the provisions of paragraph 5 of Art. 122 EPC."

142   This decision is no longer relevant under EPC2000. Further processing is now available where the r.70(1) time limit is missed and re-establishment is available if the further processing time limit is not observed.

G6/92 – *Re-establishment/DURIRON (consolidated with G5/92)*

143   See under G5/92 above.

G9/92 – *Non-appealing party/BMW (consolidated with G4/93)*

144   Headnote (1): "If the patent proprietor is the sole appellant against an interlocutory decision maintaining a patent in amended form, neither the Board of Appeal nor the non-appealing opponent as a party to the proceedings as of right under Art. 107(2) EPC may challenge the maintenance of the patent as amended in accordance with the interlocutory decision."

145   Headnote (2): "If the opponent is the sole appellant against an interlocutory decision maintaining a patent in amended form, the patent proprietor is primarily restricted during appeal proceedings to defending the patent in the form in which it was maintained by the Opposition Division in its interlocutory decision. Amendments proposed by the patent proprietor as a party to the proceedings as of right under Art. 107(2) may be rejected as inadmissible by the Board of Appeal if they are neither appropriate nor necessary."

146   This case examines the situation where a patent is maintained in amended form during opposition proceedings and only one of the parties appeals. The principle of reformatio in peius applies such that the non-appealing party may not make requests more favourable to itself then the decision of the Opposition Division. The Enlarged Board (by majority) felt that the subject matter of proceedings is the appeal itself and not a general re-examination. Further, it would be unfair if one party did not comply with the time limit for appeal but was still allowed, effectively, to appeal the decision. The subject matter of Headnote (2) was further elucidated in G1/99.

G10/92 – *Divisional application*

147   Headnote: "Under the amended version of r.25 EPC in force since 01 October 1988 an applicant may only file a divisional application on the pending earlier European patent application up to the approval in accordance with r.51(4) EPC."

148   This decision is no longer relevant. A divisional application may now be filed up until (but not including) the date of mention of grant in the Bulletin.

G1/93 – *Limiting feature/ADVANCED SEMICONDUCTOR PRODUCTS*

149   Headnote (1): "If a European patent as granted contains subject matter which extends beyond the content of the application as filed within the meaning of Art. 123(2) EPC and which also limits the scope of protection conferred by the patent, such a patent cannot be maintained in opposition proceedings unamended, because the ground for opposition under Art. 100(c) EPC prejudices the maintenance of the patent. Nor can it be amended by deleting such limiting subject-matter from the claims, because such amendment would extend the protection conferred, which is prohibited by Art. 123(3) EPC. Such a patent can, therefore, only be maintained if there is a basis in the application as filed for replacing such subject-matter without violating Art. 123(3) EPC."

150   Headnote (2): "A feature which has not been disclosed in the application as filed but which has been added to the application during examination and which, without providing a technical contribution to the subject-matter of the claimed invention, merely limits the protection conferred by the patent as granted by excluding protection for part of the subject-matter of the claimed invention as covered by the application as filed, is not to

be considered as subject-matter which extends beyond the content of the application as filed within the meaning of Art. 123(2) EPC. The ground for opposition under Art. 100(c) EPC therefore does not prejudice the maintenance of a European patent which includes such a feature."

This decision confirmed that an inescapable trap lurks for the unwary applicant who   151
makes a limiting amendment during grant proceedings which adds subject matter. Such an offending amendment would likely have to be replaced with an even more limiting amendment for which there was clear basis. The reasoning of Headnote (2) sits uncomfortably with the reasoning in later decisions G2/98 and G2/10 but an undisclosed disclaimer that meets the conditions set out in G1/03 would certainly be an example of such an amendment (see T768/20 which comes to the conclusion that an undisclosed disclaimer is the only kind of amendment that would be allowable under G1/93, deadnote 2).

G2/93 – *Hepatitis A virus/UNITED STATES OF AMERICA II*

Headnote: "The information concerning the file number of a culture deposit according   152
to r.28(1)(c) EPC may not be submitted after expiry of the time limit set out in r.28(2)(a) EPC." [NB. Rule 28 EPC 1973 is now r.31 EPC2000.]

An application must be sufficient at its filing date: any deficiency cannot be later rem-   153
edied. Thus, if the sufficiency of a disclosure depends on access to a culture, the relevant deposit must be made on or before the filing date (r.31(1)(a) EPC) and information identifying the deposit must be supplied (r.31(1)(c) EPC) in time for inclusion in the publication of the application (r.31(2) EPC).

G3/93 – *Priority interval*

Headnote (1): "A document published during the priority interval, the technical contents   154
of which correspond to that of the priority document, constitutes prior art citable under Art. 54(2) EPC against a European patent application claiming that priority, to the extent such priority is not validly claimed."

Headnote (2): "This also applies if a claim to priority is invalid due to the fact that the   155
priority document and the subsequent European patent application do not concern the same invention because the European application claims subject matter not disclosed in the priority document."

The Art. 89 effect on Art. 54, whereby the patentability of a claim is to be judged as   156
of the priority date, thus only applies where priority is validly claimed in respect of "the same invention" (Art. 87(1) EPC). See G2/98, where the concept of "the same invention" was fully considered. Publication of the contents of a priority application during the priority year can, therefore, have unfortunate consequences for any claims based on subject matter added at the filing date – such claims must be inventive over the priority disclosure.

G4/93 *(consolidated with G9/92)*

See above under G9/92.   157

G5/93 – *Re-establishment/NELLCOR*

Headnote: "The provisions of Art. 122(5) EPC apply to the time limits provided for in   158
r.104b(1)(b)(i) and (ii) EPC in conjunction with Arts. 157(2)(b) and 158(2) EPC. This notwithstanding, Euro-PCT applications may be re-established in the time limit for paying the national fee provided for in r.104b EPC in all cases where re-establishment of rights was applied for before decision G3/91 was made available to the public." [NB. All these references are to EPC1973].

As previously decided in G3/91, Art. 122(5) EPC1973 was seen to apply to payment of   159
the national fee for entering the EPO regional phase since it was the equivalent of the filing and designation fees which were both explicitly mentioned in Art. 122(5) EPC1973. No restitutio was therefore possible if these fees were not paid in time. This decision is a good example of the application of the "good faith" principle whereby nobody should suffer a disadvantage when relying on the established practice of the EPO when such practice changes. This decision is no longer relevant under EPC2000 since further processing is

available if the national fee (now simply filing fee) is not paid in due time. Re-establishment is available if the further processing time limit is not observed.

G7/93 – Late amendments/WHITBY II

160 Headnote (1): "An approval of the text submitted by an applicant pursuant to r.51(4) EPC does not become binding once a communication in accordance with r.51(6) has been issued. Following issue of such a communication under r.51(6) EPC and until issue of a decision to grant the patent, the Examining Division has a discretion under r.86(3), second sentence, EPC, whether or not to allow amendment of the application." (NB. r.51(4) EPC1993 is now r.71(3) EPC2000 and there is no equivalent of the r.51(6) EPC 1973 referred to in this headnote. Rule 86(3) EPC1973 is now r.137(3) EPC2000).

161   Headnote (2): "When exercising such discretion following issue of a communication under r.51(6) EPC, an Examining Division must consider all relevant factors. In particular it must consider and balance the applicant's interest in obtaining a patent which is legally valid in all of the designated States, and the EPO's interest in bringing the examination procedure to a close by the issue of a decision to grant the patent. Having regard to the object underlying the issue of a communication under r.51(6) EPC, which is to conclude the granting procedure on the basis of the previously approved text, the allowance of a request for amendment at that late stage in the granting procedure will be an exception rather than the rule."

162   Headnote (3): "Reservations under Art. 167(2) EPC do not constitute requirements of the EPC which have to be met according to Art. 96(2) EPC." [NB. Art. 167(2) EPC1973 is deleted in EPC2000 and Art. 96(2) EPC1973 has become Art. 94(3) EPC2000.]

163   This decision was taken at a time when a text was agreed under r.51(4) EPC1973 and claim translations/grant fees were dealt with under r.51(6) EPC1973. However, the principles established are still important. The Enlarged Board decided that Art. 113(2) (EPO to decide only on text approved by applicant) did not give the applicant a right to amend. Any amendment under r.137(3) is only admitted with the consent of the Examining Division. Equally, the Examining Division is not bound in any way by the text as approved and can authorise amendments prior to the issue of a decision to grant. Discretion will only be exercised in favour of the applicant as an exception rather than a rule at such a late stage of the grant procedure. The Examining Division must balance the applicant's interest in obtaining a valid patent against the EPO's interest in bringing grant proceedings to a close. Typically, amendments should be allowed which do not involve reopening of substantive examination.

G8/93 – Withdrawal of opposition/SERWANE II

164 Headnote: "The filing by an opponent, who is sole appellant, of a statement withdrawing his opposition immediately and automatically terminates the appeal proceedings, irrespective of whether the patent proprietor agrees to termination of those proceedings and even if in the Board of Appeal's view the requirements under the EPC for maintaining the patent are not satisfied."

165   It was the opinion of the Enlarged Board that withdrawal of the opposition by the opponent and sole appellant could only mean he wished to withdraw the appeal which was examining whether any ground of opposition might prejudice maintenance of the patent. The rest follows from G7/91 and G8/91 (see above).

G9/93 – Opposition by patent proprietor/PEUGEOT AND CITROEN

166 Headnote: "A European patent cannot be opposed by its own proprietor."

167   The Enlarged Board overruled G1/84, holding that "any person" must be interpreted in the context of the EPC as a whole to exclude the patentee since, as determined in G9/91 and G10/91, opposition proceedings are essentially contentious proceedings involving two opposed parties. In the interests of equity and good faith the decision did not apply to pending self-oppositions. The non-availability of self-opposition created the need for the limitation/revocation proceedings of Art. 105a EPC2000.

G10/93 – Scope of examination in ex parte appeal/SIEMENS

Headnote: "In an appeal from a decision of an Examining Division in which a European   168
patent application was refused, the Board of Appeal has the power to examine whether
the application or the invention to which it relates meets the requirements of the EPC.
The same is true for requirements which the Examining Division did not take into consideration in the examination proceedings or which it regarded as having been met. If there
is reason to believe that such a requirement has not been met, the board shall include this
ground in the proceedings."

The Enlarged Board contrasted ex parte examination appeals where the grounds for   169
refusal under Art. 97(2) EPC are comprehensive and the appeal can only improve the
position of the applicant whose application has been refused with inter partes opposition
appeals where the grounds for opposition are limited and in the event of the patent being
upheld in amended form the applicant could have his position improved or made worse.
Whether an additional matter should be ruled on by the Board or remitted to the first
instance for examination was a matter of judgement depending on the facts of each case.

G1/94 – Intervention/ALLIED COLLOIDS

Headnote: "Intervention of the assumed infringer under Art. 105 EPC is admissible dur-   170
ing pending appeal proceedings and may be based on any ground for opposition under
Art. 100 EPC."

The convenience of having centralised revocation being balanced by the complication   171
and delay to the appeal proceedings, the Enlarged Board was most swayed by the travaux
preparatoires which indicated that intervention was contemplated during the appeal stage.
The Board further considered that the intervener should be given the unfettered right to
raise any ground of opposition. However, in view of G10/91, if a fresh ground is raised
then the case should be remitted to the first instance unless there are special reasons to
decide otherwise, such as the agreement of the patentee. The decision does not address
the important question of whether the intervener should be allowed to attack any independent claim not opposed in the original notice of opposition, which is still an undecided
point of law. Later decision G3/04 adds to this decision, confirming that the intervener
does not obtain appellant status.

G2/94 – Representation/HAUTAU II

Headnote (1): "A Board of Appeal has a discretion to allow an accompanying person   172
(who is not entitled under Art. 134(1) or (7) EPC to represent parties in proceedings before the EPO) to make submissions during oral proceedings in ex parte proceedings, in
addition to the complete presentation of a party's case by the professional representative."
(NB. Art. 134(7) EPC1973 is now Art. 134(8) EPC2000.)

Headnote (2): "(a) In ex parte proceedings a professional representative should request   173
permission for the making of such oral submissions in advance of the day appointed for
oral proceedings. The request should state the name and qualifications of the person for
whom permission is requested, and should specify the subject matter of the proposed
oral submissions. The Board of Appeal should exercise its discretion in accordance with
the circumstances of each individual case. The main criterion to be considered is that the
Board should be fully informed of all relevant matters before deciding the case. The Board
should be satisfied that the oral submissions are made by the accompanying person under
the continuing responsibility and control of the professional representative. (b) During either ex parte or inter partes proceedings, a Board of Appeal should refuse permission for a
former member of the boards of appeal to make oral submissions during oral proceedings
before it, unless it is completely satisfied that a sufficient period of time has elapsed following termination of such former member's appointment to the boards of appeal, so that
the Board of Appeal could not reasonably be suspected of partiality in deciding the case if
it allowed such oral submissions to be made. A Board of Appeal should normally refuse
permission for a former member of the Boards of Appeal to make oral submissions during
oral proceedings before it, until at least three years have elapsed following termination of
the former member's appointment to the boards of appeal. After three years have elapsed,
permission should be granted except in very special circumstances."

G1/95 – Fresh grounds for opposition/DE LA RUE (consolidated with G7/95)

174   Headnote: "In a case where a patent has been opposed on the grounds set out in Art. 100(a) EPC, but the opposition has only been substantiated on the grounds of lack of novelty and lack of inventive step, the grounds of unpatentable subject matter based on Art. 52(1) and (2) EPC (i.e. non-invention) is a fresh ground for opposition and accordingly may not be introduced into the appeal proceedings without the agreement of the patentee."

175   The Enlarged Board decided that a ground is an individual legal basis and Art. 100(a) describes a collection of individual grounds rather than one single ground with different aspects. See also below under G7/95. See G10/91 for the criteria to be considered in assessing whether a new ground may be raised in opposition or opposition appeal proceedings.

G2/95 – Replacement of application documents/ATOTECH

176   Headnote: "The complete documents forming a European patent application, that is the description, claims and drawings, cannot be replaced by way of a correction under r.88 EPC by other documents which the applicants had intended to file with their request for grant." (NB. r.88 EPC1973 is now r.139 EPC2000.)

177   This decision follows very straightforwardly from G3/89 and G11/91 in that the subject matter that may not be extended under Art. 123(2) is that contained in the claims, description and drawings accorded a filing date under Art. 80.

G3/95 – Inadmissible referral

178   Headnote (1): "In decision T356/93 (OJ EPO 1995, 545) it was held that a claim defining genetically modified plants having a distinct, stable, herbicide-resistance genetic characteristic was not allowable under Art. 53(b) EPC because the claimed genetic modification itself made the modified or transformed plant a 'plant variety' within the meaning of Art. 53(b) EPC."

179   Headnote (2): "This finding is not in conflict with the findings in either of decisions T49/83 (OJ EPO1984, 112) or T19/90 (OJ EPO 1990, 476)."

180   Headnote (3): "Consequently, the referral of the question: 'Does a claim which relates to plants or animals but wherein specific plant or animal varieties are not individually claimed contravene the prohibition on patenting in Art. 53(b) EPC if it embraces plant or animal varieties?' to the Enlarged Board of Appeal by the President of the EPO is inadmissible under Art. 112(1)(b) EPC."

181   The question as to the extent of the exclusion under Art. 53(b) EPC was finally addressed in G1/98 – see below.

G4/95 – Representation/BOGASKY

182   Headnote (1): "During oral proceedings under Art. 116 EPC in the context of opposition or opposition appeal proceedings, a person accompanying the professional representative of a party may be allowed to make oral submissions on specific legal or technical issues (including facts, evidence or argument) on behalf of that party, otherwise than under Art. 117 EPC, in addition to the complete presentation of the party's case by the professional representative."

183   Headnote (2): "(a) Such oral submissions cannot be made as a matter of right, but only with the permission of and under the discretion of the EPO. (b) The following main criteria should be considered by the EPO when exercising its discretion to allow the making of oral submissions by an accompanying person in opposition or opposition appeal proceedings: (i) The professional representative should request permission for such oral submissions to be made. The request should state the name and qualifications of the accompanying person, and should specify the subject-matter of the proposed oral submissions. (ii) The request should be made sufficiently in advance of the oral proceedings so that all opposing parties are able properly to prepare themselves in relation to the proposed oral submissions. (iii) A request which is made shortly before or at the oral proceedings should in the absence of exceptional circumstances be refused, unless each opposing party agrees to the making of the oral submissions requested. (iv) The EPO should be satisfied that oral submissions by an accompanying person are made under the continuing responsibility and control of the professional representative. (c) No special

criteria apply to the making of oral submissions by qualified patent lawyers of countries which are not Contracting States to the EPC."

G6/95 – *Interpretation of Rule 71a(1) EPC vis-à-vis the Boards of Appeal*

Headnote: "Rule 71a(1) EPC does not apply to the Boards of Appeal." (NB. r.71a EPC1973 is now r.116 EPC2000.)   184

When this decision was taken, the rules of procedure of the Boards of Appeal made   185
the communication provided for in r.116(1) optional, depending on the facts of the case (Art. 15(1) RPBA2007). Such rules of procedure were adopted by the Presidium under Art. 23(4) and approved by the Administrative Council. The Enlarged Board decided that the Administrative Council must be presumed to know the limits of its own power and that it therefore did not intend to amend r.116 EPC so as to conflict with the RPBA (Art. 164(2) makes the provisions of the EPC superior to the provisions of the Implementing Regulations). Since then, the rules of procedure of the Boards of Appeal have been amended and a communication equivalent to the r.116(1) communication is now mandatory (Art. 15(1) RPBA2020).

G7/95 – *Fresh grounds for opposition/ETHICON (consolidated with G1/95)*

Headnote: "In a case where a patent has been opposed under Art. 100(a) EPC, on the   186
ground that the claims lack an inventive step in view of documents cited in the notice of opposition, the ground of lack of novelty based on Art. 52(1) and Art. 54 EPC is a fresh ground for opposition and accordingly may not be introduced into the appeal proceedings without the agreement of the patentee. However, the allegation that the claims lack novelty in view of the closest prior art document may be considered in the context of deciding upon the ground of lack of inventive step."

In consolidated cases G1/95 and G7/95 "grounds for opposition" under Art. 100(a)   187
were interpreted as individual legal bases for objection, e.g. "invention", "novelty", "inventive step" and "industrial application". In the context of G10/91, a fresh ground was seen as one which was neither raised and substantiated in the notice of opposition nor introduced into the proceedings by the Opposition Division under Art. 114(1). It had been held in G10/91 that a new ground may not be introduced at the appeal stage without the agreement of the patentee. So, if lack of inventive step was the only ground substantiated during opposition then lack of novelty may not, in principle, be argued during appeal. However, it was seen that determining whether the claimed invention had any novel features over the closest prior art document was an inherent part of determining inventive step. Thus, the novelty of the claim over the closest prior art document (NB. not any other document) could be considered in appeal proceedings and if there was a lack of novelty the claim must inherently lack inventive step and thus would be rejected for lack of inventive step (NB. not lack of novelty).

G8/95 – *Correction of decision to grant/US GYPSUM II*

Headnote: "An appeal from a decision of an Examining Division refusing a request under   188
r.89 EPC for correction of the decision to grant is to be decided by a technical Board of Appeal." (NB. r.89 EPC1973 is now r.140 EPC2000.)

Article 21(3) EPC determines that an appeal from a decision of an Examining Division   189
will be heard by a technical Board of Appeal when the decision concerns the refusal or grant of a European patent (as opposed to a Legal Board of Appeal). An appeal against a decision to refuse correction of a decision to grant was seen to "concern the grant of the patent". Whether or not the decision terminates proceedings was seen to be key.

G1/97 – *Request with a view to revision/ETA*

Headnote (1): "In the context of the EPC, the jurisdictional measure to be taken in response to requests based on the alleged violation of a fundamental procedural principle and aimed at the revision of a final decision of a Board of Appeal having the force of res judicata should be the refusal of the requests as inadmissible."   190

191   Headnote (2): "The decision on admissibility is to be issued by the Board of Appeal which took the decision forming the subject of the request for revision. The decision may be issued immediately and without further procedural formalities."

192   Headnote (3): "This jurisdictional measure applies only to requests directed against a decision of a Board of Appeal bearing a date after that of the present decision."

193   Headnote (4): "If the Legal Division of the EPO is asked to decide on the entry in the Register of European Patents of a request directed against a decision of a Board of Appeal, it must refrain from ordering that the entry be made if the request, in whatever form, is based on the alleged violation of a fundamental procedural principle and aimed at the revision of a final decision of a Board of Appeal."

194   The Enlarged Board considered that there was no mechanism under the EPC for the review of a decision of a Board of Appeal, even where a procedural violation had occurred. Nevertheless the Enlarged Board urged the legislator to create such a mechanism and this has now been provided by Art. 112a EPC2000. Before this decision, instead of such a request for review being deemed inadmissible (see Headnotes 2 and 3) an administrative rejection had been issued to the same effect.

G2/97 – Good faith/UNILEVER

195   Headnote: "The principle of good faith does not impose any obligations on the Boards of Appeal to notify an applicant that an appeal fee is missing when the notice of appeal is filed so early that the appellant could react and pay the fee in time, if there is no indication – either in the notice of appeal or in any other document filed in relation to the appeal – from which it could be inferred that the appellant would, without such notification, inadvertently miss the time limit for payment of the appeal fee."

196   The EPO does not have any duty to warn a party that it has not paid a fee when it is not possible for the EPO to know whether the party has made a mistake or is merely waiting to pay the fee at a later date.

G3/97 – Opposition on behalf of a third party/INDUPACK (consolidated with G4/97)

197   Headnote (1): "(a) An opposition is not inadmissible purely because the person named as opponent according to r.55(a) EPC is acting on behalf of a third party (i.e. as a strawman). (b) Such an opposition is, however, inadmissible if the involvement of the opponent is to be regarded as circumventing the law by abuse of process. (c) Such a circumvention of the law arises, in particular, if: (i) the opponent is acting on behalf of the patent proprietor; (ii) the opponent is acting on behalf of a client in the context of activities which, taken as a whole, are typically associated with professional representatives, without possessing the relevant qualifications required by Art. 134 EPC. (d) However, a circumvention of the law by abuse of process does not arise purely because (i) a professional representative is acting in his own name on behalf of a client; (ii) an opponent with either a residence or principle place of business in one of the EPC Contracting States is acting on behalf of a third party who does not meet this requirement." (NB. r.55(a) EPC is now r.76(2)(a) EPC2000.)

198   Headnote (2): "In determining whether the law has been circumvented by abuse of process, the principle of the free evaluation of evidence is to be applied (i.e. on case by case basis, no special rules to be applied). The burden of proof is to be borne by the person alleging that the opposition is inadmissible. The deciding body has to be satisfied on the basis of clear and convincing evidence that the law has been circumvented by abuse of process (i.e. more than on balance of probabilities)."
        See below under G4/97 for comment.

G4/97 – Opposition on behalf of a third party/GENENTECH (consolidated with G3/97)

199   Headnotes (1) and (2): Identical to G3/97 (see above).

200   Headnote (3): "The admissibility of an opposition on grounds relating to the identity of an opponent may be challenged during the course of the appeal, even if no such challenge has been raised before the Opposition Division."

The Enlarged Board decided that in principle it was allowable for a strawman to file 201
an opposition on behalf of another party. Such a procedure would only be unallowable if
a further provision of the EPC was being circumvented (e.g. a strawman cannot act on
behalf of the proprietor as this would amount to self-opposition – see G9/93). No special
interest is necessary to act as an opponent since every member of the public has an interest
to the extent that the ability to carry out certain acts is restricted by the patent. The Enlarged Board also decided that the decision should be applied to all pending proceedings
since there was no valid legitimate expectation to protect on the basis of past case law.

G1/98 – Transgenic plant/NOVARTIS II

Headnote (1): "A claim wherein specific plant varieties are not individually claimed is 202
not excluded from patentability under Art. 53(b) EPC even though it may embrace plant
varieties."

Headnote (2): "When a claim to a process for the production of a plant variety is exam- 203
ined, Art. 64(2) EPC is not to be taken into consideration."

Headnote (3): "The exception to patentability in Art. 53(b), first half-sentence, EPC 204
applies to plant varieties irrespective of the way in which they were produced. Therefore,
plant varieties containing genes introduced into an ancestral plant by recombinant gene
technology are excluded from patentability."

The Enlarged Board held that Art. 53(b) excluded plant varieties rather than plants and 205
existed to exclude double protection via a patent and a plant breeders right. Therefore, anything that could not be protected under UPOV should be patentable, including the claim
in dispute, directed to a genetically modified plant, which neither expressly or implicitly
defined a plant variety according to UPOV.

G2/98 – Requirement for claiming priority of the "same invention"

Headnote: "The requirement for claiming priority of 'the same invention', referred to in 206
Art. 87(1) EPC means that priority of a previous application in respect of a claim in a European patent application in accordance with Art. 88 EPC is to be acknowledged only if
the skilled person can derive the subject matter of the claim directly and unambiguously,
using common general knowledge, from the previous application as a whole."

The alternative (i.e. allowing priority where a feature not disclosed in the priority ap- 207
plication has been inserted which merely limits scope and is not related to function and
effect) was seen to be dangerously subjective and changeable during prosecution in the
light of fresh prior art. The strict approach was seen to be consistent with the Paris Convention and Arts. 87–89 EPC.

G3/98 – Six-month period/UNIVERSITY PATENTS (consolidated with G2/99)

Headnote: "For the calculation of the six-month period referred to in Art. 55(1) EPC, the 208
relevant date is the date of the actual filing of the European patent application; the date of
priority is not to be taken account of in calculating this period."

As part of the analysis in this decision, the Enlarged Board differentiated the terms 209
"filing of the application" which is the date that the applicant files documents complying
with Art. 80/r.40 and "date of filing" which is the date given to the application after examination under Art. 90(1) and, for instance, determines the term of the patent under Art. 63.

G4/98 – Designation fees

Headnote (1): "Without prejudice to Art. 67(4) EPC, the designation of a Contracting 210
State party to the EPC in a European patent application does not retroactively lose its
legal effect and is not deemed never to have taken place if the relevant designation fee has
not been paid within the applicable time limit."

Headnote (2): "The deemed withdrawal of the designation of a Contracting State pro- 211
vided for in Art. 91(4) EPC takes effect upon expiry of the time limits mentioned in
Art. 79(2), r.15(2), r.25(2) and r.107(1) EPC, as applicable, and not upon expiry of the
period of grace provided for by r.85a EPC." [NB. Art. 91(4) EPC1973 is now r.39(2)
EPC2000, Art. 79(2) EPC1973 is now r.39(1) EPC2000, r.15(2) EPC1973 is now r.17(3)
EPC2000, r.25(2) EPC1973 is now r.36(4) EPC2000, r.107(1) EPC1973 is now r.159(1)

EPC2000 and the grace period of r.85a EPC1973 no longer exists (further processing is available instead.)]

G1/99 – Reformatio in peius/3M

212   Headnote: "In principle, an amended claim, which would put the opponent and sole appellant in a worse situation than if it had not appealed, must be rejected. However, an exception to this principle may be made in order to meet an objection put forward by the opponent/appellant or the Board during the appeal proceedings, in circumstances where the patent as maintained in amended form would otherwise have to be revoked as a direct consequence of an inadmissible amendment held allowable by the Opposition Division in its interlocutory decision. In such circumstances, in order to overcome the deficiency, the patent proprietor/respondent may be allowed to file requests, as follows: (i) in the first place, for an amendment introducing one or more originally disclosed features which limit the scope of the patent as maintained; (ii) if such a limitation is not possible, for an amendment introducing one or more originally disclosed features which extend the scope of the patent as maintained, but within the limits of Art. 123(3) EPC; (iii) finally, if such amendments are not possible, for deletion of the inadmissible amendment but within the limits of Art. 123(3) EPC."

213   This decision considered in more detail the position in Headnote (2) of G9/92 where the opponent is sole appellant and in particular the meaning of "appropriate nor necessary" in relation to amendments. In the view of the Enlarged Board, equity demands that the proprietor should not lose his patent where he has not appealed against a decision taken by the Opposition Division to maintain a patent in a form considered by the Board of Appeal to be invalid, the invalidity only being curable by increasing the scope of protection vis-à-vis the interlocutory decision. In particular, the opponent always has another chance to contest validity at the national level.

G2/99 – Six-month period/DEWERT (consolidated with G3/98)

214   See above under G3/98.

G3/99 – Admissibility of joint opposition or joint appeal/HOWARD FLOREY

215   Headnote (1): "An opposition filed in common by two or more persons, which otherwise meets the requirements of Art. 99 EPC and r.1 and r.55 EPC is admissible on payment of only one opposition fee." (NB. r.1 EPC1973 is now r.3 EPC2000 and r.55 EPC1973 is now r.76(2) EPC2000.)

216   Headnote (2): "If the opposing party consists of a plurality of persons, an appeal must be filed by the common representative under r.100 EPC. Where the appeal is filed by a non-entitled person, the Board of Appeal shall consider it not to be duly signed and consequently invite the common representative to sign it within a given time limit. The non-entitled person who filed the appeal shall be informed of this invitation. If the previous common representative is no longer participating in the proceedings, a new common representative shall be determined pursuant to r.100 EPC." (NB. r.100 EPC1973 is now r.151 EPC2000.)

217   Headnote (3): "In order to safeguard the rights of the patent proprietor and in the interests of procedural efficiency, it has to be clear throughout the procedure who belongs to the group of common opponents or common appellants. If either a common opponent or appellant (including the common representative) intends to withdraw from the proceedings, the EPO shall be notified accordingly by the common representative or by a new common representative determined under r.100(1) EPC in order for the withdrawal to take effect." (NB. r.100 EPC1973 is now r.151 EPC2000.)

The situation where several natural or legal persons file an opposition in common is anticipated by r.151(1) EPC.

G1/02 – Formalities Officers' powers

218   Headnote: "Points 4 and 6 of the Notice from the Vice-President Directorate-General 2 dated 28 April 1999 (OJ, 1999 506) do not conflict with provisions of a higher level."

This decision overruled T295/01, which had suggested that formalities Officers could   219
never decide on the admissibility of an opposition, only the Opposition Division being
competent. A formalities Officer can decide on admissibility where there are no technical
or legal difficulties.

G2/02 – *Priorities from India/ASTRAZENECA (consolidated witth G3/02)*

Headnote: "The TRIPs Agreement does not entitle the applicant for a European patent   220
application to claim priority from a first filing in a State which was not at the relevant date
a member of the Paris Convention but was a member of the WTO/TRIPs Agreement."

The Legal Board of Appeal had referred a question asking whether a Euro-PCT ap-   221
plication which claimed the priority of an earlier application filed in a WTO country not
party to the Paris Convention was entitled to that priority claim in the regional phase. The
priority right should not in principle have been recognised since Art. 87(1) EPC1973 only
referred to Paris Convention countries. The Enlarged Board confirmed that TRIPS was
not applicable to the EPC, Art. 87(1) was determinative, and such a priority claim would
not therefore be recognised. Now, however, under EPC2000, priority rights originating
in non-Paris Convention WTO countries are explicitly recognised by Art. 87(1) EPC.

G3/02 – *Priorities from India/ASTRAZENECA (consolidated witth G2/02)*

See above under G2/02.   222

G1/03 – *Disclaimer/PPG (consolidated with G2/03)*

Headnote (1): "An amendment to a claim by the introduction of a disclaimer may not   223
be refused under Art. 123(2) EPC for the sole reason that neither the disclaimer nor the
subject-matter excluded by it from the scope of the claim have a basis in the application
as filed."

Headnote (2): "The following criteria are to be applied for assessing the allowability of   224
a disclaimer which is not disclosed in the application as filed:
2.1   A disclaimer may be allowable in order to:
      (1) restore novelty by delimiting a claim against state of the art under Article 54(3)
      and (4) EPC; (NB. Article 54(4) EPC1973 has been deleted in EPC2000 but still
      applies to applications filed under EPC1973)
      (2) restore novelty by delimiting a claim against an accidental anticipation under Ar-
      ticle 54(2) EPC; an anticipation is accidental if it is so unrelated to and remote from
      the claimed invention that the person skilled in the art would never have taken it into
      consideration when making the invention; and
      (3) disclaim subject-matter which, under Articles 52 to 57 EPC, is excluded from
      patentability for non-technical reasons.
2.2   A disclaimer should not remove more than is necessary either to restore novelty or
      to disclaim subject-matter excluded from patentability for non-technical reasons.
2.3   A disclaimer which is or becomes relevant for the assessment of inventive step or
      sufficiency of disclosure adds subject-matter contrary to Article 123(2) EPC.
2.4   A claim containing a disclaimer must meet the requirements of clarity and concise-
      ness of Article 84 EPC."

This case concerned the extent to which a disclaimer, having no basis in the application as   225
filed, may be introduced during prosecution in order to distinguish over novelty-destroying prior art. Disclaimers are always allowable when they restore novelty over a 54(3)
document. In the case of an Art. 54(2) document a disclaimer is only allowed where the
anticipation is accidental, i.e. the prior art reference is so remote and unrelated to the
subject matter of the invention that it would never have been taken into account by the
skilled person in making the invention. Disclaimers are also allowable to exclude subject matter which is classed as non-patentable for non-technical, policy-related reasons
(particularly under Art. 53(c), Art. 53(a) and Art. 57 EPC) where the claim covers some
embodiments which fall under the relevant exclusion and some which don't. In all cases,
no more than the novelty-destroying part of the prior art or the non-patentable embodiments may be removed from the claim. The rationale is that, in line with previous case law
(e.g. T170/87, T597/92), a disclaimer cannot make a non-inventive teaching inventive. A

disclaimer may therefore only be used when inventive step is not an issue. How the new definition of "accidental" will be applied in practice is evolving. Many decisions such as T134/01 and T782/03 have taken a very strict view – the prior art must not even be in the same technical field as the claimed invention. The validlty of this decision was confirmed by later decision G1/16 which held that no additional criteria are to be applied in assessing the compliance of an undisclosd disclaimer with Art. 123(2) EPC (i.e. that later decision G2/10 only applies to disclosed disclaimers).

G2/03 – Disclaimer/GENETIC SYSTEMS (consolidated with G1/03)

226   See above under G1/03.

G3/03 – Reimbursement of the appeal fee/HIGHLAND

227   Headnote (1): "In the event of interlocutory revision under Art. 109(1) EPC, the department of the first instance whose decision has been appealed is not competent to refuse a request of the appellant for reimbursement of the appeal fee."

228   Headnote (2): "The board of appeal which would have been competent under Art. 21 EPC to deal with the substantive issues of the appeal if no interlocutory revision had been granted is competent to decide on the request."

229   The first instance division that allows interlocutory revision must therefore decide if they think a request for reimbursement of the appeal fee should be granted. If they decide it is then they have the power to order reimbursement. However, if they think it isn't then they must remit the case to a Board of Appeal who will make the final decision on reimbursement.

G1/04 – Diagnostic methods

230   Headnote (1): "In order that the subject-matter of a claim relating to a diagnostic method practised on the human or animal body falls under the prohibition of Art. 52(4) EPC, the claim is to include the features relating to: (i) the diagnosis for curative purposes stricto sensu representing the deductive medical or veterinary decision phase as a purely intellectual exercise, (ii) the preceding steps which are constitutive for making that diagnosis, and (iii) the specific interactions with the human or animal body which occur when carrying those out among these preceding steps which are of a technical nature." (NB. Art. 52(4) EPC1973 is now Art. 53(c) EPC2000.)

231   Headnote (2): "Whether or not a method is a diagnostic method within the meaning of Article 52(4) EPC may neither depend on the participation of a medical or veterinary practitioner, by being present or by bearing the responsibility, nor on the fact that all method steps can also, or only, be practised by medical or technical support, the patient himself or herself or an automated system. Moreover, no distinction is to be made in this context between essential method steps having diagnostic character and non-essential method steps lacking it." (NB. Art. 52(4) EPC is now Art. 53(c) EPC2000)

232   Headnote (3): "In a diagnostic method under Art. 52(4) EPC, the method steps of a technical nature belonging to the preceding steps which are constitutive for making the diagnosis for curative purposes stricto sensu must satisfy the criterion 'practised on the human or animal body'." (NB. Art. 52(4) EPC is now Art. 53(c) EPC2000)

233   Headnote (4): "Article 52(4) EPC does not require a specific type and intensity of interaction with the human or animal body; a preceding step of a technical nature thus satisfies the criterion 'practised on the human or animal body' if its performance implies any interaction with the human or animal body, necessitating the presence of the latter." (NB. Art. 52(4) EPC1973 is now Art. 53(c) EPC2000)

234   The Enlarged Board has given the diagnostic methods exclusion a narrow interpretation in line with its purpose. The only diagnostic methods excluded are those that include both a data collection step and a step in which a course of therapy is proposed on the basis of that data. Moreover, each of the data collection steps must be practiced on the human or animal body, in the sense that they must require its presence. The case for broadening the exclusion, made in T964/99, was thus rejected and the old status quo, whereby a method of generating interim results for use in diagnosis was regarded as patentable, was re-established.

G2/04 – Transfer of opposition/HOFFMAN-LA ROCHE

Headnote (1): "(a) The status as an opponent cannot be freely transferred. (b) A legal per- 235
son who was a subsidiary of the opponent when the opposition was filed and who carries
on the business to which the opposed patent relates cannot acquire the status as opponent
if all its shares are assigned to another company."

Headnote (2): "If, when filing an appeal, there is a justifiable legal uncertainty as to 236
how the law is to be interpreted in respect of the question of who the correct party to
the proceedings is, it is legitimate that the appeal is filed in the name of the person whom
the person acting considers, according to his interpretation, to be the correct party, and
at the same time, as an auxiliary request, in the name of a different person who might,
according to another possible interpretation, also be considered the correct party to the
proceedings."

This decision confirmed that an opposition cannot be freely assigned but may be trans- 237
ferred as a result of universal succession (e.g. from a deceased opponent to his/her heir
(r.84(2) EPC) or in the takeover of a company, or the relevant assets of a company, by another legal entity (G4/88)). Where, however, company A, which has a legally independent
subsidiary B, files an opposition relating to a business area in which company B operates,
the opposition may not be transferred from A to a company which buys subsidiary B. The
opposition would have been transferable if: (a) it had been filed in the name of subsidiary
company B; or (b) B had not had its own legal status but had merely been a department of
company A. Where a holding company files an opposition on behalf of a legally distinct
subsidiary it is thus safer to file the opposition jointly in both names.

The decision also established that if, when filing an appeal, there is justifiable legal un- 238
certainty as to who the correct party to the proceedings is, it is legitimate for the appeal
to be filed in the name of the person whom the person acting considers to be the correct
party, and at the same time, as an auxiliary request, in the name of a different person who
might, according to another possible interpretation, also be considered the correct party
to the proceedings.

G3/04 – Intervention/EOS

Headnote: "After withdrawal of the sole appeal, the proceedings may not be continued 239
with a third party who intervened during the appeal proceedings."

The Enlarged Board had previously decided that intervention during opposition appeal 240
proceedings was possible (G1/94) but there was some doubt about the intervener's procedural status in this situation. This decision has made it clear that the intervener attains
the status of an opponent under Art. 105(2) EPC and is a party to the appeal proceedings
of right under Art. 107 EPC. The intervener does not, however, have the status of an appellant since he was not adversely affected by the decision taken. No appeal fee therefore
needs to be paid. It also follows, from decision G7/91, that withdrawal of a sole appeal
will terminate the proceedings, the consent of the intervener not being required.

G1/05 – Divisional/ASTROPOWER (consolidated with G1/06)

Headnote: "So far as Article 76(1) EPC is concerned, a divisional application which at its 241
actual date of filing contains subject-matter extending beyond the content of the earlier
application as filed can be amended later in order that its subject-matter no longer so
extends, even at a time when the earlier application is no longer pending. Furthermore,
the same limitations apply to these amendments as to amendments to any other (non-di-
visional) applications."

The Enlarged Board decided that Art. 76(1) is a substantive provision that must be 242
complied with before a divisional application can be granted but not a requirement that
must be met at the filing date. Compliance must therefore be considered by the Examining Division and the applicant must be give a chance to amend where deficiencies exist.
Since a divisional application is a new application which is separate and independent from
the parent, it is irrelevant whether the parent application is pending or not when such
amendments are made. The Enlarged Board also endorsed the principle of the prohibition
of double patenting but emphasised that this prevented the grant of a second patent for
the same subject matter and not the filing of a divisional application with identical claims
to the parent. It was confirmed that a divisional application is either entitled to the filing

date of the parent or it is not entitled to any filing date – there is no other alternative, i.e. it cannot take the date on which it was itself filed.

G1/06 – Sequences of divisionals/SEIKO (consolidated with G1/05)

243   Headnote: "In the case of a sequence of applications consisting of a root (originating) application followed by divisional applications, each divided from its predecessor, it is a necessary and sufficient condition for a divisional application of that sequence to comply with Article 76(1), second sentence, EPC that anything disclosed in that divisional application be directly and unambiguously derivable from what is disclosed in each of the preceding applications as filed."

244   The Enlarged Board found nothing in the EPC to prevent one divisional application being divided from another. A sequence of divisional applications is therefore possible. However, the operation of Art. 76(1) EPC ensures that the filing date of the original application can only be recognised if the subject matter of a member of the sequence was disclosed in every preceding member of the sequence without being abandoned at any point. Subject matter which is omitted at some point in the sequence cannot be later added back and new subject matter which is introduced at some point cannot be maintained further down the sequence. No other requirements, however, exist – it does not matter whether previous members of the sequence did not comply with Art. 76(1) or whether they were refused or withdrawn.

G2/06 – Stem Cells/WARF

245   Headnote (1): "Rule 28(c) EPC (formerly Rule 23d(c) EPC) applies to all pending applications, including those filed before the entry into force of the rule."

246   Headnote (2): "Rule 28(c) EPC (formerly Rule 23d(c) EPC) forbids the patenting of claims directed to product which – as described in the application – at the filing date could be prepared exclusively by a method which necessarily involved the destruction of the human embryos from which the said products are derived, even if the said method is not part of the claims."

247   Headnote (3): "In the context of the answer to question 2 it is not of relevance that after the filing date the same products could be obtained without having to recur to a method necessarily involving the destruction of human embryos."

248   The Enlarged Board confirmed in this decision that r.28(c) (and, by extension of the reasoning used, r.28 in general) applies to all European patent applications, including those filed before its entry into force. The Enlarged Board further decided that where the claims of a European patent application relate to a new product which, at the filing date of the patent application, could only be obtained by destroying human embryos, the application contravenes r.28(c) and must be refused. This is the case even where advances in technology mean that the claimed product can be obtained without destroying human embryos at a later date. The Enlarged Board held that the question to be considered was not whether the claims themselves included the destruction of human embryos as a technical feature but whether practicing the invention defined by the claims would inevitably involve such destruction. The Enlarged Board also refused to make a referral to the ECJ since such a referral is not contemplated under the EPC and the ECJ has no role to play in interpreting the EPC.

G1/07 – Method for treatment by surgery/Medi-Physics Inc

249   Headnote (1): "A claimed imaging method, in which, when carried out, maintaining the life and health of the subject is important and which comprises or encompasses an invasive step representing a substantial physical intervention on the body which requires professional medical expertise to be carried out and which entails a substantial health risk even when carried out with the required professional care and expertise, is excluded from patentability as a method for treatment of the human or animal body by surgery pursuant to Art. 53(c) EPC."

250   Headnote (2a): "A claim which comprises a step encompassing an embodiment which is a 'method for treatment of the human or animal body by surgery' within the meaning of Art. 53(c) EPC cannot be left to encompass that embodiment."

Headnote (2b): "The exclusion from patentability under Art. 53(c) EPC can be avoided   251
by disclaiming the embodiment, it being understood that in order to be patentable the
claim including the disclaimer must fulfil all the requirements of the EPC and, where
applicable, the requirements for a disclaimer to be allowable as defined in decision G1/03
and G2/03 of the Enlarged Board of Appeal."

Headnote (2c): "Whether or not the wording of the claim can be amended so as to omit   252
the surgical step without offending against the EPC must be assessed on the basis of the
overall circumstances of the individual case under consideration."

Headnote (3): "A claimed imaging method is not to be considered as being a 'treatment   253
of the human or animal body by surgery' within the meaning of Art. 53(c) EPC merely
because during a surgical intervention the data obtained by the use of the method immediately allow a surgeon to decide on the course of action to be taken during a surgical
intervention."

The Enlarged Board found that surgery is not defined by the purpose of the treatment   254
but by the nature of the treatment so that the exclusion covers surgical methods that are
for non-therapeutic purposes such as for cosmetic purposes. Any method incorporating
even one surgical step is excluded from patentability. However, the concept of 'surgery'
is to be given a narrow meaning which is consistent with the purpose of the exclusion: it
does not cover interventions which are minor and involve no substantial health risks and
no professional medical skills.

G2/07 – *Essentially biological processes/Plant Bioscience Limited (consolidated with G1/08)*

Headnote (1): "A non-microbiological process for the production of plants which con-   255
tains or consists of the steps of sexually crossing the whole genomes of plants and of subsequently selecting plants is in principle excluded from patentability as being 'essentially
biological' within the meaning of Art. 53(b) EPC."

Headnote (2): "Such a process does not escape the exclusion of Art. 53(b) merely be-   256
cause it contains, as a further step or as part of any of the steps of crossing and selection, a
step of a technical nature which serves to enable or assist the performance of the steps of
sexually crossing the whole genomes of plants or of subsequently selecting plants."

Headnote (3): "If, however, such a process contains within the steps of sexually cross-   257
ing and selecting an additional step of a technical nature, which step by itself introduces a
trait into the genome or modifies a trait in the genome of the plant produced, so that the
introduction or modification of that trait is not the result of the mixing of the genes of
the plants chosen for sexual crossing, then the process is not excluded from patentability
under Art. 53(b) EPC."

Headnote (4): "In the context of examining whether such a process is excluded from   258
patentability as being 'essentially biological' within the meaning of Art. 53(b) EPC, it is
not relevant whether a step of a technical nature is a new or known measure, whether it is
trivial or a fundamental alteration of a known process, whether it does or could occur in
nature or whether the essence of the invention lies in it."

The Enlarged Board of Appeal decided that the definition of r.26(5) EPC was some-   259
what self-contradictory since crossing and selection are not actually natural phenomena
in the sense that they occur without human intervention. A consideration of the legislative
history of this provision was also unhelpful. So, on the basis of Art. 53(b) and its legislative history alone, the Enlarged Board established the principle, largely in agreement with
the previous case law, that a process is not essentially biological if it involves a technical
step which directly changes the DNA content of a plant rather than relying on crossing
and selection to make such a change. Such a technical effect does not have to fulfil any
further criteria, e.g. it is irrelevant whether it is a new or known step.

G1/08 – *Essentially biological processes/State of Israel (consolidated with G2/07)*

Identical headnote and reasoning to G2/07.   260

G2/08 – Dosage Regimen/Abbott Respiratory LLC

261   Headnote (1): Where it is already known to use a medicament to treat an illness, Art. 54(5) EPC does not exclude that this medicament be patented for use in a different treatment by therapy of the same illness.

262   Headnote (2): Such patenting is also not excluded where a dosage regime is the only feature claimed which is not comprised in the state of the art.

263   Headnote (3): Where the subject matter of a claim is rendered novel only by a new therapeutic use of a medicament, such claim may no longer have the format of a so-called Swiss-style claim as instituted by G 5/83. A time limit of three months after publication of the present decision in the OJ of the EPO is set in order that future applicants comply with this new situation.

264   This decision validated earlier case law that had allowed second medical use claims where the same disease was being treated in a different way, e.g. by treating of a different population of animals (T19/86, T233/96), by utilising a different route of administration (T51/93) or by using a different dosage regimen (T1020/03). Decision G2/08 was published in the OJ on 28 October 2010 (see Notice from the EPO dated 20 September 2010, [2010] O.J. 514). Swiss style claims are therefore no longer acceptable in applications with a priority date (or filing date if no priority is claimed) of 29 January 2011 or later (more than three months after the publication of G2/08 in the OJ – see point 7.1.4 of the decision).

G3/08 – Patentability of programs for computers

265   Headnote: "The referral of 22 October 2008 of points of law to the Enlarged Board of Appeal by the President of the EPO is inadmissible under Article 112(1)(b) EPC."

266   The Enlarged Board declined to answer questions referred by the President of the EPO on the basis that the decisions cited as conflicting were, in fact, a legitimate development of the case law in a fast-evolving technical field.

G4/08 – Langue de la procedure/MERIAL

267   Headnote (1): "If an international patent application has been filed and published under the PCT in one official language of the EPO, it is not possible, on entry into the European phase, to file a translation of the application into one of the other two EPO official languages."

268   Headnote (2): "In written proceedings on a European patent application or on an international application in the regional phase, EPO departments cannot use an EPO official language other than the language of the proceedings used for the application pursuant to Article 14(3) EPC."

269   In this case a Euro-PCT application in the French language was to be prosecuted in the regional phase by an English-speaking European patent attorney who filed a translation into English when entering the regional phase. It was confirmed in the decision that the language of the proceedings cannot be changed in this way when the Euro-PCT is filed in an official language of the EPO and that the EPO must use the language of the proceedings in communicating with the applicant in writing.

G1/09 – Pending application/SONY Deutschland GmBH

270   Headnote: "In the case where no appeal is filed, a European patent application which has been refused by a decision of the Examining Division is thereafter pending within the meaning of r.25 EPC1973 (now r.36(1) EPC2000) until the expiry of the time limit for filing a notice of appeal."

271   When an application is refused, in written or oral proceedings, a divisional application may therefore validly be filed within two months of the notification of the decision, whether an appeal is filed or not. The Enlarged Board, in their reasoning, interpreted 'pending (earlier) European patent application' in the specific context of r.25 EPC1973 (now r.36(1) EPC2000) to mean an application in respect of which substantive rights are still in existence. They further established that in the case of a refusal, such substantive rights continue to exist while an appeal is possible and only terminate when the decision to refuse becomes final on expiry of the appeal period. A distinction is to be made

between whether proceedings are pending, on the one hand, and whether the application is pending on the other.

G1/10 – *Request to correct patent/FISHER-ROSEMOUNT*

Headnote (1): "Since Rule 140 EPC is not available to correct the text of a patent, a patent 272
proprietor's request for such a correction is inadmissible whenever made, including after the initiation of opposition proceedings."

The Enlarged Board decided that although the text of a patent (description, claims 273
and drawings) is an integral part of the decision to grant, it cannot be corrected under r.140 EPC once the decision has been taken since this would prejudice legal certainty for third parties. It is therefore important for applicants to thoroughly check the text proposed for grant according to r.71(3) EPC and to correct any obvious mistakes under r.139 EPC before grant.

G2/10 – *Disclaimer/SCRIPS Research Institute*

Headnote (1): "An amendment to a claim by the introduction of a disclaimer disclaiming 274
from it subject matter disclosed in the application as filed infringes Art. 123(2) EPC if the subject-matter remaining in the claim after the introduction of the disclaimer is not, be it explicitly or implicitly, directly and unambiguously disclosed to the skilled person using common general knowledge, in the application as filed."

Headnote (2): "Determining whether or not that is the case requires a technical assess- 275
ment of the overall technical circumstances of the individual case under consideration, taking into account the nature and extent of the disclosure in the application as filed, the nature and extent of the disclaimed subject matter and its relationship with the subject-matter remaining in the claim after amendment."

The Enlarged Board of Appeal refused to lay down any general rules by which it could 276
be decided whether the disclaiming of a positive embodiment of the invention amounts to added subject matter or not. It rejected the validly of the general proposition that if an application discloses a general teaching and a specific embodiment, the general subject matter minus the specific embodiment is inevitably disclosed. It also rejected the proposition that the disclaimer of a positive embodiment always adds subject matter. Instead, it is to be considered whether the remaining subject matter of the claim was directly and unambiguously disclosed in the application as filed, which will depend on the facts of the case. Later decision G1/16 confirmed that this decision only applies to disclosed disclaimers and that the compliance of undisclosed disclaimers with Art. 123(2) EPC should continue to be assessed using the criteria established by G1/03.

G1/11 – *Jurisdiction of the Board of Appeal/Bauer*

Headnote: "For the examination of an appeal against a decision of the Examining Division 277
to not refund search fees under Rule 64(2) EPC, which has not been adopted together with a decision on the grant of a European patent or the refusal of a European patent application, a Technical Board of Appeal is competent."

According to Art. 21(3) EPC, decisions of the Examining Division taken in grant pro- 278
ceedings are reviewed by a technical Board of Appeal where the decision concerns the refusal of a European patent application or grant of a European patent and by a legal Board of Appeal in all other cases. A decision solely concerned with whether additional search fees should be refunded under r.64(2) EPC is not concerned with grant or refusal of the application but involves a highly technical assessment relating to unity of invention. The Enlarged Board found that Art. 21(3) did not deal specifically with the allocation of appeals resulting from decisions under r.64(2) EPC, creating a legal loophole, which was to be filled by reference to the legislative intent: boards of appeal should have the requisite skills to deal with the relevant issues without involving external experts so that a technical board of appeal was required where a technical assessment was necessary.

G1/12 – *Identity of the appellant/Zenon Technology Partnership*

Headnote (1): "The answer to reformulated question (1) – namely whether when a notice 279
of appeal, in compliance with Rule 99(1)(a) EPC, contains the name and address of the

appellant as provided in Rule 41(2)(c) EPC and it is alleged that the identification is wrong due to an error, the true intention having been to file on behalf of the legal person which should have filed the appeal, is it possible to correct this error under Rule 101(2) EPC by a request for substitution by the name of the true appellant – is yes, provided the requirements of Rule 101(1) EPC have been met."

280   Headnote (2): "Proceedings before the EPO are conducted in accordance with the principle of free evaluation of evidence. This also applies to the problems under consideration in the present referral."

281   Headnote (3): "In cases of an error in the appellant's name, the general procedure for correcting errors under Rule 139, first sentence, EPC is available under the conditions established by the case law of the boards of appeal."

282   The Enlarged Board decided that the key point was establishing the true intention of the appellant and, quoting from T97/98, held that a deficiency in the name of the appellant can be corrected if "its correction does not reflect a later change of mind as to whom the appellant should be but on the contrary only expresses what was intended when filing the appeal".

G2/12 – *Tomatoes II/State of Israel (consolidated with G2/13)*

283   Headnote (1): "The exclusion of essentially biological processes for the production of plants in Article 53(b) EPC does not have a negative effect on the allowability of a product claim directed to plants or plant material such as a fruit."

284   Headnote (2): "In particular, the fact that the only method available at the filing date for generating the claimed subject-matter is an essentially biological process for the production of plants disclosed in the patent application does not render a claim directed to plants or plant material other than a plant variety unallowable."

285   Headnote (3): "In the circumstances, it is of no relevance that the protection conferred by the product claim encompasses the generation of the claimed product by means of an essentially biological process for the production of plants excluded as such under Article 53(b) EPC."

286   According to the Enlarged Board, the exception to patentability of Art. 53(b), relating to a process for preparing plants, applies only to process claims and cannot have any effect on the patentability of a product claim to a plant per se. However, this decision only applies to applications filed before 01 July 2017 as a result of changes to r.28(2) EPC coming into force on that date and later decision G3/19.

G2/13 – *Broccoli II/Plant Bioscience Limited (consolidated with G2/12)*

287   Headnote (1): "The exclusion of essentially biological processes for the production of plants in Article 53(b) EPC does not have a negative effect on the allowability of a product claim directed to plants or plant material such as plant parts."

288   Headnote (2a): "The fact that the process features of a product-by-process claim directed to plants or plant material other than a plant variety define an essentially biological process for the production or plants does not render the claim unallowable."

289   Headnote (2b): "The fact that the only method available at the filing date for generating the claimed subject-matter is an essentially biological process for the production of plants disclosed in the patent application does not render a claim directed to plants or plant material other than a plant variety unallowable."

290   Headnote (3): "In the circumstances, it is of no relevance that the protection conferred by the product claim encompasses the generation of the claimed product by means of an essentially biological process for the production of plants excluded as such under Article 53(b) EPC."

291   This decision only applies to applications filed before 01 July 2017 as a result of changes to r.28(2) EPC coming into force on that date and later decision G3/19.

G1/13 – *Party status/Sasol Technology*

292   Headnote (1): "Where an opposition is filed by a company which subsequently, under the relevant national law governing the company, for all purposes ceases to exist, but that company is subsequently restored to existence under a provision of that governing

national law, by virtue of which the company is deemed to have continued in existence as if it had not ceased to exist, all these events taking place before a decision of the Opposition Division maintaining the opposed patent in amended form becomes final, the European Patent Office must recognise the retroactive effect of that provision of national law and allow the opposition proceedings to be continued by the restored company."

Headnote (2): "Where, in the factual circumstances underlying Question 1, a valid appeal is filed in due time in the name of the non-existent opponent company against the decision maintaining the European patent in amended form, and the restoration of the company to existence, with retroactive effect as described in Question 1, takes place after the expiry of the time limit for filing the notice of appeal under Article 108 EPC, the Board of Appeal must treat the appeal as admissible."   293

The Enlarged Board of Appeal considered that so far as the EPC is concerned, the existence and non-existence of legal entities is exclusively a matter of national law.   294

G1/14 – *Appeal inadmissible or deemed not filed/Tenneco*

The following question was referred to the Enlarged Board following the late-filing of an appeal (case T1553/13): "Is an appeal inadmissible or deemed not to have been filed if the appeal is filed and the appeal fee is paid after expiry of the appeal period under Art. 108(1) EPC?"   295

The Enlarged Board of Appeal found that the referral was inadmissible. It was not necessary to answer the referred question since in case T1553/13 the appeal was not in fact filed out of time. This was due to the fact that the appealed decision had been sent by the courier service UPS rather than by registered mail and was not therefore properly notified in accordance with the text of r.126(1) in force at the time (hence German law applied to determine the date of notification under r.126(4) EPC).   296

Referral G2/14, concerning the same point of law, was concolidated with G1/14 but the underlying European patent application was deemed withdrawn and hence the appeal procedure and the referral were terminated without a decision. However, this point of law was final addressed and answered in G1/18.   297

G3/14 – *Examination of clarity objections/Freedom Innovations*

Headnote: "In considering whether, for the purposes of Article 101(3) EPC, a patent as amended meets the requirements of the EPC, the claims of the patent may be examined for compliance with the requirements of Article 84 EPC only when, and then only to the extent that the amendment introduces non-compliance with Article 84."   298

The Enlarged Board settled the divergence in the case law by deciding that the established jurisprudence should prevail over more recent decisions such as T1459/05. Since lack of clarity is not a ground of opposition, the examination of clarity in opposition proceedings is strictly limited to a lack of clarity arising directly from an amendment made during the opposition proceedings. The simple combination of an independent claim and one of its dependent claims cannot introduce a lack of clarity if both claims were present in the patent as granted.   299

G1/15 – *Partial priority/Infineum*

Headnote: "Under the EPC, entitlement to partial priority may not be refused for a claim encompassing alternative subject matter by virtue of one or more generic expressions or otherwise (generic 'OR'-claim) provided that said alternative subject-matter has been disclosed for the first time, directly, or at least implicitly, unambiguously and in an enabling manner in the priority document. No other substantive conditions or limitations apply in this respect."   300

The Enlarged Board found that in the case of a claim that generically covers a number of different embodiments, partial priority must always be recognised for those embodiments that are disclosed in an earlier application from which priority is claimed. This is the case regardless of whether the alternatives are explicitly stated in the claim or not and regardless of the number of alternatives present. Thus, the patentability of any subject matter falling within the scope of a claim which was disclosed in the priority application is to be   301 judged at the priority date. In this way the problem of so-called "poisonous priority" is avoided.

G1/16 – Disclaimer/OLED

302   Headnote: "For the purposes of considering whether a claim amended by the introduction of an undisclosed disclaimer is allowable under Art. 123(2) EPC, the disclaimer must fulfil one of the criteria set out in point 2.1 of the order of decision G1/03. The introduction of such a disclaimer may not provide a technical contribution to the subject-matter disclosed in the application as filed. In particular, it may not be or become relevant for the assessment of inventive step or for the question of sufficiency of disclosure. The disclaimer may not remove more than necessary either to restore novelty or to disclaim subject-matter excluded from patentability for non-technical reasons."

303   The Enlarged Board decided that the compliance of undisclosed disclaimers with Art. 123(2) EPC should continue to be examined solely according to the criteria established by decision G1/03 and that G2/10 applies only to disclosed disclaimers.

G1/18 – Filing an appeal

304   Headnote (1): "An appeal is deemed not to have been filed in the following cases:
   (a)   where notice of appeal was filed within the two-month time limit prescribed in Art. 108, first sentence, EPC and the appeal fee was paid after expiry of that two-month time limit;
   (b)   where notice of appeal was filed after expiry of the two-month time limit presecribed in Art. 108, first sentence, EPC and the appeal fee was paid after expiry of that two-month time limit;
   (c)   where the appeal fee was paid within the two-month time limit prescribed in Art. 108, first sentence, EPC, for filing notice of appeal and notice of appeal was filed after expiry of that two-month time limit."

305   Headnote (2): "In the cases referred to in answers 1(a) to (c), reimbursement of the appeal fee is to be ordered ex officio."

306   Headnote (3): "Where the appeal fee was paid within or after the two-month time limit prescribed in Art. 108, first sentence, EPC for filing notice of appeal and no notice of appeal was filed at all, the appeal fee is to be reimbursed."

307   Following the failure of referrals G2/14 (no decision necessary since applicaton deemed to be withdrawn) and G1/14 (referral inadmissible), the President of the EPO used his powers under Art. 112(1)(b) EPC to refer the relevant point of law to the Enlarged Board. The decision reached by the Enlarged Board is self-explanatory – in line with the literal wording of the first sentence of Art. 108, unless a notice of appeal is filed within the two month appeal period and the appeal fee is also paid within this period there is no appeal in existence and the appeal fee, if paid, must be refunded.

G1/19 – Pedestrian simulation/Bentley Systems (UK) Limited

308   Headnote (1): "A computer-implemented simulation of a technical system or process that is claimed as such can, for the purpose of assessing inventive step, solve a technical problem by producing a technical effect going beyond the simulation's implementation on a computer."

309   Headnote (2): "For that assessment it is not a sufficient condition that the simulation is based, in whole or in part, on technical principles underlying the simulated system or process."

310   Headnote (3): "The answers to the first and second questions are no different if the computer-implemented simulation is claimed as part of a design process, in particular for verifying a design."

311   The Enlarged Board decided that inventions involving a computer simulation should be assessed under Art. 56 in the same way as any other computer-implemented invention according to the Comvick approach, i.e. only features contributing to the technical character of the invention are considered in deriving the objective technical problem which has been solved.

G2/19 – Right to be heard and correct venue

Headnote (1): "A third party within the meaning of Art. 115 EPC who files an appeal   312
against a decision to grant a European patent does not have the right to have its request for
the reopening of grant proceedings, on the basis that the claims lack clarity (Art. 84 EPC),
heard orally before a Board of Appeal. Such an appeal does not have suspensive effect."

Headnote (2): "The holding of oral proceedings before the Boards of Appeal in Haar is   313
not contrary to Art. 113(1) and Art. 116(1) EPC."

The Enlarged Board considered firstly that the claims of a granted patent may not be   314
attacked on the basis they lack clarity (G3/14) and secondly that a third party is not a
party to grant proceedings and has no right of appeal. Such an appeal is therefore inevitably inadmissible and can be dismissed without holding oral proceedings.

G3/19 – Pepper (follow-up to "Tomatoes II" and "Broccoli II")

Headnote: "Taking into account developments after decisions G2/12 and G2/13 of the   315
Enlarged Board of Appeal, the exception to patentability of essentially biological processes for the production of plants or animals in Art. 53(b) EPC has a negative effect
on the allowability of product claims and product-by-process claims directed to plants,
plant material or animals, if the claimed product is exclusively obtained by means of an
essentially biological process or if the claimed process features define an essentially biological process. This negative effect does not apply to European patents granted before 01 July 2017 and European patent applications which were filed before that date and
are still pending."

The Enlarged Board decided for a dynamic interpretation of Art. 53(b) according to   316
which changes to the implementing regulations can result in this article being applied in
a different manner if the new interpretation is consistent with the meaning of the article.
Decisions G2/12 and G2/13 had decided that Art. 53(b) should be interpreted in such a
way that claims to plants per se are patentable even if the only way of making them is
using an essentially biological process. As a result, new r.28(2) was introduced by the
Administrative Council, coming into force on 01 July 2017, specifically excluding such
inventions from patentability. Decision G3/19 decided that this new rule validly changed
the meaning of Art. 53(b) as of 01 July 2017 but has no effect on the validity of applications filed before this date and patents granted in respect of such applications.

G4/19 – Double patenting/Societe des Produits Nestle S.A.

Headnote (1): "A European patent application can be refused under Art. 97(2) and   317
Art. 125 EPC if it claims the same subject-matter as a European patent which has been
granted to the same applicant and does not form part of the state of the art pursuant to
Art. 54(2) and (3) EPC."

Headnote (2): "The application can be refused on that legal basis, irrespective of wheth-   318
er it a) was filed on the same date as, or b) is an earlier application or a divisional application (Art. 76(1) EPC) in respect of, or c) claims the same priority (Art. 88 EPC) as the
European patent application leading to the European patent already granted."

In this decision, the Enlarged Board confirms the obiter remarks in G1/05 that double   319
patenting is in principle prohibited under the EPC. The discussion does not deal with the
effect of the prohibition in post-grant proceedings and assumes that the applicant is the
same, the subject matter is the same and there are overlapping designations. The Enlarged
Board finds that Art. 125 EPC provides a legal basis for the prohibition of double patenting since it covers procedural provisions which also involve a substantive examination.
It finds that the travaux preparatoires support the view that the legislator intended to
prohibit double patenting under Art. 125 EPC. The Enlarged Board finds that double patenting always applies whenever a second application claims subject matter already granted
to the same applicant, said subject matter having the same effective date in both cases. It
does not therefore matter whether the second application has the same filing date as the
granted patent or not, overruling T1423/07.

G1/21 – Oral proceedings by videoconference/Andrew AG

320   Headnote: "During a general emergency impairing the parties' possibilities to attend in-person oral proceedings at the EPO premises, the conduct of oral proceedings before the boards of appeal in the form of a videoconference is compatible with the EPC even if not all of the parties to the proceedings have given their consent to the conduct of oral proceedings in the form of a videoconference."

321   In answering the question posed, the Enlarged Board restricted itself to considering oral proceedings before the Boards of Appeal in the context of a pandemic infectious disease. It found that the holding of oral proceedings by videoconference was compatible with the EPC but that such proceedings were not as satisfactory as an in-person hearing. As a result, oral proceedings by videoconference should only be imposed on a party who prefers an in-person hearing if there are good reasons for doing so – an in-person hearing should be the default option.

G2/21 – Plausibility/Sumitomo

Headnote (1): "Evidence submitted by a patent applicant or proprietor to prove a technical effect relied upon for acknowledgement of inventive step of the claimed subject-matter may not be disregarded solely on the ground that such evidence, on which the effect rests, had not been public before the filing date of the patent in suit and was filed after that date." Headnote (2): "A patent applicant or proprietor may rely upon a technical effect for inventive step if the skilled person, having the common general knowledge in mind, and based on the application as originally filed, would derive said effect as being encompassed by the technical teaching and embodied by the same originally disclosed."

The Enlarged Board found that:

(1) There are no exceptions to the principle of free evaluation of evidence but this does not necessarily mean that a technical effect may be relied by on an applicant or proprietor if the only evidence for it rests on post-published data.

(2) The important question underlying all the conflicting case law is whether the skilled person could have derived the technical effect relied on from the technical teaching of the application documents.

(3) A lack of sufficiency exists for a second medical use invention if there is no proof of the therapeutic effect in the application and this cannot be remedied with post-published evidence – but this principle does not apply to the determination of inventive step.

(4) A technical effect may therefore be relied on if it is "encompassed" by the technical teaching of the application, "embodies" the same invention and does not change the "nature" of the invention. In this case post-published data may be used to prove the technical effect occurs.

(5) These rules are rather abstract but this is inevitable in establishing a general principle that applies a cross a number of different technical fields.

1.7   Miscellaneous points of interest

322   Of course, it is not possible in a book of this size to cover, in depth, all the interesting provisions of the EPC and PCT and the unusual scenarios that may arise in their application. The following sections are therefore no more than a miscellaneous bundle of matters that are topical, or have been observed to be particularly popular subject matter for the EQE or are particularly difficult for many candidates to grasp.

1.7.1   *Divisional applications*

323   The issues surrounding when, where and how to file a divisional application have now been considerably simplified by the abolition of the time limits that applied until April 2014. However, several topics of interest remain.

324   According to Art. 76(1) and r.36(1) EPC, a divisional application may only be filed if the parent application on which it is based is pending. A regular European patent application is pending from the day on which it is filed, if a filing date can be accorded. If a filing date cannot be accorded then the application is not dealt with as a European patent application and, in effect, never existed (Art. 90(2) EPC). In the case of a Euro-PCT application, although the application is equivalent to a European patent application from its

date of filing (Art. 11(4) PCT), it can only be considered to be pending within the meaning of r.36(1) EPC when it has entered the regional phase and is subject to processing by the EPO (J18/09).

A European patent application ceases to be pending when it is granted, refused, with- 325 drawn or deemed withdrawn. When it is granted, an application ceases to be pending for the purposes of r.36(1) on the day on which the grant takes effect, i.e. the day on which the mention of grant is published in the European Patent Bulletin under Art. 97(3) EPC. A divisional application may be filed up until the day before the publication of the mention of grant according to J7/04 which confirmed the interpretation previously established by the Guidelines (A-IV, 1.1.1). A divisional filed on the day on which the mention of grant is published is too late and the EPO will issue a loss of rights communication pursuant to r.112(1) EPC stating that the proposed divisional cannot be treated as such.

Since the requirement for the parent application to be pending is a condition which 326 must be met and does not represent a time limit to be complied with, none of the saving measures of EPC relating to time limits may be employed if the divisional is filed on or after the date on which the grant takes effect. Neither re-establishment nor the r.133 EPC procedure for excusing the late filing of a document may be employed, as confirmed by J18/04. Whilst it is possible to appeal a decision to grant, the suspensive effect of the appeal (Art. 106(1) EPC) does not have the effect of making the patent a pending application again according to J28/03. This decision established that a divisional would only be possible if the appeal were successful and the decision to grant was set aside. There is therefore no effective remedy if a divisional application is filed after the grant of the parent has taken effect. It would be possible, of course, to request a decision under r.112(2) EPC in response to the loss of rights communication and file an appeal in order to have a Board of Appeal review the correctness of the Receiving Section's determination that the parent was already granted but the appeal will not, once again, have the effect of making a divisional application possible unless the Receiving Section has made a factual mistake, the suspensive effect in this case only applying to the decision on the loss of rights and not the decision to grant.

In the case of a decision to refuse an application, the decision takes effect as soon as it 327 is announced, in the case of oral proceedings, or when it is notified, in the case of written proceedings (G12/91). When announced in oral proceedings, the decision is subsequently notified in writing (r.111(1) EPC). In either case, the decision may be challenged, by filing an appeal, within two months of notification of the decision in writing (Art. 108 EPC, T390/86). For the purposes of r.36(1), the application ceases to be pending, surprisingly, not when the decision to refuse takes effect but when the period for filing an appeal has expired (G1/09). Thus, in the case of refusal, if it is too late to file an appeal then it is too late to file a divisional application. If an appeal is filed in time (by filing a notice of appeal and paying the appeal fee) then the suspensive effect of the appeal (Art. 106(1) EPC) means that the application remains pending and can be divided for as long as the appeal proceedings are pending (as confirmed by J28/03). If grounds of appeal are validly filed then appeal proceedings are pending until a decision to reject the appeal or that the appeal is inadmissible takes effect or the appeal is withdrawn. However, according to J23/13, applying the principles of G1/09, if no grounds of appeal are filed then the application ceases to be pending for the purposes of r.36(1) EPC at the end of the four month period of Art. 108 for filing grounds of appeal. Note that according to the logic of decision T517/97, appeal proceedings cease immediately on receipt of a letter withdrawing the appeal and a divisional application filed later on the same day would already be too late. If the appeal is allowed and first instance proceedings are resumed then a divisional remains possible. Since an appeal fee is refunded if the appeal is withdrawn before filing of the statement of grounds of appeal and before the period for filing that statement has expired (r.103(1) EPC), it is possible to extend the period in which a divisional can be filed following a refusal by up to four months from the notification of the decision at no extra cost. Note that if a decision of a Board of Appeal is challenged by a petition for review, this does NOT have the effect of suspending the decision of the Board of Appeal (Art. 112a(3) EPC) and an application cannot become pending again in this way unless appeal proceedings are re-opened.

The withdrawal of an application by the applicant takes effect as soon as it is received 328 by the EPO or announced in oral proceedings and cannot be retracted unless it was filed by mistake and can be corrected under r.139 EPC before the public becomes aware of it. A soon as the withdrawal of the application takes effect the application ceases to be pending and a divisional application is no longer possible. According to Guidelines A-IV, 1.1.1, a divisional can be filed on or before the day on which the notice of withdrawal is received.

329   Deemed withdrawal of an application occurs by operation of law when the applicant does not meet a time limit for carrying out some act at the EPO (e.g. paying a fee or filing a document). The attendant loss of rights is subsequently notified to the applicant under r.112(1) EPC. The application ceases to be pending for the purposes of r.36(1) EPC at the moment of deemed withdrawal (J4/11). Thus, when the relevant act can no longer be validly carried out, a divisional application is no longer possible. The loss of rights may be reversed by applying either further processing or re-establishment, as the case may be. In either case, if the remedy is successful then the legal consequences of the failure to observe the time limit shall be deemed not to have ensued, the application will be pending once more and a divisional application can again be filed. The applicant can also ask for a decision on the loss of rights under r.112(2) and have that decision reviewed by filing an appeal. In this case, the suspensive effect of the appeal does **not** mean that the application is pending again – the appeal suspends the effect of the decision taken under r.112(2) EPC but does not in any way affect the deemed withdrawal that took effect at an earlier date. Only if the EPO has got the facts wrong and the appeal is allowed will the application be pending once more.

330   New language provisions were introduced applying to divisional applications filed on or after 01 April 2010. Before this date, a divisional had to be filed in the language of the proceedings for the earlier application on which it was based, without exception. Under the new r.36(2) EPC, an applicant who has filed an application in a language other than English, French or German can also file a divisional in that language prior to filing a translation into the language of proceedings for the earlier application within two months. The use of the correct language is essential for the divisional application to be recognised as such. According to J3/14, a divisional application filed in a language not accepted under r.36(2) EPC is not treated as a divisonal application (or as any kind of European patent application) by analogous application of Art. 90(2) EPC and there is no remedy available other than to re-file the divisional application in an admissible language if the parent application is still pending.

331   Apart from being filed at the right time and in the right language, a divisional application must be filed by the right person or persons. The substantive rights in a European patent application belong to the inventor or his successor in title (Art. 60(1) EPC) and, as far as the EPO is concerned, the applicant is entitled to exercise these rights (Art. 60(3) EPC). A joint application in the name of two or more natural or legal entities is possible (Art. 58 and 59 EPC). The applicant is named in the request (Art. 78(1) and r.41(1)(c) EPC) and recorded in the European patent register (Art. 127 and r.143(f) EPC). Since a divisional relates to part of the subject matter disclosed in the parent, it is the **registered applicant** for the parent who owns the rights to that subject matter and is entitled to file a divisional. A divisional application must therefore be filed by the applicant or applicants that are named on the EPO register in respect of the parent from which it is divided. If it is filed in the name of a different applicant, or in the case of joint applicants, in the names of some but not all the applicants, it is not validly filed (J2/01). If a European patent application has been assigned from registered applicant A to new owner B, this change of applicant must therefore be registered at the EPO before a divisional application is filed in the name of B. The only exception is in the case of universal succession of rights (T15/01, T425/05). In such cases, the change of ownership is immediately effective vis-à-vis the EPO without any formal registration of the change since the previous applicant ceases to exist. Thus, if applicant A dies, a divisional may be filed in the name of his heir B even before a change of applicant has been registered. The same applies where a legal entity is the applicant and ceases to exist through take-over by a second legal entity.

332   A divisional application is associated with two different filing dates. Firstly, there is the date on which the documents making up the divisional application comply with Art. 80 and r.40(1) EPC, what might be called the "actual" filing date. This date is important since it is used to calculate whether the divisional has met the pendency requirement of r.36(1) EPC. It is also important for establishing which text of the EPC applies to the divisional application – an actual filing date of 13 December 2007 or later, for example, means that

EPC2000 applies to the divisional application in full. If a divisional application does not comply with the pendency requirement of r.36(1) EPC then it cannot be considered to be a divisional application. Neither can it be considered to be a regular European patent application (see G1/05, point 11.1 of the Reasons). A loss of rights communication is sent pursuant to r.112(1) EPC indicating that the documents filed cannot be treated as a divisional application.

However, the divisional application is also entitled to another filing date if certain requirements are met. If the content of the divisional does not extend beyond the content of the parent application it is divided from then, according to Art. 76(1) EPC, the divisional application is deemed to have been filed on the filing date of the parent application and to benefit from any right to priority that the parent application is entitled to (so long as the right to priority is still valid on the "actual" filing date of the divisional). This date, which might be called the "deemed" filing date, is important for all other purposes, including, for example, the assessment of the state of the art under Art. 54(2) EPC, the calculation of renewal fee due dates and the calculation of the patent term under Art. 63(1) EPC. Furthermore, the "actual" filing date can never be used for these purposes, even if the divisional application is not entitled to its "deemed" filing date by contravention of Art. 76(1) EPC (containing added subject matter vis-à-vis the parent). A divisional application can never be considered to be a regular European patent application with an "actual" date of filing that applies for all purposes. It is either a divisional application with a deemed filing date or it is in contravention of Art. 76(1) and must be refused under Art. 97(2) EPC.   333

The requirement under Art. 76(1) EPC, that a divisional application may only be filed in respect of subject-matter that does not extend beyond the content of the parent application, is therefore a substantive requirement that is assessed by the Examining Division under Art. 94(1) EPC in the same way as novelty and inventive step. It is irrelevant whether the divisional complies with Art. 76(1) or not on its "actual" filing date. If it does not comply then this will be noted as an objection in the first communication from the Examining Division and the applicant will have a chance to amend the application in order to make it compliant. If the objection is not properly overcome then the application will be refused. Throughout the proceedings until that point, it is assumed that either the application complies with Art. 76(1) and is entitled to the "deemed" filing date or else that it will eventually comply with Art. 76(1) and become entitled to the "deemed" filing date. The "deemed" filing date is therefore used for all necessary purposes in the meantime such as, for example, calculating the date of publication under Art. 93(1)(a) EPC and is entered in the register as the filing date pursuant to Art. 127 and r.143(1)(b) EPC (see Guidelines A-IV, 1.2.1).   334

These matters are discussed extensively in Enlarged Board of Appeal decision G1/05. A divisional application does not have to comply with Art. 76(1) on filing but must be compliant before grant. Therefore, the applicant must always be given a chance to bring the application into line with Art. 76(1) during substantive examination. Since a divisional application, once it has an "actual" filing date, is a separate application from the parent, the status of the parent (e.g. whether it is still pending) when such amendment is made is irrelevant.   335

Whether it is possible for the applicant to amend a divisional application in order to bring it into line with Art. 76(1) EPC will, of course depend on the facts of the case. It must be borne in mind that any such amendment must comply with Art. 123(2) and, in post-grant proceedings, Art. 123(3) EPC. Whilst Art. 76(1) is judged by comparing the disclosure of the divisional application as filed with the disclosure of the parent application as filed, the allowability of any amendment under Art. 123(2) EPC is judged by comparing the disclosure of the divisional application as amended with the disclosure of the divisional application as filed. It is possible for an inescapable trap to be created by the mutual action of these two differing requirements. Thus, if the divisional does not comply with Art. 76(1) EPC because an extra feature has been added to the main independent claim as compared to the parent application, it may be relatively easy to delete it without offending against Art. 123(2) EPC (assuming extra sections have not been added to the description suggesting this feature is essential). However, if the divisional does not comply with Art. 76(1) EPC because an essential feature of the main claim has been deleted, it will not be possible to add this feature back (assuming there is no separate basis in the description) without contravening Art. 123(2) EPC. The claim cannot be maintained as   336 it is (Art. 76(1) EPC), nor can it be amended to cure the deficiency (Art. 123(2) EPC). Similarly, if a divisional application does not comply with Art. 76(1) because an extra feature has been added to the main independent claim and the application is granted in this form, it will not be possible to delete this feature during opposition proceedings without contravening Art. 123(3) EPC.

337   Where a chain of two or more divisional applications exists, Art. 76(1) is complied with if, at the time a further divisional application is filed, its subject matter has been disclosed in each previous member of the sequence including the original European patent application at the head of the chain and this subject matter has not been abandoned in any of those previous applications at that time (e.g. by deleting claims without any indication that protection by means of a divisional might still be pursued, J15/85). This means that a divisional application should always include the whole disclosure of the parent application from which it is divided in order to maintain the maximum flexibility for filing further divisional applications. Once subject matter is omitted in one member of a chain it may not then be re-introduced further down the sequence. If new subject matter is introduced at some point in the chain then it contravenes Art. 76(1) for the divisional application in which it is introduced and every further member of the sequence. It is irrelevant, however, whether each previous member of the sequence complied with Art. 76(1) EPC. It is possible to validly base a divisional on a previously filed divisional that is eventually refused for non-compliance with Art. 76(1) EPC. Consider the following scenarios.

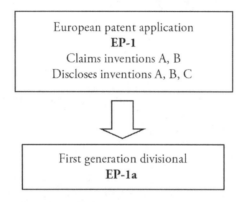

Figure 1

338   **Scenario 1**: Following a unity objection, EP-1 is amended so that the claims only refer to invention A, the applicant reserving the right to file a divisional for invention B. EP-1a is filed with claims relating to invention B and the same description as EP-1.

339   In this scenario, EP-1a complies with Art. 76(1). Further, the applicant is entitled to file a further divisional, based on EP-1a or EP-1, directed to invention C.

340   **Scenario 2**: Following a unity objection, EP-1 is amended so that the claims only refer to invention A, without reserving the right to file a divisional for invention B. EP-1a is filed with claims relating to invention B and the same description as EP-1.

341   In this scenario, EP-1a may not comply with Art. 76(1) since it relates to subject matter that, at its filing date, had been abandoned in EP-1 according to J15/85. A further divisional application based on EP-1a directed to invention C can still be filed since it is irrelevant for these purposes whether the previous member of the sequence complies with Art. 76(1) or not. The further divisional based on EP-1a, however, cannot relate to invention B for the same reasons. Similarly, a further divisional directed to invention C can be based on EP-1.

342   Scenario 3: Following a unity objection, EP-1 is amended so that the claims only refer to invention A, the applicant reserving the right to file a divisional for invention B. EP-1a is filed with claims relating to invention B and a description relating solely to invention B.

343   In this scenario, EP-1a complies with Art. 76(1) EPC. However, a further divisional relating to invention C may not be based on EP-1a since EP-1a no longer discloses this subject matter. A divisional relating to invention C could still be based on EP-1.

344   **Scenario 4**: Following a unity objection, EP-1 is amended so that the claims only refer to invention A, the applicant reserving the right to file a divisional for invention B. EP-1a is filed with claims relating to invention B and a description that includes the disclosure of EP-1 relating to inventions A, B and C as well as a new disclosure of invention D.

In this scenario, EP-1a does not comply with Art. 76(1) in view of the added disclo-   345
sure of invention D. A further divisional directed to invention C can still be filed based
on EP-1a since it is irrelevant for these purposes whether the previous member of the
sequence complies with Art. 76(1) or not. A divisional directed to invention C could also
be based on EP-1. However, a divisional directed to invention D, based on EP-1a, would
not comply with Art. 76(1) EPC since this subject matter was not present in the original
application EP-1.

It is therefore desirable, as mentioned above, for a divisional application to include   346
all the subject matter disclosed in the parent from which it is divided in order to ensure
that any further divisional that might be required complies with Art. 76(1) EPC. No
matter should therefore be deleted from the description when the divisional is filed. It
may also be desirable to file the same claims if they contain subject matter not disclosed
in the description though care must be taken to ensure the correct invention is searched.
It is possible to amend the claims after receipt of the search report under Art. 123(1) and
r.137(2) but such amended claims may not relate to unsearched subject matter which does
not combine with the originally claimed invention or group of inventions to form a single
general inventive concept (r.137(5) EPC). If all the subject matter of the original claims
is to proceed to grant in the parent application, it is therefore better to at least add new
claims relating to the subject matter for which a second patent is required and to add them
at the front of the claim set so that they are the claims searched first in the event of a unity
objection (r.64(1) EPC).

It is important to note that decisions G1/05 and G4/19 have upheld the principle of the   347
prohibition of double patenting. According to this principle, an applicant is not entitled
to the grant of a second patent for subject matter **that he has already been granted**. From
this it can be deduced that the principle only applies (1) when a patent has been granted;
(2) when the proprietor to which the patent was granted is the same as the applicant for
the further application (such as a divisional); (3) where the designated states overlap; and
(4) where the further application claims **identical** subject matter to that already granted.
The identical subject matter in the patent and application must also have the same effective
date or else one would be prior art to the other. With regard to point (4), the case law is
not entirely consistent but the majority view is that the prohibition of double patenting
only applies to an identical combination of features, i.e. when both a granted claim and a
claim proposed for grant are novelty destroying **to each other**.

However, the prohibition of double patenting does not prevent the filing of a divisional   348
application with identical claims to the parent from which it is derived. At the point the
divisional is filed the parent cannot be granted and so the principle of the prohibition of
double patenting does not yet apply. Either of the parent or divisional could be amended
or withdrawn to avoid double patenting. Thus, only when an applicant proposes claims
for grant in a divisional that have already been granted in the parent should an objection
of double patenting be raised. The applicant must then have a chance to amend the application before the divisional is refused. Note that a double patenting objection could
not be overcome by limiting the patent under Art. 105a EPC since the subject matter
concerned has already been granted and cannot be granted again. The prohibition of double patenting forbids the grant of a second patent for subject matter that has already been
granted, not the maintenance of two patents claiming the same subject matter.

1.7.2 *The prior art effects of a published European patent application*

When a European patent application is published, prior art is created in several different   349
ways at the same time. First of all, the content of the published application enters the
state of the art as of its date of publication, for the purposes of novelty and inventive step
(Art. 54(2) EPC). This is the case for any published document, including a published
patent application. The information published includes the description, claims, drawings
and abstract – r.68(1) EPC). Secondly, the content of the description, claims and drawings
enters the state of the art as of its date of filing, or in certain cases as of a claimed priority
date, for the purposes of novelty only (Art. 54(3) EPC). The abstract is excluded in this
case (Art. 85 EPC). Thirdly, the publication of the application makes available, as of the
publication date, most of the content of the EPO file by file inspection (Art. 128(4) EPC).
Additional information may enter the state of the art in this way under Art. 54(2) EPC,

such as the content of a priority document, the written opinion of the Search Division and any letter from the applicant. Some documents, however, are excluded from file inspection under r.144 EPC. Fourthly, if the published application is a divisional application, or a replacement application under Art. 61(1) EPC, and the earlier application from which it has been divided or which it replaces has not yet been published, then the file of the earlier application becomes available for inspection as well (Art. 128(5) EPC). This may happen when a request for early publication of the divisional or replacement application has been made.

350   In the case of a Euro-PCT application, the content of the published application also enters the state of the art under Art. 54(2) as of its date of publication. A **potential** prior art effect under Art. 54(3), is also created at the same time but does not immediately come into effect – it is held in abeyance until a filing fee has been paid to the EPO and, if the application was published in a language other than English, French or German, a translation into one of those languages has been supplied to the EPO (Art. 153(5) and r.165 EPC). The application file held by the International Bureau is also made available on publication (r.94.1 PCT) though any documents relating to international preliminary examination are excluded at this stage. For applications filed after 01 April 2014, the written opinion of the International Searching Authority is, however, available for inspection.

351   It is the Art. 54(3) prior art effect which is most interesting and which creates most difficulty. This provision gives effect to the first-to-file principle articulated by Art. 60(2) EPC – the person to first file a European patent application for any particular subject matter is entitled to a patent for it. If inventor A files a European patent application EP-A for invention X a day before inventor B files a European patent application EP-B for the same invention then inventor/applicant A will be able to obtain a patent, assuming all relevant requirements are met, whereas inventor/applicant B will not since, on publication, the description, claims and drawings of EP-A will become prior art for the purposes of assessing the novelty of EP-B. If they both file their applications on the same day, on the other hand, neither will be prior art citable against the other and they may both obtain a European patent and prevent each other from exploiting the invention.

352   Where the priority of one or more previous applications is validly claimed, the assessment of the Art. 54(3) prior art effect of a published European patent application becomes more complicated. Subject matter which was added on filing the European patent application and is not disclosed in any of the applications from which priority is claimed enters the state of the art as of the filing date. Subject matter which is disclosed in the European patent application and also disclosed in one or more of the applications from which priority is claimed enters the state of the art as of the filing date of the earliest priority application in which it was disclosed. Subject matter which was disclosed in one or more of the priority documents and omitted from the European patent application does not enter the state of the art at all under Art. 54(3) though it may enter the state of the art under Art. 54(2) as of the publication date by file inspection if the relevant priority document is in the file at that point.

353   Consider the following scenarios in which PRD means priority date, FD means filing date and PLD means publication date:

354   **Scenario 1:**

| **PRD-EP2** | **FD-EP2** | **PLD-EP2** | *PRD-EP1* | *FD-EP1* | *PLD-EP1* |

The published disclosure of EP2 is prior art for all claims of EP1 under Art. 54(2) EPC.

355   **Scenario 2:**

| **PRD-EP2** | **PD-EP2** | *PRD-EP1* | **PLD-EP2** | *FD-EP1* | *PLD-EP1* |

The published disclosure of EP2 is prior art for EP1 under Art. 54(2) EPC for those claims of EP1 that are not entitled to priority and prior art under Art. 54(3) EPC for those claims of EP1 that are entitled to priority.

356   **Scenario 3:**

| **PRD-EP2** | *PRD-EP1* | **FD-EP2** | *FD-EP1* | **PLD-EP2** | *PLD-EP1* |

The published disclosure of EP2 is prior art for EP1 under Art. 54(3) EPC for all those claims of EP1 that are not entitled to priority and also those claims in EP1 that are entitled to priority to the extent that the disclosure of EP2 is itself entitled to priority.

Scenario 4: 357

PRD-EP1   **PRD-EP2**   *FD-EP1*   **FD-EP2**   *PLD-EP1*   **PLD-EP2**

The published disclosure of EP2 is prior art under Art. 54(3) EPC only for those claims of EP1 that are not entitled to priority and only to the extent that the subject matter in EP2 is itself entitled to priority.

Priority rights, of course, can also be invalid for formal reasons or can be lost for formal 358 reasons. If priority has been claimed, for example, by a person not entitled to exercise the priority right, or if priority has been claimed from an application which is not a first filing for the subject matter it discloses, then the priority claim is invalid ab initio and all the subject matter of the published European patent application will enter the state of the art under Art. 54(3) as of the filing date. In other circumstances, the priority claim can be valid on filing the European patent application but be lost at some later date or can be withdrawn by the applicant. In particular, the priority claim is lost according to Art. 90(5) EPC if the applicant fails to file a certified copy of the priority document when invited to do so under Art. 90(4) and r.59 EPC. In these circumstances it is almost always going to be the case that priority will be lost after publication since a deficiency will only exist on expiry of the r.53(1) time limit of 16 months from the priority date claimed and the period specified under r.59 must be at least two months according to r.132(2) EPC. Withdrawal of the priority claim, on the other hand, is most likely to take place before publication, in order to delay it. With a Euro-PCT application, it is also possible to envisage withdrawal of the priority claim after publication in order to delay national/regional phase entry.

The question therefore arises: what is the effect of losing a priority claim before or after 359 publication of a European patent application on the Art. 54(3) effect of that publication? The Art. 54(3) effect comes into being at the point of publication – after all, if the application does not publish there is no Art. 54(3) effect at all. If the right to priority is lost before publication it is therefore not taken into account – all subject matter enters the state of the art under Art. 54(3) EPC as of the filing date of the application. If the priority claim is lost after publication, on the other hand, the answer is not so clear. Once an Art. 54(3) prior art effect has been created as of the priority date, can it then be re-dated to the filing date? In fact, the only answer we have is given by the Guidelines (G-IV, 5.1.1) which state that loss of a priority claim after publication makes **no difference** to the Art. 54(3) effect of the application. The status of the priority claim on publication is therefore completely decisive – once created, an Art. 54(3) prior art effect may not vary. This is in the interest of legal certainty.

The following scenarios are illustrative. In each case, applicant A files a European pat- 360 ent application EP-A claiming the priority of earlier application P1. The European application EP-A proceeds to publication. Applicant B files European patent application EP-B without a priority claim and it is likewise published in due course. EP-A and EP-B both disclose, and have a single claim directed to, invention X.

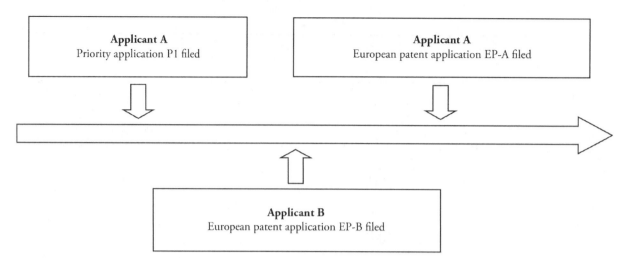

Figure 2

361 **Scenario 1**: P1 discloses invention X and EP-A validly claims its priority on publication. The patentability of EP-A is to be assessed at the filing date of P1 since the priority claim is valid and EP-B is not prior art under Art. 54(3) EPC. The patentability of EP-B is to be assessed at its filing date and EP-A is prior art under Art. 54(3) and Art. 89 EPC since the priority claim is valid. Applicant A gets a patent.

362 **Scenario 2**: P1 does not disclose invention X. The patentability of EP-A is to be assessed at its filing date since the priority claim is not valid and EP-B is prior art under Art. 54(3) EPC. The patentability of EP-B is to be assessed at its filing date and EP-A is not prior art under Art. 54(3) and Art. 89 EPC since the priority claim is not valid. Applicant B gets a patent.

363 **Scenario 3**: P1 discloses invention X but EP-A is filed beyond the end of the priority year. The patentability of EP-A is to be assessed at its filing date since the priority claim is not valid and EP-B is prior art under Art. 54(3) EPC. The patentability of EP-B is to be assessed at its filing date and EP-A is not prior art under Art. 54(3) and Art. 89 EPC since the priority claim is not valid. Applicant B gets a patent.

364 **Scenario 4**: P1 discloses invention X but the priority claim is withdrawn one month after the filing of EP-A to delay publication. The patentability of EP-A is to be assessed at its filing date since the priority claim has been withdrawn and EP-B is prior art under Art. 54(3) EPC. The patentability of EP-B is to be assessed at its filing date and EP-A is not prior art under Art. 54(3) and Art. 89 EPC since the priority claim was withdrawn when EP-A was published. Applicant B gets a patent.

365 **Scenario 5**: P1 discloses invention X but a certified copy is not filed in time and the priority claim is lost one month after publication. The patentability of EP-A is to be assessed at its filing date since the priority claim has been lost and EP-B is prior art under Art. 54(3) EPC. The patentability of EP-B is to be assessed at its filing date and EP-A is prior art under Art. 54(3) EPC since when EP-A was published the priority claim was valid. Neither applicant gets a patent.

366 The prior art effect of one European patent application against another is therefore complicated and sometimes leads to surprising results. Although Art. 60(2) EPC seems to promise that a single applicant who is the first to file will obtain the rights to any particular invention, the way Art. 54(3) EPC works means that it is possible for two applicants to obtain a patent (if they file on the same day) or for neither applicant to obtain a patent (see scenario 5 above). Another result that many find surprising is that European patent applications within the same family can be prior art to each other if one loses its right to claim priority. This can occur between a parent and a divisional application, for example, or between two divisional applications, or between a first European patent application and a later European patent application claiming the priority of the first. In each case, the two applications are separate applications which, on publication, generate prior art under Art. 54(3) which is potentially relevant to the other should a priority right be lost. On the other hand, if priority is validly claimed, such applications cannot have a novelty-destroying effect on each other following decision G1/15 which teaches that partial priority must always be recognised. Consider the following scenarios:

Scenario 1: A first European patent application EP-1 discloses a composition contain-   367
ing 5 % of substance X. A second European patent application EP-2, claiming the priority of the first, discloses two compositions containing either 5 % or 6 % of substance X
and has a claim to a composition containing 5 or 6 % of substance X. Both applications
publish.

Scenario 2: A first European patent application EP-1 discloses a composition contain-   368
ing 5 % of substance X. A second European patent application EP-2, claiming the priority
of the first, discloses two compositions containing either 5 % or 10 % of substance X
and has a claim to a composition containing 2 to 15 % of substance X. Both applications
publish.

Scenario 3: An first international application PCT-1 discloses a composition contain-   369
ing 5 % of substance X. A second international application PCT-2, claiming the priority
of PCT-1, discloses two compositions containing either 5 % or 6 % of substance X and
has a claim to a composition containing 5 or 6 % of substance X. Both applications publish and enter the EPO regional phase. The priority claim for PCT-2 is lost since a certified
copy of the priority document is not filed in due time following a request under r.163(2)
EPC.

In scenario 1, the claim of EP-2 encompasses two discrete embodiments. These differ-   370
ent embodiments can have different priority dates and their patentability can be assessed
differently (Art. 88(2) EPC, second sentence and G2/98, point 6.7). The first embodiment
(5 %) is entitled to the priority date and its patentability is to be assessed at that date.
EP-1 is not prior art under Art. 54(3) since its disclosure has the same effective date. The
second embodiment (6 %) is not entitled to the priority date and its patentability is to
be assessed at the filing date. EP-1 is state of the art under Art. 54(3) EPC but does not
include the relevant disclosure. The claim is patentable.

In scenario 2, the same analysis applies. Even though the claim of EP-2 encompasses   371
a limitless number of embodiments contained in a continuous range, partial priority still
applies for those embodiments disclosed in EP-1 according to G1/15. The two embodiments in this case are (1) 5 % of substance X (which is entitled to the priority date) and
(2) everything in the range 2 to 15 % other than 5 % (which is not entitled to the priority
date).

In scenario 3, the priority claim has been lost so that the patentability of both claimed   372
embodiments in PCT-2 is to be judged at its filing date. PCT-1 is therefore state of the art
under Art. 54(3) EPC and is novelty destroying to the claim. The claim must be amended
by deleting the 5 % embodiment.

Another point to which careful attention needs to be paid when assessing the state of   373
the art under Art. 54(3) EPC is the filing date of the application (or patent) whose patentability (or validity) is being considered. If that application or patent has a filing date on or
after 13 December 2007 then any prior art under Art. 54(3) EPC is novelty-destroying to
the application (or patent) as a whole, for all its designated states and extension states. **Note
that the filing date of the prior art European application is irrelevant**, it is the filing
date of the European application/patent whose validity is being considered that counts.
If, on the other hand, the application or patent whose patentability or validity is being
considered has a filing date before 13 December 2007 then Art. 54(4) and r.23a EPC1973
continue to apply and any prior art under Art. 54(3) EPC will only be novelty-destroying
in respect of states whose designation/extension was valid on publication of the prior art
application and for which designation/extension fees were paid.

Just as with priority, when assessing how many states are validly designated by a Euro-   374
pean patent application that is prior art according to Art. 54(3) EPC1973, it is the status
of the designations at the point of publication that is determinative. If the designation of a
state is withdrawn by the applicant before publication then the published application does
not have any Art. 54(3) prior art effect for this designation under EPC1973. If, on the other hand, the designation of a state is withdrawn after publication then the published application still maintains an Art. 53(3) prior art effect in respect of this state under EPC1973
since it was effective at the point when the prior art effect came into being. However,
Art. 54(4) and r.23a EPC1973 make this effect conditional on the payment of designation
fees, just as the prior art effect of a Euro-PCT application under Art. 54(3) EPC is determined at the point of publication but conditional on the payment of a filing fee. Under

EPC1973 it was possible to pay designation fees individually for up to 6 states – payment of 7 fees was sufficient to designate all states. The following scenarios may therefore arise:

375   **Scenario 1**: State designated on publication and designation fee paid – prior art effect under Art. 54(3) EPC1973 is effective for that state.

376   **Scenario 2**: State not designated on publication and designation fee paid – prior art effect under Art. 54(3) EPC1973 is not effective for that state.

377   **Scenario 3**: State designated on publication and designation fee not paid – prior art effect under Art. 54(3) EPC1973 is not effective for that state.

378   **Scenario 4**: State not designated on publication and designation fee not paid – prior art effect under Art. 54(3) EPC1973 not effective for that state.

379   **Scenario 5**: State designated on publication and designation fee paid, designation of state withdrawn after publication – prior art effect under Art. 54(3) EPC1973 is effective for that state.

380   It should be noted that EPC2000 applies without exception to a divisional application filed on or after 13 December 2007, even if Art. 54(4) EPC1973 continues to apply to the parent application from which it is divided (see Point 1 of the Notice from the EPO dated 20.9.2007–O.J. [2007] 504). If the subject matter of a European patent application filed before 13 December 2007 needs to be divided at some point after 13 December 2007 (e.g. in response to a lack of unity objection) the prior art needs to be evaluated carefully before a decision is taken on which way to divide the subject matter since any Art. 54(3) prior art would apply to the divisional application as a whole but the parent application only in respect of validly designated states. For instance, consider the following scenarios in which European patent application EP-2 claims two non-unitary inventions X and Y for which two search fees are paid. The state of the art includes prior European right EP-1 which discloses invention X and is published in due course.

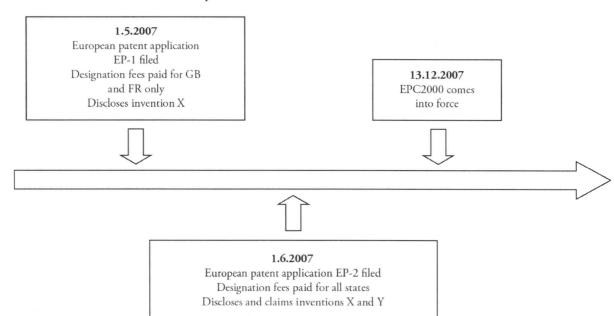

Figure 3

381   **Scenario 1**: Divisional application for invention X filed 1.12.2007, invention Y pursued in EP-2. In this case, Art. 54(4) EPC1973 applies to EP-2 and its divisional. The divisional can be granted for all states except GB and FR and EP-2 can be granted for all states.

382   **Scenario 2**: Divisional application for invention Y filed 1.12.2007, invention X pursued in EP-2. In this case, Art. 54(4) EPC1973 applies to EP-2 and its divisional. EP-2 can be granted for all states except GB and FR and its divisional can be granted for all states.

383   **Scenario 3**: Divisional application for invention X filed 1.1.2008, invention Y pursued in EP-2. In this case, Art. 54(4) EPC1973 applies to EP-2 but not to its divisional. EP-2 can be granted for all states but its divisional cannot be granted for any states. No protection for invention X in any state is possible.

384   **Scenario 4**: Divisional application for invention Y filed 1.1.2008, invention X filed pursued in EP-2. In this case, Art. 54(4) EPC1973 applies to EP-2 but not to its divisional.

EP-2 can be granted for all states except GB and FR and its divisional can be granted for all states.

Note that r.87 EPC1973 also continues to apply to applications filed before 13 Decem-   385
ber 2007, in addition to Art. 54(4) and r.23a EPC1973, since it may be necessary to have different claims (and possibly a different description) where Art. 54(3) prior art exists that is relevant to some designated states and not others.

Two further interesting points can be made concerning prior art according to Art. 54(3)   386
EPC. Firstly, when an application is unconditionally withdrawn prior to publication but publishes anyway (e.g. where the notice of withdrawal is received after the technical preparations for publication are complete), the published application does not have any prior art effect under Art. 54(3) according to J5/81. It does, of course, still have a prior art effect under Art. 54(2) as a published document. Secondly, if a European patent application is filed in a language which is not an official language of the EPO it is this original text that becomes state of the art under Art. 54(3) on publication and not the translation into the language of the proceedings that is actually published (see Guidelines A-VII, 7). This is consistent with the fact that the translation can always be brought into line with the original text at any time (Art. 14(2) EPC).

1.7.3   Renewal fees

The requirement to pay renewal fees in respect of a pending European patent application   387
is easily overlooked since renewal fees are more usually associated with post-grant pro- ceedings. Special attention should therefore be paid to the need to pay renewal fees when answering paper D questions in the EQE: even if a question does not refer explicitly to the need to pay a renewal fee it may disclose the filing date of a European patent application from which a due date should be apparent. The payment of renewal fees also involves several unique features that can be difficult to understand and which lend themselves to the drafting of exam questions.

Most fees payable under the EPC fall due on the date on which the action giving rise to   388
their payment occurs (the due date) but can be paid at a later time within a defined period. This due date is usually the first day on which the relevant fee may be paid – if it is paid earlier then the payment will be without legal basis and it will be refunded. For example, the filing of a European patent application gives rise to the need to pay a filing fee and a search fee and these fees fall due on the day on which the application is filed. The filing and search fees must then be paid within a time limit of one month from the filing of the application.

The payment of renewal fees, however, is very different in several respects! For a regu-   389
lar European patent application, the first renewal fee falls due on the last day of the month containing the second anniversary of the filing date (Art. 86(1) and r.51(1) EPC) – note that the filing date applies here regardless of whether priority is claimed or not. Further renewal fees are due at the end of the month containing each subsequent anniversary until the application is granted (Art. 86(1) EPC). These fees are referred to below as 'regular' renewal fees. Instead of a period being provided for the payment of a regular renewal fee following the due date, it must be paid on the due date itself to be in time! For this reason, it **is** possible to pay a regular renewal fee before its due date, in contrast to most other fees, but no earlier than six months before in the case of the first renewal fee for the third year of pendency and no earlier than three months before in the case of all subsequent fees (Art. 86(1) and r.51(1) EPC). The EPC provisions relating to renewal fees are therefore unique and the situation becomes further complicated by the fact that different kinds of renewal fee due date can occur, as will be discussed below.

The important point to appreciate straight away is that **there is no time limit for the**   390
payment of a regular renewal fee. It must be paid on the date on which it falls due or up to three months earlier (up to six months earlier in the case of the first renewal fee). This means that none of the EPC provisions relating to time limits, such as extension to account for closed days (Art. 120 and r.134(1) EPC), further processing (Art. 121 and r.135 EPC), re-establishment (Art. 122 and r.136 EPC) and excused late filing (Art. 120 and r.133 EPC) may be applied to a regular renewal fee due date. However, confusingly, if a regular renewal fee due date falls on a day on which one of the EPO filing offices is not open for business, the renewal fee may still be paid without surcharge on the first day on

which all of the filing offices are open – this is not by application of r.134(1) EPC but a special allowance made by the case law (J4/91) by analogy with r.134(1) EPC. The renewal fee due date is not actually changed or extended by this allowance which is actually a short grace period.

391   When considering the earliest point at which a regular renewal fee may be paid, it is important to remember that the three or six months of r.51(1) EPC is not a time limit either and merely represents a condition which must be met – it does not define a starting point and a term from which an end may be calculated but, conversely, defines an endpoint from which a starting point may retrospectively be calculated. The principles of Art. 120 and r.131 do not therefore apply. In fact, the EPO considers that since a regular renewal fee is due at the end of a particular month, the earliest that the renewal fee can be paid is the end of the third or sixth month previous, regardless of the number of days in the two months concerned (Guidelines A-X, 5.2.4). Thus, for example, a second renewal fee due on 30 April can be paid from 31 January onwards; a second renewal fee due on 31 May can be paid from 28/29 February onwards (depending on whether a leap year is concerned or not); a second renewal fee due on 30 June can be paid from 31 March onwards.

392   All this would be complicated enough on its own but the situation is further confused by the fact that renewal fee due dates do not necessarily fall at the end of a month in all cases. Several different kinds of due date may be encountered under the EPC depending on the kind of European patent application being considered and the prosecution history of the application. For instance, for a Euro-PCT application, the first renewal fee may fall due under r.51(1) during the international phase of the application. This can happen if no priority is claimed or only partial use is made of the priority year. In these circumstances, a time limit for paying the renewal fee **is** provided under the EPC – it must be paid within the 31 month time limit for entering the regional phase (Art. 86(1) and r.159(1)(g) EPC). The provisions relating to time limits, such as r.134(1) EPC apply here in the usual way, so that if the last day of the period falls on a day on which one of the filing offices of the EPO is shut for business then the due date becomes the next day on which they are all open. Furthermore, the due date is deemed not to actually fall due under r.51(1). Instead, its falling due is postponed to the end of the r.159(1) 31 month time limit (Guidelines A-X, 5.2.4). So, in this case, the renewal fee must be paid within a time limit and the end of the time limit determines the due date! Thus, as with a regular renewal fee, payment must be made **before or on** the due date to be in time.

393   A further kind of due date can arise when a divisional application is filed. Any renewal fees that have already fallen due for the **parent** application at the time the divisional is filed (including a fee falling due on the day the divisional is filed) will fall due in respect of the **divisional** application on its date of filing (Art. 86(1) and r.51(3) EPC). In contrast to the situation with a regular due date, it is not possible here to pay the renewal fee up to three months earlier – it is not possible to pay a fee for an application that does not exist yet! Such a fee would be paid without legal basis and refunded. For the same reason, a renewal fee is refunded if the application for which it is paid becomes withdrawn before the due date (Guidelines A-XI, 10.1.1). To avoid the situation that the renewal fee would have to be paid on its due date, no earlier and no later, the EPC provides a time limit for paying the fee that **starts** at the due date and is four months long (Art. 86(1) and r.51(3) EPC). All the provisions associated with time limits apply to this four month period in the usual way.

394   The situation arising with renewal fees that have fallen due before a divisional application is filed is mirrored in two other circumstances; firstly when rights are re-established under Art. 122 following the deemed withdrawal or refusal of an application and a renewal fee would have fallen due at a time at which the application was not pending and secondly where proceedings are re-opened before a Board of Appeal following a successful petition under Art. 112a EPC and a renewal fee would have fallen due at a time when the application was finally refused. In the first case the due date is the date of notification of the decision to re-establish the application (Art. 86(1) and r.51(4) EPC) and in the second case the due date is the date of notification of the decision of the Enlarged Board of Appeal concerning the petition (Art. 86(1) and r.51(5) EPC). Once again, in these two cases, it is not possible to pay such a renewal fee up to three months before the due date since the application is not be pending at that time and so a four month time limit commencing at the due date is provided for paying the fee.

The date of notification in these two cases will be the date of written notification cal-   395
culated as usual under Art. 119 and r.126(2) EPC. Notification is deemed to take place on
the 10th day following the date that the decision bears, unless it is delivered later.

In all of these latter three cases (divisional, re-establishment, petition), the EPC also   396
provides that any further regular renewal fee that falls due during the four month period
is also to be paid within that time limit rather than on its due date, in order to avoid an
applicant being taken by surprise by events occurring almost immediately after the application is filed or revived (Art. 86(1) and r.51(3), 51(4) and 51(5) respectively).

One further kind of due date can arise. When proceedings have been interrupted under   397
r.142(1) EPC and a renewal fee has fallen due under r.51(1) following the date of interruption, the due date for that renewal fee is deemed to be the date of resumption of proceedings (J902/87). In these cases, the EPO decides on a date of resumption that it is at some
point in the future and notifies the applicant well in advance. The fee may therefore be
paid up to three months preceding the date of resumption that is set and no special time
limit for its payment is provided. The situation here is the same as for a regular renewal fee
though the due date falls on an appointed day rather than at the end of a particular month.
The earliest date for payment should probably be calculated in this case as the day of the
month having the same number as the day of resumption in the third month before the
month in which proceedings are resumed (no information in the Guidelines).

If a renewal fee is not validly paid on or before the due date, or within the time limit   398
provided, as the case may be, there is no immediate loss of rights (and hence, for example, neither further processing nor re-establishment apply to the four month time limit).
Instead, the fee can be paid late, with a surcharge, within a time limit of six months that
runs from the **due date** in all cases (Art. 86(1) and r.51(2) EPC). In the case of a regular
renewal fee due date that falls at the end of a particular month, the six month grace period
is calculated according to the unique formula of J4/91 and expires on the last day of the
sixth month from the month in which the anniversary of the filing date falls (or, where a
filing office is closed on this day, the next day when all the filing offices are open). In the
case where a renewal fee for a Euro-PCT application must be paid within the 31 month
time limit for entering the EPO regional phase, the six month grace period is calculated as
an aggregate time limit running from the expiry of the 31 month period (J1/89, Guidelines
A-X, 5.2.4). In the case where the renewal fee can be paid within a four month time limit
(divisional, re-establishment or petition), the six month grace period runs **concurrently**
with the four-month period (both being calculated from the due date) so that it is effectively reduced to a two-month period. In the case where a renewal fee falls due on a date
of resumption of proceedings, the six month grace period runs from the resumption date
and is calculated according to Art. 120(b) and r.131(4) in the usual way. The surcharge in
all cases amounts to 50 % of the unpaid renewal fee (Art. 2(1)(5) RRF).

If a six month grace period for paying a renewal fee late with surcharge is running (1)   399
when an application is refused or deemed withdrawn and the application is later successfully re-established under Art. 122, or (2) when an application is finally refused by
a Board of Appeal and appeal proceedings are re-opened following a successful petition
to the Enlarged Board of Appeal, the six-month grace period begins again as calculated
from the new due date (notification of the decision on re-establishment or the decision of
the Enlarged Board of Appeal, r.51(4)(b) or 5(b) EPC respectively). If a six-month grace
period for paying a renewal fee late with surcharge is running when proceedings are interrupted, on the other hand, only the part of the period that had not yet expired at the
date of interruption is available as calculated from the new due date (date of resumption
of proceedings, J902/87).

If a renewal fee remains unpaid when the six month grace period expires, the European   400
patent application is deemed withdrawn (Art. 86(1) and r.51(2) EPC). Further processing
may not be used since it is excluded under r.135(2) EPC. Re-establishment is therefore
possible if the relevant grace period was missed despite all due care required by the circumstances having been taken. The one year time limit of r.136(2) EPC is calculated as
an aggregate time limit from the expiry of the grace period. Amendments were made to
r.51(2) EPC, coming into force on 01 January 2017, to make it clear that the deemed withdrawal takes place at the end of the six month grace period. This was necessary following decision T1402/13 which had found that under the previous wording of r.51 deemed
withdrawal took place at the due date.

401   One other grace period established by the EPC in relation to renewal fees can be mentioned – any renewal fee due to a national office in respect of a European patent that falls due within two months of the date on which its grant takes effect can be paid within that two month period without surcharge (Art. 141(2) EPC). All other aspects relating to the payment of renewal fees for the granted patent are matters for national law to decide and details may be found in Table VI of the national law book. Note that while the EPO requires a renewal fee in respect of the 3rd and each subsequent year of pendency, this is not true of all the EPC Contracting states. Austria only requires a fee for the 6th and each subsequent year, for example, and Italy for the fifth and each subsequent year – one cannot therefore assume that national fees will be required immediately in all designated states after grant. Furthermore, other states (e.g. Croatia, Czech Republic, Hungary) deem the due date to fall on the anniversary of the filing date rather than the end of the month containing the anniversary and Cyprus considers the due date to be the date preceding the anniversary date!

Various arrangements for the payment of renewal fees under the EPC are summarised in the following table.

402

Kind of renewal fee	Due date for payment	Can be paid earlier than due date?	Can be paid within a time limit?	Expiry of six month grace period
Second and each subsequent anniversary of the filing date	Last day of the month containing the anniversary	Yes, up to three months before due date (up to six months for the first renewal fee)	No	Last day of sixth month from month containing anniversary
Originally falls due in the international phase	Last day of 31 month period of r.159(1)	Probably up to three months before the expiry of the r.159(1) time limit (no information in Guidelines)	Yes, within 31 month period of r.159(1)	Six-month aggregate time limit calculated from end of 31 month period
Already due for the parent on filing a divisional	On the day of filing of the divisional application	No	Yes, within four months of the filing of the divisional application	Six months from the filing of the divisional application
Falls due for a divisional within 4 months of filing	Last day of the month containing the anniversary	Yes, up to three months before due date as long as application pending	Yes, within four months of the filing of the divisional application	Last day of sixth month from month containing anniversary
Fell due when application subject to re-establishment was withdrawn or refused	Date of notification of decision to re-establish rights in the application	No	Yes, within four months of the notification of the decision	Six months from notification of the decision
Falls due within four months of notification of decision to re-establish	Last day of the month containing the anniversary	Yes, up to three months before due date as long as application pending	Yes, within four months of the notification of the decision	Last day of sixth month from month containing anniversary
Fell due when application finally refused and proceedings reopened before Board of Appeal	Date of notification of the decision to re-open proceedings	No	Yes, within four months of the notification of the decision	Six months from notification of the decision
Falls due within four months of notification of decision to reopen proceedings before Board of Appeal	Last day of the month containing the anniversary	Yes, up to three months before due date as long as application pending	Yes, within four months of the notification of the decision	Last day of sixth month from month containing anniversary
Fell due at a time following interruption of proceedings	On the date of resumption of proceedings	Yes, up to three months before the date of resumption	No	Six months from the date of resumption

The following detailed examples concerning the payment of renewal fees under the EPC may be helpful.

Scenario 1: A European patent application is filed on 08 March 2017.
The first renewal fee, in respect of the third year, is due on 31 March 2019 (Sunday) and   403
can be paid up until Monday 01 April 2019 without surcharge according to J4/91. It can
be paid from Sunday 30 September 2018 onwards. The six month period for paying the
fee late with surcharge would expire on Monday 30 September 2019 according to J4/91.

Scenario 2: A European patent application is filed on 15 March 2017. A divisional application is filed on 24 January 2020.

The first renewal fee for the parent application is due on 31 March 2019 (Sunday) and   404
can be paid on Monday 01 April 2019 without surcharge according to J4/91. It may be
paid from Sunday 30 September 2018 onwards. It may also be paid late with surcharge
until 30 September 2019 (Monday).

The second renewal fee for the parent application is due on Tuesday 31 March 2020.   405
It can be paid from 31 December 2019 onwards. It may be paid late with surcharge until
Wednesday 30 September 2020.

The first renewal fee for the divisional is due on its filing date, 24 January 2020. It can-   406
not be paid earlier since this would be without legal basis. It may be paid within the four
month period ending 24 May 2020 (Sunday) extended under r.134(1) EPC until Monday 25 May 2020. It may be paid late with surcharge during the period commencing Tuesday 26 May 2014 and expiring six months from the due date on Friday 24 July 2020.

The second renewal fee for the divisional is due on Tuesday 31 March 2020. It may   407
be paid from the filing date of the divisional application (24 January 2020) onwards.
Since it falls due within four months from the divisional filing date, it may be paid late
without surcharge until 24 May 2020 (Sunday) extended under r.134(1) EPC until Monday 25 May 2020. It may be paid late with surcharge until Wednesday 30 September 2020.

Scenario 3: A PCT application designating the EPO is filed on 06 June 2016 without a
claim to priority.

The first renewal fee would have fallen due during the international phase   408
on 30 June 2018. It must therefore be paid to the EPO during the 31 month time limit
which expires 06 January 2019 (Sunday), extended under r.134(1) EPC to Monday 07 January 2019. It can be paid from 07 July 2018 onwards. It may also be paid late with surcharge during the six month period that expires Sunday 07 July 2019, extended under
r.134(1) EPC until Monday 08 July 2019.

Scenario 4: A European patent application is filed on 04 February 2019. It is refused for   409
lack of inventive step by the Examining Division. On Appeal, the Board of Appeal takes
a decision dated 20 September 2022 to uphold the decision of the Examining Division
without appointing oral proceedings as requested by the applicant. A petition for review
by the Enlarged Board of Appeal is successful and the Enlarged Board takes a written
decision dated 19 November 2023 to set aside the decision of the Board of Appeal and
reopen appeal proceedings. The decision is received by the applicant three days later.

The first renewal fee falls due on 28 February 2021 (Sunday) but can be paid with-   410
out surcharge on Monday 01 March 2021 It can be paid late with surcharge until
Tuesday 31 August 2021.

The second renewal fee falls due on Monday 28 February 2022 It can be paid late with   411
surcharge until Wednesday 31 August 2022.

The third renewal fee falls due following the decision taken by the Board of Appeal to   412
uphold the decision of the Examining Division. It is therefore due on notification of the
decision of the Enlarged Board, which is deemed under r.126(2) EPC to be 29 November 2023. It can be paid within four months of this date, i.e. until 29 March 2024, extended
under r.134(1) EPC until Tuesday 02 April 2024. It can also be paid with surcharge from
Wednesday 03 April 2024 until Wednesday 29 May 2024.

The fourth renewal falls due on Wednesday 28 February 2024 which is within the   413
four month period of r.51(5)(a) EPC. It can therefore be paid without surcharge until 02 April 2024. It can also be paid with surcharge until 31 August 2024 (Saturday) extended under r.134(1) until Monday 02 September 2024.

414   **Scenario 5**: A European patent application is filed on 04 May 2016 claiming an earlier priority. The applicant misses the due date for the payment of the first renewal fee. The applicant also misses the period set for responding to the first communication from the Examining Division under Art. 94(3) EPC and the application is deemed withdrawn on 06 June 2018. The applicant intends to respond to the first communication from the Examining Division using further processing but misses the deadline despite showing all required due care. His rights are re-established by a written decision dated 13 May 2019.

415   The first renewal fee falls due on Thursday 31 May 2018. It can be paid late with surcharge until Friday 30 November 2018. Since the six-month period for paying the renewal fee late is running when the application is deemed withdrawn, that period begins again as of notification of the decision on re-establishment.

416   Notification of that decision is deemed to have occurred on 23 May 2019 according to r.126(2) EPC and the six month period therefore expires on 23 November 2019 (Saturday) extended until Monday 25 November 2019 under r.134(1) EPC.

417   The second renewal fee falls due on Friday 31 May 2019. This is within four months of the date of notification of the decision to re-establish rights. It can therefore be paid within the four month period ending Monday 23 September 2019 without surcharge. It can also be paid with surcharge until 30 November 2019 (Saturday) extended until Monday 02 December 2019 under r.134(1) EPC.

1.7.4   *Incorporation by reference*

418   The Patent Law Treaty was adopted at Geneva on 01 June 2000 and allows applicants to incorporate by reference the description and drawings of a previous application in order to obtain a filing date (Art. 5(7) PLT) rather than filing these documents directly and to file late a missing part of the description or a drawing that is contained in an application from which priority is claimed without necessarily changing the filing date (Art. 5(6)(b) PLT). The PLT regulations specify certain further requirements that contracting states may insist upon (r.2 PLT), such as, for example, that missing part of the description or missing drawing must be completely contained in the priority document. The EPO was a signatory to the PLT and EPC2000 was drafted to be fully compliant with it so that European patent applications filed on or after 13 December 2007 benefit from the options provided by Art. 5 and r.2 PLT. The PCT regulations have also been amended so that international applications filed on or after 01 April 2007 can benefit from the possibility of incorporation by reference, but not in the same way.

419   Art. 5 and r.2 PLT offer contracting states some flexibility in how generously or strictly the provisions relating to incorporation by reference are to be implemented. Moreover, the PLT lays down **minimum** rights for applicants and patentees and contracting states are free to provide more generous provisions if they wish (Art. 2(1) PLT). Because of this, the way in which applicants can incorporate part or all of the description and drawings under the EPC and the PCT differs significantly. The way in which incorporation by reference works under the PCT is also influenced by the fact that according to Art. 11(1)(iii)(e) a claim and a description are both required for the award of a filing date whereas under the EPC (Art. 80 and r.40) a claim is no longer required.

420   Under the EPC, incorporation by reference for the purposes of a filing date (Art. 80, r.40(2) and r.40(3) EPC) is dealt with separately from incorporation by reference for the purposes of adding missing parts or correcting erroneously filed parts (Art. 80, r.56(3) and r.56a(4) EPC) and different requirements apply. Thus, for instance, the description and drawings of **any previous application** can be incorporated for the purposes of obtaining a filing date whereas a missing drawing or part of the description may only be incorporated from a priority-claiming application. Under the PCT, on the other hand, incorporation by reference for the purposes of obtaining a filing date is subject to the same requirements as incorporation by reference for the purposes of adding missing parts (Art. 11(1)(iii) and r.20.6(a) PCT) – in both cases, for example, only an application from which priority is being claimed may be used. Under the PCT, elements and parts of the application must be provisionally incorporated on the filing date from an application from which priority is claimed on that date and the incorporation is confirmed at a later date.

421   Thus, under the PCT, incorporation by reference for the purposes of obtaining a filing date can only be based on an application from which priority is claimed whereas, under

the EPC, incorporation by reference for the purposes of obtaining a filing date can be based on any earlier application. Priority must be claimed on the filing date of the application under the PCT or incorporation by reference is not possible, whereas, for European patent applications filed before 01 November 2022, a priority claim may be added after the filing date in order to incorporate missing parts by reference. However, for applications filed on or after 01 November 2022, the incorporation of a missing part by reference or the correction of an erroneously filed part by reference under the EPC may only be based on an application whose priority was claimed on on the filing date. The applicant must specifically reserve the right to incorporate by reference on filing under the PCT, whereas under the EPC the applicant may indicate at a date later than the filing date that missing parts are incorporated by reference.

These fundamental differences and other more subtle differences are highlighted in the following comparative tables.

Table 1: General requirements

Requirement	EPC	PCT	
Must the relevant formalities section apply incorporation by reference?	Yes, the Receiving Section must proceed according to r.40, r.56 and r.56a EPC.	No, several receiving Offices have filed reservations under r.20.8(a) PCT and will not award a filing date or maintain a filing date by incorporating the content of a previously filed application.	422
Must the relevant substantive examining section apply incorporation by reference?	Yes, the Examining Division must recognise the provisions of r.40, r.56 and r.56a EPC.	No, several designated Offices have filed reservations under r.20.8(b) PCT and will not recognise a filing date awarded on the basis of incorporation by reference	

Table 2: Requirements relating to the award of a filing date

Requirement	EPC	PCT	
Can the description and drawings be incorporated from any previous application?	Yes, r.40(1)(c) EPC refers to "a previously filed application".	No, only from an application from which priority is claimed according to r.4.18 PCT.	423
Does priority from a previous application have to be claimed on filing?	No, the presence of a priority claim is irrelevant since any previous application can be used.	Yes, according to r.4.18, priority must be claimed on the date the international application is filed.	
Does the filing date of the previous application have to be indicated to receive a filing date?	Yes, according to r.40(2) EPC this is an essential element for a filing date.	Yes, since a priority claim must indicate the date on which the previous application was filed according to r.4.10(a)(i) PCT.	
Does the number of the previous application have to be indicated to receive a filing date?	Yes, according to r.40(2) EPC this is an essential element for a filing date.	Uncertain – depends on the meaning of "claims priority" in r.4.18. A priority claim must indicate the number of the previous application according to r.4.10(a)(ii) PCT. However, according to Art. 4(D)(1) PC, applicable by virtue of Art. 8(2)(a) PCT, a declaration of priority only need indicate the date and state of the earlier application and the absence of the number does not invalidate a priority claim according to r.26*bis*.2(c) PCT.	
Does the filing office for the previous application have to be indicated to receive a filing date?	Yes, according to r.40(2) EPC this is an essential element for a filing date.	Yes, since a priority claim must indicate the filing office of the previous application according to r.4.10(a)(iii)–(v) PCT.	

Requirement	EPC	PCT
Does the application as filed have to contain an indication that parts are incorporated by reference to receive a filing date?	Yes, according to r.40(2) EPC it is essential to indicate that the reference to a previous application replaces the description and drawings for a filing date to be awarded.	Yes, according to r.4.18 PCT the application as filed must include a statement that the incorporation of an element or part of the application may be confirmed at a later date.
Can the description be incorporated by reference separately from the drawings?	No, according to r.40(2) EPC any reference to a previous application replaces both the description and drawings.	Yes, under r.20.3(a)(ii), the applicant may confirm the incorporation of the description separately. The drawings may be filed separately either on the filing date or as the incorporation of a missing part under Art. 14(2) and r.20.5(a) PCT.
Can the claims also be incorporated by reference?	Yes, according to r.57(c), EPC the claims may, optionally, also be incorporated along with the description and drawings. A claim is not required, however, for a filing date.	Yes, according to r.20.3(a)(ii) PCT, the claims may also be incorporated by reference. At least one claim is required for a filing date (Art. 11(1)(iii)(e) PCT).
Must a hard copy of the incorporated part be filed at some point in order to obtain a filing date?	No, there is no requirement under the EPC to file the incorporated part in hard copy.	Yes, according to r.20.6(a)(i) PCT a sheet or sheets embodying the incorporated element must be filed within a two month period. If it is not filed, the application is not treated as an international patent application (r.20.4 PCT).
Must a certified copy of the previous application be filed?	Yes, according to r.40(3), EPC a **certified copy** of the previous application must be filed within two months. It can also be filed late within a further two month period (r.55 EPC) without affecting the filing date. Otherwise, the application is not dealt with as a European patent application (Art. 90(2) EPC).	No, according to r.20.6(a)(ii) PCT a **copy** of the application is required within a two month period but it does not have to be certified. If it is not filed, the application is not treated as an international patent application (r.20.4 PCT).
Must a translation of the previous application be filed?	Yes, if the previous application is not in English, French or German. It must be filed within two months but can also be filed late within a further two month period (r.58). Otherwise, the application is deemed withdrawn (Art. 14(2) EPC).	Yes, if the previous application is not in the language in which the international application is filed (r.20.6(a)(iii) PCT) a translation is required within a two month period. If it is not filed, the application is not treated as an international patent application (r.20.4 PCT).

Table 3: Requirements relating to the incorporation of missing parts

Requirement	EPC	PCT
Can a missing part of the description be incorporated by reference?	Yes (r.56(2) EPC).	Yes (r.20.5(a) PCT).
Can a missing drawing be incorporated by reference?	Yes (r.56(2) EPC), but not part of a drawing (Guidelines A-II, 5.3).	Yes (r.20.5(a) PCT).
Can a missing claim be incorporated by reference?	No (r.56(2) EPC).	Yes (r.20.5(a) PCT).
Can a missing part be incorporated from any previous application?	No, only from an application from which priority is claimed (r.56(3) EPC).	No, only from an application from which priority is claimed (r.20.5(a) and r.4.18 PCT).

424

Requirement	EPC	PCT
Does priority from a previous application have to be claimed on filing?	No, for applications filed earlier than 01 November 2022, but it must be claimed no later than the request for incorporation by reference is made (r.56(3) EPC, Guidelines A-II, 5.4.1). Yes, for applications filed on or after 01 November 2022.	Yes (r.20.5(a) and r.4.18 PCT).
Does the application as filed have to contain an indication that parts are incorporated by reference to incorporate a missing part?	No	Yes (r.20.5(a) and r.4.18 PCT).
Must a hard copy of the incorporated part be filed at some point in order to incorporate a missing part?	No	Yes (r.20.6(a)(i) PCT).
Must a certified copy of the previous application be filed?	No, only a copy is required under r.56(3)(a) EPC.	No, only a copy is required under r.20.6(a)(ii) PCT.
Must a translation of the previous application be filed?	Yes, if the earlier application is not in English, French or German (r.56(3)(b) EPC).	Yes, if the previous application is not in the language in which the international application is filed (r.20.6(a)(iii) PCT).
Must the missing part be completely contained in the earlier application?	Yes (r.56(3) EPC).	Yes (r.4.18 PCT).
Must the applicant indicate where the missing part is contained in the earlier application?	Yes (r.56(3)(c) EPC).	Yes (r.20.6(a)(iv) PCT).

1.7.5   The filing of an application and its filing date

The date on which documents satisfying the requirements of Art. 80 and r.40 EPC are 425 filed at the EPO, or a national office which allows the filing of European patent applications, is the date on which the filing of the application takes place. This date is important since it determines various time limits within which acts must be carried out. For example, a filing fee and a search fee must be paid "within one month of filing" a European patent application (r.38(1) EPC). If an application is filed in a language other than English, French or German, a translation into one of those languages must be filed "within two months of filing the European patent application" (r.6(1) EPC).

The filing date allocated to the application following an examination under Art. 90(1) 426 EPC may differ from this date of filing the application (see G3/98, point 2.2 of the reasons). Most often, these two dates are the same, but this is not necessarily the case. Firstly, it is possible to file the application with an express request that a later date (e.g. the date of the accession of a new state or the date on which a change in the law takes place) be accorded under Art. 90(1) as the filing date (see, for example, J18/90). Secondly, a missing part of the description or a missing drawing may be filed at a later date under r.56 or an erroneously filed part of the application may be corrected under r.56a and this may result in a change in the filing date first allocated to the application. Thirdly, for a divisional application, the filing date accorded can only be the date of filing of the parent application by operation of Art. 76(1) EPC.

Whilst some time limits start with the date on which the filing of the application takes 427 place, as discussed above, many other time limits are calculated from the filing date. For example, missing parts can be filed of the applicant's own volition under r.56(2) EPC "within two months of the date of filing", a priority claim can be corrected under r.52(3) EPC "until the expiry of four months from the date of filing accorded to the European patent application", the application will be refused if the designation of the inventor is not made under r.60(1) EPC "within 16 months of the date of filing of the application" and the publication of the application takes place as soon as possible "after the expiry of a period of 18 months from the date of filing" under Art. 93(1)(a) EPC. Furthermore, the state of the art under Art. 54(2) includes everything made available to the public before the "date of filing of the European patent application" and the term of a patent under Art. 63(1) EPC is "20 years from the date of filing of the application". Finally, renewal fees are due under r.51(1) EPC on the last day of the month containing the anniversary of "the date of filing of the European patent application".

428   Unfortunately, the Guidelines do not make a clear distinction between the date on which the filing of the application takes place and the date of filing of the application. Guidelines A-III, 13.1, for example, refers to the time limit for paying the filing and search fees for a regular European patent application as being one month from the "filing date" and the time limit for paying the same fees for a divisional application being one month from the "date of filing" of the divisional. In both cases it would be more accurate to refer to these time limits being calculated from the date on which the filing of the application takes place, as was made clear in decision G3/98. In this decision the Enlarged Board decided that for a European application to comply with Art. 55 EPC (part of the state of the art to be disregarded), the relevant disclosure must have taken place no earlier than six months before the filing of the European patent application (not the filing date or priority date).

1.7.6 *Filing of documents – Languages and fee reductions*

429   Under EPC2000, a European patent application may be filed in any language (Art. 14(2) EPC). Three cases may be distinguished: (1) the application is filed in an official language of the EPO (English, French or German – Art. 14(1) EPC); (2) the application is filed in an official language of a contracting state to the EPC other than an official language of the EPC; and (3) the application is filed in a language which is not the official language of any contracting state to the EPC.

430   In case (1), no translation is required and the language of application as originally filed becomes the language of the proceedings (Art. 14(3) EPC). The original text is the authentic text of the application (Art. 70(1) EPC) and is used for the purposes of deciding whether an amendment goes beyond the disclosure of the application as filed (Art. 123(2) EPC) and for assessing the extent of the disclosure made available to the public under Art. 54(3) EPC. No reduction in the filing fee is available to the applicant.

431   In case (2), a translation into an official language of the EPO must be filed within two months of the filing of the original text (Art. 14(2) and r.6(1) EPC). The language used for this translation becomes the language of the proceedings (Art. 14(3) EPC). Although this translation is considered to be the authentic text of the application in proceedings before the EPO (Art. 70(1) EPC), its legal effect is provisional and conditional. If the translation contains errors vis-à-vis the original text (e.g. additions, omissions or translation errors) then it may be brought into conformity with the original text at any point during proceedings before the EPO (Art. 14(2) EPC). The only limit to this otherwise unfettered freedom to correct defects in the translation is that the protection conferred by a patent may not be extended during opposition proceedings (Art. 123(3) EPC). Furthermore, the original text is to be regarded as the "application as filed" (Art. 70(2) EPC) and hence to be used for the purposes of deciding whether an amendment goes beyond the disclosure of the application as filed (Art. 123(2) EPC) and for assessing the extent of the disclosure made available to the public under Art. 54(3) EPC (see Guidelines A-VII, 7).

432   If the applicant is a natural or legal person having residence or a principle place of business within a Contracting State having the language of the original text as an official language, or a national of such a State living abroad, then the filing fee is reduced by 30 % if the applicant has a certain status (r.6(3) and RRFArt. 14(1) EPC). Since a reduction is applied in this situation rather than a refund being credited, only 70 % of the filing fee needs to be paid. Note that the applicant is the beneficiary of the fee reduction and hence it is the residence and nationality of the applicant that must be considered, not the residence or nationality of any representative (T149/85). Furthermore, the fee reduction is available if the original text and the translation are both filed simultaneously but not if the translation into an official language of the EPO is filed first and the "original" text is filed later (G6/91) – this situation would fall within case (1) above. Since only a description is now necessary in order to obtain a filing date, it is the language of the description that determines whether a reduction is available or not (G6/91, Guidelines A-X, 9.2.2 and A-II, 4.1.3.1). The reduction applies to both the fixed (RRFArt. 2(1)(1)) and the

variable (RRFArt. 2(1)(1a)) elements of the filing fee as well as any additional part of the filing fee due in respect of a second or further generation divisional application (Guidelines A-X, 9.2.2). According to J4/18, in the case of joint applicants, each one must be a natural person or entity within the meaning of r.6(4) EPC, as specified in r.6(7) EPC, but only one of them needs to be a person defined by Art. 14(4) for the fee reduction to apply.

Case (3) is exactly the same as case (2) except that no reduction in the filing fee is available.   433

Consider the following scenarios: 434

Scenario 1: A European patent application is filed in German by an English applicant resident in France.

The language of the proceedings is German, no translation is required and the filing fee is not reduced.

Scenario 2: A European patent application is filed in Swedish by the Swedish representative of an English applicant resident in France.

A translation into an official language of the EPO is required and the filing fee is not reduced.

Scenario 3: A European patent application is filed in Swedish by the Swedish representative of a Swedish applicant resident in France.

A translation into an official language of the EPO is required and the filing fee is reduced.

Scenario 4: A European patent application is filed in Swedish by the French representative of a French applicant resident in Sweden.

A translation into an official language of the EPO is required and the filing fee is reduced.

Scenario 5: A European patent application is filed in Portuguese by a Brazilian applicant resident in Brazil.

A translation into an official language of the EPO is required and the filing fee is not reduced.

Scenario 6: A European patent application is filed in Portuguese by a Brazilian applicant resident in Spain.

A translation into an official language of the EPO is required and the filing fee is not reduced.

Scenario 7: A European patent application is filed in Portuguese by a Brazilian applicant resident in Portugal.

A translation into an official language of the EPO is required and the filing fee is reduced.

Scenario 8: A European patent application is filed in Portuguese by a Portuguese applicant resident in Brazil.

A translation into an official language of the EPO is required and the filing fee is reduced.

A Euro-PCT application may be filed in any language that is accepted by the competent receiving Office for the filing of PCT applications (Art. 3(4)(i) and r.12.1 PCT). A translation may be necessary for the purposes of international search (r.12.3(a) PCT) or international publication (r.12.4(a) PCT). If the Euro-PCT application is published in English, French or German then no translation needs to be provided to the EPO and the language of the publication becomes the language of the proceedings in the regional phase. Neither will any translation be accepted in this situation – the applicant has no ability to change the language of the proceedings (G4/08). If the Euro-PCT application is published in Arabic, Chinese, Japanese, Korean, Portuguese, Russian or Spanish then a translation into an official language of the EPO is necessary on regional phase entry (Art. 153(4) EPC) and the language of this translation becomes the language of the proceedings (Art. 14(3) EPC). The filing fee is not reduced for an Art. 14(4) person since r.6(3) only refers to a person filing a European patent application and not to a person entering the regional phase of a Euro-PCT application.   435

Whilst the application may be filed in any language, specific language requirements apply from that point onwards and a document filed in a non-admissible language will be considered not to have been filed at all (Art. 14(1) EPC, Guidelines A-VII, 5). Once the language of the proceedings has been determined by the choice of language in which the European patent application is filed or into which it is translated, this language is, unless a   436 specific exception is provided, to be used by the applicant and the EPO in all proceedings relating to the application and resulting patent (Art. 14(3) EPC). As far as exceptions are concerned, these differ as between the EPO and a party to the proceedings and as between written proceedings and oral proceedings.

437   As far as the written stage of proceedings is concerned, the EPO must always use the language of the proceedings (G4/08). A party to the proceedings, on the other hand, such as the applicant, has more flexibility and may use any official language of the EPO (r.3(1) EPC) except where amendments to the application are concerned in which case the language of the proceedings is mandatory (r.3(2) EPC). Supporting documentation, such as evidence, may be in any language but the EPO may require a translation which, once again, may be in any official language of the EPO (r.3(2) EPC).

438   For certain applicants, certain documents may also be filed in a language that is not an official language of the EPO (Art. 14(4) EPC). These applicants are natural or legal persons having residence or a principle place of business within a Contracting State having a language other than English, French or German as an official language and nationals of such a state living abroad. They may file documents that must be filed **within a time limit** in such an official language of that state. A translation of the document into any of the EPO official languages must then be filed within a period of one month (r.3(1) and r.6(2) EPC), with the usual caveat that amendments must always be translated into the language of the proceedings (r.3(2) EPC). In the case where the document is a notice of appeal, a statement of grounds of appeal or a petition for review, the translation may be filed up until the end of the period for filing that document, if it expires later (r.6(2) EPC). If the party concerned does not have the right to use an Art. 14(4) language or the translation is not filed in time then the original document is deemed not to have been filed (Art. 14(4) EPC).

439   Almost all documents that the applicant may have to file have an associated time limit and fall within the bounds of Art. 14(4). An example of a document that the applicant does not have to file within a time limit is a request for accelerated examination. A document that can be filed at any time should always be filed in an official language of the EPO or else it may be deemed not to have been filed. Equally, applicants that do not fall within the group of applicants defined by Art. 14(4) must always use an official language of the EPO. Thus a Brazilian applicant resident in Brazil must use an official language of the EPO whereas a Portuguese applicant resident in Brazil or a Brazilian applicant resident in Portugal is entitled to use Portuguese. As discussed above, the nationality and residence of the applicant's representative is of no relevance. It may be that the applicant changes at some point in the proceedings. In such cases, it is the residence and nationality of the new applicant that is taken into account in assessing the language requirements for filing documents from that point onwards.

440   Some documents that the applicant must file within a time limit are associated with the payment of a fee. In the case of a request for examination an applicant having the necessary status can take advantage of the Art. 14(4) option to use an official language of a Contracting State and is entitled to a 30 % reduction of the examination fee (r.6(3) and RRFArt. 14(1) EPC). As with the filing fee, the reduction is available as long as the translation required under Art. 14(4) and r.6(2) EPC is filed later than or at the same time as the request for examination in the non-EPO language. The document that must be filed in an official language of a Contracting State (G6/91) is either a letter from the applicant containing a statement that the applicant requests examination or the EPO request form that bears a pre-printed statement to this effect in English, French and German. The language in which subsequent documents relating to the examination proceedings, such as the response to an Art. 94(3) communication, is filed in is irrelevant. According to J4/18, in the case of joint applicants, each one must be a natural person or entity within the meaning of r.6(4) EPC, as specified in r.6(7) EPC, but only one of them needs to be a person defined by Art. 14(4) for the fee reduction to apply.

441   The request for examination is not deemed to have been filed until the associated fee has been paid (Art. 94(1) EPC). This means that it is actually possible to file the request for examination in English, French or German, then file the same request in an official language of a Contracting State as per Art. 14(4) EPC and pay 70 % of the relevant fee. This is because the relevant document is not deemed filed until the fee is paid and the document in the qualifying Art. 14(4) language has been filed at the time the fee is paid and

hence is on file no later than the translation into an EPO official language is filed (G6/91). This is particularly important since, as mentioned above, the request for examination is pre-printed in English, French and German on the EPO Request form the use of which is mandatory if the application is to proceed beyond the stage of formalities examination (Art. 90(3), r.57(b) and r.41(1) EPC). As long as the examination fee has not been paid, it is therefore still possible to file the same request in an Art. 14(4) language and benefit from the fee reduction. This may be important where the applicant has changed and an applicant that qualifies for the fee reduction under Art. 14(4) has replaced an applicant that did not qualify. It may be noted that the pre-printed request for examination may also be withdrawn whilst the examination fee remains unpaid (J28/86).

Consider the following scenarios:

Scenario 1: A French applicant, resident in France, files a European patent application 442 using EPO Request form 1001 and paying the examination fee. The application is transferred to a Danish applicant shortly after publication.

The examination fee must be paid in full. A valid request for examination is made on the 443 filing date and the applicant is not entitled to the reduction at this point.

Scenario 2: A French applicant, resident in France, files a European patent application 444 using EPO Request form 1001 without paying the examination fee. The application is transferred to a Danish applicant shortly after publication, the tranfer is registered and automatic direct debiting is requested. The Danish applicant requests examination in Danish before expiry of the r.70(1) time limit.

Assuming the applicant declares he has the necessary status (r.6(6) EPC), the EPO 445 should automatically withdraw 70 % of the examination fee from the Danish applicant's deposit account on the last day of the r.70(1) period. At this point the applicant is qualified under Art. 14(4) to receive the r.6(3) discount and the request for examination in Danish becomes effective when the fee is paid, the request for examination in French not having become effective before this point.

Scenario 3: A French applicant, resident in France, files a European patent application 446 using EPO Request form 1001 without paying the examination fee. The application is transferred to a Danish applicant shortly after publication. The Danish applicant requests examination in Danish and pays the examination fee on the same day.

Assuming the applicant declares he has the necessary status (r.6(6) EPC), only 70 % of 447 the examination fee is due since at the time examination is requested by paying the fee the translation into Danish is on file. A request for examination in French has not taken effect earlier than this.

Scenario 4: A French applicant, resident in France, files a European patent application 448 using EPO Request form 1001 without paying the examination fee. The application is transferred to a Danish applicant shortly after publication. The Danish applicant pays the examination fee immediately and requests examination in Danish on the last day of the r.70(1) period.

The examination fee is due in full. A valid request for examination is made at the point 449 the fee is paid and the request for examination in Danish is filed later.

Third party observations must always be filed in an official language of the EPO since 450 there is no time limit for filing such observations and hence Art. 14(4) does not apply (r.114(1) EPC). Third party observations filed in Swedish are therefore deemed not to have been filed (Art. 14(4) EPC). They will, however, be put on file and the arguments they contain and/or documents they cite may be introduced into the proceedings by the EPO or, in inter partes proceedings, by another party.

Equally, a request for a stay of proceedings under r.14(1) EPC following the institution 451 of entitlement proceedings before a national authority must be filed in an official language of the EPO since there is no time limit for filing such a request and Art. 14(4) does not apply. If the request for a stay is refused then the third party can appeal. A notice of appeal is a document that must be filed within a time limit and Art. 14(4) EPC does apply – hence the third party could use an Art. 14(4) language if he was qualified to do so based on his nationality or residence.

When a European patent is granted, opposition proceedings and limitation/revocation 452 proceedings are possible. The opponent and proprietor operate under the same language regime in written proceedings as the applicant and may use any official language of the EPO (r.3(1) EPC) except where amendments to the application are concerned in which case the language of the proceedings is mandatory (r.3(2) EPC). A notice of opposition is a document that must be filed within a time limit and an opponent may therefore make use of the option to file the opposition in an official language of a Contracting State as per Art. 14(4) EPC (if he is a qualifying person) and then file a translation in an EPO official language within a one month period or within the opposition period if that expires later (r.6(2) EPC). Note that in post-grant proceedings, further processing is not available as a remedy if the time limit is not observed. Nor is re-establishment available to an opponent unless appeal proceedings are pending.

453   There is no time limit for filing a request for limitation or revocation and hence Art. 14(4) does not apply. However, the Implementing Regulations have been specifically amended in order extend the possibilities offered by Art. 14(4) to the filing of these documents. According to r.92(1), a request for limitation or revocation may therefore also be filed in an official language of a Contracting State **regardless of the residence or nationality of the proprietor**. A translation into an official language of the EPO must be filed within a one month period as usual (r.92(1) and r.6(2) EPC).

454   In oral proceedings, both a party to the proceedings and the EPO have a different degree of flexibility in deviating from the language of the proceedings. In fact, if the parties and the EPO agree then **any language** may be used (r.4(4) EPC) though the minutes must be recorded in an official language and amendments must be both made and recorded in the minutes in the language of proceedings (r.4(6) and r.3(2) EPC). If there is no such agreement then a party is nevertheless entitled to use any official language of the EPO, as is the case with written proceedings, but in this case only if at least one month's notice is given so that the EPO can arrange for translation into the language of the proceedings or if the party provides such translation itself (r.4(1) and r.4(5) EPC). A party may also use an official language of a Contracting State if he provides translation into the language of the proceedings himself (r.4(1) EPC). The EPO is itself entitled in oral proceedings to use any official language of the EPO as long as it provides translation into the language of the proceedings (r.4(2) and r.4(5) EPC) whereas, as pointed out above, it has no such flexibility in written proceedings.

1.7.7   *Filing of documents – other considerations*

455   The filing of documents is fundamental aspect of all proceedings under the EPC and the requirements that determine whether a document is validly filed or not are therefore frequently examined in the EQE. Certain considerations such a the calculation of any time limit that applies and the choice of language have already been considered. Other aspects of importance are (1) the person entitled to file the document; (2) the place at which the document is filed; (3) the means chosen to file the document; and (4) the need for a signature.

456   A natural or legal person who is resident in a Contracting State or has a principle place of business in a Contracting State, regardless of nationality, has the choice of either representing himself before the EPO or acting through a professional representative, a legal practitioner or an employee (Art. 133 EPC). A natural person may obviously represent themselves as such whereas a legal person must represent themselves through a person entitled to exert the will of the relevant company or organisation such as a director.

457   If a representative of any kind is to be used then the representative will need to be both authorised and appointed. Being authorised is simply a matter of having been given the right by the relevant natural or legal person to act on their behalf. Such authorisation may be verbal or written but in certain cases the EPO will require written evidence that authorisation has been granted. A written authorisation may be specific for one or more applications/patents/oppositions or may be a general authorisation that is valid for all proceedings. Appointment is a matter of telling the EPO who the representative is – this can be done by the relevant natural or legal person in which case the authorisation is implicit or by the representative in which case explicit evidence of authorisation may be required. The natural or legal person may, for example, file an application or an opposition and appoint a representative in the request or accompanying letter or the representative may file the application or opposition himself, appointing himself as representative. Once a representative has been properly appointed, the EPO must address all correspondence to that representative rather than the natural or legal person (r.130(1) EPC).

The situations in which a written, signed authorisation is required are determined by the President of the EPO (r.152(1) EPC; Decision dated 12.7.2007, [2007] O.J. Special Edition No. 3 L1). A professional representative is only obliged to file an authorisation or refer to a general authorisation (1) where there is a change of professional representative, the two representatives are not members of the same association, and the previous representative has not terminated his appointment; and (2) where the EPO has any specific reason to doubt the professional representative's entitlement to act. Employees and legal practitioners, on the other hand, always need to file an authorisation. If a required authorisation is not filed, or a reference to a general authorisation made, then the EPO will write to the representative who has appointed himself and request that the deficiency be remedied within a time limit set by the EPO (r.152(2) EPC). In the case where a second professional representative is appointed, the request for an authorisation may be disregarded if the first representative terminates his appointment within the period set. Otherwise, if the deficiency is not remedied in due time then any procedural steps taken by the purported representative, other than the filing of an application, will be deemed not to have been taken (r.152(6) EPC). So, for example, if an opposition is filed by a legal practitioner without an authorisation and the authorisation is not filed following a request from the EPO, the opposition is deemed not filed.

Any representative needs to be appropriately qualified for the role. In the case of a professional representative, the person concerned must have been entered on the list maintained by the EPO (Art. 134(1) EPC). In the case of a legal practitioner, the person concerned must have a legal qualification in a Contracting State and a place of business in that State and be entitled to act as a professional representative in patent matters in that State (Art. 134(8) EPC). In the case of an employee, the person concerned must be directly employed by the legal entity that is acting before the EPO (Art. 133(3) EPC) – it is not sufficient that he is employed by a different legal entity that is under common ownership. Any act that is purportedly carried out by a person not qualified to act as a representative is formally invalid (J28/86). However, this does not usually lead to an immediate loss of rights since the EPO will usually treat the document as having been wrongly signed and issue an invitation to correct the deficiency under r.50(3) EPC (T665/89). If the document is re-submitted bearing the signature of an authorised representative within the time limit set then the document will be deemed to have been properly filed on the original date of receipt. If the deficiency is not corrected in time, however, the document will be deemed not to have been filed.

A natural or legal person who is not resident in a Contracting State and has no principle place of business in a Contracting State has fewer choices with respect to representation (Art. 133(2) EPC). Such a person must be represented by a professional representative or a legal practitioner in order to carry out any act other than the filing of a European patent application (Art. 133(2) EPC), the entry of a Euro-PCT application into the regional phase or the payment of a fee (Guidelines A-X, 1). Any other act carried out by a natural or legal person requiring representation is formally invalid. However, as discussed above, this does not usually lead to an immediate loss of rights since the EPO will usually treat the document as having been wrongly signed (e.g. signed by the applicant instead of the representative) and issue an invitation to correct the deficiency under r.50(3) EPC (T665/89).

Sometimes there may be joint applicants, proprietors or opponents. Such a group of persons must always act though a common representative determined under Art. 133(4) and r.151(1) EPC. The various ways in which a group of persons may be commonly represented is very complicated and an exact interpretation of the law is difficult to come by, either in the case law or the Guidelines. The following is offered as one credible interpretation. The first question to ask is: do any of the members of the group require professional representation? If the answer to this question is "yes" then it is mandatory to appoint a professional representative or legal practitioner as common representative since it is an absolute requirement that a natural or legal person not having their residence or principle place of business in a Contracting State must be represented (r.133(2) EPC). If no representative is appointed by the group acting as a whole (e.g. according to r.41(3) EPC), or the first-named member of the group acting independently (r.151(1) EPC second sentence), then the EPO will ask the party requiring representation to appoint one and this person will be the common representative.

458

459

460

461

462   Where no members of the group require professional representation then one of them may act as common representative on behalf of the group as a whole. Thus, if Mr A and Mr B are both inventors and not legally qualified in any way, Mr A could not represent Mr B before the EPO for an application filed in the name of Mr B but Mr A can represent both himself and Mr B before the EPO for an application filed in the name of Mr A and Mr B jointly. This follows by virtue of Art. 133(1) EPC which provides that, save for the requirement of Art. 133(2) EPC, no applicant (whether joint or single) is compelled to appoint a professional representative. Any of the applicants/opponents may be chosen as common representative and named as such in the request (r.41(3)) or notice of opposition. If none is named in this way then the first named applicant/opponent is deemed to be common representative. The common representative determined in this way has the choice of conducting proceedings himself before the EPO or appointing a professional representative or legal practitioner to conduct proceedings on his behalf. He may also name an employee to act on his behalf. According to Art. 133(3) EPC, natural or legal persons having their residence or principle place of business in a Contracting State may be represented by an employee and no distinction is made between single and joint applicants. Thus, whilst the employee of one legal entity may not act as representative for an application filed in the name of a different legal entity in the case of a single applicant (no provision has been made in the Regulations re. Art. 133(2) second sentence), an employee may act as common representative where an application is filed jointly in the name of his own employer and a different legal entity.

463   When considering where a document may be filed, one must distinguish between new European patent applications on the one hand and all other documents on the other. For new European patent applications (i.e. excluding divisional applications and replacement applications filed under Art. 61(1)(b) EPC) there is a choice between filing at one of the EPO filing offices and with the competent authority of a Contracting State that is willing to accept the application on behalf of the EPO. The filing offices of the EPO are Munich, the Hague and Berlin (r.35(1) EPC). Of the Contracting States, all allow the filing of European patent applications except for San Marino, the Netherlands and Belgium (National Law Book, Table II). There is no nationality or residency requirement so that, for instance, a European patent application could be filed at the French Intellectual Property Office by a German applicant resident in Austria, but each office is free to specify the conditions under which applications will be accepted. For instance, filing by facsimile or electronically is not permitted by the Estonian office and the Norwegian office will only accept applications filed in Norwegian, English, French or German. The application receives as filing date the date on which it is received by the EPO filing office or the competent national authority. If a European patent application is filed at a place not competent to receive it (e.g. the Netherlands patent office, the patent office of an extension state or the Vienna office of the EPO), it cannot be accorded a filing date. If, as a matter of courtesy, it is forwarded to an EPO filing office, it can only be accorded as filing date the date on which it reaches that filing office.

464   All other applications and documents, including European divisional applications, replacement applications filed under Art. 61(1)(b), documents concerning the entry into the regional phase of a Euro-PCT application, documents relating to the prosecution of a European patent application, oppositions, requests for a stay of proceedings, requests for the limitation or revocation of a European patent, appeals and petitions for review must be filed directly at an EPO filing office. If such an application or document is filed anywhere else (e.g. at a national patent office or the Vienna office of the EPO), it cannot be accorded a date of receipt. If, as a matter of courtesy, it is forwarded to an EPO filing office, it can only be accorded as date of receipt the date on which it reaches that filing office (Decision of the President dated 03.01.2017, [2017] O.J. A11, Art. 1(2)).

465   In terms of the means chosen to file a document, there are three options: (1) a document may be filed in writing, either by hand, by post or by utilising some kind of delivery service; (2) a document may be filed by facsimile; or (3) a document may be filed electronically. No other means of communication, such as telegram, telex or e-mail may be used (r.2(1) EPC and Decision of the President dated 20.02.2019, [2019] O.J. A18). The only exception is that e-mail is acceptable and indeed must be used during telephone consultations and during interviews and oral proceedings held by videoconference to file

all documents including authorisations (Decision of the President dated 13 May 2020, [2020] O.J. A71). Documents filed by such other means of communication are deemed not received.

All documents may be filed in writing both at the EPO and, in the case of a new ap- 466
plication, at the competent authority of a Contracting State (r.35(1) EPC, r.2(1) EPC and Decision of the President dated 03 January 2017, [2017] O.J. A11). The EPO filing offices are available for this purpose 24 hours a day, 365 days a year having either an automated mail box or a porter service. This also applies to international applications (r.89*bis*.1(a) PCT).

All documents **other than authorisations and priority documents** may be also filed 467
at the EPO by facsimile (r.2(1) EPC and Decision of the President dated 20.2.2019, [2019] O.J. A18). Competent national authorities are free to choose whether they allow the filing of new European patent applications by facsimile or not. A confirmation copy in writing does not have to be filed unless the EPO specifically requests one. If the confirmation copy of a European patent application is not filed within the two month period set the application will be refused (Decision of the President dated 20.2.2019, [2019] O.J. A18 Art. 7). In all other cases, if a requested confirmation copy is not filed within the two month time limit set then the original fax is deemed not received. If a facsimile is received over two days (i.e. starting before midnight on one day and finishing after midnight on the subsequent day) then the date of receipt is, in principle, the day on which the transmission finishes. In the case of an application, the part arriving after midnight can be renounced in order to obtain the earlier filing date (Art. 5(2) of the President's decision) but in the case of any other document this is not possible (Art. 5(3) of the President's decision and T858/18).

International patent applications may also be filed at the EPO by facsimile but a con- 468
firmation copy in writing is always required in this case (r.92.4(a) PCT and Decision of the President dated 20.2.2019, [2019] O.J. A18 Art. 2). If the confirmation copy is not supplied and an invitation from the EPO is ignored then the international application is considered to be withdrawn (r.92.4(g) PCT).

Applications and subsequent documents may be filed electronically using EPO Online 469
Filing (OLF), Online Filing 2.0, the web-form filing service or the EPO Contingency Upload Service (see Decision of the President dated 03 May 2023, [2023] O.J. A48) except that priority documents may only be filed electronically if they have been digitally signed by the issuing authority in a manner acceptable to the EPO and may not in any case be filed by web-form filing. Many other exceptions exist for web-form filing. Although authorisations must be supplied as an original according to the Decision of the President dated 12.7.2007 ([2007] O.J. Special Edition No. 3 L1), it seems that the EPO will nevertheless accept the electronic filing of authorisations (other than by web form filing). No confirmation copy is required in the case of electronic filing. Competent national authorities are free to choose whether they allow the filing of new European patent applications electronically or not.

International applications and documents relating thereto may also be filed electron- 470
ically at the EPO (r.89*bis*.1(a) PCT and Decision of the President dated 03 May 2023, [2023] O.J. A48). No confirmation copy is required.

The request accompanying a European patent application must be signed by each of the 471
applicants or their representative (r.41(2)(h) EPC). If it not properly signed, the EPO will request that the deficiency is corrected under r.58 EPC. If the deficiency is not corrected then the application is refused (Art. 90(5) EPC). Equally, all later documents concerning the application (including a notice of opposition, a notice of appeal, a request for limitation/revocation and a petition for review) must be signed (r.50(3) EPC). If an unsigned document is filed (or a document is filed with the signature of a person not entitled to file it), the EPO will request that the deficiency is corrected under r.50(3) EPC. If the deficiency is corrected then the document maintains its original date of receipt. If it is not corrected then the document is deemed not to have been filed.

Third party observations, on the other hand, do not have to be signed to be taken into 472
account. In fact, they can even be filed anonymously in many cases. This is because, according to decision T1336/09, r.50(3) EPC only applies to parties to proceedings before the EPO and, since somebody who files third party observations does not become a party to the proceedings (Art. 115 EPC), the requirement for a signature does not apply. This

interpretation was not, however, adopted by the Board in T146/07, which considered that r.50(3) applies to all documents filed in writing. Nevertheless, the latter decision concerned inter partes proceedings in which one party may try to gain a procedural advantage by filing observations under Art. 115 late in the proceedings that it would either not have been entitled to file as a party to the proceedings (in view of their late filing) or the filing of which as a party to the proceedings would have led to an award of costs. Thus, according to the current case law, third party observations filed anonymously in inter partes proceedings may be deemed not filed whereas third party observations filed anonymously in ex parte proceedings will likely be deemed filed. Even when deemed not filed, third party observations still form part of the prosecution file and it is still possible for a party to the proceedings to adopt the relevant arguments as part of its own case (T735/04).

1.7.8   The prohibition of reformatio in peius

473   According to Enlarged Board of Appeal decisions G9/92 and G1/99, reformatio in peius is prohibited under the legal framework of the EPC. Reformatio in peius is not addressed at all in the articles and rules of the EPC but its prohibition may be considered to be a generally recognised principle of procedural law falling within the ambit of Art. 125 EPC. According to the prohibition of reformation in peius, a party that appeals a decision of a first instance department as sole appellant should not end up in a worse position than if they had not appealed at all.

474   Reformatio in peius only has relevance in opposition proceedings where the patent is maintained in amended form since it is only in this situation that a sole appellant's position can be made both better and worse. Consider the following scenarios:

475   **Scenario 1**: Application refused by the Examining Division.
The applicant is adversely affected and may appeal. The applicant has lost his application and his position cannot be made worse on appeal.

476   **Scenario 2**: Patent revoked by the Opposition Division.
The patentee is the adversely affected party and may appeal. The patentee has lost his patent and his position cannot be made worse on appeal.

477   **Scenario 3**: Opposition rejected by the Opposition Division.
The opponent is the adversely affected party and may appeal. The opponent has achieved nothing and his position cannot be made worse on appeal.

478   **Scenario 4**: Patent maintained in amended form by the Opposition Division.
Both the patentee and the opponent are adversely affected (assuming the opponent requested revocation and the patentee requested rejection of the opposition) and may appeal. The opponent's position may be made worse if the patent is maintained as granted or in a form broader than that upheld by the opposition division. The patentee's position may be made worse if the patent is revoked or maintained in a form narrower than that upheld by the opposition division.

479   It is thus only in scenario 4 that the appellant's position may be made worse and the principle of reformation in peius needs to be considered. However, the principle applies only where one of the patentee and opponent **does not appeal** (or where both appeal but one of the appeals is withdrawn). If both parties appeal then they are both contesting the decision and have the right to argue that the other party should be put in a worse position. However, a non-appealing party is implicitly indicating satisfaction with the outcome of the first instance proceedings and is not asking for anything going beyond the decision taken. Consider the following scenarios:

480   **Scenario 4a**: Patent maintained in amended form by the Opposition Division. Both parties appeal.
Both parties are expressing dissatisfaction with the decision reached by the Opposition Division and in each case the appeal is filed in order to seek a more favourable outcome that by definition will put the other party in a worse position.

481   **Scenario 4b**: Patent maintained in amended form by the Opposition Division. Only the patentee appeals.
The patentee is filing an appeal in order to seek a broader scope of protection that that allowed by the Opposition Division. The opponent, by not filing an appeal, is indicating that he agrees with the decision of the opposition division and does not think that the patent should be limited any further.

Scenario 4c: Patent maintained in amended form by the Opposition Division. Only the   482
opponent appeals.

The opponent is filing an appeal in order to seek restriction of the scope of the patent
beyond the scope allowed by the Opposition Division. The patentee, by not filing an appeal, is indicating that he agrees with the decision of the opposition division and does not
think the patent should be maintained with a broader scope.

Scenario 4d: Patent maintained in amended form by the Opposition Division. Both   483
parties appeal but the opponent withdraws his appeal shortly after filing the grounds of
appeal.

The patentee is filing an appeal in order to seek a broader scope of protection that that
allowed by the Opposition Division. The opponent, by withdrawing his appeal, is indicating that he agrees with the decision of the opposition division and does not think that
the patent should be limited any further.

It is thus in scenarios 4b, 4c and 4d that the principle of the prohibition of reformatio in   484
peius applies. In scenario 4b and scenario 4d, the opponent is not allowed to make any requests that seek to limit the scope of the patent as compared with the form upheld by the
Opposition Division (and neither is the Board of Appeal allowed to challenge that decision). The appeal proceedings are solely for the purpose of giving the patentee the chance
to seek broader protection and the opponent can only challenge the maintenance of the
patent in a form broader than that upheld by the Opposition Division. In scenario 4c, the
patentee is not allowed to make any requests that seek to expand the scope of the patent as
compared with the form upheld by the Opposition Division. The appeal proceedings are
solely for the purpose of giving the opponent a chance to seek further limitation or revocation of the patent and the patentee must defend the patent as upheld by the Opposition
Division or in a narrower form.

These are the principles established by G9/92. The reasoning behind these principles   485
is that the purpose of an appeal is to seek rectification of the decision taken – appeal proceedings are not a continuation of the first instance proceedings in which re-examination
of all the issues is conducted. It is the appellant who brings the appeal into existence who
determines the scope of those proceedings on the basis of the requests made. Other parties
become parties as of right and may present arguments that call into question the requests
of the appellant but they may not present arguments that call into question the decision
itself since they have not appealed that decision. For the same reasons, if the sole appellant
withdraws his appeal, proceedings are immediately terminated regardless of the opinion
of the other parties and the Board of Appeal (G7/91).

However, the application of this principle in scenario 4c, could lead to an inequita-   486
ble result if the Board of Appeal agreed with the opponent that the form of the patent
maintained by the Opposition Division was unallowable and the relevant objection could
only be overcome by the patentee by proposing amended claims with a broader scope.
Typically, for example, this could arise where the claims upheld by the Opposition Division were considered to contain added subject matter contrary to Art. 123(2) EPC in
view of the introduction of a limiting feature. Such a request would be contrary to the
principle of the prohibition of reformatio in peius. On the other hand, if the request was
not allowed, the patent would have to be revoked despite the fact that it may disclose
patentable subject matter.

This scenario was considered in G1/99. It was held that as a narrow exception, refor-   487
matio in peius does not apply when the **only** way in which a patent can be amended to
make it valid is to increase the scope of protection beyond the scope maintained by the
Opposition Division. Even then, where more than one amendment is possible, only the
amendment that increases the scope of protection to the least extent possible is allowable – the removal of a limiting feature so that the patent is upheld as granted should only
be allowed as worst case scenario when no other options exist.

As a concrete example, consider a patent directed to a process for making a compound   488
wherein, according to the sole novel feature, the temperature must be held at 150–275°C.
The patent is maintained in amended form by the Opposition Division with a temperature range of 225–275°C in view of an inventive step objection raised by the opponent
(the advantages of the invention are allegedly not obtained at lower temperatures). The
lower limit of the amended range (225°C) is based on Fig. 1, a graph plotting yield against
temperature. Only the opponent appeals, requesting complete revocation of the patent.

The Board of Appeal agrees with the opponent's objection that the claim as maintained contains added subject matter, the lower limit of the range not being unambiguously derivable from the graph. Consider the following scenarios:

Scenario 1: The patent does not contain any other preferred features relating to the temperature range.

489   In this case, the only way of amending the patent to provide a claim that is allowable under Art. 123(2) is to revert to the scope of the patent as granted. Reformatio in peius must be tolerated.

Scenario 2: The description indicates that the reaction is preferably carried out at T=220–250°C.

490   In this case, the patentee is not allowed to defend the patent in the form it was granted but must defend it with the temperature range 220–250°C. Although this represents reformatio in peius to an extent (the range 220–225°C goes beyond the scope of the patent as maintained), it is the less harmful amendment from the opponent's perspective.

Scenario 3: The description indicates that the reaction is preferably carried out at T=220–250°C, most preferably at 250–260°C.

491   In this case, the patentee is not allowed to defend the patent in the form it was granted or using the temperature range T=220–250°C since it is possible to introduce a more limiting amendment (T=250–260°C) that narrows protection vis-à-vis the patent as maintained by the Opposition Division.

492   It should be noted that the principle of the prohibition of reformatio in peius does not always apply if the factual situation has changed on appeal as compared to the first instance proceedings. If a patentee does not file an appeal, for example, then he is taken to have indicated that he is satisfied with the decision of the opposition division and does not wish to seek broader protection. If, in these circumstances, the opponent introduces new facts and/or arguments in his grounds of appeal that render the patent as maintained by the opposition division no longer defensible then reformatio in peius should not be applied since the opponent has introduced new elements which undermine the assessment of the interlocutory decision made by the patentee. This was recognised in G1/99 where it was stated that "if the patent cannot be maintained for reasons which were not raised at first instance, the non-appealing proprietor deserves protection for reasons of equity". Thus, if the opponent objects in his grounds of appeal for the first time that a feature introduced to limit the patent in opposition proceedings introduces a lack of clarity or introduces added subject matter (or the Board of Appeal raises such an objection for the first time) then the principle of the prohibition of double patenting may not apply and the proprietor may be allowed to delete that feature (see, for example, T974/10). Equally, if a new novelty-destroying document is introduced on appeal which makes the validity of the priority claim a key issue, the proprietor should be allowed to delete a limiting amendment made in first instance proceedings which had the effect of taking away the entitlement of the claims to priority (T1843/09).

1.7.9   *The nature of opposition proceedings – in what way do they differ from grant proceedings?*

493   Opposition proceedings offer an opportunity to members of the public to contest the grant of a European patent and demonstrate why, in part or in full, the patent does not meet one of a number of key criteria for patentability, allowing the European Patent Office an opportunity to amend its grant decision as appropriate. A new character, the opponent, has entered the stage to join the proprietor and the EPO and the fact that multiple parties are involved means that opposition proceedings have a fundamentally different character as compared with grant proceedings. In grant proceedings, the applicant and the EPO (as represented by an Examining Division) are discussing whether a patent should be granted and, if so, on what terms. The EPO has a single relationship with the applicant to manage and takes a very active role in the discussion: it carries out its own search, makes its own objections where appropriate and may suggest amendments that it considers would overcome those objections. In opposition proceedings, on the contrary, the EPO has two relationships to manage as recognised in the following terms in G9/91: "Post grant opposition proceedings under the EPC are in principle to be considered as contentious proceedings between parties normally representing opposite interests, who

should be given equally fair treatment" (Reasons 2). As a result, the EPO (as represented by an Opposition Division) takes a less active, less investigative role in opposition proceedings than it does in grant proceedings, predominantly playing the role of an arbiter seeking to resolve a dispute between two quarrelling parties in the most equitable manner possible. On the other hand, there is an overriding interest in maintaining only valid patents and so the Opposition Division does not take an entirely passive role – there is a balance to be struck. If the Opposition Division finds itself in a situation in which it is impossible to resolve a particular matter in favour of either party, for example in the case of conflicting and equally valid experimental results, then the benefit of the doubt is given to the proprietor since the opponent always has a second chance to have the patent revoked in national revocation proceedings (Guidelines D-V, 2.2; G9/91, Reasons 18).

Another important point to appreciate is that opposition proceedings are not an opportunity to re-open examination proceedings with an additional party at the table and discuss whether the decision to grant a patent was correct in all its aspects. Opposition proceedings are entirely separate proceedings with a much more limited agenda. The question to be answered is no longer what scope, if any, a patent should be granted with, bearing in mind all the requirements of the EPC, but whether a particular patent, granted with a defined scope, should be restricted or revoked on the basis that it does not meet one of the specific grounds of Art. 100 EPC. Both parties are constrained as compared to grant proceedings: the patentee may not ask for his patent to be maintained any more broadly than the original decision to grant (Art. 123(3) EPC) and the opponent may not object to the patent on any ground other than those specified in Art. 100 EPC.   494

These important principles shape the nature of opposition proceedings from the outset, influencing even the composition of the Opposition Division which is to conduct them. According to Art. 19(2) EPC only one of the three members of the Opposition Division may have been a member of the Examining Division that granted the contested patent and that member may not be the chairman. This different composition recognises that the proceedings are not a continuation or re-opening of the grant proceedings but new, different proceedings that should be conducted by a newly composed panel and that it would not be a fair treatment of the two opposing parties if the panel was composed wholly or mainly of members who had already taken a decision that the patent and invention to which it relates meet the requirements of the EPC.   495

According to Art. 99(1) EPC, any person may oppose a European patent. However, despite its clear, literal meaning, this term has been interpreted by the Enlarged Board of Appeal in light of the important principles established above to mean any person other than the patent proprietor (G9/93). This is because opposition proceedings are contentious proceedings conducted by two parties representing different interests whose dispute is heard and decided upon by the EPO. Such proceedings depend on the participation of two different parties – to allow the proprietor to oppose his own patent would institute proceedings akin to grant proceedings in which the proprietor and the Opposition Division decided together the text with which the patent should be maintained. Neither may the proprietor circumvent this requirement by inducing another person to file an opposition on his behalf against his own patent (G3/97). Of course, there is no need for a proprietor to act in this way since separate limitation or revocation proceedings are open to him under Art. 105a(1) EPC. There is otherwise no limitation on who may oppose a European patent – there is no need, for example, to show that the opponent's activities are in any way limited by the rights conferred by the patent.   496

In order for an opposition to be admissible under r.77(1) EPC, the opponent must, within the nine month opposition period of Art. 99(1) EPC, indicate the extent to which the patent is opposed (i.e. whether revocation as a whole is sought or whether only the deletion of certain claims is sought or whether the scope of protection of the patent is to be limited to a certain specified point) and the grounds according to Art. 100 which prejudice the validity of the patent, as well as giving an indication of the facts and evidence relating to those grounds (r.76(2)(c) EPC). If no opposition is filed within the nine month time limit then the EPO has no jurisdiction to amend the patent in any way. The jurisdiction of the Opposition Division is therefore brought into being by the notice of opposition and, given its restricted investigative role, the Opposition Division should therefore conduct the proceedings primarily within the framework established by that notice (G9/91). Indeed, if the extent of the opposition is partial in the sense that the validity of one or   497 more of the independent claims of the patent is not called into question then the Opposition Division has no right to consider the validity of those independent claims (and their dependent claims) at all (G9/91). Only the validity of the independent claims that are included within the initial scope of the opposition may be considered, along with the validity of any dependent claims whose validity is also prima facie in doubt. In relation to grounds of opposition, the Opposition Division is allowed a somewhat more investigative role and may consider any ground of opposition, even if it was not raised by the opponent within the opposition period, and even if it is not raised by the opponent at all, if that ground would prejudice maintenance of the patent. According to G10/91, the Opposition Division should first conduct a prima facie assessment of whether the new ground would prejudice the maintenance of the patent before deciding whether to admit it into the proceedings or not. Thus the degree to which the Opposition Division investigates matters of its own motion (Art. 114(1) EPC) is carefully balanced in view of its role as an impartial arbiter on the one hand and the desirability of only upholding valid patents on the other.

498   As already mentioned, those grounds for opposition that may be raised by the opponent are strictly limited and do not include many of the grounds for refusal that the Examining Division may cite – opposition proceedings are not a rerun of grant proceedings. It is not a ground of opposition, for example, that the patent lacks unity of invention according to Art. 82 EPC and, even if the claims of the patent are amended during opposition proceedings to introduce a lack of unity (e.g. by splitting a single independent claim into two or more narrower independent claims in response to a novelty objection), this cannot be objected to by the opponent or the Opposition Division (G1/91). Neither is lack of clarity under Art. 84 a ground of opposition. If the claims of the patent are amended by simply deleting claims or combining dependent claims then this may not be objected to under Art. 84 either since the remaining subject matter was effectively disclosed in the claims of the patent and such an objection would therefore be tantamount to using lack of clarity as a ground of opposition (G3/14). On the other hand, if the claims are amended by introducing a new feature from the description, which is itself unclear or which introduces a lack of clarity, then an objection under Art. 84 is a valid objection against maintenance of the patent. In this case it is the amendment that is being objected to rather than the granted patent. In deciding that amended claims may, in such instances, be objected to under Art. 84 but amended claims may never be objected to under Art. 82 EPC, the Enlarged Board of Appeal has considered in each case the purpose behind the different objections. Claims must be clear so that third parties can understand the scope of patents and avoid trespassing on other people's intellectual property – this applies to patents as granted by the Examining Division and patents as maintained in amended form by the Opposition Division. On the other hand, unity of invention has a less substantive more administrative function which is of primary importance in grant proceedings – to ensure sufficient search and examination fees are paid and that published patent documents can be efficiently searched.

499   Because the grounds of opposition are limited, and in keeping with the desirability of treating parties equally in contentious proceedings, the ability of the proprietor to amend his patent is similarly restricted. Thus, according to r.80 EPC, the patent may only be amended if such amendment is occasioned by a ground of opposition under Art. 100 EPC. This means that to the extent an opponent is able to contest the validity of the patent, the proprietor is able to amend the patent to meet that objection but no other amendment is allowed; each amendment must be justified by the nature of the proceedings. Whether the actual objection has been raised or not is unimportant: if the objection is possible then the corresponding amendment is admissible. This prevents the proprietor, for example, from strengthening his patent by adding new dependent claims that correspond to commercially utilised features of the invention, whilst giving him the freedom to propose a text for maintenance of the patent which cannot be successfully contested by the opponent. The proprietor is further limited in opposition proceedings by compliance with Art. 123(3) EPC – nothing may infringe the patent as maintained in opposition proceedings which did not infringe the patent as granted in order to protect legal certainty for third parties. The Opposition Division, in contrast to the Examining Division, will not propose amendments which it believes would lead to the maintenance of a valid patent since this would not be compatible with its duty to treat the parties equally. It is for the proprietor to propose amendments, for the opponent to make comments on their admissibility and

allowability and for the Opposition Division to decide on the matter having heard both parties.

The proprietor is given a chance to respond to the notice of opposition by filing obser-   500
vations and/or amending the patent within a period of four months (r.79(1) and r.132(2) EPC; Guidelines D-IV, 5.2). Any new grounds and evidence filed after the expiry of the opposition period by the opponent and any new requests for amendment filed after expiry of this four month period by the proprietor are in principle late filed and their admissibility can be contested by the other party (Art. 114(2) EPC). In conducting the opposition proceedings in a manner that is fair to both parties, the Opposition Division will balance a range of different criteria when deciding on the admissibility of such late filed submissions. In the case of new grounds and evidence, the primary criterion will be their prima facie relevance to the decision to be taken – if they are prima facie relevant then they should be taken into account regardless of their lateness in view of the desirability of only maintaining valid patents (Guidelines E-VI, 2). In relation to late filed requests, the primary criterion will be their prima facie allowability, i.e. whether they are suitable to overcome outstanding objections without introducing any further ground for objection (Guidelines E-VI, 2.2, referring to H-II, 2.7.1). Other factors to be taken into account include any reasons that objectively justify the late filing, the state of the proceedings (i.e. the need to bring proceedings to a timely conclusion) and the attitude of the other party or parties.

One aspect of the procedure that serves to illustrate the fact that opposition proceedings   501
are separate proceedings and not a continuation of grant proceedings is the lack of binding precedent. There is no binding effect of decisions taken during grant proceedings on the freedom of the Opposition Division to decide on the opposition. The Opposition Division may decide, for example, that the patent as granted lacks novelty over a document cited in the European search report which the Examining Division fully considered and found to not be prejudicial to novelty. Furthermore, a decision of a Board of Appeal during grant proceedings is binding on the Examining Division under Art. 111(2) EPC but is not binding on the Opposition Division in subsequent opposition proceedings (T167/93). Equally, the contentious nature of opposition proceedings is illustrated by the fact that oral proceedings before the Opposition Division are usually open to the public whereas oral proceedings before the Examining Division are not (Art. 116(3) and (4) EPC). Grant proceedings are a closed negotiation between the applicant and Examining Division, both in written and oral proceedings, to which other parties and the public at large have no access (with the exception of the right to file written third party observations). In opposition proceedings, on the other hand, the public has already been admitted through the participation of the opponent as a party and there is no reason why oral proceedings should not be generally publicly accessible.

Sometimes, the need to try and ensure only valid patents are upheld takes precedence   502
over the need to respect the contentious nature of the proceedings and the Opposition Division is allowed a more investigational role. This is most clearly demonstrated in the situation in which the opposition is withdrawn (r.84(2) EPC). If the proceedings were truly contentious then it would be logical to assume that withdrawal of the opposition would lead to their immediate termination. If the EPO has no competence to examine the patent but for the filing of the opposition then the withdrawal of the opposition should once more remove that competence. However, this is not the case. If the opposition is withdrawn then the Opposition Division may nevertheless continue the opposition proceedings of its own motion, invoking its general power under Art. 114(1) EPC. As usual, however, there is a balance to be struck – proceedings are not always continued. The Opposition Division must take a prima facie view on the likelihood of the patent being limited in some way on the basis of the proceedings as they stand at the moment of withdrawal. If, for example, the proprietor has already resiled from the patent as granted and requested that the patent be maintained in amended form then the proceedings will likely continue. Equally, if the opponent has shown convincingly that the claims of the granted patent lack novelty over a new prior art document and the Opposition Division does not require the further participation of the opponent from an evidentiary perspective then proceedings are also likely to be continued. In exceptional cases, the Opposition Division may also take a more investigational role by carrying out its own search but there must be a clear justification for this (Guidelines D-VI, 5). The contentious nature of opposition

proceedings usually demands impartiality and inhibits the Opposition Division from taking any steps to improve the position of either side by proposing allowable amendments on behalf of the proprietor or citing further prior art documents on behalf of the opponent.

503   Opposition proceedings must be terminated by means of a decision. Grant proceedings, on the other hand, may be terminated by a decision (to refuse the application or grant a patent) or else by withdrawal or deemed withdrawal of the application. However, in opposition proceedings the patent may not be withdrawn or deemed withdrawn. The patent may lapse by its withdrawal (surrender) in the Contracting States or non-payment of a renewal fees but in this case it leaves rights outstanding which the opponent has a legitimate interest in contesting (Art. 68 and r.84(1) EPC). Equally, the patent is granted and in force and in no sense can be deemed withdrawn – if no response to a communication from the Opposition Division is filed by the proprietor then no immediate loss of rights occurs, though the Opposition Division may be able to take an adverse decision without giving the proprietor any further right to comment. The opposition may be withdrawn, as discussed above, but this does not terminate proceedings since the Opposition Division may continue of its own motion. There is no deemed withdrawal of the opposition in the same way as there is no deemed withdrawal of the patent. If no response to a communication from the Opposition Division is filed by the opponent, the Opposition Division simply moves forward with the proceedings in an appropriate manner bearing in mind the right of the opponent to be heard (Art. 113(1) EPC). The Opposition Division must therefore terminate the proceedings by taking a decision either that the opposition is inadmissible; that the opposition is allowable and the patent is revoked; that the opposition is rejected and the patent is maintained as granted; that the patent as amended meets the requirements of the EPC and is to be upheld in that form if no appeal is filed and formal requirements are met; or that the opposition proceedings are terminated. A decision to simply terminate the proceedings is appropriate, for example, if the patent has lapsed in all states and the opponent does not wish to continue the proceedings (r.84(1) EPC) or an earlier and admissible request under Art. 105a(1) to revoke the patent has been filed by the proprietor.

1.7.10 The nature of appeal proceedings – in what way do they differ from first instance proceedings?

504   Appeal proceedings allow a party to proceedings before the EPO that has been adversely affected by a decision of the Receiving Section, an Examining Division, an Opposition Division or the Legal Decision to have an independent review of the correctness of the decision taken (Art. 106(1) and Art. 107 EPC). Adversely affected in this sense means that the party has been denied what it has requested or, where more than one request has been made, that it has been denied its main request. So, for example, an applicant who has requested the grant of a patent and had his application refused by the Examining Decision or Receiving Section is adversely affected; a proprietor who has requested maintenance of his patent as granted and has had the patent revoked or considered to meet the requirements of the EPC only in an amended form by the Opposition Division is adversely affected; an opponent who has requested revocation of a patent and has had his opposition rejected or the patent maintained in an amended form by the Opposition Division is adversely affected; an applicant whose application has been deemed withdrawn and who has had a request for re-establishment refused by the Examining Division or Receiving Section is adversely affected; and a third party who has had his request for a stay of proceedings refused by the Legal Division, following the commencement of an entitlement dispute, is adversely affected. On the other hand, the proprietor who defends an opposition on the basis of restricted claims is not adversely affected by a decision to maintain the patent in that amended form even though the opposition has been partly successful and an opponent who indicates that he has no objections to the maintenance of a patent in a certain form is not adversely affected by a decision to maintain the patent in that form even though the patent has not been revoked.

505   It therefore necessarily follows that appeal proceedings do not exist independently but are based on proceedings that have already taken place before what is commonly termed a "first instance" department of the EPO (Receiving Section, Examining Division,

Opposition Division or Legal Division). A key point to appreciate in understanding how appeal proceedings work is that appeal proceedings are not a continuation of those first instance proceedings, i.e. they are not a chance to have another go by restarting grant or opposition proceedings to see if a better effort can be made to obtain the desired outcome. On the contrary, they are for the purpose of reviewing whether the actual decision taken by the first instance department was correct, taking into account the requests, facts and evidence on which that decision was based (Art. 12(2) RPBA). This means that the appeal is primarily based on the decision itself and those requests, facts, objections and pieces of evidence discussed in that decision and not on different requests, facts, objections and pieces of evidence that could have formed part of the decision if they had been introduced during first instance proceedings but were not. Whilst new requests and documents are sometimes introduced at the appeal stage there must always be a justification for their introduction, nothing going beyond the framework of the decision itself can be introduced as of right. This central concept has important consequences for the way in which appeal proceedings are conducted as will be discussed below.

A second important principle that informs the way appeal proceedings are conducted   506
is that the review of the decision is judicial in nature, i.e. conducted by a body equivalent to a court of law. The departments of the EPO are listed in Art. 15 EPC and no special distinction is made between the first instance departments and the Boards of Appeal. However, Art. 23(3) EPC establishes the legal independence of the Boards of Appeal within the EPO: a decision taken by a Board of Appeal is to be based on the legal framework established by the EPC itself and not influenced by any administrative instructions applying to the first instance departments such as the Guidelines for Examination or any other instructions issued by the President of the EPO. In order to preserve this independence, the Boards of Appeal and the Enlarged Board of Appeal are now organised in a completely separate unit within the EPO with its own President who answers only to the Administrative Council not to the President of the EPO (r.12a(1) and (2) EPC). So the three key roles within the patent system in the Contracting States, the legislature that drafts and amends the law, the patent office that administers the grant of patents under that law and the courts that review decisions of the patent office are mirrored in the EPO by the Administrative Council, the first instance departments of the EPO and the Boards of Appeal respectively. Because the Boards of Appeal have an independent, judicial role within the EPO, the way that they operate is influenced by the general principles of procedural law applying to national courts (as recognised under Art. 125 EPC).

Appeal proceedings are initiated by the filing of a notice of appeal and the payment   507
of an appeal fee within a period of two months following notification of the decision (Art. 108 EPC). Further processing is not applicable to this time limit (Art. 121(4) EPC) and re-establishment is therefore available for an applicant or proprietor who missed the time limit in spite of all due care required by the circumstances having been taken. However, no remedy exists for a party other than an applicant or proprietor, most notably for an opponent.

Once appeal proceedings have been initiated, the appellant must file grounds of appeal   508
within a period of four months following notification of the decision in order for the appeal to be admissible (Art. 108 and r.101(1) EPC). Further processing is also excluded for this time limit (Art. 121(4) EPC) and re-establishment is therefore available if the appellant is an applicant or proprietor and the time limit was missed in spite of all due care required by the circumstances having been taken. Perhaps more surprisingly, and despite the clear wording of Art. 122(1) EPC, it was decided by the Enlarged Board of Appeal in case G1/86 that re-establishment is also available for an opponent if the four month time limit is not complied with. This result follows directly from the notion that a Board of Appeal is a judicial body that must apply general principles of law recognised by courts in the Contracting States: "The Contracting States to the EPC recognise the principle that all parties to proceedings before a court must be accorded the same procedural rights" (G1/86, Reasons 13) and "the Boards act as courts, with the task of ensuring that the provisions of the EPC do not conflict with the law when applied in practice. The principle of equal treatment of parties to court proceedings must therefore also be applied to proceedings before the Boards of Appeal of the EPO" (G1/86, Reasons 14).

Once grounds of appeal have been filed, and assuming all the requirements relating to   509
admissibility have been complied with, the Board of Appeal will examine whether the

appeal is allowable or not. As a first step, any other party to the appeal proceedings will be given the opportunity to comment on the grounds of appeal. Such a party could be a party as of right, who decided not to file an appeal or was not adversely affected by the decision, or another appellant. The appeal proceedings are then based on the decision taken, the grounds of appeal filed by the appellant or appellants and the comments filed by all parties in response (Art. 12(1) RPBA), with the exception of any request, fact, objection or evidence that the Board decides to hold inadmissible on the basis that it was not submitted or maintained during first instance proceedings, or was submitted but not admitted in those proceedings, and was therefore not considered in the decision which is the subject of the appeal (Art. 12(6) RPBA). This power of the Board to exclude from the appeal proceedings requests and documents which were not considered in the decision is a direct reflection of the fact that appeal proceedings exist in order to review the correctness of a decision which has been taken by a first instance department and not an opportunity to start those first instance proceedings a second time.

510   Should the appeal be withdrawn at any time, then the appeal proceedings are immediately terminated, assuming there is only one appellant in the proceedings – if this is not the case then the appeal proceedings continue for the remaining appellant or appellants with the withdrawing party still a party as of right (G7/91, G8/91). This is in contrast, for example, to the right of an Opposition Division to continue opposition proceedings even if all of the opponents have withdrawn their oppositions (r.84(2) EPC) and is another reflection of the fact that first instance proceedings are administrative in nature whereas appeal proceedings are judicial in nature. An administrative body such as an Examining Division or Opposition Division examines the facts of its own motion in accordance with Art. 114(1) EPC (albeit with certain limitations in the case of an Opposition Division) whereas a judicial body in civil litigation is bound by the requests of the party that has initiated the legal process, i.e. it may not decide more than it has been asked to decide. If the appellant withdraws an appeal then it is asking the court to put the matter aside and avoid taking any decision and the court is bound by this request. This principle is also sometimes referred to as the principle of party disposition, as explained in G8/91: "a public authority or a court normally may not continue proceedings if the procedural act which gave rise to the proceedings (such as the filing of an appeal) has been retracted" (Reasons 5). The Enlarged Board went on to find that "Whereas the opposition procedure is a purely administrative procedure, the appeal procedure must be regarded as a procedure proper to an administrative court" and that no reasons could be found for making an exception to the principle of party disposition.

511   In its substantive examination of the appeal, the procedure of the Board of Appeal is further influenced by the overriding principle that the appeal is a judicial review of a particular decision. For example, in opposition appeal proceedings, a Board of Appeal may not introduce new grounds of appeal without the consent of the patent proprietor (G10/91). Again, this contrasts with the more administrative procedure before the Opposition Division in which new grounds of appeal may be introduced by the Opposition Division if they prejudice the maintenance of the patent (Art. 114(1) and r.81(1) EPC). In case G10/91 the Enlarged Board came to its conclusion by considering both the judicial nature of appeal proceedings and the need to conduct appeal proceedings primarily within the framework of the contested decision. It was held that "The purpose of the appeal procedure inter partes is mainly to give the losing party the possibility of challenging the decision of the Opposition Division on its merits. It is not in conformity with this purpose to consider grounds for opposition on which the decision of the Opposition Division has not been based. Furthermore, in contrast to the merely administrative character of the opposition procedure, the appeal procedure is to be considered as a judicial procedure ... Such procedure is by its very nature less investigative than an administrative procedure" (Reasons 18).

512   In opposition appeal proceedings a further important principle is applied in recognition of their judicial character, the principle of the prohibition of reformatio in peius (G9/92, G1/99). Reformatio in peius occurs when a decision is amended during appeal proceedings such that the appealing party ends up in a worse situation then if he or she had not appealed at all. This would be contrary to the appellant's request on which the appeal proceedings are based (and would contradict the judicial principle of party disposition as referred to above). The application of the prohibition of reformation in peius is explained

in more detail in section 1.7.8 but for the present purposes it is enough to note that where a European patent is maintained in amended form by an Opposition Division and only one of the parties appeals, the appellant should not (with some exceptions) end up in a worse position as a result of the appeal. This principle is not expressed in the EPC at all but is derived from the procedural law generally applied by the courts of the Contracting States (Art. 125 EPC) and is applicable in proceedings before the Boards of Appeal in view of the fundamentally judicial nature of these proceedings.

When taking a decision on an appeal, the Board may step into the shoes of the first   513
instance department and take a decision on its behalf or may remit the matter back to the first instance for further prosecution (Art. 111(1) EPC). Because the purpose of the appeal proceedings is to review the actual decision which has been taken by the first instance department, the Board of Appeal is less likely to take a decision on an issue that has not been considered in that decision and much more likely to remit the matter for further prosecution so that the further issue can be considered by the first instance. For instance, if a European patent application has been refused solely for non-compliance with Art. 123(2) EPC and the Board of Appeal finds that the claims before it meet the requirements of that provision, it is likely to remit the matter back to the Examining Division for other issues such as novelty and inventive step to be considered rather than examining those issues itself for the first time.

In some situations, when examining an appeal, the Board of Appeal may decide to   514
introduce a ground, document or request which takes the appeal proceedings outside the framework of the decision whose correctness is being considered. In this case as well, since it is contrary to the primary purpose of appeal proceedings to consider matters going beyond the contested decision, it is more likely that a Board of Appeal will refer the matter back to the first instance department rather than take a decision on it itself. For instance, as noted above, a new ground of appeal may be admitted into opposition appeal proceedings if it would prima facie prejudice maintenance of the patent and the proprietor agrees to its introduction (G9/91). In this situation, the Board of Appeal is likely to remit the opposition proceedings back to the Opposition Division to consider the new ground rather than deciding on the matter itself (G9/91, Reasons 18). Equally, if a valid intervention is filed during opposition appeal proceedings, the intervener is entitled to raise new grounds of opposition and in this situation the proprietor cannot prevent their introduction (G1/94). The Board of Appeal should, absent special reasons for proceeding otherwise, remit the opposition proceedings back to the Opposition Division for consideration of the new ground (G1/94, Reasons 13). In appeal proceedings following a decision taken by an Examining Division to refuse a European patent application, the Board of Appeal is, in principle, entitled to raise any ground that would preclude the grant of a patent, whether it was raised by the Examining Division or not. Once again, however, the application is more likely to be remitted to the Examining Division for further investigation of the new ground if it was not discussed in the contested decision (G10/93, Reasons 5).

1.7.11 Entering the EPO regional phase with a Euro-PCT application

The term "entering the regional phase" is frequently used in common parlance to describe   515
the process by which the international phase of a Euro-PCT application is terminated and the processing of the application by the EPO commences. Such processing may start by default on expiry of the 31 month regional phase entry deadline of r.159(1) EPC or earlier on the basis of a specific request made by the applicant. In each case, a set of procedural acts needs to be carried out by the applicant in order to start such processing. If one or more of these acts remains uncompleted then the EPO will not process the application, whether a request for early processing has been made or not and, in many cases, the Euro-PCT application will be deemed withdrawn when the 31 month deadline expires. Being able to pinpoint the point in time at which the international phase ends and regional phase processing of the application by the EPO commences can be important for various reasons. For example, it determines the earliest date on which a valid divisional application may be filed according to r.36(1) EPC. Equally, it determines the point at which the international patent application, or some associated right such as a priority right, can be withdrawn centrally at the International Bureau without having any effect on the European part of that application (r.90bis.6(a) PCT).

516   Processing of a Euro-PCT application by the EPO is thus dependent on two separate factors: on the one hand the EPO must be able to process the application and on the other hand the EPO must be willing to process the application. The ability of the EPO to process the application is limited by Art. 23 PCT which specifies that the EPO as a designated office may only process and examine the application when the 31 month time limit has expired unless the applicant has expressly asked for processing to begin at an earlier date. Therefore, absent an explicit request for early processing from the applicant, the EPO must wait until the 31 month regional phase entry deadline has expired before assessing whether the relevant acts necessary to start regional processing have been carried out by the applicant and whether it is therefore willing to process the application. If it finds that the relevant acts have been carried out then processing commences or, if it finds out that one or more relevant acts remain uncompleted then it will not process the application and, in many cases, the application will be deemed withdrawn instead. If an earlier explicit request for processing is made by the applicant then the EPO will assess whether the acts necessary to start regional processing at that time (which may be different from the acts that would have been necessary at the expiry of the 31 month deadline) have been met or not. If they have been met then the EPO will commence early processing of the application. If they have not been met then early processing will not commence until the deficiency is remedied, and the application will once again not be processed at all but, in many cases, be deemed withdrawn if the deficiency is not remedied before the expiry of the 31 month time limit.

517   There is no limit on how early the processing of an international patent application by the EPO may begin. In principle, it may start at any time after the international patent application is filed. The PCT and the EPC merely provide time limits within which certain acts must be carried out in order to avoid the Euro-PCT application becoming deemed withdrawn, though the relationship between the carrying out of these acts and the processing of the application by the EPO is not properly explained. Thus, according to the Art. 24(1)(iii) PCT, the applicant must carry out certain acts at the EPO within a specified time limit in order to avoid the effect of the international application as a European patent application ceasing and the Euro-PCT application being considered withdrawn. The relevant acts are the furnishing of a copy of the application, unless such a copy has already been transmitted by the International Bureau under Art. 20 PCT, the furnishing of any prescribed translation, the furnishing of data identifying the inventor, where required under national law, and the payment of a national fee (Art. 22(1) PCT). The relevant time limit is the expiry of 30 months from the priority date or any later date allowed by national law. The EPC does indeed specify a later time limit of 31 months from the priority date (r.159(1) EPC). The requirement to supply, where applicable, a translation and pay a national (here the filing fee) are mirrored in r.159(1)(a) and (c) EPC. However, further requirements for entering the regional phase are also specified in r.159(1) EPC: a designation fee, a search fee and a renewal fee may need to be paid (r.159(1)(d)(e)(g)), and a request for examination may need to be filed (r.159(1)(f), itself requiring the payment of an examination fee), all depending on the circumstances, in order to avoid the application being deemed withdrawn (r.160(1) EPC) or, in the case of the renewal fee, to avoid payment of an additional surcharge (r.51(2) EPC); the documents on which the grant procedure are to be based must be specified (though no penalty exists for not doing so); and any relevant certificate of exhibition according to Art. 55(2) and r.25 must be filed in order to avoid the disclosure of the invention at the exhibition being considered as prior art under Art. 54(2) EPC.

518   There is no mention in r.159(1) EPC of the requirements in Art. 22(1) PCT that a copy of the international application be provided and that data concerning the inventor be furnished. On the other hand, as mentioned above, there are a number of additional requirements set out in r.159(1) EPC that are not mentioned in Art. 22(1) PCT. So what exactly are the essential acts that must be carried out for the EPO to be willing to start processing a Euro-PCT application? A summary is provided in the following Table of all the requirements of Art. 22(1) and r.159(1) EPC, indicating whether they are essential for the processing of the Euro-PCT application by the EPO or not, what the consequences of non-fulfilment are and when that consequence takes effect.

519

Requirement	Listed in Art. 22(1) PCT?	Listed in r.159(1) EPC?	Essential for processing by EPO?	Consequence of not taking action
Furnish copy of international application (unless Art. 20 communication has occurred)	YES	NO	NO	NONE
Furnish translation of international application, if not published in EN, FR or DE	YES	YES r. 159(1)(a) EPC	YES	No early processing and deemed withdrawal under r.160(1) EPC at 31 m deadline
Pay national fee (= filing fee)	YES	YES r.159(1)(c) EPC	YES	No early processing and deemed withdrawal under r.160(1) EPC at 31 m deadline
Furnish data concerning inventor (if not already part of the international application)	YES	NO	NO	If not provided with request for early processing or within 31 m deadline, invitation is sent under r.163(1) EPC
Specify documents on which grant proceedings are to be based	NO	YES r.159(1)(b) EPC	YES	NONE (other than that no processing of the application will be carried out)
Pay designation fee if normal period under r.39 EPC has expired	NO	YES r.159(1)(d) EPC	YES	No early processing and deemed withdrawal under r.160(1) EPC at 31 m deadline
Pay search fee if supplementary European search required	NO	YES r.159(1)(e) EPC	YES	No early processing and deemed withdrawal under r.160(1) EPC at 31 m deadline
File request for examination and pay examination fee if normal period under r.70(1) EPC has expired	NO	YES r.159(1)(f) EPC	YES	No early processing and deemed withdrawal under r.160(1) EPC at 31 m deadline
Pay renewal fee if it has already fallen due under r.51(1) EPC	NO	YES r.159(1)(g) EPC	YES	No early processing, must be paid with surcharge after 31 m deadline, deemed withdrawal under Art. 86(1) and r.51(2) on expiry of 6 m grace period
File, where applicable, certificate of exhibition	NO	YES	NO	Disclosure of invention taken into account under Art. 54(2) EPC

Since early processing by the EPO can be requested at any point from the filing of the international application onwards, a copy of the international application may or may not have been transmitted to the EPO by the International Bureau under Art. 20(1) PCT at the time such a request is made by the applicant. Under normal circumstances, no Art. 20(1) communication takes place before international publication (r.47.1 PCT). One might assume, therefore, based on the wording of Art. 22(1) PCT that the EPO would not begin to process a Euro-PCT application if a request for early processing was made before

520

it had received a copy of the international application from the International Bureau unless furnished with a copy by the applicant. However, this is not the case and no such requirement is specified in r.159(1) EPC. This is because the Art. 20(1) PCT communication can be made earlier than international publication if the applicant or the EPO informs the International Bureau that a request for early processing has been made (r.47.1(a) in conjunction with r.47.4 or r.61.2(d) PCT). Furnishing a copy of the international application is therefore never a requirement for early processing of a Euro-PCT application by the EPO since either the EPO is already in possession of a copy or else it begins to process the application and requests the International Bureau to provide it with a copy thereof (see Guidelines E-IX, 2.1.2 and E-IX, 2.7).

521   Similarly, it could be inferred from Art. 22(1) PCT that the applicant would always have to supply to the EPO the name and other data concerning the inventor for processing of the Euro-PCT application to begin. Again, this is not a mandatory requirement under the EPC and is not listed in r.159(1) EPC. Instead, processing begins regardless and the requirement to provide indications concerning the inventor is dealt with subsequently under r.163(1) and (6) EPC – if the data is not provided within two months of notification of the deficiency then the application is refused. The filing of a translation, where necessary, and the payment of the national (filing) fee, in all cases, are, however, mandatory acts for processing of the application to begin and are listed under both Art. 22(1) PCT and r.159 EPC. The EPO will not start processing the application until both of these acts have been carried out and will not process the application at all if the 31 month time limit expires and one of them remains outstanding – the application is instead deemed withdrawn according to r.160(1) EPC.

522   Mandatory acts specified in r.159(1) EPC that are not required by Art. 22(1) PCT include the payment of the search fee, where a supplementary European search is required (Art. 153(7) EPC), and the payment of a designation fee and the filing of a request for examination, if the usual period for carrying out these acts – six month period from publication of the international search report – has already expired (Art. 153(6), r.39(1) and r.70(1) EPC). In the case of the request for examination, of course, two acts are necessary, the filing of a written request to this effect and the payment of the examination fee (Art. 94(1) EPC). Once again, the EPO will not start processing the application until all of these acts have been carried out and will not process the application at all if the 31 month time limit expires and one of them remains outstanding – the application is instead deemed withdrawn according to r.160(1) EPC.

523   According to r.159(1)(b), it is a further mandatory act for processing to begin that the applicant specifies the documents on which the grant procedure is to be based. Curiously, however, the application is not deemed to be withdrawn if this act is not carried out by the expiry of the 31 month time limit. Indeed, no sanction is provided by the EPC for not carrying out this act within the prescribed time limit which would tend to indicate that it is, in fact, not a mandatory act required to start processing of the application – one could imagine that processing on the basis of the international application as filed could begin in the absence of any other indication. Nevertheless, point 6 of the notice of the EPO dated 21 February 2013 (O.J. [2013] 156), insists that this is indeed an act required before processing of the application can begin. On the basis of the available information from the EPO, we must therefore assume that early processing will not begin until the relevant documents for grant have been specified. Normal processing after the 31 month time limit has expired, however, will proceed on the basis of the international application as published according to Guidelines E-IX, 2.1.1, even if the applicant has not specified which documents are to be taken into account.

524   According to r.159(g) EPC, it is also a mandatory act for processing to begin that the applicant pays any renewal fee that has already fallen due under r.51(1) EPC (last day of the month containing the second anniversary of the filing date). A renewal fee may fall due before expiry of the 31 month period of r.159(1) EPC if no priority is claimed or a priority period of less than seven months is claimed. On expiry of the 31 month time limit, if such a renewal fee has still not been paid, then it must be paid with surcharge under r.51(2) EPC and processing will be further delayed until the fee and surcharge have both been paid. Eventually, on expiry of the aggregate six month time limit of r.51(2) EPC, the application will be deemed withdrawn under Art. 86(1) EPC if the renewal fee or surcharge remain unpaid.

Finally, although r.159(h) EPC seems to make processing of the application contingent 525
on the filing of a certificate of exhibition, in cases where the applicant has requested a
disclosure of the invention in the six months prior to the filing of the application to be excluded from the state of the art under Art. 55(1)(b) and (2) EPC, this is apparently not the
case. Referring to point 13 of the notice from the EPO cited above (O.J. [2013] 156) and
Guidelines E-IX, 2.8, early processing will commence regardless of whether a required
certificate is filed or not but, in the absence of the certificate, the disclosure at the exhibition will be taken into account under Art. 54(2) EPC during grant proceedings.

Having established which acts, in principle, need to be carried out such that the EPO is 526
willing to process the international application, deciding which of them will apply in any
particular set of circumstances depends on a range of factors including the time at which
the applicant gives the EPO the authority to process the application, the date on which the
international search report is published (and hence the deadline for paying the designation
fee and filing a request for examination), the language in which the application is filed and
published (and hence whether a translation is required) and whether the EPO acted as
international searching authority or not (and hence whether a search fee must be paid).

Note that when a request for early processing is validly filed, the 31 month deadline 527
of r.159(1) EPC no longer applies to any acts which were not necessary to initiate early
processing because they were not yet due – such acts must then be carried out at the time
when they fall due under the provisions relating to a direct filed European patent application. Specifically, this applies to the payment of the designation fee, the filing of a request
for examination and the payment of the first renewal fee.

The following scenarios illustrate some of the circumstances that may arise in practice.

Scenario 1:

In this scenario, an international patent application is filed in English at the EPO on Tues- 528
day 02 January 2018 claiming the priority of a national application filed 12 months earlier on Monday 02 January 2017. The application is published shortly after the expiry
of 18 months from the priority date on Thursday 05 July 2018 along with the international
search report. The normal period for paying the designation fee and requesting examination under r.39(1) and r.70(1) EPC, respectively, therefore expires on Monday 07 January 2019. The first renewal fee falls due under r.51(1) EPC on Friday 31 January 2020.
The 31 month deadline for entering the regional phase under r.159(1) EPC expires on
Friday 02 August 2019. The scenario can be summarised in schematic form as follows:

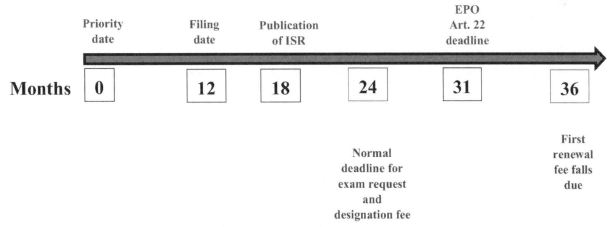

Figure 4

Because the application has been filed in English and no translation is required for inter- 529
national search or international publication (ISA = EPO), no translation will be required
for entering the regional phase under r.159(1)(a) EPC. Furthermore, because the EPO
will act as International Searching Authority, no supplementary European search will be
carried out on regional phase entry and no search fee will be due under r.159(1)(e) EPC.

The acts that must be carried out in order for the EPO to process the application early
are as follows:

From 02 January 2018 until 07 January 2019: Request early processing, pay the filing 530
fee and specify the documents on which grant proceedings are to be based. Note that the

payment of the designation fee and the request for examination will now both fall due on 07 January 2019 and action must be taken on this day or earlier to avoid the application being deemed withdrawn under r.39(2) and Art. 94(2) EPC respectively.

531   **From 08 January 2019 until 02 August 2019:** Request early processing, pay the filing fee, pay the designation fee, request examination and specify the documents on which grant proceedings are to be based.

532   **On 03 August 2019:** the EPO is free to process the application without any request for early processing being required and will assess whether the filing fee has been paid, the designation fee has been paid and a request for examination has been filed. If these requirements have been met then it will process the application by examining other requirements and, should they be met, by sending a communication pursuant to r.161(1) EPC. If one of these requirements remains uncompleted then the application will be deemed withdrawn and a loss of rights communication pursuant to r.112(1) EPC will be dispatched. The first renewal fee must be paid by 31 January 2020 in order to avoid surcharge.

Scenario 2:

533   In this scenario, an international patent application is filed in Japanese at the Japanese Patent Office on Tuesday 02 January 2018 claiming the priority of a national application filed 12 months earlier on Monday 02 January 2017. The application is published shortly after the expiry of 18 months from the priority date on Thursday 05 July 2018 but the international search is delayed and the international search report is published late on Thursday 16 May 2019. The normal period for paying the designation fee and requesting examination under r.39(1) and r.70(1) EPC, respectively, therefore expires on Monday 18 November 2019. The first renewal fee falls due under r.51(1) EPC on Friday 31 January 2020. The 31 month deadline for entering the regional phase under r.159(1) EPC expires on Friday 02 August 2019. The scenario can be summarised in schematic form as follows:

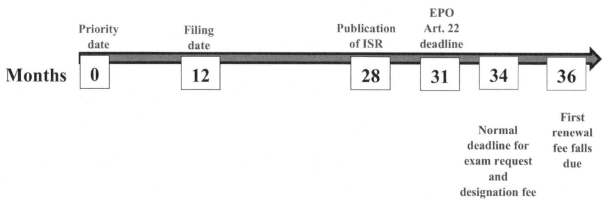

Figure 5

534   Because the application has been filed in Japanese and no translation is required for international search or international publication (ISA = JPO), a translation into English, French or German will be required for entering the regional phase under r.159(1)(a) EPC. Furthermore, because the JPO will act as International Searching Authority, a supplementary European search will be carried out on regional phase entry and a search fee will be due under r.159(1)(e) EPC.

The acts that must be carried out in order for the EPO to process the application early are as follows:

535   **From 02 January 2018 until 02 August 2019:** Request early processing, pay the filing fee and search fee, file a translation and specify the documents on which grant proceedings are to be based.

536   **On 03 August 2019:** the EPO is free to process the application without any request for early processing being required and will assess whether the filing fee and search fee have been paid and a translation has been filed. If these requirements have been met then it will process the application by examining other requirements and, should they be met, by sending a communication pursuant to r.161(1) EPC. If one of these requirements remains uncompleted then the application will be deemed withdrawn and a loss of rights

communication pursuant to r.112(1) EPC will be dispatched. Note that the payment of the designation fee and the request for examination will now both fall due on 18 November 2019 and action must be taken on this day or earlier to avoid the application being deemed withdrawn under r.39(2) and Art. 94(2) EPC respectively. The first renewal fee must be paid by 31 January 2020 to avoid a surcharge.

Scenario 3:

In this scenario, an international patent application is filed in English at the EPO on Monday 02 January 2017 without any claim to priority. The application is published shortly after the expiry of 18 months from the priority date on Thursday 05 July 2018 along with the international search report. The normal period for paying the designation fee and requesting examination under r.39(1) and r.70(1) EPC, respectively, therefore expires on Monday 07 January 2019. The first renewal fee falls due under r.51(1) EPC on 31 January 2019. The 31 month deadline for entering the regional phase under r.159(1) EPC expires on Friday 02 August 2019. The scenario can be summarised in schematic form as follows: 537

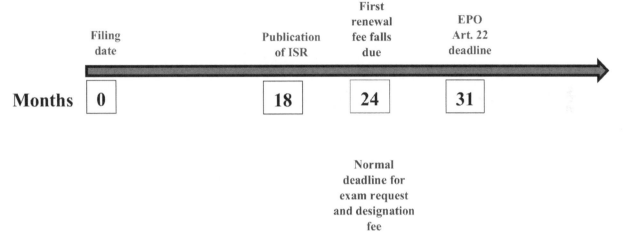

Figure 6

Because the application has been filed in English and no translation is required for international search or international publication (ISA = EPO), no translation will be required for entering the regional phase under r.159(1)(a) EPC. Furthermore, because the EPO will act as International Searching Authority, no supplementary European search will be carried out on regional phase entry and no search fee will be due under r.159(1)(e) EPC. 538

The acts that must be carried out in order for the EPO to process the application early are as follows:

From 02 January 2017 until 07 January 2019: Request early processing, pay the filing fee and specify the documents on which grant proceedings are to be based. Note that the payment of the designation fee and the request for examination will now both fall due on 07 January 2019 and action must be taken on this day or earlier to avoid the application being deemed withdrawn under r.39(2) and Art. 94(2) EPC respectively. Note also that payment of the first renewal fee will now fall due on 31 January 2019 and must be paid on this day or earlier to avoid the payment of a surcharge. 539

From 08 January 2019 until 31 January 2019: Request early processing, pay the filing fee, pay the designation fee, request examination and specify the documents on which grant proceedings are to be based. Note that payment of the first renewal fee will now fall due on 31 January 2019 and must be paid on this day or earlier to avoid the payment of a surcharge. 540

From 01 February until 02 August 2019: Request early processing, pay the filing fee, pay the designation fee, request examination, pay the first renewal fee and specify the documents on which grant proceedings are to be based. 541

On 03 August 2019: the EPO is free to process the application without any request for early processing being required and will assess whether the filing fee has been paid, the designation fee has been paid, a request for examination has been filed and the first renewal fee has been paid. If these requirements have been met then it will process the 542 application by examining other requirements and, should they be met, by sending a communication pursuant to r.161(1) EPC. Should any of these acts other than the payment of the first renewal fee remain uncompleted then the application will be deemed withdrawn and a loss of rights communication pursuant to r.112(1) EPC will be dispatched. If the first renewal fee has not been paid then it must be paid with surcharge by Monday 03 February 2020 or the application will be deemed withdrawn.

Scenario 4:

543   In this scenario, an international patent application is filed in English at the EPO on Monday 02 January 2017 without any claim to priority. The application is published shortly after the expiry of 18 months from the priority date on Thursday 05 July 2018 but the international search is delayed and the international search report is published late on Thursday 18 October 2018. The normal period for paying the designation fee and requesting examination under r.39(1) and r.70(1) EPC, respectively, therefore expires on Thursday 18 April 2019. The first renewal fee falls due under r.51(1) EPC on 31 January 2019. The 31 month deadline for entering the regional phase under r.159(1) EPC expires on Friday 02 August 2019. The scenario can be summarised in schematic form as follows:

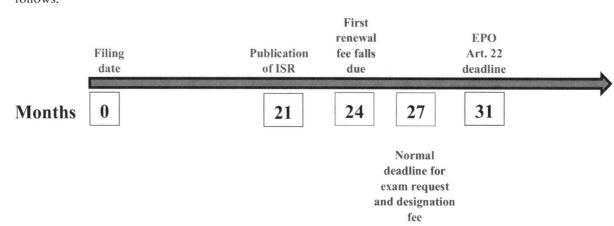

Figure 7

544   Because the application has been filed in English and no translation is required for international search or international publication (ISA = EPO), no translation will be required for entering the regional phase under r.159(1)(a) EPC. Furthermore, because the EPO will act as International Searching Authority, no supplementary European search will be carried out on regional phase entry and no search fee will be due under r.159(1)(e) EPC.

The acts that must be carried out in order for the EPO to process the application early are as follows:

545   **From 02 January 2017 until 31 January 2019:** Request early processing, pay the filing fee and specify the documents on which grant proceedings are to be based. Note that payment of the first renewal fee will now fall due on 31 January 2019 and must be paid on this day or earlier to avoid the payment of a surcharge. Note also that the payment of the designation fee and the request for examination will now both fall due on 18 April 2019 and action must be taken on this day or earlier to avoid the application being deemed withdrawn under r.39(2) and Art. 94(2) EPC respectively.

546   **From 01 February 2019 until 18 April 2019:** Request early processing, pay the filing fee, pay the first renewal fee and specify the documents on which grant proceedings are to be based. Note that the payment of the designation fee and the request for examination will now both fall due on 18 April 2019 and action must be taken on this day or earlier to avoid the application being deemed withdrawn under r.39(2) and Art. 94(2) EPC respectively

547   **From 19 April 2019 until 02 August 2019:** Request early processing, pay the filing fee, pay the designation fee, request examination, pay the first renewal fee and specify the documents on which grant proceedings are to be based.

548   **On 03 August 2019:** the EPO is free to process the application without any request for early processing being required and will assess whether the filing fee has been paid,

the designation fee has been paid, a request for examination has been filed and the first renewal fee has been paid. If these requirements have been met then it will process the application by examining other requirements and, should they be met, by sending a communication pursuant to r.161(1) EPC. Should any of these acts other than the payment of the first renewal fee remain uncompleted then the application will be deemed withdrawn and a loss of rights communication pursuant to r.112(1) EPC will be dispatched. If the first renewal fee has not been paid then it must be paid with surcharge by Monday 03 February 2020 or the application will be deemed withdrawn.

1.7.12   Interlocutory aspects of EPO procedure

The word "interlocutory" refers to a measure which is preliminary or interim and is used   549
in European practice to refer to preliminary decisions which do not terminate proceedings (interlocutory decisions) and the intermediate review process by which first instance departments have a chance to set aside a decision which is the subject of an appeal (interlocutory review).

Interlocutory decisions are explicitly contemplated in the EPC by Art. 106(2) which   550
refers to decisions that do not terminate proceedings and specifies that these decisions are only subject to appeal if specifically designated as such. Decisions can therefore be divided into three categories:

(a)   A final decision that terminates proceedings – such a decision is always subject to appeal.

(b)   An interlocutory decision that does not terminate proceedings and which is made subject to appeal.

(c)   An interlocutory decision that does not terminate proceedings and which is not made subject to appeal.

Decisions falling in category (a) include the decision of an Examining Division to refuse   551
or grant a patent and the decision of an Opposition Division to revoke a patent or reject an opposition. Decisions falling in category (b) may include the decision of an Examining Division to change the filing date of a patent application on the basis that an added part was not completely contained in the earlier application from which priority is claimed (see Guidelines C-III, 1.1.1) and the decision of an Opposition Division that a certain text of a patent meets the requirements of the EPC (Guidelines D-VI, 7.2.1). An example of a decision falling within category (c) may be a decision that an allegation of partiality made by the applicant against a member of the Examining Division is unjustified and the composition of the division should not be changed. In the case of interlocutory decisions of kinds (b) and (c) it simply falls to the competent EPO department to decide whether the decision should be subject to appeal or not, based on a determination of whether such an intermediate review would make the proceedings more or less efficient as a whole (Guidelines E-X, 3). If the nature of the decision means that the way in which the remainder of the proceedings will be conducted will vary considerably depending on whether the decision is upheld or not, and if the procedure is still in its early stages, then an appealable interlocutory decision may be more efficient – even though the procedure will have to be suspended pending the outcome of the appeal. If, on the other hand, the procedure is already well advanced and will likely continue in the same manner regardless of whether the interlocutory decision is upheld or not then an appealable decision would be less sensible. In the case of the example given above under category (c), for example, the possibility for such an interlocutory decision to be made appealable or not is explicitly recognised in decision G5/91 (see Headnote 2). In such a situation, there is clearly an advantage in taking an appealable interlocutory decision since if the allegation of impartiality is upheld on appeal then the relevant member of the Examining Division will have to be replaced and the application re-examined by the newly constituted division.

It is in opposition proceedings that an appealable interlocutory decision is most fre-   552
quently encountered. If an Opposition Division considers that the opposition is to be rejected since none of the cited grounds prejudice maintenance of the patent as granted then it can issue a final decision to this effect immediately since no amendment of the patent is necessary. Such a decision terminates the proceedings and is therefore subject to appeal. Equally, if an Opposition Division considers that none of the requests presented by the proprietor are allowable then it can take a final decision to revoke the patent since, in this

case as well, no amendment of the patent is required. Such a decision also terminates the proceedings and is subject to appeal. If, however, an Opposition Division considers that the cited grounds prevent maintenance of the patent as granted but that the patent can be maintained in an amended form which complies with the requirements of the EPC then it has two possible ways of proceeding:

553   **Option 1:** The Opposition Division could invite the proprietor to file translations of the amended claims and pay the prescribed fee under r.82(2) EPC and then take a decision under Art. 101(3)(a) EPC maintaining the patent as amended. This would be a final decision subject to appeal within a period of two months from its notification (Art. 108 EPC). In the meantime, the decision would be mentioned in the European Patent Bulletin and re-validation would be necessary in those states requiring a translation of the new claims or the whole patent (Art. 65(1) EPC). If appeal proceedings take place then they could end with the revocation of the patent, the maintenance of the patent as granted, the maintenance of the patent in the form maintained by the Opposition Division or the maintenance of the patent in an amended form different from that maintained by the Opposition Division. In the case of revocation, the filing of amended claims and revalidation process would turn out to have been pointless. In the case that the patent was maintained as granted or in a new form, the filing of amended claims and revalidation process would not only turn out to have been pointless but would have to be repeated! The chances of this procedure being procedurally highly inefficient are therefore high.

554   **Option 2:** The Opposition Division could take an interlocutory decision that the patent as amended meets the requirements of the EPC and make the decision subject to appeal. If no appeal was filed then the decision would become final and the Opposition Division could request the filing of claim translations and the payment of the prescribed fee before taking a final, non-appealable decision to maintain the patent in amended form. No appeal would be possible since none of the parties would be adversely affected, having implicitly agreed to the text of the patent by not appealing the interlocutory decision. If appeal proceedings take place then, as before, they could end with the revocation of the patent, the maintenance of the patent as granted, the maintenance of the patent in the form maintained by the Opposition Division or the maintenance of the patent in an amended form different from that maintained by the Opposition Division. In all cases, the procedure is much more efficient since only one set of claims translation is to be filed and only one re-validation process is necessary. This is therefore the procedure that is adopted in practice.

555   No such interlocutory decision subject to appeal needs to be taken by an Examining Division when, for example, it decides in oral proceedings that a certain text of the application meets the requirements of the EPC. The decision to grant a patent, which will be taken following the completion of the formalities under r.71(3) EPC, is highly unlikely to be subject to appeal and there is therefore no compelling reason to have the decision reviewed by a Board of Appeal prior to the filing of claim translations and payment of the printing fee. In this case the Examining Division can simply take an interlocutory decision that it intends to grant a patent based on the application documents filed during the oral proceedings and continue the procedure in writing.

556   An appealable interlocutory decision may also be taken in opposition proceedings at a much earlier stage. An opposition is only subject to substantive examination if it is admissible (Art. 101(1) EPC). If it is not clear to the Opposition Division whether the opposition is admissible or not because a potential deficiency exists and the applicable point of law has not been previously decided then it may issue an interlocutory decision on admissibility which is subject to appeal. This can certainly be justified in terms of procedural efficiency since, if the opposition is inadmissible, no further examination will be necessary.

557   In many cases, the applicant for a European patent may ask for a decision on a particular matter and the Examining Division will have to decide whether to make its interlocutory decision subject to separate appeal or not. Frequently, this concerns the refund of fees. For example, the applicant may ask for the refund of a search fee under Art. 9(2) RRF where the EPO has already carried out a search on an application from which priority is claimed. If there is disagreement on the amount of the refund then then an interlocutory decision will be issued which is usually made subject to appeal (Guidelines A-X, 10.2.1). A similar situation arises where the applicant requests the refund of additional search fees paid in response to a finding by the Search Division that the claims of the application lack unity of invention (Guidelines C-III, 3.4). An appealable interlocutory decision will be

taken unless the application is at a stage where a final decision can already be taken and the decision on the refund included as an auxiliary matter (as an example, see T2441/18). Such an interlocutory decision led to Enlarged Board of Appeal decision G1/11. In that case the Examining Division actually issued an appealable interlocutory decision refusing the refund of search fees a month before taking a decision to grant the application. The subject matter of the referral to the Enlarged Board was whether a legal or technical board of appeal should review the matter – the Enlarged Board of appeal decided that the technical board of appeal was competent. A refund of the further processing fee may be requested when the use of further processing has been necessitated by the refusal of the Examining Division to extend a time limit and the applicant considers that the Examining Division has not exercised its discretion in a reasonable way. In this case also an appealable interlocutory decision is usually taken (Guidelines E-VIII, 1.6 and J37/89).

If the Legal Division has decided to stay proceedings under r.14(1) or r.78(1) EPC following the initiation of entitlement proceedings and this is contested by the applicant or patent proprietor, respectively, then the Legal Division will take an interlocutory decision on the matter which is subject to appeal (Guidelines A-IV, 2.2.3 and D-VII, 4.1.2).   **558**

Interlocutory decisions are also a feature of appeal proceedings when a point of law needs to be clarified by the Enlarged Board of Appeal before a decision can be taken (Art. 112(1)(a) EPC). The Board of Appeal will take an interlocutory decision, setting out the facts of the case and containing full reasoning as to why clarification from the Enlarged Board of Appeal is required. The decision will then conclude with the questions that need to be answered rather than a final order dealing with the appeal. Following a decision from the Enlarged Board of Appeal dealing with the referred questions, the appeal procedure is re-opened and a final decision can be taken.   **559**

Interlocutory revision under Art. 109 EPC is another "interim" measure which in this case is inserted between the filing of an appeal by a party to first instance proceedings and its examination by a Board of Appeal. When grounds of appeal have been filed they are first forwarded to the first instance department that took the decision so that it can consider the arguments and/or amendments made and consider whether the grounds on which the decision was based are overcome or not. Just as in the case of an interlocutory decision, interlocutory revision serves the purpose of making the proceedings more efficient as a whole. If the procedure can be resumed before the first instance department since the grounds of appeal successfully deal with the objections on which the appealed decision was based then the decision can be set aside immediately by the first instance department and there is no need for a Board of Appeal to be involved at all. If, on the other hand, the grounds of appeal do not fully deal with those objections then the file is passed on to the Board of Appeal in the usual way. Then first instance department has a three month period in which it can apply interlocutory revision which starts with the filing of the grounds of appeal and when this period has expired proceedings before the Board of Appeal commence (Art. 109(2) EPC).   **560**

There is one very important restriction on the scope of the interlocutory revision procedure: it does not apply where the appellant is opposed by another party to the proceedings. This means that it only usually applies in grant proceedings in which the applicant is the only party. Thus, for example, when an application is refused by the Examining Division because the claimed invention lacks novelty over the cited prior art and the applicant files an appeal, either amending the claims of his main request so that they are clearly novel or else providing convincing arguments showing that the claims on which the decision was based are themselves novel, then the Examining Division should apply interlocutory revision, set aside the decision to refuse the application and resume examination. However, in opposition proceedings, the proprietor is usually opposed by one or more opponents and under these circumstances interlocutory revision cannot be applied. If the Opposition Division takes a decision to revoke the patent because the sole request of the proprietor lacks novelty over the cited prior art and the proprietor files an appeal including a new request which is clearly novel then the Opposition Division will not usually be able to apply interlocutory revision and the matter must be considered directly by a Board of Appeal. The only exception would be where all of the opponents have withdrawn their oppositions when the grounds of appeal are filed. In this case the proprietor is no longer opposed by another party and interlocutory revision would once more become possible.   **561**

Even if all oppositions have been withdrawn the proceedings can be continued by the Opposition Division with the proprietor as the single unopposed party (r.84(2) EPC).

1.8   Transitional provisions EPC1973/EPC2000

562   In order to quote the correct basis when answering a D1 question, it is necessary to know whether EPC1973 or EPC2000 applies in any given situation.

563   The first point to determine is when the relevant European patent application (or Euro-PCT application) was filed (NB: any claimed priority date is irrelevant).

564   If the application was filed on or after December 13, 2007 then EPC2000 applies in its entirety and no further investigation is necessary (Art. 7(1) of revision act). Naturally, EPC2000 also applies in its entirety to any patent which has arisen from the grant of such an application.

565   In the case of divisional applications, it is the actual filing date of the divisional which counts and not the date of the parent application to which the divisional is entitled under Art. 76(1) EPC (see Point 1 of the Notice from the EPO dated 20.9.2007–O.J. [2007] 504).

566   If the application concerned was filed before December 13, 2007, then the question as to whether EPC1973 or EPC2000 applies in any given situation must be answered according to which EPC Article is relevant. If one of the Implementing Regulations is relevant then it is necessary to decide which Article of the EPC that particular Regulation is implementing (J10/07, J3/06).

567   The first question to be asked is: can I apply the relevant Article of EPC2000? The transitional provisions (Art. 7(1) of the revision act and Art. 1 of the decision of the AC of 28.6.2001) answer this question for us – the following provisions of EPC2000 are applicable to applications filed before December 13, 2007 (and the granted patents they lead to):

568

Article of EPC2000	Corresponding EPC2000 Regulations	Comments
Art. 14(3)–(6)	r.3–7	
Art. 51	RRF	
Art. 52		
Art. 53	r.26–34	
Art. 54(3) and (4)		
Art. 54(5)		Only applies to pending applications for which a decision to grant has not been taken.
Art. 61	r.14–18	
Art. 65		
Art. 67		
Art. 68		
Art. 69 and Protocol		
Art. 70		
Art. 86	r.51	
Art. 88	r.52–54	
Art. 90	r.55–60	
Art. 92	r.61–66	
Art. 93	r.67–69	
Art. 94	r.70–71	
Art. 97	r.71–72	
Art. 98	r.73–74	
Art. 99	r.75–76	
Art. 101	r.77–86	
Art. 103	r.87	

Article of EPC2000	Corresponding EPC2000 Regulations	Comments
Art. 104	r.88	
Art. 105	r.89	
Art. 105a–105c	r.90–96	
Art. 106	r.97–98	
Art. 108	r.99, 103	
Art. 110	r.100–101	
Art. 112a	r.104–110	Only in respect of decisions taken on or after 13.12.2007
Art. 115	r.114	
Art. 117	r.117–123, 124(part)	
Art. 119	r.125–130	
Art. 120	r.131–134, 142	
Art. 121	r.135	In so far as the time limit for requesting further processing has not expired on 13.12.2007
Art. 122	r.136	In so far as the time limit for requesting re-establishment has not expired on 13.12.2007
Art. 123	r.137–140	
Art. 124	r.141	
Art. 127	r.143	
Art. 128	r.144–147	
Art. 129		
Art. 133	r.151–152	
Art. 135	r.155–156	
Art. 137		
Art. 138		
Art. 141		
Art. 150–153	r.157–r.165	Except for protest procedures where BoA still has competence under Art. 154(3) and Art. 155(3) EPC1973

The following provisions of EPC2000 do not therefore apply to applications filed before December 13, 2007 and the granted patents they lead to:

Article of EPC2000	Corresponding EPC2000 Regulations	Comments	
Art. 1–13			569
Art. 14(1)–(2) and (7)–(8)			
Art. 15	r.9		
Art. 16–18	r.8, 10, 11	Provisionally applies as of 29.11.00	
Art. 19–36	r.12–13		
Art. 37–38		Provisionally applies as of 29.11.00	
Art. 39–41			
Art. 42		Provisionally applies as of 29.11.00	
Art. 43–49			
Art. 50		Provisionally applies as of 29.11.00	
Art. 54(1)–(2)			
Art. 55–60	r.25		

Article of EPC2000	Corresponding EPC2000 Regulations	Comments
Art. 62–64	r.19–21	
Art. 66		
Art. 71–85	r.22–24, r.35–50	
Art. 87		
Art. 89		
Art. 91		
Art. 95–96		
Art. 100		
Art. 102		
Art. 107		
Art. 109		
Art. 111–112	r.102	
Art. 112a		To decisions taken before 13.12.2007
Art. 113–114	r.111–113	
Art. 116	r.115–116, 124(part)	
Art. 118		
Art. 125–126		
Art. 130–132	r.148–150	
Art. 134–134a	r.153–154	
Art. 136		
Art. 139–140		
Art. 142–149a		
Art. 154–178		

The following provisions of EPC1973 therefore continue to apply to applications filed before December 13, 2007 and the granted patents they lead to:

570

Article of EPC1973	Corresponding EPC1973 Regulations	Comments
Art. 1–13		
Art. 14(1)–(2) and (8)–(9)		
Art. 15		
Art. 16–18		Applies up to 29.11.00
Art. 19–36		
Art. 37–38		Applies up to 29.11.00
Art. 39–41		
Art. 42		Applies up to 29.11.00
Art. 43–49		
Art. 50		Applies up to 29.11.00
Art. 54(1)–(2)		
Art. 54(4)	r.23a, r.87	
Art. 55–60	r.23	
Art. 62–64	r.17–19	
Art. 66		

Article of EPC1973	Corresponding EPC1973 Regulations	Comments
Art. 71–85	r.20–22, 24–27, 29–36	
Art. 87		
Art. 89		
Art. 90(3)		Deemed withdrawal of application when search/filing fee not paid or translation not filed.
Art. 91(4)		Deemed withdrawal of designation when fee not paid
Art. 100		
Art. 107		
Art. 109		
Art. 111–112	r.66(2)	
Art. 113–114	r.68–70	
Art. 116	r.71–71a	
Art. 118		
Art. 125–126		
Art. 130–132	r.97–99	
Art. 134	r.102	
Art. 139–140		
Art. 142–149		
Art. 154(3) and Art. 155(3)		BoA still has competence for protest procedure

Some important points to bear in mind:

(a)   Art. 54(4) EPC1973 and r.23a EPC1973 continue to apply to applications filed be-   571
fore December 13, 2007 and the patents which these applications lead to. When the
state of the art is assessed for such applications, prior art citable under Art. 54(3)
EPC is only relevant for those States which the earlier European right validly designates. This means that r.87 EPC1973, allowing a different text of the application
and patent for different states where a European prior right is only relevant to some
states, also continues to apply.

(b)   Art. 54(5) EPC2000 (new second medical use claim format) applies to applications   572
pending on December 13, 2007 where a decision to grant had not yet been taken. If
a decision to grant had been taken on December 12, 2007 or earlier then Art. 54(5)
EPC2000 does not apply and a claim in the format prescribed by this provision will
be interpreted as a first medical use claim under Art. 54(5) EPC1973.

(c)   Art. 87(1) EPC2000 (priority can be claimed from a filing in a WTO country) does   573
not apply to applications filed before December 13, 2007. Remember it is the date of
the European patent application which counts and not that of the priority application. A European patent application filed before December 13, 2007 can only validly
claim priority from a previous application filed in a Paris Convention country.

1.9   Worked examples – Paper D1 2012

The following worked examples are included to show how the short legal questions in   574
Paper D could be approached and answered. The answers given are not intended to be
complete or perfect but representative of the kind of answers that should lead to a high
pass mark in the exam. In each case, some comments that might occur on a first reading of
the question have been noted followed by an analysis of how the correct legal provisions
could have been identified, a discussion of the where the marks would likely have been
allocated in the marking schedule, a possible answer and comments on the question as a
whole.

Question 1 (6 marks): On 29 December 2011 you received a decision dated 27 Decem-   575
ber 2011 refusing your European patent application.[1.1] The last sentence of the decision

reads as follows: "As all the features of the independent claim are known from the prior art document D1, the application is refused for lack of novelty, Art. 56 EPC".[1.2] On 26 January 2012 you received a correction of the decision according to Rule 140 EPC for the same application.[1.3] The correction is dated 24 January 2012.[1.4] Only the last sentence was changed to "As all the features of the independent claim are known from the prior art document D1, the application is refused for lack of novelty, Art. 54 EPC".[1.5] Your client has not yet decided whether to file an appeal, but intends to take this decision in the next few weeks.[1.6] However, he will call you this morning to discuss the further procedure.[1.7] What will you advise your client?[1.8]

576   1.1   When an application is refused by the Examining Division we should immediately realise that it has ceased to be pending, and the only way in which we could obtain a patent would be to appeal the decision or file a divisional application within the appeal period. According to Art. 108 EPC, the time limit for filing an appeal is two months from notification of the decision. Notification here is less than 10 days so the deemed notification period of r.126(2) EPC applies – the decision is deemed notified on 06 January 2012 (note that before 01 November 2023, a 10 day notification period applied which is no longer the case). The period therefore expires · on 06 March 2012 – a Tuesday which just happens to be today! We therefore understand immediately that, in principle, an appeal should be filed today if required.

1.2   The citation of Art. 56 is clearly a mistake since the rest of the sentence clearly refers to a lack of novelty for which the legal basis would be Art. 54 EPC. Furthermore, this is an obvious mistake in the sense that the reader would automatically know both that a mistake was present and what the correction should be. The presence of this mistake should lead the well-prepared candidate to two possible legal consequences: (1) Decisions can be corrected under r.140; and (2) Mistakes in decisions sometimes render them invalid (e.g. where it is not consistent with the decision as previously given orally or is inappropriately signed).

1.3   We should find nothing surprising in this sentence given our knowledge of the EPC – see comment 1.2. The Examining Division has identified the mistake of its own motion and issued a correction.

1.4   The point of the question should now start to become clear: we have a decision and a corrected decision with different dates: from which date does the appeal period start? If it remains the date of the original decision we need to file an appeal today. If not, we can wait until later. From a purely psychological perspective, it is more likely that the answer to a question will require urgent action today!

1.5   Thus the obvious mistake has been corrected in the expected manner. Such a correction of an obvious mistake does not actually alter the informational content of the decision, it merely makes explicit what was already implicit.

1.6   The EQE is meant to test your ability to practice as a patent attorney. That will frequently involve advising a client who has little knowledge of patent law and the legal consequences of events and correcting his false assumptions. The client cannot afford to take a decision in the next few weeks if an appeal needs to be filed today. Again, even without knowing the legal situation properly, you could come to the conclusion that an appeal needs to be filed today just from a knowledge of the way examiners tend to think.

1.7   So if an appeal needs to be filed today you will have the chance to take instructions from your client this morning and file the appeal this afternoon – see how the pieces of the question are starting to fit together like a jigsaw puzzle to create a coherent picture.

1.8   This is the question that must be answered. Make sure you answer this question rather than just writing lots of things that you know about the filing of an appeal and the correction of decisions.

577   Legal analysis: Does the correction of an obvious mistake in a decision (as explicitly allowed by r.140 EPC) reset the period for filing an appeal? The answer to this question may not be apparent to even a well prepared candidate since it is not a situation that arises often. In the exam, we have a small amount of time to find the answer if we know where to look. First, consider the Articles and Rules. Art. 113–114 and Implementing Regulation r.111 deal with decisions. Nothing of interest here. Nothing either in r.140 cited in the

question. Nothing in those provisions refer to a decision of the President or a provision of national law. So the answer must be found in the Guidelines or the case law. The relevant parts of the Guidelines would be time limit for filing an appeal (E-XII, 6) and corrections under r.140 (H/VI/3) – nothing of interest here except for the comment that corrections are retrospective in effect. In the case law book, however, the section relating to r.140 discloses both that corrections under r.140 are retrospective in effect (T212/88) and that decisions are not re-dated as a result (T116/90).

Where are the marks? It seems likely there would be marks in this case for identifying   578
the original decision as triggering the appeal deadline, calculating the deadline, advising the client that an appeal, if needed, must be filed today, specifying the concrete steps to be taken and identifying further acts necessary (filing grounds). Less obviously, the examiner's report indicates that marks would have been available for advising the client that the appeal fee would be refunded if he changed his mind before the grounds for appeal were filed and the deadline for filing them had expired. There is nothing in the question that provides a direct stimulus for providing this information.

Possible answer: The wrong citation of Art. 54 in the original decision is an obvious   579
mistake within the meaning of r.140 EPC that can be corrected by the Examining Division. The effect of this correction is retrospective and no re-dating of the decision is necessary according to the case law (see T 212/88 and T116/90). The appeal deadline is therefore to be calculated from the date of the original decision. Deemed notification under Art. 126(2) EPC is 06 January 2012 (note that at the time of the question a 10 day notification period applied which is no longer the case after 01 November 2023) and the two month period of Art. 108 EPC expires today, 06 March 2012 (Art. 120(b) and r.131(2) and (4) EPC). The client must therefore decide **today** whether an appeal is to be filed or not. If an appeal is to be filed, a written notice of appeal must be filed today specifying the name and address of the appellant, an indication of the decision impugned and a request that the decision be set aside and a patent granted (Art. 108 and r.99(1) EPC). It may be filed electronically or by fax (r.2(1) EPC and decisions of the President dated 12 July 2007 and 10 November 2015) at any of the EPO filing offices. The appeal fee must also be paid today (Art. 108 EPC). Grounds setting out why the appeal should be allowed (r.99(2) EPC) must be filed within the four month deadline of Art. 108 EPC which will expire 06 May 2012, extended under r.134(1) to 07 May 2012 (Art. 120(b) and r.131(2) EPC). If the client changes his mind about the appeal later on, the appeal fee will be refunded if the appeal is withdrawn before the filing of the statement of grounds and before the four-month period for filing the grounds has expired (r.103(1)(b) EPC).

Comment: It is unfair, and unusual, to find a question such as this as the first question   580
in the D paper. Normally, the first question will be relatively straightforward and involve only a knowledge of the Articles and Rules of the EPC or perhaps a decision of the Enlarged Board of Appeal in order to settle candidates nerves. This question, on the other hand, required a deep knowledge of the case law that only a minority of candidates would possess.

Question 2 (6 marks): For European patent application EP1, filed in English,[2.1] the   581
first communication from the examining division under Art. 94(3) and Rule 71(1), (2) EPC dated 13 December 2007[2.2] raised only a lack of clarity objection.[2.3] On 14 December 2009 a divisional application DIV1 of EP1 was filed in the same language as EP1 at the EPO in Munich.[2.4] On 30 September 2010 a further divisional application DIV2 of EP1 was filed in the same language as EP1 at the EPO in Berlin.[2.5] The partial search report for DIV1 dated 06 October 2011 contained a statement regarding lack of unity.[2.6] However, no additional search fee was paid.[2.7] EP1 and DIV2 were withdrawn on 28 January 2011.[2.8] (a) What were the filing requirements for divisional applications DIV1 and DIV2?[2.9] (b) Is it still possible to validly file further divisional applications?[2.10]

2.1   No translation required, English is the language of the proceedings.   582
2.2   This communication is notable for triggering the time limit for filing a voluntary divisional application under Art. 76(1) and r.36(1)(a) EPC that applied at the time of the exam. The time limit would have expired 23 December 2009. However, the law only entered into force on 01 April 2010 and, under the transitional provisions, voluntary divisionals could still be filed until 01 October 2010 (see decision of the Administrative Council dated 25 March 2009, [2009] O.J. 296).
2.3   Usually a relatively easy objection to overcome.

2.4   Assuming that EP1 was still pending on 14 December 2009, the divisional application seems to have been validly filed since no time limit applied at this time and the language of filing is admissible. Munich is a valid filing office.

2.5   Assuming EP1 was still pending on 30 September 2010, this divisional also seems to have been validly filed since it was filed within the grace period allowed under the translational provisions and was filed in an admissible language. Berlin is a valid filing office.

2.6   This does not trigger a further time limit for filing a divisional application since r.36(1)(b) in force at the time specified communications from the Examining Division.

2.7   With the consequence that only the searched invention may be prosecuted in DIV1 unless the lack of unity is successfully contested before the Examining Division.

2.8   Good circumstantial evidence that EP1 was pending when the two divisional applications were filed. Withdrawal is immediate and irrevocable such that these applications can no longer lead to any patent rights. Nor can they be further divided.

2.9   This is a fairly open-ended question. The fact that these two applications were filed either side of the amendments to r.36 taking effect implies that the question is primarily probing candidate's knowledge of the amendments and their effect.

2.10 This is a nice straightforward question which should be relatively simple to answer.

583   Legal Analysis: The question is clearly testing candidates' knowledge of the amendments to r.36 EPC that came into force on 01 April 2010. The result of these amendments was to introduce a time limit for filing divisional applications. Both DIV1 and DIV2 seem to have been correctly filed though the legal requirements applying to them are different. In relation to part (b) we must consider whether any applications are pending (and can therefore be divided) and whether a time limit under r.36(1)(a) or (b) is still running, or may be triggered in the future.

584   Where are the marks? The points that need to be made seem to be quite straightforward since the questions are fairly specific. The only ambiguity concerns what 'filing requirements' may mean. The term would tend to suggest those requirements which are necessary to achieve a filing date, any subsequent requirements which are triggered by the filing date but not necessary for obtaining it not being included. Payment of fees, for example, would not be included since they are not necessary for obtaining a filing date and it is unlikely that marks would be available for any discussion of them.

585   Possible answer: (a) DIV1 was filed on 14 December 2009 under Art. 76(1) and r.36 EPC2000 as in force before 01 April 2010. Accordingly, no time limit applied to the filing of this divisional application; according to r.36(1) EPC in force at the time it was sufficient that the parent application was pending at the time of division. This seems to have been the case given the later withdrawal of EP1. It was also a requirement according to r.36(2) EPC in force at the time that the divisional application was filed in the language of proceedings of the parent, in this case English. This condition was also complied with. The divisional was filed in Munich which is a valid filing office of the EPO (see decision of the President dated 12 July 2007). It therefore seems that DIV1 was properly filed. DIV2 was filed on 30 September 2010 under Art. 76(1) and r.36 EPC as in force from 01 April 2010 onwards. Accordingly, a time limit for the filing of a voluntary divisional applied expiring 24 months from notification of the first communication from the examining division. This time limit would have expired 23 December 2009 (Art. 120(b), r.126(2) and r.131(2) EPC). However, according to the decision of the Administrative Council dated 25 March 2009 ([2009] O.J. 296) divisional applications could still be filed until 01 October 2010 where the time limit had expired. DIV2 was therefore filed in time. It is still a requirement under new r.36(1) EPC that the parent application is pending when the divisional is filed – this seems to have been the case for DIV2 given the later withdrawal of EP1. It is also a requirement according to new r.36(2) EPC that a divisional application is filed in the language of proceedings of the parent application, in this case English. The divisional was filed in Berlin which is a valid filing office of the EPO and complies with new r.36(2) EPC. (b) Only a pending European patent application can be divided. The only application which is currently subject to division is therefore DIV1. The time limit for filing a voluntary divisional from DIV1 under r.36(1)(a) EPC has already expired (01 October 2010 – see above). A time limit under r.36(1)(b) has not yet been triggered since no communication from the Examining Division has been received

(the unity objection was made by the Search Division). If a communication from the Examining Division for DIV1 containing a unity objection issues then a new 24 month time limit for the filing of a divisional application will be triggered (the subject of the divisional application does not have to be associated with the unity objection). In the absence of such a communication, a further divisional will not be possible.

Comment: In order to answer this question candidates were required to have knowledge of r.36 as in force before 01 April 2010. At the time of the exam the new law had been in force for almost two years and the transitional period had expired some 18 months previously. It is unusual for D1 questions to require a detailed historical knowledge of this kind and this question could be argued to be somewhat unfair. It nevertheless illustrates the enormous breadth of knowledge that candidates need to possess to be sure of being able to answer all the questions. How far back such a historical perspective should stretch is unclear but it would certainly be unwise not to have a firm grasp of the main transitional provisions relating to EPC2000. Note that the time limit of r.36(1) was abolished as of April 2014.

Question 3 (5 marks): On 05 October 2010 your Spanish client filed a PCT application[3.1] in Spanish[3.2] with the Spanish Patent and Trade Mark Office (SPTO).[3.3] No priority was claimed.[3.4] Due to a lack of unity objection, which the client accepts, only the first invention was searched by the SPTO.[3.5] However, your client wants a search to be carried out by the EPO on the second invention before deciding on entry into the national/regional phase but does not want to file a new application.[3.6] (a) Is this possible?[3.7] (b) If so, what steps have to be taken?[3.8]

3.1   Numerous time limits are triggered by the filing of a PCT application which could be relevant in this question. Marks are usually available for correctly calculating them. A Spanish client is a national of a PCT contracting state and eligible to file a PCT application.

3.2   Spanish is a language of publication for a PCT application but a translation would be required if the EPO were to act as ISA, IPEA or designated office.

3.3   This is a competent receiving Office for a Spanish applicant.

3.4   This confirms that the filing date is to be used for the calculation of time limits referred to in comment 3.1.

3.5   So the Spanish PTO acted as ISA rather than the EPO.

3.6   So it is necessary to consider what kinds of search the EPO will carry out on an international patent application that has already been the subject of an international search before entry into the regional phase (at which point a supplementary European search report would be drawn up).

3.7   If the answer to this question was 'no' then the question would not make any sense and it would be impossible to award 5 marks for the answer. It is therefore already abundantly clear, without using any legal knowledge, that the answer must be 'yes'.

3.8   The bulk of the marks are going to be available for accurately setting out what needs to be filed, where, when and at what cost.

Legal Analysis: It is necessary to consider the kinds of search offered by the EPO. European and additional European searches, carried out by the Search Division or Examining Division for a regular European patent application, are clearly not relevant here. Neither is a supplementary European search a possible solution given the requirement stipulated by the client that the search results are available prior to regional phase entry. The international search has already been carried out so the EPO will not be able to act as International Searching Authority. Neither will the EPO be able to carry out an international-type search according to Art. 15(5) PCT since these are carried out on national applications rather than international applications. Only one option remains: a supplementary international search. This option is available and meets the requirements specified by the client.

Where are the marks? There is unlikely to be more than half a mark for saying 'Yes' in answer to part (a). The marks for this question will be earned for identifying the concrete steps that need to be taken by the client, the time-limit(s) for doing so and the institution before which the steps need to be taken.

Possible answer: (a) Yes, it is possible to request the EPO to draw up a supplementary international search report according to r.45*bis* PCT since it did not act as International

Searching Authority and has indicated that it is competent in the circumstances specified in the question (r.45*bis*.9 PCT and Annex E of the Agreement between the EPO and the IB ([2010] O.J. 304). (b) A request for a supplementary international search must be filed with the International Bureau (r.45*bis*.1(b)) before the expiration of 19 months from the priority date (r.45*bis*.1(a) PCT). In this case the 19 month period expires Saturday 05 May 2012 (Art. 47(1) and r.80.2 PCT) and is extended until Monday 07 May 2012 (Art. 47(1) and r.80.5 PCT). The request must contain the necessary indications laid down by r.45*bis*.1(b) PCT and be accompanied by a translation of the international application into English, French or German, which are the only languages accepted by the EPO as Supplementary International Searching Authority (r.45*bis*.1(c) PCT and Annex E of the Agreement between the EPO and the IB ([2010] O.J. 304)). The request should also contain an indication that the supplementary search should be directed towards the subject matter which was not searched by the International Searching Authority (r.45*bis*.1(d) PCT). A supplementary search fee (r.45*bis*.3(a), currently 1875 euros as specified in Art. 2(1)(2) of the EPC Rules Relating to Fees) and a supplementary search handling fee (r.45*bis*.2(a) PCT, currently 200 Swiss Francs as specified in the PCT Schedule of Fees) must also be paid within one month of the filing of the request (r.45*bis*.2(c) and r.45*bis*.3(c) PCT).

592   Comment: This is a fair question, based on recent amendments to the PCT Regulations. The answer to the question should have been relatively easy to spot and the marks relatively easy to accumulate. It would, in fact, have made a much better opening question for the paper than Question 1 or Question 2. Note that the time limit for filing a request for a supplementary international search report has now been extended to 22 months from the priority date. The agreement between the EPO and the IB, quoted in the answer above, is furthermore not the current version.

593   **Question 4 (4 marks):** Company X filed a draft of a scientific paper as a European patent application EP-X at the EPO.[4.1] The draft describes compositions of the class A. The EPO accorded to application EP-X a date of filing of 20 December 2009.[4.2] On 15 February 2010, company X filed, for EP-X, a claim directed to product A1, which was not described in the draft paper.[4.3] On 17 November 2010 company X filed an international application PCT1 at the USPTO with the description of EP-X and the same claim as above, claiming priority from EP-X.[4.4] Company X received from the USPTO an international search report indicating only a single document which discloses product A1.[4.5] This document was made available to the public in March 2010.[4.6] (a) Is it possible to obtain valid patent protection via the claim directed to product A1 if PCT1 enters the European phase? (b) How could the situation be different for PCT1 if the draft paper had disclosed A1?

594   4.1   It is not necessary to file a claim in order to obtain a filing date under the EPC (Art. 80 and r.40 EPC) and so the scientific paper is sufficient basis for the application. Claims will be required in due course and must not extend in subject matter beyond what was originally disclosed (Art. 123(2) EPC).

        4.2   The filing date could be relevant to a number of different issues which may be important in answering the question, including: extent to which EPC2000 applies, Contracting States that are designated, effective date for patentability, first renewal fee due date, due date for payment of search fee and filing fee. Which, if any, of these are important will be determined by the further facts of the question.

        4.3   Claims were filed in this case within two months of the filing of the application. There is no time limit in which they must be filed calculated from the filing date. If not filed, the EPO eventually sends an invitation to correct according to r.58 EPC but it seems the applicant has avoided the need for such an invitation by filing the claims before the EPO has taken any action. However, the claims as filed are not allowable according to Art. 123(2) EPC since they relate to subject matter which extends beyond the content of the application as filed.

        4.4   The second application is filed within the priority year and by the same applicant so in these respects the priority claim is valid. A claim is a necessary element of a PCT application if a filing date is to be awarded. In this case, the claim relates to subject matter which is not disclosed in the earlier application and hence the priority claim is not valid from a substantive point of view according to Art. 87(1) EPC and G2/98.

4.5   Hence the claim to product A1 will lack novelty under the EPC if this disclosure was made available to the public earlier than the effective date to which the claim is entitled, which in this case is the filing date of the PCT application.

4.6   Hence the claim to product A1 lacks novelty.

Legal Analysis: This is a straightforward question which demands a basic knowledge relating to the validity of a priority claim and its effect in assessing the state of the art along with an appreciation of what constitutes the content of the application as filed under Art. 123(2) EPC. The application as filed is the content of the description, claims and drawings on the basis of which a filing date is awarded. The only way in which the content of the application as filed can change is through the late filing of missing parts of the description or drawings under r.56 EPC, either with or without redating of the application. Missing claims, however, may not be added under r.56 EPC. Claims are either present on the filing date, in which case they form part of the application as filed, or are missing, in which case they do not. In any case, the operation of r.56 EPC is beyond the facts of this question. When an application obtains a filing date, it generates a right of priority for the subject matter associated with that filing date (assuming this is the first filing of that subject matter). This means that the patentability of a later application validly claiming the priority of the first will be judged at the priority date rather than the filing date by operation of Art. 89 EPC. However, the priority claim is only valid if the subject matter claimed in the later application is directly and unambiguously derivable from the content of the earlier application (requirement for same invention under Art. 87(1) EPC, G2/98). [595]

Where are the marks? There are four marks for this question, probably two marks each for the two scenarios. These marks should be easily collected by a simple explanation of the legal principles involved and their application to the facts. [596]

Possible answer: (a) No, it will not be possible to obtain a patent directed to product A1 if PCT1 enters the European phase. The validity of the claim to product A1 in PCT-1 is to be assessed at the filing date (17 November 2010) unless a validly priority claim exists (Art. 54 and Art. 89 EPC). The priority year for EP-X (expiring Monday 20 December 2010) has been respected and the priority right was correctly exercised by company X. Furthermore, EP-X appears to have been a first filing for the subject matter it discloses. However, EP-X does not disclose product A1. The filing of the claim to product A1 on 15 February represented an unallowable amendment of EP-X (Art. 123(2)) and cannot add subject matter to EP-X as filed. The priority claim is therefore not in respect of the same invention (Art. 87(1), G2/98) and is not valid. Hence the validly of the PCT-1 claim is to be judged as of 17 November 2010 and it lacks novelty under Art. 54(2) over the cited document which was made available earlier in March 2010. (b) In this case, EP-X discloses product A1 and the priority claim from PCT-1 is valid in respect of product A1. This means that the validity of the claim to product A1 is to be assessed at the priority date of 20 December 2009 and, in this case, the document made available in March 2010 is not part of the state of the art. It should therefore be possible to obtain a granted patent for product A1 if PCT1 enters the regional phase. [597]

Comment: This is a fair question based on fundamental principles of disclosure, priority and novelty and one which any candidate capable of practising as a patent attorney should have been able to answer correctly. [598]

Question 5 (5 marks): International application PCT-CN was filed in Chinese in September 2010 with the Chinese State Intellectual Property Office (SIPO).[5.1] In March 2011 the applicant received the international search report from SIPO.[5.2] In May 2011 the applicant filed with the International Bureau amended claims together with a brief statement explaining the amendments.[5.3] The application will be published next week.[5.4] (a) Which parts of the publication will be in what language(s)? (b) Will a French translation of the abstract be publicly available from WIPO?[5.5] [599]

5.1   The application has been filed in a language accepted by the receiving Office which is also a language of publication. A translation will be required for entry into the EPO regional phase. The filing date is given, which can lead to a range of legal consequences as discussed in comments 3.1 and 4.2. [600]

5.2   The search report has been drawn up well within the time limit prescribed by Art. 18(1) and r.42 PCT that allows International Searching Authorities at least nine months from the priority date (which, under the PCT, means the filing date in the absence of a priority claim – Art. 2 PCT).

5.3   The claims and statement have been filed according to Art. 19 PCT which gives applicants the chance to amend the claims (but not the description) following receipt of the International Search Report and have the amended claims published with the application. The time limit (r.46.1) is the later of 16 months from the priority date (January 2012) and two months from transmittal of the International Search Report (May 2011) and is clearly met in this case.

5.4   Given the priority date of September 2010 (which in this case is the filing date) we would expect publication sometime in March 2012 so, given that today is 06 March 2012, the facts of the question make sense.

5.5   If we can quickly identify the PCT provisions relevant to publication of the application, this question should be easy to answer accurately.

601   Legal Analysis: The first part of the question does not demand any difficult legal analysis. It is all about identifying specific PCT provisions (relevant to the publication of the application) and applying these provisions directly to the specific facts of the question (application filed in Chinese, no translation yet available, Art. 19 amendments filed) in order to generate the answer. The second part of the question, on the other hand, is very difficult to find any answer for. Clearly, in the present case, none of the application will be published in French. On the other hand, from a purely psychological perspective, it is highly likely that the answer to the second part of the question is 'yes' since it is so specifically worded, referring to the French language. Candidates would therefore have to consider whether any information relating to published applications is made available by WIPO independently from the international publication itself. Very well-prepared candidates may then be led to consider the PCT Gazette and the provisions of r.86 PCT.

602   Where are the marks? It should not be difficult to identify the points for which marks are available in this question. We need to (i) identify what parts of a PCT application are published, bearing in mind the amendment and statement that have been filed (ii) establish what language of publication will be used for each part given the PCT application has been filed in Chinese (and not subsequently translated for search) and (iii) give relevant legal basis.

603   Possible answer: (a) The application will be published in Chinese since this was the language the application was filed in and it is a language of publication (r.48.3(a) PCT). The elements published in Chinese will be: (i) a standardised front page containing bibliographic information, the abstract and and accompanying figure or figures (r.48.2(a)(i)); (ii) the description (r.48.2(a)(ii); (iii) the claims (r.48.2(a)(iii)); (iv) any drawings (r.48.2(a) (iv); and (v) the international search report (r.48.2(a)(v)). However, the following parts of the publication will also be published in English: (i) the international search report; (ii) the title of the invention; and (iii) the abstract and any text matter pertaining to the figure or figures accompanying the abstract (r.48.3(c) PCT). In this case the publication will include both the original claims and the claims as amended as well as the statement relating to the amendments (r.48.2(a)(vi) and (f) PCT). (b) Yes. The PCT Gazette contains details relating to each published international application including bibliographic information, the abstract and any drawing accompanying the abstract (Art. 55(4) and r.86.1(i) PCT). This information is published in both English and French (r.86.2(a) PCT).

604   Comment: The first part of this question is very reasonable but the second part requires the retrieval of obscure information which is rather academic and which many practising European Patent Attorneys would not know where to find.

605   **Question 6 (6 marks):** On 28 October 2010 your client filed an Italian application IT1 for invention Inv1 and an Italian application IT2 for invention Inv2.[6.1] Inv1 and Inv2 are unitary.[6.2] On 28 October 2011 your client duly filed a European application EP1 describing and claiming inventions Inv1 and Inv2.[6.3] EP1 claims the priority of IT1 only.[6.4] Your client has discovered a document D published on 8 August 2011 disclosing Inv1 and Inv2.[6.5] Your client wants to use EP1 to obtain Europe-wide protection for both Inv1 and Inv2. What do you advise your client?[6.6]

606   6.1   There is nothing unusual about filing two applications for different inventions on the same day. The filing date could be of interest for numerous reasons as previously discussed. As this stage it just needs to be noted.

6.2 This is unusual however – it is normally preferable to file all unitary subject matter in a single application to save costs though good reasons sometimes exist for doing otherwise.

6.3 The European application has been filed on the 12 month anniversary of the filing of the Italian applications and is therefore in time to validly claim priority. It seems that all applications have been filed in the name of the client and that EP1 was therefore filed by the person owning the right to claim priority. It makes sense to combine inventions Inv1 and Inv2 in the same European application if they are unitary.

6.4 This is a nonsensical course of action and therefore one which it is likely will need reversing in order to safeguard the applicant's interests. At the moment, only claims in EP-1 directed to Inv1 will be entitled to the priority date. We should already be thinking about the options under European procedure for adding priority claims later than the filing of an application.

6.5 This disclosure is before the filing date of EP-1 and will therefore be novelty-destroying for any claim to Inv2 which is currently only entitled to the filing date. On the other hand, it is after the priority date which Inv2 would be entitled to if EP-1 also claimed the priority of IT2. The need to add this priority claim is now well-established by the question.

6.6 The client must be advised to add a priority claim to IT2 if this is indeed possible. Chances are it must be given the fact that 6 marks are available for the question.

Legal Analysis: Under EPC2000 it is now possible to add a priority claim until 16 months   607
from the earliest priority date claimed (so that it is in time for publication) – r.52(2) EPC.
We must therefore calculate this deadline and, if it is still running, add the inexplicably
omitted priority declaration. If it is not then we still have the possibility of adding the
priority claim as a correction of the request under r.139 EPC if the technical preparations
for publication have not yet been completed – this was the only option under EPC1973
and should still be available under EPC2000.

Where are the marks? There are a number of marks for this question but it can easily be   608
appreciated where they lie: the effective dates for Inv and Inv 2 need to be calculated, the
effect of the prior art considered and the need for a new priority claim from IT2 appreciated. Then, the possible ways of adding the missing priority claim needs to be described
and evaluated.

Possible answer: EP1 has been filed within 12 months from the filing of IT1 and by   609
the same legal entity (Art. 87(1) EPC). It is in respect of the same invention (Inv1) and it
is presumed that IT1 is a first filing of this subject matter (Art. 87(1) EPC, G2/98). The
priority claim therefore appears to be valid and the patentability of any claim in EP1
directed to Inv1 should be assessed as of 28 October 2010 (Art. 54 and Art. 89 EPC).
Document D is therefore not comprised in the state of the art and a patent for Inv1 can
be expected. However, EP1 does not claim priority from IT2 and Inv2 is not disclosed
in IT1, from which priority is validly claimed. The effective date for Inv2 is therefore the
filing date of EP1, 28 October 2011. Document D is therefore comprised in the state of
the art in respect of any claim in EP1 directed to invention Inv2 and such a claim would
lack novelty (Art. 54(2) EPC). It is therefore imperative, if granted claims directed to Inv2
are also to be obtained, that a priority claim to IT2 be added to EP1 so that Document D
is no longer comprised in the state of the art. It is now possible according to Art. 88(1)
and r.52(2) EPC to add a priority claim until the expiry of 16 months from the earliest
priority date claimed. This period expires Tuesday 28 February 2012. Hence the period
has expired. Furthermore, further processing is ruled out by Art. 121(4) and r.135(2) EPC.
Re-establishment (Art. 122, r.136 EPC) would in principle be applicable but the client
would have to show that the deadline had been missed in spite of all due care required
by the circumstances having been taken (Art. 122(1) EPC) and no relevant circumstances
are described by the client. It may still, however, be possible to add the priority claim in
the form of a correction to the request under r.139 EPC. Importantly, since the request
is concerned, the mistake does not have to be an 'obvious' one. However, we will need to
show that there was always an intention to claim priority from IT2 and such an intention
may already be implied by the inclusion of Inv2 in the claims and description of EP1. Such
correction will usually only be allowed if the request for correction is received before
the technical preparations for publication are complete so that a warning that a priority

claim is to be added can be included in the publication (see case law book VII/A/6.2 and lead cases cited therein such as J3/91). In the present case, the earliest date that the application could be published is Saturday 28th April 2012 (18 months from the earliest priority date claimed, Art. 93(1)(a) EPC). The technical preparations for publication are complete 5 weeks before this date (r.67(1) EPC and Decision of the President dated 12 July 2007), i.e. Saturday 24th March 2012. There therefore appears to be ample time to request the addition of a declaration of priority from IT2 as a correction of the request under r.139 and it is likely that this request will be successful and that claims directed to Inv2 will also be granted in EP1.

Comment: This is a generally fair question with a number of marks that can be steadily accumulated.

610   **Question 7 (4 Marks):** Your client has developed the following way of diagnosing an illness:[7.1] (a) Carrying out a known method of biopsy by a medical practitioner to extract a liver tissue sample from a patient;[7.2] (b) carrying out a novel and inventive method for diagnosing the illness on the basis of the tissue sample in an analysing liquid.[7.3] Your client has informed you that the way in which the tissue sample is obtained is not an essential feature of his development.[7.4] Your client wants you to file a European patent application. Discuss the patentability of his development according to the EPC.[7.5]

611   7.1   This question demonstrates that candidates must have a general appreciation of the patentability of inventions across the technical fields. Chemists and biologists must have an awareness, for example, of the patentability of computer-implemented inventions and those working in the mechanical and electrical fields must have an awareness of patentability in the biomedical field. The word 'diagnosing' should automatically bring to mind the exclusion under Art. 53(c) EPC of diagnostic methods practised on the human or animal body and the lead case law G1/04.

7.2   It is clear that the first step of the diagnostic method may also be excluded as a method for treatment of the human or animal body by surgery and the case law relevant to surgical methods such as the recent G1/07 should also be brought to mind.

7.3   This step sounds much more promising as a candidate for patent protection! Aside from being novel and inventive, it does not involve any interaction with the human or animal body – but can it be separated from the biopsy step and is it nevertheless a method of diagnosis?

7.4   This sounds promising for separating the biopsy step from the analysis step.

7.5   A summary of the main provisions and case law and the application of those relevant principles to the facts of the client's invention is clearly signposted.

612   Legal Analysis: Both steps of the method seem at first sight to be excluded by Art. 53(c) EPC – step (a) as a surgical method and step (b) as a diagnostic method. Applying the principles of G1/07, step (a) does indeed seem to be an excluded surgical method since a biopsy is an invasive step which involves a substantial health risk. Applying the principles of G1/04, on the other hand, step (b) does not amount to a diagnostic method since a technical step is included which is not practiced on the human or animal body. Furthermore, it is legitimate to separate the two steps since the first step is not an essential feature vis-à-vis the second step. The second step therefore embodies a patentable invention.

613   Where are the marks? The marks are available here for correctly summarising the relevant legal provisions (Art. 53(c), G1/04 and G1/07), applying that law to the facts of the question and arriving at the legal consequence that step (b) of the method represents a patentable invention.

614   Possible answer: According to Art. 53(c) EPC, methods for treatment of the human or animal body by surgery are not patentable. A surgical method in this sense has been defined in G1/07 as one involving an invasive step representing a substantial physical intervention on the body which requires professional medical expertise and which entails a substantial health risk. A biopsy would therefore seem to be a surgical method and, according to G1/07, any method incorporating a biopsy will be excluded from patentability. However, step (a) is not an essential feature of the invention as a whole and it may therefore be possible to claim step (b) on its own since this step seems to be novel and inventive. According to Art. 53(c) EPC, diagnostic methods practised on the human or animal body are also excluded from patentability. However, it has been decided by G1/04 that this exclusion only applies when each essential technical step of the method is

practised on the human or animal body, i.e. requires its physical presence. Since, in this case, step (b) is carried out on a tissue sample, it is not carried out on the human or animal body within the meaning of G1/04 and is not therefore an excluded diagnostic method. It would therefore be possible to obtain a patent under the EPC for the subject matter of step (b) of the method described by the client.

Comment: This is a straightforward question requiring the application of clear legal   615
principles to a clear set of facts. It may have been more challenging to those who work outside the biomedical area but a knowledge of Enlarged Board of Appeal case law is clearly important regardless of technical speciality.

Question 8 (5 marks): European patent application EP1 was published   616
on 10 March 2010.[8.1] In reply to a communication of the examining division, the applicant filed amended claims containing improved subject-matter in June 2011.[8.2] This improved subject-matter is new and inventive over the originally disclosed subject-matter and, in itself, is sufficiently disclosed according to Art. 83 EPC.[8.3] On 09 December 2011 the applicant filed a second European patent application EP2 describing and claiming the improved subject-matter.[8.4] Can the applicant obtain valid protection for the improved subject-matter via EP1 or EP2?

8.1   A published European patent applications has entered the state of the art under both   617
      Art. 54(2) and Art. 54(3) EPC and provides provisional protection for the applicant,
      amongst other things.

8.2   It is perfectly reasonable to amend the claims by introducing further technical fea-
      tures which solve a more impressive problem and bring novelty and inventive step
      to the claim as long as there is basis for such features in the application as filed.

8.3   What does this sentence mean? Is the 'originally disclosed subject matter' the sub-
      ject matter which was originally claimed and is the 'improved' subject matter one of
      the embodiments originally only disclosed in the description? Or is this 'improved'
      subject matter a new development which was invented after the filing of the appli-
      cation and hence not disclosed at all? The latter interpretation fits better with the
      wording of the question since the 'improved' subject matter is said to be new and
      inventive over what was originally 'disclosed' rather than over what was originally
      'claimed' but some doubt remains in my mind, especially since it is difficult to im-
      agine how the 'improved' subject matter could be sufficiently disclosed if it is not
      discussed. The question is particularly confusing since the 'improved' subject matter
      is described as 'sufficiently disclosed', albeit in the context of Art. 83 rather than
      Art. 123(2). The drafting of the question is poor and it may be sensible to include in
      the answer a short discussion on interpretation.

8.4   This sentence also supports the interpretation that the 'improved' subject matter was
      not originally disclosed (even if it is somehow enabled by the original disclosure)
      since the filing of a new application would be pointless if the 'improved' subject
      matter had been part of the publication of EP1.

Legal Analysis: The key difficulty here is interpreting what the question means. The ques-   618
tion seems to be proposing a scenario according to which the applicant is claiming subject matter not originally disclosed in EP1 but which, somehow, is enabled by the disclosure of EP1. Presumably, EP1 must disclose a general concept and embodiment E1 and the 'improved' subject matter must be an embodiment E2 which could be made and used by the skilled person by applying common general knowledge along with the detailed disclo- sure of E1. According to this interpretation it is therefore clear that Art. 123(2) is contra- vened and the claim in EP1 to this 'improved' subject matter is unallowable. The applicant has also filed a new application EP2 for the 'improved' subject matter. The publication of EP1 would not seem to represent a problem if the 'improved' subject matter is both novel and inventive in relation to its disclosure. However, the key point to be appreciated is that the filing date of EP2 is some six months following the filing of the amended claims for EP1, said claims including the 'improved' subject matter. Since EP1 is published, these claims would be immediately subject to file inspection and hence available to the public. The claims of EP2 must therefore lack novelty.

Where are the marks: Once the question has been properly interpreted and understood,   619
the answer required is relatively easy to spot. The marks are available for indicating why

no patent protection is possible via EP1 (Art. 123(2)) and EP2 (Art. 54(2)). There are no 'hidden' points to be made.

620   Possible answer: Regardless of whether the improved subject matter is enabled by the disclosure of EP1, it seems from the facts of the question that it was not disclosed in EP1 as filed. Claims to this improved subject matter therefore extend beyond the content of the application as filed and contravene Art. 123(2) EPC. It will thus not be possible to obtain patent protection for the improved subject matter via EP1. Application EP2 was filed after the publication of EP1. However, the improved subject matter is known to be novel and inventive over the disclosure of EP1 so this is not a problem. Unfortunately, EP2 was also filed some six months following the disclosure of the improved subject matter to the EPO in the form of new claims for EP1. Since at the time the new claims were filed, EP1 had already been published, these claims would have been immediately made available to the public according to Art. 54(2) EPC through file inspection (Art. 128(4) and r.144 EPC and Decision of the President of the EPO dated 12 July 2007). Claims to the improved subject matter in EP2 will therefore lack novelty over this disclosure and no patent protection will be possible.

621   Comment: This question is, unfortunately, poorly drafted and many candidates would likely have lost many or all marks through an inability to understand the question rather than an inability to be able to apply the relevant legal principles correctly. This is a shame.

Chapter 2: Paper D Part II - Legal Opinion

2.1 General comments

In the second part of paper D of the EQE (from 2013 onwards), the candidate must an- 622
swer one or more longer questions in which a more complicated set of facts needs to be
analysed in order to advise a client on questions of validity and infringement (Part II: Legal Opinion; Art. 1(4) RQEQPR, r.26(1) IPREQE). These longer questions correspond
to the kind of questions posed in the D2 paper of the EQE up to and including 2012 and
the overall content and style of the questions have not changed at all in the new format –
the only change is that the length of the question(s) has decreased in order to take into
account the reduced time allocated to the exam as a whole. Whereas a typical D2 paper
may have included one very complicated long question and one much less complicated
long question, the new D paper is more likely to have one moderately complicated long
question or two much less complicated long questions. The number of marks allocated to
this part of paper D will vary between 40 % and 60 % of the marks allocated to paper D
as a whole (notice from the Examination Board dated 13 March 2019).

Having answered several short legal questions in paper D, the candidate must signifi- 623
cantly change gear when addressing the long question or questions. These questions do
not involve applying specific, diverse (and often esoteric) legal provisions to a narrow-
ly-framed set of facts. Rather, they involve applying largely the same, well-known legal
provisions (patentable subject matter, priority, novelty, inventive step, ownership) to a
complicated and broadly-framed set of inter-related facts in order to provide realistic advice to a client trying to use intellectual property rights to further his or her commercial
aims (r.26(3) IPREQE). Providing detailed legal basis is no longer important; providing
useful advice that will bring the clients commercial strategy into harmony with the intellectual property rights owned by himself and others is crucial.

The client will have made some inventions relevant to the business that he or she carries 624
out. In almost all cases, one or more patent applications will have been filed relating to
these inventions. In some papers, these applications will be facing significant prosecution
issues: an important part of the answer in such situations will be advice on how such issues
can be addressed in order to get useful patents granted, either by recovering rights lost
by applying procedural remedies or by making substantive claim amendments in view
of prior art. Sometimes, an application will not yet have been filed for at least some embodiments of the client's inventions. In this case the answer must include advice on what
filing strategy would be appropriate and what kind of claims could be filed. The client is
also very likely to have a competitor who has also filed patent applications. In these cases
it will be necessary to assess the validity of these patent rights and advise the client how
such rights might limit his freedom to operate commercially. This advice might include
reference to actions necessary to neutralise infringement threats by, for example, opposing granted patents or filing third party observations in respect of pending applications. It
might also include advice relating to a licensing or cross-licensing solution to the problem.

As in the real world, the client and his competitor will likely have taken advantage of 625
the possibility to maximise patent term by claiming priority. The ability to correctly assess the validity of priority claims is absolutely vital in this paper and it is very rare that a
long Paper D question does not involve some issue relating to a priority claim. Sometimes
a priority claim will be wholly invalid by virtue of the priority application not being a
first filing or the applicant for the later application not being legally entitled to claim the
priority of the earlier application. Even more often, a priority claim will only be partially
valid by virtue of the second application claiming subject matter not disclosed in the earlier application and different effective dates will apply to different claims. Whether the 12
month term has been respected or whether a lack of compliance with the 12 month term
can be excused is also often relevant.

Apart from correctly assessing priority in order to assign effective dates to various 626
claims and/or unclaimed subject matter, these long questions also invariably involve identifying the state of the art relevant to those effective dates and assessing patentability in
light of one or more disclosures. Considering whether one or more disclosures were actually made available to the public (e.g. by virtue of an implicit or explicit confidentiality)

and understanding the differing effects of Art. 54(2) and Art. 54(3) prior art are important aspects of this.

627   Other issues which sometimes need addressing are ownership and sufficiency. Occasionally the competitor will have filed a patent application based on information obtained from the client under confidence: the operation of Art. 55 to limit the prior art effect of such an application and the possibilities for the client to contest ownership of the application will need to be explored in these cases. Sometimes the client will have filed an application which apparently lacks the information necessary to allow a skilled person to carry out the claimed invention – whether a cross-reference to another document, a publication which is state of the art or common general knowledge of some kind could be applied to compensate for the deficiency may be important.

628   In these longer D questions the technology on which the client's inventions is based is likely, in common with the other EQE papers, to be of a simple mechanical nature which all candidates can understand regardless of technical background (tennis rackets (2008) and bicycle components (2011) are typical examples). Indeed, candidates are expected to ignore any specialist knowledge of the technology that they may have (r.22(3) IPREQE). However, occasionally the subject matter will stray into a more chemical or electronic field and it is important for all candidates to have a basic grasp of what subject matter is patentable across the technical spectrum. For instance, the 2000 D2 paper concerned pharmaceutical formulations and proteins isolated from a fermentation and the 2009 paper concerned the use of organic compounds as agrochemicals for controlling snails and slugs. It is therefore important for candidates to have an outline knowledge of the patentability of compounds and their uses including an appreciation that methods of treatment by surgery and therapy are excluded subject matter and specific first and second medical use claims are available instead. It is also important, for example, to understand what a selection invention is and how the patentability of such inventions is judged. On the other side of the coin, the 2004 D2 paper concerned imagine enhancement software and chips for use in digital cameras and the 2010 D2 paper concerned technology for use in the fishing industry comprising electronic circuits and filters. It is therefore equally important for candidates to have a broad appreciation of the patentability of computer-implemented inventions and whether, for example, a claim to a signal conveying information is a presentation of information as such.

629   They key to obtaining a high mark in this part of the legal paper is to remember that the answer is not being addressed to a legal expert, as the answers to the short questions are, but to a client who is interested in making and selling things. Whilst some of the marks are awarded for analysing the legal situation correctly, many others are available for providing sensible, pragmatic, commercially-focussed advice to the client. The commercial aims of the client need to be taken into consideration – there is no point analysing the patentability of subject matter which the client is not interested in pursuing because it is too expensive to manufacture. The stated preferences of the client also need to be taken into consideration – there is no point in taking legal action against a third party that the client considers to be a friend and collaborator except as a last resort. The cost implications of the advice given should also be measured against the facts of the question – expensive litigation may not be appropriate for a small client who has limited financial means. It is likely that when the paper has been fully analysed there will be at least some valid patent rights belonging to the competitor that cover at least some of the commercial embodiments being considered by the client in at least some countries. Sometimes the situation will be more extreme and the competitor will have a dominating patent covering all embodiments. The client, on the other hand, will also have something that the competitor wants. Always therefore consider negotiation as one way forward for the client and the possibility of licensing or cross-licensing. Much better than mentioning cross-licensing in general terms, however, is to propose some concrete manner in which markets, or commercial embodiments could be shared under such a license, always bearing in mind the requirements of competition law! Where the client has options, set them out along with their pros and cons and, where appropriate, express a value judgement as to which is the better course of action.

630   Because the answer to a longer paper D question is addressed to a client, it seems that candidates lose many marks for failing to make what might be termed "obvious" points in the answer. It is important to highlight in the answer the messages that such a client

actually wants to hear: what can he make and sell without infringing any third party patent rights, what are the consequences of infringement (preliminary injunction, permanent injunction, damages etc), what can he prevent the competitor from doing, what actions are necessary to preserve legal rights and within what time frame, what are the cost implications, what license terms should he propose? The Examination Committee has made it clear that no marks are awarded for citing legal basis in these longer questions. This does not mean, however, that it is not a good idea to cite legal basis where it is known or easily accessible. On the contrary, citing brief legal basis for your conclusions in the form of an Article, Rule or decision helps to build a sense of credibility and enhances the impression that your answer will make in the mind of the examiner. It is not recommended, however, to spend much time looking for legal basis.

Under the current eEQE format the legal opinion is allocated 55 marks and must be   631
completed in one session lasting 3 hours 20 minutes. About half this time should be spent analysing the question and elucidating the answer, the other half being devoted to writing the answer. Previous comments on time management made in relation to the shorter questions are also relevant here: if sufficient time is allocated to analysing the paper properly then it should not take too long to write the answer in a concise and effective manner. Most of the points made in answering the paper before a full analysis has been completed, on the other hand, are likely to be off-point or plain wrong and are unlikely to score many marks.

2.2 How to tackle each question

The key difficulty with the longer D questions is not working out which legal provi-   632
sions to apply but trying to come to terms with the amount of information that needs to be assimilated. There is far too much information to be analysed at once and unless a candidate has a strategy for organising logically and breaking down this information into manageable parts then he or she is likely to panic and flounder. The key strategy is therefore to divide and conquer. Information from different parts of the paper relevant to a single issue needs to be collated, organised and analysed separately to come to an individual conclusion on each specific point. All these conclusions can then be brought back together again in order to generate some coherent advice in relation to the situation as a whole. The key information that needs to be gathered at the end relates to which party will own patent rights for each embodiment of the technology discussed in the paper, in each territory of interest. This information can only be obtained by working though a list of issues is a logical manner for each of those embodiments (i.e. has an application been filed; does the applicant own the rights to the invention; is the application pending; has the embodiment been claimed; what is the effective date; what prior art exists; is the claim novel; is the claim inventive; is the application sufficient). And these issues can only be addressed when all the information in the question has been ordered and can be readily accessed – for which purpose a timeline is a very helpful tool. Tackling the question in the systematic way suggested below should reduce the amount of thinking required in the exam, help to prevent panic and minimise the chances of a key piece of information or key issue being overlooked.

2.2.1 Preparing a time line

Before individual points of interest can be analysed (e.g. the patentability of a particular   633
claim) the information in the question needs to be organised in an accessible way. Frequently, the important facts are not presented in chronological order. Furthermore, facts relevant to a particular issue may be scattered throughout the text. The easiest way to remedy this, while at the same time becoming familiar with the legal situation presented by the question, is to construct a time line.

First of all, read through the question once and gain a general understanding of the   634
facts. Try and consider the possible reasons why each piece of information is being presented – generally, nothing is superfluous in this paper and each sentence signifies something important. The first time you read the paper through it will not be possible to fully appreciate the significance of each piece of information since its relationship with other facts will need to be established to put it properly in context. Nevertheless, it is worth

nothing some of the points which come to mind. Practising with past papers will help to increase awareness of which points are particularly important. The worked example presented below for the 2012 D2 paper may also be helpful. Pieces of information which at first sight do not seem to have any relevance or importance are often particularly significant when combined with other information in the paper, just like two pieces of a jigsaw can come together to create an identifiable image.

635   Next, read through the question a second time, noting all dates in a list on a separate sheet of paper. These dates will frequently correspond to some event associated with the prosecution of a patent application (e.g. priority date, filing date, publication date, grant date) or a disclosure of some kind (e.g. the publication of a document or application or the oral disclosure of a piece of information). The date of the exam is an important date to add since it is the date on which relevant advice needs to be provided. Before beginning to draft a time line it is important to have some appreciation of the span of time that it needs to encompass in order to be able to produce a neat, legible diagram at the first attempt. The value of the time line is greatly enhanced if it is clear, well laid-out and legible. Hence starting with a simple list of dates rather than constructing a time line ab initio has value. This list of dates can then be expanded by introducing further dates which are implicit from the facts of the question and which may be important to the answer. For instance, a first filing (or a second filing disclosing new subject matter) implies a 12 month priority period and a publication date, a PCT filing implies 30 and 31 month national/regional phase entry deadlines, a patent grant implies opposition and validation periods. Note that the publication of a European patent application will simultaneously generate two disclosures – an Art. 54(2) disclosure on the publication date and an Art. 54(3) disclosure on the filing or priority date. The expanded list of dates can then be put into order and assembled along a time line. It is helpful to use a large A3 sheet of paper for this purpose in order to have plenty of space to play with. Be sure, when adding additional deadlines to the list, to bear in mind r.134(1) EPC and the possibility of deadlines being extended by one or more days to compensate for the EPO being closed.

636   Lastly, complete the time line by going through the paper a third time and noting the key information associated with each date on the time line. It is often useful to add a further level of organisation by arranging information relevant to a particular application or applicant in a particular column or down a particular axis on the time line. Aligning all the possible disclosures of information in this way can also be helpful. Bringing all the information relevant to a particular issue as close as possible together is a key strategy in analysing the paper.

637   Creating a proper time line will require the investment of a significant amount of time, perhaps up to 30 minutes. Once again, it is important to stress that this is not time wasted. The mental discipline involved in creating such a tool will mean that the facts of the question will become much clearer in your mind and the elements of a possible answer will start to crystallise. The active process of gathering and ordering the facts of the question is a much more powerful aid to comprehension then the passive process of simply reading through the question.

2.2.2 *Analysing the paper by considering the patentability of each invention*

638   A typical longer D question will revolve around inventions that your client and his competitor have made in a particular technical field. Some of these inventions will have been made the subject of patent applications and some may not. In the latter scenario, where no application has been filed, it is often the case that the relevant invention has been, or will soon be, disclosed in some manner and the clients rights will need protecting by the timely filing of an application. Where an application has been filed, it is usual for some inventions to have been claimed and others to have been merely disclosed in the description. It is also common for some inventions to have been disclosed in a priority application and others added at the filing date. When talking of different "inventions" in this context, we are referring to different embodiments of the same general inventive concept as well as separate inventions not having unity – inventive subject matter in its broadest context.

639   The patentability and ownership of all this subject matter needs to be considered separately. Perhaps the easiest way of doing this is to fill out a pre-prepared table that can be brought into the exam specifically for this purpose. It can contain headings as a reminder

in order to make sure that all the possibly relevant issues are being considered, minimising the amount of thinking necessary in the exam itself, helping to create a calm sense of order and logical thought processes. One very important reminder, however: **no pre-prepared materials may be handed in as part of the answer** (Point I.9(c) ICEQE). The answer itself must be written in its entirety on the day of the exam using the paper supplied in the exam (Point III.22(c) ICEQE). No marks can be awarded for any part of the answer presented using pre-prepared materials however correct it is. So, such a table can only be used in the analysis phase and must not be presented as part of the answer. A suitable table may have the following general layout:

Subject matter	Ownership	Prosecution status	Effective date	Prior art	Novelty and inventive step	Sufficiency and other matters	Conclusion

640

Subject matter can then be arranged in the left hand column sorted by (1) Who has made the invention; (2) Whether an application has been filed or not; and (3) whether the subject matter is claimed or only disclosed. Ownership will not usually be an issue since the person filing the application is most likely the person entitled to be granted a patent – but occasionally it is an issue and having a column relating to this issue prompts you to consider the matter. If the prosecution status is withdrawn or deemed withdrawn without legal remedy or finally refused then the analysis can stop at this point – no rights are going to be obtained unless a new application can be filed (which of course must be considered). The effective date will be a filing date or a priority date and an accurate determination of priority will be necessary at this point. The prior art can then be determined by reference to the time line: consider disclosures of all kinds before the effective date. Of course, in the case of subject matter which is not yet the subject of a patent application, the columns relating to ownership and prosecution status can be ignored and the effective date will be the date of the exam since that is the earliest date an application could be filed. Based on the prior art, a determination of patentability can then be made. Sufficiency should also be raised as a possible issue though it rarely is and other matters that could prevent the grant of a patent may also arise from time to time (e.g. clarity, added subject matter) but are even rarer.

641

The results of this analysis (conclusion) will show who owns or can obtain valid patent rights in relevant countries in respect of each embodiment of each invention. This is the key information that can be used to advise the client since it determines which commercial options are available. Your answer will also contain a summary of all the analysis carried out in completing the table (but not the table itself!).

642

2.2.3 *Points to consider when an application for an invention has been filed*

The theft of an invention is more commonplace in the unprincipled world of the EQE than in real life. Consider firstly, therefore, whether the applicant (usually one of the client's competitors) has the right to be granted a patent as the inventor or his successor in title. If the answer is no then several steps can be taken. Firstly, an application could be made to the court of a Contracting State for an entitlement decision (the Protocol on Recognition, part of the EPC, determines which Contracting State must be used). Consider whether the known evidence is persuasive.

643

Once such an application has been made, proceedings before the EPO can be stayed under r.14 EPC, but only after publication of the European patent application. Action can be taken no earlier than entry into the regional phase in the case of a PCT application. During the stay of proceedings a check should be made to see if renewal fees have been paid. Anybody can validly pay a due renewal fee and thus keep the application pending. After grant it is also possible to stay any opposition proceedings which are ongoing according to r.78 EPC if the proprietor is not entitled. However, the Protocol on Recognition does not apply after grant and entitlement actions must therefore be commenced in each designated Contracting State.

644

645   Following a positive final decision on entitlement from the national court, the wronged party can choose under Art. 61 EPC to prosecute the application itself if it is still pending or file a new application in its place (it does not matter for the purpose of filing a new application if the application has lapsed, G3/92). Alternatively, the entitled person can request that the application be refused – worth considering if the application is worth little (e.g. if the client has his own application with a similar content and an earlier date).

646   If negotiation is possible then an assignment of the application containing the stolen material would be more straightforward for everybody. Care should be taken in alerting the third party if they are likely to be hostile since they may accelerate the grant procedure. For any material that the client is not entitled to, the filing of a divisional application may be best, or a free license could be granted to the competitor. In general, joint ownership of patents is likely to cause problems and is not to be recommended. In any case, consideration should be given to filing an application immediately on behalf of the client since the prior application may not, pursuant to Art. 55 EPC, be prior art. Note that if an invention is "stolen" and the thief files a patent application, it is the publication of that application and not its filing date which constitutes the disclosure for the purposes of Art. 55(1) EPC.

647   Having addressed the issue of entitlement, consider the status of the application and what steps need to be taken to keep it alive. Sometimes a translation will have been filed in an inappropriate language or necessary fees will not have been paid (e.g. a renewal fee). Sometimes a priority document (or a translation thereof) will not have been filed. In the unusual circumstance that an application cannot be rescued, consider the filing of another application claiming its priority if there is any priority right from which to benefit.

648   Having established the legal status of the application, and assuming that it is not irrevocably flawed, assess what subject matter is disclosed in the application and could be claimed. In particular, identify any possibly patentable subject matter that has not been claimed. Then, determine the effective date for the assessment of patentability. This will be the filing date or a priority date where priority has been validly claimed. The validity of a priority claim is frequently an important issue. The first point is to ensure that the priority period is correctly calculated with reference to r.134(1) and (3) EPC.

649   A priority claim is not valid where: (1) the claimed invention is not clearly and unambiguously derivable from the priority document (Art. 87(1) EPC and G2/98); (2) priority is claimed from an application which is not the first qualifying application for that subject matter (Art. 87(1) and (4) EPC); (3) a declaration of priority was not filed in due time (r.52(2) EPC) or added to the request as a correction before publication (r.139 EPC); (4) the applicant is not the applicant for the priority application or, where appropriate, his successor in title when the priority-claiming application is filed (Art. 87(1) EPC); (5) the application was filed outside the priority period (only excusable under r.133 EPC (posted/ sent in time) or Art. 122 (re-establishment)); (6) the previous application was not an application for an invention in the sense of Art. 87 EPC (e.g. it was a design application); (7) the priority application was not filed in an appropriate country (Art. 87(1) EPC); (8) a copy of the priority application was not filed within the appropriate time limit (Art. 90(5) EPC); or (9) a translation (where necessary) of the priority document was not filed (r.53(3) EPC).

650   Having established the effective date of the subject matter in the application, assess novelty and inventive step in respect of this subject matter on the basis of any known disclosures and hence establish what valid claims might be granted.

651   Consider all the events described in the question before the effective date of the application and consider whether any of them rank as a publication, an oral public disclosure or a prior use. Consider all co-pending EP and PCT applications as potential Art. 54(3) art. Consider whether any disclosure should be discounted on the basis of the Art. 55 six-month period (or 12-month US grace period for US applications) or on the basis that it was covered by any express or implied term of confidence. In the case of an oral disclosure or prior use, consider if there is enough proof available (note that these disclosures do not form part of International Preliminary Examination).

Consider possible amendments that would be necessary and allowable in view of the prior art.

652   Assess patentability on other grounds such as sufficiency. Where an application is insufficient per se, consider whether any other disclosure prior to the filing date or in a referenced document could be considered to make it sufficient or whether a further

application claiming priority from the insufficient application should be filed with additional information included to improve the situation (though the priority claim may obviously be invalid for lack of enablement).

Finally, summarise which granted claims might be obtained and in respect of which 653 states such patent rights would be available. Where a national patent application has been used as a priority basis for a European patent application don't forget to consider the possibility of the national application being prosecuted to grant.

2.2.4 *Points to consider where an application for an invention has not been filed*

Consider how much of the material is patentable and formulate a filing strategy for the 654 patentable material. If possible, the answer should include a description of what claims will be allowable – which is where your knowledge of what can be claimed in different technical areas becomes important.

In some cases the new matter may be associated with another invention for which an 655 application has already been filed and the new application could include the contents of the filed application, claiming its priority (or be filed as a continuation in part application in the US). Consider who the applicant should be. Where it is too late to obtain assignments of the priority right, file in joint names and assign later.

Take into account the six-month non-prejudicial disclosure period under the EPC and the US (12 months) grace period if necessary.

For broadest coverage, file via the PCT and file national patents in non-PCT countries. 656 A PCT application will be particularly useful where the commercial importance of the case will not be known for some time and where limited funding is available.

Consider incorporating features disclosed in competitor applications, provided that 657 this information has not been acquired in confidence, applied to the client's own novel subject matter.

Consider what the language of filing should be in respect of the fee reduction available to applicants from EPC Contracting States that have an official language other than French, English and German.

2.2.5 *What national rights are therefore obtainable by the client and might be used to keep competitors off the market?*

Based on your analysis of any inventions made by the client for which patent applications 658 have been filed (who owns them, what claims are likely to be granted in which States) and for which patent applications have not been filed (what granted patents a sensible filing strategy might lead to) it should now be possible to assess what rights the client has or may expect to obtain in countries of commercial importance and advise him how to get these rights and what he can do with them. It should be clear from the question which countries are of importance – these are the markets in which the client's competitors are making and selling infringing products and the markets in which the client expects to commercialise his invention. If patent protection can be obtained in the state in which a competitor is manufacturing then this could be particularly significant.

The advice will include sections on how to get back stolen patent rights, how to rescue 659 applications and prosecute them to grant, how to amend invalid claims and what further applications need to be filed. The balance will vary markedly from year to year, depending on the facts presented in the paper.

Where a granted patent is needed to take action against an infringer, and a relevant ap- 660 plication exists, consider accelerating proceedings. In order for the client to claim damages back to publication, analyse the search report and suggest the filing of amendments, if necessary, so that the claims of the published application are patentable. Translations of published claims should be filed where necessary and a copy of the application served on any infringer. Consider amending to a narrow claim covering the infringement which will be granted straightforwardly and filing a divisional application to other material.

2.2.6 *What national rights are therefore obtainable by any competitor which might limit your client's commercial freedom?*

661   Based on your analysis of any patentable inventions made by third parties you should also be in a position to assess, in important countries (i.e. the ones that the client says are important to him), what rights exist, or could be obtained, which could be used against your client.

662   Where a relevant European patent exists, consider filing an opposition if the opposition period has not yet expired or intervening in any ongoing opposition where infringement proceedings have been initiated against the client. National revocation actions are also possible.

663   Where relevant European patent applications exist, a file watch should be set up to monitor their progress to grant. An opposition can be filed on grant. It is often worthwhile filing observations (Art. 115 EPC) if a novelty-destroying reference is available which has not been cited in the search report. However, filing observations is not as effective where inventive step or sufficiency is concerned since the party filing the observations is not a party to the proceedings and cannot assert its case properly. There is no formal mechanism under the PCT for handling third-party observations but it is nevertheless possible to make observations on an international application via the WIPO website between publication of the application and 28 months from the priority date. Such observations are transmitted to relevant international authorities and designated offices.

664   If a competitor and the client both hold relevant rights that could be used against each other, advise your client about the possibility of cross-licensing, explaining what claims/rights could be licensed by each party for which territories, depending on what would suit the client's commercial aims best.

2.2.7 *Answering the paper*

665   Rather than just asking for general advice, it is most likely that the facts of the question will be followed by a series of specific questions posed by the client. It is best to structure your answer in line with these questions since they have been set as a guide to the answer required and it will be easier for the examiner to award marks if your answer is aligned with the marking schedule. However, it is also important to ensure that you identify and answer any questions which are implicit in the paper and make sure that you address any misunderstandings of patent law or false assumptions on the part of the client which are evident from the question. Within these limits, structure your answer as described above in respect of each invention, grouping together related inventions in a sensible way. Summarise the important points of the legal analysis that you have carried out in order to arrive at the relevant conclusions regarding valid patent protection before advising what the consequences are and what action could be taken to improve the position.

666   Remember that your answer is primarily addressed to a notional client and should include concrete advice on how to proceed in respect of obtaining patent rights relevant to his commercial activities and/or dealing with a third-party patent right relevant to his commercial activities. The advice should preferably be tailored to the nature of the commercial activities in which the client is engaged (i.e. what he is making or selling and where his main markets are) – it may help to summarise the client's commercial objectives in the answer. Whilst it is useful to describe different options the client may have and summarise their relative merits, you should always come to some conclusion regarding which course of action is preferred. Make sure you specifically correct any false assumptions made by the client in his instructing letter.

Do not use any pre-prepared materials as part of the answer (Points I.5 and I.9(c) ICEQE)!

667   Make sure that all parts of the answer are legible! Remember that the person marking your script will likely be tired after a day at work and keen to get through your answer as quickly as possible. He or she may not be reading your script in mother tongue. If your answer is well structured and easily legible then it will be much easier to award marks. This is succinctly expressed in the Examiner's Report for the 1993 paper: "Scripts that cannot be read cannot be marked" (see also Point III.22(a) ICEQE). Be sure to use simple, grammatically correct language and not to use any abbreviations whose meaning may be obscure to others. On the other hand, answers should be brief and to the point – there are

no marks for using beautiful, full sentences and an answer in memo-format using bulleted points is quite acceptable.

Finally, make sure you get all the marks allocated for addressing basic points in the analysis and advice. In the analysis, consider the validity of each priority claim and indicate, for example, when priority periods are extended under r.134(1) EPC. Do not make the assumption that these points are obvious and can be ignored. When assessing the novelty of a patent claim, consider all potential disclosures before the effective date of the claim and indicate their relevance. If a disclosure has been made in confidence and is therefore not state of the art, indicate this in your answer rather than glossing over the point as too obvious to mention. When it comes to the advice, indicate to the client which activities each competitor patent right can be used to prevent him pursuing and the territories that this applies to. Marks are likely to be available for making all these obvious points, as can be inferred from reading the model solutions published by the Examination Committee each year and they should not be missed.

2.3   Relevant timeline events for European and Euro-PCT applications

When constructing a time line, it may be worth considering one or more of the following time limits and due dates.

2.3.1   Regular European patent application

Filing date – 6 months	Disclosures not taken into account under Art. 55(1)
Filing date + 1 month	Filing fee and search fee due
Filing set of claims + 1 month	Claims fees due
Filing date + 2 months	Translation in EPO official language due
	Deadline for filing certified copy of referenced application
	Deadline for filing translation of referenced application
	Deadline for filing missing parts voluntarily
Filing date + 4 months	Certificate of display at international exhibition due
	Priority claim can be corrected until now
Filing date + 12 months	Priority period ends for first filing
Filing date/priority date + 16 months	Designation of inventor due
	Depository institution and accession number to be identified
Priority date + 16 months	Deadline for adding or correcting a priority claim under r.52(2)
	Certified copy of priority document is due
Publication date – 5 weeks	Technical preparations for publication complete
Filing date/priority date + 18 months	Publication of application (and possibly SR)
Publication of SR + 6 months	Request for examination, payment of examination fee
	Payment of designation, validation and extension fees
	Filing of comments/corrections in response to written opinion
	Last chance for voluntary amendment
Invitation + 6 months	Confirmation of wish to proceed to examination, response to written opinion, filing of amendments as of right
Filing date + 24 months	Renewal fee for third year due at end of month
Grant + 3 months	Validation period ends for most states
Grant + 9 months	Opposition period ends

2.3.2   *European patent application filed via the PCT*

671	Filing date + 1 month	International fee, transmittal fee and search fee due
		Translation of the application due where necessary
	Filing date + 2 months	Deadline for incorporation by reference where no invitation sent
	Filing date + 4 months	Can add/correct a priority claim
	Filing date + 12 months	Priority year ends for first filing
	Priority date + 16 months	Can add/correct a priority claim
	Filing date/priority date + 16 months	Art. 19 amendments due (or transmittal of ISR + 2 m if later)
		Certified copy of priority application due
	Publication date – 15 days	Technical preparations for publication due
	Filing date/priority date + 18 months	Publication of the application (and possibly SR)
	Filing date/priority date + 19 months	Demand must be filed in order to delay national phase entry for some states
	Filing date/priority date + 20 months	National phase entry date for some countries
	Filing date/priority date + 22 months	Deadline for filing demand (or transmittal of ISR + 3 months if later)
		Deadline for requesting supplementary international search
	Filing date/priority date + 26 months	Deadline for requesting rectification of a mistake
	Filing date/priority date + 28 months	IPER to be established
	Filing date/priority date + 30 months	National/regional phase entry date for some countries
		Deadline for withdrawal of application, designation, priority claim
		Deadline for recordal of changes re. applicant etc with IB
	Filing date/priority date + 31 months	National/regional phase entry date for most countries

2.4   Aspects of US and Japanese patent law

672   According to the examination syllabus for the EQE, candidates are expected to have a general knowledge of US and Japanese patent law (Art. 13(2)(b) REQEPR). This knowledge is often probed in the longer D questions where a client may have commercial interests that stretch across the globe. The following paragraphs highlight some of the main differences between the EPC and US patent law. For most important purposes, Japanese and European law are similar enough to conclude that the outcome will be the same.

673   The situation in the US has now been considerably complicated by the coming into force of the America Invents Act, moving to a first inventor-to-file system for new applications but retaining the first-to-invent regime for applications already filed. For applications filed before 16 March 2013, the first-to-invent law continues to apply. For applications filed on or after 16 March 2013 which do not claim the priority of an application filed before that date or the benefit of the filing date of an application filed before that date, the new first inventor-to-file law applies. For other applications, so-called "transition" applications, the new law applies if they contain, or contained at any time, a claim with an effective date on or after 16 March 2013; otherwise the old law applies.

674   Under the old first-to-invent law in the US, the right to a patent for an invention belonged to the person who first conceived the invention and diligently reduced it to

practice. There was therefore no provision similar to Art. 54(3) EPC. Instead, where two parties had co-pending applications directed to the same subject matter, ownership was decided in complicated legal proceedings called interference proceedings in which evidence was presented as to which party made the invention first. Under the new law, the definition of prior art has been adjusted such that the person with the earliest effective filing date will be entitled to a patent.

According to the old law an applicant was entitled to a patent even if there was a public   675
disclosure of the invention within the 12 months preceding the filing of the application in the US, whether or not that disclosure originated from the inventor of that application, as long as the invention was made before the disclosure (35 USC 102(b) applying before 16 March 2013). This is known as the grace period. The grace period still exists under the new law but, in substantially all cases, only applies to disclosures made by the applicant himself.

Under the old law, if the invention was known or used by others in the US, or patented   676
or described in a printed publication in the US or a foreign country, before the invention thereof by the applicant for the patent, the applicant was not entitled to a patent (35 USC 102(a)). Under the new law there is no distinction made between use of the invention in the US and use abroad.

Whereas in Europe and Japan the applicant should be the inventor or his legal suc-   677
cessor, under the law applying in the US before 16 September 2012, the applicant had to always be the inventor. Subsequent assignment of the application to the legal owner occured during prosecution of the application. A PCT application designating the US should therefore have included the inventors as applicants for the US designation. For international applications filed on or after 16 September 2012, it is no longer required that the inventors be named as applicants. Instead, the person who owns the rights to the invention may be indicated as the applicant for the U.S. designation.

In the US there is no restriction on the filing of patent applications in respect of com-   678
puter-implemented inventions, business methods, or methods of medical treatment. In Europe there is a need to show that the invention has technical character or addresses a technical problem.

In the US, infringement is judged by the doctrine of equivalents whereby the scope of   679
a granted patent includes all obvious equivalents of claim features (except where a means plus function formulation is used – in which case the equivalents are only those of the features disclosed in the description). This doctrine is limited by prosecution history estoppel. This means that any limiting amendment to a claim made by an applicant during prosecution may, in certain circumstances, be seen to bar the application of the doctrine of equivalents to the limited features.

In the US it is possible to file a continuation in part (CIP) application whereby a pend-   680
ing application is re-filed with additional subject matter included. The patentability of the new matter is judged as of the date of filing of the CIP application. It is not possible under the EPC, on the other hand, to file a divisional or replacement application with additional subject matter.

A US application must disclose the best mode, that is to say the best way of carrying   681
out the invention known to the inventor at the time of filing the application. This applies under the new and old law but under the new law it is no longer a defence to infringement to show that the best mode was not disclosed.

There is also a duty of candour in the US which means that any relevant prior art   682
known to the inventor must be disclosed to the US Patent and Trademark Office. Failure to comply with these requirements can render a US patent unenforceable.

2.5 Notes on claiming priority

The validity of a priority claim is frequently an issue in both the short and long questions   683
in EQE Paper D but particularly in the case of the latter. There is very seldom a year in which no question of priority arises in the longer questions. This is because priority claims are an important aspect of real-life practice as a patent attorney and because candidates often find the substantive aspects of priority difficult to fully grasp. Commenting on priority issues in 1995, the Examination Committee said in its report: "This is a major issue for the correct handling of a client's patent matters and any candidate who cannot

deal with this is not fit to practise." Assessing whether a candidate is fit to practise is, of course, the overarching purpose of the EQE (Art. 1(1) REQEPR). In the following sections some notes are provided on issues which commonly cause confusion.

2.5.1   Relevance of the Paris Convention to European and Euro-PCT applications

684   For international applications, the Paris Convention is directly applicable by virtue of Art. 8 PCT. The Patent Co-operation Treaty, however, also contains its own supplementary set of provisions which extend the minimum provisions set by the Paris Convention and allow, for instance, priority claims to be added after the filing date (r.26*bis*) as well as recognising priority rights originating in WTO member countries which are not members of the Paris Convention (r.4.10). Re-establishment where the priority period is not observed is also possible (r.26*bis* EPC).

685   In contrast, the European Patent Convention does not apply the Paris Convention but instead contains its own priority code in Arts 87–89. However, these provisions must be consistent with the Paris Convention. The preamble to the EPC indicates that the EPC is a special agreement within the meaning of Art. 19 of the Paris Convention and that article only allows such special agreements to the extent that they do not contravene the provisions of the Paris Convention. The Paris Convention can therefore be used in interpreting the meaning of Arts. 87–89 EPC. The EPC also contains provisions, similar to the PCT, extending beyond the minimum rights laid out in the Paris Convention.

686   For a Euro-PCT application the situation is therefore somewhat complicated. During the international phase the Paris Convention, supplemented by the provisions of the PCT, applies directly. During the regional phase, Arts. 87–89 EPC (which are consistent with the Paris Convention) apply and some PCT provisions continue to apply, imposing certain obligations on Contracting States during the national/regional phase, such as the need to give the applicant a chance to produce a priority document not furnished in the international phase (r.17.1 PCT). Although during the regional phase the provisions of the PCT override the provisions on the EPC in cases of conflict (Art. 150(2) EPC), the substantive (as opposed to procedural) aspects of a priority claim are provisions relating to patentability in which national law is unfettered by the provisions of the PCT (Art. 27(5) PCT). Thus, for instance, for an application filed before the coming into force of EPC 2000, a priority claim originating in a WTO member state not a party to the Paris Convention might have been valid during the international phase but would subsequently be invalid in the European regional phase (see G2/02).

687   The relevant basis to be quoted when answering a question relating to the priority claim of a Euro-PCT application, and whether the Paris Convention is relevant basis, will therefore depend on whether the application is in the international phase or the regional phase.

2.5.2   The importance of naming the correct applicant

688   According to Article 4(A)(1) of the Paris Convention and Art. 87(1) EPC, the right to claim priority belongs to a person who has filed a patent application or his successor in title. When priority is claimed, it must be claimed by this entitled person for the priority claim to be valid – if priority is claimed by a person not legally entitled to claim it then it cannot be valid.

689   The person who has filed an application is the **named applicant**, not necessarily the inventor or even the person who is entitled to be granted a patent and certainly not a licensee or another legal entity that is associated with the applicant in some way. If a first filing (e.g. a national patent application) is therefore made with legal entity A as the applicant, the subsequent filing claiming its priority (e.g. a European patent application or Euro-PCT application) must also name A as an applicant in order for the priority claim to be valid (unless there has been a succession of title in the meantime). Equally, if a first filing is made with the inventor as applicant, the subsequent filing claiming its priority must also name the inventor as applicant in order to for the priority claim to be valid (unless there has been a succession of title in the meantime).

690   When there is a succession in title, i.e. the rights in the first filing are assigned to another party, the legal situation becomes a little more vague since neither the Paris Convention nor the EPC contains any provisions specifying either the provisions under which the

validity of such a transfer of title is to be assessed or the time period during which such a transfer is effective. We must therefore turn to case law for assistance. Decisions of the Boards of Appeal and the national courts of EPC contracting states have been fairly consistent on two points: firstly that the relevant transfer of rights must have been effected before the filing of the second application to be effective, and secondly that a transfer of rights after the filing of the second application which purports to have retroactive effect cannot be taken into account (e.g. T577/11, T1201/14). Thus, if the priority right is claimed by somebody not entitled to exercise it at that point then the priority claim is invalid and this deficiency cannot later be cured (unless the priority year is still pending and a third application can be filed naming the correct applicant). It should also be noted that the transfer of rights must include the transfer of the right to claim priority and not just the transfer of the first application per se (these two rights can be assigned independently).

Where decisions have not been so uniform is in establishing which law the validity of   691
a transfer needs to be assessed under and therefore the formal requirements it needs to comply with (e.g. does it need to be in writing, does it need to have been registered with a patent office, does it need to be signed by both parties or only one?). As a result, these issues are unlikely to arise in the EQE. If they do then a party would be best advised either (1) not to assign the priority right during the priority year and to file in the name of the original applicant; or (2) to execute a written assignment signed by both parties and registered at the patent office that specifically states the law under which it is to be interpreted and complies with all the formal requirements of that law.

2.5.3 The importance of the "first filing"

A priority right comes into being when an application disclosing certain subject matter   692
is allocated a filing date in a Paris Convention country (Art. 87(1) EPC; Art. 4A(2) Paris Convention), whatever the subsequent fate of the application (Art. 87(2) EPC; Art. 4A(3) Paris Convention), i.e. whether it is withdrawn or refused, before or after publication.

The filing of an application for certain subject matter in a Paris Convention country   693
is thus a very important event since it determines the period (12 months from the filing date) during which further applications may be filed validly claiming priority in respect of that subject matter. In principle (subject to the narrow exception outlined below) no **subsequent application disclosing the same subject matter may be used by the relevant applicant to claim priority in respect of that subject matter**. The Paris Convention (Art. 4C(2)) and the European Patent Convention (Art. 87(1)) both dictate that **priority may only be claimed from the first filing of any particular subject matter**.

2.5.4 The limited circumstances in which priority may be claimed from a second or subsequent filing

Priority may validly be claimed from the second filing of certain subject matter only if: 694
(a) the first and second applications were made in or in respect of the same state; (b) at the date of filing the second application the first application had already been withdrawn, abandoned or refused, without being open to public inspection and without leaving any rights outstanding (including the right to claim priority); and (c) at the date of filing the second application, the priority of the first application had not already been claimed (Art. 87(4) EPC; Art. 4C(4) Paris Convention). If one or more of these criteria are not met then priority for the subject matter in question may only be claimed from the first application; a claim to priority for this subject matter from the second application will be invalid. If all these criteria are met, then priority for the subject matter in question may only be claimed from the second application; a claim to priority from the first application will be invalid. At any given time, only one application can exist for a given subject matter from which priority may validly be claimed in order to prevent the so-called strategy of "rolling" priority in which successive filings of the same subject matter are made in order to give the applicant a choice of which priority period to use.

Where a first application is filed in a non-Paris Convention state which is a WTO mem-   695
ber and the same application is later filed in a Paris Convention state it is not clear how the law would be interpreted. In principle, it should be possible to file a European patent application validly claiming the priority of both, the first priority claim being guaranteed by

Art. 87(1) EPC2000 and the second by the Paris Convention with which Arts 87–89 EPC must be in conformity. This anomaly has been introduced by the amendments to the EPC and PCT introducing the right to claim priority from a first filing in a WTO state without making any corresponding amendments to the Paris Convention.

2.5.5   *Illustrative examples of how priority works in relation to the first filing*

696   (A) Application P1 is filed in a Paris Convention country (e.g. Germany) containing subject matter X. European application E1, claiming subject matter X, is filed within 12 months claiming priority from P1.

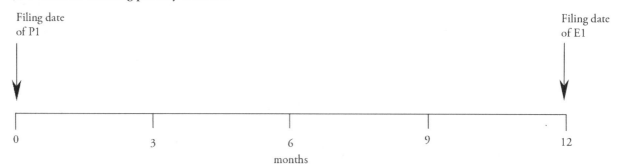

Figure 8

The priority claim is valid (at least in principle; there are many formal requirements which must also be satisfied).

697   (B) Application P1 is filed in a Paris Convention country (e.g. Germany) containing subject matter X. An identical application P2 is filed three months later in another Paris Convention country (e.g. France), while P1 is still pending. European application E1 is filed within 12 months of P2 claiming its priority.

Figure 9

The priority claim is not valid since P2 was not the first filing and the conditions of Art. 87(4) EPC have not been complied with. In the exam, P2 could be referred to as a US continuation application which therefore cannot be the first filing for the subject matter concerned.

698   (C) Application P1 is filed in a Paris Convention country (e.g. Germany) containing subject matter X. An application P2 is filed three months later in another Paris Convention country (e.g. France), while P1 is still pending, containing subject matters X and Y. European application E1 is filed within 12 months of P2 claiming its priority.

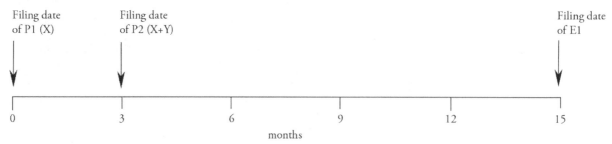

Figure 10

The priority claim is valid in respect of subject matter Y but not valid in respect of subject matter X for which P2 is not the first filing. In the exam P2 could be a US

continuation-in-part of earlier US application P1 and only the extra subject matter would
be entitled to the priority date.

(D) Application P1 is filed in a Paris Convention country (e.g. Germany) containing   699
subject matter X. The application is withdrawn leaving no rights outstanding and an identical application P2 is filed immediately after the withdrawal of P1 in the same Paris Convention country. European application E1 is filed within 12 months of P2, claiming its priority.

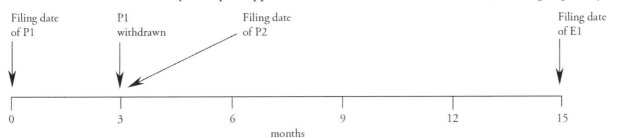

Figure 11

The priority claim is valid since under Art. 87(4) EPC P2 replaces P1 as the application
from which priority is to be claimed.

(E) Application P1 is filed in a Paris Convention country (e.g. Germany) containing   700
subject matter X. The application is withdrawn leaving no rights outstanding and an identical application P2 is filed immediately after the withdrawal of P1 in a different Paris
Convention country (e.g. France). European application E1 is filed within 12 months of
P2, claiming its priority.

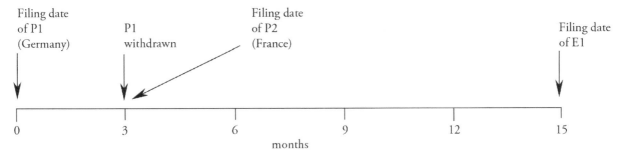

Figure 12

The priority claim is not valid since P2 was not re-filed in the same country as P1 and
Art. 87(4) EPC does not therefore apply. P1 remains the first filing from which priority
must be claimed.

(F) Application P1 is filed in a Paris Convention country (e.g. Germany) containing   701
subject matter X. The application is withdrawn leaving no rights outstanding and an identical application P2 is filed the next day in the same Paris Convention country. European
application E1 is filed within 12 months of P1, claiming its priority.

Figure 13

The priority claim is not valid since, according to the last sentence of Art. 87(4) EPC, P2
replaces P1 as the application from which priority can be claimed (see also PC Art. 4C(4)).
The priority claim is not invalid simply because P1 was withdrawn – once an application
has obtained a filing date its subsequent fate (withdrawn, deemed withdrawn, refused,
granted etc) is irrelevant to its status as a priority right (Art. 87(3) EPC). Here, the priority

claim is invalid because P1 was not only withdrawn, but was withdrawn leaving no rights outstanding and all the other criteria of Art. 87(4) were complied with such that P2 takes its place as the first filing from which priority may validly be claimed. Note that this interpretation is not universally shared, particularly amongst US practitioners, but is in line with a strict interpretation of the relevant provisions that can be expected in the EQE.

702   (G) Application P1 is filed in a Paris Convention country (e.g. Germany) containing subject matter X. Three months later an identical application P2 is filed in the same Paris Convention country. Application P1 is then withdrawn, leaving no rights outstanding. European application E1 is filed within 12 months of P2, claiming its priority.

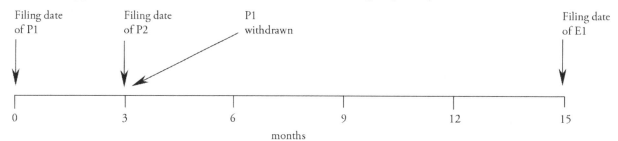

Figure 14

The priority claim is not valid since under P1 should have been withdrawn before the filing of P2 according to Art. 87(4) EPC.

703   (H) Application P1 is filed in a Paris Convention country (e.g. Germany) containing subject matter X and is published early at the applicant's request after six months. Four months later application P1 is withdrawn, leaving no rights outstanding. An identical application P2 is then filed in the same Paris Convention country. European application E1 is filed within 12 months of P2, claiming its priority.

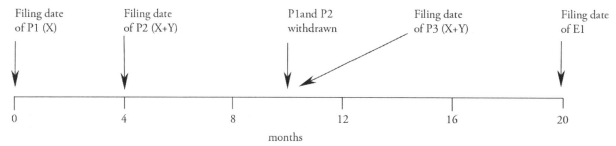

Figure 15

The priority claim is not valid since P1 was published and therefore open to public inspection before it was withdrawn.

704   (I) Application P1 is filed in a Paris Convention country (e.g. Germany) containing subject matter X. Four months later application P2 is filed in the same country claiming priority from P1 and disclosing subject matters X and Y. Six months later applications P1 and P2 are withdrawn, leaving no rights outstanding. An application P3, identical to P2 is then filed in the same Paris Convention country. European application E1 is filed within 12 months of P3, claiming its priority.

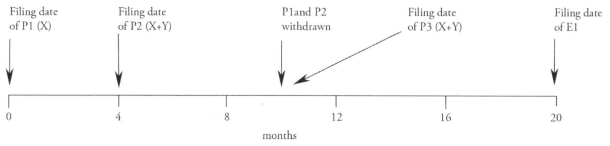

Figure 16

The priority claim is not valid for subject matter X since P3 is not the first application for this subject matter. Art. 87(4) EPC does not apply since P1 has already served as the basis for a priority claim in respect of X before it was withdrawn. The priority claim is valid in respect of subject matter Y.

2.5.6   Examples of questions relating to the claiming of priority from a first filing in the EQE

Paper D2, 2001: A competitor of the client (Niffy Shoe liners Ltd) has filed a European   705
application NF-EU1 on August 1, 1999 claiming the priority of Irish application NF-IE1
filed on October 15, 1998. Both applications are identical and describe (i) product A, (ii)
a new class of polymers having moisture-absorbent properties, (iii) a process for making
the polymers as fibres, (iv) use of the fibres as a shoe liner. However, Niffy have already
filed a previous European application NF-EU2 on September 30, 1998 claiming the priority of Irish application NF-IE2 filed on October 1, 1997. Both of these applications are
also identical and disclose (i) product A, (ii) the new class of polymers, (iii) the process for
making the polymers as fibres, (iv) use of fibres of product A as a shoe liner.

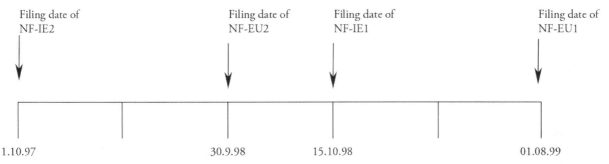

Figure 17

Therefore, the NF-EU1 is not entitled to claim the priority of NF-IE1 to the extent that it   706
claims any subject matter already disclosed in NF-IE2 and NF-EU2 since NF-IE1 is not
the first filing of this subject matter in a Paris Convention country. So, the patentability of
product A, the new class of polymers and the new process, in so far as they are claimed in
NF-EU1, will be judged at the filing date of NF-EU1, June 1, 1999.

    Paper C, 2000: The patent being opposed (EP-0712647) was filed as an application   707
on February 20, 1995 and claims the priority of a US application (US163946) filed on
March 10, 1994. In his letter, the client reveals that the priority application is in fact a continuation of an earlier US application filed on September 7, 1989, which has been withdrawn.

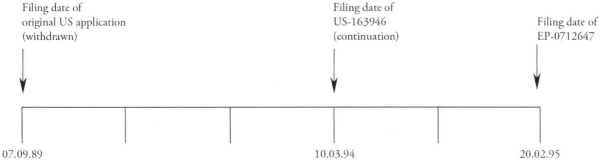

Figure 18

The priority claim from US-163946 is completely invalid and the patentability of all the   708
claims of EP-0712647 must be assessed as of its filing date 20.02.95. This is because a continuation application has the same text as its parent application and the parent application
must be pending at the time the continuation application is filed. Therefore, US-163946 is
not the first filing of the subject matter it contains and Art. 87(4) EPC does not apply
since the original US application was not withdrawn at the time the continuation application was filed.

2.6   Worked example – Paper D2 2012

The following sections show how a typical Paper D long question could be analysed and   709
answered using the 2012 Paper D2 as subject matter.

2.6.1   *First reading and initial thoughts*

710   The first step in answering this question is to read through the paper and note points of interest. The analysis below illustrates some of the points which could have been appreciated on a careful first reading. Some of the most important points should be noted on the paper itself so that they are not later overlooked. Where the paper is divided into two mutually exclusive parts, as in the present case, each should be analysed and answered separately.

Membrain AG

Wassergasse 12

A-1030 Vienna

6 March 2012[1.1]

Dear Mrs. Patent Attorney

711   [0001] We are a medium-sized[1.2] manufacturer of products[1.3] for the treatment of water, said products comprising membranes.[1.4] Our main production facilities are located in Vienna, Austria,[1.5] and from there we export our products to emerging countries,[1.6] where the market for water treatment is rapidly growing.

712   1.1   Dates are of particular significance in a D2 paper. The first important date is the date of the exam. This is the date on which all advice needs to be given without further contact with the client and the earliest priority date for any further patent application that needs to be filed disclosing new subject matter. All dates should be highlighted for later ordering and transfer to a timeline.

1.2   In answering the long paper D questions, candidates are expected to provide useful real-world advice to their clients, taking into account the preferences the client has indicated and the constraints that the client is likely to suffer from. Relevant information concerning the client's status should therefore be borne in mind. A 'medium-sized' client may have the resources to pursue modest litigation that a smaller company would not.

1.3   If your client is a manufacturer of products then his entire business could be under threat if patent rights covering these products or the process used to make the products exists in the country where the products are made. Ensuring freedom to operate in the country of manufacture is therefore paramount.

1.4   The technology on which the question is based is likely to be of a simple mechanical nature that is readily comprehensible to all candidates, much the same as in Paper C. However, it is occasionally in one of the electrical or chemical fields and candidates should ensure that they are aware, at least in broad terms, of the relevant EPC provisions and case law concerning the patentability of such inventions (e.g. computer software, plants, medical uses).

1.5   See 1.2 above. Country of manufacture is Austria. The business is particularly sensitive to third party patent rights here.

1.6   Main markets in which goods are sold are emerging markets. When thinking of obtaining patent protection in several countries across the world, the candidate should immediately consider the desirability of a PCT application, particularly for the purpose of delaying translation costs while keeping options open.

713   [0002] For the filtering out of fine solid particles present in waste water, modules are known[2.1] that comprise a bundle B of hollow fibre membranes, i.e. hollow tubular fibres whose walls act as a membrane. These modules are adapted to be connected, via a holder for holding the fibres, to a pump in order to draw water from the outside into the interior of the hollow fibre membranes. The membranes are usually made of ceramics of class C, but may also be made of a special class of polymers P.[2.2] These modules are adapted to be immersed in waste water but suffer from the problem of incrustation with particles if the waste water surrounding the modules does not flow, but stagnates. In order to obviate this problem, we have developed a membrane module that can be immersed in stagnant waste water. Our module comprises, in addition to the known bundle B of hollow fibre membranes, a specially designed nozzle N that is adapted to inject air bubbles into the bundle B, thereby removing incrustations on the fibres which decreases the frequency of cleaning and prolonging the life time of the module.[2.3, 2.4]

2.1 Prior art over which any of the client's inventions will have to be new and inventive. 714

2.2 Alternative embodiments are a significant element in the longer D questions and often have a different status. Very often different embodiments will be entitled to different effective dates and have a different patentability assessment or else some will fall within the scope of third party patent rights and some will not. Alternatively, some embodiments may not yet have been claimed or even disclosed. Assessing these differences and advising the client of their significance and the actions which may result is frequently important.

2.3 Very often it is useful, when trying to understand the question, to have some idea of what the client's technology and its features would actually look like in real life. A simplistic sketch is often very helpful.

2.4 This is the client's first invention. It is always important to consider what claims might be available. Here, the idea of using a nozzle in combination with the bundle of hollow fibre membranes seems to be novel and the unexpected advantages of decreased incrustation and longer life could support an inventive step. Furthermore, the nozzle N is presumably itself novel (being 'specially designed') and would be inventive by virtue of its use in the module.

[0003] On 31 July 2009[3.1] we[3.2] filed a European patent application EP-1[3.3] without 715
claims.[3.4] Its description comprises a general part and a part describing a single embodiment and referring to the drawings.[3.5] The general part discloses a module comprising a bundle B of hollow fibre membranes and the specially designed nozzle N for injecting air into the bundle B in order to remove incrustations on the fibre bundle.[3.6] It is stated in this part that the membranes and the nozzle N may be made of any suitable material and in particular that the membranes may be made of ceramics class C and the nozzle N may be made of stainless steel.[3.7] The part describing the embodiment and referring to the drawings discloses a module comprising bundle B of hollow fibre membranes made of ceramics of class C and the specially designed nozzle N made of stainless steel.[3.8] It is stated that it is essential for this embodiment that the specially designed nozzle N is made of stainless steel and that the membranes are made of ceramics of class C.[3.9] It is further stated that this provides a reliable module having a prolonged life as the nozzle can be readily immersed in waste water without corroding.[3.10] EP-1 was subsequently abandoned.[3.11 3.12]

3.1 Important date to highlight. The filing date will be important for assessing the pa- 716
tentability of any subject matter disclosed in EP-1 which becomes the subject matter of a claim. It also determines what states can be designated in application EP-1 – it is a common trick in D2 papers to have filing dates that falls before the dates of accession of important contracting states. It may also be relevant for calculating renewal fee due dates. And it determines the patent term if it is necessary to choose between applications which claim the same subject matter but have different filing dates. Lastly, it determines the extent to which EPC2000 applies which is particularly important in assessing the state of the art under Art. 54(3) EPC.

3.2 It is important to note the applicant when a first filing is made since only this applicant or a successor in title is entitled to claim priority. Here we presume that the applicant is Membrain AG.

3.3 The fundamental task in answering a D2 question is to establish what patent rights the parties are entitled to in various countries. Combined with the filing date (see 3.1), this information allows us to establish which countries patent protection may be obtained in.

3.4 Claims are not needed for a filing date under EPC2000 and this application was filed after 13 December 2007. However, claims are required if the application is to proceed to publication and must be properly based on the content of the application as filed in line with Art. 123(2) EPC.

3.5 These are separate parts of the disclosure and it would not usually be permissible to combine features from the general and specific embodiments without contravening Art. 123(2) EPC – intermediate generalisation.

3.6 This is the first combination of features which could form the basis for a claim and the patentability of which will likely have to be assessed as part of the answer.

3.7 Two more claimable embodiments of the invention are disclosed whose patentability will have to be considered: (1) a module comprising a bundle B of hollow fibre membranes made from ceramics class C and the specially designed nozzle N; and (2) a module comprising a bundle B of hollow fibre membranes and the specially designed nozzle N made of stainless steel. It is arguable whether there is also basis for a module comprising a bundle B of hollow fibre membranes made from ceramics class C and the specially designed nozzle N made from stainless steel – this seems to represent a combination of preferred features for which no unambiguous basis exists.

3.8   So the other part of the description discloses the most preferred embodiment of the invention for which the earlier part of the description only arguably provided basis – the patentability of this specific combination of features will also have to be assessed.

3.9   It is not at all clear what this statement means – it seems to contradict the earlier part of the description if it means that only this combination of materials provides a workable system since, if this is so, claims based on the earlier subject matter would lack sufficiency. An alternative interpretation is that all embodiments are workable but the combination of these two materials provides an embodiment that works particularly well.

3.10 The second interpretation of 3.9 seems most likely – the use of ceramics class C with stainless steel provides a particularly preferred embodiment of the invention with further advantages.

3.11 It is not clear what is meant by "abandoned" in this context. Was the application withdrawn by the client or allowed to become deemed withdrawn for failure to pay fees or file claims in response to an invitation from the Receiving Section? When an application is withdrawn, the legal effect is immediate and irrevocable whereas an application that is deemed withdrawn is subject to legal remedies that can rescue it. In the present case, the time that has elapsed means that the effect will likely be the same in each case: the client will not be able to obtain any patent protection from EP-1. Furthermore, if EP-1 was abandoned before publication then it will not provide any prior art effect under Art. 54(3) against any competitor's European patent applications. This must be assumed since the application was filed without any claims and would not therefore have proceeded to publication without further action being taken. It may, however, serve as the basis for a priority claim since, once an application has a filing date, its subsequent fate is irrelevant to its status as a priority basis (Art. 87(3) EPC). If it has been withdrawn leaving no rights outstanding and without serving as the basis for a priority claim then it may also have been possible to re-file it and restart the priority period. Which of these speculations is valid should be clarified by the remaining parts of the question.

3.12 One of the significant parts of this paragraph is what is **not** stated. We have been told that the membranes may be made of any suitable material and that one such suitable material is the class of polymers P. However, this has NOT been disclosed in EP-1. There are therefore two potential inventions which the client has made but not filed an application for: (1) a module comprising a bundle B of hollow fibre membranes made from polymers of class P and the specially designed nozzle N; and (2) a module comprising a bundle B of hollow fibre membranes made from polymers of class P and the specially designed nozzle N made of stainless steel. Furthermore, there is no claim to the nozzle N itself or to the nozzle N made of stainless steel. Spotting such subject-matter and proposing ways in which the client could improve his position by filing one or more subsequent applications is frequently an important part of paper D. Sometimes, as in this case, the subject matter will not have been yet included in a patent application: a filing strategy is required. In other cases, subject matter will have been included in the description but not claimed: a prosecution strategy involving amendments and/or divisional applications or a filing strategy for further applications claiming the priority of the first will be required. In other cases still, the subject matter will be lost since another party will have filed on it – it is almost always the case that a competitor will have rights to some subject matter of importance to the client in this paper.

717 [0004] On 03 May 2010[4.1] we[4.2] filed a PCT application[4.3] PCT-1 containing the same description as EP-1.[4.4] PCT-1 claims priority from EP-1[4.5] and contains a claim directed to a module comprising the specially designed nozzle N and a bundle B of hollow fibre

membranes.[4.6] The claim does not specify the material of the membranes and the material of the nozzle N.[4.7] The purpose of filing PCT-1 was to obtain patent protection in emerging countries such as Brazil and India.[4.8] PCT-1 was published in February 2011.[4.9]

4.1   Another important date to be highlighted: the filing date of a patent application. See   718
      comment 3.1 for the significance of a filing date.

4.2   Presumably, "we" in this context means Membrain AG. Any priority claim made in relation to EP-1 should therefore be valid from the formal perspective of whether the applicant is entitled to exercise the priority right.

4.3   A PCT application may provide protection with a wide geographical coverage. The 30 m and 31 m national and regional phase entry dates will be important to calculate. It would have been important to name the inventors as applicants for the purposes of the US designation when this PCT application was filed. It is important to bear in mind the other unique requirements of a PCT application such as the need for a claim to establish a filing date and the requirements for incorporating elements by reference. However, none of these points are likely to attract marks in the answer unless there are specific facts in the question which cast doubt on whether the client has proceeded in the correct manner.

4.4   EP-1 did not have any claims so the description of PCT-1 is identical to the whole disclosure of EP-1. This is important in deciding whether claimed subject matter is entitled to the priority date of EP-1 and the date at which subject matter published in PCT-1 enters the state of the art under Art. 54(3) EPC. In this case it does not seem that any new subject matter has been disclosed in PCT-1 that would start a new priority year – in other papers, however, this is frequently the case.

4.5   It is important to assess the validity of any purported priority claim from a formal and substantive angle and include this information in the answer. Here, the priority period would have expired on 31 July 2010 but this was a Saturday and hence the priority period was extended until Monday 02 August 2010. The filing date of PCT-1 was clearly filed in good time to claim priority.

4.6   A claim is important for a filing date. The patentability of the claim is, in principle, to be assessed as of the filing date of EP-1 since the priority claim looks to be valid (same subject matter, correct applicant, within priority year, EP-1 was first filing).

4.7   It is not clear at this stage why we are being told this. The claim relates to subject matter already disclosed in the priority document and represents the broadest claim the applicant may be entitled to so it is not surprising in any way. This sentence may be alluding to the 'essential' nature of the materials ceramics class C and stainless steel that was disclosed in the specific embodiment of EP-1 – see point 3.9 – but we need to know more to come to any conclusion.

4.8   This seems reasonable in view of the client's commercial interest in these countries (see point 1.6). However, the client should also be interested in protection in European countries where his manufacturing facilities are situated (for instance, the regionalisation of PCT-1 may provide an important prior art effect under Art. 54(3) which may nullify a potential freedom to operate threat) and where any competitors are manufacturing (stopping a competitor manufacturing could prevent worldwide sales for a period of time). Pay special attention in the D paper to actions that the client could have taken and might normally be expected to have taken but has instead ignored – it may be possible to improve the client's position by carrying out these actions, possibly by using some kind of legal remedy. You should in due course be adding the 31 month regional phase entry date for PCT-1 to your timeline and noticing that it has expired (29 February 2012) but is subject to further processing.

4.9   PCT-1 has been published and is therefore prior art under Art. 52(2) EPC as of its date of publication. Whether it becomes prior art according to Art. 54(3) EPC or not, as from its filing/priority date, depends on whether the EPO regional phase is entered or not. It seems that the client currently has no intention of doing this which should again be noted as a potential way of improving the client's position (see point 4.8).

[0005] In June 2010, our research engineers tested other nozzles[5.1] available on the market   719
which are intended for aerating waste water.[5.2] These nozzles are described in the Handbook of Waste Water Aeration[5.3] published in December 2009[5.4], which states that they are

suitable for injecting air into small interstices.[5.5] The tests revealed that, although suitable for injecting air bubbles into the fibre bundle, these nozzles are not as effective as our specially designed nozzle N.[5.6] As they are cheaper than our specially designed nozzle N, we nevertheless considered using them in our modules.[5.7] In order to secure our rights in Europe, on 02 August 2010[5.8] we filed a European patent application EP-2 claiming priority from EP-1.[5.9] To obtain the broadest patent protection possible, in the general part of the description of EP-2 we replaced the term "specially designed nozzle N" with the term "means for injecting air into the fibre bundle".[5.10] The part describing the embodiment shown in the drawings was left unchanged.[5.11] Claim 1 of EP-2 is directed to a module comprising a bundle B of hollow fibre membranes and means for injecting air into the fibre bundle.[5.12] Claim 1 does not specify the material of the membranes.[5.13] Dependent claim 2 is directed to the module comprising bundle B of hollow fibre membranes made of ceramics class C and the specially designed nozzle N made of stainless steel.[5.14]

720   5.1   Further research is likely to lead to further inventions or to broaden the scope of inventions already made.

5.2   These nozzles are known and therefore could not be claimed per se unlike, possibly, nozzle N. The fact that they are known for aerating waste water does not seem to prejudice the inventiveness of their use in a module containing a fibre bundle even though it is in the same technical field.

5.3   This sounds like a publication which is representative of the common general knowledge. It is prior art which will need to be taken into account in assessing the patentability of various inventions. In your answer, you should comment on the relevance of each piece of prior art which is identified in the question since there are often marks allocated for this.

5.4   Important date for timeline. It may be useful to have disclosures identified on your timeline in a separate colour and/or aligned on a particular axis.

5.5   This is a relevant disclosure which should be taken into account. However, although the nozzles are known to be useful for injecting air into small interstices and one would imagine that fibre bundles are well known to have such interstices, the fact that the bubbles are able to prevent incrustation would still seem to be an unexpected technical effect supporting an inventive step, in the absence of further motivation in the art.

5.6   This confirms the inventiveness of the nozzle N per se – it gives unexpectedly superior results compared with standard known nozzles.

5.7   This reminds us again to pay attention to our client's commercial aims. It is no use obtaining protection for an invention which is too expensive to be commercially viable. Patent protection for products which the client actually intends to sell, on the other hand, would be highly desirable. EP-1 and PCT-1 do not cover the use of these embodiments so further patent filings would be necessary if they haven't already been made.

5.8   New important date for the timeline – filing date of a patent application. Unlike PCT-1, this will only lead to rights in Europe. Further filings may be necessary in other markets of interest such as Brazil and India.

5.9   Presumably the 'we' in this sentence means Membrain AG so that the applicant is entitled to claim priority. At first sight the date of filing appears to be beyond the priority year (02 Aug vs. 31 July) but inspection of the calendar shows that 31 July 2010 was a Saturday and that EP-2 was filed in time. These are points which will need to be made in the answer since marks are almost always available for such analysis.

5.10 This is new subject matter that has been disclosed for the first time and two consequences arise: (1) Any claim based on this subject matter will not be entitled to the priority date but must be assessed for patentability at the filing date of EP-2; and (2) a new priority year has been triggered in respect of this subject matter. It is somewhat ambiguous whether the further parts of the general disclosure in EP-1 are also included, i.e. that the means for injecting air can be Nozzle N, that the membranes and the nozzle N may be made of any suitable material and that the membranes may be made of ceramics class C and the nozzle N may be made of stainless steel. If this turns out to be important then the consequences of both scenarios should be explored in the answer.

5.11 Any claim based on this subject matter will still be entitled to the priority date and will be assessed for patentability at 31 July 2009.

5.12 Patentability to be assessed at 02 August 2010 – see comment 5.10.

5.13 The significance of this is not immediately obvious but, for example, the novelty of the claim would be compromised by a disclosure of a system incorporating membranes made of either ceramics class C or polymers class P. Further, if an inventive step is to be based on the advantages of either of these materials then the claim would need to be appropriately restricted. Also potentially relevant for sufficiency – see comment 3.9.

5.14 Patentability to be assessed at 31 July 2009 – see comment 5.11.

[0006] The search reports of EP-2 and PCT-1 did not reveal any relevant documents,[6.1]   721
but in the written opinion for PCT-1 an objection pursuant to Art. 6 PCT was raised.[6.2]
According to the examiner, it is essential that the hollow fibre membranes are made of
ceramics class C, but this feature is missing from the independent claim.[6.3] The international search report for PCT-1 including the written opinion was transmitted on 11 August 2011.[6.4] EP-2 is still pending.[6.5]

6.1 This tends to indicate that the claims of these applications are novel and inventive.   722
However, it is possible that Art. 54(3) prior art relevant to novelty exists which was not published at the time the searches were carried out. It is also possible that a non-published disclosure has taken place or a publication exists which is not searchable by the EPO. The patentability of these applications will need to be considered carefully by analysis of the completed timeline which will identify all possible disclosures.

6.2 Art. 6 PCT states that the claims must define the matter for which protection is sought, be clear and concise and be fully supported by the description.

6.3 This is one of the possible conclusions identified in comment 3.9 though it is not clear why the examiner has focussed on the material of the membranes and ignored the material of the nozzle N. However, on the face of it, the objection does not seem to be well founded since the description of PCT-1 explicitly states that the membranes may be made of any suitable material and the client has indicated that polymers of class P are a suitable alternative. The examiner is not aware of this latter point which may be used as an argument to counter the objection.

6.4 Another date for the timeline. This is an unusual date to highlight since it has no special significance in itself. Its inclusion in the paper should give rise to a consideration of what other dates or events it may trigger. These include the deadline for making claim amendments under Art. 19 PCT (at least two months from the date of transmittal of the ISR according to r.46.1 PCT) and the deadline for filing a demand for international preliminary examination (at least three months from the date of transmittal of the ISR is allowed according to r.54*bis*.1(a) PCT).

6.5 The fact that EP-2 is still pending today (06 March 2012) means that (1) it must have been published (sometime in February 2011); (2) a request for examination must have been filed; (3) divisional applications are possible if a relevant time limit has not expired (a time limit for the filing of divisional applications existed at the date of the question which has since been scrapped); and (4) the application can be prosecuted to grant to obtain rights for the client.

[0007] On 10 November 2011, we filed a demand for international preliminary examination of PCT-1[7.1] at the EPO[7.2] and paid the corresponding fee.[7.3] In our submissions accompanying the demand, we did not amend PCT-1, but rather explained why it is not essential that the hollow fibres are made of ceramics of class C.[7.4] We included experimental data showing that our specially designed nozzle N also works with hollow fibres made of the class P.[7.5] We also included an extensive description of our recently developed hollow fibre membranes that are made of polymers of the class P and are coated with a special coating K.[7.6] We are convinced that these new hollow fibre membranes will revolutionise the hollow fibre membrane market[7.7] as they are as stiff as ceramic membranes, but are less vulnerable to vibrations, in particular those generated by air bubbles injected into the bundle.[7.8] Moreover, their production costs are very low compared to ceramic hollow fibre membranes.[7.9]

724   7.1   Another date for the timeline. The demand appears to have been filed within the three month time limit from transmittal of the international search report (see comment 6.4). It is possible that there will be a mark for pointing this out.

      7.2   This is the right place to file the demand – directly with the competent International Preliminary Examining Authority (Art. 31(6)(a)). An Austrian PCT applicant must use the EPO as International Searching Authority and International Preliminary Examining Authority by virtue of the Protocol on Centralisation.

      7.3   In fact, two fees are due: a handling fee for the benefit of the International Bureau and a Preliminary Examination Fee for the benefit of the International Preliminary Examining Authority (Art. 31(5), r.57.1 and r.58.1 PCT). However, it is unlikely any marks will be available for pointing this out – in the context of the question as a whole it is clear that international preliminary examination is ongoing so the fees must have been paid and 'fee' here must be taken to refer to the aggregate of the two fees. It is important in these long questions to take a realistic rather than a pedantic approach.

      7.4   This seems like a reasonable argument from what we have already been told. See comments 3.9 and 6.3.

      7.5   This is what we would expect based on the client's previous comments. See comment 6.3. It reinforces the mystery surrounding the omission of this information from the description of EP-1 – this omission could be potentially damaging. See comment 3.12. Furthermore, if this information becomes publicly available via file inspection, the client will NO LONGER be able to file a patent application for it. It is important in this paper to consider ALL possible disclosures of information and comment on them in the answer. This passage should have stirred thoughts relating to the confidentiality of international preliminary examination and the limits of such confidentiality.

      7.6   This is another new invention which has not been the subject of a patent application yet – see comment 3.12. In this case the invention has already been disclosed in some manner which could be very damaging – see comment 7.5. It may be possible to claim the polymers coated with special coating K per se as well as a module comprising them, either without a nozzle, with a standard nozzle, with a special nozzle N or with a special nozzle N made of stainless steel.

      7.7   This is now a very serious matter indeed: subject matter which is of high commercial importance has been potentially disclosed without the filing of a patent application. Dealing with this mess will clearly be an important aspect in answering the paper.

      7.8   This is a problem which has been solved in a non-obvious way since it seems unlikely that it could have been predicted that the coating would have led to these advantages. The subject matter described in comment 7.6 seems to be associated with an inventive step but is it still novel given its disclosure to the EPO?

      7.9   Just reinforcing again the commercial importance of the new subject matter which is in a perilous position and emphasising that the candidate must propose all possible measures to ensure the client obtains the best protection possible for this subject matter by rectifying the mistakes the client has already made to the greatest extent possible.

725   [0008] We have not received an international preliminary examination report (IPER) for PCT-1 yet.[8.1] As we are interested in having a positive IPER, we have contacted the examiner at the EPO, who has agreed to give us a personal interview, tomorrow, at the EPO premises.[8.2] PCT-1 has entered the national phase only in those emerging countries that we are interested in, which include Brazil and India.[8.3] As we had also filed EP-2 and no objection concerning it was raised in the extended European search report, we did not enter the regional phase before the EPO for PCT-1.[8.4]

726   8.1   In respect of each sentence in the paper you must ask yourself: why am I being told this information? This is especially the case when the information appears on its face to be superfluous. Why should it matter whether the IPER has been established yet, or whether it will be established next week or next year? Its content would seem to be more important than the date on which it is established. It is very important with an apparently superfluous fact such as this to consider carefully any legal consequences that it gives rise to, particularly in the context of the question. The context here is the

previous paragraph which tells us that important subject matter has been disclosed to the EPO as IPEA which would be state of the art if subject to file inspection. In this context, the key legal consequence of the IPER not being established is that, according to Art. 38(1) and r.94.3 PCT, public access to the international preliminary examination file is prohibited. Nearly all long D questions contain a sentence like this that includes a seemingly trivial piece of information which gives rise to a very important legal consequence which is highly relevant to the answer.

8.2 The more obvious but less important point here is that we still have a chance to obtain a positive IPER. The less obvious but much more important point, following on from the last comment, is that the IPER will not be established until tomorrow at the earliest which means that any information that could be obtained by inspection of the international preliminary examination file for PCT-1 will not be state of the art for a patent application filed today or tomorrow.

8.3 This sentence immediately directs us to consider whether it would have been wiser to nationalise PCT-1 in any other countries and, if so, whether this is still possible. Hence the 30 and 31 month dates for national and regional phase entry must be calculated and added to the list of dates from which a timeline will be constructed.

8.4 This sentence focuses our minds particularly on the EPO: is EP-2 deficient in any way that would have made it preferable to regionalise PCT-1 at the EPO? If so, has the 31 month deadline for regionalisation of PCT-1 at the EPO expired yet? If it has, is any remedy available? All this will become clear when the timeline has been constructed and analysed. What we can say already is that EP-2 is not entitled to its priority date for all matter claimed and may be to subject to different prior art than PCT-1. When different aspects of the paper start to fit together like this in the manner of a jigsaw, you can be confident your analysis is heading in the right direction. The key point at this stage is to realise that the client is not a patent expert and is making decisions based on a superficial analysis of the legal situation (no objection for EP-2 in the ISR) – always pay attention to decisions of this nature that have been made by the client and expect some of them to be naive and based on a mistaken appreciation of the legal situation.

[0009] Watergate Inc. from the US are our main competitor[9.1] in the emerging countries and have their production sites in the US.[9.2] As we knew that they had also been investigating how to solve the problem of incrustations in fibre bundle modules, we became concerned when we read a communication first posted on their website on 30 July 2010[9.3] stating that they had filed a US patent application on 30 April 2010.[9.4] The communication mentioned that the application relates to a hollow fibre membrane bundle module for waste water treatment comprising a nozzle for injecting air into the bundle for incrustation removal.[9.5] Moreover, the communication stated that Watergate would soon also start manufacturing their products in Europe.[9.6] We have since then also found out that on 2 May 2011[9.7] Watergate filed a European patent application EP-WG[9.8] by reference to[9.9] and claiming priority from US-WG[9.10] filed on 30 April 2010.[9.11] EP-WG and US-WG have been published.[9.12] US-WG discloses a module comprising hollow fibre membranes made of polymer of class P, and a nozzle that is identical to our specially designed nozzle N and that is preferably made of stainless steel.[9.13] Claim 1 of US-WG is directed to a module comprising a bundle B of hollow fibre membranes and the specially designed nozzle N. Claim 1 does not specify the material of the membranes and the material of the nozzle.[9.14] Dependent claim 2 is directed to a module comprising the nozzle N and a bundle B of hollow fibre membranes made of polymers of class P.[9.15]   727

9.1 In almost all of these long D questions the client will have a competitor working on   728 similar inventions who will have filed patent applications. In the usual scenario, the patent rights of the client and competitor will overlap in some way and, when the analysis has been done, both parties will be entitled to some patent rights affecting the other's freedom to operate in key markets. Most commonly, the candidate will be expected to propose some form of cross-licensing as the best way of furthering the client's commercial aims.

9.2 So it seems that some patent rights in the US would be useful in addition to rights in Europe and emerging markets.

9.3 Date for the timeline – in this case a public disclosure the effect of which will need to be assessed vis-à-vis any patent claims belonging to Membrain with a later effective date. The possibility of such a disclosure was foreseen in comment 6.1. The case law relating to matters of proof in relation to internet citations will have to be considered.

9.4 Another date for the timeline. A US patent application may not directly affect Membrain's freedom to operate in Europe and emerging countries but it could serve as a priority right for further applications which do. Its publication may also be prior art relevant to come of Membrain's filings. At this stage we must await confirmation that Watergate have actually filed a US patent application on this date.

9.5 This disclosure already seems to be potentially novelty-destroying to the broad claim of EP-2 if it has an earlier effective date.

9.6 So some patent rights in Europe covering their products could seriously hamper their ability to supply markets worldwide.

9.7 Further date for the timeline – filing date of a new application.

9.8 A direct threat to the client's ability to manufacture products in Austria and supply markets in developing countries. We will have to consider carefully what valid rights this application might give rise to and advise the client accordingly as to what he can and cannot do.

9.9 Filing by reference means that the content is identical so that any priority right will be valid. Not clear whether both the claims and description have been incorporated by reference – it would be natural to assume so in the absence of further information. Any assumptions which are necessary should be noted in the answer.

9.10 The priority claim looks to be too late, as with EP-2 (priority date 30 April 2010; filing date 02 May 2011). However, once again, referring to the calendar we find that 30 April 2011 was a Saturday so that filing on 02 May 2011 was in time. This point will need to be made in the answer. We don't have enough information to decide whether the application was filed in the right name to claim priority as we are not sure what legal entity the US inventors have assigned their rights to in the priority year.

9.11 Confirming the statement made on Watergate's website.

9.12 Two new disclosures entering the state of the art under Art. 54(2) EPC and one under Art. 54(3) EPC. We will need to calculate the likely date of publication if we are not told in order to assess the prior art effect of these disclosures on the client's patent rights.

9.13 This is the disclosure of the application which may have a prior art effect on any of the client's patent claims with a later effective date. It sounds highly relevant to the client's technology, the only difference being the use of membranes made of polymers P rather than ceramics C.

9.14 This claim is clearly relevant to many of the client's products and we will need to look at its validity very carefully. Hopefully for the client there will be prior art which will render it invalid.

9.15 This claim is equally worrisome for the client since it is narrower and therefore potentially more likely to be valid and yet it covers the products incorporating membranes of polymer P which the client has lately realised to be of immense commercial importance (when incorporating coating K) – see comments 7.6–7.9. Its validity will likewise have to be carefully considered. The fact that the client has not filed on (and therefore disclosed under Art. 54(2) and/or Art. 54(3)) any products incorporating polymer P turns out to have been potentially a big mistake.

729 [0010] We are presently manufacturing modules with specially designed nozzles N made of stainless steel and with hollow fibre membranes made of ceramics of class C.[10.1] We are, however, also producing modules comprising the specially designed nozzle N made of other materials and hollow fibre membranes made of polymers of class P without the coating K.[10.2] The latter modules are not as reliable as the first ones, but can be produced at much lower costs.[10.3] We are planning to manufacture and sell modules in which the specially designed nozzle N is replaced by nozzles available on the market that are cheaper but less effective.[10.4]

Please advise us on the following questions:[10.5]

1) What is the legal status[10.6] of our patent rights and those of Watergate?

2) What do you advise us concerning our recently developed membranes comprising the special coating K?[10.7]

3) What can be done to improve our patent rights and what would be our resulting position vis-à-vis Watergate?[10.8]

10.1 Whilst in the answer we will be trying to suggest measures which improve the client's situation in all respects it is obviously most important to try and improve the client's position in relation to his current commercial aims. Assessing whether the client is free to manufacture and sell this module and whether he can prevent others from doing the same in order to be able to charge a premium price are therefore of paramount importance.   730

10.2 Ditto comment 10.1. We must assess the legal situation for this product and comment on it specifically in the answer.

10.3 See comment 5.7. The client is running a business and is more interested in what he can and can't do in relation to commercially viable products than an academic assessment of rights he could obtain covering commercially non-viable products.

10.4 Ditto comments 10.1 and 10.3.

10.5 Most recent long D questions have included specific questions that the candidate is expected to answer. These questions may not directly address all the points which need to be made in a full answer but it may be wise to structure your answer in line with these questions in order to better align your answer with the marking schedule and make it easier for the person marking your paper to find the points for which marks are available in your answer. At a minimum, the questions asked must be directly addressed at some point in your answer.

10.6 Note that "legal status" in this context does not have the narrow meaning of prosecution status (pending, withdrawn, deemed withdrawn, granted etc). It means the rights that can be expected to be granted and enforced. Thus, in order to answer this question it will be necessary to consider prosecution status, ownership, validity of priority claim, effective date of subject matter claimed (or which could be claimed), prior art, novelty, inventive step, sufficiency and possibly other matters.

10.7 The question here is how to improve Membrain's position vis-à-vis subject matter which has not yet been the subject of a patent application – what new filings might lead to valid, enforceable patent rights that provide a competitive edge for the client.

10.8 The question here is how to improve Membrain's position vis-à-vis filed patent applications and how best to use these patent rights to provide a competitive edge for the client.

[0011] We also need your advice on another urgent matter. Since 2008 we have been producing and selling filter cartridges comprising a different kind of membranes, known as Q-membranes, for the production of drinking water from sea water.[11.1] Our Q-membranes are made of polymer Alpha and contain 4 % of a compound R that is used to control the pore size of the membranes. Polymer Alpha has been used in the past for Q-membranes.[11.2] We thought it was commonly known in the art, at the latest by the end of 2005, to use compound R to control the pore size of the membranes. In 2007 we carried out extensive tests that did not reveal any technical effect that would go beyond the expected pore size control.[11.3] For these reasons we did not apply for patent protection for our Q-membranes or for the filter cartridges.[11.4]   731

11.1 This part of the question is clearly completely separate from the first part and should be read, analysed and answered separately.   732

11.2 It therefore seems that Q-membranes per se and Q-membranes made of polymer Alpha are both known and may not be the subject of patent protection. Statements of facts such as this should be accepted at face value unless contradicted by any further information.

11.3 These, on the other hand, are the subjective opinions of the client who is not skilled in patent matters and whose research may not have been exhaustive. They should therefore be treated with caution until we have some objective evidence to back them up.

11.4 Clearly it would have been better to at least publish this information in order to ensure freedom to operate. The earliest disclosure will be the date of the first sale in 2008.

733 [0012] We were therefore very surprised when on 6 February 2012[12.1] Watergate instituted infringement proceedings against us before an Austrian court based on a European patent validated in Austria. This patent, EP-CART, was filed on 23 March 2006[12.2] without claiming priority.[12.3] The single claim[12.4] of EP-CART is directed to a Q-membrane made of polymer Alpha characterised by 1–5 % of compound R.[12.5] The subject matter of the claim is directly and unambiguously derivable from the application as filed.[12.6] The description states that the problem to be solved by the compound R is the control of pore size.[12.7] The search report cited only category A documents, among others document D1, published in 1999, which discloses a Q-membrane made of polymer Alpha.[12.8]

734 12.1 First date in this part of the paper, about a month ago. Since this part of the question is very short, a formal time line may not be as important as it was in the first part of the question. The significance of this date is not clear but one date associated with the institution of infringement proceedings is the three month intervention time limit.

12.2 Another date to note, this time the filing date of a patent application. Since the resulting patent is being asserted against the client, one possible defence will be an invalidity attack and hence the filing date is important. The filing date of a European patent also has many other important consequences which should be considered – see comment 3.1.

12.3 Hence the validity of all claims is to be assessed at the filing date of 23 March 2006.

12.4 Having only one claim simplifies the situation immensely and is common in paper D.

12.5 Hence the claim has three integers for the purposes of analysing its novelty: (1) It must be a Q membrane; (2) it must be made of polymer Alpha; and (3) it must comprise 1–5 % of compound R. What is ambiguous is whether 'made of polymer alpha' implies that, apart from compound R, no other material is present or whether it implies that at least some polymer Alpha is present. An interpretation may need to be developed and justified as part of the answer.

12.6 In Paper D, clear statements such as these are usually to be accepted at face value and not questioned. This statement is telling us that the claim cannot be attacked for containing subject matter going beyond the content of the application as filed contrary to Art. 123(2) EPC. No marks will be available for discussing Art. 123(2) and candidates should therefore not waste any time considering it. However, since this information is coming from a client who is not skilled in patent matters we should not automatically assume it is correct if other information comes to light which tends to contradict it.

12.7 This is the technical effect which the client identified as being known by the end of 2005. If the client is correct then the claim may well lack an inventive step unless the 1–5 % range would not have been obvious. However, we lack any objective evidence to validate the client's opinion at this point.

12.8 This is worrying since it tends to contradict the client's opinion that the use of compound R to control pore size was well known by the end of 2005. Perhaps it was well known internally at Membrain AG but this information was never made available to the public.

735 [0013] From a file inspection we have found out that Dialab GmbH, an Austrian company, had validly filed before the EPO an opposition against EP-CART[13.1] on the sole ground that the subject-matter of the only claim extends beyond the content of the application as filed.[13.2] It appears from the file that the opposition division rejected the opposition[13.3] in a decision announced during oral proceedings held on 02 December 2011 followed by a written reasoned decision dated 27 February 2012.[13.4] We believe that the decision is correct.[13.5]

736 13.1 Has the opposition period already ended so that we are too late to file an opposition ourselves? We do not know yet. If the opposition period has expired then intervention may be possible since the client has been sued. Alternatively, national revocation proceedings in Austria would be possible.

13.2 This attack is likely doomed to failure based on what the client has already said – see comment 12.6.

13.3 So the opposition period is over. Only intervention and revocation proceedings are possible.

13.4 Two more dates to consider. Firstly, the opposition proceedings were terminated on 02 December 2011. Since these proceedings are no longer pending, intervention is no longer possible unless an appeal is filed. The appeal period runs from the second date, the notification of the decision. Adding a ten day notification period (r.126(2) EPC) and a two month appeal period (Art. 108 EPC) gets us to Tuesday 08 May 2012. So an appeal is still possible and, if an appeal is filed, intervention will be possible.

13.5 This is entirely consistent with what the client has said in the previous paragraph (see comments 12.6 and 13.2).

[0014] Triggered by the infringement proceedings, we consulted our copy of the Encyclo-   737
paedia of Membrane Technologies, a standard handbook in the field of membrane technology.[14.1] The encyclopaedia was published on 23 March 2006[14.2] and teaches that it is common to use between 1 and 5 % of compound R to control the pore size in membranes made of polymers.[14.3]

14.1 Handbooks are usually considered to reflect the common general knowledge of the   738
skilled person and hence an ideal source of information with which to show a claim lacks an inventive step.

14.2 Another important date. This is somewhat later than the "end of 2005" previously cited by the client and is actually the same date as the filing date of EP-CART. The legal consequence of this is that the disclosure is not prior art which can be cited against the patent under Art. 54 EPC. However, crucially, it may be cited as **evidence** of the common general knowledge of the skilled person at the filing date of the patent under Art. 56 EPC.

14.3 Along with the previous information that Q membranes made of polymer Alpha were known, this represents a good validity attack with which to defend the infringement proceedings.

[0015] By mere coincidence, our sales manager Franz S. recently met Wolfgang M., the   739
sole owner of Dialab GmbH, at a cocktail party.[15.1] According to Wolfgang, Dialab deals with analytics, i.e. analysing samples sent from hospitals and clinics. Dialab wants to use a membrane covered by the claim or EP-CART for a new and promising analytics application.[15.2] This is why they filed the opposition against EP-CART. Wolfgang is very upset by the decision of the opposition division and asked Franz whether Membrain and Dialab could work together to have the patent revoked.[15.3]

4) In view of the opposition and infringement proceedings, what are the options and corresponding actions to be taken before the EPO?[15.4]

15.1 It sounds like a good personal relationship may have developed over a few drinks   740
that will facilitate the co-operation of the client Membrain AG with the opponent Dialab.

15.2 Since Membrain AG and Dialab are not competitors, they have everything to gain by co-operating and nothing to lose.

15.3 If there was no way of co-operating then the question would not make sense. It is therefore for the candidate to apply his or her legal knowledge relating to opposition/intervention to the facts of the question in order to identify the manner in which these parties could co-operate and identify the concrete steps that need to be taken. A well prepared candidate will remember immediately that there are Enlarged Board of Appeal decisions relating to intervention and that these decisions may have some relevance to the answer. Enlarged Board of Appeal decisions are much loved by examiners since they interpret important points of law which usually have important practical consequences and they often establish an interpretation of the EPC which is not evident from the wording of the Articles and Rules themselves.

15.4 This is a nice straightforward question which can be answered directly without drawing up any complicated timelines or undertaking any complicated analysis. A few notes should suffice to collect the relevant points in the right order and the question can then be answered directly.

Yours sincerely
J. Strauss
CEO Membrain AG

2.6.2   *Generating a list of dates (Q1–3)*

741   The first part of the paper, relating to bundles of hollow fibres, is much too complicated to answer without a systematic analysis of the facts facilitated by the construction of a time line. Focussing on this part alone and ignoring the second part for the time being, the candidate should read though the question again and make a list of important dates. Each date should be accompanied by a brief description identifying its significance. This list will not yet be in chronological order. It may be possible to order the dates chronologically as they are being noted but it is difficult to do so with this paper, as with most long D questions, since the dates are not presented chronologically in the paper. To attempt to prepare a chronological list in one step can therefore be counterproductive, involving much crossing-out and messy amendment.

06 March 2012 – Date of the exam
31 July 2009 – Filing date of EP-1
03 May 2010 – Filing date of PCT-1
February 2011 – Publication date of PCT-1 (presumably early in the month since
P+18 m = 31 January 2011)
June 2010 – Testing of standard nozzles
December 2009 – Publication of handbook disclosing standard nozzles
02 August 2010 – Filing date of EP-2
11 August 2011 – Transmittal of ISR for PCT-1
10 November 2011 – Demand for international preliminary examination of PCT-1
filed
and disclosure to EPO of nozzle + polymers P and polymers P + coating K
07 March 2012 – interview at EPO re. international preliminary examination of PCT-1
30 July 2010 – Watergate internet disclosure of bundle + nozzle
30 April 2010 – Filing date of US-WG
02 May 2011 – Filing date of EP-WG

2.6.3   *Chronological list of dates (Q1–3)*

742   The dates should now be ordered so that a time line can be generated with the correct span of dates. In reality in the exam it is not necessary to drawn up a new list, the dates can be ordered by writing numbers next to them to save time.

31 July 2009 – Filing date of EP-1
December 2009 – Publication of handbook disclosing standard nozzles
30 April 2010 – Filing date of US-WG
03 May 2010 – Filing date of PCT-1
June 2010 – Testing of standard nozzles
30 July 2010 – Watergate internet disclosure of bundle + nozzle
02 August 2010 – Filing date of EP-2
February 2011 – Publication date of PCT-1 (presumably early in the month since
P+18 m = 31 January 2011)
02 May 2011 – Filing date of EP-WG
11 August 2011 – Transmittal of ISR for PCT-1
10 November 2011 – Demand for international preliminary examination of PCT-1
filed
and disclosure to EPO of nozzle + polymers P and polymers P + coating K
06 March 2012 – Date of the exam
07 March 2012 – interview at EPO re. international preliminary examination of PCT-1

2.6.4   *Expanded chronological list of dates (Q1–3)*

743   Before starting to draw up a timeline, it is wise to add further important dates that will need to be considered. This is to make sure that the timeline has an appropriate span.

Otherwise, there may not be any space later on to add further dates in the future. Four additional dates have been identified in the list below.

31 July 2009 – Filing date of EP-1

December 2009 – Publication of handbook disclosing standard nozzles

30 April 2010 – Filing date of US-WG

03 May 2010 – Filing date of PCT-1

June 2010 – Testing of standard nozzles

30 July 2010 – Watergate internet disclosure of bundle + nozzle

02 August 2010 – Filing date of EP-2

February 2011 – Publication date of PCT-1 (presumably early in the month since P+18 m = 31 January 2011)

February 2011 – Also publication date of EP-2

02 May 2011 – Filing date of EP-WG

11 August 2011 – Transmittal of ISR for PCT-1

30 October 2011 – 18 month (publication) date for US-WG and EP-WG

10 November 2011 – Demand for international preliminary examination of PCT-1 filed

and disclosure to EPO of nozzle + polymers P and polymers P + coating K

31 January 2012 – 30 month national phase entry date for PCT-1

31 February 2012 – 31 month national phase entry date for PCT-1

06 March 2012 – Date of the exam

07 March 2012 – interview at EPO re. international preliminary examination of PCT-1

2.6.5   *Drawing up a timeline (Q1–3)*

Now it is possible to draw up a timeline which includes all of the relevant dates that have been established and brief details of the events associated with each of them. When the basic features of the timeline have been established, the candidate should read through the question once more and add important information. It is often helpful to line up events relating to the same subject (e.g. the same patent application) along a single axis in order to better organise the numerous facts in manner that is more easily comprehensible. It may, for example, be helpful to line up all possible disclosures along a single axis as has been done in the timeline below. The use of colour-coding is also very helpful, e.g. to distinguish between disclosures and events relating to patent applications and/or to distinguish between events relevant to different legal entities.

744

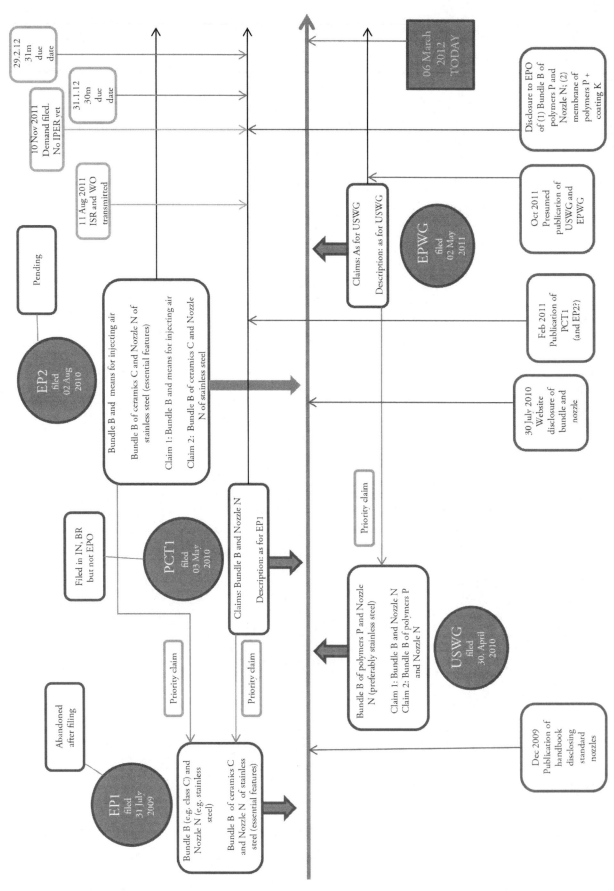

Figure 19

2.6.6   *Analysis of patent rights (Q1–3)*

It is now possible to analyse the various patent rights which have or could be created and   745
to decide which parties will be entitled to which rights in which territories. This information will then lead to a consideration of how strong the client's position is and consequently his likely commercial options. This is conveniently done in the form of a table and
a suitable table with relevant headings can be prepared in advance of the exam and filled
in on the day – remember, however, that such pre-prepared materials cannot form part of
the answer and should only be used for the purposes of analysis (Point I.9(c) ICEQE).

Application	Prosecution status	Subject matter	Effective date	Prior art	Likely protection
EP1	Abandoned	Description: (1) Module comprising bundle B and nozzle N (2) Module comprising bundle B of ceramics class C and nozzle N (3) Module comprising bundle B and nozzle N made of stainless steel (4) Module comprising bundle B made of ceramics of class C and nozzle N made of stainless steel	31 July 2009	None	None
PCT-1	Pending in India and Brazil, deemed withdrawn EPO (subject to further processing), other national phases may be possible to salvage	Claims: (1) Module comprising bundle B and nozzle N. Description: (1) Module comprising bundle B made of ceramics of class C and nozzle N (2) Module comprising bundle B and nozzle N made of stainless steel (3) Module comprising bundle B made of ceramics of class C and nozzle N made of stainless steel	31 July 2009 31 July 2009 31 July 2009 31 July 2009	None	All disclosed subject matter in India, Brazil and (if needed) Europe and (possibly) elsewhere
EP-2	Pending	Claims: (1) Module comprising bundle B and means for injecting air (2) Module comprising bundle B made of ceramics of class C and nozzle N made of stainless steel Description: not clear whether preferred features (ceramics class C, nozzle N) present or not	02 August 2010 31 July 2010	PCT-1 if enters regional phase (Art. 54(3)) EP-WG (Art. 54(3)) Website disclosure Handbook disclosure None	Claim 1 will lack novelty over website disclosure (if enabled and proven), over EP-WG and over PCT-1 if it enters the regional phase. No protection. Claim 2 patentable (but must avoid double patenting with PCT-1 if it enters regional phase).
US–WG	Assumed pending	Claims: (1) Module comprising bundle B and nozzle N (2) Module comprising bundle B made of polymers of class P and nozzle N Description: Module comprising bundle B made of polymers of class P and nozzle N made of stainless steel	30 April 2010 30 April 2010 30 April 2010	Handbook disclosure PCT-1 publication?	Handbook only discloses standard nozzles so all claims should be patentable over it. Effect of PCT-1 is to be assessed under national law.

Application	Prosecution status	Subject matter	Effective date	Prior art	Likely protection
EP-WG	Assumed pending	Claims: (1) Module comprising bundle B and nozzle N (2) Module comprising bundle B made of polymers of class P and nozzle N Description:	30 April 2010 30 April 2010	PCT-1 if enters regional phase (Art. 54(3)) – would destroy novelty of claim 1 but not claim 2	Only claim 2
		Module comprising bundle B made of polymers of class P and nozzle N made of stainless steel	30 April 2010	EP-2 in so far as it validly claims priority (Art. 54(3)) – destroys the novelty of claim 1 but not claim 2. Handbook disclosure.	
Not yet claimed	–	Nozzle N	–	Publications of PCT-1, EP-2 and EP-WG all disclose nozzle N so no new application possible.	Protection only possible if basis for claiming nozzle N in PCT-1 and/or EP2. Would seem likely.
Not yet claimed	–	Nozzle N made of stainless steel	–	Publications of PCT-1, EP-2 and EP-WG all disclose nozzle N so no new application possible.	Protection only possible if basis for claiming nozzle N made of stainless steel in PCT-1 and/or EP2. Would seem likely.
Not yet claimed	–	(1) Membranes made of polymers of class P with special coating K (2) Module comprising (1) with nozzle (3) Module comprising (1) with nozzle N (4) Module comprising (1) with nozzle N made of stainless steel	–	No prior art relevant to coating K as long as international preliminary examination file remains confidential	Patentable – new application should be filed today or tomorrow.

2.6.7   Possible answer (Q1–3)

746   An answer can now be written. A possible answer could be worded as follows.

(a) Legal status of patent rights belonging to Membrain and Watergate

747   **EP-1** has been "abandoned". It is not clear if it was withdrawn or allowed to become deemed withdrawn. Since it was filed without claims, however, it must be assumed that the application did not publish and is therefore not prior art under Art. 54(2) or Art. 54(3) EPC. In the case of withdrawal the effect is immediate and irrevocable. Given the time that has elapsed it must also be assumed that no legal remedy is available in the case of deemed withdrawal (1 year maximum for reestablishment). No patent rights will therefore arise from EP-1. However, EP-1 created a valid priority basis since it was accorded a filing date (no claims required for a filing date under Art. 80 and r.40 EPC2000) and its subsequent fate is irrelevant (Art. 87(3) EPC).

748   **PCT-1** is pending in India and Brazil. The 31 month time limit for entering the EPO regional phase expired on 29 February 2012 so that the application is deemed withdrawn as far as the EPO is concerned. This was only a matter of days ago and hence it will be possible to validly enter the EPO regional phase using further processing within two months of notification of loss of rights. Entering the EPO regional phase would mean that patent protection would be possible and that PCT-1 would become prior art under Art. 54(3) EPC. It may also be possible to enter the regional/national phase late in other countries such as the US depending on the provisions of national law.

749   PCT-1 has a single claim to a module comprising nozzle N and a bundle B of hollow fibre membranes. The priority claim from EP-1 appears to be valid (both applications filed by Membrain, within priority year, same subject matter, EP-1 a first filing). The validity of this claim is therefore to be assessed as of 31 July 2009. The search report for PCT-1 did not reveal any relevant documents and no other prior art is apparent from the client's letter. The claim therefore appears to be valid. Further claims could be added directed to a module comprising (i) nozzle N made of stainless steel and bundle B of hollow fibre membranes; (ii) nozzle N and bundle B of hollow fibre membranes made of ceramics C; and (iii) nozzle N made of stainless steel and bundle B of hollow fibre membranes made of ceramics C. Validity for this subject matter is the same. However, double patenting in Europe with respect to EP-2 is to be avoided: in respect of duplicated subject matter it would be better to obtain patent protection from EP-2 in order to benefit from a longer patent term.

750   The objection under Art. 6 PCT does not seem well founded in view of the fact that the description clearly states that the membranes may be made of any suitable material and Membrain has provided evidence that this is in fact the case. The objection should be withdrawn.

751   It is also noted that the nozzle N is new and superior to standard nozzles disclosed in the Handbook of waste water Aeration. It should be possible to include claims in PCT-1 to the nozzle per se (and to the nozzle when made of stainless steel) if there is basis for doing so in the application as filed. A new application claiming the nozzle is no longer possible in view of the publications of PCT-1, EP-2, US-WG and EP-WG.

752   **EP-2** is pending. The formal requirements of the priority claim from EP-1 appear to be met. The applicant appears to be Membrain in each case. The 12 month priority period for EP-1 ended on 31 July 2010 which was a Saturday and hence the priority period was extended until Monday 02 August 2010, the filing date of EP-2. EP-1 was also the first filing of the subject matter it discloses.

753   Regarding claim 1 of EP-2, this subject matter was not disclosed in EP-1 and hence the priority claim is not valid. Its validity is therefore to be assessed as of 02 August 2010. EP-1 is not potential prior art since it was seemingly abandoned before publication. The publication of the handbook in December 2009, whilst Art. 54(2) state of the art, is not relevant since the use of a nozzle in the context of a bundle of hollow fibre membranes and the advantageous effects of this arrangement are not disclosed. PCT-1 will be novelty-destroying prior art under Art. 54(3) EPC if it enters the EPO regional phase since it discloses both bundle B and nozzle N which is a means for injecting air. The website disclosure of 30 July 2010 is also novelty-destroying under Art. 54(2) EPC since it discloses a hollow fibre membrane bundle and a nozzle which is a means for injecting air – this is subject to the assumptions that the disclosure is enabling and that its date and content

can be properly established (website disclosures are subject to a higher level of proof than other written disclosures). Finally, EP-WG is novelty-destroying prior art under Art. 54(3) EPC since it has been published and it validly claims priority from US-WG in respect of its disclosure of a module comprising a bundle B and nozzle N (see below). Claim 1 of EP-2 is therefore not patentable and will not lead to any valid and enforceable patent rights.

Regarding claim 2 of EP-2, this subject matter was disclosed in EP-1 (the single embodiment) and hence the priority claim is valid. Its validity is therefore to be assessed as of 31 July 2009. This claim is therefore patentable (see analysis for PCT-1 above). 754

It is not clear whether there is sufficient basis in the description of EP-2 to add claims to a module comprising (i) bundle B of hollow fibre membranes and nozzle N; (ii) bundle B of hollow fibre membranes made of ceramics C and nozzle N; and (iii) bundle B of hollow fibre membranes and nozzle N made of stainless steel. If there is, these claims should added during prosecution (they have unity by virtue of nozzle N). Otherwise, they should be prosecuted to grant as part of PCT-1 (see above). 755

As with PCT-1, it may be possible to introduce a claim to the nozzle N per se and to the nozzle N when made of stainless steel.

US-WG is assumed to be pending. It is a first filing and its claims are to be assessed for validity as of 30 April 2010. The publication of the handbook in December 2009 is not relevant prior art (see above). The only other prior art is the publication of PCT-1 which claims the priority of EP-1 (filed 31 July 2009), the effect of which needs to be assessed under US national law. Expert advice will be necessary here but it is my preliminary opinion that the section 102(e) effect of PCT-1 will only apply as of its filing date since priority is not claimed from a US application. The claims of US-WG must therefore be assumed to be patentable. 756

EP-WG is assumed to be pending. It validly claims priority from US-WG. The 12 month priority period expires 30 April 2011 which is a Saturday so the filing of EP-WG on Monday 02 May was in time. US-WG would have been filed in the name of the inventors; in the absence of further information it is assumed that they assigned their rights to Watergate who then filed EP-WG. US-WG was a first filing and is in respect of the same subject matter as EP-WG. The validity of EP-WG is therefore to be assessed as of 30 April 2010. In Europe, PCT-1 will be Art. 54(3) prior art if it enters the regional phase and will destroy the novelty of claim 1 of EP-WG. EP-2 is in any case Art. 54(3) prior art to the extent that it validly claims priority. The priority claim is valid for the subject matter of claim 2 of EP-2 which therefore destroys the novelty of claim 1 of EP-WG. Only claim 2 of EP-WG is therefore patentable. 757

(b) Advice concerning recently developed membranes comprising the special coating K

No patent application has yet been filed for the membranes made of polymers of class P coated with coating K. Membranes made of polymers of class P are known from the publications of US-WG and EP-WG. Membranes made of polymers P coated with coating K are novel over this disclosure and the coating seems to confer advantageous properties which could not have been predicted from the known art (stiff but nevertheless less vulnerable to vibrations). However, the coated membranes have been disclosed in a letter to the EPO dated 10 November 2011 – if this disclosure has been made available to the public then a claim to the coated membranes will lack novelty. The demand for international preliminary examination was filed in time (within three months of the date of dispatch of the International Search Report, r.54*bis*.1(a) PCT). The letter was sent with the demand for international preliminary examination and forms part of the file of international preliminary examination which may not, according to Art. 38(1) PCT be made available by the International Preliminary Examining Authority to anybody except to an elected office once the International Preliminary Examination Report has been established. Once it has established the International Preliminary Examination Report, the EPO will make the file available to itself as elected office and will then, as an elected office, make documents in the file available to the public by file inspection as it would make the file of any published European patent application available (r.94.3 PCT, [1999] O.J. 329 and [2003] O.J. 382). It is therefore imperative that a new application directed to the coated membranes be filed before the EPO establishes an International preliminary Examination Report for PCT-1. Since the examiner has granted Membrain an interview tomorrow, tomorrow is 758 the first day on which the IPER could be established and the letter made available to the public. The application should therefore be filed tomorrow at the latest in order to guarantee patentability. Claims should be included directed to hollow fibre membranes made of polymers of the class P and coated with special coating K, to a module comprising such membranes, to such a module additionally comprising a means for injecting air, e.g. a nozzle, the nozzle N or the nozzle N made of stainless steel. This application can then be abandoned and further applications filed 12 months later claiming its priority in order to maximise patent term. Consider also filing a US application as soon as possible to ensure the greatest prior art effect in the US and obtain patent protection where Watergate are manufacturing. In view of the client's worldwide markets, a PCT application should be considered. It is impossible at this stage to know whether valid patent rights will be obtained since the extent of the prior art (particularly under Art. 54(3) is not yet known.

(c) Steps to be taken to improve Membrain's patent rights and resulting position vis-à-vis Watergate?

759   The steps to be taken by Membrain in order to improve its patent rights include the following:

(i) File a patent application (first filing) tomorrow latest (07 March 2012) directed to invention of hollow fibre membranes made of polymers of the class P coated with special coating K.

(ii) Attend meeting with EPO examiner re. PCT-1 on 07 March 2012 and present arguments to overcome Art. 6 PCT objection and obtain positive IPER

760   (iii) Enter EPO regional phase (further processing) with PCT-1 in order to obtain protection for any subject matter for which there is no basis in EP-2 (to be assessed when actual documents are available) – see item (v) below.

(iv) Enter national phase with PCT-1 in other countries of interest where national law allows – particularly in US where Watergate have production facilities.

761   (v) Amend EP-2 by deleting claim 1 and introducing claims, if there is basis to do so, to (i) bundle B of hollow fibre membranes and nozzle N; (ii) bundle B of hollow fibre membranes made of ceramics C and nozzle N; and (iii) bundle B of hollow fibre membranes and nozzle N made of stainless steel. For any subject matter that lacks sufficient basis, prosecute these claims in PCT-1 (see item (iii) above).

(vi) Introduce claims to nozzle N per se and nozzle N made of stainless steel in EP-2 and PCT-1 is there is sufficient basis.

(vii) File third party observations at the EPO indicating that claim 1 of EP-WG lacks novelty over the publication of EP-2. File opposition on grant if observations are not taken into account.

(viii) Engage US agent to assess the validity of US-WG in view of the publication of PCT-1.

762   (ix) Prosecute PCT-1 to grant in countries of interest, introducing additional claims for which there is basis in the description: (i) nozzle N made of stainless steel and bundle B of hollow fibre membranes; (ii) nozzle N and bundle B of hollow fibre membranes made of ceramics C; and (iii) nozzle N made of stainless steel and bundle B of hollow fibre membranes made of ceramics C.

The position vis-à-vis Watergate for various commercial embodiments is as follows:

763   (i) **Module comprising bundle B of membranes made of ceramics of class C and nozzle N made of stainless steel** Membrain will be able to use patent rights resulting from prosecution of EP-2 and PCT-1 to prevent Watergate making and selling this embodiment in EPC contracting states and extension states (40 countries), India, Brazil and possibly in other countries such as the US. Membrain will be free to sell this embodiment in Europe and other countries except perhaps the US (validity of claim 1 of US-WG to be assessed).

(ii) **Module comprising bundle B of membranes made of ceramics of class C and nozzle N made of other material** Same situation as for (i).

764   (iii) **Module comprising bundle B of membranes made of ceramics of class C and a standard nozzle** No patent rights will protect this embodiment – it will be possible for all parties to manufacture and sell it in all territories

765   (iv) **Module comprising bundle B of membranes made of polymers of class P and nozzle N made of stainless steel** Membrain will be able to use patent rights resulting from prosecution of EP-2 and PCT-1 to prevent Watergate making and selling this embodiment in EPC contracting states and extension states (40 countries), India, Brazil and possibly in

other countries such as the US. However, Watergate will also be able to use patent rights resulting from US-WG and EP-WG to prevent Membrain manufacturing and selling this embodiment in the US and EPC contracting and extension states.

(v) **Module comprising bundle B of membranes made of polymers of class P and nozzle N made of other material** Same situation as for (iv).

(vi) **Module comprising bundle B of membranes made of polymers of class P and a standard nozzle** Same situation as for (iii).

(vii) **Module comprising bundle of membranes made of polymers of class P and special coating K and nozzle N made of stainless steel** Membrain should be able to use patent rights resulting from the new planned filing to prevent the manufacture and sale of this embodiment worldwide. However, Watergate will also be able to use EP-WG and US-WG to prevent the manufacture and sale of this embodiment in the US and EPC contracting and extension states.

766

(viii) **Module comprising bundle of membranes made of polymers of class P and special coating K and nozzle N made of other material** Same situation as for (vii).

(ix) **Module comprising bundle of membranes made of polymers of class P and special coating K and a standard nozzle** Membrain should be able to use patent rights resulting from the new planned filing to prevent the manufacture and sale of this embodiment worldwide. They should also be free to sell this embodiment worldwide.

767

The most promising commercial embodiments for Watergate to pursue are therefore (i), (ii) and (ix) since they should be free to sell these embodiments without infringing Watergate's patent rights and should also be able to prevent competition in important markets using their own patent rights. Embodiments (iii) and (vi) should be avoided since Membrain will not be able to stop cheap generic products from competitors and will not be able to charge a premium price. In relation to embodiments (iv), (v), (vii) and (viii), Membrain will have to consider negotiating an agreement with Watergate if they want to sell them. Some form of cross-license could be possible allowing both parties to sell the embodiments in different countries or market segments or sell different embodiments worldwide. Care should be taken to ensure the terms of any such agreement comply with competition laws in the US and Europe.

768

2.6.8   Possible answer (Q4)

The second part of the question can be answered more or less without any formal analysis, just based on the notes made from reading through the question. A possible answer could be worded as follows.

769

European patent EP-CART is being asserted against Membrain AG. It does not seem that there is an valid non-infringement argument since Membrain have been selling filter cartridges comprising Q membranes made from polymer Alpha and 4 % compound R which fall within the claim of EP-CART directed to a Q-membrane made of polymer Alpha and 1–5 % compound R. It is therefore necessary for Membrain, in order to defend itself, to show that EP-CART is invalid and have the patent revoked.

770

In order to seek revocation of a European patent it is possible to file an opposition at the EPO or to file national revocation actions In the courts of states in which the patent has been validated. Opposition proceedings are more useful since the patent as a whole can be revoked in a single procedure. However, an opposition must be filed within nine months of the grant of the patent taking effect. In the present case, this deadline has clearly been missed since an opposition has already been filed and examined, such examination not being possible until the opposition period has expired. Furthermore, there are no legal remedies by which the failure to file an opposition in time could be excused.

771

On the other hand, if opposition proceedings are already in existence, it is possible for a third party to take part in those proceedings by filing observations according to Art. 115 EPC or, in certain cases, by intervening. Intervention is far more effective since, if admissible, it is treated as an opposition and the intervener becomes a party to the proceedings (Art. 105(2) EPC). In the present case, an intervention would be possible if opposition proceedings were pending since Membrain has been sued for infringing the patent (Art. 105(1) EPC). Intervention needs to be filed by three months from the institution of proceedings, this period expiring 06 May 2012 (Sunday), extended until Monday 07 May 2012 under r.134(1) EPC, so the time limit has not yet expired. In the present

772

case, however, opposition proceedings are not pending since they were terminated by a decision to reject the opposition on 02 December 2012. This means that an intervention would not be admissible (G4/91).

773   If, on the other hand, the opponent Dialab was to file an appeal against the decision to reject the opposition, the effect of that decision would be suspended and opposition proceedings would be pending again, allowing the filing of an intervention (G1/94). The two-month appeal period starts from notification of the written decision and will hence expire on 08 May 2012 so it is not yet too late. It is possible, in appeal proceedings, for an intervention to raise any new ground of opposition (G1/94) so that Membrain would be able to raise the ground of lack of inventive step even though this ground was not raised during the opposition proceedings by Dialab. The most likely outcome of this would be that the case would be remitted to the opposition division so that the new ground could be considered by both instances of the EPO. If this happens then Membrain will have full rights as an opponent. If, however, the case is not remitted then Membrain would assume the status of an opponent and a party as of right to the appeal proceedings and it would be important for Dialab not to withdraw the appeal since this would automatically terminate proceedings and render the decision of the opposition division final (G3/04).

774   It seems, from the opinion of the client and the decision of the opposition division, that the ground of added subject matter cannot be properly supported and is unlikely to lead to the revocation of the patent (this should nevertheless be verified). The ground of lack of inventive step, on the other hand, seems to be well supported by the evidence and may well lead to revocation. The Encyclopaedia article was published on the filing date to which the patent is entitled and is therefore not prior art according to Art. 54 EPC. Nevertheless, being a standard handbook, it is good evidence of the common general knowledge of the skilled patent at that date. Given that, according to the client, the use of Q membranes made of polymer Alpha was well known at the filing date of the patent (and this is supported by document D1) and that the common general knowledge of the skilled person at that date indicated the use of 1–5 % of compound R was useful in controlling the pore size in polymer membranes, it would have been obvious to the skilled person to make the claimed invention. This is especially true since, according to the client, the presence of compound R does not give rise to any unexpected advantageous effect going beyond its control of pore size. If such an effect is identified by Watergate, it can in any case be argued that the skilled person would necessarily use compound R anyway to achieve pore size control and that the additional effect is merely a bonus.

775   It appears to be in the best interests of both Membrain and Dialab to co-operate in order to obtain revocation of EP-CART since they are not competitors, having different commercial interests, and would both benefit from such revocation. Therefore, the following specific actions should be taken:

(i) Dialab must file a notice of appeal against the decision of the opposition division to reject the opposition by the deadline of 08 May 2012 and pay the appeal fee.

776   (ii) Following the filing of the notice of appeal, Membrain must file a notice of intervention in the opposition appeal proceedings and pay the opposition fee. The notice of intervention must be filed as a reasoned written statement introducing the ground of lack of inventive step and fully substantiating it by referring to D1 which discloses Q-membranes made of polymer Alpha and citing the Encyclopaedia of Membrane Technologies as evidence that the common general knowledge of the skilled person at the filing date of the patent included the motivation to include 1–5 % of compound R in order to control pore size. All the formal requirements for the filing of an opposition should be observed. The intervention must be filed by Monday 07 May 2012 at the latest and include evidence showing that the infringement proceedings in Austria were initiated on 06 February 2012.

777   (iii) Unless the case is remitted to the opposition division, Dialab must make sure that their appeal is maintained since Membrain only obtain the status in the appeal proceedings as a non-appealing opponent and party as of right. Therefore, the appeal must be properly substantiated by the filing of grounds arguing why the decision of the opposition division in relating to added subject matter was wrong and Dialab must under no circumstances withdraw the appeal. The grounds of appeal must be filed within the four month deadline expiring Monday 09 July 2012.

(iv) Membrain should then ask the Austrian court to suspend the infringement proceedings pending the decision of the Board of Appeal to revoke the patent.

(v) If the Austrian court is not minded to stay proceedings, or if the eventual outcome   778
of the appeal is to uphold the patent, then Membrain will have to defend the infringement
proceedings with a counterclaim for invalidity based on the lack of inventive step (or
choose to settle by negotiation, possibly using patent rights relating to water-treatment
modules discussed in the first part of the question as an incentive).

It should be noted that it would not be sufficient for Dialab themselves to raise the   779
ground of lack of inventive step as part of the grounds of appeal since in opposition appeal
proceedings, a new ground of opposition raised by an opponent or the Board of Appeal
may only be admitted into the proceedings with the consent of the patentee (G10/91).

Chapter 3: Pre-examination - Legal Questions

3.1 Overview

780   The pre-examination, held in 2012 for the first time, differs fundamentally from the papers of the main exam by virtue of its multiple choice format. This means that answering the paper is a straightforward affair, it being necessary to simply select true or false for each question posed. There is no need to cite any legal basis and no notes to the examiner will be taken into account. Indeed, anything presented by the candidate as part of his or her answer other than multiple choice answer sheet will be ignored. Problems can arise, therefore when the candidate considers that the question is in some way ambiguous and that the answer is neither clearly 'true' nor 'false' but may be either depending on the nature of some additional clarification or fact which is absent. There is no way out of such a dilemma and the candidate must nevertheless choose what he or she considers to be the most likely interpretation and answer the question on that basis. As already noted, there is no point in trying to write a note to the examiner explaining the interpretation adopted since it will be ignored. This means that the Examining Committee bears a greater burden than ever in drafting the pre-examination to make sure that the questions are phrased with complete clarity and exactness in all three official languages.

781   The knowledge necessary to answer the legal questions in this paper is essentially that required to tackle Part I of Paper D but at a lower level. It seems that, for example, only Enlarged Board of Appeal case law is being tested. Indeed, most questions can be accurately answered with a knowledge of the Articles and Rules of the EPC and PCT. Furthermore, the issues examined have been for the most part fundamental ones relating to admissible languages, requirements for a filing date, priority rights, search procedure, divisional applications, fees and time limits. These are the areas on which the candidate should therefore clearly concentrate.

782   The exam contains 10 questions on legal topics and 10 questions on claim analysis. Since all the questions are worth the same marks, is makes sense to allocate time evenly throughout the paper. Under the current eEQE format the paper is split into four 70 minute sections each containing 5 questions which helps in allocating time evenly. As noted for other papers, it is important to tackle all questions in order to maximise one's chances of success – the difference here is that an answer can easily be provided even when a lack of time does not permit a consideration of the question by simply guessing. However, unfortunately, if the paper was completed entirely using guesswork, it would statistically only garner some 14 % of the marks in view of the weighted marking schedule (5 marks for all 4 sub-parts correctly answered; 3 marks for three sub-parts correctly answered; 1 mark for 2 sub-parts correctly answered; 0 marks in other cases).

783   Bearing all this in mind, one of the most important considerations in answering the paper is to ensure that for each sub-part of each question, one single answer 'true' or 'false' has been clearly selected. It is certainly worth reserving some time at the end of the exam to check through the answer sheet and make sure this is the case. From this point of view, it is critically important that a soft pencil is used to complete the answer sheet so that any mistakes can be easily and completely erased.

784   The pass mark for the pre-examination has been very high, indicating that the challenges posed by this exam are very much more modest than those posed by the main exam. In the first exam held in 2012 about 40 % of the candidates managed to score over 90 % and several attained a maximum mark.

    As from the 2014 exam, the pass mark has been raised from 50 % to 70 % (see amended r.6(2) IPREQE).

3.2 Worked examples

785   Using the 2012 paper, the following examples show the legal reasoning necessary to answer the kind of legal questions found in the pre-examination.

786   **Question 1:** Bikeparts AS is a Danish company based in Copenhagen. Bikeparts AS validly filed a Japanese patent application JP-X on 11 March 2011 at the Japanese Patent Office in the Japanese language for invention X. Today, 5 March 2012, it is desired to file a European patent application EP-X at the EPO claiming the priority of JP-X for invention X.

For each of the statements 1.1–1.4, indicate on the answer sheet whether the statement is true or false:

1.1 EP-X can be filed in Danish
1.2 EP-X can be filed in Korean
1.3 EP-X can be filed in Japanese
1.4 If EP-X is not filed in one of the official languages of the EPO, then a translation into an official language of the EPO must be filed within a time limit of one month.

Legal reasoning: According to Art. 14(2) EPC, a European patent application may be filed in any language but, if it is not filed in an official language of the EPO, it must be translated into an official language in accordance with the Implementing Regulations. The official languages of the EPO are English, French and German (Art. 14(1) EPC). The time limit for filing the Art. 14(2) translation is two months from the filing of the application (r.6(1) EPC).   787

Answer: 788

1.1 True – a European patent application can be filed in any language including Danish.
1.2 True – a European patent application can be filed in any language including Korean.
1.3 True – a European patent application can be filed in any language including Japanese.
1.4 False – the relevant time limit is two months long.

Comment: Simple question based on knowledge of an important Article and its Implementing Regulation. A perfect question for settling nerves at the start of the examination.

Question 2: Mr X validly filed a German patent application on 06 April 2011. He intends to claim priority of this first application in a later European patent application. For each of the statements 2.1–2.4, indicate on the answer sheet whether the statement is true or false: 789

2.1 Mr X can validly claim priority if he files the European patent application on 10 April 2012.
2.2 The priority declaration must be made at the latest on 10 August 2012.
2.3 If Mr X had filed a German Utility model application instead of a German patent application, it would have been possible to claim priority from the German utility model application.
2.4 Mr X can claim priority from the German patent application even if the German patent application is abandoned before filing of the European patent application.

Legal reasoning: A 12 month period is specified by Art. 87(1) EPC for a priority claim which expires 06 April 2012 (as calculated under Art. 120(b) and r.131(4) EPC). This is Good Friday and the EPO is shut. It opens again for business on Tuesday 10 April 2012. Hence the priority period is extended under r.134(1) EPC until 10 April 2012. According to Art. 88(1) and r.52(2) EPC a declaration of priority may be made at any time until the expiry of 16 months from the earliest priority date, this period expiring on Monday 06 August 2012 (Art. 120(b) and r.131(4) EPC). Priority claims based on patent applications and utility model applications are both recognised according to Art. 87(1) EPC. Once the German patent application has been accorded a filing date it is a valid priority basis according to Art. 87(2) and (3) EPC and its subsequent fate (whether withdrawn, deemed withdrawn, refused or granted) is irrelevant according to Art. 87(3) EPC.   790

Answer: 791

2.1   True – the priority period ends on 10 April 2012.
2.2 False – the period for filing a declaration of priority ends on 06 August 2012.
2.3 True – priority may be claimed from both a patent application and a utility model application.
2.4 True – once it has been accorded a filing date, the subsequent fate of an application has no effect on its status as a valid priority basis.

Comment: Another simple question based on knowledge of an important article and its implementing regulation.

Question 3: Today, 05 March 2012, applicant Z wishes to file a PCT application with the EPO without claiming priority. Applicant Z has filed no other patent application for his invention. For each of the statements 3.1–3.4, indicate on the answer sheet whether the   792

statement is true or false: One of the elements that the EPO as receiving Office has to receive today in order to accord today's date as the filing date for the PCT application is ...
3.1   .. the description.
3.2   .. the abstract.
3.3   .. one or more claims.
3.4   .. the title of the invention.

793   Legal reasoning: According to Art. 11(1) PCT, both a part which appears on the face of
it to be a description and a part which appears on the face of it to be a claim or claims are
necessary for the award of a filing date. An abstract and a title, on the other hand, are not
listed as elements which are essential for the award of a filing date.

794   Answer:
   3.1   True – a part of the application which appears to be a description is necessary for a
          filing date under the PCT.
   3.2   False – an abstract is not necessary for a filing date under the PCT.
   3.3   True – a part of the application which appears to be a claim or claims is necessary for
          a filing date under the PCT.
   3.4   False – a title is not necessary for a filing date under the PCT.

795   Comment: Another simple question based on the knowledge of a key article. The question would have been somewhat ambiguous if the priority of an earlier application had
been claimed since, in this case, an indication under r.4.18 that the incorporation of the
claims and description by reference would be later confirmed could have been filed instead of the claims and description themselves. Happily, the explicit lack of a priority
claim removes this potential ambiguity.

796   **Question 4:** A PCT application was filed with the EPO. As the International Searching
Authority, the EPO considered that the application was not unitary. The invention first
mentioned in the claims was searched and an invitation to pay two additional international search fees was sent to the applicant last week. The third invention, which has not yet
been searched, is the only invention that the applicant would like to pursue in the European phase before the EPO. For each of the statements 4.1–4.4, indicate on the answer sheet
whether the statement is true or false:
   4.1   In the international PCT phase, the applicant can file a protest with the EPO and
          request that a full search is made. The protest is free of charge, but it has to be sup-
          ported by arguments.
   4.2   The applicant can timely pay one additional search fee for the third invention to be
          searched in the international PCT phase. In the European phase, the applicant can
          limit the application to the third invention.
   4.3   The applicant can ignore the invitation. In the European phase, the applicant can file
          a divisional application directed to the third invention.
   4.4   The applicant can ignore the invitation. In the European phase, the applicant will
          again receive an invitation to pay additional search fees.

797   Legal reasoning: When the International Searching Authority considers that the claims
lack unity of invention, it invites the applicant to pay further fees within a one month
period (Art. 17(3)(a) and r.40.1(ii) PCT). The applicant has the option of paying the extra
fees, paying them under protest (r.40.2(c) PCT) or not paying them. The International
Searching Authority establishes a search report based on the first invention made in the
claims and, if any further fees have been paid, on those further parts of the application
to which the fees relate (Art. 17(3)(a) PCT). A protest may be made subject to the payment of a protest fee (r.40.2(e) PCT) and the EPO, when acting as International Searching
Authority, charges such a fee (r.158(3) EPC and Art. 2(1)(21) RRF). If the EPO acted as
International Searching Authority, no supplementary European search report is drawn
up on entry into the European regional phase (Art. 153(7) EPC and Decision of the Administrative Council dated 28 October 2009, [2009] O.J. 594). At the time of the question,
if the EPO as designated Office agreed with the decision on unity of invention that it
took when acting as International Searching Authority then the applicant could only pursue an invention which had been the subject of the International Search Report (r.164(2)
EPC). Naturally, other inventions could be made the subject of one or more divisional

applications (Art. 76(1) EPC). New r.164 in force from 01 November 2014 has completely changed the legal position in relation to this question.

Answer (as of the date of the exam): 798
4.1 False – a protest is not free of charge when the EPO acts as International Searching Authority.
4.2 True – additional search fees may be paid in respect of one or more of the supplementary inventions identified by the International Searching Authority and the search report will be extended accordingly. Any invention which has been the subject of the international search may be prosecuted before the EPO as designated Office.
4.3 True – Payment of additional fees is optional. The applicant always has the possibility of filing divisional applications in the regional phase.
4.4 False – because the EPO acted as International Searching Authority, no supplementary European search report will be drawn up and hence no search fee of any kind is required.

Comment: Another straightforward question based on important and well-known procedure under the PCT and EPC. The ability to have a further search on non-unitary subject matter on entry into the regional phase, when the EPO acts as International Searching Authority, was removed with the coming into force of EPC2000 but was then reintroduced as of 01 November 2014. This is an example of where the answer to a past question changes over time – care should always be taken with model solutions to past questions as a result. 799

Question 5: On 01 February 2010 Document US1 was published. US1 discloses inventive 800 feature A but not inventive feature B. On 01 June 2010 your client filed European patent application EP1 disclosing inventive feature B but not feature A. On 01 June 2011 your client filed European patent application EP2 claiming priority from EP1. EP2 has the following claims: Claim 1 is directed to feature B; claim 2 is directed to the combination of features B and A. EP1 was published in December 2011. The combination of features B and A would be obvious if the skilled person were aware of the disclosures of EP1 and US1. For each of the statements 5.1–5.4, indicate on the answer sheet whether the statement is true or false:
5.1 The subject-matter of claim 2 of EP2 lacks inventive step
5.2 If EP2 had not claimed priority from EP1, the patentability of claim 1 of EP2 would not change.
5.3 A valid novelty objection can be made using EP1 against claim 1 of EP2.
5.4 The subject-matter of claim 2 of EP2 is novel.

Legal reasoning: This question concerns the patentability of the two claims of a Euro- 801 pean patent application EP2. There are two potential items of prior art: (1) Feature A is Art. 54(2) prior art in view of the publication of US1 on 01 February 2010 and is citable for novelty and inventive step; (2) Feature B is potentially Art. 54(3) prior art since it is disclosed in a separate European patent application with an earlier filing date and a later publication date. However, EP2 claims priority from EP1 which complicates the matter. Claim 1 of EP2 is directed to Feature B. This subject matter was disclosed in EP1 and hence the priority claim is valid. Its effective date is therefore 01 June 2010 and only US1 is state of the art. Since US1 only discloses Feature A, claim 1 of EP2 is certainly novel and, since there is no information in the question to the contrary, probably inventive. Claim 2 of EP2 is not entitled to the priority date since feature B was not disclosed in EP1 (Art. 87(1) EPC). Its effective date is therefore 01 June 2011. US1 is therefore prior art under Art. 54(2) but, for the same reasons given in relation to claim 1, this claim is novel and inventive. EP1 is prior art under Art. 54(3) but does not disclose the combination of features A and B and does not therefore destroy the novelty of the claim. Hence claims 1 and 2 are both patentable. If EP2 had not claimed the priority of EP1 then the effective date of claim 1 would have been 01 June 2011 and EP1 would be prior art under Art. 54(3) EPC. Since EP1 discloses Feature B, claim 1 would lack novelty in this scenario.

802   Answer:

5.1   False – only feature A is state of the art and whilst we know the combination of features A and B would be obvious if both were known, there is no information in the question to suggest that the combination is obvious over A alone.

5.2   False – since EP2 claims priority from EP1, the effective date of claim 1 is the filing date of EP1 and the claim is novel. If EP2 did not claim priority from EP1, the effective date of claim 1 would be 01 June 2011 and it would lack novelty over EP1.

5.3   False – The effective date of claim 1 of EP2 is the filing date of EP1 so EP1 cannot be state of the art under Art. 54(2) or Art. 54(3) EPC.

5.4   True – the combination of features A and B is not described in either in US1 or EP1.

803   Comment: This is the first question in this paper with some ambiguity. The candidate must decide whether the combination of Features A and B is obvious over the disclosure of Feature A alone without any information in the question that directly addresses the point. However, prima facie one must consider that bringing two different features together is not obvious. We are also told in the question that the combination of features A and B would be obvious if both were individually known, allowing us to make the inference that the combination would not be obvious if one of them was not known. Coming to the correct decision should therefore have been reasonably straightforward. Otherwise, the question addresses important issues of novelty and priority in a readily comprehensible manner.

804   **Question 6:** A divisional application EP-D was filed on 10 February 2012 with the EPO. The parent application EP-P was filed on 14 December 2010 and was still pending on 10 February 2012. The claims of EP-D contain subject-matter that was not originally disclosed in the parent application. For each of the statements 6.1–6.4, indicate on the answer sheet whether the statement is true or false:

6.1   The subject-matter that is common to EP-D and EP-P is deemed to have the date of filing of 14 December 2010 and the remaining subject-matter of EP-D is deemed to have 10 February 1012 as its date of filing.

6.2   EP-D is deemed to have 10 February 2012 as its date of filing.

6.3   It is mandatory for EP-D to have the same set of claims as EP-P.

6.4   During examination the applicant can amend EP-D so that it does not extend beyond the content of EP-P as originally filed, provided that the amended EP-D does not extend beyond the content of EP-D as originally filed.

805   Legal reasoning: In the present question the divisional EP-D complies with r.36(1) EPC since the parent application was pending when it was filed and it was filed within 14 months of the filing of the parent and therefore certainly within 24 months of the first communication from the Examining Division (note this time limit has now been abolished). According to Art. 76(1) EPC, however, a divisional application may only be filed in respect of subject matter which does not extend beyond the content of the earlier application as filed (i.e. beyond the disclosure of the parent application from which it is divided). If this provision is complied with then the divisional benefits from the filing date of the parent. If it is not complied with then the divisional must be refused. A divisional may not, however, be awarded as a filing date the day on which it was actually filed (G1/05, Reasons 11.1). Neither may different parts of the same application (whether a divisional or otherwise) be awarded different filing dates (G1/05, Reasons 11.1). Compliance with Art. 76(1) is a requirement with which the divisional must comply in order to be granted; it is not a requirement which the divisional as filed must comply with and the divisional may be amended later in order to achieve compliance (G1/05, Reasons 7). There is no requirement for a divisional application to have the same set of claims as the parent; within the limits set by Art. 76(1) EPC, the divisional application may claim any subject matter disclosed in the earlier application from which it is divided.

806   Answer:

6.1   False – a divisional application may only be awarded the filing date of the parent from which it is divided.

6.2   False – EP-D contains subject matter which extends beyond the content of the earlier application and may only be awarded the filing date of EP-P when this subject matter is removed.

6.3 False – a divisional application may claim any subject matter disclosed in the earlier application.

6.4 True – a divisional may be amended in order to achieve compliance with Art. 76(1) EPC but the requirements of the EPC relating to amendment, including Art. 123(2) EPC, must be respected.

Comment: A straightforward question requiring knowledge of an important article and an important decision of the Enlarged Board of Appeal which provides an interpretation of that article. Note that the time limit of r.36(1) EPC was abolished as of 01 April 2014.

Question 7: A European patent application is filed today, 05 March 2012. It contains 1 abstract page, 28 description pages, 5 drawing pages and 4 claims pages. The application has 19 claims. Three of the 19 claims are independent claims. The applicant wishes to proceed with all claims. For each of the statements 7.1–7.4, indicate on the answer sheet whether the statement is true or false:

7.1 Claims fees are due for 3 claims only.
7.2 If the application is filed online, no additional fee for pages has to be paid.
7.3 If the application is filed by post, the additional fee for three pages has to be paid.
7.4 If no claims fees are paid, the application will be deemed withdrawn.

Legal reasoning: According to r.45(1) EPC, a claims fee is due for the 16th and each subsequent claim in an application. If a claims fee is not paid in time, there is a grace period for late payment (r.45(2) EPC). If a claims fee not paid within the grace period, then the claim for which it was due is deemed abandoned (r.45(3) EPC). According to Art. 78(2) EPC, a filing fee is due on filing a European patent application. This fee comprises a fixed element and a variable page-related fee which is payable for the 36th and each subsequent page in the application. Both these elements are to be paid regardless of how the application is filed, though the fixed element is reduced if the application is filed online (Art. 2(1) (1) RRF).

Answer:
7.1 False – in this case four claims fees are due.
7.2 False – three page fees are due regardless of how the application is filed.
7.3 True – three page fees are due regardless of how the application is filed.
7.4 False – if no claims fees are paid then claims 16–19 will be deemed withdrawn.

Comment: A straightforward question concerning important fees due on filing.

Question 8: The publication of the mention of the grant of a European patent was made on 22 June 2011. The European patent includes independent claim 1 directed to a product and independent claim 2 directed to a process. The two claims are not linked by a single general inventive concept. Your client wants the opposition division to revoke the patent in its entirety but so far he has found state of the art that anticipates the subject-matter of product claim 1 only. For each of the statements 8.1–8.4, indicate on the answer sheet whether the statement is true or false:

8.1 A notice of opposition must be filed at the latest by 22 March 2012.
8.2 If an opposition is filed against claim 1 only, the opposition can be extended by the opponent to claim 2 after the expiry of the opposition period.
8.3 The statement setting out the grounds for opposition must be filed at the latest by 22 May 2012.
8.4 As claims 1 and 2 are not linked by a single general inventive concept, lack of unity of invention is a valid ground for opposition.

Legal reasoning: According to Art. 99(1), an opposition must be filed within nine months of the publication of the mention of the grant of a European patent in the European Patent Bulletin which, in this case, expires Thursday 22 March 2012 (Art. 120(b) and r.131(4) EPC). An opposition must be filed as a written, reasoned statement including a statement of the extent to which the European patent is opposed and of the grounds on which the opposition is based, as well as an indication of the facts and evidence that support these grounds (Art. 99(1) and r.76(1) and 2(c) EPC). Once the opposition period has expired, the opposition may not be extended to cover any independent claim which was not

originally attacked (G9/91). The grounds on which an opposition may be based are specified in Art. 100 EPC and do not include lack of unity of invention (confirmed by G1/91).

812   Answer:
      8.1   True – the opposition period expires, in this case, on 22 March 2012.
      8.2   False – an opposition may not be extended to cover an independent claim which was
            not opposed during the opposition period.
      8.3   False – an opposition must be substantiated during the opposition period which
            expires 22 March 2012.
      8.4   False – lack of unity of invention is not a ground of opposition.

      Comment: A straightforward question based on important aspects of opposition proce-
      dure established by the articles, rules and Enlarged Board of Appeal case law relating to
      opposition.

813   **Question 9:** Your British client buys a French company with all its assets including and
      international application PCT1 directed to a first invention and a French application FR2
      directed to a second invention. Both applications are in the French language. PCT1 was
      filed in December 2009 and FR2 was filed in April 2011. Neither application claims an
      earlier priority. Your client wants to pursue both inventions as European patent applica-
      tions, by entering the European phase with PCT1 and by filing a European application
      EP-FR claiming the priority from FR2. However, he would prefer that the language of the
      European proceedings of both applications be English. For each of the statements 9.1–9.4,
      indicate on the answer sheet whether the statement is true or false:
      9.1   Upon entry of PCT1 into the European phase before the EPO, your client can file
            a translation of PCT1 into English, and English will become the language of the
            proceedings.
      9.2   A European patent application validly claiming priority from FR2 can be filed in
            English.
      9.3   Today, on 05 March 2012, it is no longer possible to validly claim priority from FR2
            for a European patent application.
      9.4   The applicant can file EP-FR in French and then validly file a European divisional
            application of EP-FR in English.

814   Legal reasoning: The official languages of the EPO are English, French and German
      (Art. 14(1) EPC) and proceedings in relation to a European patent application are primar-
      ily conducted in one of these languages (Art. 14(3) EPC – language of the proceedings). A
      European patent application must therefore either be filed in one of these languages or, if
      filed in a different language, be translated into one of them within two months of the filing
      date (Art. 14(2) and r.6(1) EPC). Whether priority is claimed or not has no bearing on this.
      In the case of a divisional application, this must be filed in (or translated into) the lan-
      guage of the proceedings of the parent application (Art. 76(1) and r.36(2) EPC) – it is not
      possible to use an official language of the EPO different to that of the parent. In the case
      of a Euro-PCT application which is published in a language which is not an official lan-
      guage of the EPO, a translation into English, French or German must be supplied to the
      EPO within 31 months of the priority date for the regional phase to proceed (Art. 153(4)
      and r.159(1)(a) EPC). Where the Euro-PCT application has been published in an official
      language of the EPO, on the other hand, no translation is required and, furthermore, it is
      not possible to change the language of the proceedings by filing one (G4/08). The priority
      period for FR2 will expire sometime in April 2012 (Art. 87(1), Art. 120(b) and r.131(4)
      EPC).

815   Answer:
      9.1   False – since PCT1 was published in an official language of the EPO, no translation
            is required and none may be filed in order to change the language of the proceedings.
      9.2   True – a European patent application may be filed in any language regardless of
            whether it claims priority or not.
      9.3   False – the priority period does not expire until sometime in April 2012 and must
            therefore still be pending on 05 March 2012.
      9.4   False – a divisional application must be filed in, or translated into, the language of the
            proceedings for the parent application.

Comment: A straightforward question requiring a knowledge of the articles and rules 816 relating to filing languages for European, European divisional and Euro-PCT applications along with a decision of the Enlarged Board of Appeal interpreting one of these provisions.

Question 10: The applicant did not respond to a communication issued by the examining 817 division setting a two month time limit for bringing the description into conformity with the amended claims. The EPO issued a notice of loss of rights by registered mail dated 23 November 2011. On Saturday 4 February 2012 the applicant discovered the notice of loss of rights in an unrelated file. For each of the statements 10.1–10.4, indicate on the answer sheet whether the statement is true or false:

10.1 The time limit for requesting further processing expired on 03 February 2012.

10.2 The time limit for requesting re-establishment of rights expires on 06 April 2012.

10.3 For requesting further processing of a European patent application following failure to observe a time limit, the applicant must have taken all due care required by the circumstances to observe the time limit.

10.4 To save the application, it is sufficient to timely:

– file at the EPO a request for re-establishment of rights in respect of the time limit for requesting further processing;

– pay the fees for re-establishment of rights and for further processing; and

– demonstrate that all due care required by the circumstances to observe the time limit was taken.

Legal reasoning: Further processing must be requested within two months of notification 818 of loss of rights (Art. 121(2) and r.135(1) EPC). This period expires, in the present case, on Friday 03 February 2012 (Art. 120(b), r.126(2), and r.131(4) EPC). Further processing is requested by paying the further processing fee and requires the completion of the omitted act (Art. 121(2) and r.135(1) EPC) – there is no requirement to show that any care was taken. If the further processing deadline is missed despite all due care required by the circumstances having been taken then re-establishment is possible (Art. 122(1) EPC). The time limit for requesting re-establishment is the earlier of two months from the removal of the cause of non-compliance with the further processing deadline and one year from the expiry of the further processing deadline (Art. 122(2) and r.136(1) EPC). In the present case, the removal of the cause of non-compliance was Saturday 04 February 2012 such that the two month period ends on Wednesday 04 April 2012 (Art. 120(b) and r.131(4) EPC). The one year period ends on Sunday 03 February 2013 extended to Monday 04 February 2013 (Art. 120(b), r.131(3) and r.134(1) EPC). The re-establishment deadline is therefore Wednesday 04 April 2012. In order to request re-establishment, it is necessary to file a request in writing, pay the fee, state the grounds and facts on which it is based and complete the omitted act (Art. 122(2), r.136(1) and r.136(2) EPC). In the present case, completing the omitted act means filing a valid request for further processing which necessitates paying the further processing fee and filing an amended description (Art. 121(2) and r.135(1) EPC).

Answer: 819

10.1 True – the further processing time limit did expire on 03 February 2012.

10.2 False – the re-establishment time limit expires on 04 April 2012.

10.3 False – there is no requirement to show that all due care required by the circumstances was taken in order to request further processing – this requirement applies to re-establishment.

10.4 False – one additional requirement must be met which is the filing of an amended description.

Comment: This is a straightforward question requiring a knowledge of the articles and rules relating to further processing and re-establishment.

PART B - THE EPC

Chapter 4: The EPC and EPO

4.1   European patents

Preamble	The Contracting States,	820

DESIRING to strengthen co-operation between the States of Europe in respect of the protection of inventions,

DESIRING that such protection may be obtained in those States by a single procedure for the grant of patents and by the establishment of certain standard rules governing patents so granted,

DESIRING, for this purpose, to conclude a Convention which establishes a European Patent Organisation and which constitutes a special agreement within the meaning of Article 19 of the Convention for the Protection of Industrial Property, signed in Paris on 20 March 1883 and last revised on 14 July 1967, and a regional patent treaty within the meaning of Article 45, paragraph 1, of the Patent Cooperation Treaty of 19 June 1970, HAVE AGREED on the following provisions.

PC Art. 19 The countries of the Union (as established by the Paris Convention) have the right to make separately between themselves special agreements for the protection of industrial property, as long as these agreements do not contravene the provisions of the Paris Convention.

PCT Art. 45(1) Any treaty providing for the grant of regional patents ("regional patent treaty"), and giving to all persons who, according to Art. 9, are entitled to file international applications the right to file applications for such patents, may provide that international applications designating or electing a party to both the regional patent treaty and the present Treaty may be filed as applications for such patents.

Art. 1 The EPC establishes a system of law, common to the Contracting States, for the grant of patents for invention.

Art. 2(1) Patents granted by virtue of the EPC are called European Patents.

4.2   The European Patent Organisation

4.2.1   *Foundation of the Organisation*

Art. 4(1) The EPC establishes a European Patent Organisation, referred to in the EPC as the Organisation. It has administrative and financial autonomy. — 821

4.2.2   *Structure of the Organisation*

Art. 4(2) The two organs of the Organisation are: 822
(a) the European Patent Office; and
(b) the Administrative Council.

Art. 5(1)(3) The Organisation has legal personality and is represented by the President of the European Patent Office.

Art. 6(1) The Organisation has its seat in Munich.

4.2.3   *Purpose of the Organisation*

Art. 4(3) The task of the Organisation is to grant European Patents. This is carried out by the European Patent Office, supervised by the Administrative Council.   823

4.3   The European Patent Office and its employees

4.3.1   *Location of the European Patent Office and its sub-offices*

Art. 6(2) The European Patent Office is based in Munich and has a branch at The Hague.   824

Art. 7 By decision of the Administrative Council, sub-offices of the European Patent Office may be created if need be, for the purpose of information and liaison, in the Contracting States and with intergovernmental organisations in the field of intellectual property, subject to the approval of the Contracting State or organisation concerned.

PonC Art. 3(a)(b)	A sub-office of the EPO, under the direction of The Hague, is located in Berlin, its duties being determined by the Administrative Council.
OJ	The Berlin sub-office is a filing office within the meaning of Art. 75(1)(a) EPC (Decision of the President dated 03 January 2017, [2017], A11, Art. 1(1)).
OJ	A sub-office in Vienna was set up in 1991 ([1990] O.J. 492). This is not a filing office within the meaning of Art. 75(1)(a) and patent applications filed there are forwarded to one of the filing offices. The filing date in this case is the date of receipt by the filing office (Decision of the President dated 03 January 2017, [2017] O.J. A11, 1(2)).
G2/19	Headnote (2): "The holding of oral proceedings before the Boards of Appeal in Haar is not contrary to Art. 113(1) and Art. 116(1) EPC."

4.3.2   President of the European Patent Office and his duties

825	Art. 10(1)	The European Patent Office is managed by the President who is responsible for its activities to the Administrative Council.
	Art. 10(2)	To this end, the President has, in particular, the following functions and powers: (a) he must take all necessary steps, including the adoption of internal administrative instructions and the publication of guidance for the public, to ensure the functioning of the European Patent Office; (b) unless the EPC provides otherwise, he must prescribe which acts are to be performed at the European Patent Office in Munich and its branch at The Hague respectively; (c) he may place before the Administrative Council any proposal for amending the EPC and any proposal for general regulations or decisions which come within the competence of the Administrative Council; (d) he must prepare and implement the budget and any amending or supplementary budget; (e) he must submit a management report to the Administrative Council each year; (f) he must exercise supervisory authority over EPO staff; (g) subject to Art. 11, he must appoint and promote EPO employees; (h) he must exercise disciplinary authority over the employees other than those referred to in Art. 11, and may propose disciplinary action to the Administrative Council with regard to employees referred to in Art. 11, paragraphs as 2 and 3; and (i) he may delegate his functions and powers.
	Comment	The Guidelines for Examination are adopted by the President exercising his power under Art. 10(2)(a).
	Art. 10(3)	The President is assisted by a number of Vice-Presidents. If the President is absent or indisposed, one of the Vice-Presidents takes his place in accordance with the procedure laid down by the Administrative Council.

4.3.3   Appointment of senior EPO employees

826	Art. 11(1)	The President of the European Patent Office is appointed by the Administrative Council.
	Art. 11(2)	The Vice-Presidents are appointed by the Administrative Council after the President has been consulted.
	Art. 11(3)	The members, including the Chairmen, of the Boards of Appeal and of the Enlarged Board of Appeal, are appointed by the Administrative Council, on a proposal from the President of the European Patent Office. They may be reappointed by the Administrative Council after the President of the European Patent Office has been consulted.
	Art. 11(4)	The Administrative Council exercises disciplinary authority over the employees referred to in Art. 11(1) to (3).

4.3.4   Employees not to disclose or make use of confidential information

827	Art. 12	The employees of the European Patent Office are bound, even after the termination of their employment, neither to disclose nor to make use of information which by its nature is a professional secret.

4.3.5   *Disputes between the Organisation and the employees of the European Patent Office*

Art. 13(1) Employees and former employees of the European Patent Office or their successors in ti-   828
tle may apply to the Administrative Tribunal of the International Labour Organisation in
the case of disputes with the European Patent Organisation in accordance with the Statute
of the Tribunal and within the limits and subject to the conditions laid down in the Service
Regulations for permanent employees or the Pension Scheme Regulations or arising from
the conditions of employment of other employees.

Art. 13(2) An appeal is only admissible if the person concerned has exhausted such other means of
appeal as are available to him under the Service Regulations, the Pension Scheme Regulations or the conditions of employment.

4.4   The departments of the European Patent Office

4.4.1   *The departments entrusted with the procedure*

Art. 15   For implementing the procedures laid down in the EPC, the European Patent Office   829
comprises:
(a) a Receiving Section;
(b) Search Divisions;
(c) Examining Divisions;
(d) Opposition Divisions;
(e) a Legal Division;
(f) Boards of Appeal; and
(g) an Enlarged Board of Appeal.

4.4.2   *Administrative structure of the EPO*

r.9(1)   The EPO is divided administratively into Directorates-General, to which the departments   830
set out in Art. 15(a) to (e), and the services set up to deal with legal matters and the internal
administration of the Office, are assigned.

Comment   The Boards of Appeal and Enlarged Board of Appeal are organised separately in a Board
of Appeal Unit headed by its own president in order to ensure their independence – see
section 4.10.2 below.

r.9(2)   Each Directorate-General is directed by a Vice-President. The assignment of a Vice-President to a Directorate-General is decided upon by the Administrative Council, after the
President of the EPO has been consulted.

Comment   As currently configured, Directorate General 1 (DG1, Patent Granting Process) includes
the Receiving Section, Search Divisions, Examining Divisions, and Opposition Divisions.
Directorate General 2 (DG2, Corporate Services) comprises various administrative staff
including human resources, finance and procurement. Directorate General 3 (DG3, Legal
and International Affairs) comprises, amongst other things, the Legal Division.

r.11(1)   Technically qualified examiners acting as members of the Search, Examining or Opposition Divisions are assigned to Directorates. The President of the EPO allocates duties to
these Directorates by reference to the international classification.

4.5   The Receiving Section

Art. 16   The Receiving Section is responsible for the examination on filing and the examination as   831
to formal requirements of European patent applications.

r.10(1)   The Receiving Section is responsible for the examination on filing and the examination as
to formal requirements of a European patent application up to the time when the Examining Division becomes responsible for the examination of the European patent application
under Art. 94(1).

r.11(2)   The President of the EPO may also allocate further duties to the Receiving Section.

4.6   The Search Divisions

Art. 17   The Search Divisions are responsible for drawing up European search reports.   832
r.11(2)   The President of the EPO may also allocate further duties to the Search Divisions.

r.11(3)	The President of the EPO may entrust to employees who are not technically or legally qualified examiners the execution of duties falling to the Search Divisions and involving no technical or legal difficulties.
OJ	See Decision of the President dated 12 December 2013 ([2014] O.J. A6) and Decision of the President dated 23 November 2015 ([2015] O.J. A104).
Guidelines	See B-I,2. A Search Division normally consists of one examiner who will usually become the first examiner in the Examining Division. In some cases, however, where an application spans different technical fields, the Search Division may be expanded to 2 or 3 examiners.

4.7   The Examining Divisions

833	Art. 18(1) r.10(2)	An Examining Division is responsible for the examination of European patent applications. Subject to r.10(3) and (4), the Examining Division is responsible for the examination of a European patent application under Art. 94(1), from the time when a request for examination is filed.
	r.10(3)	If a request for examination is filed before the European Search Report has been transmitted to the applicant, the Examining Division will, subject to r.10(4), be responsible from the time when the EPO receives the indication under r.70(2) (that the applicant wishes to proceed further).
	r.10(4)	If a request for examination is filed before the European Search Report has been transmitted to the applicant, and if the applicant has waived the right under r.70(2), the Examining Division will be responsible from the time when the search report is transmitted to the applicant.
	Guidelines	See A-VI, 2.4 and C-II, 1. The contents of the dossier which is transferred from the Receiving Section to the Examining Division is specified.
	Art. 18(2)	An Examining Division consists of three technically qualified examiners. However, before a decision is taken on a European patent application, its examination is, as a general rule, entrusted to one member of the Examining Division. Oral proceedings are before the Examining Division itself. If the Examining Division considers that the nature of the decision so requires, it is enlarged by the addition of a legally qualified examiner. In the event of parity of votes, the vote of the Chairman of the Division is decisive.
	Guidelines	See C-VIII
	Art. 33(3)	The Administrative Council is competent to decide that one examiner is enough in certain cases, though it has not yet done so.
	T714/92	If a decision is not signed by the correct members of the Examining Division it must be set aside and a substantial procedural violation has occurred.
	T1088/11	A decision to enlarge the Division must be taken by the original 3-member panel. It is possible, in principle, for the Division to be reduced in size back to its original composition but a decision to this effect must be taken by the expanded 4-membered Division as a whole. If it is not clear from the public file that this decision to return to a three-membered panel was taken correctly then a substantial procedural violation has occurred. See also Guidelines C-VIII, 7.
	G5/91	Headnote (1): Although Art. 24 EPC applies only to members of the Boards of Appeal and of the Enlarged Board of Appeal, the requirement of impartiality applies in principle also to employees of the departments of first instance of the EPO taking part in decision making activities affecting the rights of any party.
	Comment	So, the decision of an Examining Division or Opposition Division can be appealed on the basis of lack of impartiality. Article 125, which requires that the EPO takes into account the principles of procedural law generally recognised in the Contracting States, provides a legal basis for this decision. If a Board of Appeal finds that there was a lack of impartiality a substantial procedural violation has occurred and the decision at first instance is void.
	Guidelines	See E-XI. A lack of impartiality can occur for subjective reasons (member of the division has a personal interest in the case) or objective reasons (party has good reasons to suspect partiality). An objection must be made as soon as possible and must be substantiated. Any substantiated objection is decided on by the immediate superior of the members of the division and the relevant member is either replaced or else reasons are provided with the final decision as to why the objection was not upheld. Such reasoning may then be appealed along with the decision itself.

r.11(2)	The President of the EPO may also allocate further duties to the Examining Divisions.
r.11(3)	The President of the EPO may entrust to employees who are not technically or legally qualified examiners the execution of duties falling to the Examining Divisions and involving no technical or legal difficulties.
OJ	See Decision of the President dated 12 December 2013 ([2014] O.J. A6), Decision of the President dated 23 November 2015 ([2015] O.J. A104) and Decision of the President dated 14 June 2020 ([2020] O.J. A80).

4.8 The Opposition Divisions

Art. 19(1)	An Opposition Division is responsible for the examination of oppositions against any European patent.	834
Art. 19(2)	An Opposition Division consists of three technically qualified examiners, at least two of whom must not have taken part in the proceedings for grant of the patent to which the opposition relates. An examiner who has taken part in the proceedings for the grant of the European patent cannot be the chairman. Prior to the taking of a final decision on the opposition, the Opposition Division may entrust the examination of the opposition to one of its members. Oral proceedings are before the Opposition Division itself. If the Opposition Division considers that the nature of the decision so requires, it is enlarged by the addition of a legally qualified examiner who must not have taken part in the proceedings for grant of the patent. In the event of parity of votes, the vote of the Chairman of the Division is decisive.	
Comment	According to current EPO policy it is preferable that none of the members of the opposition division should have taken part in grant proceedings.	
Case law	See T390/86, T243/87 and related cases in the Case Law book. Where the composition of an Opposition Division is wrong, any decision taken is void ab initio and a substantial procedural violation has occurred.	
T1088/11	A decision to enlarge the Division must be taken by the original 3-member panel. It is possible, in principle, for the Division to be reduced in size back to its original composition but a decision to this effect must be taken by the expanded 4-membered Division as a whole. If it is not clear from the public file that this decision to return to a three-membered panel was taken correctly then a substantial procedural violation has occurred.	
G5/91	Headnote (1): Although Art. 24 EPC applies only to members of the Boards of Appeal and of the Enlarged Board of Appeal, the requirement of impartiality applies in principle also to employees of the departments of first instance of the EPO taking part in decision making activities affecting the rights of any party.	
Comment	See comment and Guidelines reference above under Section 4.7.	
r.11(2)	The President of the EPO may also allocate further duties to the Opposition Divisions.	
r.11(3)	The President of the EPO may entrust to employees who are not technically or legally qualified examiners the execution of duties falling to the Opposition Divisions and involving no technical or legal difficulties.	
OJ	See Decision of the President dated 12 December 2013 ([2014] O.J. A6), Decision of the President dated 23 November 2015 ([2015] O.J. A104) and Decision of the President dated 14 June 2020 ([2020] O.J. A80).	
G1/02	Headnote: Points 4 and 6 of the Notice from the Vice-President Directorate-General 2 dated April 28, 1999 ([1999] O.J. 506) do not conflict with provisions of a higher level.	
Comment	This decision overruled T295/01, which had suggested that formalities officers could never decide on the admissibility of an opposition, only the Opposition Division being competent.	
Guidelines	See D-II	

4.9 The Legal Division

Art. 20(1)	The Legal Division is responsible for decisions in respect of entries in the Register of European Patents and in respect of registration on, and deletion from, the list of professional representatives.	835
Art. 20(2)	Decisions of the Legal Division are taken by one legally qualified member.	
r.11(2)	The President of the EPO may also allocate further duties to the Legal Division.	

OJ	The Legal Division has sole responsibility for various entries and deletions in the European Patent Register (procedure where the applicant or proprietor is not entitled, interruption and resumption of proceedings, registration and cancellation of licenses and other rights, registration of transfers and changes of name, rectification of the designation of an inventor) and the Register of Representatives (professional representatives, associations, legal practitioners, general authorisations). See Decision of the President dated 21 November 2013, [2013] O.J. 600.
OJ	In his role under Art. 10(2)(a) to ensure proper functioning of the EPO, the President has decided (decision of 21 November 2013) that some duties of the Legal Division can be entrusted to formalities officers, e.g. registration of transfers that can be granted directly. Any decision, however, must be taken by the Legal Division.
OJ	See Decision of the President dated 20 May 2022 ([2022] O.J. A69) – members of the Legal Division carry out the tasks entrusted to the EPO concerning unitary patents.

4.10   The Boards of Appeal and the Enlarged Board of Appeal

4.10.1   Composition of the Board of Appeal

836	Art. 21(1)	The Boards of Appeal are responsible for the examination of appeals from the decisions of the Receiving Section, Examining Divisions, Opposition Divisions and Legal Division.
	Art. 21(2)	For appeals from a decision of the Receiving Section or the Legal Division, a Board of Appeal consists of three legally qualified members.
	Art. 21(3)	For appeals from a decision of an Examining Division, a Board of Appeal consists of: (a) two technically qualified members and one legally qualified member, when the decision concerns the refusal of a European patent application or the grant, limitation or revocation of a European patent and was taken by an Examining Division consisting of less than four members; (b) three technically qualified members and two legally qualified members, when the decision was taken by an Examining Division consisting of four members or when the Board of Appeal considers that the nature of the appeal so requires (e.g. where there are mixed technologies or difficult legal or technical issues arise); or (c) three legally qualified members in all other cases.
	Comment	(a) and (b) are known as Technical Boards of Appeal (whose decisions are listed under the letter "T") whereas (c) is known as the Legal Board of Appeal (whose decisions are listed under the letter "J").
	Art. 21(4)	For appeals from a decision of an Opposition Division, a Board of Appeal consists of: (a) two technically qualified members and one legally qualified member, when the decision was taken by an Opposition Division consisting of three members; (b) three technically qualified members and two legally qualified members, when the decision was taken by an Opposition Division consisting of four members or when the Board of Appeal considers that the nature of the appeal so requires (e.g. where there are mixed technologies or difficult legal or technical issues arise).
	RPBA Art. 9	If a Board of Appeal consisting of two technically qualified members and one legally qualified member considers that the nature of the appeal requires that the Board should consist of three technically qualified members and two legally qualified members, the decision to enlarge the Board shall be taken at the earliest possible stage in the examination of that appeal.
	G2/90	Headnote (1): Under Art. 21(3)(c) EPC, the Legal Board of Appeal is competent only to hear appeals against decisions taken by an Examining Division consisting of fewer than four members when the decision does not concern the refusal of a European patent application or the grant of a European patent. In all other cases, i.e. those covered by Art. 21(3) (a), 3(b) and (4) EPC, the Technical Board of Appeal is competent. Headnote (2): The provisions relating to competence in Art. 21(3) and (4) EPC are not affected by r.9(3) EPC (i.e. whether the decision is delegated to a formalities officer or not).
	Comment	Note that r.9(3) has been renumbered as r.11(3) under EPC2000. The Enlarged Board felt that since only duties involving no legal difficulties could be entrusted to a formalities officer, an appeal from such a decision should rightly be entrusted to the Technical Board of Appeal and no special considerations applied to change the normal operation of Art. 21(3) and (4) concerning which appeals are allocated to which Board.

G8/95	Headnote: An appeal from a decision of an Examining Division refusing a request under r.89 EPC for correction of the decision to grant is to be decided by a Technical Board of Appeal.
Comment	An appeal against a decision to refuse correction of a decision to grant was seen to "concern the grant of the patent" in contrast, for instance, to a decision to refuse a correction of a designation under r.88. Whether or not the decision terminates proceedings was seen to be key. Note that r.88 and r.89 have been renumbered as r.139 and r.140 EPC2000.
G1/11	Headnote: For the examination of an appeal against a decision of the Examining Division to not refund search fees under Rule 64(2) EPC, which has not been adopted together with a decision on the grant of a European patent or the refusal of a European patent application, a Technical Board of Appeal is competent.
r.12(6)	The Administrative Council may allocate duties under Art. 134a(1)(c) to the Boards of Appeal (concerning disciplinary power of the European Patent Institute or European Patent Office over professional representatives).
RPBA Art. 8(1)	If the composition of a Board is changed after oral proceedings, the parties shall be informed that, at the request of any party, fresh oral proceedings shall be held before the Board in its new composition. Fresh oral proceedings shall also be held if so requested by the new member and if the other members of the Board in the particular appeal have given their agreement.
RPBA Art. 8(2)	Each new member shall be bound to the same extent as the other members by an interlocutory decision which has already been taken.
RPBA Art. 8(3)	A member who is unable to act after the Board has already reached a decision on the appeal shall not be replaced. If the Chair in a particular appeal is unable to act, the member of the Board having the longer or longest service on the Boards of Appeal or, in the case where members have the same length of service, the elder or eldest member, shall sign the decision on behalf of the Chair.

4.10.2   Organisation of the Boards of Appeal

r.12a(1)	The Boards of Appeal and the Enlarged Board of Appeal, including their registries and support services, shall be organised as a separate unit (the "Boards of Appeal Unit") and be directed by the President of the Boards of Appeal. The Chairman of the Enlarged Board of Appeal shall act as President of the Boards of Appeal. The President of the Boards of Appeal shall be appointed by the Administrative Council on a joint proposal made by Committee established under r.12c(1) and the President of the EPO. If the President of the Boards of Appeal is absent or indisposed, one of the members of the Enlarged Board of Appeal shall take his place in accordance with the procedure laid down by the Administrative Council.
r.12a(2)	The President of the Boards of Appeal shall manage the Boards of Appeal Unit and, to this end, have the functions and powers delegated to him by the President of the EPO. In exercising the delegated functions and powers, the President of the Boards of Appeal shall be responsible solely to the Administrative Council and shall be subject to its hierarchical and disciplinary authority.
r.12a(3)(4)	Further provisions specify the preparation of a budget and the provision of services.
r.12b	An autonomous authority exists within the Boards of Appeal Unit called the Presidium of the Boards of Appeal which consists of the President of the Boards of Appeal, who acts as chairman, and twelve members of the Boards of Appeal, six being Chairmen and six being other members. The Presidium adopts a code of conduct for members of the Boards of Appeal, advises on amendments to the Rules of Procedure of the Boards of Appeal and Enlarged Board of Appeal and advises the President of the Boards of Appeal on matters in general.
RPBA Art. 6	The Presidium delegates tasks involving no legal or technical difficulties to Registrars (e.g. inspection of files, issuance of summons to oral proceedings, further processing requests). A Registrar conducts a preliminary examination of admissibility and reports to the Chairman.
r.12c	A committee within the Administrative Council called the Boards of Appeal Committee advises the Administrative Council and the President of the Boards of Appeal on matters concerning the Boards of Appeal Unit and adopts the Rules of Procedure of the Boards of Appeal and the Enlarged Board of Appeal.

837

r.12d	The President of the Boards of Appeal proposes the membership of the Boards of Appeal and Enlarged Board of Appeal for appointment and reappointment by the Administrative Council.
OJ	See OJ [2018] A63. The President of the EPO has delegated some of his functions and powers under Art. 10(2), Art. 11(3) and (5) and Art. 48(1) EPC to the President of the Boards of Appeal in so far as they relate to the Boards of Appeal and its staff.

4.10.3   Enlarged Board of Appeal

838	Art. 22(1)	The Enlarged Board of Appeal is responsible for: (a) deciding points of law referred to it by Boards of Appeal pursuant to Art. 112; (b) giving opinions on points of law referred to it by the President of the European Patent Office under the conditions laid down in Art. 112; and (c) deciding on petitions for review of decision of the Boards of Appeal under Art. 112a.
	Art. 22(2)	For giving decisions or opinions under Art. 22(1)(a) and (b), the Enlarged Board of Appeal consists of five legally qualified members and two technically qualified members. In proceedings under Art. 22(1)(c), the Enlarged Board of Appeal consists of three or five members as laid down in the Implementing Regulations. In all proceedings, a legally qualified member is the Chairman.
	r.13	Before the beginning of each working year, the members of the Enlarged Board of Appeal appointed under Art. 11(3) designate the regular and alternate members of the Enlarged Board of Appeal in proceedings under Art. 22(1)(a) and (b) and the regular and alternate members of the Enlarged Board of Appeal under Art. 22(1)(c). Decisions may only be taken if at least five members are present, including the Chairman of the Enlarged Board of Appeal or his deputy; in the event of parity of votes the Chairman or his deputy has the casting vote. Abstentions are not considered as votes.
	Art. 11(5)	The Administrative Council, after consulting the President of the EPO, may also appoint as members of the Enlarged Board of Appeal legally qualified members of the national courts or quasi-judicial authorities of the Contracting States, who may continue their judicial activities at the national level. They are appointed for a term of three years and may be reappointed.

4.10.4   Independence and exclusion of Board of Appeal members

839	Art. 23(1)	The members of the Enlarged Board of Appeal and of the Boards of Appeal are appointed for a term of five years and may not be removed from office during this term, except if there are serious grounds for such removal and if the Administrative Council, on a proposal from the Enlarged Board of Appeal, takes a decision to this effect. Nevertheless, the term of office of members of the Boards ends if they resign or are retired in accordance with the service regulations for permanent employees of the EPO.
	Art. 23(2)	The members of the Boards may not be members of the Receiving Section, Examining Divisions, Opposition Divisions or of the Legal Division.
	Art. 23(3)	In their decisions the members of the Boards are not bound by any instructions and comply only with the provisions of the Convention.

4.10.5   Adoption of Rules of Procedure by the Boards of Appeal and the Enlarged Board

840	Art. 23(4)	The Rules of Procedure of the Boards of Appeal and the Enlarged Board of Appeal are adopted in accordance with the provisions of the Implementing Regulations. They are subject to the approval of the Administrative Council.
	r.12c(2)	The Rules of Procedure of the Boards of Appeal and the Enlarged Board of Appeal are adopted by the Boards of Appeal Committee of the Administrative Council based on a proposal from the President of the Boards of Appeal.
	OJ	See Decision of the Administrative Council dated 25 March 2015 ([2015] O.J. A35) for the current version of the Rules of Procedure of the Enlarged Board of Appeal. See Decision of the Administrative Council dated 26 June 2019 ([2019] O.J. A63) for the current version of the Rules of Procedure of the Boards of Appeal.
	G6/95	The Rules of Procedure of the Boards of Appeal have higher status than the Implementing Regulations in cases of conflict.

RPBA Art. 23	The Rules of Procedure are binding upon the Boards of Appeal, provided that they do not lead to a situation which would be incompatible with the spirit and purpose of the Convention.

4.10.6 Exclusion and objection

Art. 24(1)	Members of the Boards of Appeal or of the Enlarged Board of Appeal may not take part in a case if they have any personal interest, or if they have previously been involved as representatives of one of the parties, or if they participated in the decision under appeal.	841
Art. 24(2)	If, for one of the reasons mentioned in Art. 24(1), or for any other reason, a member of a Board of Appeal or of the Enlarged Board of Appeal considers that he should not take part in any appeal, he must inform the Board accordingly.	
Art. 24(3)	Members of a Board of Appeal or of the Enlarged Board of Appeal may be objected to by any party for one of the reasons mentioned in Art. 24(1), or if suspected of partiality. An objection is not admissible if, while being aware of a reason for objection, the party has taken a procedural step. No objection may be based upon the nationality of members.	
T1028/96	If a member of the Board of Appeal in a particular case has already given a decision in that same case on substantially the same issue, that member's impartiality may be challenged (e.g. in opposition appeal where the same issue was the subject of appeal during examination).	
RPBA Art. 3	Another member of the Board may also object to a fellow member.	
Art. 24(4)	The Boards of Appeal and the Enlarged Board of Appeal decide as to the action to be taken in the cases specified in Art. 24(2) and (3) without the participation of the member concerned. For the purposes of taking this decision the member objected to is replaced by his alternate.	
Comment	A decision on admissibility under the terms of Art. 24(3) is taken with the Board as originally assembled. If the objection is admissible then the Board will decide on its substantive merits with the alternate member replacing the objected member.	
T190/03	Exclusion can be justified on subjective grounds (i.e. where a party to the proceedings has evidence justifying partiality) or on objective grounds (i.e. where the circumstances indicate partiality). An objective risk of partiality cannot arise at the beginning of proceedings when the Board has not yet performed any procedural steps and in particular does not arise from the Board having allegedly made procedural errors in previous decisions.	
G1/05	The Enlarged Board of Appeal in this case had to decide on two possible exclusions. One of the parties to the proceedings was represented by a law firm in which both the husband and son of one of the members of the EBA were partners. The Enlarged Board did not consider this relationship prima facie to be a valid ground for exclusion but since the member concerned had requested her own exclusion it was granted since she was considered to know best whether a suspicion of bias could arise. Another member was objected to by one of the parties on the basis of the position he had taken as a Board of Appeal member considering similar issues to those before the Enlarged Board. This request for exclusion was refused.	
r.144(a)	Documents relating to exclusion or objection are not part of the public file.	

4.11 The Administrative Council

Art. 26–36	Detailed provisions concerning the composition and functioning of the Administrative Council are set out in Arts. 26–36. It consists of representatives from all the Contracting States (Art. 26) and meets at least once a year (Art. 29). Most importantly, it is competent to amend the time limits set out in the EPC, the Implementing Regulations and Rules Relating to Fees in their entirety and, subject to certain conditions, Arts. 52–141 and 150–158 in order to bring them into line with an international treaty relating to patents (e.g. a substantive patent law treaty) or EU legislation relating to patents (e.g. the unitary patent regulations) (Art. 33).	842

Chapter 5: The Invention

5.1 What is not an invention for the purposes of the EPC?

5.1.1 Requirement for technical subject matter

843 Case law

According to the case law of the Board of Appeal, an invention within the meaning of Art. 52(1) EPC must have technical character (e.g. T931/95). This implicit requirement can be derived, in particular from r.42(1) (description to specify technical field and disclose invention so technical problem solved by the invention can be understood) and r.43(1) (claims to define invention in terms of technical features). Examples of subject matter not having a technical character are given in Art. 52(2) and (3) but these examples do not represent an exhaustive list (T163/85).

The required technical character may be provided by a technical effect achieved by the invention (e.g. T1173/97) or by the fact that technical considerations were necessary to carry out the invention (T769/92). In assessing technical character a claim must be judged as a whole (T26/86, T931/95, T258/03), the so-called contribution approach whereby only novel features of the claim are considered is not used. A mix of technical and non-technical features is therefore allowable in a claim (T26/86, T209/91). In such cases, however, the features that do not contribute to the technical character of the invention may not be used to define an effect from which an objective technical problem may be derived – such features may actually form part of the objective problem itself (T258/03).

Guidelines See G-I, 1 and G-II, 1–2

5.1.2 Discoveries

844 Art. 52(2)(3)

To the extent that a European patent application relates to a discovery as such, it is not regarded as containing patentable subject matter.

r.29(1) Thus, in the field of biotechnology, the human body, at the various stages of its formation and development, and the simple discovery of one of its elements, including the sequence or partial sequence of a gene, cannot constitute patentable inventions.

r.27(a) However, biotechnological inventions are patentable if they concern biological material which is isolated from its natural environment or produced by means of a technical process even if it previously occurred in nature.

r.29(2) Thus, an element isolated from the human body or otherwise produced by means of a technical process, including the sequence or partial sequence of a gene, may constitute a patentable invention, even if the structure of that element is identical to that of a natural element.

Guidelines See G-II, 3.1. A new property of a material is a discovery but the practical application of that property is an invention. The mere finding that a substance, microorganism, gene etc occurs in nature is a discovery but if it is isolated and found to be associated with a technical effect then it becomes an invention (e.g. a substance which has antibiotic properties, a microorganism that produces an antibiotic, a gene useful in gene therapy).

5.1.3 Scientific theories and mathematical methods

845 Art. 52(2)(3)

To the extent that a European patent application relates to a scientific theory or a mathematical method as such, it is not regarded as containing patentable subject matter.

T208/84 A mathematical method as such is seen to be a method practised on numbers and having a numerical outcome whereas a mathematical method used in a technical process carried out on a physical entity, and resulting in a change to that entity, is not a mathematical method as such.

Guidelines See G-II, 3.2–3.3. A scientific theory is a generalised form of a discovery.

5.1.4 Aesthetic creations

846 Art. 52(2)(3)

To the extent that a European patent application relates to an aesthetic creation as such, it is not regarded as containing patentable subject matter.

T119/88

A disc sleeve of a particular colour was said to have the technical benefit of reducing fingerprints. However, this effect was not directly related to the colour specified in the claim which was essentially aesthetic in character. The application was therefore refused.

Guidelines

G-II, 3.4. An aesthetic creation is an article defined solely in terms of features which are non-technical and appreciated in a subjective sense. An invention, however, defined in terms of technical features, may nonetheless be aesthetically pleasing.

5.1.5 *Scheme, rule or method for performing a mental act*

Art. 52(2)(3)

To the extent that a European patent application relates to a scheme, rule or method for performing a mental act as such, it is not regarded as containing patentable subject matter. 847

Guidelines

See G-II, 3.5. A scheme for learning a language is an abstract, intellectual activity that is excluded.

5.1.6 *Scheme, rule or method for playing games*

Art. 52(2)(3)

To the extent that a European patent application relates to a scheme, rule or method for playing games as such, it is not regarded as containing patentable subject matter. 848

Guidelines

See G-II, 3.5. A game in this sense is an abstract entity defined entirely in terms of rules.

5.1.7 *Scheme, rule or method for doing business*

Art. 52(2)(3)

To the extent that a European patent application relates to a scheme, rule or method for doing business as such, it is not regarded as containing patentable subject matter. 849

Case law

If a method for doing business has technical character then it is not a method of doing business as such (T931/95). A computer system set up to carry out a method generally in the category of "doing business" is allowable where technical considerations are necessary for its implementation (T769/92 – improved screen display). An apparatus constituting a physical entity would not be excluded even if the method it was set up to run was excluded (T931/95, T1002/92) although since all the features of the claim that do not contribute to the technical character of the invention (e.g. an aim to be achieved in a non-technical field) are ignored when assessing inventive step, it may well be obvious (T931/95, T641/00, T172/03).

Guidelines

See G-II, 3.5 and G-VII, 5.4

5.1.8 *Computer programs*

Art. 52(2)(3)

To the extent that a European patent application relates to a program for a computer as such, it is not regarded as containing patentable subject matter. 850

Case law

Computer-related inventions must have technical character (T931/95), which may be provided by a further technical effect (i.e. other than the usual physical interactions between any software and the computer running it) achieved by the invention (e.g. T1173/97). A claim to a technical process carried out under the control of a program or a claim to a computer set up to operate in accordance with a program for controlling that technical process is allowable (T208/84). Furthermore, where a program produces a further technical effect, it may in principle be claimed in the form of a record on a carrier or as a program per se (T1173/97).

G3/08

The Enlarged Board declined to answer questions concerning computer programs referred by the President of the EPO on the basis that the decisions cited as conflicting were, in fact, a legitimate development of the case law in a fast-evolving technical field.

G1/19

Headnote (1): A computer-implemented simulation of a technical system or process that is claimed as such can, for the purpose of assessing inventive step, solve a technical problem by producing a technical effect going beyond the simulation's implementation on a computer.

Comment

The Enlarged Board decided that inventions involving a computer simulation should be assessed under Art. 56 in the same way as any other computer-implemented invention according to the Comvick approach, i.e. only features contributing to the technical character of the invention are considered in deriving the objective technical problem which has been solved.

Guidelines	See G-II, 3.6. Any subject matter that uses technical means (e.g. includes a computer) is an invention within the meaning of Art. 52(1) EPC (but see above under 5.1.7 for the way in which inventive step may be considered).

5.1.9   *Presentation of information*

851 Art. 52(2)(3)	To the extent that a European patent application relates to a presentation of information as such, it is not regarded as containing patentable subject matter.
T163/85	A TV signal characterised by certain physical parameters was not seen to be a presentation of information as such whereas if it had been characterised by its informational content it would have been.
T1149/97	A claim to a record carrier bearing functional data is not objectionable as a presentation of information.
T858/02	An electronic message is not automatically excluded from patentability as a presentation of information. This will depend on whether the message is defined by its structure or its content.
Guidelines	See G-II, 3.7. A presentation of information defined solely by the content of the information is excluded. Features relating to the graphic design of a user interface are not patentable unless they achieve a technical effect, e.g. by making a machine earlier to use.

5.2   **What inventions are barred from patentability?**

5.2.1   *Morality exemption*

852 Art. 53(a)	European patents cannot be granted in respect of inventions the commercial exploitation of which would be contrary to "ordre public" or morality, provided that the exploitation is not deemed to be so contrary merely because it is prohibited by law or regulation in some or all of the Contracting States.
r.28	Under Art. 53(a), a European patent will not be granted in respect of biotechnological inventions which, in particular, concern the following: (a) processes for cloning human beings, (b) processes for modifying the germ line genetic identity of human beings, (c) uses of human embryos for industrial or commercial purposes, (d) processes for modifying the genetic identity of animals which are likely to cause them suffering without any substantial medical benefit to man or animal, and also animals resulting from such processes.
G2/06	The Enlarged Board confirmed in this decision that r.28(c) (and, by extension of the reasoning used, r.28 in general) applies to all European patent applications, including those filed before its entry into force. The Enlarged Board further decided that where the claims of a European patent application relate to a new product which, at the filing date of the patent application, could only be obtained by destroying human embryos, the application contravenes r.28(c) and must be refused. This is the case even where advances in technology mean that the claimed product can be obtained without destroying human embryos at a later date. The Enlarged Board held that the question to be considered was not whether the claims themselves included the step of destroying a human embryo but whether practicing the invention defined by the claims would inevitably involve such destruction.
T315/03	The exclusions in r.28 represent specific instances of the general exclusion of Art. 53(a). The exclusions are to be judged at the filing/priority date though relevant evidence may have been published later. Note that r.28 was previously r.23d under EPC1973.
Case law	Whether an invention is contrary to ordre public or morality is a matter of balancing the advantages and disadvantages – benefit to mankind versus any cruelty to animals or risk to the environment (T19/90). Ordre public includes public security and a consideration of possible environmental hazards but such hazards must be properly substantiated to be persuasive (T356/93). The morality question is to be judged on the basis of conventionally accepted standards of European culture (T356/93).
Guidelines	See G-II, 4.1. Inventions likely to induce riot or public disorder or lead to criminal behaviour are excluded, e.g. an anti-personnel mine. However, the mere possibility of an invention being abused is not relevant where the invention can equally be exploited legitimately (G-II, 4.1.2). See also G-II, 4.2.2 – a screening method for compounds carried out on animals would be contrary to Art. 53(a) unless humans were excluded or it related exclusively to a clinical trial of an experimental medication carried out with informed consent. See also G-II, 5.3 for biotech exclusions.

5.2.2 Plant varieties

Art. 53(b)	European patents will not be granted in respect of plant varieties.	853
r.26(4)	Plant variety means any plant grouping within a single botanical taxon of the lowest known rank, which grouping, irrespective of whether the conditions for the grant of a plant variety right are fully met, can be: (a) defined by the expression of the characteristics that results from a given genotype or combination of genotypes; (b) distinguished from any other plant grouping by the expression of at least one of the said characteristics; and (c) considered as a unit with regard to its suitability for being propagated unchanged (this corresponds to the UPOV definition).	
r.27(b)	Without prejudice to r.28(2), biotechnological inventions concerning plants are patentable if the technical feasibility of the invention is not confined to a particular plant variety.	
G1/98	Headnote (1): A claim wherein specific plant varieties are not individually claimed is not excluded from patentability under Art. 53(b) EPC even though it may embrace plant varieties. Headnote (2): When a claim to a process for the production of a plant variety is examined, Art. 64(2) EPC is not to be taken into consideration. Headnote (3): The exception to patentability in Art. 53(b), first half-sentence, EPC applies to plant varieties irrespective of the way in which they were produced. Therefore, plant varieties containing genes introduced into an ancestral plant by recombinant gene technology are excluded from patentability.	
Comment	The Enlarged Board held that Art. 53(b) excluded plant varieties rather than plants and existed to exclude double protection via a patent and a plant breeders right. Therefore, anything that could not be protected under UPOV should be patentable, including the claim in dispute, which was directed to a genetically modified plant which neither expressly or implicitly defined a plant variety according to UPOV. The conclusions from this decision have now been codified as r.26(4) and r.27(b) EPC.	
r.28(2)	Under Art. 53(b), European patents shall not be granted in respect of plants exclusively obtained by means of an essentially biological process.	
Comment	Enlarged Board decisions G2/12 and G2/13 decided that Art. 53(b) should be interpreted in such a way that claims to plants per se are patentable even if the only way of making them is using an essentially biological process. As a result, new r.28(2) was introduced by the Administrative Council, coming into force on 01 July 2017. Decision G3/19 decided that this new rule validly changed the meaning of Art. 53(b) as of 01 July 2017 but has no effect on the validity of applications with a filing/priority date before 01 July 2017 and patents granted in respect of such applications.	
G3/19	Headnote: Taking into account developments after decisions G2/12 and G2/13 of the Enlarged Board of Appeal, the exception to patentability of essentially biological processes for the production of plants or animals in Art. 53(b) EPC has a negative effect on the allowability of product claims and product-by-process claims directed to plants, plant material or animals, if the claimed product is exclusively obtained by means of an essentially biological process or if the claimed process features define an essentially biological process. This negative effect does not apply to European patents granted before 01 July 2017 and European patent applications which were filed before that date and are still pending.	
Guidelines	See G-II, 5.2 and 5.4.1.	

5.2.3 Animal varieties

Art. 53(b)	European patents will not be granted in respect of animal varieties.	854
r.27(b)	Without prejudice to r.28(2), biotechnological inventions concerning animals are patentable if the technical feasibility of the invention is not confined to a particular animal variety.	
Case law	The exclusion applies to certain categories of animals but not to animals as such (T19/90). The Examining Division in the Oncomouse case ([1992] O.J. 588) decided that no accepted definition of animal variety exists. However, neither "rodent" nor "mammal" were felt to be specific enough to amount to an animal variety. The Opposition Division in the Oncomouse case ([2003] O.J. 473) also felt that "mouse" did not amount to an animal variety, indicating that a particular "strain" of mice might. The Board of Appeal (T315/03) decided that G1/98 (see above under Plant varieties) should be applied as far as possible. Thus, a claim can be granted if it embraces many varieties as long as it is not directed at a single animal variety.	

r.28(2)	Under Art. 53(b), European patents shall not be granted in respect of animals exclusively obtained by means of an essentially biological process.
Comment	Enlarged Board decisions G2/12 and G2/13 decided that Art. 53(b) should be interpreted in such a way that claims to plants per se are patentable even if the only way of making them is using an essentially biological process. By extrapolation, one may assume that the same principle applies to animals. As a result, new r.28(2) was introduced by the Administrative Council, coming into force on 01 July 2017. Decision G3/19 decided that this new rule validly changed the meaning of Art. 53(b) as of 01 July 2017 but has no effect on the validity of applications with a filing/priority date before 01 July 2017 and patents granted in respect of such applications.
G3/19	Headnote: Taking into account developments after decisions G2/12 and G2/13 of the Enlarged Board of Appeal, the exception to patentability of essentially biological processes for the production of plants or animals in Art. 53(b) EPC has a negative effect on the allowability of product claims and product-by-process claims directed to plants, plant material or animals, if the claimed product is exclusively obtained by means of an essentially biological process or if the claimed process features define an essentially biological process. This negative effect does not apply to European patents granted before 01 July 2017 and European patent applications which were filed before that date and are still pending.
Guidelines	See G-II, 5.2 and 5.4.

5.2.4   *Essentially biological processes*

855	Art. 53(b)	European patents will not be granted in respect of essentially biological processes for the production of plants or animals; this provision does not apply to microbiological processes or the products thereof.
	r.26(5)	A process for the production of plants and animals is essentially biological if it consists entirely of natural phenomena such as crossing or selection.
	Case law	Whether a process is "essentially" biological is to be judged on the basis of the totality of human intervention and its effect on the final result (T320/87). A process involving the essential technical step of transforming plant cells with recombinant DNA was not essentially biological since human intervention was necessary and had a decisive impact on the result (T356/93).
	G2/07, G1/08	Headnote (1): A non-microbiological process for the production of plants which contains or consists of the steps of sexually crossing the whole genomes of plants and of subsequently selecting plants is in principle excluded from patentability as being "essentially biological" within the meaning of Art. 53(b) EPC.
		Headnote (2): Such a process does not escape the exclusion of Art. 53(b) merely because it contains, as a further step or as part of any of the steps of crossing and selection, a step of a technical nature which serves to enable or assist the performance of the steps of sexually crossing the whole genomes of plants or of subsequently selecting plants.
		Headnote (3): If, however, such a process contains within the steps of sexually crossing and selecting an additional step of a technical nature, which step by itself introduces a trait into the genome or modifies a trait in the genome of the plant produced, so that the introduction or modification of that trait is not the result of the mixing of the genes of the plants chosen for sexual crossing, then the process is not excluded from patentability under Art. 53(b) EPC.
		Headnote (4): In the context of examining whether such a process is excluded from patentability as being "essentially biological" within the meaning of Art. 53(b) EPC, it is not relevant whether a step of a technical nature is a new or known measure, whether it is trivial or a fundamental alteration of a known process, whether it does or could occur in nature or whether the essence of the invention lies in it.

Comment	The Enlarged Board of Appeal decided that the definition of r.26(5) EPC was somewhat self-contradictory since crossing and selection are not actually natural phenomena in the sense that they occur without human intervention. A consideration of the legislative history of this rule was also unhelpful. So, on the basis of Art. 53(b) and its legislative history alone, they established the principle, largely in agreement with the previous case law, that a process is not essentially biological if it involves a technical step which directly changes the DNA content of a plant rather than relying on crossing and selection to make such a change. Such a technical effect does not have to fulfil any further criteria, e.g. it is irrelevant whether it is a new or known step.
Comment	Decisions G2/12 and G2/13 decided that the exclusion of Art. 53(b), while excluding essentially biological processes for the production of plants, did not prevent the grant of a product claim for a plant even if such a plant could only be produced by means of an essentially biological process. The Administrative Council then introduced new r.28(2) EPC, in force as of 01 July 2017, which specifically excluded such product claims. Finally, decision G3/19 decided that this new rule validly changed the meaning of Art. 53(b) as of 01 July 2017 but has no effect on the validity of applications with a filing/priority date before 01 July 2017 and patents granted in respect of such applications. See above under plant varieties and animal varieties.
Case law	"Microbiological" refers to generally unicellular organisms too small to be seen with the eye, including bacteria, yeasts, fungi, algae, protozoa, human cells, animal cells and plant cells. The products of microbiological processes include new microorganisms as well as chemical products (T356/93). However, the processes of genetic engineering are not identical to microbiological processes (G1/98).
Guidelines	See G-II, 5.4.2 and 5.5

5.2.5   *Method of treatment or diagnosis exclusion – general points*

Art. 53(c)	European patents will not be granted for methods for treatment of the human or animal body by surgery or therapy and diagnostic methods practised on the human or animal body. However, this exclusion does not apply to products, in particular substances or compositions, for use in any of these methods.	856
Comment	Note that under EPC1973, such methods were deemed to lack industrial applicability under Art. 57 but are now specifically excluded from patentability under Art. 53(c).	
G5/83	Headnote (1): A European patent with claims directed to the use may not be granted for the use of a substance or composition for the treatment of the human or animal body by therapy.	
Comment	The Enlarged Board felt that there was no substantive difference, for the purposes of the EPC, between a use claim and a method claim and thus that a claim to the use of a substance or composition for treatment were excluded in the same way as a method claim (see below for allowable second medical use format).	
Case law	The purpose of these exclusions is to prevent non-commercial and non-industrial medical and veterinary activities from being restrained by patent rights (G5/83) and they should be construed narrowly according to this purpose (T385/86). A claim which contains any element excluded by Art. 53(c) is excluded from patentability. Whether the feature is technical or not is irrelevant (T82/93) (cf. claims excluded under Art. 52(2), (3)).	
Guidelines	See G-II, 4.2.	

5.2.6   *Method of treatment of the human or animal body by therapy*

T58/87	Therapy is any non-surgical treatment designed to cure, alleviate, remove or lessen the symptoms of, or prevent or reduce the possibility of contracting, any malfunction of the body.	857

Case law

Therapy includes both curative and prophylactic treatment (e.g. immunisation) (T19/86, T290/86) and all methods of alleviating pain (T144/83, T81/84). Whether the treatment is performed by a medical practitioner or vet is not conclusive but can be indicative (T24/91, T329/94). For instance, it makes no difference if the therapeutic treatment is applied by a farmer as opposed to a vet (T116/85). If therapy occurs during a treatment, that treatment is excluded even though therapy might not be the main purpose of the treatment (e.g. T780/89 – immunisation increases meat production; T438/91 – prevention of scours increases animal weight; T290/86 – eliminating plaque prevented caries and other dental disease). Therapy includes internal and external treatment, e.g. of ectoparasites (T116/85). Cosmetic treatments are not excluded (T144/83) as long as therapy is not inherently also taking place (T290/86, T1077/93). The claim must be worded so as to exclude any therapeutic treatment. Methods of contraception are also allowable in principle since pregnancy is not an illness and its prevention is not therapy (T820/92) though acts performed in the personal sphere may not be considered capable of industrial application in the ordinary sense (T74/93).

Method claims are allowed where there is no functional relationship between the effect of the method on a therapeutic apparatus and the therapeutic effect produced by the apparatus (e.g. pacemaker cases T426/89 and T789/96 and T245/87 Siemens/Flow measurement). Equally, an allowable method can interact with the human body (e.g. facilitating the flow of blood to an extraction point) as long as no therapeutic purpose exists (T329/94). Prevention of accidents and possible harm or death (e.g. a mother pig smothering her piglets) is not therapy (T58/87).

Guidelines

See G-II, 4.2, specifically G-II, 4.2.1.2. The treatment of animals to achieve purely non-therapeutic advantages (e.g. quality of meat or yield of wool) is not excluded.

5.2.7   *Method of treatment of the human or animal body by surgery*

858 G1/07

Headnote (1): A claimed imaging method, in which, when carried out, maintaining the life and health of the subject is important and which comprises or encompasses an invasive step representing a substantial physical intervention on the body which requires professional medical expertise to be carried out and which entails a substantial health risk even when carried out with the required professional care and expertise, is excluded from patentability as a method for treatment of the human or animal body by surgery pursuant to Art. 53(c) EPC.

Headnote (2a): A claim which comprises a step encompassing an embodiment which is a "method for treatment of the human or animal body by surgery" within the meaning of Art. 53(c) EPC cannot be left to encompass that embodiment.

Headnote (2b): The exclusion from patentability under Art. 53(c) EPC can be avoided by disclaiming the embodiment, it being understood that in order to be patentable the claim including the disclaimer must fulfil all the requirements of the EPC and, where applicable, the requirements for a disclaimer to be allowable as defined in decision G1/03 and G2/03 of the Enlarged Board of Appeal.

Headnote (2c): Whether or not the wording of the claim can be amended so as to omit the surgical step without offending against the EPC must be assessed on the basis of the overall circumstances of the individual case under consideration.

Headnote (3): A claimed imaging method is not to be considered as being a "treatment of the human or animal body by surgery" within the meaning of Art. 53(c) EPC merely because during a surgical intervention the data obtained by the use of the method immediately allow a surgeon to decide on the course of action to be taken during a surgical intervention.

Case law

Surgery is not defined by the purpose of the treatment but by the nature of the treatment so that the exclusion covers surgical methods that are for non-therapeutic purposes such as for cosmetic purposes or fertility treatment (T35/99, G1/07). Any method incorporating even one surgical step is excluded from patentability (G1/04, G1/07). However, the concept of 'surgery' is to be given a narrow meaning which is consistent with the purpose of the exclusion: it does not cover interventions which are minor and involve no substantial health risks and no professional medical skills (G1/07). Furthermore, where a treatment results in an animal inevitably dying, the fact that the treatment includes a surgical step does not exclude it (T182/90). An act performed on an implant which has become part of the human body is a surgical treatment (T24/91). However, acts performed on prostheses are not excluded.

Guidelines

See G-II, 4.2, specifically G-II, 4.2.1.1. Examples of excluded surgical methods include the injection of a contrasting agent into the heart, catheterisation and endoscopy. Examples of non-excluded methods include tattooing, piercing, hair removal by optical radiation and micro-abrasion of the skin.

5.2.8   Diagnostic method practiced on the human or animal body

G1/04

Headnote (1): In order that the subject-matter of a claim relating to a diagnostic method   859
practised on the human or animal body falls under the prohibition of Article 52(4) EPC (NB. Now Art. 53(c)), the claim is to include the features relating to: (i) the diagnosis for curative purposes stricto sensu representing the deductive medical or veterinary decision phase as a purely intellectual exercise, (ii) the preceding steps which are constitutive for making that diagnosis, and (iii) the specific interactions with the human or animal body which occur when carrying those out among these preceding steps which are of a technical nature.

Headnote (2): Whether or not a method is a diagnostic method within the meaning of Article 52(4) EPC (NB. Now Art. 53(c)) may neither depend on the participation of a medical or veterinary practitioner, by being present or by bearing the responsibility, nor on the fact that all method steps can also, or only, be practised by medical or technical support staff, the patient himself or herself or an automated system. Moreover, no distinction is to be made in this context between essential method steps having diagnostic character and non-essential method steps lacking it.

Headnote (3): In a diagnostic method under Article 52(4) EPC (NB. Now Art. 53(c)), the method steps of a technical nature belonging to the preceding steps which are constitutive for making the diagnosis for curative purposes stricto sensu must satisfy the criterion 'practised on the human or animal body'.

Headnote (4): Article 52(4) EPC (NB. Now Art. 53(c)) does not require a specific type and intensity of interaction with the human or animal body; a preceding step of a technical nature thus satisfies the criterion 'practised on the human or animal body' if its performance implies any interaction with the human or animal body, necessitating the presence of the latter.

The Enlarged Board has given the diagnostic methods exclusion a narrow interpretation in line with its purpose. The only diagnostic methods excluded are those that include both a data collection step and a step in which a course of therapy is proposed on the basis of those data. Moreover, each of the data collection steps must be practiced on the human or animal body, in the sense that they must require its presence. A method for generating interim results that can be used in diagnosis is therefore patentable.

Guidelines

See G-II, 4.2.1.3. According to the EPO interpretation of G1/04 a diagnostic method has steps relating to (i) an examination phase involving the collection of data, (ii) the comparison of these data with standard values, (iii) the finding of any significant deviation (i.e. a symptom) during the comparison, and (iv) the attribution of the deviation to a particular clinical picture. All of the steps must be present in the claim for the exclusion to be applied. In addition, for the exclusion to apply all technical aspects of steps (i) to (iii) (usually just step (i)) must be practiced on the human or animal body. Thus, methods which involve no more than obtaining information from the human or animal body (e.g. X-ray investigations, MRI studies, blood pressure measurements) are not excluded.

5.3   What is a patentable invention?

860   Art. 52(1)   European patents are granted for any inventions, in all fields of technology, which are susceptible of industrial application, which are new and which involve an inventive step.

5.4   Which inventions are susceptible of industrial application?

861   Art. 57   An invention is considered as susceptible of industrial application if it can be made or used in any kind of industry, including agriculture.

r.29(3)   The industrial application of a sequence or a partial sequence of a gene must be disclosed in the patent application.

T18/09   In order to comply with Art. 57, an application relating to a new gene sequence must disclose enough information to allow its practical exploitation. The identification of the protein encoded by the gene as part of a known family may be enough if the function of the other members of the family is known and reliable predictions may be made. Any objections under Art. 57 EPC must give rise to serious doubts and be substantiated by verifiable facts in the same way as an objection under Art. 83 EPC.

Guidelines   See G-III. Industry is to be understood broadly to include any physical activity having a technical character, i.e. belonging to the useful/practical arts as opposed to the aesthetic arts. A claim specifying the intended function or purpose of an invention alleged to operate in a manner contrary to well-established physical laws is not susceptible of industrial application.

5.5   Which inventions are new?

5.5.1   Definition of novelty

862   Art. 54(1)   An invention is considered to be new if it does not form part of the state of the art.

5.5.2   The state of the art includes earlier disclosures

863   Art. 54(2)   The state of the art is held to comprise everything made available to the public by means of a written or oral description, by use, or in any other way, before the date of filing (or priority date – Art. 89) of the European patent application of interest.

G3/93   Headnote (1): A document published during the priority interval, the technical contents of which correspond to that of the priority document, constitutes prior art citable under Art. 54(2) EPC against a European patent application claiming that priority, to the extent such priority is not validly claimed.

G3/93   Headnote (2): This also applies if a claim to priority is invalid due to the fact that the priority document and the subsequent European patent application do not concern the same invention because the European application claims subject matter not disclosed in the priority document.

Comment   Thus, the Art. 89 effect only applies where priority is validly claimed in respect of "the same invention" (see also G2/98).

Guidelines   See G-IV. Disclosures in all languages are state of the art but the applicant may dispute, with reasons, the relevance of a document published in a language other than English, French or German in which case the examiner must obtain a translation (a machine translation is sufficient) to pursue the matter further (G-IV, 4).

Comment   A disclosure enters the state of the art if it is made available the day before the filing (or priority) date of a European patent application or earlier. A disclosure made on the filing (or priority) date itself is not part of the state of the art. Note that if a disclosure is made on a day on which the EPO is closed (e.g. a Sunday), a filing date must be secured on that same day if the document is not to enter the state of the art (this can be achieved by fax filing, electronic filing or by using one of the automated post boxes at EPO filing offices). If a European application is filed on the next day when the EPO is open then the previous disclosure will form part of the state of the art. This is because in the case of a first filing there is no time limit running which can be extended according to r.134(1) EPC. If, on the other hand, a priority application has already been filed and the priority period ends on an EPO closed day on which a disclosure is to be made then the European application can safely be filed on the first day on which the EPO is open again since the priority period is extended according to r.134(1) EPC and priority is still validly claimed.

5.5.3   *The state of the art includes the contents of earlier European patent applications*

Art. 54(3)	The state of the art also comprises the (whole) content of European patent applications as filed, the dates of filing (or priority – Art. 89) of which are prior to the date of filing (or priority – Art. 89) of the European patent application of interest and which were published on or after that date.
Art. 54(4)1973	For applications filed before the coming into force of EPC2000 (referring to the application whose novelty is being assessed), however, such matter is only taken to be prior art in so far as a Contracting State designated in respect of the later application, was also designated in respect of the earlier application as published and to the extent that designation fees pursuant to Art. 79(2) were paid (Art. 54(4) and r.23a EPC1973 – both deleted in EPC2000). See Decision of the Administrative Council of 28 June 2001 on the transitional provisions under Article 7 of the Act revising the European Patent Convention of 29 November 2000, Article 1(1).
Comment	For applications filed on or after the coming into force of EPC2000 (referring to the application whose novelty is being assessed), any Art. 54(3) prior art applies to all States regardless of how many States are validly designated in the European prior right.
Art. 153(5)	An international application only becomes Art. 54(3) art if it is published in English, French or German under the PCT procedure (Art. 153(3)) or supplied to the EPO in one of these languages on regional phase entry (Art. 153(4)) and the filing fee due under r.159(1)(c) is paid (r.165).
OJ	Note that none of the other requirements for regional phase entry need to be complied with (Notice from the EPO dated 21 June 2021; [2021] O.J. A51). International applications not entering the EPO regional phase which nevertheless constitute prior art under Art. 54(3) EPC are noted in the European Patent Bulletin. See also Guidelines G-IV, 5.2.
Art. 85	The content of the abstract is to be disregarded when applying Art. 54(3).
J5/81	Where an application has been withdrawn before publication but published anyway (e.g. because technical preparations were complete) it does not form part of the state of the art under Art. 54(3) but has an Art. 54(2) effect from the date of publication.
T550/88	National prior rights are not citable under Art. 54(3).
Guidelines	See G-IV, 5.1. The content of the earlier application includes any matter disclaimed (with the exception of unworkable embodiments), matter properly referenced and prior art properly described. It does not include the priority document. Changes after publication, such as the withdrawal of a designation, the withdrawal of a priority claim or the loss of a priority claim, have no effect on the operation of Art. 54(3) (G-IV, 5.1.1). Conversely, loss of a right of priority before publication does affect the extent of the 54(3) effect.
Art. 70(2)	Where a European patent application is filed in a language other than English, French or German, the text in this original language is relevant for determining its disclosure as prior art under Art. 54(3) and not the later translation into an EPO official language. Any mistakes in the translation are always correctable (Art. 14(2)) and do not limit the prior art effect. See Guidelines A-VII, 7.
r.87 EPC1973	For an application filed before the coming into force of EPC2000, where an Art. 54(3) document exists in respect of only some designated States, the application and corresponding patent may have different claims and, if the EPO agrees, a different description and drawings for different States, as an exception to the unity requirement of Art. 118.

5.5.4   *Under what circumstances is something "made available to the public"?*

Case law	Information is made available when at least one member of the public can access it and is not under any duty of confidentiality (T482/89). However, disclosure in confidence (either implicit or explicit) does not make information available, even if in the form of a lecture (T838/97). The public in this context is the public at large and is not limited to the "skilled" public who are experts in the relevant technical field (T953/90).

864

865

The fact of availability is enough – there is no requirement for a document to have been consulted by a member of the public as long as the possibility was there. In T381/87 the presence of a book on a library shelf made its contents available and in T750/94 the fact that a document was known to be available on demand from a publisher was enough. However, T314/99 suggests that in some cases a publication must be catalogued to make it truly available. Likewise, a single sale of an article makes it part of the state of the art (T1022/99). However, sending a document using a postal service before the filing date is not enough – it must be received before that date (T381/87). Equally, giving permission to publish is not enough (T842/91). Documents do not have to be available for free to enter the state of the art (T1030/00).

The burden of proof always lies on the party alleging the lack of novelty (e.g. T193/84) and the standard of proof is usually "on the balance of probability" (e.g. T729/91). In cases of prior use, however, where the evidence is in the hands of the person alleging the prior use, there is usually a more considerable burden of proof to be discharged by an opponent (T472/92 – "up to the hilt") and full details along the lines of when/what/how/where/whom must be provided (T93/89 and T472/92). The same considerations also apply in the case of a public lecture (T1212/97) where the evidence of the lecturer alone is not sufficient. Furthermore, it cannot be assumed that a written disclosure based on an earlier oral disclosure contains the same information (T153/88).

OJ

The extent to which internet publications are considered to be state of the art has been the subject of an EPO notice (see [2009] O.J. 456). In general, the first instance departments apply a standard of proof akin to 'balance of the probabilities' in deciding whether an internet disclosure is state of the art (see also Guidelines G-IV, 7.5.2). Some Board of Appeal decisions such as T1134/06 have demanded a standard more akin to 'beyond all reasonable doubt' whereas others (e.g. T2227/11) have applied the "balance of the probabilities" standard and yet others (e.g. T545/08) have found little difference between these standards in practice – the disclosure must be shown convincingly to have occurred rather than just being probable.

Guidelines

See G-IV, 1 and 7. Where a document which is itself not state of the art describes the contents of an earlier oral presentation (which is state of the art), EPO first instance departments will assume in the first instance that the document gives a true account of the oral presentation – this is not in line with Board of Appeal case law (see above).

5.5.5   *Judging the content of what has been made available*

866   G1/92

Headnote (1): The chemical composition of a product is state of the art when the product as such is available to the public and can be analysed and reproduced by the skilled person, irrespective of whether or not particular reasons can be identified for analysing the composition.

Headnote (2): The same principle applies mutatis mutandis to any other product.

Case law

Availability of a product thus frequently makes available its composition and structure but not any properties that depend on further action being taken (e.g. a particular use). However, the principle of G1/92 may not apply where the information is hidden or deeply buried in the product made available. For example, in T301/87 a gene sequence was not made available since it only existed as part of a very large library and in T461/88 information on a microchip in a printing machine would have required complex reverse-engineering to obtain.

In the case of a publication, the document must be considered in its entirety and particular passages must be read in context (T56/87, T89/87). Where a disclosure (e.g. an abstract) is clearly erroneous (e.g. by reference to a fuller disclosure) its teaching must be discounted (T77/87, T1080/99). The content of a document should be interpreted as of its date of publication (T677/91).

The inevitable result of carrying out instructions in the prior art is also part of its disclosure (T666/89). For instance, where a disclosure refers to a chemical compound and proposes that it may be used as a starting material in a particular process, the inevitable product of using that process in combination with the identified starting material is also disclosed.

Normally, documents may not be combined when assessing novelty. However, where a further document is clearly referred to, the contents of the further document specifically identified can be incorporated if it was available at the publication date of the first document (T153/85). Where one document refers to separate embodiments, these may not be combined without any relevant cross-reference.

The disclosure of something as part of a negative teaching (e.g. disclosure of X in the context "don't use X") does not make it available (T26/85).

The disclosure in the prior art must be enabling to destroy novelty (T206/83), i.e. the skilled man must be able to carry out its technical teaching with no more than his common general knowledge. For instance, a chemical compound is not disclosed in an enabling way if it cannot be made on the basis of the teaching or disclosure combined with common general knowledge.

Guidelines   See sections G-IV and G-VI in general. See G-IV, 2 and G-VI, 4 for the concept of an enabling disclosure. The document must be enabled on the basis of the skilled person's common general knowledge (e.g. text books) alone. Documents may be read together in the case of an explicit cross-reference (G-IV, 8). An error in a prior art document does not affect its disclosure if the correction is obvious for the skilled person (G-IV, 9).

5.5.6   *Judging whether the content of what has been made available is prejudicial to novelty*

Case law   To destroy novelty, there must be a "clear and unmistakeable" disclosure (T450/89) of   867
all the features of the invention as claimed in combination (G2/88). Put another way, the invention must be directly and unambiguously derivable from the prior art (T204/83). Novelty is a matter of substance rather than form and the use of different wording is not enough to establish novelty (T12/81, T198/84).

What is implicit in the prior art is taken into account (T666/89) but not what is obvious from the prior art (T572/88) or what is an equivalent (T167/84). For instance, where a compound is known to be water-soluble, describing it in the form of a solution does not impart novelty (T80/96).

Guidelines   See G-IV and G-VI. Claims which include numerical ranges are construed according to the convention that the last decimal indicates the degree of accuracy, e.g. a value of 3.5 includes all measurements in the range 3.45–3.54 (G-VI, 8.1).

5.5.7   *First medical use*

Art. 54(4)   The provisions of Art. 54(2) and (3) do not exclude the patentability of any substance or   868
composition, comprised in the state of the art, for use in a method referred to in Art. 53(c), provided that its use for any such method is not comprised in the state of the art.

T128/82   A first medical use claim does not have to be restricted to the newly discovered therapeutic use but can claim all therapeutic uses. The format "Compound/composition X for use as a medicament" is usually used.

Comment   This is a narrow exception to the general rule that a 'for use' feature does not limit a product claim, being interpreted as 'suitable for use'. Note that a first medical use claim phrased in a narrow manner (e.g. Compound X for use in the treatment of cancer), which is not a second medical use claim under EPC2000 in view of the transitional provisions (see below), will still be anticipated by an earlier medical use of the same compound for a different indication.

Guidelines   See G-II, 4.2.

5.5.8   *Second medical use*

Art. 54(5)   For applications pending when EPC2000 came into force for which a decision to grant had   869
not been taken and applications filed on or later than that date, the following applies (See Decision of the Administrative Council of 28 June 2001 on the transitional provisions under Article 7 of the Act revising the European Patent Convention of 29 November 2000, Article 1(3)): The provisions of Art. 54(2) and (3) do not exclude the patentability of any substance or composition, comprised in the state of the art, for any specific use in a method referred to in Art. 53(c), provided that such use is not comprised in the state of the art.

Comment	This new provision of Art. 54(5) EPC2000 means that a claim in the form "Compound/ composition X for use in the treatment of disease Y" is now available when a second medical use invention is made, i.e. when a compound or composition already known to be useful in therapy is found to have a further therapeutic use. This is a further exception to the general rule that a 'for use' feature does not limit a product claim, being interpreted as 'suitable for use'.
G5/83	For applications pending when EPC2000 came into force for which a decision to grant had been taken, the Swiss style form of second medical use claim approved in G5/83 remains valid. Headnote (2): A European patent may be granted with claims directed to the use of a substance or composition for the manufacture of a medicament for a specified new and inventive therapeutic application. The Enlarged Board decided that since under Art. 54(5) EPC1973 (NB. now Art. 54(4) EPC2000), a use-limited product claim was novel by virtue of the use feature, so a use-limited process claim (i.e. use of a substance/composition for the manufacture of a medicament for treatment) could be seen to be novel by virtue of the use feature and hence Swiss-style claims would be novel even if the process described was already known.
G2/08	Headnote (3): Where the subject matter of a claim is rendered novel only by a new therapeutic use of a medicament, such claim may no longer have the format of a so-called Swiss-style claim as instituted by G 5/83. A time limit of three months after publication of the present decision in the OJ of the EPO is set in order that future applicants comply with this new situation.
OJ	Decision G2/08 was published in the OJ on 28 October 2010 (see Notice from the EPO dated 20 September 2010, [2010] O.J. 514). Swiss style claims are therefore no longer acceptable in applications with a priority date (or filing date if no priority is claimed) of 29 January 2011 or later (more than three months after the publication of G2/08 in the OJ – see point 7.1.4 of the decision).
Comment	Thus, depending on the filing date/priority date and date of the decision to grant, a European patent application and patent may be entitled to use Swiss style second medical use claims only, Art. 54(5) style second medical use claims only or both of these claim formats.
G2/08	Headnote (1): Where it is already known to use a medicament to treat an illness, Art. 54(5) EPC does not exclude that this medicament be patented for use in a different treatment by therapy of the same illness. Headnote (2): Such patenting is also not excluded where a dosage regime is the only feature claimed which is not comprised in the state of the art.
Case law	This decision G2/08 validated earlier case law that had allowed second medical use claims where the same disease was being treated in a different way, e.g. by treating of a different population of animals (T19/86, T233/96), by utilising a different route of administration (T51/93) or by using a different dosage regimen (T1020/03).
Case law	Normally the new medical use will concern a newly identified disease state. See T4/98 for a discussion of the features necessary in a second medical use claim (information regarding the disease, substance and subject to be treated). According to T241/95, a defined condition must be included in the claim, the selective occupancy of a receptor not being a second medical use in itself. Where there is a new technical effect underlying the new use, a second medical use claim is allowable even if the means of realisation are known – here removal of dental plaque versus inhibiting tooth decay by reducing enamel solubility (T290/86 – same reasoning as Mobil, G2/88). However, when only new information about the old use has been discovered, e.g. an explanation of how it works, this cannot be a further technical effect supporting a further second medical use claim (T254/93). It is not possible to use the second medical use claim format in relation to an apparatus (e.g. an instrument) as the apparatus is not consumed during treatment but can be used repeatedly (T227/91).
Guidelines	See G-VI, 7.1. Helpful examples are provided illustrating the way in which independent and dependent claims should be drafted to comply with Art. 54(5) EPC.

5.5.9 Second non-medical use

G2/88 Headnote (3): A claim to the use of a known compound for a particular purpose, which 870 is based on a technical effect which is described in the patent, should be interpreted as including that technical effect as a functional technical feature, and is accordingly not open to objection under Art. 54(1) EPC provided that such technical feature has not previously been made available to the public.
Here, the new use was the use of a known compound, used in the same way to achieve a different purpose (reducing friction – previous purpose was rust inhibition). The Enlarged Board reasoned that the claim should be construed to include the functional feature of attaining the new technical effect. This technical feature was inherent in the prior art but not made available, by inevitable result or description. Second non-medical use claims are therefore allowable, even if the new use was inherent (but secret) in a prior art use.

G6/88 Essentially the same decision was given in this case where the known use was the use of a compound for influencing plant growth whereas the new use was the use of the same compound for controlling fungi.

Case law For a valid second non-medical use claim there must be a new technical effect underlying a new purpose that has not been previously made available. A new technical effect which relates to the purpose already known will not establish novelty. In T958/90 the applicant had discovered that the technical effect underlying the known use (use of compounds as sequestering agents) was merely present to a hitherto unknown extent and there was no new invention. Similarly, in T279/93 the applicant had merely shown that the known use (use of a compound in a process) had the advantage of leading to fewer impurities. In T892/94 an explanation of the mechanism underlying the known use was the contribution made by the new invention (that it was the esterase activity of the compounds that led to their deodorising activity) and this was not sufficient to make the claim novel.

Guidelines See G-VI, 7.2

5.5.10 Abusive disclosure exemption

Art. 55(1)(a) For the application of Art. 54 a disclosure of the invention is not taken into considera- 871 tion if it occurred no earlier than six months preceding the filing of the European patent application and if it was due to, or in consequence of an evident abuse in relation to the applicant or his legal predecessor.

Comment The "no earlier than" language was chosen carefully so as to include the publication of Art. 54(3) documents after the filing date of the application in question. Thus, Art. 55(1) (a) applies to Art. 54(2) and Art. 54(3) prior art, the "disclosure" of the invention being in each case its publication. Note that there is no time limit in the sense in which this term is used in the EPC but a condition which is either fulfilled or not. So, if the six-months following an abusive disclosure ends on a day on which the EPO is closed for business (e.g. a Sunday), it is not extended under r.134(1) to the next day on which the EPO is open – a European application must be filed on the closed day itself or earlier if the disclosure is not to be taken into account.

G3/98 Headnote: "For the calculation of the six-month period referred to in Art. 55(1) EPC, the relevant date is the date of the actual filing of the European patent application; the date of priority is not to be taken account of in calculating this period." Proceedings were consolidated with G2/99.

T585/92 There is no evident abuse when a government department accidentally publishes a patent application earlier then the date requested by the applicant since the term implies some intent to cause harm or reasonable expectation that harm would ensue.

Guidelines See G-V.

5.5.11 Exhibition exemption

Art. 55(1)(b) For the application of Art. 54 a disclosure of the invention is not taken into consideration 872 if it occurred no earlier than six months preceding the filing of the European patent application and if it was due to, or in consequence of the fact that the applicant or his legal predecessor displayed the invention at an official, or officially recognised, international exhibition falling within the terms of the Convention on international exhibitions signed at Paris on November 22, 1928, and last revised on November 30, 1972.

Comment	See comment above under "abusive disclosure exemption" regarding the "no earlier than" language.
Art. 55(2)	In the case of Art. 55(1)(b), the exemption only applies if the applicant states, when filing the European patent application, that the invention has been so displayed and files a supporting certificate within the time limit and under the conditions laid down in the Implementing Regulations.
Comment	There is no remedy if the statement is not made on the filing date except perhaps to file another application if the six-month condition would still be met.
r.25	The period for filing the certificate is four months from the filing of the application. The certificate must have been issued at the exhibition by the authority responsible for the protection of intellectual property and must state that the invention was actually displayed there. It must also state the opening date of the exhibition and, where the first disclosure of the invention did not coincide with the opening date of the exhibition, the date of the first disclosure. The certificate must be accompanied by an identification of the invention, duly authenticated by the above-mentioned authority.
Art. 121	Further processing is possible if the four-month time limit is missed.
RRF Art. 2(1)(12)	The further processing fee is € 290 in this case.
Art. 122	Re-establishment would be possible if the further processing time limit was missed in spite of all due care having been shown.
G3/98	See comments above under "abusive disclosure exemption" regarding the fact that the six months condition applies to the filing date and not to any priority date.
OJ	Exhibitions which qualify as relevant international exhibitions are published in the Official Journal.
Guidelines	See A-IV, 3 and G-V, 4. The applicant is notified according to r.112(1) if the certificate is not filed in time in order to trigger the further processing period.

5.5.12   *Novelty of selection inventions*

873

Guidelines	The disclosure in the prior art of a general term does not, in principle, destroy the novelty of a subsequent claim to a specific embodiment falling within the general term but described at a lower order of generality (see Guidelines G-VI, 5 – the disclosure of "metal" would not destroy the novelty of a later claim to "copper"). The subsequent claim embodies a selection invention.
Case law	Selection inventions are most common in the chemical field. The lead case is T12/81. Here it was decided that the disclosure of a list of starting materials in combination with a list of potential processes made available the product of each process when carried out in respect of each starting material. However, it was acknowledged that when two starting materials had to be chosen from lists of some length, any particular product would be new. This concept was extended analogously in T7/86 to a prior art generic formula with multiple substituents where selection of any particular compound by choosing a substituent from each of at least two lists represents a novel selection.
	Specific chemical compounds are thus novel unless there is a direct and unambiguous prior disclosure of the same compound in the form of a technical teaching (T181/82, T296/87), the same applying to enantiomers where only the racemate is known (T296/87). However, with overlapping generic formulae the situation is less clear (T133/92, T12/90).
	A sub-range selected from a broader range disclosed in the prior art is novel if it is: (a) narrow; (b) removed from the preferred part of the prior art range; and (c) is a purposive as opposed to an arbitrary selection, i.e. has some new property associated with it (T279/89). More recent case law, however, has cast doubt on whether the third criterion (c) should be considered in the context of novelty (T1233/05 and T230/07). T1688/20 even proposes abandoning this test altogether as it is so subjective and applying a simple disclosure test. Another strand of case law seeks to assess novelty in the context of overlapping ranges by considering whether the skilled person would seriously contemplate working in the area of overlap (T666/89).
Guidelines	See G-VI, 5 and 8. The third part of the three-part test of T279/89 is now not to be applied by first instance departments. A selected subrange is novel if it is merely narrow and sufficiently far removed from specific examples.

5.6   Which inventions involve an inventive step?

5.6.1   Definition of inventive step

Art. 56   An invention is considered to involve an inventive step if, having regard to the state of the   874
art, it is not obvious to a person skilled in the art. However, for this purpose, the state of
the art does not include documents within the meaning of Art. 54(3).

5.6.2   Problem-solution approach

r.42(1)   The problem-solution approach is derived from r.42(1) which states that the description   875
must, inter alia, specify the technical field to which the invention relates and disclose
the invention, as claimed, in such terms that the technical problem and its solution can
be understood. This is a mandatory requirement of the description (T26/81). The problem-solution approach is used by the EPO universally in assessing inventive step.

Case law   The first step in applying the problem-solution approach is to identify the closest pri-
or art. This is the piece of prior art that, in retrospect, represents the most promising
springboard for making the invention (T254/86) and is usually the piece of art out of
those pieces of art aimed at solving the same problem as the invention that requires the
minimum structural modification (T606/89). Where the invention is a new process for
making a known compound, the closest prior art will be a known process for making the
compound (T641/89).

The second step is to assess the technical results achieved by the invention in relation to
the closest prior art and hence derive the objective problem that the invention has solved,
i.e. (1) what is the difference between the prior art and the claim, (2) what technical effect
is associated with the difference, and (3) the problem will be providing means delivering
such an effect. Only those features which contribute to the solution (T37/82) and which
distinguish over the prior art (T192/82) can contribute to an inventive improvement and
be used in deriving the objective technical problem. Furthermore, only features which
contribute to the technical character of the invention can be taken into account (T641/00).
The objective technical problem will often be the problem disclosed in the application
(T495/91) but may be different where the closest prior art has changed (T13/84). It is
possible to provide data during prosecution showing that a more challenging problem
has been solved (T1/80, T184/82) as long as the new problem is consistent with the application as a whole and the skilled person would derive the underlying technical effect
as being encompassed by original technical teaching (G2/21, T184/82). The formulated
problem should include no pointer to the solution (T229/85), although a non-technical
feature of a claim (e.g. an aim to be achieved in a non-technical field) may form part of the
problem (T641/00).

The third step in the problem-solution approach is to assess whether the solution to the
objective problem proposed by the invention would have been obvious to the skilled
person at the filing/priority date on the basis of his common general knowledge or on
the basis of a further piece of prior art that can be legitimately combined with the closest
prior art (see below).

G2/21   Headnote (2): A patent applicant or proprietor may rely upon a technical effect for inventive step if the skilled person, having the common general knowledge in mind, and based
on the application as originally filed, would derive said effect as being encompassed by the
technical teaching and embodied by the same originally disclosed invention.

Comment	Enlarged Board found that:
	(1) There are no exceptions to the principle of free evaluation of evidence but this does not necessarily mean that a technical effect may be relied by on an applicant or proprietor if the only evidence for it rests on post-published data.
	(2) The important question underlying the conflicting case law is whether the skilled person could have derived the technical effect relied on from the technical teaching of the application documents.
	(3) A lack of sufficiency exists for a second medical use invention if there is no proof of the therapeutic effect in the application and this cannot be remedied with post-published evidence – but this principle does not apply to the determination of inventive step.
	(4) A technical effect may therefore be relied on if it is "encompassed" by the technical teaching of the application, "embodies" the same invention and does not change the "nature" of the invention. In this case post-published data may be used to prove the technical effect occurs.
	(5) These rules are rather abstract but this is inevitable in establishing a general principle that applies a cross a number of different technical fields.
Guidelines	See G-VII, 5.

5.6.3   *The skilled person and common general knowledge*

876 Case law	The skilled person can be a person or a team (e.g. T141/87, T424/90) but has no inventive capacity (T39/93). The skilled person usually works in the same field as that in which the problem is formulated (T422/93) but if the problem prompts the skilled man to seek a solution in another technical field then the skilled person is in the latter field (T32/81).
	Common general knowledge includes encyclopaedias, textbooks, dictionaries and handbooks (T890/02) and may even include specific patents/publications in very new fields (T51/87).
	In general, whether a source is classed as common general knowledge is a unique assessment to be made for each technical area based on the practice of skilled people and, for example, includes generally available databases in the field of gene technology (T890/02).
Guidelines	See G-VII, 3

5.6.4   *Considerations when asking whether the invention is obvious*

877 Case law	Inventive step is to be assessed at the priority date or filing date of the application (T241/81, T268/89, T772/94). Hindsight is to be avoided (hence the absence of any pointer to the solution when formulating the objective technical problem) and the invention is to be judged from the closest prior art looking forwards, not from the invention looking backwards (T181/82).
	When assessing obviousness it is not a question of whether the skilled man could have made the invention but whether he would have done so in the expectation of some improvement or advantage (T2/83, T265/84).
	Documents may only be combined if it would have been obvious to the skilled man to do so (e.g. T142/84) and as long as there is no conflict between them (T2/81, T39/82).
Guidelines	G-VII, 6 (combining prior art documents), G-VII, 8 (no hindsight analysis)

5.6.5   *Inventive step based on an unexpected advantage*

878 Case law	Unforeseeable advantages achieved by a new invention may indicate an inventive step (T2/81, T39/82) and even a small increase in yield (e.g. 0.5 %) can be taken into account if commercially significant (T38/84). Where comparative tests are necessary to substantiate such an advantage, the closest structural prior art must be chosen for data generation (T181/82). Where inventive step relies on an unexpected technical effect, this property must extend to everything embraced by the claim scope (T939/92).
	However, where there is an obvious advantage to combining features, further unexpected advantages are merely a bonus and cannot be used to justify inventive step (T21/81, T936/96). Equally, if only one way forward exists for the skilled man (one-way street) a resulting advantage is irrelevant (T192/82, T69/83).
Guidelines	See G-VII, 10. Any unexpected effect relied upon must be associated with the characterising features of the invention.

5.6.6   *Further indicators of inventive step*

Case law

An inventive step may be present where there is no reasonable expectation of success   879
(T386/94). Secondary indications of inventive step include a long-felt want (T109/82,
T271/84), overcoming a prejudice (T18/81) and commercial success (T191/82, T677/91).
Sometimes, the discovery of an unrecognised problem can be non-obvious in itself, even
where the solution is immediately apparent when the problem is recognised (T2/83) but
not if the problem could have been posed by one of ordinary skill in the art, particularly
if arising during routine use of a known object (T109/82).

Guidelines

See G-VII, 10

Chapter 6: The Application

6.1 Elements of the application

880   Art. 78(1)   A European patent application must contain the following elements: (a) a request for the grant of a European patent; (b) a description of the invention; (c) one or more claims; (d) any drawings referred to in the description or the claims; (e) an abstract; and satisfy the requirements laid down in the Implementing Regulations.

r.49(1)   A translation submitted under Art. 14(2) or r.40(3) is deemed to be a document making up the European patent application.

6.2 General and physical requirements of the application

6.2.1 Prohibited matter

881   r.48(1)   A European patent application may not contain:
(a) statements or other matter contrary to "ordre public" or morality;
(b) statements disparaging the products or processes of any third party, or the merits or validity of applications or patents of any such party. Mere comparisons with the prior art are not considered disparaging per se;
(c) any statement or other matter obviously irrelevant or unnecessary under the circumstances.

r.48(2)(3)   See under publication and examination of formal requirements for the consequences of including prohibited matter.

Guidelines   See A-III, 8 and F-II, 4.4 and 7. Prohibited matter includes statements constituting an incitement to riot, racial, religious or other discriminatory propaganda and grossly obscene matter.

6.2.2 Presentation of the application documents

882   r.49(2)   The President of the EPO determines the presentation requirements of documents making up the application.

OJ   The application documents must comply with numerous requirements (see Art. 2 of Decision of the President dated 25 November 2022 ([2022] O.J. A113).

6.3 Requirements relating to the request

883   Art. 78(1)(a)   A European patent application must contain a request for grant.

6.3.1 Use of a specified form

884   r.41(1)   A form drawn up by the EPO must be used. This is Form 1001, available in several formats from the EPO website.

6.3.2 Drawings not allowed

885   r.49(2)   The President of the EPO determines the presentation requirements of documents making up the application.

OJ   The request should not contain drawings (see Art. 2(8) of Decision of the President dated 25 November 2022 ([2022] O.J. A113).

6.3.3 Petition for grant

886   r.41(2)(a)   The request must contain a petition for the grant of a European patent.

6.3.4 Details of the applicant

887   r.41(2)(c)   The request must state the name, address and nationality of the applicant and the State in which his residence or principal place of business is located.

Names of natural persons must be indicated by the person's family name and given names, the family name being indicated before the given names. Names of legal persons, as well as bodies equivalent to legal persons under the law governing them, must be indicated by their official designations.

Addresses must be indicated in accordance with the applicable customary requirements for prompt postal delivery. They must comprise all the relevant administrative units, including the house number, if any. It is recommended that fax and telephone number are indicated.

J2/01

For a divisional application the applicant(s) must be the registered applicant(s) for the parent application (unless a universal succession of rights has occurred). This cannot be remedied after filing the notional divisional application (unless as the correction of an obvious error).

Guidelines

See A-III, 4.2.1. Full details for each applicant must be provided.

6.3.5   Details of any representative

r.41(3)

Where there is more than one applicant, the request should preferably contain the appointment of one applicant or representative as common representative.   888

r.41(2)(d)

If a representative has been appointed, his name and the address of his place of business must be specified using the same format specified for the applicant details.

6.3.6   Designation of the inventor

Art. 81

A European patent application must designate the inventor.   889

r.19(1)

The designation of the inventor must be filed in the request (as confirmed by r.41(2)(j)) when the applicant and the inventor are the same. In the alternative, the designation of the inventor must be filed in a separate document.

Comment

See separate section below (Requirements relating to the designation of the inventor) for further details.

6.3.7   Title of the invention

r.41(2)(b)

The request must contain the title of the invention which must clearly and concisely state   890
the technical designation of the invention and must exclude all "fancy names".

Guidelines

See A-III, 7 and F-II, 3. No personal names, fancy names, non-technical terms, the expression 'etc', vague terms or trade marks/names should be used. The EPO will redraft the title of its own motion and without consulting the applicant if necessary – the Examining Division is ultimately responsible for the wording of the title but the Search Division will redraft it for inclusion in the published application where required.

6.3.8   Priority claim

r.41(2)(g)

Where applicable, the request must contain a declaration claiming the priority of an earlier   891
application and indicating the date on which and the country in or for which the earlier application was filed.

Comment

See separate section below (Requirements relating to a priority claim) for further details. A declaration of priority does not have to be made on filing.

6.3.9   Indication of divisional status

r.41(2)(e)

Where appropriate, the request must state that the application is a divisional application   892
and indicate the number of the earlier European patent application.

Guidelines

See A-IV, 1.3.2. If these indications are deficient, they may be corrected under r.58.

6.3.10   Indication that application is a replacement application

r.41(2)(f)

In all cases covered by Art. 61(1)(b) (new application filed because applicant had no right   893
to the original application) the request must state the number of the original application.

6.3.11   Figure of the drawings to be published with the abstract

894   r.47(4)   Where the application contains drawings, the applicant should indicate the figure, or, exceptionally, figures, which should accompany the abstract when it is published.

6.3.12   List of documents accompanying the request

895   r.41(2)(j)   The request must include a list of accompanying documents which also indicates the number of sheets of the description, claims, drawings and abstract filed with the request.

6.3.13   Signature

896   r.41(2)(h)   The request must contain the signature of the applicant or his representative (a failure to sign is correctable following an invitation under r.58).

r.2(2)   Where the EPC provides that a document must be signed, the authenticity of the document may be confirmed by handwritten signature or other appropriate means the use of which has been permitted by the President of the EPO. A document authenticated by such other means will be deemed to meet the legal requirements of signature in the same way as a document bearing a handwritten signature which has been filed in paper form.

Guidelines   Where there is more than one applicant, each (or the representative of each) must sign (A-III, 4.2.2 and A-VIII, 3.4)

6.3.14   Correction of the request

897   J21/94   Correction of the request is possible when the wrong request is filed with an application.

6.4   Requirements relating to the description

898   Art. 78(1)(b)   A European patent application must contain a description of the invention.

6.4.1   Need for a sufficient disclosure

899   Art. 83   A European patent application must disclose an invention in a manner sufficiently clear and complete for it to be carried out by a person skilled in the art.

G2/93   Sufficiency must be complied with at the filing date.

T1173/00   The decisive issue is whether the invention is sufficiently disclosed such that an average person skilled in the art, with knowledge of the patent and on the basis of that person's common general knowledge, could have carried it out.

Case law   The disclosure is sufficient if the invention can be carried out without undue burden (T435/91). A reasonable amount of trial and error (T226/85) and the occasional lack of success (T14/83) are not fatal but the skilled man must not be expected to rely on chance events (T727/95). Common general knowledge may be used to supplement the disclosure of an application (T171/84, T51/87) and this includes the contents of textbooks (T206/83) but not usually patent applications (T206/83) unless special circumstances, e.g. a new field of technology, prevail (T51/87). However, a comprehensive search should not be necessary (T206/83). It should be possible to perform the invention over the entire area of the claims (T409/91) and in this respect the disclosure of a single example may (e.g. Oncomouse, T19/90) or may not be enough (T409/91). If the claims cover many alternatives, the presence of a few non-working embodiments is not objectionable (G1/03). Objections under Art. 83 should only be raised where there are serious doubts substantiated by verifiable facts (T409/91 and T694/92).

r.31   Where a sample of biological material is necessary to practice the invention a deposit must be made before the filing date and certain information must be supplied in time for publication in order for the application to be sufficient (see below under Section 6.11.2).

Guidelines	See F-II, 4.1 and F-III. The description can reference other documents in order to properly comply with the sufficiency requirement but may not incorporate them by reference. Such a statement must be deleted during examination – the content of the referenced document can be imported into the description if necessary and if certain criteria are satisfied but Art. 123(2) must be carefully respected. See G-III, 1 and F-III, 3 – a claim to a machine that allegedly operates contrary to a well-established physical law (e.g. a perpetual motion machine), lacks sufficiency of disclosure. Where the successful performance of the invention is dependent on chance a lack of sufficiency also results.	

6.4.2   Content of the description

r.42(1)	The description must: (a) specify the technical field to which the invention relates; (b) indicate the background art which, as far as known to the applicant, can be regarded as useful for understanding the invention, for drawing up the European Search Report and for the examination, and, preferably, cite the documents reflecting such art; (c) disclose the invention, as claimed, in such terms that the technical problem (even if not expressly stated as such) and its solution can be understood, and state any advantageous effects of the invention with reference to the background art; (d) briefly describe the figures in the drawings, if any; (e) describe in detail at least one way of carrying out the invention claimed, using examples where appropriate and referring to the drawings, if any; and (f) indicate explicitly, when it is not obvious from the description or nature of the invention, the way in which the invention is industrially applicable.	900
T11/82	Pursuant to r.42(1)(b), prior art references must be added later where they are not in the application as filed.	
T407/87	The requirement under r.42(1)(e) is part of the more general requirement under Art. 83 for a sufficient disclosure. The lack of a detailed specific example is not necessarily fatal.	
r.29(3)	The industrial application of a sequence or partial sequence of a gene must be disclosed in the patent application.	
r.30	The description must include a sequence listing where the nature of the invention so requires.	
Guidelines	See F-II, 4. Background art which has not been acknowledged and which is identified during examination must be added to the description – this does not contravene Art. 123(2) since it is not subject matter relating to the invention. Any document which is citable only under Art. 54(3) must be acknowledged as such.	

6.4.3   Order of presentation of the content of the description

r.42(2)	The description must be presented in the manner and order specified in r.42(1), unless, owing to the nature of the invention, a different presentation would afford a better understanding or be more concise.	901
Guidelines	See F-II, 4.10.	

6.4.4   Description not to contain drawings

r.49(2)	The President of the EPO determines the presentation requirements of documents making up the application.	902
OJ	The description may not contain drawings but may contain chemical or mathematical formulae and tables (see Art. 2(8) of Decision of the President dated 25 November 2022 ([2022] O.J. A113).	
Guidelines	See A-IX, 11.	

6.5   Requirements relating to the claims

Art. 78(1)(c)	A European patent application must contain one or more claims.	903

6.5.1   *Requirement for clarity, conciseness and support*

904 Art. 84	The claims must be clear and concise and be supported by the description.
T1020/98	Clarity should not be confused with simplicity. A claim may be complex but clear. In particular, a Markush formula is the most concise way of defining a group of chemical compounds.
T3087/19	This decision, along with the majority of the case law, considers that Art. 84 imposes a requirement that the description must be amended in order to be in conformity with any claims agreed for grant.
Guidelines	See F-IV, 3.8 – a claim to an apparatus limited by the manner in which it is used lacks clarity. See also F-IV, 4 – claims should be clear in themselves without recourse to the description. A lack of clarity may result from inconsistency between the claims and the description (F-IV, 4.3), statements implying that the protection sought goes beyond the wording of the claims (F-IV, 4.4), the omission of essential features in the claims (F-IV, 4.5), the use of relative terms such as "thin" (F-IV, 4.6), the use of terms such as "about" and "approximately" (F-IV, 4.7) and the use of trade marks as technical features (F-IV, 4.8). See F-IV, 5 for conciseness. See F-IV, 6 for support.

6.5.2   *Claims to define matter the applicant seeks to protect*

905 Art. 84	The claims must define the matter for which protection is sought.
r.43(1)	Such a definition of the matter for which protection is sought must be in terms of the technical features of the invention.
Guidelines	See F-IV, 2.1.

6.5.3   *Situations in which two-part form is required*

906 r.43(1)	Wherever appropriate, claims must contain: (a) a statement indicating the designation of the subject matter of the invention and those technical features which are necessary for the definition of the claimed subject matter but which, in combination, form part of the prior art; and (b) a characterising part, beginning with the expression "characterised in that" or "characterised by", and specifying the technical features for which, in combination with the features stated under (a), protection is sought.
T13/84	The pre-characterising portion is normally based on the structurally closest prior art rather than the closest prior art for determining inventive step.
T170/84	The two-part form is not always appropriate. This is particularly true in the field of chemistry.
Guidelines	See F-IV, 2.2–2.3. Where the only relevant prior art is an Art. 54(3) citation, the two-part form should not be used. The relevant art should however be clearly acknowledged in the description.

6.5.4   *Number and type of claims allowed*

907 r.43(5)	The number of claims must be reasonable in consideration of the nature of the invention claimed.
r.43(2)	In particular, without prejudice to Art. 82 (unity of invention), the inclusion of more than one independent claim in the same category (product, process, apparatus or use) is only allowed if the subject matter of the application involves one of the following: (a) a plurality of interrelated products; (b) different uses of a product or apparatus; or (c) alternative solutions to a particular problem, where it is not appropriate to cover these alternatives by a single claim.
OJ	See [2002] O.J. 113 for further explanation. Note in particular that it is incumbent on the applicant to justify the presence of multiple claims in the same category, even where the requirements of r.43(2)(a), (b), or (c) are met.
r.43(3)	Any claim stating the essential features of an invention may be followed by one or more claims containing particular embodiments of that invention.

r.43(4)	A dependent claim must contain, if possible at the beginning, a reference to the claim whose features it includes and then state the additional features. A dependent claim directly referring to another dependent claim is also admissible. All dependent claims referring back to a single previous claim, and all dependent claims referring back to several previous claims, must be grouped together to the extent and in the most appropriate way possible.
Guidelines	See F-IV, 3.2 for examples of independent claims in the same category that are allowable. See F-IV, 3.3 for procedure under r.43(2). See F-IV, 3.4 and 3.5 for dependent claims. See F-IV, 5 for number of claims.

6.5.5   *Numbering of the claims*

r.43(5)	If there are two or more claims, they must be numbered consecutively in Arabic numerals.	908

6.5.6   *Omnibus claims generally not allowed*

r.43(6)	Except where absolutely necessary, claims may not rely on references to the description and drawings in specifying the technical features of the invention. In particular, they shall not contain such expressions as "as described in part … of the description", or "as illustrated in figure … of the drawings".	909
T150/82	The onus is on the applicant to demonstrate that an exceptional situation justifying the use of an omnibus claim prevails.	
Guidelines	See F-IV, 4.17.	

6.5.7   *References in claims to reference signs in figures*

r.43(7)	Where the application contains drawings which include reference signs, the technical features specified in the claims should preferably be followed by such reference signs relating to those features, placed in parentheses, if the intelligibility of the claim can thereby be increased. Such reference signs may not be construed as limiting the claim.	910
Guidelines	See F-IV, 4.19.	

6.5.8   *Unity of invention*

Art. 82	A European patent application must relate to one invention only or to a group of inventions so linked as to form a single general inventive concept.	911
r.44(1)	Such a group of inventions is taken to be so linked when there is a technical relationship among the inventions involving one or more of the same or corresponding special technical features, i.e. those features which define a contribution which each of the claimed inventions, considered as a whole, makes over the prior art.	
r.44(2)	It doesn't matter, when determining whether a group of inventions is so linked, whether they are in separate claims or alternatives within a single claim.	
Guidelines	See B-VII, 1 and F-V. The requirement for unity of invention is to ensure that sufficient fees are paid to cover the EPO's workload and that the subject matter of a patent is readily comprehensible for third parties. However, interconnected matter should not be split up needlessly. When evaluating unity of invention, prior art citable only under Art. 54(3) and accidental anticipations citable under Art. 54(2) should not be taken into account (F-V,3.1)	

6.5.9   *Allowability of disclaimers*

T4/80	Disclaimers are allowed where the subject matter cannot be described positively.	912
Comment	Disclaimers present on the filing of an application are of course not subject to the restrictions imposed by the Enlarged Board of Appeal Decisions G1/03 and G2/03. See below under amendment for the rules governing the introduction of an undisclosed disclaimer during prosecution.	
Guidelines	See F-IV, 4.19.	

6.5.10   *Functional features*

| 913 | Case law | Functional features are allowable, where necessary in order to obtain a fair scope of protection. The functional language can cover known or future variants (T292/85) and, as long as some suitable variants are known, some of the variants covered may be unsuitable or unavailable (T292/85). |
| | Guidelines | See F-IV, 6.5. |

6.5.11   *Claims not to contain drawings*

914	r.49(2)	The President of the EPO determines the presentation requirements of documents making up the application.
	OJ	The claims may not contain drawings but may contain chemical or mathematical formula and, if the subject matter makes their use desirable, tables (see Art. 2(8) of Decision of the President dated 25 November 2022 ([2022] O.J. A113).
	Guidelines	See F-IV, 2.4.

6.6   Requirements relating to the abstract

915	Art. 78(1)(e)	A European patent application must contain an abstract.
	Art. 85	The abstract serves for use as technical information; it may not be taken into account for any other purpose, in particular not for the purpose of interpreting the scope of the protection sought nor for the purpose of applying Art. 54(3).
	r.47(5)	It should therefore be drafted so that it constitutes an efficient instrument for the purposes of searching in the particular technical field. In particular, it should make it possible to assess whether consultation of the European patent application itself is necessary.
	r.47(1)	The abstract must indicate the title of the invention.
	r.47(2)	The abstract must contain a concise summary of the disclosure as contained in the description, the claims and any drawings; the summary must indicate the technical field to which the invention pertains and must be drafted in a way which allows the clear understanding of the technical problem, the gist of the solution of that problem through the invention and the principal use or uses of the invention. The abstract must, where applicable, contain the chemical formula which, among those contained in the application, best characterises the invention. It must not contain statements on the alleged merits or value of the invention or on speculative applications thereof.
	r.47(3)	The abstract should preferably not contain more than 150 words.
	r.47(4)	Where the application contains drawings, the applicant must indicate the figure, or exceptionally figures, of the drawings which should be published with the abstract. However, the EPO may decide to publish one or more other figures if it considers that they better characterise the invention.
	r.47(4)	Each essential feature mentioned in the abstract and illustrated by a drawing must be followed by a reference sign placed in parentheses.
	r.49(2)	The President of the EPO determines the presentation requirements of documents making up the application.
	OJ	The abstract may not contain drawings but may contain chemical or mathematical formulae and tables (see Art. 2(8) of Decision of the President dated 25 November 2022 ([2022] O.J. A113).
	Guidelines	See B-X, 7(i), F-II, 2 and F-II,Annex 1. Whilst the abstract is supplied by the applicant, the search examiner has the responsibility of deciding on its final wording and content. The search examiner may decide that no figure of the drawings should accompany the abstract, even where the applicant has proposed one or more himself. The definitive content of the abstract is transmitted to the applicant with the search report.

6.7   Requirements relating to the drawings

916	Art. 78(1)(d)	A European patent application must contain any drawings referred to in the description or claims.
	r.49(2)	The President of the EPO determines the presentation requirements of documents making up the application.
	OJ	Drawings must comply with a range of formal requirements (see Art. 1 of Decision of the President dated 25 November 2022 ([2022] O.J. A113).

Guidelines	See A-IX and F-II, 5.

6.8 Requirements relating to any priority claim

6.8.1 Relevance of the Paris Convention

Preamble	The EPC is a special agreement within the meaning of Article 19 of the Convention for the Protection of Industrial Property, signed in Paris on 20 March 1883 and last revised on 14 July 1967.	917
PC Art. 19	The countries of the Union (as established by the Paris Convention) have the right to make separately between themselves special agreements for the protection of industrial property, as long as these agreements do not contravene the provisions of the Paris Convention.	
Comment	Unlike the situation under the PCT, which specifically applies it, the Paris Convention is not directly applicable under the EPC, in the sense of being part of the law, since the EPC contains its own complete priority code. However, this code must be consistent with the Paris Convention which can therefore be used to interpret it (see J15/80, G3/93, G2/98).	

6.8.2 Who may make a claim to priority?

Art. 87(1)	The priority right is enjoyed by a person who has duly filed in, or for a certain State (see below) a certain kind of application (see below) and his successors in title.	918
T1201/14	Since neither the EPC nor the Paris Convention specify any rules for determining a valid succession of title, national law must be applied.	
Comment	It is, however, as discussed in T1201/14 and other decisions, not entirely clear which national law should apply: the national law applying to a relevant agreement, the national law of the country in which the invention was made, the national law of the country in which the priority application was filed, the national law of the country in which the parties to the agreement reside or the national law of the country in which the priority claim is being examined.	
Case law	As stated in T1201/14 and numerous other decisions concerning priority, if priority is claimed by a person who is not entitled at that point to claim it (not being the applicant for the earlier application or his valid successor in title) then the priority claim is invalid and this cannot subsequently be remedied, for example by putting in place a retrospective assignment of rights.	

6.8.3 Length of priority period

Art. 87(1)	A right of priority exists during a period of 12 months from the date of filing of the first application.	919
r.134(1)	If the priority period ends on a day on which one of the filing offices of the EPO is not open for business then it is extended until the first day on which all of the filing offices of the EPO are open, regardless of the EPO filing office with which the European patent application is actually filed.	
r.134(3)	Equally, if a European patent application is to be filed at a national office and that office is not open for business on the last day of the priority period then the priority period is extended for filing at that office until the first day on which it is open again.	
r.133	The priority year may be deemed complied with even if the filing date is more than 12 months from the priority date when documents have been sent to the EPO in good time.	
Art. 122	Re-establishment is possible if an applicant fails to comply with the priority year. No such remedy was available under EPC1973. However, according to r.136(1), the request must be filed in writing within two months of the expiry of the priority period (which may be longer than 12 months by virtue of r.134(1)).	
Art. 121(4)	Further processing is not available if the priority period is not complied with.	
Guidelines	See A-III, 6.1. A European patent application may not claim the priority of an application filed on the same day that the European patent application is filed. Such a priority claim is disregarded (unless it is a mistake that is corrected).	

6.8.4   *Priority claim to be in respect of the same invention*

920 Art. 87(1)

The claims of the subsequent application that claims priority must be in respect of the same invention as that disclosed in the earlier application.

Art. 88(3)

If one or more priorities are claimed in respect of a European patent application, the right of priority covers only those elements of the European patent application which are included in the application or applications whose priority is claimed.

Art. 88(4)

If certain elements of the invention for which priority is claimed do not appear among the claims formulated in the previous application, priority may nonetheless be granted, provided that the documents of the previous application as a whole specifically disclose such elements.

G2/98

Headnote: The requirement for claiming priority of 'the same invention', referred to in Art. 87(1) EPC means that priority of a previous application in respect of a claim in a European patent application in accordance with Art. 88 EPC is to be acknowledged only if the skilled person can derive the subject matter of the claim directly and unambiguously, using common general knowledge, from the previous application as a whole.

The alternative (i.e. allowing priority where a feature not disclosed in the priority application has been inserted which merely limits scope and is not related to function and effect) was seen to be dangerously subjective and changeable during prosecution in the light of fresh prior art. The strict approach was seen to be consistent with the Paris Convention and Arts 87–89 EPC.

T81/87

The priority document must also be an enabling disclosure of the claimed invention for a priority claim to be valid.

Guidelines

See F-VI, 2.2.

6.8.5   *What kind of application may be used as a basis for claiming priority?*

921 Art. 87(1)

The priority application must be an application for a patent, a utility model or a utility certificate in or for:
(a) any State party to the Paris Convention for the Protection of Industrial Property; or
(b) any member of the World Trade Organisation; or
(c) any State recognised by virtue of an agreement made under Art. 87(5).

Art. 87(5)

If the first filing has been made with an industrial property authority which is not subject to the Paris Convention for the Protection of Industrial Property, or the Agreement Establishing the World Trade Organisation, Art. 87(1)–(4) apply if that authority, according to a communication issued by the President of the EPO, recognises that a first filing made with the EPO gives rise to a right of priority under conditions and with effects equivalent to those laid down in the Paris Convention.

Guidelines

No communication from the President of the EPO under Art. 87(5) has ever been made (A-III, 6.2).

EPC1973

Art. 87(1) EPC1973 only recognised a priority claim in respect of a previous application filed in or for a Paris Convention country – priority rights based on applications filed in WTO countries were not recognised – see G2/02 below. This law continues to apply to all applications filed before the coming into force of EPC2000 and corresponding patents.

G2/02

Headnote: The TRIPS agreement does not entitle the applicant for a European patent application to claim priority from a first filing in a State which was not at the relevant date a member of the Paris Convention but was a member of the WTO/TRIPS agreement (joined with G3/02). This decision was taken under Art. 87(1) EPC1973 and does not apply to European patent applications filed after the coming into force of EPC2000.

J15/80

A design application such as a German Geschmacksmuster does not give rise to a priority right under the terms of Art. 87(1).

OJ

The EPO recognises a US provisional application as being a valid earlier application for the purposes of claiming priority (see Notice from the EPO dated 26 January 1996, [1996] O.J. 81 and Guidelines A-III, 6.2).

Art. 87(2)

Every filing that is equivalent to a regular national filing under the national law of the State where it was made or under bilateral or multilateral agreements, including the EPC, is recognised as giving rise to a right of priority.

Art. 87(3)

By a regular national filing is meant any filing that is sufficient to establish the date on which the application was filed, whatever may be the outcome of the application.

Art. 87(4) Priority may normally only be claimed from the first filing of any particular subject matter but a subsequent application in respect of the same subject matter as a previous first application and filed in or for the same State is considered as the first application for the purposes of determining priority, provided that, at the date of filing the subsequent application, the previous application has been withdrawn, abandoned or refused, without being open to public inspection and without leaving any rights outstanding, and has not served as a basis for claiming a right of priority. The previous application may not thereafter serve as a basis for claiming a right of priority.

Guidelines See A-III, 6.2 and F-VI, 1.4. The previous application may be a national application, an application filed under a regional patent treaty such as the EPC, or an international application filed under the PCT. A member of the WTO is not necessarily a state as such, but can be a region with special status such as Taiwan.

6.8.6   *Procedure for claiming priority – declaration*

Art. 88(1) An applicant for a European patent desiring to take advantage of the priority of a previous application must file a declaration of priority in accordance with the Implementing Regulations.   922

r.52(1) The declaration must indicate the date of the previous filing, the State party to the Paris Convention or Member of the World Trade Organisation in or for which it was made and the file number. This provision applies mutatis mutandis in the case of Art. 87(5) (other State from which a priority claim is recognised).

r.52(2)(4) The declaration can be made at any time within 16 months from the earliest priority date claimed but should preferably be made on filing the European application and may not be made after a request for early publication under Art. 93(1)(b) has been made.

r.52(3)(4) Furthermore, the applicant may correct a declaration of priority at any time within 16 months from the earliest priority date claimed, or, where the correction would cause a change in the earliest priority date claimed, within 16 months from the corrected earliest priority date, whichever 16-month period expires first, provided that such a correction may be submitted until the expiry of four months from the date of filing accorded to the European patent application. Again, however, no correction may be made after a request for early publication under Art. 93(1)(b) has been made.

Comment A priority claim may thus only be added within 16 months from the earliest priority date (which could be the added date). However, a priority date may be corrected within the later of: (1) four months from the filing date, and (2) the earlier of (the original priority date + 16 months) and (the new priority date + 16 months). Under EPC1973 it was only possible to add a priority claim as a correction of the request under r.139 EPC (r.88 EPC1973) and a correction in that sense meant that the applicant acted contrary to his original intention. The r.139 mechanism still applies but now the applicant can also add a priority claim under r.52(2) even if he just changes his mind. Correction under r.139 is generally possible if received in time for a warning to be included in the published application that the priority claim could change, and in rare circumstances even later.

Art. 121 Further processing is ruled out in respect of the r.52(2) and r.52(3) time limits.

Art. 122 Re-establishment, however, is available.

Guidelines See A-III, 6.5 and F-VI, 3.2. If the declaration of priority is made subsequent to filing the request, a corrected request will not be required. The filing of a certified copy, if it contains the relevant information, will be seen as an implicit declaration of priority.

See A-III, 6.5.3. The date of the previous application and the State in or for which it was filed are the essential elements of the declaration. If one of these elements is missing then the declaration has not been made. The lack of the file number, on the other hand, can be rectified on notification by the EPO under Art. 90(4)/r.58 (as of right) or under r.139 (if the conditions established by the relevant case law are met).

See A-IV, 1.2.2. For a divisional application, no explicit declaration is necessary in order for the divisional to enjoy the right of priority to which the parent is entitled.

r.52(5) The particulars in the declaration of priority are published with the application and the patent.

6.8.7   Procedure for claiming priority – certified copy

923   Art. 88(1)   An applicant desiring to take advantage of the priority of a previous application must also file any other document required under a provision of the Implementing Regulations.

r.53(1)(2)   A copy of the previous application must be filed within 16 months of the earliest priority date claimed. This copy, and the date of filing of the previous application, must be certified as correct by the authority with which the application was filed. The copy will be deemed to be duly filed if a copy of that application available to the EPO is to be included in the file of the European patent application under the conditions determined by the President of the EPO.

OJ   See Decision of the President dated 13 November 2021 ([2021] O.J. A83). The applicant may request the EPO to include in the file, free of charge, any priority document available from the WIPO Digital Access Service (DAS) if the necessary access code is provided. Furthermore, the EPO will obtain a priority document, without being requested and free of charge, and include it in the file, if it is a European patent application or an international application filed with the EPO as receiving Office. If, however, a priority document cannot be included in the file, it will not be deemed to have been filed. If the priority document cannot be included in the file because the applicant has not filed a request for the EPO to retrieve it from DAS or it is not available to the EPO from DAS, the EPO will invite the applicant to file a copy pursuant to r.53(1) EPC.

Comment   For European applications filed before 01 July 2020 and Euro-PCT applications entering the EPO regional phase before that date the EPO would have automatically obtained a copy of any Japanese priority application but a request must now be made for the EPO to retrieve it via DAS or else it must be filed by the applicant. The lack of automatic inclusion also applies if the Japanese priority application could not be included in the file by 31 December 2021 (Notice of the EPO dated 31 March 2020; [2020] O.J. A58). For European applications filed before 01 January 2022 and Euro-PCT applications entering the European regional phase before that date the EPO would likewise have automatically obtained a copy of any Chinese, Korean or US priority application but a request must now be made for the EPO to retrieve it via DAS or else it must be filed directly by the applicant. The lack of automatic inclusion also applies if the relevant Chinese, Korean or US priority application could not be included in the file by 30 June 2023 (Notice of the EPO dated 13 November 2021; [2021] O.J. A84).

OJ   See Notice from the EPO dated 18 October 2018 ([2018] OJ A79). Details are provided concerning the generation of a Digital Access Service (DAS) code for a first filing at the EPO. The code is available only to the applicant and stored in the non-public part of the application file. See also Notice from the EPO dated 22 February 2019 ([2019] OJ A27) – this service is also extended to international applications filed with the EPO as receiving Office.

OJ   Where the application claiming priority is a divisional application or a replacement application (Art. 61(1)(b)), there is no need to file a copy of the priority document if it was filed during the prosecution of the parent application (see Decision of the President dated 12 July 2007, [2007] O.J. Special Edition No. 3 B2). See also Guidelines A-IV, 1.2.2 – if the priority document has not been filed in respect of the parent at the time when the divisional is filed then it must be filed for both applications or filed first for the parent along with a letter in respect of the divisional drawing attention to that filing.

OJ   A priority document is one of the few documents which cannot be filed by fax (see Decision of the President dated 20 February 2019, [2019] O.J. A18). A priority document may be filed electronically using EPO Online Filing (OLF) or Online Filing 2.0 if it has been digitally signed by the issuing authority in a manner acceptable to the EPO (see Decision of the President dated 03 May 2023, [2023] O.J. A48). A priority document may under no circumstances be filed using the web-form filing service or the EPO Contingency Upload Service. If filed by an inappropriate means the priority document is considered not to have been received.

Guidelines   See A-III, 6.7 and F-VI, 3.3.
J11/95   The priority document must be sent to the correct file to have been received in time.
r.54   Where the previous application is a European patent application, a certified copy can be obtained from the EPO. See Guidelines A-XI, 6.

RRFArt. 3(1)	The amount of the administrative fee for providing a certified copy is fixed by the President of the EPO and is currently € 115 (see decision of the President dated 17 January 2023, [2023] O.J. A3).
RRFArt. 4(1)(2)	Where a due date is not specified for the payment of a fee, either in the EPC or the PCT, or their regulations, it falls due on the date of receipt of the request for the service incurring the fee concerned. However, the President of the EPO may decide that such services may be carried out without advance payment.

6.8.8   *Procedure for claiming priority – translation*

r.53(3)	If the previous application is not in one of the official languages of the European Patent Office, and the validity of the priority claim is relevant to the determination of the patentability of the invention concerned, the EPO will invite the applicant for or proprietor of the European patent to file a translation of that application into one of the official languages within a period to be specified.	924
r.132(2)	The period will be from two to six months (see Guidelines below).	
r.53(3)	Alternatively, a declaration may be submitted that the European patent application is a complete translation of the previous application.	
OJ	Where the application claiming priority is a divisional application or a replacement application under Art. 61(1)(b), there is no need to file the translation of the priority application if it was filed during prosecution of the parent application. (See Decision of the President dated 12 July 2007, [2007] O.J. Special Edition No. 3 B2).	
r.53(3)	If a requested translation is not supplied, the right of priority for the application or patent is lost and the applicant or proprietor is informed accordingly.	
Art. 121	In pre-grant proceedings, further processing is available to the applicant.	
Art. 122	In post-grant proceedings, re-establishment is available to the proprietor.	
Guidelines	See A-III, 6.8, F-VI, 3.4 and D-VII, 2. The EPO may demand a translation if the validity of the priority claim becomes an issue in grant or opposition proceedings. If the need for a translation is evident at the search stage an invitation is sent and the translation must be filed within the period for requesting examination under r.70(1) for confirming the applicant wishes to proceed further under r.70(2) (subject to a minimum of two months being available as per r.132(2) EPC). Otherwise an invitation is sent by the Examining Division or Opposition Division, as the case may be (and the time limit set will be four months). Since the period for supplying the translation under r.53(3) is set by the EPO, it is possible to request an extension. If further processing or re-establishment is necessary, one fee is payable for each priority document. As for any loss of rights, if the right to priority is lost a decision under r.112(2) may be requested if the EPO is in error. The declaration that the European patent application is a complete translation of the priority document is only usually valid when the description and claims are both identical. If, however, the European patent application was filed without claims then only the description needs to be identical.	

6.8.9   *Can one application claim more than one priority?*

Art. 88(2)	Multiple priorities may be claimed in respect of a European patent application, notwithstanding the fact that they originated in different countries. Where appropriate, multiple priorities may be claimed for any one claim. Where multiple priorities are claimed, time limits which run from the date of priority run from the earliest date of priority.	925
G1/15	Headnote: Under the EPC, entitlement to partial priority may not be refused for a claim encompassing alternative subject matter by virtue of one or more generic expressions or otherwise (generic "OR"-claim) provided that said alternative subject-matter has been disclosed for the first time, directly, or at least implicitly, unambiguously and in an enabling manner in the priority document. No other substantive conditions or limitations apply in this respect.	

The Enlarged Board found that in the case of a claim that generically covers a number of different embodiments, partial priority must always be recognised for those embodiments that are disclosed in an earlier application from which priority is claimed. This is the case regardless of whether the alternatives are explicitly stated in the claim or not and regardless of the number of alternatives present. Thus, the patentability of any subject matter falling within the scope of a claim which was disclosed in the priority application is to be judged at the priority date. In this way, the problem of so-called "poisonous priority" does not arise.

Guidelines   See F-VI, 1.5.

6.8.10   *Can one priority be claimed in more than one application?*

926   T15/01   Once a priority right has been generated, it may be validly claimed in one or more later European applications filed in the Convention year.

6.8.11   *Effect of priority right*

927   Art. 89   The right of priority has the effect that the date of priority counts as the date of filing of the European patent application for the purposes of Art. 54(2) and Art. 54(3) (state of the art) and Art. 60(2) (right to a European patent).

G3/93   This effect only applies when the claimed invention is directly and unambiguously derivable from the priority document. Where this is not the case, a document published by the applicant in the priority year and having the same content as the priority document will be citable against the later claim.

6.8.12   *Obligation to file copies of search results when claiming priority*

928   r.141(1)   See under section 25.15. The applicant has an obligation to file copies of search results relating to the priority application.

6.9   Requirements relating to the designation of the inventor

929   Art. 81   A European patent application must designate the inventor. If the applicant is not the inventor or is not the sole inventor, the designation must contain a statement indicating the origin of the right to the European patent.

r.19(1)   The designation of the inventor must be filed in the request (as confirmed by r.41(2)(j)) when the applicant and the inventor are the same. In the alternative, the designation of the inventor must be filed in a separate document – the designation must state the family name, given names and country and place of residence of the inventor, contain the statement referred to in Art. 81 and bear the signature of the applicant or his representative.

r.2(2)   Where the EPC provides that a document must be signed, the authenticity of the document may be confirmed by handwritten signature or other appropriate means, the use of which has been permitted by the President of the EPO. A document authenticated by such other means will be deemed to meet the legal requirements of signature in the same way as a document bearing a handwritten signature which has been filed in paper form.

r.19(2)   The EPO does not verify the accuracy of the designation of the inventor.

OJ   See Notice from the EPO dated 22 February 2021 ([2021] O.J. A12). Following the entry into force of amended r.19 EPC on 01 April 2021, the full name and address of each inventor is no longer required, only their country and place of residence. Equally, the EPO no longer notifies the inventors of their designation.

r.21   A designation of the inventor may be corrected if the correction is appropriately authorised. See section 22.1.3.

Guidelines   See A-III, 5. See also A-IV, 1.5 – a separate designation of the inventor is required for a divisional application. The country and place of residence of the inventor specified may be that of the inventor's employer.

J8/20   The inventor must be a person with legal capacity (and not, for example, a machine embodying artificial intelligence).

6.10 Language requirements of the application

6.10.1 Acceptable languages of filing

Art. 14(2)	A European patent application may be filed in any language, regardless of the residence or nationality of the applicant.
Guidelines	See A-VII, 1

930

6.10.2 Requirement for a translation

Art. 14(1)(2)	If the application is not filed in one of the official languages of the EPO (i.e. English, French or German), it must be translated into one of the official languages in accordance with the Implementing Regulations.
r.6(1)	The translation must be filed within two months of filing the European patent application.
r.135(2)	Further processing does not apply to the r.6(1) time limit but there is, in any case, no direct loss of rights.
r.57(a)/r.58	The absence of a required translation is a formal deficiency that may be corrected (see Chapter 8).
Art. 14(2)	If a required translation is not filed in due time, the application is deemed to be withdrawn.
r.5	The EPO may require the applicant to supply a certificate indicating that the translation corresponds to the original text within a period to be specified.
Art. 14(2)	Throughout proceedings before the EPO, the translation may be brought into conformity with the application as filed.
Guidelines	The exception to this rule is that no amendment may be made in post-grant proceedings that extends the protection of the patent contrary to Art. 123(3) (A-VII, 7).
r.49(1)	A translation submitted under Art. 14(2) is deemed to be a document making up the European patent application.
Art. 70(2)	Where a translation is required under Art. 14(2), the text as originally filed is the "application as filed" within the meaning of the Convention and is therefore the basis for determining whether the subject matter of the application or patent extends beyond the content of the application as filed.
r.7	However, unless evidence is provided to the contrary, the EPO will, for the purposes of determining whether the subject matter of a European patent application or European patent extends beyond the content of the European patent application as filed, assume that the translation referred to in Art. 14(2) is in conformity with the original text of the application.

931

6.10.3 Languages of filing under EPC1973

Comment	European patent applications had to be filed in an official language of the European Patent Office (English, French and German) under EPC1973 the only exception being that residents and nationals of Contracting States having an official language other than English, French and German could use such a national language instead and file a translation into an EPO official language. If an application was filed in one of the languages specified by Art. 14(2) EPC1973 by an applicant who did not possess the relevant residence/nationality a date of filing could not be accorded (J9/01, J6/05).

932

6.10.4 Languages accepted if filing at a national office

NatLaw	Some national offices have specific language requirements (see book on national law, Table II).

933

6.10.5 Language of a divisional application or a replacement application

Art. 76(1)	A divisional application must be filed in accordance with the Implementing Regulations.
r.36(2)	A divisional application must be in the language of the proceedings for the earlier patent application. If the earlier patent application was not filed in an official language of the EPO, the divisional application may be filed in the language of the earlier application but a translation into the language of the proceedings for the earlier application must be filed within two months of the filing of the divisional application.
Art. 61(2)	Art. 76(1) applies to a replacement application mutatis mutandis.

934

J3/14	If a divisional application (or, applying Art. 61(2) a replacement application) is filed in a language other than one specified by r.36(2) then it will not be dealt with as a European (divisional) patent application by analogous application of Art. 90(2). No remedy is possible.
r.57(a)/r.58	The absence of a required translation is a formal deficiency that may be corrected (see Chapter 8).
r.135(2)	Further processing is not possible in respect of the r.36(2) time limit. However, the absence of a translation is a formal defect that can be corrected under r.58 EPC.
Guidelines	See A-IV, 1.3.3 and A-VII, 1.3.

6.11   Requirements relating to biotechnological inventions

6.11.1   *Sequence listings*

935 r.30(1)	If nucleotide or amino acid sequences are disclosed in a European patent application, the description must contain a sequence listing conforming to the rules laid down by the President of the European Patent Office for the standard representation of nucleotide and amino acid sequences.
OJ	See Decision of the President dated 28 April 2011 ([2011] O.J. 372) for applications filed before 01 July 2022 and Decision of the President dated 09 December 2021 ([2021] O.J. A96) for applications filed on or after 01 July 2022. The description must contain a sequence listing which is to be filed in electronic form (as a TXT file before the 2022 change and as an XML file afterwards). A paper copy is not required. The sequence listing is published with the application and patent as part of the description. Where a divisional application is filed on or after 01 July 2022, a sequence listing in the divisional must comply with the new XML standard, even if a sequence listing in TXT format was validly filed for the parent application (see Notice from the EPO dated 09 December 2020 ([2021] O.J. A97).
r.30(3)	See section 8.4.8 for the consequences of not filing a required sequence listing at the filing date.
r.30(2)	A sequence listing filed after the date of filing shall not form part of the description.
Guidelines	See A-IV, 5 and F-II, 6. No sequence listing is required if the application merely refers to a sequence that can be retrieved from a publicly available database. If a sequence listing in the correct format has been filed in respect of a parent application, a further listing does not need to be filed in respect of its divisional in order to satisfy the requirements of r.30 but from the point of view of disclosure, it must be filed again if it is to form part of the divisional application as filed.

6.11.2   *Deposit of biological material*

936 r.31–34	There are specific requirements relating to the deposit of biological material.
Case law	Rule 31 is only important where the written description is not in itself sufficient (T361/87). This being the case, a deposit is necessary at the filing date (corresponding to the filing of the written description) and the culture must be available at the publication date (corresponding to the publication of the description). Certain information regarding the deposit must therefore be supplied in time for publication. An "expert option" may be used to restrict the availability of the deposit before grant of the patent.
	Usually, the applicant and depositor must be the same (T118/87). If this is not the case then suitable measures need to be taken to ensure the sample is freely available.
OJ	See Notice from the EPO dated 07 July 2010 ([2010] O.J. 498) in general and [2017] O.J. A60 specifically with reference to the recognition of experts under r.32.
G2/93	Headnote: The information concerning the file number of a culture deposit according to r.28(1)(c) EPC may not be submitted after expiry of the time limit set out in r.28(2)(a) EPC. NB. these Rules are now r.31(1)(c) and r.31(2)(a) under EPC2000.
	The Enlarged Board decided that Art. 83 (sufficiency of disclosure) must be complied with at the filing date. The later provision of the file number must be able to be linked to information in the application as filed showing the deposit has been made. The indication of the file number is instrumental in enabling a person to carry out the invention and must be provided by the time limit set by the legislator to ensure it is included in the application as published.

r.135(1)	Further processing is not available where the r.31(2) time limit is missed.
Guidelines	According to A-IV, 4.1, re-establishment would not be available either since "a lack of disclosure cannot be remedied by way of re-establishment under Art. 122".
Guidelines	See A-IV, 4 and F-III, 6.

6.12 Special requirements for divisional applications

Art. 76(1) To be awarded the filing date of its parent application (and any right of priority enjoyed 937
by the parent application), a divisional application must not contain subject matter extending beyond the content of the parent application as filed.

G1/05 However, a divisional application which contains subject matter extending beyond the content of the parent application on its filing date can later be amended to comply with Art. 76(1). Such amendment may take place whether the parent application is still pending or not.

Guidelines See A-IV, 1.2.1 – the compliance of a divisional application with Art. 76(1) is assessed by the Examining Division during substantive examination and not by the Receiving Section. During formal examination by the Receiving Section, the divisional application is provisionally awarded the filing date of the parent application if it complies with the usual requirements of Art. 80/r.40. See also C-IX, 1.4 – if the applicant does not amend a divisional application so as to comply with Art. 76(1) then the divisional application is refused pursuant to Art. 97(2). It is not possible for a divisional application which does not comply with Art. 76(1) to be awarded the date on which it was actually filed as a filing date (as confirmed in G1/05).

See also A-IV, 1.2.2 – the divisional cannot enjoy the parent application's right to priority if that priority right has been lost before the filing of the divisional. One or more priority rights that the divisional benefits from can subsequently be withdrawn if desired. There is no need to explicitly claim the parent application's priority rights when filing the divisional application – they apply automatically.

G1/06 It is possible for a divisional application to be itself divided from a divisional application. For this second or further generation divisional application to comply with Art. 76(1) and be awarded the filing date of the original "root" application, each preceding application in the sequence of divisionals must have disclosed the subject matter contained in that divisional. What was claimed in the previous members of the sequence is irrelevant.

Guidelines See C-IX, 1.1. Once a divisional application has been filed, it comes quite separate from the parent application from which it has been divided. For example, the prosecution of a divisional is not stayed pending the outcome of opposition proceedings concerning the parent.

Case law It is possible for a divisional application to be filed with a description identical to that of the parent application (T441/92). Indeed, the claims may also be identical, but in this case one or both of the two applications will require amendment since the EPO will not grant two patents for the same subject matter (Guidelines G/IV/5.4, G1/05). There is no question of the subject matter of the divisional becoming abandoned in respect of the parent application (T118/91).

Chapter 7: Filing a European Patent Application

7.1 Who is entitled to file a European patent application?

938 Art. 58	A European patent application may be filed by any natural or legal person, or any body equivalent to a legal person by virtue of the law governing it.
Art. 59	A European patent application may also be filed either by joint applicants or by two or more applicants designating different Contracting States.
Comment	Note that a common representative must be appointed – r.151 – and a single text maintained – Art. 118.
Comment	In contrast to the situation under the PCT, anybody of any nationality or residence can file a European patent application.

7.2 Where may a European patent application be filed?

7.2.1 Where to file a regular European patent application

939 Art. 75(1)	A European patent application may be filed: (a) at the European Patent Office; or (b) if the law of a Contracting State so permits, at the central industrial property office or other competent authority of that State. An application filed in this way has the same effect as if it had been filed on the same date at the European Patent Office.
r.35(1)	European patent applications may be filed in writing with the European Patent Office in Munich, The Hague or Berlin, or the authorities referred to in Art. 75(1)(b).
Comment	Divisional and replacement applications must be filed directly with the EPO – see below
OJ	Applications may be filed directly with the EPO at any of the filing offices specified in r.35(1) (see decision of the President dated 03.01.2017, [2017] O.J. A11). The Berlin office, being a sub-office of The Hague, is such a filing office. However, the Vienna sub-office is not a filing office. Applications may be filed in Munich at the EPO Pschorrhofe building or at the Isar building.
Guidelines	See A-II, 1.1
NatLaw	See Table II for information on whether a particular country allows the filing of European applications with its national authority and, if so, what languages are accepted. Only San Marino, the Netherlands and Belgium refuse to allow the filing of a European application at their national patent offices under any circumstances (other than where national security issues exist). Italy will only allow the filing of a European patent application at its national office if it claims the priority of a national Italian application.
r.134(3)	The extension of time limits in the case of shut days and mail interruptions (r.134(1) and (2)) applies to national offices in the same way that it applies to the EPO.
Comment	The extension of time limits under r.134 may have the effect of extending the priority period (see section 6.8.3).

7.2.2 Where to file a divisional application

940 Art. 76(1)	Divisional applications must be filed directly with the EPO in accordance with the Implementing Regulations.
r.36(2)	Divisional applications must be filed with the EPO in Munich, The Hague or Berlin.
Guidelines	See A-IV, 1.3.1. A divisional filed at a national office may be forwarded to an EPO filing office out of courtesy but will not be awarded a filing date under Art. 80 until it arrives there.

7.2.3 Where to file a replacement application under Art. 61(1)(b)

941 Art. 61(2)	Art. 76(1) applies to replacement applications mutatis mutandis.
Art. 76(1)	Divisional applications (and therefore replacement applications) must be filed directly with the EPO in accordance with the Implementing Regulations.
r.36(2)	Divisional applications (and therefore replacement applications) must be filed directly with the EPO in Munich, The Hague or Berlin.
Guidelines	See A-IV, 2.5.

7.2.4 Restrictions on the filing of European patent applications under national law

Art. 75(2)	In spite of Art. 75(1) (European application can be filed at the EPO), national law may 942 contain legislative or regulatory provisions which, in any Contracting State: (a) govern inventions which, owing to the nature of their subject matter, may not be communicated abroad without the prior authorisation of the competent authorities of that State, or (b) prescribe that each application is to be filed initially with a national authority or make direct filing with another authority subject to prior authorisation.
NatLaw	See Table II for such restrictions imposed by national law.

7.2.5 Procedure where the application is filed with a national office – time limit for forwarding to the EPO

Art. 77(1)	The central industrial property office of a Contracting State is obliged to forward to the 943 European Patent Office any European patent application filed with it or any another competent authority in that State, in accordance with the Implementing Regulations.
r.37(1)	Such an application must be forwarded in the shortest time compatible with the national law relating to the secrecy of inventions in the interests of that State and the national office must take all appropriate steps to ensure that the application is forwarded within: (a) six weeks of filing where the subject of the application is evidently not liable to secrecy under the national law; or (b) four months of filing, or, where priority has been claimed, 14 months of the date of priority, where the application requires further examination as to its liability to secrecy.
Art. 77(2)	A European patent application, the subject of which has been made secret, is not forwarded to the European Patent Office.
Art. 77(3)	A European patent application not forwarded to the EPO in due time is deemed to be withdrawn.
r.37(2)	Due time in this context is within 14 months of filing or, if priority has been claimed, within 14 months of the claimed date of priority.
r.37(2) J3/80	If the application is deemed withdrawn in this way, all fees are refunded. No re-establishment of rights was available under Art. 122 EPC1973 where the time limit for forwarding was missed since the applicant is not responsible for complying with the time limit. This case law would seem to be equally applicable to Art. 121 EPC2000 which would be the equivalent remedy.
Art. 135	Conversion is, however, possible in these circumstances.
Guidelines	See A-II, 1.6.

7.3 Manner of filing the application

7.3.1 Filing in writing by post or by hand

r.35(1)	The application may be filed in writing with any of the Art. 75 authorities. 944
r.1	In written proceedings before the EPO, the requirement to use the written form is satisfied if the content of the documents can be reproduced in a legible form on paper.
r.2(1)	In proceedings before the EPO, documents may be filed by delivery by hand or by postal services. The President of the EPO lays down the details and conditions and, where appropriate, any special formal or technical requirements for the filing of documents.
Guidelines	See A-II, 1.1. It is possible to file out of hours using automated mail boxes in Munich and Berlin or via the porter at The Hague.

7.3.2 Filing by fax

r.2(1)	In proceedings before the EPO, documents may be filed by means of electronic com- 945 munication. The President of the EPO lays down the details and conditions and, where appropriate, any special formal or technical requirements for the filing of documents. In particular, he may specify that confirmation must be supplied. If such confirmation copy of a European patent application is not supplied in due time, the European patent application will be refused.

OJ	European patent applications may be filed with the EPO (and those national offices which so allow) by fax. The applicant may be invited to file a confirmation copy but this is no longer routinely required (Decision of the President dated 20.2.2019, [2019] O.J. A18). The application is refused in the case that a requested confirmation copy is not filed within the two month period set. If the application is received in a transmission running past midnight then the date of receipt is, in principle, the second day when the transmission is complete but the applicant has the opportunity of renouncing the part received after midnight in order to get the earlier filing date.
Art. 121	If the application is refused in the case that no requested confirmation copy is filed, further processing would be available.
Guidelines	See A-II, 1.2.1 for a list of national offices which accept fax filing.

7.3.3   Filing electronically

946 r.2(1)	In proceedings before the EPO, documents may be filed by means of electronic communication. The President of the EPO lays down the details and conditions and, where appropriate, any special formal or technical requirements for the filing of documents. In particular, he may specify that confirmation must be supplied. If such confirmation is not supplied in due time, the European patent application will be refused.
OJ	See Decision of the President dated 03 May 2023 ([2023] O.J. A48). European patent applications may be filed in electronic form, both with the EPO and with competent national authorities which allow electronic filing. Such electronic filing may be carried out using EPO Online Filing (OLF), Online Filing 2.0, the web-form filing service or the EPO Contingency Upload Service.
Guidelines	See A-II, 1.2.2

7.3.4   Filing by other means

947 OJ	No other means of filing (e.g. telegram, teletex, email) are allowed (Decision of the President dated 20.2.2019, [2019] O.J. A18, Art. 1(3) and Guidelines A-II, 1.3). If filed by such means, an application will not be treated as such and no date of filing will be accorded.

7.4   Filing a Divisional application

7.4.1   Up to what point in time can a divisional application be filed?

948 Art. 76(1)	All details relating to the filing of a divisional application are to be found in the Implementing Regulations.
r.36(1)	The applicant may file a divisional application relating to any pending earlier European patent application.
Comment	Between 01 April 2010 and 31 March 2014, there was also a time limit specified in r.36(1) according to which a divisional application could only be filed within one of two 24 month time limits. The time limit came into force on 01 April 2010 but all divisional applications were allowed if they were filed before 01 October 2010, regardless of whether the time limit had expired or not (see Decision of the Administrative Council dated 25 March 2009, [2009] O.J. 296). The current version of r.36(1) came into force on 01 April 2014 and applies to all divisional application filed on or after that date (no special transitional provisions were provided – see Notice from the EPO dated 08 January 2014, [2014] O.J. A22).

7.4.2   A divisional application may be filed in respect of any pending earlier European patent application

949 OJ	The 'earlier' application in the sense of r.36(1) is the direct predecessor of the divisional if there is a chain (see Notice from the EPO dated 20 August 2009, [2009] O.J. 481).
J18/09	A Euro-PCT application only starts to be pending when it has validly entered the regional phase so that the EPO is responsible for processing it and grant proceedings are initiated (see also Guidelines A-IV, 1.1.1 and E-IX, 2.4.1). See section 38.12 for further comment.
Comment	An application is pending up until the point at which a decision to grant or refuse takes effect or the application is withdrawn or deemed to be withdrawn.
J7/04	In the case of a decision to grant, the application is pending up to, but not including, the date of the mention of grant (see also J28/03, Guidelines A-IV, 1.1.1).

G1/09	Headnote: In the case where no appeal is filed, a European patent application which has been refused by a decision of the Examining Division is thereafter pending within the meaning of r.25 EPC1973 (r.36(1) EPC2000) until the expiry of the time limit for filing a notice of appeal.
Comment	When an application is refused, in written or oral proceedings, a divisional application may therefore validly be filed within two months of the notification of the decision, whether an appeal is filed or not.
J28/03	When an application has been refused, the filing of an appeal, having suspensive effect, deprives the decision of its effect and a divisional may validly be filed from this point onwards until the appeal proceedings are terminated, regardless of the manner in which they are terminated. In the case where a decision to grant is appealed, however, the suspensive effect does not work in the same way and a divisional application may only be filed if the appeal is successful.
J23/13	However, in the case where a valid appeal is filed but no grounds are filed within the four month time limit of Art. 108, a divisional application may only be filed up until the expiry of that four month period.
J18/04	The requirement of r.36(1) that the parent application is pending is a condition which must be fulfilled and does not represent a time limit within the meaning accorded to that term under the EPC. It is not therefore possible to use re-establishment to file a divisional application after the grant of an application takes effect. Nor would it be possible to use r.133 to excuse the late arrival of a divisional application at the EPO.
Guidelines	By the same reasoning, further processing would not be applicable (A-IV, 1.1.1, citing J10/01).
Comment	If an application becomes deemed withdrawn, it is possible to request a decision on the matter pursuant to r.112(2) and appeal this decision. However, it is not possible to then validly file a divisional application unless the appeal is successful (or the decision under r.112(2) finds the application is not deemed withdrawn after all) since the suspensive effect only applies to the decision which is taken regarding the deemed withdrawal and not to the deemed withdrawal itself.
Guidelines	If a loss of rights is cured using further processing or re-establishment, the application is deemed to have always been pending and a divisional is possible once more (see Guidelines A-IV, 1.1.1).
J4/11	In the case of deemed withdrawal, the application ceases to be pending immediately and a divisional application may not be validly filed during the period in which a request for further processing or re-establishment could be filed or during the pendency of such a request if it is refused. Only if the request is granted and the loss of rights is deemed not to have occurred is a divisional possible.
Guidelines	See A-IV, 1.1. When a divisional application is filed at a time when the parent is not pending the EPO will dispatch a r.112(1) communication to the would-be applicant saying that the purported application cannot be treated as a divisional application. An appealable decision can be requested under r.112(2) EPC. Any fees paid are refunded when the loss of rights becomes final.
Guidelines	See A-IV, 1.1.1 in general for the pendency requirement. In the case where a renewal fee is not paid, the application is pending until the expiry of the six month grace period as stated in r.51(2). A divisional is not possible during a stay of proceedings under r.14(1). See also C-IX, 1.1. When an application is withdrawn by the applicant, a divisional application may be filed on or before the day on which the declaration of withdrawal is received by the EPO.

7.4.3 *On what kind of application can a divisional be based?*

G1/06	A divisional application can be divided from a regular European patent application or from an application which is itself a divisional.	950

7.4.4   Who is entitled to file a divisional application?

951 J2/01	Where the parent application has been filed jointly by two or more applicants and the requirements of Art. 61 or r.22(3) have not been met (i.e. no non-entitlement finding has been made and no recordal of a transfer has taken place), the right to file a divisional application is only available to these joint applicants and not to one alone or fewer than all of them.
J7/21	However, in the case of universal succession of title (as opposed to assignment), the new owner can file a divisional in his own name without first registering the change.
Guidelines	See A-IV, 1.1.3. If the divisional application is filed by an applicant who is not entitled to file it, it will not be dealt with as a European (divisional) patent application, applying Art. 90(2) EPC by analogy, and the EPO will send a loss of rights communication pursuant to r.112(1) EPC.

7.5   Filing a replacement application

952 Art. 61(1)	Please refer to Chapter 22.

7.6   Requirement to pay a filing fee, a search fee and claims fees

7.6.1   Filing fee

953 Art. 78(2)	A European patent application is subject to the payment of a filing fee.
r.38(2)	The filing fee has a fixed component and a variable page-related component for applications having more than 35 pages.
RRFArt. 2(1)(1)	The filing fee is (i) € 105 where the European patent application or, if required, its translation, is filed online in character-coded format; (ii) € 135 where the European patent application is filed online but the application or, where required, its translation, is not filed in character-coded format; and (iii) € 285 in other cases.
RRF Art. 2(3)	The President of the EPO determines the formats referred to in RRF Art. 2(1) and RRF Art. 2(2) and may specify the conditions under which a document is deemed to have been filed online in character-coded format.
RRF Art. 2(4)	Fee levels which relate to a means of electronic communication or a format referred to in RRF Art. 2(1) or Art. 2(2) shall not apply until a date set by the President of the Office.
OJ	See Decision of the President dated 12 December 2018 ([2019] O.J. A3) and Notice from the EPO dated 24 January 2019 ([2019] O.J. A6). New RRF Art. 2(4) applies as of 01 April 2019 to item (i) of RRF Art. 2(1)(1) and the € 105 filing fee will not apply for the time being.
RRFArt. 2(1)(1a)	The variable component is € 17 for the 36th and each subsequent page.
OJ	See [2009] O.J. 118 for the manner in which the number of pages in the application is to be calculated. Pages of the request do not count. Neither do pages of any sequence listing that complies with WIPO Standard ST.25 and that is presented as a separate part of the description.
Guidelines	See A-III, 13. The additional fee is calculated on the basis of the pages of the description, claims, and drawings with one page added in respect of the abstract. The application in the language of filing is used for the calculation. Where the content of the application changes under r.56 or r.56a, the additional fee is calculated on the basis of the documents present at the expiry of the time limit under r.38(3).
r.38(1)	The fixed component of the filing fee must be paid within one month of filing the European patent application.
r.38(3)	The variable component of the filing fee must be paid within one month of filing the European patent application or one month of filing the first set of claims or one month of filing the certified copy referred to in r.40(3), whichever period expires last.
G3/98	The filing of a European patent application is the date on which the applicant first lodges documents complying with r.40 EPC (see also G2/99).
r.38(4)	The Rules relating to fees may provide for an additional fee as part of the filing fee in the case of a divisional application filed in respect of any earlier application which is itself a divisional application.
RRFArt. 2(1)(1b)	The additional fee is € 235 for a second generation divisional, € 480 for a third generation divisional, € 715 for a fourth generation divisional and € 955 for a fifth or subsequent generation divisional.

Guidelines	See A-IV, 1.4.1.1 for an explanation of which generation a divisional belongs to.
RRFArt. 4(1)	The filing fee (including fixed and variable components) may be paid from the date the application is filed (the due date). See also Guidelines A-X, 5.2.1.
Comment	For the consequences of non-payment, see Chapter 8.
r.37(2)	The filing fee is refunded if the application is not forwarded to the EPO by a national office within 14 months from the filing or priority date.

7.6.2   *Reduction of the filing fee if using an official language of a contracting state*

r.6(3)–(7)	Where the applicant is a natural or legal person having a residence or principle place of business within a Contracting State having an official language other than English, French or German, or a national of such a State resident abroad, and the application is filed in an official language of that State, the filing fee is reduced in accordance with the Rules relating to Fees. However, the reduction only applies if the applicant is a small or medium-sized company (the definition of which is found in Commission recommendation 2003/361/ EC of 6 May 2003, see Official Journal of the EU, L/124/p36 of 20 May 2003), a natural person, or a non-profit organisation, university or public research organisation. The applicant must declare himself to be such a person or entity and provide evidence if required by the EPO. In the case of multiple applicants, each one must be a qualifying person or entity.	954
OJ	See Notice from the EPO dated 10 January 2014 ([2014] OJ A23). Changes in status of an organisation will not retrospectively affect a reduction already taken advantage of – the status of the applicant at the time of filing is determinative. If the EPO becomes aware that a fee should have been paid in full since the applicant did not have the necessary status, the fee will be deemed not to have been paid, the application will be deemed withdrawn and further processing will be necessary.	
Comment	New r.6(3)–(7) entered into force on 01 April 2014 and applies to direct European patent applications filed on or after that date. Under the previous version of the rule, a reduction of 20 % applied to all applicants having the necessary residency/nationality regardless of their status.	
RRFArt. 14(1)	The reduction is 30 % of the filing fee.	
Comment	Note that this is a reduction rather than a refund.	
T149/85	The nationality/residency of the applicant is determinative, not that of the representative.	
G6/91	The fee reduction is allowed where the "essential item" of the first act in filing is in an official non-EPO language and the necessary translation is filed no earlier than simultaneously.	
J4/18	In the case of joint applicants, each one must be a natural person or entity within the meaning of r.6(4) EPC, as specified in r.6(7) EPC, but only one of them needs to be a person defined by Art. 14(4) for the fee reduction to apply.	
Guidelines	See A-X, 9.2.2. Under EPC2000, the essential item is the description. The reduction applies to all parts of the filing fee including any element payable in respect of the number of pages of the application or in respect of a divisional application.	
Guidelines	See A-II, 4.1.3.1. Where the applicant has incorporated the description by reference, the fee reduction applies if the previous application is in an appropriate language. The reduction also applies if only the description is incorporated by reference and the claims are added later in the language of translation.	
NatLaw	See Table II for the official languages of the Contracting States.	

7.6.3   *Search fee*

Art. 78(2)	A European patent application is subject to the payment of a search fee.	955
RRFArt. 2(1)(2)	The search fee is € 1460 for applications filed on or after July 1, 2005 and € 1000 for applications filed before that date (for a divisional application, the date of filing of the divisional, rather than the date of filing of the parent, is determinative – see Notice from the EPO dated 20 March 2020 ([2020] OJ A30).	
r.38(1)	The search fee must be paid within one month of filing the European patent application.	
G3/98	The filing of a European patent application is the date on which the applicant first lodges documents complying with r.40 EPC (see also G2/99).	
RRFArt. 4(1)	The search fee may be paid from the date the application is filed (the due date). See also Guidelines A-X, 5.2.1.	
Comment	For the consequences of non-payment, see Chapter 8.	

r.37(2)	The search fee is refunded if the application is not forwarded to the EPO by a national office within 14 months from the filing or priority date.
RRFArt. 9(1)	The search fee paid for a European search will be fully refunded if the European patent application is withdrawn or refused or deemed to be withdrawn at a time when the office has not yet begun to draw up the search report.
OJ	See also Notice from the EPO dated 29 January 2013 – the date on which searching activity starts is now stored electronically in the application file and clearly indicated in the European Patent Register.
RRFArt. 9(2)	Where the European Search Report is based on an earlier search report prepared by the EPO on an application whose priority is claimed or an earlier application within the meaning of Art. 76 or r.17 the EPO will refund the applicant, in accordance with a Decision of the President, an amount which depends on the type of the earlier search and the extent to which the EPO benefits from the earlier search report when carrying out the subsequent search.
OJ	See Decision of the President dated 17 January 2023 ([2023] O.J. A4). The refund varies between 17.5 % and 100 % depending on the kind of search relied on, the availability of a written opinion and the extent to which it is of benefit (full or partial). See also Guidelines A-X, 10.2.1 – if there is disagreement concerning the amount of the refund the applicant can request an appealable interlocutory decision on the matter which is issued by the Receiving Section or Examining Division depending on who is responsible for the application at the time.
Guidelines	See A-III, 13.

7.6.4   Claims fees

956	r.45(1)	For the 16th and each subsequent claim in the application, a claims fee is due.
	RRFArt. 2(2)(15)	Each claims fee is € 265 for European applications filed before April 1, 2009 and international applications entering the regional phase before that date.
	RRFArt. 2(1)(15)	Each claims fee is € 265 for claims in the range 16–50 and € 660 for the 51st and each subsequent claim for European applications filed on or after April 1, 2009 and international applications entering the regional phase on or after date.
	r.45(2)	Claims fees are due within one month of filing the first set of claims.
	Comment	The first set of claims could be filed on the filing date or later – if the claims are incorporated by reference, as allowed by r.57(c), then the filing date is the relevant date.
	RRFArt. 4(1)	The claims fees can be paid from the day the first set of claims is filed (the due date). See also Guidelines A-X, 5.2.5.
	Comment	For the consequences of non-payment, see Chapter 8.
	r.37(2)	Claims fees are refunded if the application is not forwarded to the EPO by a national office within 14 months from the filing or priority date.
	J6/96	The number of claims fees due is to be calculated at the end of the normal period for payment.
	r.71(6)	Further claims fees may be payable after allowance of the application.
	Guidelines	See A-III,9 – when erroneously filed claims are corrected under r.56a(3) or (4), claims fees are calculated based on the original set of claims. See C-V, 1.4 – claims fees are not refunded if the number of claims is reduced during prosecution.

7.6.5   Fees for divisional applications

957	Art. 76(1)	A divisional application must be filed in accordance with the Implementing Regulations.
	r.36(3)	The filing fee and search fee must be paid within one month of filing the divisional application. If these fees are not paid in due time then the application is deemed to be withdrawn.
	Comment	For the consequences of non-payment, see Chapter 8.
	r.45	Claims fees are payable in the normal way (see above).
	Art. 86(1)	Renewal fees in respect of previous years may be payable – see section on renewal fees under common provisions.
	Guidelines	See A-IV, 1.4.

7.6.6   Fees for replacement applications

958	r.17(2)	The filing fee and search fee must be paid within one month of filing the new application.

Comment	For the consequences of non-payment, see Chapter 8.
r.51(6)	No renewal fees are payable in respect of the year of filing of the replacement application and in respect of past years.
Guidelines	See A-IV, 2.5.
r.45	Claims fees are payable in the normal way (see above).

7.7 Designation of Contracting States

Art. 3	The grant of a European patent may be requested for one or more of the Contracting States.	959
Art. 79(1)	All the Contracting States party to the EPC at the time of filing of the application are deemed to be designated in the request according to EPC2000.	
Comment	This provision only applies to applications filed after EPC2000 came into force. Under EPC1973, the State or States in which protection was sought had to be designated in the request. The current 39 Contracting States are:	

Contracting State	Entry into force of the EPC	Contracting State	Entry into force of the EPC
AL (Albania)	01.05.2010	IT (Italy)	01.12.1978
AT (Austria)	01.05.1979	LI (Liechtenstein)	01.04.1980
BE (Belgium)	07.10.1977	LT (Lithuania)	01.12.2004
BG (Bulgaria)	01.07.2002	LU (Luxembourg)	07.10.1977
CH (Switzerland)	07.10.1977	LV (Latvia)	01.07.2005
CY (Cyprus)	01.04.1998	MC (Monaco)	01.12.1991
		ME (Montenegro)	01.10.2022
CZ (Czech Republic)	01.07.2002	MK (North Macedonia)	01.01.2009
DE (Germany)	07.10.1977	MT (Malta)	01.03.2007
DK (Denmark)	01.01.1990	NL (Netherlands)	07.10.1977
EE (Estonia)	01.07.2002	NO (Norway)	01.01.2008
ES (Spain)	01.10.1986	PL (Poland)	01.03.2004
FI (Finland)	01.03.1996	PT (Portugal)	01.01.1992
FR (France)	07.10.1977	RO (Romania)	01.03.2003
GB (United Kingdom)	07.10.1977	RS (Serbia)	01.10.2010
GR (Greece)	01.10.1986	SE (Sweden)	01.05.1978
HR (Croatia)	01.01.2008	SI (Slovenia)	01.12.2002
HU (Hungary)	01.01.2003	SK (Slovak Republic)	01.07.2002
IE (Ireland)	01.08.1992	SM (San Marino)	01.07.2009
IS (Iceland)	01.11.2004	TR (Turkey)	01.11.2000

J30/90	The EPC must be in force in a Contracting State on the filing date of the application for that State to be designated, whether the application is initiated under the EPC or PCT.
J18/90	If the applicant purports to designate a State which is not yet eligible, the EPO will write and ask if the applicant wishes to post-date the application's filing date to make the designation effective.
Art. 79(3)	The designation of a Contracting State may be withdrawn at any time up to the grant of the European patent (i.e. the date the grant takes effect).
Art. 76(2)	In the case of a European divisional application, all the Contracting States designated in the earlier application at the time of filing the divisional are deemed to be designated.
Comment	Therefore, only Contracting States whose designation is still current at the time of filing of the divisional, may be designated in the divisional (see also J19/96 and Guidelines A-IV, 1.3.4).
Art. 149(1)	A group of Contracting States may decide that they may only be designated jointly.

Comment   This is the case with Switzerland and Liechtenstein.
Guidelines   See A-III, 11.

7.8   Extension of a European patent

960   OJ   A European patent may be extended to Bosnia and Herzegovina ([2004] O.J. 619). All
                 legal basis in relation to the extension of the European patent is found in the extension
                 agreement rather than the EPC and the EPC only applies to the extent specified in the
                 relevant agreement (see J14/00, J4/05 and J22/10).
                 Extension agreements with Albania ([1995] O.J. 803 and [1996] O.J. 82), Croatia ([2004]
                 O.J. 117), Latvia ([1994] O.J. 201 and [1995] O.J. 345), Lithuania ([1994] O.J. 201 and
                 [1994] O.J. 527), Macedonia ([1997] O.J. 345), Montenegro ([2010] O.J. 10), Slovenia
                 ([1994] O.J. 75 and [1999] O.J. 183), Romania ([1994] O.J. 746 and [1996] O.J. 601) and
                 Serbia ([2004] O.J. 563, formerly Serbia and Montenegro) terminated when the EPC came
                 into force for these States.

Extension State	Entry into force of extension agreement	Last day of extension agreement
AL (Albania)	01.02.1996	30.04.2010
BA (Bosnia and Herzegovina)	01.12.2004	
HR (Croatia)	01.04.2004	31.12.2007
LT (Lithuania)	05.07.1994	30.11.2004
LV (Latvia)	01.05.1995	30.06.2005
ME (Montenegro)	01.03.2010	30.09.2022
MK (North Macedonia)	01.11.1997	31.12.2008
RO (Romania)	15.10.1996	28.02.2003
RS (Serbia)	01.11.2004	30.09.2010
SI (Slovenia)	01.03.1994	30.11.2002

Guidelines   See A-III, 12.1. Under an extension agreement, extension is deemed requested on filing
                 for all European patent applications filed after the coming into force of the agreement and
                 must be confirmed by the payment of an extension fee within the time limit for payment
                 of the designation fee. If an extension fee is not paid, then the request for extension is
                 deemed withdrawn. In the case of a Euro-PCT application, the relevant national office
                 must be designated in respect of the PCT application. For a divisional application, ex-
                 tension is deemed to be requested if the respective request is still effective for the parent
                 application at the time the divisional is filed. Since EPC provisions only apply if specified
                 in the relevant extension agreement, there is no appeal, further processing or re-estab-
                 lishment concerning an extension and it is not possible to maintain a different text for an
                 extension state (r.138).
Guidelines   See A-III, 12.3. An extension may be withdrawn at any time but a validly paid extension
                 fee is not refunded.

7.9   Validation of a European patent

961   OJ   A European patent may be validated in Morocco ([2015] O.J. A20 and [2016] O.J. A5),
                 Moldova ([2015] O.J. A85), Tunisia ([2017] O.J. A85) and Cambodia. As with extension
                 states, all legal basis is found in the relevant validation agreement and national law rather
                 than in the EPC (for example, see Art. 50.1 to 50.5 of Moroccan law No. 17–97).

Validation State	Entry into force of validation agreement
MA (Morocco)	01 March 2015
MD (Republic of Moldova)	01 November 2015
TN (Tunisia)	01 December 2017
KH (Cambodia)	01 March 2018

Guidelines

See A-III, 12.1. Under the validation agreements, validation is deemed requested on filing for all European patent applications filed after the coming into force of the agreement and must be confirmed by payment of a validation fee within the same time limit that the designation fee is due. If a validation fee is not paid, then the request for validation is deemed withdrawn. In the case of a Euro-PCT application, the relevant national office must be designated in respect of the PCT application. For a divisional application, validation is deemed to be requested if the respective validation request is still effective for the parent application at the time the divisional is filed. Since EPC provisions only apply if specified in the relevant agreement, there is no appeal, further processing or re-establishment concerning a validation and it is not possible to maintain a different text for a validation state (r.138).

Guidelines

See A-III, 12.3. A validation request may be withdrawn at any time but a validly paid validation fee is not refunded.

7.10   Requirement to file copies of search results relating to a priority application

r.141(1)

See under section 24.15. The applicant should file copies of search results relating to any application whose priority is claimed along with the European patent application (unless they are to be automatically included in the file by the EPO).   962

Chapter 8: Examination on Filing

8.1 Procedure on receipt of a new application

963 r.35(2) The authority with which the application is filed (i.e. the EPO or national authority) marks the documents making up the application with the date of receipt and issues, without delay, a receipt to the applicant which states at least the application number, the nature and number of the documents and the date of their receipt.

r.35(3) If the application is filed with an Art. 75(1)(b) authority (i.e. a national authority), that authority will, without delay, inform the EPO of the receipt of the application, and, in particular, the nature and date of receipt of the documents, the application number and any priority date claimed.

r.35(4) When the EPO has received a new application which has been forwarded by the industrial property office of a Contracting State, it informs the applicant accordingly, indicating the date of receipt at the EPO.

Guidelines See A-II, 3.1 and 3.2. The EPO will no longer issue an acknowledgement of receipt by fax. For online filings, receipt is acknowledged electronically during the submission session.

8.2 Examination as to whether a filing date can be accorded

8.2.1 Requirements for a filing date

964 Art. 90(1) The EPO examines, in accordance with the Implementing Regulations, whether a filing date can be accorded to the application.

r.10(1) The Receiving Section is responsible.

Case law The filing date is the date on which documents are actually received, either at a national office (J18/86) or directly at the EPO (J4/87). No discretion exists to excuse postal delays. A filing date later than the date of receipt, e.g. to allow for the designation of new Contracting States or to benefit from the advantages of a new form of the EPC coming into effect, can be given, but only if this is made clear at the time of filing (J14/90, J18/90, [2007] O.J. 504).

Art. 80 The date of filing of a European patent application is the date on which the requirements laid down in the Implementing Regulations are satisfied.

r.40(1) The date of filing of a European patent application is the date on which the documents filed by the applicant contain:
(a) an indication that a European patent is sought;
(b) information identifying the applicant or allowing the applicant to be contacted; and
(c) a description or reference to a previously filed application.

Guidelines See A-II, 4.1.2. If there are multiple applicants, the condition of r.40(1)(b) need only be met in respect of one of them for the award of a filing date. Any kind of information allowing the applicant to be contacted will suffice including the name and address of the applicant's representative, a fax number or a post office box number. The indication a patent is sought could be explicit or implicit.

r.40(2) A reference to a previously filed application under r.40(1)(c) must state the filing date and number of that application and the office with which it was filed. Such reference must also indicate it replaces the description and any drawing.

r.57(c) The reference may also, optionally, indicate that the claims are incorporated by reference.

Guidelines See A-II, 4.1.3.1. The previous application does not have to be an application from which priority is claimed. It can be a patent application or a utility model application.
See A-IV, 1.3.1. A divisional application can be filed by reference to the parent.

Comment An application for the protection of an invention is presumably implied so that a design application would not be accepted.

8.2.2 Need for a certified copy of the previous application if filing by reference

965 r.40(3) Where the application contains a reference under r.40(2), a certified copy of the previously filed application must be filed within two months of filing the application – r.53(2) applies mutatis mutandis.

r.53(2)	A copy of the previously filed application will be deemed to be duly filed if a copy of that application is available to the EPO and is to be included in the file of the European patent application under the conditions determined by the President of the EPO.
OJ	See Notice from the EPO dated 14 September 2009 ([2009] O.J. 486. Applicants do not have to file a certified copy where previous application is a European patent application or an international application filed with the EPO as receiving Office. The same rules apply to divisional applications filed by reference and a certified copy is required under the same conditions even if e.g. the previous application is an international application filed with a receiving Office other than the EPO which is pending before the EPO.
Guidelines	See also A-II, 4.1.3.1. If a certified copy of the priority document has already been filed to satisfy the requirements of r.53(1) EPC it does not need to be filed again.
r.135(2)	Further processing is not available in respect of the r.40(3) time limit.
r.55	There is no immediate loss of rights if the certified copy is not filed in time since the EPO issues an invitation to correct the deficiency (see section 8.2.4).
Comment	The lack of a certified copy prevents the according of a filing date (since no description has been filed in its absence). See below.

8.2.3   *Need for a translation of the previous application if filing by reference*

r.40(3)	Where the previously filed application is not in an official language of the EPO, a translation thereof in one of these languages must be filed within two months of filing the application – r.53(2) applies mutatis mutandis.	966
OJ	See Notice from the EPO dated 14 September 2009 ([2009] O.J. 486) – no translation is necessary if it is already available to the EPO since a copy is added to the file free of charge (see also Guidelines A-II, 4.1.3.1).	
r.135(2)	Further processing is not available in respect of the r.40(3) time limit.	
r.58	The applicant has a chance to correct the deficiency caused by a missing translation (see below).	
Comment	The lack of a translation is a formal deficiency which does not prevent the according of a filing date (since a European patent application can be filed in any language).	

8.2.4   *Procedure where a filing date cannot be accorded*

Art. 90(4)	Where the EPO notices there are deficiencies which may be corrected, it gives the applicant a chance to correct them.	967
r.55	If there is a deficiency under: (a) r.40(1)(a) (no indication a patent is sought); (b) r.40(1)(c) (no description or reference to a previously filed application); (c) r.40(2) (missing filing date, number or State for a previously filed application or indication that it replaces the description and any drawings); or (d) r.40(3) first sentence (no certified copy of a previous application filed within the two month time limit); the EPO informs the applicant of the deficiency and advises that the application will not be dealt with as a European patent application unless the deficiency is remedied within two months.	
r.55	If the applicant remedies the deficiencie(s) he is informed of the filing date.	
Guidelines	See A-II, 4.1.4 and 4.1.5. This means, in the case of deficiencies (a), (b) and (c), that the filing date awarded will be the date on which the deficiency is corrected. However, in the case of deficiency (d) (no certified copy), correction results in the original filing date being maintained.	
Art. 90(2)	If a filing date cannot be accorded, the application is not dealt with as a European patent application.	
Guidelines	See A-II, 4.1.4. If a filing date cannot be accorded then any fees paid are refunded.	
Art. 87(3)	In the case a filing date cannot be accorded, no priority right is generated.	
r.135(2)	Further processing is ruled out in respect of the r.55 time limit.	

Art. 122

Re-establishment is, however, available. In the case of re-establishment, the filing date accorded should be the date on which the omitted act is completed in the case of one of deficiencies (a), (b) and (c) noted above. In one of these cases it is therefore cheaper and more certain to simply re-file the application rather than to request re-establishment. However, in the case of deficiency (d) above, the original filing date is maintained and re-establishment is therefore a useful remedy.

Guidelines

See A-II, 4.1.4. Where there is insufficient information for the EPO to contact the applicant, it is unable to send a communication pursuant to r.55 EPC. However, if the applicant corrects the defect of his own initiative within two months of the receipt of the original documents, a filing date is awarded. If a filing date cannot be accorded, the EPO notifies the applicant of the loss of rights under r.112(1) and the applicant may request an appealable decision under r.112(2) (if the EPO is mistaken regarding the facts) or request reestablishment (if the time limit was missed in spite of all due care having been taken), or else refile the application.

Comment

Note that where the description and drawings are incorporated by reference and a required translation of the previous application is not supplied in time then the deficiency is dealt with under Art. 90(3) and r.57(a) – this is not a requirement for according a filing date since applications can be filed in any language.

8.2.5   *Filing date in the case of a divisional application or replacement application*

968   Art. 76(1)

In so far as a divisional application only contains subject matter which does not extend beyond the content of the earlier application as filed, it will be deemed to have been filed on the date of filing of the earlier application and will have the benefit of any right to priority.

Art. 61(2)

The provisions of Art. 76(1) apply mutatis mutandis to a new application filed under Art. 61(1)(b).

8.3   Filing date where pages of the application are subsequently filed

8.3.1   *Adding missing parts of the description and missing drawings with redating of the application*

969   r.56(1)

If the examination under Art. 90(1) reveals that (1) a part of the description, or (2) a drawing referred to in the description or claims appears to be missing, the EPO will invite the applicant to file the missing part of the description or the missing drawing within two months. The applicant may not, however, invoke the omission of such a communication.

Guidelines

See A-II, 5.3 – a drawing here means a single numbered figure. Only where a whole figure is missing can r.56 be used.

r.56(2)

If a missing part of the description, or a missing drawing, is filed later than the date of filing, but within two months of the date of filing or, if a communication is issued under r.56(1) or under r.56a(1), within two months of that communication, the application will be re-dated to the date on which the missing parts of the description or missing drawings were filed. The EPO will inform the applicant accordingly.

Comment

Thus, the applicant can file missing parts either in response to an invitation from the EPO or of his own motion.

Comment

Note that under r.56, it is not possible to reinstate claims if they have been accidentally left out, only drawings and parts of the description. Thus, if some particular subject matter was contained only in the claims and these claims were accidentally left out on filing then this subject matter is lost from the application and protection can only be obtained for it by re-filing.

r.56(4)

If the applicant:
(a) fails to file the missing parts of the description or the missing drawings within the period under r.56(1) or r.56(2); or
(b) withdraws under r.56(6) any missing part of the description or missing drawing filed under r.56(2);
any reference referred to in r.56(1) will be deemed to be deleted, and any filing of the missing parts of the description or missing drawings will be deemed not to have been made. The EPO will inform the applicant accordingly.

r.56(6)	Within one month of the notification referred to in the last sentence of r.56(2), the applicant may withdraw the missing parts of the description or the missing drawings filed, in which case the re-dating will be deemed not to have been made. The EPO will inform the applicant accordingly.
r.135(2)	Further processing is ruled out in respect of the r.56 time limits.
Art. 122	Re-establishment, however, is available.

8.3.2   Adding missing parts of the description and missing drawings without redating of the application – applications filed before 01 November 2022

r.56(3)	If the missing parts of the description or missing drawings are filed within the period under r.56(2), and the application claims the priority of an earlier application, the date of filing will, provided that the missing parts of the description or the missing drawings are completely contained in the earlier application, remain the date on which the requirements laid down in r.40(1) were fulfilled, where the applicant so requests and files, within the period under r.56(2):	970

(a) a copy of the earlier application, unless such copy is available to the EPO under r.53(2) (i.e. is available to the EPO and is to be included in the file of the European patent application under the conditions determined by the President of the EPO – see Guidelines A-II, 5.4.3, and section 6.8.7);

(b) a translation of the earlier application in an official language of the EPO, if it is not in such a language, unless such a translation is available to the EPO under r.53(3) (i.e. where the EPO has asked for a translation since the validity of the priority claim is important); and

(c) an indication as to where the missing parts of the description or the missing drawings are completely contained in the earlier application and, where applicable, in the translation thereof.

Guidelines	For a request under r.56(3) to be successful, a valid priority claim must exist. Such a claim may be made or later up to the point that the request under r.56(3) is filed. See A-II, 5.4.1. "Completely contained" means that the relevant drawing or text must be identical to a drawing or text in the priority document (or its translation where one is required) (A-II, 5.4.2). Identical for these purposes means containing the same text.

The copy of the priority document does not need to be certified for the purposes of r.56 (A-II, 5.4.3). Further, a copy will be automatically be placed in the file by the EPO is available to according to r.53(2) and the corresponding decision of the President. If the priority document is in a different official language of the EPO from the application as filed, a translation is not required according to r.56(3)(b) – however, the EPO will nevertheless not recognise that the missing part is 'completely contained' in the earlier application unless a translation of the relevant parts of the priority application into the language of the proceedings is filed (A-II, 5.4.4). A translation of the full document is not required. Alternatively, a declaration that the relevant parts are already an exact translation would be sufficient.

J27/10	It is not possible to replace the description originally filed with the description of the priority document under r.56. This provision allows the description originally filed to be completed by adding missing parts and not to be amended by changing, replacing or deleting parts originally filed. It should be clear from the description as originally filed that the sections filed under r.56 were actually missing.
r.56(5)	If the applicant fails to comply with the requirements referred to in r.56(3)(a)–(c) within the period under r.56(2), the application will be re-dated to the date on which the missing parts of the description or missing drawings were filed. The EPO will inform the applicant accordingly.
r.56(6)	Within one month of the notification referred to in r.56(5), the applicant may withdraw the missing parts of the description or the missing drawings filed, in which case the re-dating will be deemed not to have been made. The EPO will inform the applicant accordingly.
r.135(2)	Further processing is ruled out in respect of the r.56 time limits.
Art. 122	Re-establishment, however, is available.

Guidelines

Even where the Receiving Section determines that the conditions laid down in r.56(3) are met regarding "completely contained", this can be challenged later in the procedure during substantive examination and a communication under r.56(5) issued re-dating the application (unless the missing parts are withdrawn under r.56(6)). It is not clear if the deficiency could be corrected by amending the subsequently filed matter. The applicant may request a decision on the matter of redating which allows of separate appeal. See B-XI, 2.1 and C-III, 1.1.1.

8.3.3 Adding missing parts of the description and missing drawings without redating of the application – applications filed on or after 01 November 2022

971   r.56(3)

If the missing parts of the description or missing drawings are filed within the period under r.56(2), and the application claims the priority of an earlier application on the date on which the requirements laid down in r.40(1) were fulfilled, the date of filing will, provided that the missing parts of the description or the missing drawings are completely contained in the earlier application, remain the date on which the requirements laid down in r.40(1) were fulfilled, where the applicant so requests and files, within the period under r.56(2):
(a) a copy of the earlier application, unless such copy is available to the EPO under r.53(2) (i.e. is available to the EPO and is to be included in the file of the European patent application under the conditions determined by the President of the EPO – see Guidelines A-II, 5.4.3, and section 6.8.7);
(b) a translation of the earlier application in an official language of the EPO, if it is not in such a language, unless such a translation is available to the EPO under r.53(3) (i.e. where the EPO has asked for a translation since the validity of the priority claim is important); and
(c) an indication as to where the missing parts of the description or the missing drawings are completely contained in the earlier application and, where applicable, in the translation thereof.

Comment

For a request under r.56(3) to be successful, in this case, a valid priority claim must have been made on the filing date allocated to the application. It cannot be added later.

Guidelines

"Completely contained" means that the relevant drawing or text must be identical to a drawing or text in the priority document (or its translation where one is required) (A-II, 5.4.2). Identical for these purposes means containing the same text.
The copy of the priority document does not need to be certified for the purposes of r.56 (A-II, 5.4.3). Further, a copy will be automatically be placed in the file by the EPO is available to according to r.53(2) and the corresponding decision of the President. If the priority document is in a different official language of the EPO from the application as filed, a translation is not required according to r.56(3)(b) – however, the EPO will nevertheless not recognise that the missing part is 'completely contained' in the earlier application unless a translation of the relevant parts of the priority application into the language of the proceedings is filed (A-II, 5.4.4). A translation of the full document is not required. Alternatively, a declaration that the relevant parts are already an exact translation would be sufficient.

J27/10

It is not possible to replace the description originally filed with the description of the priority document under r.56. This provision allows the description originally filed to be completed by adding missing parts and not to be amended by changing, replacing or deleting parts originally filed. It should be clear from the description as originally filed that the sections filed under r.56 were actually missing.

r.56(5)

If the applicant fails to comply with the requirements referred to in r.56(3)(a)–(c) within the period under r.56(2), the application will be re-dated to the date on which the missing parts of the description or missing drawings were filed. The EPO will inform the applicant accordingly.

r.56(6)

Within one month of the notification referred to in r.56(5), the applicant may withdraw the missing parts of the description or the missing drawings filed, in which case the re-dating will be deemed not to have been made. The EPO will inform the applicant accordingly.

r.135(2)

Further processing is ruled out in respect of the r.56 time limits.

Art. 122

Re-establishment, however, is available.

Guidelines	Even where the Receiving Section determines that the conditions laid down in r.56(3) are met regarding "completely contained", this can be challenged later in the procedure during substantive examination and a communication under r.56(5) issued re-dating the application (unless the missing parts are withdrawn under r.56(6)). It is not clear if the deficiency could be corrected by amending the subsequently filed matter. The applicant may request a decision on the matter of redating which allows of separate appeal. See B-XI, 2.1 and C-III, 1.1.1.

8.3.4   Replacing erroneously filed application documents, or parts thereof, with or without redating – applications filed on or after 01 November 2022

r.56a(1)	If the examination under Art. 90(1) reveals that the description, claims or drawings, or parts of those application documents appear to have been erroneously filed, the EPO will invite the applicant to file the correct application documents or parts within two months. The applicant may not, however, invoke the omission of such a communication.
r.56a(2)	If correct application documents or parts referred to in r.56a(1) are filed on or before the date of filing so as to correct the application, those correct application documents or parts shall be included in the application and the erroneously filed application documents or parts shall be deemed not to have been filed. The EPO will inform the applicant accordingly.
r.56a(3)	If correct application documents or parts referred to in r.56a(1) are filed later than the date of filing, but within two months of the date of filing, or, if a communication is issued under r.56(1) or r.56a(1), within two months of that communication, the application will be re-dated to the date on which the correct application documents or parts were filed. The correct application documents or parts shall be included in the application and the erroneously filed application documents or parts shall be deemed not to have been filed. The EPO will inform the applicant accordingly.
Comment	Thus the applicant can file correct application documents or parts thereof either in response to an invitation from the EPO or of his own motion.
Guidelines	See A-II,6.2 (and Notice from the EPO dated 23 June 2022 ([2022] O.J. A71) – whether documents were erroneously filed depends only on the applicant's statement as to what was intended – no evidence is required.
r.56a(4)	If the correct application documents or parts are filed within the period under r.56a(3), and the application claims priority of an earlier application on the date on which the requirements laid down in r.40(1) were fulfilled, the date of filing shall, provided that the correct application documents or parts are completely contained in the earlier application, remain the date on which the requirements laid down in r.40(1) were fulfilled, where the applicant so requests and files, within the period under r.56a(3): (a) a copy of the earlier application, unless such copy is available to the EPO under r.53(2) (i.e. is available to the EPO and is to be included in the file of the European patent application under the conditions determined by the President of the EPO – see Guidelines A-II, 5.4.3, and section 6.8.7); (b) a translation of the earlier application in an official language of the EPO, if it is not in such a language, unless such a translation is available to the EPO under r.53(3) (i.e. where the EPO has asked for a translation since the validity of the priority claim is important); and (c) an indication as to where the correct application documents or parts are completely contained in the earlier application and, where applicable, in the translation thereof. If these requirements are fulfilled, the correct application documents or parts shall be included in the application and the erroneously filed application documents or parts shall remain in the application.
OJ	Both the erroneously filed and corrected documents will be published if r.56a(4) applies. The erroneously filed parts may later be removed by amending the application during grant proceedings as along as Art. 123(2) is respected (Notice from the EPO dated 23 June 2022, [2022] O.J. A71).
r.56a(5)	If the applicant: (a) fails to file the correct application documents or parts within the period under r.56a(1) or r.56a(3); or

972

	(b) withdraws under r.56a(7) any correct application documents or parts filed under r.56a(3);
	any filing of the correct application documents or parts shall be deemed not to have been made and the erroneously filed application documents or parts shall remain in the application or be restored to the application. The EPO will inform the applicant accordingly.
r.56a(6)	If the applicant fails to comply with the requirements referred to in r.56a(4)(a)–(c) within the period under r.56a(3), the application shall be re-dated to the date on which the correct application documents or parts were filed. The filing of the erroneously filed application documents or parts shall be deemed not to have been made. The EPO will inform the applicant accordingly.
r.56a(7)	Within one month of the notification referred to in the last sentence of r.56a(3) or r.56a(6), the applicant may withdraw the correct applications documents or parts filed, in which case the re-dating will be deemed not to have been made. The EPO will inform the applicant accordingly.
r.56a(8)	If the applicant files correct application documents or parts under r.56a(3) or r.56a(4) after the EPO has begun to draw up the search report, the EPO shall invite the applicant to pay a further search fee within one month. If the search fee is not paid in due time, the application shall be deemed to be withdrawn.
RRFArt. 2(1)(2)	The search fee is € 1460.
r.135(2)	Further processing is ruled out in respect of the time limits of r.56a(1) and r.56a(3)-(7). Re-establishment is therefore available.
r.135(2)	Further processing is, however, available for the one-month time limit of r.56a(8).
OJ	Whether the application is redated or not, all documents filed during the procedure will be available, in principle, for file inspection (Notice from the EPO dated 23 June 2022, [2022] O.J. A71 – see also Guidelines A, II-6.3). However, erroneously filed documents which are not considered to form part of the application as filed may be excluded from file inspection if the applicant submits a reasoned request.
Guidelines	See A-II,6.

8.4   Procedure where a filing date can be accorded – examination of formal requirements

973	Art. 90(3)/r.57	If a filing date can be accorded, the EPO next examines whether certain formal requirements have been satisfied.
	r.10(1)	The Receiving Section is responsible.
	OJ	See Decision of the President dated 12 July 2007 ([2007] O.J. Special Edition No. 3 F2). Examination of formal requirements under Art. 90(3) can be entrusted to a formalities officer.
	J19/13	Any formal deficiencies that are detected during substantive examination will be notified by the Examining Division and require correction at that stage. However, if any formal deficiencies remain when the patent is granted, they do not affect the validity of the patent (such deficiencies are "cured" by the grant).

8.4.1   Determination as to whether any necessary translation has been filed

974	Art. 90(3)	The EPO examines, in accordance with the Implementing Regulations, whether the requirements of Art. 14 have been satisfied.
	r.57(a)	The EPO examines whether a translation of the application required under Art. 14(2) or r.36(2) second sentence (if the application is not filed in English, French or German) or under r.40(3) second sentence (if a previous application relied on for obtaining a filing date is not in English, French or German) has been filed in due time.
	Art. 90(4)	Where the EPO notices there are deficiencies which may be corrected, it gives the applicant a chance to correct them.
	r.58	If there is a deficiency, the EPO informs the applicant accordingly and invites him to correct it within a period of two months.
	Art. 14(2)	If the translation is not filed in due time in response to the invitation, the application is deemed to be withdrawn.
	r.135(2)	Further processing is ruled out in respect of the r.58 time limit.
	Art. 122	Re-establishment, however, is available.
	Guidelines	See A-III, 14.

8.4.2 Request, description, claims, drawings and abstract

Art. 90(3)	The EPO examines, in accordance with the Implementing Regulations, whether the provisions of Art. 78 have been satisfied (i.e. whether the application contains a request, description, one or more claims, any drawings referred to in the description and claims and an abstract, and whether each satisfies the requirements laid down in the Implementing Regulations).
r.57(b)	The EPO examines whether the request for grant satisfies the requirements of r.41.
r.57(c)	The EPO examines whether the application contains one or more claims in accordance with Art. 78(1)(c), or a reference to a previously filed application in accordance with r.40(1)(c), r.40(2) and r.40(3) indicating that it also replaces the claims.
r.57(d)	The EPO examines whether the application contains an abstract in accordance with Art. 78(1)(e).
r.57(i)	The EPO examines whether the application meets the requirements laid down in r.49(1) and the applicable requirements prescribed by the President of the EPO under r.49(2) (presentation of the application documents).
OJ	According to Art. 4(1) of Decision of the President dated 25 November 2022 ([2022] O.J. A113) the EPO examines under r.57(i) whether the requirements of Article 1 of that decision (form and content of the drawings) and Article 2 of that decision (presentation of the application documents) have been complied with. According to Art. 4(2) and Art. 4(3) of the same decision, the Receiving Section examines whether the requirements set out in Art. 1(1), Art. 1(2)(a) to (h), Art. 2(1)-(7), Art. 2(8) sentences 1–3 and 5–6 and Art. 2(11) of that decision have been complied with but only the extent necessary for the purpose of ensuring a satisfactory reproduction or a reasonably uniform publication of the application under r.68(1) EPC.
OJ	See Notice from the EPO dated 25 November 2022 ([2022] O.J. A114 for more information). The EPO as a whole examines the requirements of Articles 1 and 2 of the Decision of the President dated 25 November 2022 (form and content of the drawings and presentation of the application documents). More technical requirements are considered by the Examining Division during substantive examination (i.e. Article 1(2)(i), Article 1(2)(j), Article 2(8) fourth sentence, Article 2(9), Article 2(10). The other requirements are considered by the Receiving Section during the formalities examination, but only to the extent necessary for the purposes of ensuring a satisfactory reproduction or a reasonably uniform publication of the application.
Art. 90(4)	Where the EPO notices there are deficiencies which may be corrected, it gives the applicant a chance to correct them.
r.58	If there is a deficiency, the EPO informs the applicant accordingly and invites him to correct it within a period of two months. The description, claims and drawings may only be amended to an extent sufficient to remedy the deficiency.
Art. 90(5)	If any such deficiency is not corrected, the European patent application is refused.
r.135(2)	Further processing is ruled out in respect of the r.58 time limit.
Art. 122	Re-establishment, however, is available.
J18/08	As an alternative to re-establishment, it would be possible to appeal the decision to refuse the application and correct the deficiency when filing grounds for appeal. According to Guidelines E-XII, 7.4.4, the Receiving Section should apply interlocutory revision.
Guidelines	See A-III, 3.2 – the examination of physical requirements at this stage is primarily to ensure that a reasonably uniform publication is possible. See also A-III, 15 – claims filed after the filing date must of course comply with Art. 123(2). Late filed claims must be in the language of the proceedings (r.3(2)). If any claims are filed on filing the application then additional claims may not be added during the formalities examination (r.137(1)). Where an application has been filed by reference it is of course the certified copy of the previous application or its translation which must comply with the physical requirements. See also A-III, 1.1 – the Receiving Section will check whether the request has been signed or not.

8.4.3 Designation of the inventor

Art. 90(3)	The EPO examines, in accordance with the Implementing Regulations, whether the requirements of Art. 81 have been satisfied.
r.57(f)	The EPO examines whether the designation of the inventor has been made in accordance with r.19(1).

975

976

Art. 90(4)	Where the EPO notices there are deficiencies which may be corrected, it gives the applicant a chance to correct them.
r.60(1)	If the designation of the inventor has not been made in accordance with r.19, the EPO will inform the applicant that the European patent application will be refused unless the designation is made within 16 months of the date of filing of the application or, if priority is claimed, of the date of priority, this period being deemed to have been observed if the information is communicated before completion of the technical preparations for the publication of the European patent application.
r.60(2)	Where, in a divisional application or a new application under Art. 61(1)(b), the designation of the inventor has not been made in accordance with r.19, the EPO will invite the applicant to make the designation within a period to be specified.
r.132(2)	Such a period is never less than two months, usually no more than four months and in certain circumstances up to six months. It may be extended on request.
Art. 90(5)	If any deficiency is not corrected, the European patent application is refused.
Art. 121	Further processing is possible.
RRFArt. 2(1)(12)	The further processing fee is € 290 in this case.
Art. 122	Re-establishment would be possible if the further processing time limit was missed in spite of all due care having been taken.
Guidelines	See A-III, 5.4 and 5.5. An incorrect designation of the inventor can later be corrected under r.21 (see section 22.1.3). Even if a request for early publication is made, the applicant still has the 16 month time limit to file the designation of the inventor.

8.4.4   Priority claim

977

Art. 90(3)	The EPO examines, where appropriate, and in accordance with the Implementing Regulations, whether the requirements of Art. 88(1) have been satisfied.
r.57(g)	The EPO examines, where appropriate, whether the requirements laid down in r.52 (declaration of priority) and r.53 (priority document) concerning the claim to priority have been satisfied.
Art. 90(4)	Where the EPO notices there are deficiencies which may be corrected, it gives the applicant a chance to correct them.
r.59	If the file number of the previous application under r.52(1) or the copy of that application under r.53(1) have not been filed in due time, the EPO will inform the applicant accordingly and invite him to file them within a period to be specified.
r.132(2)	Such a period is never less than two months, usually no more than four months and in certain circumstances up to six months. It may be extended on request.
Art. 90(5)	If any deficiency is not corrected, the right of priority will be lost for the application.
r.135(2)	Further processing is ruled out in respect of the r.59 time limit.
Art. 122	Re-establishment, however, is available.
Guidelines	See A-III, 6.5.3. The date of the previous application and the State in or for which it was filed must be made on filing or within the r.52 time limit or the right to priority is lost (Art. 4(D)(1) PC). The lack of the file number or certified copy of the previous application can, however, be rectified on notification by the EPO under Art. 90(4).

8.4.5   Representation and authorisation

978

Art. 90(3)	The EPO examines, where appropriate, and in accordance with the Implementing Regulations, whether the requirements of Art. 133(2) have been satisfied (natural or legal persons not having their residence or principal place of business in a Contracting State must be represented by a professional representative).
r.57(h)	The EPO examines, where appropriate, whether the requirements of Art. 133(2) have been satisfied.
Art. 90(4)	Where the EPO notices there are deficiencies which may be corrected, it gives the applicant a chance to correct them.
r.58	If there is a deficiency, the EPO informs the applicant accordingly and invites him to correct it within a period of two months.
Guidelines	See A-III, 2. The EPO also checks whether any required authorisation has been filed.
r.152(3)	Where the requirements of Art. 133(2) have not been satisfied, the EPO will specify the same period for the appointment of a representative and the filing of an authorisation (see section 23.3).

Art. 90(5)	If any deficiency is not corrected, the European patent application is refused.
r.135(2)	Further processing is ruled out in respect of the r.58 time limit.
Art. 122	Re-establishment, however, is available.
J18/08	As an alternative to re-establishment, it would be possible to appeal the decision to refuse the application and appoint a representative when filing the grounds of appeal. According to Guidelines E-XII, 7.4.4, the Receiving Section should apply interlocutory revision.

8.4.6 Filing and search fees

Art. 90(3)	The EPO examines, in accordance with the Implementing Regulations, whether any additional requirements laid down in the Implementing Regulations have been satisfied.	979
r.57(e)	The EPO examines whether the filing fee and search fee have been paid in accordance with r.17(2) (for a replacement application), r.36(3) (for a divisional application) or r.38 (for a regular application).	
Art. 78(2)	If the filing fee or the search fee is not paid in due time, the application is deemed to be withdrawn.	
Art. 121	Further processing is possible where the time limit for paying the filing or search fee is missed.	
RRFArt. 2(1)(12)	The further processing fee is 50 % of the unpaid fees.	
Art. 122	Re-establishment is possible if the further processing time limit is missed despite all due care required by the circumstances having been taken.	
Guidelines	See A-III, 13.	

8.4.7 Claims fees

Guidelines	See A-III, 1.2. The Receiving Section also checks at this stage whether claims fees have been paid.	980
r.45(2)	If claims fees are not paid in due time, the EPO will send a communication to the applicant pointing out the deficiency and they may still be validly paid within one month of notification of this communication.	
r.45(3)	If claims fees are still not paid in time, the relevant claims are deemed to be abandoned.	
Art. 121	Further processing is available if claims are deemed to be abandoned.	
RRFArt. 2(1)(12)	The further processing fee is 50 % of the unpaid claims fees.	
Art. 122	If the further processing time limit is missed despite all due care having been taken then re-establishment is possible.	
Guidelines	See A-III, 9. If the fees paid are insufficient the EPO will, where necessary, ask the applicant to indicate for which claims fees have been paid. Features of claims which have been deemed abandoned for failure to pay claims fees may not be reintroduced into the application (i.e. as a later claim amendment) if they are not also present in the description (as per J15/88) – it is necessary to file a divisional application to obtain protection for such subject matter.	

8.4.8 Sequence listings

Art. 90(3)	The EPO examines, in accordance with the Implementing Regulations, whether any requirements laid down in the Implementing Regulations have been satisfied.	981
r.57(j)	The EPO examines whether the application meets the requirements laid down in r.30 (requirements relating to sequence listings).	
Art. 90(4)	Where the EPO notices there are deficiencies which may be corrected, it gives the applicant a chance to correct them.	
r.30(3)	Where a sequence listing complying with the appropriate requirements is missing, the EPO will invite the applicant to furnish such a sequence listing and pay a late furnishing fee within a time limit of two months.	
Guidelines	See A-III, 1.2 and A-IV, 5 – since the time limit is set in the EPC it is not extensible.	
RRFArt. 2(1)(14a)	The late furnishing fee is € 255.	
Art. 90(5)	If any deficiency is not corrected, the European patent application is refused.	
r.30(3)	If the required sequence listing is not filed or the late furnishing fee is not paid, the application is refused.	

Art. 121   Further processing is possible. Two fees may be due since two omitted acts may be involved; a fee of € 290 will be due if the sequence listing has not been furnished in time and 50 % of the late furnishing fee will be due if this fee has not been paid in time (RR-FArt. 2(1)(12)).

Art. 122   Re-establishment would be possible if the further processing time limit was missed in spite of all due care being shown.

r.30(2)   A sequence listing filed after the date of filing does not form part of the description.

J7/11   If a corrected sequence listing contains further errors not previously notified to the applicant then the EPO must issue a further r.30(3) invitation rather than refusing the application. See also Guidelines A-IV, 5.

OJ   See Decision of the President dated 09 December 2021 ([2021] O.J. A96). The late-filed sequence listing must be accompanied by a statement to the effect that it does not include matter which goes beyond the content of the application as filed.

8.4.9   Other matters

982   Guidelines   See A-III, 1.2. The Receiving Section also checks at this stage whether the title complies with the requirements of r.41(2)(b), whether a certificate of exhibition has been filed pursuant to r.25 and whether information relating to a biological deposit pursuant to r.31(1) has been supplied.

Chapter 9: The Search Report and Opinion

9.1 The EPO must draw up a search report for each European patent application

Art. 92

The EPO will, in accordance with the Implementing Regulations, draw up and publish a European Search Report in respect of the European patent application and on the basis of the claims, with due regard to the description and any drawings.   983

Guidelines

See B-III, 3. The scope of the search should be broader than the literal meaning of the claims in accordance with Art. 69 and its Protocol. The search is performed on the basis of the claims as filed since amendments are not allowed under r.137(1) prior to receipt of the search report. Claims for which claims fees have not been paid are not searched.

9.2 Procedure where a plurality of independent claims exist

r.62a(1)

If the EPO considers that the claims as filed to not comply with r.43(2) (unallowable plurality of independent claims in the same category), it will invite the applicant to indicate, within a period of two months, the claims complying with r.43(2) on the basis of which the search is to be carried out. If the applicant fails to provide such an indication in due time, the search will be carried out on the basis of the first claim in each category.   984

r.135(2)
Art. 122
Guidelines

Further processing is ruled out for the time limit of r.62a(1)
Re-establishment is therefore available in principle (see Guidelines B-VIII, 4.2.1).
See B-VIII, 4. The applicant may indicate which independent claim is to be searched or maintain one or more independent claims in the same category and explain why they meet the requirements of r.43(2). If the Search Division is not convinced by such arguments it will proceed to search the independent claim of lowest number and indicate its reasoning in the search opinion. Claims deemed abandoned due to the non-payment of claims fees cannot be selected for the search. A late-filed reply is included in the file for consideration by the Examining Division.

9.3 Procedure where a meaningful search is not possible

r.63(1)

If the EPO considers that the European patent application fails to such an extent to comply with the EPC that it is impossible to carry out a meaningful search regarding the state of the art on the basis of all or some of the subject-matter claimed, it will invite the applicant to file, within a period of two months, a statement indicating the subject-matter to be searched.   985

r.63(2)

If the statement submitted by the applicant pursuant to r.63(1) is not filed in due time, or if it is not sufficient to overcome the deficiency noted under r.63(1), the EPO will either issue a reasoned declaration stating that the European patent application fails to such an extent to comply with the EPC that it is impossible to carry out a meaningful search regarding the state of the art on the basis of some or all of the subject-matter claimed or, as far as is practicable, draw up a partial search report. The reasoned declaration or the partial search report shall be considered, for the purposes of subsequent proceedings, as the European search report.

r.135(2)
Art. 122
T1242/04

Further processing is ruled out for the time limit of r.63(1).
Re-establishment is therefore available in principle (see Guidelines B-VIII, 3.2.1).
The provision of r.63 must be interpreted narrowly – the inability to conduct a search will only apply in exceptional cases where, for example, the entire claim set lacks technical character.

Guidelines

An incomplete search may result when the claims relate, in part, to subject matter which is not a technical invention within the meaning of Art. 52(1) and (2) EPC (G-II, 2) or to subject matter which is contrary to ordre public or morality (G-II, 4.1).

Guidelines

If a document cited in the application by the applicant is not available to the EPO and is essential for understanding the invention and carrying out a proper search, the applicant will be invited under r.63 to file a copy (see B-IV, 1.3).

Guidelines	See B-VIII, 3. An incomplete search may result from the claims lacking proper support from an insufficient disclosure (very broad claims), clarity (e.g. claims limited by an inappropriate parameter) or conciseness (e.g. burdensome number of claims or number of alternatives within a claim). A meaningful search may also be precluded where the claims clearly violate Art. 123(2), having been filed later than the filing date, or Art. 76(1) in the case of a divisional (B-VIII, 6). According to B-III, 3.2.1, no invitation under r.63(1) is issued in respect of an omnibus claim. According to B-VIII, 2.1 and 3.1, an invention relating to a method of treatment should be searched fully if it is based on the second medical use of a compound. A late-filed reply is included in the file for consideration by the Examining Division (B-VIII, 3.2.1).
OJ	See Notice from the EPO dated 15 October 2009 ([2009] O.J. 533). No amendment is possible at this stage of proceedings (r.137(1)) but the applicant can refer to particular embodiments in the description or suggest improved claim wording and the claims can later be brought into line with what is searched (see also Guidelines H-II, 5 and B-VIII,3.2.2). See also Notice from the EPO dated 01 October 2007 ([2007] O.J. 592) – an application relating to a method of doing business may result in the issuance of a reasoned declaration rather than a search report.

9.4   Procedure where the application lacks unity

986	r.64(1)	If the EPO considers that the application does not comply with the requirement of unity of invention, it will draw up a partial search report on those parts of the application which relate to the invention, or the group of inventions within the meaning of Art. 82, first mentioned in the claims. It will then inform the applicant that for the European Search Report to cover other inventions, a further search fee must be paid, in respect of each invention involved, within a period of two months.
	RRFArt. 2(1)(2)	The search fee is € 1460 for applications filed on or after 01 July 2005. For applications filed before 01 July 2005, the fee is € 1000.
	Art. 106(1)	It is not possible to appeal the request for further fees (no appeal is possible from a decision of the Search Division).
	r.64(1)	The European Search Report will be drawn up for the parts of the application relating to inventions in respect of which search fees have been paid.
	r.135(2)	Further processing is ruled out in respect of the r.64(1) time limit.
	Art. 122	Re-establishment should therefore be available in principle.
	r.64(2)	Any additional fees paid will be refunded if, during examination of the application, the applicant requests a refund and the Examining Division finds that the demand for extra fees was not justified.
	Guidelines	See B-VII. The search examiner informs the applicant that a lack of unity exists and accompanies the communication with a copy of the partial search report and an invitation to pay extra fees. Care must be taken by users of the automatic direct debiting procedure since all additional fees will be debited by the EPO at the end of the two month period unless instructed otherwise. If a full search can be easily completed despite the lack of unity then an invitation to pay extra fees is not sent but the search report will still indicate non-compliance with Art. 82.
	OJ	See [2017] O.J. A20. From 01 April 2017 onwards a partial search report issued under r.64(1) will be accompanied by a written opinion relating to the searched subject matter, including reasoning concerning the lack of unity (see also Guidelines B-XI,5). Before this date a written opinion was only sent to the applicant along with the European search report itself. The "partial" written opinion is for information only and no response is required or taken into account.

9.5   Establishing of the definitive content of the abstract

987	r.66	Upon drawing up the search report, the EPO also determines the definitive content of the abstract and transmits it to the applicant together with the search report.
	Guidelines	See B-X, 7(i) and F-II, 2. Whilst the abstract is supplied by the applicant, the search examiner has the responsibility of deciding on its final wording and content. The search examiner may decide that no Figure should accompany the abstract, even where the applicant has proposed one or more himself.

9.6   Patent classification used by the EPO

r.8

The EPO will use the classification referred to in Art. 1 of the Strasbourg Agreement   988
concerning the International Patent Classification of March 24, 1971. This classification
(under r.8) is referred to in the EPC as the international classification.

9.7   Accelerated search

OJ

See [2015] O.J. A93. As from 01 July 2014 the EPO tries to issue a search report within   989
six months of the filing date (or expiry of the r.161(2) period for Euro-PCT applications
where a supplementary European search is necessary) as standard and no further acceleration is possible. For such a Euro-PCT application, a communication under r.161(2) and
r.162(2) can be waived in order to further expedite the procedure. Clearly, the applicant
must co-operate in order to ensure the fastest search, particularly where a communication
under r.62a, r.63 or r.64 has been issued, and all formal requirements of the application
must be complied with.

OJ

See [2016] O.J. A66. If the EPO receives an enquiry from the applicant concerning the
processing of the file on Form 1012, it will take action to ensure that the extended or partial European search report is issued within a period of one month from receipt of the enquiry if the relevant search report has not been issued within six months of the filing date
(for applications filed on or after 01 June 2014) or within a period of six months from the
date of the enquiry if the relevant search report has not yet been issued (for applications
filed before 01 June 2014 which claim priority).

9.8   The European Search Report

9.8.1   Content of the search report

r.61(1)

The search report mentions those documents, available to the EPO at the time of drawing   990
up the report, which may be taken into consideration in deciding whether the invention
to which the European patent application relates is new and involves an inventive step.

r.61(2)

Each citation is referred to the claims to which it relates. Where appropriate, relevant parts
of the documents cited are identified.

r.61(3)

The search report distinguishes between cited documents published before the claimed
priority date, between the claimed priority date and the date of filing, and on or after the
date of filing.

r.61(4)

Any document which refers to an oral disclosure, a use or any other means of disclosure
which took place before the date of filing of the European patent application are mentioned in the European Search Report, together with an indication of the date of publication, if any, of the document and the date of the non-written disclosure.

r.61(6)

The search report also contains the classification of the subject matter of the application
in accordance with the international classification (see r.8 above).

OJ

From 1982 onwards, search reports have also included, in an annex, information on the
patent families of cited applications or patents ([1982] O.J. 448). From 1999, the annex has
also listed "family members" and their publication dates ([1999] O.J. 90).

Guidelines

See B-X. A prior art document is cited in category "X" if it prejudices novelty or inventive
step when taken alone, "Y" if it prejudices inventive step in combination with another
document in the same category or "A" if it does not prejudice novelty or inventive step
but merely defines the state of the art. An "O" document refers to a non-written disclosure, a "P" document was made available during the priority period, a "T" document is
useful for understanding the invention, an "E" document is potentially relevant under
Art. 54(3), a "D" document was cited in the application as filed and an "L" document is
cited as evidence for a relevant assertion (e.g. which casts doubt on a priority claim, or
which establishes the publication date of another citation, or which is relevant to the issue
of double patenting).

9.8.2   Language of the search report

r.61(5)

The search report is drawn up in the language of the proceedings.   991

9.8.3   Additional copies of citations

992	RRFArt. 3(1)	The amount of the administrative fee is fixed by the President of the EPO.
	OJ	The amount is € 115 (see decision of the President dated 17 January 2023, [2023] O.J. A3).

9.9   The extended European Search Report

993	Guidelines	The extended European Search Report is made up of two components: the European search report and a search opinion (B-XI, 1).
	r.62(1)	The European Search Report is accompanied by an opinion on whether the application and the invention to which it relates seem to meet the requirements of the EPC, unless a communication under r.71(1) or r.71(3) can be issued.
	Guidelines	See B/XI. A communication under r.71(1) or r.71(3) can be issued directly where a valid request for examination has been filed before transmittal of the European search report and the applicant has waived the right to a communication under r.70(2) asking him whether he wishes to proceed to examination or not. In this case, no search opinion is issued (B-XI, 7). Where the application was not re-dated on the basis that the content of a late-filed part was completely contained in the priority document and the search examiner disagrees with opinion of the Receiving Section, the opinion will indicate that re-dating will probably be necessary during substantive examination (B-XI, 2.1). If the claims were filed later than the date of filing the application the search examiner must examine whether they meet the requirements of Art. 123(2) EPC and comment in the opinion where a deficiency is found (B-XI, 2.2). See also B-VIII, 3.3 – the search opinion will give reasons why the claims could not be meaningfully searched under r.63 where appropriate. The priority claim is usually assumed to be valid at this stage (B-XI, 4).
	r.62(2)	The opinion is not published with the search report.
	Comment	The opinion is made available to the public as part of the application file once the application is published.

9.10   Transmittal of the search report, search opinion and definitive content of the abstract

994	r.65	Immediately after it has been drawn up, the European Search Report (accompanied by the opinion pursuant to r.62(1)) is transmitted to the applicant. The EPO makes available copies of any cited documents.
	r.66	The definitive content of the abstract is also submitted to the applicant along with the search report.

9.11   Requirement to file a response to the extended European search report

995	r.70a(1)	In the opinion accompanying the European search report, the EPO gives the applicant a chance to comment on the extended European search report and, where appropriate, invites him to correct any deficiencies noted in the opinion accompanying the European search report and to amend the description, claims and drawings within the period referred to in r.70(1) (period for requesting examination).
	r.70(1)	The period is six months after the date on which the European Patent Bulletin mentions the publication of the European search report.
	r.69(2)	The period may be longer if a later date is notified to the applicant by the EPO pursuant to r.69(1) EPC and the error is not obvious.
	r.70a(2)	If the applicant has already requested examination before transmittal of the European search report (r.70(2)), or if a supplementary European search report is drawn up on a Euro-PCT application, the EPO gives the applicant a chance to comment on the extended European search report and, where appropriate, invites him to correct any deficiencies noted in the opinion accompanying the European search report and to amend the description, claims and drawings within the period specified for indicating whether he wishes to proceed further with the application under r.70(2).
	r.70(2)	The period is one which is to be specified.
	r.132(1)	Where the EPC or Implementing Regulations refer to 'a period to be specified', this period is specified by the EPO.

r.132(2)	Such a period is never less than two months, usually no more than 4 months and in certain circumstances up to six months.
Guidelines	The time limit set is six months from mention of the publication of the search report in the European patent bulletin (A-VI, 2.2).
r.132(2)	In special cases, the period may be extended on request.
Guidelines	See E-VIII, 1.6. An extension is only granted if good reasons are presented.
r.70a(3)	If the applicant neither complies with nor comments on an invitation in accordance with r.70a(1) or r.70a(2), the application is deemed to be withdrawn.
Art. 121	Further processing is possible.
RRFArt. 2(1)(12)	The further processing fee is € 290 in this case.
Art. 122	Re-establishment would be possible if the further processing time limit was missed in spite of all due care being taken.
Guidelines	See B-XI, 8. There is no requirement to respond to the extended European search report if it does not contain any objections. Procedural requests (e.g. for an interview or for oral proceedings) do not constitute a valid response to the invitation in the absence of any comments on the objections raised. Nor is a mere statement disapproving of the objections a valid response – the applicant must make comments addressing the specific objections made.

9.12   One chance for submission of voluntary amendments in response to extended European search report

Art. 123(1)	The conditions under which amendment is possible are laid down in the Regulations. 996
r.137(2)	Together with any comments, corrections or amendments made in response to communications by the EPO under r.70a(1) or (2), the applicant may amend the description, claims and drawings of his own volition.
Guidelines	See H-II,2.2. Although it does not follow from the wording of r.137(2), where no search opinion is issued, voluntary amendments may be submitted in response to the first communication from the Examining Division. This may arise, for example, where the applicant has requested examination before transmittal of the search report and also dispensed with the invitation to indicate whether he wishes to proceed with examination or not.

Chapter 10: Publication of the Application and Search Report

10.1 Timing of publication

997 Art. 93(1)(a)	A European patent application is published by the EPO as soon as possible after the expiry of a period of 18 months from the date of filing or, if priority has been claimed, from the date of priority.
Art. 93(1)(b)	Nevertheless, at the request of the applicant, the application may be published before the expiry of the period specified in Art. 93(1)(a).
Art. 93(2)	It is published simultaneously with the publication of the specification of the European patent when the decision to grant the patent becomes effective before the expiry of the period referred to in Art. 93(1)(a).
Guidelines	The publication will be delayed if the priority claim is withdrawn before the technical preparations for publication are completed (see A-VI, 1.1). See below under section 10.2 for the date on which technical preparations are completed. For a divisional application, the period under Art. 93(1)(a) has often expired when the divisional is filed (since the filing date/priority date of the parent applies) and publication takes place as soon as all formal requirements have been met (A-IV, 1.8).
Comment	At present, publication takes place every Wednesday.

10.2 No publication to take place when the application is withdrawn or refused

998 r.67(2)	The application will not be published if it has been finally refused or withdrawn or is deemed to be withdrawn before the termination of the technical preparations for publication.
r.67(1)	Such technical preparations are deemed to have been completed at a time determined by the President of the EPO.
OJ	The date is five weeks before the 18-month mark (Decision of the President dated 12 July 2007, [2007] O.J. Special Edition No. 3 D1). See also Guidelines A-VI, 1.2.
J5/81	The EPO can prevent publication, at its own discretion, even after the technical preparations are complete.
OJ	Indeed, the EPO will do its best to prevent publication where a request is received after the technical preparations are complete (see Notice from the EPO dated 25 April 2006, [2006] O.J. 406). See also Guidelines A-VI, 1.2.
Guidelines	See A-VI, 1.2. The application is still published if the application is deemed withdrawn but a request for a decision under r.112(2) is pending or a request for re-establishment is pending. The applicant is bound by an effective declaration of withdrawal but withdrawal may be made conditional on publication being avoided.
G1/09	An application is finally refused when the period for filing an appeal expires (or later if an appeal is filed).

10.3 Language and form of the publication

999 Art. 14(5)	European patent applications are published in the language of the proceedings.
r.68(2)	The President of the EPO determines the form of the publication. The same applies where the European Search Report and the abstract are published separately.
OJ	The publication is in electronic form by means of a publication server from which the application and search report can be downloaded (as from April 1, 2005) – Decision of the President dated 12 July 2007, [2007] O.J. Special Edition No. D3, and Guidelines A-VI, 1.4.

10.4 Contents of the publication

1000 r.68(1)	The publication contains the description, the claims and any drawings as filed and the abstract, or, if these documents making up the application were not filed in an official language of the EPO, a translation in the language of proceedings, and, in an annex, the European Search Report where it is available before the termination of the technical preparations for publication. If the European Search Report or the abstract is not published at the same time as the application, it is published separately.

r.62(2)	The opinion as to whether the invention and application meet the requirements of the EPC is not part of the publication (but can be inspected as part of the contents of the application file once the application has been published).
r.68(2)	The President of the EPO prescribes the data to be included in the publication. The same applies where the European Search Report and the abstract are published separately.
r.47(4)	Where the application contains drawings, the applicant must indicate the figure, or exceptionally, the figures of the drawings, which should be published with the abstract. However, the EPO may decide to publish one or more other figures if it considers that they better characterise the invention.
r.68(3)	The designated Contracting States are indicated in the publication.
Comment	For applications filed on or after 13.12.2007, all States are deemed designated on filing (Art. 79(1)) and all states will therefore be designated on publication unless the designation of one or more states is specifically withdrawn.
r.52(5)	The particulars in the declaration of priority are published with the application.
r.68(4)	If the patent claims were not filed on the date of filing of the application, this will be indicated when the application is published.
r.68(4)	If, before the termination of the technical preparations for publication of the application, the claims have been amended under r.137(2), the new or amended claims are included in the publication in addition to the claims as filed.
r.20(1)	The designated inventor is mentioned in the published European patent application, unless he informs the EPO in writing that he has waived his right to be thus mentioned.
r.20(2)	In the event of a third party filing with the EPO a final decision determining that the applicant for a European patent is required to designate him as an inventor, the provisions of r.20(1) apply.
Guidelines	See A-VI, 1.3. Where an application for correction under r.139 is pending, or has been granted, this fact is included in the publication if it would affect third parties. If a correction is authorised in time then the corrected page is included in the publication. Republication is possible if significant mistakes are corrected later. Any pages late filed according to r.56 EPC are included unless subsequently withdrawn. A request for correction under r.56a may also change the content of the publication. If the procedure under r.56 or r.56a is not finalised then a later correction of the publication may be necessary.
OJ	A list of any art cited by the applicant in the description pursuant to r.42(1)(b) is now included at the end of the published application (Decision of the President dated 12 July 2007, [2007] O.J. Special Edition No. 3 D4). A sequence listing filed with the application is published as part of the description (see Decision of the President dated 28 April 2011, [2011] O.J. 372).

10.5 Matter excluded from the publication

r.48(2)	If a European patent application contains prohibited matter within the meaning of r.48(1)(a) (statements contrary to ordre public or morality) the EPO may omit it from the application as published, indicating the place and number of words or drawings omitted.	1001
r.48(3)	Further, if a European patent application contains prohibited matter within the meaning of r.48(1)(b) (disparaging statements) the EPO may omit it from the application as published, indicating the place and number of words omitted and will furnish, on request, a copy of the passages omitted.	

Chapter 11: Request for Examination, Designation Fee, Extension Fees and Validation Fees

11.1 Communication to the applicant of the date on which the Bulletin mentions the publication of the search report

1002 r.69(1) — The EPO tells the applicant the date on which the European Patent Bulletin will mention the publication of the search report and draws his attention to the provisions of r.70(1) and Art. 94(2) (time limit for filing the request for examination; consequences of not doing so) and r.70a (requirement to file a response to extended European search report).

r.69(2) — If a date of publication is specified in the communication which is later than the actual date of publication, that later date shall be the decisive date as regards the period for filing the request for examination and the period for responding to the extended European search report, unless the error is obvious.

Comment — The error would be obvious, for example if the year was incorrectly stated.

Guidelines — See A-VI, 2.1.

11.2 Payment of the designation fee

11.2.1 Designation fee for a regular European patent application

1003 Art. 79(2) — The designation of a Contracting State is subject to the payment of a designation fee.

RRFArt. 2(1)(3) — The designation fee is € 660 for European applications filed on or after 01 April 2009 and international applications entering the regional phase on or after that date.

RRFArt. 2(2)(3) — The designation fee is € 115 per contracting state for European applications filed before 01 April 2009 and international applications entering the regional phase before that date (Switzerland and Liechtenstein counting as one designation – RRFArt. 2(2)(3a)), but fees for all states are deemed paid upon payment of 7 fees.

r.39(1) — The designation fee must be paid within six months of the date on which the European Patent Bulletin mentions the publication of the European Search Report.

RRFArt. 4(1) — According to the Guidelines (A-X, 5.2.2), the designation fee falls due on the mention of the publication of the European search report and may be paid from this point onwards. However, if it is paid earlier, it is not refunded, in contrast to most fees. Where there has been a fee increase in the meantime, the amount due is that which applies on mention of publication of the search report in the Bulletin.

r.39(2) — Non-payment of the fee leads to the European patent application being deemed withdrawn.

Art. 121 — Further processing is possible in this case.

RRFArt. 2(1)(12) — The further processing fee is 50 % of the designation fee.

Art. 122 — If the further processing time limit is missed despite all due care having been taken then re-establishment would be available.

r.39(3) — No refund of the designation fee is made apart from the case under r.37(2) where a European patent application is not forwarded to the EPO by a national authority in time.

Guidelines — See A-III, 11.

11.2.2 Designation fee for a divisional application

1004 r.36(4) — The designation fee must be paid within six months of the date on which the European Patent Bulletin mentions the publication of the search report relating to the divisional application. Since r.39(2) and (3) apply: (1) if the designation fee is not paid then the application itself is deemed withdrawn; and (2) the designation fee is not refundable.

11.2.3 Designation fee for a replacement application

1005 r.17(3) — The designation fee must be paid within six months of the date on which the European Patent Bulletin mentions the publication of the European Search Report drawn up in respect of the new application. Since r.39(2) and (3) apply: (1) if the designation fee is not paid then the application itself is deemed withdrawn; and (2) the designation fee is not refundable.

11.3 Payment of extension fees

OJ	A European patent may be extended to Bosnia and Herzegovina ([2004] O.J. 619). See section 7.8. All legal basis in relation to the extension of a European patent is found in the relevant agreement rather than in the EPC. The deadline for paying the extension fee is the same as that for paying the designation fee under the EPC.
r.39(1)	The designation fee, and hence an extension fee, must be paid within six months of the date on which the European Patent Bulletin mentions the publication of the European Search Report.
RRFArt. 4(1)	According to the Guidelines (A-X, 5.2.2), the designation fee falls due on mention of the publication of the European search report and may be paid from this point onwards (but is not refunded if paid earlier). It may be assumed that the same applies to the extension fees.
OJ	The extension fee is currently € 102.
OJ	If an extension fee is not paid in due time, then according to the extension agreements the request for extension concerned is deemed withdrawn.
OJ	If an extension fee is not paid, the extension agreements provide that the grace period of r.85a(2) EPC1973 applies, i.e. they may be paid within two months from the expiry of the normal time limit along with a surcharge of 50 %. The continuing validity of this provision has been recognised by the EPO ([2009] O.J. 603).
Comment	This is an aggregate time limit.
Guidelines	See Guidelines A-III, 12.2. Where the designation fee is not paid in time and further processing is used to remedy the consequent loss of rights, further processing may also be used to pay any missing extension fee. Further processing cannot be used, however, if the designation fee is paid in due time and only the extension fee is missing. No loss of rights is notified if an extension fee is not paid in time (though non-payment will be noted in any loss of rights communication concerning the non-payment of the designation fee) and no other EPC remedies such as re-establishment may be invoked.
RRFArt. 2(1)(12)	The further processing fee in this case will be the usual 50 % of the unpaid extension fees.
Guidelines	See A-III, 12.3. An extension may be withdrawn at any time but a validly paid extension fee is not refunded.

1006

11.4 Payment of validation fees

OJ	A European patent may be validated in Morocco ([2015] O.J. A20 and [2016] O.J. A5), Moldova ([2015] O.J. A85), Tunisia ([2017] O.J. A84 and A85) and Cambodia ([2018] O.J. A15 and A16). See section 7.9. All legal basis in relation to the validation of the European patent in these countries is found in the relevant agreement and under national law rather than in the EPC. The deadline for paying the validation fees is the same as that for paying the designation fee under the EPC.
r.39(1)	The designation fee, and hence the validation fees, must be paid within six months of the mention of the publication of the European Search Report.
RRFArt. 4(1)	According to the Guidelines (A-X, 5.2.2), the designation fee falls due on mention of the publication of the European search report and may be paid from this point onwards (but is not refunded if paid earlier). It may be assumed that the same applies to the validation fees.
OJ	The validation fee is currently € 240 for Morocco, € 200 for Moldova and € 180 for Tunisia and Cambodia.
OJ	If a validation fee is not paid in due time, then according to the validation agreements the request for validation concerned is deemed withdrawn.
OJ	If a validation fee is not paid, the validation agreements provide that a grace period applies, i.e. it may be paid within two months from the expiry of the normal time limit along with a surcharge of 50 %.
Comment	This is an aggregate time limit.

1007

Guidelines	See Guidelines A-III, 12.2. Where the designation fee is not paid in time and further processing is used to remedy the consequent loss of rights, further processing may also be used to pay any missing validation fees. Further processing cannot be used, however, if the designation fee is paid in due time and only the validation fees are missing. No loss of rights is notified if a validation fee is not paid in time (though non-payment will be noted in any loss of rights communication concerning the designation fee) and no other EPC remedies such as re-establishment may be invoked.
RRFArt. 2(1)(12) Guidelines	The further processing fee in this case will be the usual 50 % of the unpaid validation fees. See A-III, 12.3. A validation may be withdrawn at any time but a validly paid validation fee is not refunded.

11.5   Request for examination

11.5.1   *Examination must be requested*

1008	Art. 94(1)	The European Patent Office will, in accordance with the Implementing Regulations, examine, on request, whether a European patent application and the invention to which it relates meet the requirements of the EPC.
	J12/82	Paying the examination fee is not enough, a request for examination must also be filed. Such a request is built into Form 1001 so that paying the fee is the determinative factor (J25/92).
	r.70(1) Guidelines	A request for examination cannot be withdrawn See A-VI, 2.2 and C-II, 1.

11.5.2   *Time limit for requesting examination*

1009	r.70(1)	The applicant may request examination up to six months after the date on which the European Patent Bulletin mentions the publication of the European Search Report.

11.5.3   *Payment of an examination fee*

1010	Art. 94(1)	The request for examination is not deemed to be filed until the examination fee has been paid.
	RRFArt. 2(1)(6)	For European applications filed before July 1, 2005, the examination fee is € 2055, but for applications filed on or after July 1, 2005, the fee is € 1840. For international patent applications filed on or after July 1, 2005, for which no supplementary search is drawn up the fee is € 2055. For a divisional application, the date of filing of the divisional, rather than the date of filing of the parent, is determinative – see Notice from the EPO dated 06 March 2023 ([2023] OJ A28).
	RRFArt. 14(2)	Where the EPO has drawn up an International Preliminary Examination Report, the examination fee is reduced by 75 %. If the report was established on certain parts of the international application in accordance with Art. 34(3)(c) of the PCT, the fee will not be reduced if subject matter not covered by the report is also to be examined.
	Guidelines	See A-X, 5.2.2. The examination fee is due when the request for examination is filed (RRFArt. 4(1)). Since this is included in the request for grant form, it can be paid from the date of filing when this form is used.

11.5.4   *Consequences of not requesting examination*

1011	Art. 94(2)	If no request for examination has been made by the end of the period for requesting examination, the application will be deemed to be withdrawn.
	Art. 121 Guidelines	Further processing is available. See E-VIII, 2. In principle, a further processing fee in respect of a missing request for examination and a further processing fee in respect of a missing examination fee may both be due if neither act has been carried out. Since both acts have the same legal basis, however, it is considered that a single further processing fee is paid comprising one or two components as appropriate.
	Comment	However, since the request for examination is pre-printed on the request form it is highly unlikely that this act will be outstanding.
	RRFArt. 2(1)(12)	The further processing fee in respect of a missing examination fee is 50 % of the examination fee and the fee for not filing a request for examination is the standard fee.

Art. 122   Re-establishment is available if the further processing time limit is missed despite all due care required by the circumstances having been shown. A single re-establishment fee would be due regardless of the amount of the further processing fee (Guidelines E-VIII, 3.1.3).

11.5.5   Refund of the examination fee

RRFArt. 11   The examination fee is refunded: 1012
(a) in full if the European patent application is withdrawn, refused or deemed to be withdrawn before substantive examination has begun;
(b) at a rate of 50 % if the European patent application is withdrawn after substantive examination has begun and
   – before expiry of the time limit for replying to the first invitation under Art. 94(3) EPC issued by the Examining Division proper or,
   – if no such invitation has been issued by the Examining Division, before the date of the communication under r.71(3) EPC.

OJ   The current text of RRFArt. 11 entered into force on 01 July 2016. Paragraph (a) applies to all European patent applications which are withdrawn, refused, or deemed to be withdrawn on or after 01 July 2016 and paragraph (b) applies to all European patent applications for which substantive examination starts on or after 01 November 2016 (Decision of the Administrative Council dated 29 June 2016, [2016] O.J. A48).

Comment   The previous version of RRFArt. 11 provided for a full refund if the application was withdrawn, refused or deemed withdrawn before the Examining Division assumed responsibility (see r.10) and a 75 % refund if the application was withdrawn, refused or deemed withdrawn after the Examining Division had assumed responsibility but before substantive examination had begun.

J25/10   If a refund is to be refused on the basis that substantive examination has begun, the EPO must state the date on which such examination started and the nature of the act which commenced the phase of examination so that the decision taken is predicable and verifiable. The Legal Board of Appeal confirmed that work concerned with preparation of the search opinion did not count.

J9/10   The issuance of an Art. 94(3) communication on form 2001A, generated automatically by a computer and sent by a formalities officer, which merely refers generically to objections made in the search opinion, is not a legally effective step taken by the Examining Division and does not therefore represent the beginning of substantive examination.

Guidelines   See A-VI, 2.5. The date on which examination starts, when the first member begins the work preparatory to the issuance of a communication from the Division, is now clearly indicated in the the European Patent Register and available via on-line inspection of the file. Communications under Art. 94(3) sent by the Examining Division "proper" include all communications indicating that the application does not meet the requirements of the EPC and referring to deemed withdrawal under Art. 94(4) such as (i) invitations under r.137(4) (requesting the applicant indicate the basis for amendments made), (ii) the minutes of a consultation by phone/in person sent along with an invitation to correct deficiencies, (iii) any communication questioning whether a late-filed missing part of the description or drawing is completely contained in the disclosure of the priority document under r.56 and (iv) any invitation to oral proceedings which annexes a communication pursuant to Art. 94(3). However, a communication concerning a formal deficiency issued by a formalities officer, even if issued under Art. 94(3), is not a communication sent by the Examining Division "proper" and neither is a communication issued under a different legal basis such as r.164(2)(a) (asking for additional search fees), r.53(3) (asking for a translation of the priority document) or Art. 124 (asking for prior art taken into account in other proceedings relating to the same invention). Any withdrawal may be made conditional on the refund applying.

OJ   See also Notice from the EPO dated 30 June 2016 ([2016] O.J. A49) – where the first communication from the Examining Division is under r.71(3) rather than Art. 94(3), the withdrawal of the application must be received by the EPO no later than the day before the date of the communication under r.71(3) for the 50 % refund to apply.

11.5.6   Language of the request for examination – fee reduction

1013	r.6(3)–(7)	Where the applicant is a natural or legal person having a residence or principle place of business within a Contracting State having an official language other than English, French or German, or a national of such a State resident abroad, and the request for examination is filed in such an official language of that State, the examination fee is reduced in accordance with the Rules relating to Fees. However, the reduction only applies if the applicant is a small or medium-sized company (the definition of which is found in Commission recommendation 2003/361/EC of 6 May 2003, see Official Journal of the EU, L/124/ p36 of 20 May 2003), a natural person, or a non-profit organisation, university or public research organisation. The applicant must declare himself to be such a person or entity and provide evidence if required by the EPO. In the case of multiple applicants, each one must be a qualifying person or entity.
	Comment	New r.6(3)–(7) entered into force on 01 April 2014 and apply to direct European patent applications filed on or after that date and Euro-PCT applications entering the European phase on or after that date. Under the previous version of the rule, a reduction of 20 % applied to all applicants having the necessary residency/nationality regardless of their commercial status.
	OJ	See Notice from the EPO dated 10 January 2014 ([2014] OJ A23). Changes in status of an organisation will not retrospectively affect a reduction already taken advantage of – the status of the applicant at the time of requesting examination is determinative. If the EPO becomes aware that a fee should have been paid in full since the applicant did not have the necessary status, the fee will be deemed not to have been paid, the application will be deemed withdrawn and further processing will be necessary.
	Guidelines	See A-X, 9.2.3.
	RRFArt. 14(1)	The reduction available is 30 %. Note this is a reduction rather than a refund.
	J21/98	Examination is only requested when the fee is paid so the applicant can still benefit from an available fee reduction when using the request form with a pre-checked request for examination (which is printed in English, French and German) unless the fee is paid on filing. The request for examination in a non-EPO official language of a contracting state must be filed before or with the payment of the fee.
	J4/18	In the case of joint applicants, each one must be a natural person or entity within the meaning of r.6(4) EPC, as specified in r.6(7) EPC, but only one of them needs to be a person defined by Art. 14(4) for the fee reduction to apply.
	Guidelines	See A-X, 9.2.3. If the request for examination in a non-EPO language is filed later than the request for examination in an EPO language (e.g. during the r.70(1) period along with payment of the examination fee) then a translation of the request into an EPO language must be filed a second time in order to take advantage of the fee reduction (in line with G6/91, Reasons 12).

11.6   A request for examination filed before transmittal of the search report must usually be confirmed

1014	r.70(2)	If the request for examination has been filed before the European Search Report has been transmitted to the applicant, the EPO will invite the applicant to indicate, within a period to be specified, whether he wishes to proceed further with the application. In the communication, the EPO will invite the applicant to comment on the search report and to amend, where appropriate, the description, claims and drawings.
	r.132(1)	Where the EPC or Implementing Regulations refer to 'a period to be specified', this period is specified by the EPO.
	r.132(2)	Such a period is never less than two months, usually no more than four months and in certain circumstances up to six months.
	Guidelines	The time limit set is six months from publication of the search report for a direct European application (A-VI, 2.2 and C-II, 1.1) or six months from notification of the r.70(2) communication for a Euro-PCT for which a supplementary European search report is drawn up (E-IX, 2.5.3).
	r.132(2)	In special cases, the period may be extended on request.
	Guidelines	See E-VII, 1.6. An extension is only granted if good reasons are presented.
	r.70(3)	If the applicant fails to reply in due time to the invitation under r.70(2), the application will be deemed to be withdrawn.

Guidelines	See C-II, 1.1 – a response to the objections raised in the search opinion (see section 9.11) will be interpreted by the EPO as an indication that the applicant wishes to proceed further with the application even if this is not expressly stated.
Art. 121	Further processing is available.
RRFArt. 2(1)(12)	The further processing fee is € 290.
Comment	Two further processing fees may be due if no response was filed.
Art. 122	Re-establishment is available in respect of the further processing time limit if it was missed in spite of all due care having been taken.
J8/83	The issuance of a r.70(2) communication also applies to international applications in respect of which a supplementary search has been carried out.
Guidelines	The need to confirm examination can be avoided by a categorical statement before the search requesting examination whatever the outcome of the search (C-VI, 3). This can be achieved by crossing Box 5.1 on the Request Form.

11.7   Assumption of responsibility by the Examining Division

r.10(2)	Subject to r.10(3) and (4), the Examining Division is responsible for the examination of a European patent application under Art. 94(1), from the time when a request for examination is filed.
r.10(3)	If a request for examination is filed before the European Search Report has been transmitted to the applicant, the Examining Division will, subject to r.10(4), be responsible from the time when the EPO receives the indication under r.70(2) (that the applicant wishes to proceed further).
r.10(4)	If a request for examination is filed before the European Search Report has been transmitted to the applicant, and if the applicant has waived the right under r.70(2), the Examining Division will be responsible from the time when the search report is transmitted to the applicant.

1015

Chapter 12: Substantive Examination

12.1 Formal written procedure

1016 Art. 94(3)	If the examination of a European patent application reveals that the application or the invention to which it relates does not meet the requirements of the EPC, the Examining Division will invite the applicant, as often as necessary, to file his observations and, subject to Art. 123(1), to amend the application.
Guidelines	See C-V, 14. A decision to refuse the application cannot be taken solely on the basis of the search opinion and response thereto. At least one communication from the Examining Division is necessary.
Case law	The Examining Division has a discretionary power to refuse an application after a single Art. 94(3) communication, even if the applicant makes a bona fide response (see, for example, T84/82, T161/82, T162/82, T 243/89). But Art. 113(1) must be respected – the decision to refuse must be based on grounds and evidence that the applicant has had a chance to comment on and it must be clear from the decision that the applicant's arguments have been taken into account. Discretion should be exercised according to the likelihood of a patent being granted.
r.71(1)(2)	The communication will contain a reasoned statement covering, where appropriate, all the grounds against the grant of the European patent. In the communication, the Examining Division will, where appropriate, invite the applicant to correct any deficiencies noted and amend the description, claims and drawings within a period to be specified.
Case law	The applicant should be notified of each requirement of the EPC that has not been met and, in each case, of the legal and factual reasons (see, for example, T5/81, T161/82, T568/89, T20/83, T98/88).
r.132(1)	'A period to be specified' is one which is specified by the EPO.
r.132(2)	The time limit set for reply must be from two to six months, usually from two to four months.
r.132(2)	The time limit may be extended, at the discretion of the EPO, if a request for extension is submitted before its expiry.
Guidelines	See C-VI, 1 and E-VII, 1.6. The time limit should generally be set between two and four months, taking into account the amount of work the applicant will have to undertake to respond. Exceptionally it may be set at six months. An extension is usually granted if the deadline as extended does not exceed six months, even if no reasons are given. Further extensions are only granted if good reasons are presented. Good reasons may include serious illness or the need to conduct tests. Pressure of work and holiday arrangements, however, do not constitute good reasons. The acceleration of grant proceedings will cease if the applicant requests the extension of a time limit.
J37/89	This decision explains how to proceed where a valid request for extension of the time limit is not granted – request further processing and a refund of the further processing fee.
Art. 94(4)	If the applicant fails to reply in due time to any communication from the Examining Division, the application will be deemed to be withdrawn.
T685/98	A letter which does not waive or exercise the right to present comments pursuant to Art. 113(1) does not count as a reply and in these circumstances no refusal of the application is possible, the application must be deemed withdrawn.
Guidelines	See C-IV, 3. Any response that addresses even one objection, even partially, counts as a response and avoids deemed withdrawal. However, a formal request, such as for the extension of the time limit or for a consultation, does not consitute a response.
Art. 121	Further processing is possible if the application is deemed withdrawn.
RRFArt. 2(1)(12)	The further processing fee is € 290 in this case.
Art. 122	Re-establishment is possible in respect of the further processing time limit if it was missed in spite of all due care required by the circumstances having been taken.

Guidelines	See C-III, 4 and C-IV, 3. The examiner must try and reach grant or refusal in as few actions as possible and must decide on the procedure after an initial Art. 94(3) communication and response in order to achieve this objective. See F-II, 2.7 – the content of the abstract is not changed during substantive examination. See also C-III, 5 – the first communication from the Examining Division can, in exceptional circumstances, take the form of a summons to oral proceedings. This may be the case where the applicant has not amended the claims in response to the search opinion and has not overcome one or more objections made in that opinion and the examiner cannot envisage the grant of a patent. At least six months notice of the oral proceedings must be given. If the applicant files new claims and/ or arguments before the deadline for filing final submissions that respond to the objections made then the oral proceedings may be cancelled or postponed. However, such an approach is not generally appropriate (E-III, 5). See also C-VII, 2.5 – notified minutes of a telephone call with the applicant may also be considered a first communication from the Examining Division if the minutes contain fully reasoned objections and indicate a time limit for response not shorter than four months.
Guidelines	See C-III, 1.1.1. If the Examining Division disagrees with a decision taken by the Receiving Section under r.56 or r.56a that a late-filed part was completely contained in an application from which priority is claimed, the application may be re-dated unless the applicant withdraws the late-filed part. The applicant can request an interlocutory decision in order to have the matter reviewed by a Board of Appeal.

12.2 Informal consultations by telephone, videoconference or e-mail

Guidelines	See C-IV, 3 and C-VII, 2. Minor matters of disagreement and misunderstandings are often best dealt with by informal consultation. Such a consultation takes place entirely at the discretion of the examiner. A videoconference is preferred by the EPO but a telephone call is also possible. Oral statements must be made separately in writing for them to become part of the procedure. Minutes are taken by the examiner, put on file and communicated to the applicant. E-mail communication can be useful in certain circumstances but has no legal force and cannot therefore be used to perform any procedural act other than during a telephone consultation or videoconference (see below).	1017
OJ	The EPO prefers to hold consultations during grant proceedings by videoconference (see Notice from the EPO dated 22 November 2022, [2022] O.J. A106). As an exception to the general rule, during consultations and oral proceedings held by videoconference, documents, including authorisations, can and must be filed by e-mail (Decision of the President dated 13 May 2020, [2020] O.J. A71).	

12.3 Procedure of the Examining Division in the case of an incomplete search

r.62a(2)	Where the search has been restricted on the basis that the claims do not comply with r.43(2) (unallowable plurality of independent claims in the same category), the Examining Division will invite the applicant to restrict the claims to the subject-matter searched unless it finds that the objection raised by the Search Division was unjustified.	1018
r.63(3)	Where a partial search report has been drawn up pursuant to r.63(2) (application fails to such an extent to comply with the EPC that a meaningful search is not possible for all the subject-matter claimed), the Examining Division will invite the applicant to restrict the claims to the subject-matter searched unless it finds that the objection of the Search Division under r.63(1) was not justified.	
r.137(5)	Amended claims may not relate to subject-matter not searched in accordance with r.62a or r.63.	
OJ	The unsearched subject matter must therefore be excised from the claims and cannot be reintroduced. If it is not removed the application is refused. See Notice from the EPO dated 15 October 2009 ([2009] O.J. 533). See also Guidelines H-IV, 4.	
G2/92	Headnote: An applicant who fails to pay the further search fees for a non-unitary application when requested to do so by the Search Division under r.46(1) EPC (now r.64(1) EPC2000) cannot pursue that application for the subject matter in respect of which no search fees have been paid. Such an applicant must file a divisional application in respect of such subject matter if he wishes to seek protection for it.	

Comment	The Enlarged Board felt that only one examination fee is payable and so only one invention may be examined and that this invention must have been one searched by the Search Division. The applicant who pays the extra fees may not only argue for unity subsequently before the Examining Division but may also select which of the inventions is examined if they are unsuccessful in this argument. These fees are not lost since the search fees payable on any divisional application which must be filed are reduced to the extent the first search can be used.
T631/97	Whether additional fees are paid or not, the applicant has the same right to argue against the non-unity finding before the Examining Division. The only advantage of paying the extra fees is being able to choose which invention to prosecute in the parent application if such arguments are unsuccessful.
Guidelines	See H-II, 6.2. If the applicant refuses to restrict the claims to searched subject matter in view of a unity objection, the EPO will refuse the application under r.64 (for a direct filed European patent application) or r.164 (for a Euro-PCT application), in accordance with G2/92.
r.64(2)	Any additional fees paid at the search stage will be refunded if, during examination of the application, the applicant requests a refund and the Examining Division finds that the demand for extra fees was not justified.
G1/11	Headnote: For the examination of an appeal against a decision of the Examining Division to not refund search fees under Rule 64(2) EPC, which has not been adopted together with a decision on the grant of a European patent or the refusal of a European patent application, a Technical Board of Appeal is competent.
Guidelines	See C-III, 3. If the applicant asks for a refund of additional search fees and the Examining Division decides no refund is necessary, it should normally take an interlocutory decision to this effect, having respected the applicant's right to be heard, which allows of separate appeal. No refund is possible where the EPO acted as International Search Authority for a Euro-PCT application since the fees in this case were paid according to the PCT under which a separate protest procedure operates. See F-V, 11 for lack of unity during substantive examination and F-V, 13 for lack of unity in respect of the examination of a Euro-PCT application.

12.4   Further searches

1019 Guidelines	See B-II, 4.2 and C-IV, 7. The Examining Division may carry out an additional European search where one is required (e.g. because issues preventing a meaningful search by the Search Division have been resolved or the applicant has successfully argued against a lack of unity objection or an objection relating to multiple independent claims raised by the Search Division. In any case, a search for Art. 54(3) documents will be performed. If any new documents are cited, copies are sent to the applicant.

12.5   Auxiliary requests

1020 Guidelines	See H-III, 3. It is possible to make auxiliary requests pursuant to Art. 113(2) in addition to the main request in examination proceedings. If the main request is allowable, auxiliary requests are ignored. If the main request is not allowable, on the other hand, the Examining Division will consider any auxiliary requests in the sequence indicated by the applicant until an allowable request is encountered. Reasons for the non-allowability of any higher-ranking request must be given. Each auxiliary request is a request for amendment and may be considered inadmissible under r.137(3).

12.6 Double patenting

G1/05

"The Board accepts that the principle of double patenting exists on the basis that an applicant has no legitimate interest in proceedings leading to the grant of a second patent for the same subject-matter if he already possesses one granted patent therefor. Therefore, the Enlarged Board finds nothing objectionable in the established practice of the EPO that amendments to a divisional application are objected to and refused when the amended divisional application claims the same subject matter as a pending parent application or a granted parent patent" (Reasons, 13.4).

1021

G4/19

Headnote (1): "A European patent application can be refused under Art. 97(2) and Art. 125 EPC if it claims the same subject-matter as a European patent which has been granted to the same applicant and does not form part of the state of the art pursuant to Art. 54(2) and (3) EPC."

Headnote (2): "The application can be refused on that legal basis, irrespective of whether it a) was filed on the same date as, or b) is an earlier application or a divisional application (Art. 76(1) EPC) in respect of, or c) claims the same priority (Art. 88 EPC) as the European patent application leading to the European patent already granted."

Comment

In this decision, the Enlarged Board confirms the obiter remarks in G1/05 that double patenting is in principle prohibited under the EPC. The discussion does not deal with the effect of the prohibition in post-grant proceedings and assumes that the applicant is the same, the subject matter is the same and there are overlapping designations. The Enlarged Board finds that Art. 125 EPC provides a legal basis for the prohibition of double patenting since it covers procedural provisions which also involve a substantive examination. It finds that the travaux preparatoires support the view that the legislator intended to prohibit double patenting under Art. 125 EPC. The Enlarged Board finds that double patenting always applies whenever a second application claims subject matter already granted to the same applicant, said subject matter having the same effective date in both cases. It does not therefore matter whether the second application has the same filing date as the granted patent or not, overruling T1423/07.

Guidelines

See G-IV, 5.4. Where there are two applications with the same applicant, designating the same state or states, having the same effective date and claiming the same invention, only one may proceed to grant. Double patenting does not apply where the applicants are different. See also C-IX, 1.6 in respect of divisional applications.

Case law

The case law is not consistent on the scope of the prohibition of double patenting. Decision T587/98 makes it clear that a mere overlap of scope between a parent patent and a divisional is unobjectionable. However, T307/03 did not follow T587/98 and found basis in Art. 60 for the proposition that an applicant is only entitled to one grant in respect of any invention – so that the grant of a later patent having claims more broadly formulated than those of the parent patent is prohibited.

Comment

The use of the terminology 'same subject matter' should probably lead to a narrow interpretation whereby only if the subject matter of each claim is novelty-destroying to the other does double patenting exist.

12.7 Accelerated procedure

OJ

See [2015] O.J. A93 and Guidelines C-VI, 2 and E-VIII, 4.2. Accelerated examination can be requested at any time when the Examining Division has assumed responsibility and the Examining Division will make every effort to issue communications within three months of receiving the request or a subsequent response. A request for accelerated examination must be made online using Form 1005 and may only be filed once. Such requests are excluded from file inspection. Accelerated examination is terminated if the request is withdrawn or a request for the extension of a time limit is made (Guidelines E-VIII,1.6) or the application is withdrawn, deemed withdrawn or refused or a renewal fee is not paid by the due date.

1022

OJ

See [2016] O.J. A66. If the EPO receives an enquiry from the applicant concerning the processing of the file on Form 1012, it will take action to ensure that the next office action is issued within a period of one month from receipt of the enquiry if either the application concerned is subject to the PACE programme or a previous enquiry has been filed and an office action has not been issued within the committed period under the PACE programme or as stated in response to the previous enquiry, respectively.

12.8   Request for information concerning prior art

1023   Art. 124(1)

See section 25.15. The EPO has a general right to request information on prior art taken into account in other proceedings concerning the same invention (Art. 124(1) and r.141(3)) and will specifically request copies of search results generated in respect of any application whose priority is claimed if they have not been submitted already or included automatically in the file (r.141(1)–(2), r.70b(1)). Lack of a response to an invitation of this kind will result in deemed withdrawal of the application (Art. 124(2) or r.70b(2)).

12.9   Refusal of the application

1024   Art. 97(2)

If the Examining Division is of the opinion that a European patent application, or the invention to which it relates, does not meet the requirements of the EPC, it will refuse the application, unless the EPC provides for a different legal consequence.

T5/81

An application must be refused in its entirety if even one claim does not meet the requirements of the EPC (see also T11/82).

Guidelines

See C-V, 14. At least one communication pursuant to Art. 94(3) EPC must be issued before an application is refused and Art. 113(1) must be respected – see section 12.1.

Art. 106(1)

A decision to refuse a European patent application is open to appeal.

Chapter 13: Allowance and Grant

13.1 Circumstances in which a patent is granted

Art. 97(2) If the Examining Division is of the opinion that a European patent application and the in-   1025
vention to which it relates meet the requirements of the EPC, it will decide to grant a patent provided that the conditions laid down in the Implementing Regulations are fulfilled.

13.2 Approval of the text for grant, payment of fees and filing of claim translations

13.2.1 Communication from the Examining Division under r.71(3)

r.71(3)(4) Before deciding to grant a patent, the Examining Division: 1026
(a) informs the applicant of the text which it intends to grant and related bibliographic
data; and invites the applicant to:
(b) pay the fee for grant and publishing;
(c) file translations of the claims into the two official languages of the EPO other than the
language of proceedings; and
(e) pay claims fees for every claim over 15 for which a fee has not already been paid under
r.45 or r.162;
within a period of four months.

RRFArt. 2(2)(7) For European applications filed before April 1, 2009 and international applications entering the regional phase before that date, the fee for grant, including the fee for printing, is a combination of a fixed fee and an additional charge for each page more than 35.
The fixed fee is (i) € 930 for fees paid on or after 01 April 2018 where all amendments
and corrections of the application, if any, and the translations of the claims are filed online in character-coded format; or (ii) in all other cases € 1040 where the fee is paid between 01 April 2018 and a date yet to be set by the President and € 1150 where the fee is
paid on or after a date yet to be set by the President. The variable fee for the 36th and each
subsequent page is € 17.

RRFArt. 2(1)(7) For European applications filed on or after April 1, 2009 and international applications
entering the regional phase on or after that date, the fee for grant and publishing (as it is
now known) is a flat fee since the variable fee for pages more than 35 is now part of the
filing fee. The fee is (i) € 930 if all amendments and corrections of the application, if any,
and the translations of the claims are filed online in character-coded format; or (ii) in all
other cases € 1040 if paid between 01 April 2018 and a date yet to be set by the President
and € 1150 if paid on or after a date yet to be set by the President.

RRF Art. 2(3) The President of the EPO determines the formats referred to in RRF Art. 2(1) and RRF
Art. 2(2) and may specify the conditions under which a document is deemed to have been
filed online in character-coded format.

RRF Art. 2(4) Fee levels which relate to a means of electronic communication or a format referred to in
RRF Art. 2(1) or Art. 2(2) shall not apply until a date set by the President of the Office.

OJ See Decision of the President dated 12 December 2018 ([2019] O.J. A3) and Notice
from the EPO dated 24 January 2019 ([2019] O.J. A6). New RRF Art. 2(4) applies as
of 01 April 2019 to RRF Art. 2(1)(7) and RRF Art. 2(2)(7) and as a consequence the € 930
and € 1040 fees will not apply for the time being.

RRFArt. 2(2)(15) Each claims fee is € 265 for European applications filed before April 1, 2009 and international applications entering the regional phase before that date.

RRFArt. 2(1)(15) Each claims fee is € 265 for claims in the range 16–50 and € 660 for the 51st and each subsequent claim for European applications filed on or after April 1, 2009 and international
applications entering the regional phase on or after date.

Guidelines The grant and printing fee and any additional claims fees fall due on the notification of the
r.71(3) communication (A-X, 5.2.3). See also C-V, 1.4 – claims fees are not refunded if the
number of claims is reduced during prosecution.

T1255/04	If, during examination proceedings, a main and a subsidiary request have been filed and one of the subsidiary requests is allowable, the communication pursuant to r.71(3) is to be issued on the basis of the (first) allowable request and must be accompanied by an explanation of the reasons why the higher-ranking requests are not allowable and must expressly mention the applicant's right to maintain the main request and thus obtain an appealable decision (see below). See also T1181/04 and Guidelines H-III, 3.3.4 and C-V, 1.1.
T646/20	Once a response has been filed approving the text proposed for grant, the Examining Division can issue a decision to grant at any time without waiting for the 4 month period of r.71(3) to expire.
Guidelines	See H-VI, 5 – mistakes in claim translations cannot be corrected after a decision to grant has been taken under r.140 since they do not form part of that decision. They are not part of the authentic text of the patent and are provided for information only. A corrected version will, however, be published as part of the B publication if received in time. They can also be corrected if the patent is later upheld in amended form in opposition or limitation proceedings.
OJ	See Notice from the EPO dated 13 December 2011 [[2012] O.J. 52). The text proposed for grant by the EPO may contain amendments/corrections made by the Examining Division which the applicant can reasonably be expected to accept (see also Guidelines C-V, 1.1 for examples of such amendments).
r.50(1)	Rule 49(2) (governing the presentation of the application documents) applies to the translation of the claims referred to in r.71 (translation of the allowed claims).
Guidelines	See C-IV,7.2 – the results of a search for prior national rights is also attached to the r.71(3) communication in order to help the applicant decide whether a request for unitary effect is appropriate or not (a single prior national right in a state to which unitary effect applies may be novelty-destroying to the unitary patent).

13.2.2   Consequences of not responding fully to the r.71(3) communication

1027	r.71(7)	If the fee for grant and publishing or any due claims fees are not paid in due time or if the translations of the claims are not filed in due time, the application is deemed to be withdrawn.
	Guidelines	See C-V, 3 and C-V, 4.9. Deemed withdrawal is only possible in the absence of any indication from the applicant that he does not approve the text proposed for grant.
	Art. 121	Further processing is available.
	Guidelines	See C-V, 3 and C-V, 8 – the omitted act could be payment of the fee for grant and publishing, payment of claims fees, filing of claim translations, filing of proposed amendments, rejection of amendments proposed by the Examining Division or the maintenance of a high-ranking request. See also Notice from the EPO dated 13 December 2011 [[2012] O.J. 52).
	RRFArt. 2(1)(12)	The further processing fee is € 290 in respect of the acts to be performed under r.71(3) (filing of claim translations and payment of the fee for grant and publishing), whether one or both of these acts are omitted, plus an additional 50 % of any unpaid claims fees and € 290 in other cases.
	Guidelines	See E-VIII, 2 where examples are given.
	Art. 122	Re-establishment is available in respect of the time limit for further processing if it was missed in spite of all due care being shown.

13.2.3   Implicit approval of the text by payment of fees and filing of translations

1028	r.71(5)	If the applicant pays the grant and printing fees and, if necessary, the claims fees and files the translations within the period set then he will be deemed to have approved the text intended for grant and verified the bibliographic data.

13.2.4   Procedure where the proposed text is not acceptable to the applicant

1029	r.71(6)	If the applicant responds within the period set under r.71(3) by requesting reasoned amendments or corrections to the text proposed for grant, or by maintaining the latest text proposed by the applicant for grant, the Examining Division will either issue a new communication under r.71(3) if it gives its consent or will resume examination proceedings.

r.137(2)	Though it does not follow from the wording of r.137, point 7.2 of the notice from the EPO of 15 October 2009 ([2009] O.J. 533) indicates that where no search opinion is issued and the first communication from the Examining Division is under r.71(3), the applicant has the right to introduce amendments of his own volition. This is confirmed by Guidelines H-II, 2.5.3 and C-V, 4.4.
Guidelines	See C-V, 4 and H-II, 2.5. The applicant may request new amendments, request the reversal of amendments proposed by the Examining Division or, where the r.71(3) communication was based on an auxiliary request, maintain a higher-ranking request. Examination must be resumed if either the amendments are not admitted into the procedure or the amendments are admitted into the procedure but found to be unallowable. Amendments should be reasoned – if they are not reasoned, it is more likely that examination will be reopened. Examination may be reopened in some cases with an invitation to oral proceedings or the refusal of the application (Guidelines C-V, 4.7.1).
OJ	See Notice from the EPO dated 13 December 2011 [[2012] O.J. 52). Where the applicant responds according to r.71(6), he does not need to pay any fees or file any translations (see also Guidelines C-V, 4.1). The applicant may, however, voluntarily pay the fees and the amount will be credited if a further r.71(3) communication is issued (r.71a(5), Guidelines A-X, 11, C-V, 4.2, C-V, 4.8) or refunded in other cases. Any additional amount due a fee increase in the meantime must still be paid.
T2558/18	The applicant has no right to amend further under r.71(6) when a board of appeal has taken a decision indicating an allowable text for the grant of a patent and remitted the matter back to the examining division to implement the grant procedure. The decision taken is binding on the examining division under Art. 111(2) EPC and only the correction of errors pursuant to r.139 EPC is possible.

13.2.5   Refund of grant and publishing fee

r.71a(6)	If the European patent application is refused or withdrawn prior to the notification of the decision on the grant of a European patent or, at that time, deemed to be withdrawn, the fee for grant and publishing will be refunded.	1030
Guidelines	See A-X, 10.2.5 – the fee for grant and publishing is refunded but claims fees are not refunded (unless they were paid when requesting amendments in response to a r.71(3) communication and were hence not due (C-V, 4.2)).	

13.3   Between approval of the text and a decision to grant

r.71a(2)	Until the decision to grant the European patent, the Examining Division may resume the examination proceedings at any time.	1031
Guidelines	See C-V, 6.1. Resumption may be necessary where third party observations are filed, the Examining Division becomes otherwise aware of deficiencies which have been overlooked or the applicant files amendments that are admitted into the procedure (see below).	
r.71a(5)	If, in response to an invitation under r.71(3), the applicant has already paid the fee for grant and publishing, or claims fees, the paid amount will be credited if a further such invitation is issued (Guidelines A-X, 11, C-V, 4.2, C-V, 4.8).	
G7/93	Headnote (1): An approval of the text submitted by an applicant pursuant to r.51(4) EPC (now r.71(3) EPC2000) does not become binding once a communication in accordance with r.51(6) (now part of r.71(3) EPC2000) has been issued. Following issue of such a communication under r.51(6) EPC and until issue of a decision to grant the patent, the Examining Division has a discretion under r.86(3) (now r.137(3) EPC2000), second sentence, EPC, whether or not to allow amendment of the application.	

Comment	This decision (G7/93) was taken under the old law where the grant procedure was considerably different but the principles established are still important. The Enlarged Board decided that Art. 113(2) (EPO to decide only on text approved by applicant) did not give the applicant a right to amend. Any amendment under r.137(3) had to be made with the consent of the Examining Division. Equally, the Examining Division is not bound in any way by the text as approved and can authorise amendments prior to the issue of a decision to grant. Discretion will only be exercised in favour of the applicant as an exception rather than a rule at such a late stage of the grant procedure. The Examining Division must balance the applicant's interest in obtaining a valid patent against the EPO's interest in bringing grant proceedings to a close. Typically, amendments should be allowed which do not involve reopening of substantive examination.
T556/95	A request for oral proceedings must be honoured at any time while proceedings are pending, i.e. up to the decision to grant or refuse.
Guidelines	See H-II, 2.6. Further requests for amendment after approval of the text are only admitted in exceptional circumstances, e.g. to take into account prior national rights, or if they are minor changes which will not delay grant appreciably.

13.4   Decision to grant

1032	r.71a(1)	If all fees have been paid, translations of the claims in the two official languages of the EPO other than the language of the proceedings have been filed and the applicant has approved the text proposed for grant, a decision to grant the patent will be issued.
	r.71a(1)	The decision to grant the patent will state the text of the application which forms the basis for the decision.
	J7/96	Between the decision to grant and the grant taking effect there are only certain things that may be done in relation to the application. Linguistic errors, errors of transcription and obvious mistakes in the decision may be corrected under r.140, the application may be withdrawn or transferred or a designation may be withdrawn.
	Case law	Where a patent is granted with a text not approved by the applicant there is a right of appeal since the applicant is adversely affected by the decision (J12/83). Some decisions have also allowed an appeal where the applicant approved the text but that text was clearly not what either the Examining Division or the applicant intended, for example where it did not include drawings which the applicant had not withdrawn (see, for example, T408/21, T1003/19 and T2081/16 as well as diverging decision T265/20 which did not allow such an appeal).
	J28/03	When the mention of grant has been published in the bulletin, the fact that an appeal has been filed against the decision to grant does not mean that a divisional application can once more be filed – the suspensive effect on its own is not enough in this case (unlike the case where an appeal is filed against a decision to refuse). Only if the appeal is allowed does the application become pending again for the purposes of r.36(1).
	Guidelines	See C-V, 2, H-II, 2.6 and H-VI, 2.1. After a decision to grant has been taken (it is effective at the moment the decision is handed to the EPO's internal postal system or, very rarely, when announced in oral proceedings), neither amendment under Art. 123(1) nor correction under r.139 are possible. Only correction of the decision under r.140 is possible (and this cannot be used to change the text of the specification, G1/10). It would be possible, for example, to correct the bibliographic data in the decision under r.140 (H-VI, 3.2).

13.5   The decision to grant takes effect on publication of the mention of grant in the Bulletin

1033	Art. 97(3)	The decision to grant a European patent takes effect on the date on which the mention of grant is published in the European Patent Bulletin.

13.6   No publication of the mention of grant until designation or renewal fees have been paid

1034	r.71a(3)	If the designation fee becomes due after the communication under r.71(3), the mention of the grant of the European patent will not be published until the designation fee has been paid. The applicant will be informed accordingly.

r.71a(4)	If a renewal fee becomes due after the communication under r.71(3) and before the next possible date for publication of the mention of grant of the European patent, the mention will not be published until the renewal fee has been paid. The applicant will be informed accordingly.

13.7   Publication of the specification of the granted patent

Art. 98	The European Patent Office will publish the specification of the European patent as soon as possible after the mention of grant of the European patent has been published in the European Patent Bulletin.	1035
r.73(1)	The specification of the European patent includes the description, the claims and any drawings. It also indicates the period for opposing the European patent.	
r.73(2)	The President of the EPO determines the form of the publication of the specification and the data to be included.	
r.73(3)	The designated Contracting States are indicated in the specification.	
Art. 14(6)	The specification of the European patent is published in the language of the proceedings and includes a translation of the claims in the two other official languages of the European Patent Office.	
r.52(5)	The particulars in the declaration of priority are published with the granted patent.	
OJ	The European patent as granted or amended is published in electronic form by means of a publication server from which it may be downloaded (since April 1, 2005) – see Decision of the President dated 12 July 2007, [2007] O.J. Special Edition No. D3.	
r.20(1)	The designated inventor will be mentioned in the European patent specification unless the inventor informs the EPO in writing that he waives his right to be thus mentioned.	
r.20(2)	In the event of a third party filing with the EPO a final decision determining that the applicant for or proprietor of a European patent is required to designate him as an inventor, the provisions of r.20(1) apply.	
OJ	A copy of the patent can be requested to accompany the certificate ([2007] O.J. Special Edition No. 3, p. 95). Where technical information has been included in the file wrapper during prosecution, the granted patent will contain a reference to such material ([1981] O.J. 74 and Guidelines C-V, 1.5). The title of the invention is only shown on the title page and not as a heading to the description ([1984] O.J. 88). The published specification is not legally authentic (the text agreed for grant is) and any mistakes in it may readily be corrected ([1990] O.J. 260, T150/89 – see also Guidelines H-VI, 4 and C-V, 10). A list of any art cited by the applicant in the description pursuant to r.27(i)(b) is listed separately at the end of the published specification (see Decision of the President dated 12 July 2007, [2007] O.J. Special Edition No. 3 D4). A sequence listing filed with the application is published as part of the description (see Decision of the President dated 28 April 2011, [2011] O.J. 372).	
Guidelines	See C-V, 11 – the patent specification is not published where the application is withdrawn before termination of the technical preparations for publication.	

13.8   Grant to different applicants

r.72	Where different persons are recorded in the European Patent Register as applicants in respect of different Contracting States, the EPO will grant the European patent for each Contracting State accordingly.	1036

13.9   Issue of a certificate

r.74	As soon as the specification of the European patent has been published, the EPO issues to the proprietor of the patent a certificate for a European patent. The President of the EPO prescribes the content, form and means of communication of the certificate and determines the circumstances in which an administrative fee is due.	1037

OJ   The certificate is supplied as a digital file for download where the proprietor/representative has an activated Mailbox and in paper form in other cases. The certificate is issued to each proprietor where there is more than one. The supply of any additional certified copies of the certificate with the patent attached is subject to an administrative fee. The certificate must state the patent number and certify that the patent has been granted, in respect of the invention described and the States designated in the patent specification, to the persons named in the certificate. It also states the title of the invention, the date of grant and the name and address of the proprietor(s). A new certificate is issued when a patent is maintained in amended or limited form. See Decision of the President dated 17 December 2021, [2021] O.J. A94.

RRFArt. 3(1)   The amount of the administrative fee is fixed by the President of the EPO.

OJ   The amount is € 115 (see decision of the President dated 17 January 2023, [2023] O.J. A3).

13.10 Validation in contracting States

1038   See Chapter 19 (The application and patent in the Contracting States).

13.11 Registration of the granted patent

1039 OJ   A European patent (UK) may be registered in Hong Kong – a request must be filed within six months of publication of the application ([1997] O.J. 429 and [2009] O.J. 546). A European patent (UK) may also be registered in several overseas territories after grant ([2018] O.J. A97).

13.12 Validation in non-contracting States

1040 NatLaw   Note that for the extension of a European patent to one of the extension states or the validation of a European patent in a validation state to be valid, various acts in these states are necessary following the grant of the European patent (see Table IV).

Chapter 14: European Patent with Unitary Effect

14.1 Abbreviations

For the purposes of Chapter 14, the following abbreviations apply: 1041

EU1257	Articles (Art.) and Recitals (Rec.) of Regulation (EU) No EU1257/2012 of 17 December 2012 implementing enhanced cooperation in the area of the creation of unitary patent protection ([2013] O.J. 111)
EU1260	Articles (Art.) and Recitals (Rec.) of Regulation (EU) No EU1260/2012 of 17 December 2012 implementing enhanced cooperation in the area of the creation of unitary patent protection with regard to the applicable translation arrangements ([2013] O.J. 132)
UPCA	Articles (Art.) and Rules of Procedure (r.) of the Agreement on a Unified Patent Court ([2013] O.J. 287), as amended
UPG	Unitary Patent Guide published by the EPO
UPR	Rules relating to Unitary Patent Protection adopted by Decision of the Select Committee of the Administrative Council of 15 December 2015 ([2016] O.J. A39), as amended
UPRRF	Rules relating to Fees for Unitary Patent Protection adopted by the Decision of the Select Committee of the Administrative Council of 15 December 2015 ([2016] O.J. A40), as amended

14.2 Status of the Unitary Patent Regulation in relation to the PC, PCT and EPC

EU1257 Art. 1(2) This Regulation constitutes a special agreement within the meaning of Art. 142 EPC. 1042

EPC Art. 142(1) Any group of Contracting States, which has provided by a special agreement that a European patent granted for those States has a unitary character throughout their territories, may provide that a European patent may only be granted jointly in respect of those States.

EU1257 Rec.(6) The Regulation also constitutes a regional patent treaty within the meaning of Art. 45(1) PCT and a special agreement within the meaning of Art. 19 PC.

14.3 New institutions

14.3.1 Select Committee of the Administrative Council

Art. 145(1) EPC The group of Contracting States may set up a Select Committee of the Administrative 1043 Council for the purpose of supervising the activities of the special departments set up under Art. 143(2); the EPO will place at its disposal such staff, premises and equipment as may be necessary for the performance of its duties. The President of the EPO will be responsible for the activities of the special departments to the select committee of the Administrative Council.

EU1257 Art. 9(2) The participating Member States shall ensure compliance with this Regulation in fulfilling their international obligations undertaken in the EPC and shall cooperate to that end. In their capacity as Contracting States to the EPC, the participating Member States shall ensure that the governance and supervision of the activities related to the tasks referred to in EU1257 Art. 9(1) and shall ensure the setting of the level of renewal fees in accordance with EU1257 Art. 12 and the setting of the share of distribution of the renewal fees in accordance with EU1257 Art. 13 of this Regulation.

To that end they shall set up a select committee of the Administrative Council of the European Patent Organisation (hereinafter 'Select Committee') within the meaning of Art. 145 EPC.

The Select Committee shall consist of representatives of the participating Member States and a representative of the Commission as an observer, as well as alternates who will represent them in their absence. The members of the Select Committee may be assisted by advisors or experts.

Decisions of the Select Committee shall be taken with due regard for the position of the Commission and in accordance with the rules laid down in Art. 35(2) EPC.

EPC Art. 35(2) A majority of 75 % of the votes of the Contracting States represented and voting is required for decisions that the Select Committee of the Administrative Council is empowered to take.

r.2(1) UPR The Select Committee of the Administrative Council shall be competent to amend
(a) the present Rules (i.e. Rules relating to Unitary Patent Protection);

(b) the Rules relating to Fees for Unitary Patent Protection;
(c) other rules or decisions of a financial or budgetary nature;
(d) its Rules of Procedure.

r.2(2) UPR   The Select Committee of the Administrative Council shall ensure the governance and supervision of the activities related to the tasks entrusted to the EPO in accordance with r.1(1) UPR (i.e. the tasks entrusted to the EPO relating to the Unitary patent set out in EU1257 Art. 9(1)).

14.3.2   *Unitary Patent Protection Division of the EPO*

1044   Art. 143(1) EPC   The group of Contracting States may give additional tasks to the EPO.

Art. 143(2) EPC   Special departments common to the Contracting States in the group may be set up within the EPO in order to carry out the additional tasks. The President of the EPO will direct such special departments; Art. 10, paras 2 and 3 apply mutatis mutandis (President's powers and functions).

r.3 UPR   The Unitary Patent Protection Division referred to in r.4 UPR shall be managed by the President of the EPO, who shall be responsible for its activities to the Select Committee of the Administrative Council. To this end, Art. 10(2) and (3) EPC shall apply mutatis mutandis (functions and powers of the President of the EPO).

r.4(1) UPR   A Unitary Patent Protection Division is hereby established within the EPO as a special department within the meaning of Art. 143(2) EPC.

r.4(2) UPR   The tasks entrusted to the EPO in accordance with r.1(1) UPR shall be carried out under the responsibility of the Unitary Patent Protection Division.

r.4(3) UPR   Decisions of the Unitary Patent Protection Division shall be taken by one legally qualified member.

r.4(4) UPR   The President of the EPO may entrust to employees who are not legally qualified members the execution of duties falling to the Unitary Patent Protection Division and involving no legal difficulties.

EU1257 Art. 10   The expenses incurred by the EPO in carrying out the additional tasks given to it, within the meaning of Art. 143 EPC, by the participating Member States shall be covered by the fees generated by the European patents with unitary effect.

OJ   See Decision of the President dated 30 May 2022 ([2022] O.J. A69). The tasks carried out by the Unitary Patent Protection Division are allocated to the Legal Division, those tasks involving no legal difficulties being delegated to a formalities officer.

14.4   A Unitary Patent may only be granted for participating EU states in which the Unified Patent Court has jurisdiction

1045   EU1257 Art. 3(1)   A European patent granted with the same set of claims in respect of all the participating Member States shall benefit from unitary effect in the participating Member States provided that its unitary effect has been registered in the Register for unitary patent protection.

EU1257 Art. 18(2)   Furthermore, a European patent for which unitary effect is registered in the Register for unitary patent protection shall have unitary effect only in those participating Member States in which the Unified Patent Court has exclusive jurisdiction with regard to European patents with unitary effect at the date of registration.

EU1257 Art. 2(a)   "Participating Member State" means a Member State that participates in enhanced co-operation in the area of the creation of unitary patent protection by virtue of Decision 2011/167/EU or by virtue of a decision adopted in accordance with the second or third subparagraph of Art. 331(1) of the TFEU (Treaty on the Functioning of the EU), at the time the request for unitary effect as referred to in Art. 9 is made.

UPG   Different Unitary Patents may therefore have a different geographical scope depending on the number of eligible states when the unitary effect is registered (see paragraphs 23–26). The European patent may be validated as usual in participating Member States which has not yet ratified the UPCA and in non-participating EPC states (paragraphs30).

EU state	Participating Member State?	UPCA status
Austria	YES	Signed and ratified
Belgium	YES	Signed and ratified

EU state	Participating Member State?	UPCA status
Bulgaria	YES	Signed and ratified
Croatia	NO	
Cyprus	YES	Signed
Czech Republic	YES	Signed
Denmark	YES	Signed and ratified
Estonia	YES	Signed and ratified
Finland	YES	Signed and ratified
France	YES	Signed and ratified
Germany	YES	Signed and ratified
Greece	YES	Signed
Hungary	YES	Signed
Ireland	YES	Signed
Italy	YES	Signed and ratified
Latvia	YES	Signed and ratified
Lithuania	YES	Signed and ratified
Luxembourg	YES	Signed and ratified
Malta	YES	Signed and ratified
Netherlands	YES	Signed and ratified
Poland	YES	
Portugal	YES	Signed and ratified
Romania	YES	Signed
Slovakia	YES	Signed
Slovenia	YES	Signed and ratified
Spain	NO	
Sweden	YES	Signed and ratified

14.5   A unitary patent may only be granted for a European patent granted after the date of application of the Unitary Patent Regulation

EU1257 Art. 18(6)   Unitary patent protection may be requested for any European patent granted on or after   1046
the date of application of this Regulation.

EU1257 Art. 18(2)   EU1257 applies from the date of entry into force of the Unified Patent Court Agreement.

Comment   The UPCA entered into force on 01 June 2023.

14.6   A European Patent must have the same set of claims in all participating Member States to have unitary effect

EU1257 Art. 3(1)   A European patent granted with the same set of claims in respect of all the participating   1047
Member States shall benefit from unitary effect in the participating Member States provided that its unitary effect has been registered in the Register for unitary patent protection. A European patent granted with different sets of claims for different participating Member States shall not benefit from unitary effect.

r.5(2) UPR   Unitary effect shall be registered only if the European patent has been granted with the same set of claims in respect of all the participating Member States.

Comment   This means that unitary patent protection is not possible if the designation of one of the participating member states has been withdrawn or where there is a different set of claims for one participating member state to take into account a national right (r.138 EPC) or a prior European right under EPC1973 (Art. 87 EPC1973). This is the case even if the participating member state concerned does not form part of the unitary patent because the UPCA is not in force yet in that state. Furthermore, no European patent with a filing date before 01 March 2007 can benefit from unitary effect because Malta (one of the participating Member States) would not be designated.

14.7   Filing a request for unitary effect

14.7.1   Who can file a request for unitary effect?

1048   EU1257 Art. 9(1) (a)   The proprietor of the patent may request unitary effect.

r.6(1) UPR   At the request of the proprietor of the European Patent, unitary effect shall be registered by the EPO in the Register for unitary patent protection.

UPG   Unitary effect is possible when there are multiple proprietors, whether there are joint proprietors for the participating Member States or different proprietors for different participating Member States (paragraph 48).

UPG   The proprietor filing the request is the registered proprietor at the EPO in respect of those states which are to form part of the unitary patent (paragraph 51). In the case of joint proprietors, common representation applies in the usual way (since r.20(2)(l) UPR applies r.151 EPC, see paragraph 49). However the request must be signed by all the proprietors (or their representative) for a common representative to be entitled to act for them all (see paragraph 50).

14.7.2   Where should a request for unitary effect be filed?

1049   EU1257 Art. 9(1) (a)   The EPO administers requests for unitary effect.

Comment   Since r.20(2) UPR applies r.2 EPC, the usual means of filing at an EPO filing office are available. The request may not be filed with a national office.

14.7.3   What is the deadline for filing a request for unitary effect?

1050   EU1257 Art. 9(1) (g)   A request for unitary effect must be submitted no later than one month after the mention of the grant is published in the European Patent Bulletin.

r.6(1) UPR   The request for unitary effect shall be filed with the EPO no later than one month after publication of the mention of grant of the European patent in the European Patent Bulletin.

Comment   The time limit is not subject to extension

r.22(1) UPR   Re-establishment is available but must be filed within 2 months of the expiry of the time limit.

OJ   See Notice from the EPO dated 26 April 2023 ([2023] O.J. Supplementary Publication 3, pages 5–6) – A request for unitary effect can be filed at any time from issuance of a decision to grant but will not be processed until the grant of the patent takes effect. The request will not be effective if in the meantime a change of proprietor is registered without the new proprietor confirming the request.

14.7.4   What language should the request for unitary effect be filed in?

1051   EU1257 Art. 9(1) (g)   A request for unitary effect must be submitted in the language of the proceedings defined in Art. 14(3) EPC.

EU1260 Art. 3(2)   A request for unitary effect as referred to in Art. 9 EU1257 shall be submitted in the language of the proceedings (of the EPO under Art. 14(3) EPC, see Art. 2(b) EU1260).

14.7.5   Content and form of the request for unitary effect

1052   r.6(2) UPR   The request for unitary effect shall be filed in writing in the language of the proceedings and shall contain:
(a) particulars of the proprietor of the European patent making the request (hereinafter "the requester") as provided for in r.41(2)(c) EPC;
(b) the number of the European patent to which unitary effect shall be attributed;
(c) where the requester has appointed a representative, particulars as provided for in r.41(2)(d) EPC;
(d) a translation of the European patent as required under Art. 6(1), Regulation (EU) No EU1260/2012, as follows:
– where the language of the proceedings is French or German, a full translation of the specification of the European patent into English; or

	– where the language of the proceedings is English, a full translation of the specification of the European patent into any other official language of the European Union.
Comment	No fee is to be paid
Comment	The need to provide a translation according to r.6(2)(d) UPR will only apply for a limited period (see below). No other translation is required other than for the purposes of enforcement (EU1260 Art. 3(1)).
UPG	The request must be signed since r.20(2) UPR applies r.50(3) EPC (see paragraph 46).
UPG	According to paragraphs 53 to 55, the request may also indicate a place of business in one of the Member States in which the patent will have unitary effect belonging to the applicant when the application was filed (for the purposes of EU1257 Art. 7(1), unitary patent as an object of property).

14.7.6   *Chance to correct formal deficiencies where content of request is incomplete*

r.7(3) UPR	If the requirements under r.5(2) UPR are met (same set of claims) and the request for unitary effect complies with r.6(1) UPR (time limit), but fails to comply with the requirements of r.6(2) UPR (contents), the EPO shall invite the request to correct the deficiencies noted within a non-extendable period of one month. If the deficiencies are not corrected in due time, the EPO shall reject the request.	1053
r.22(6) UPR	Re-establishment of rights is ruled out for this time limit.	
UPG	There is no remedy for missing the deadline – the request will be refused (see paragraph 69). The decision may, however, be challenged at the UPC.	

14.7.7   *Decision on a request for unitary effect*

r.7(1) UPR	If the requirements under r.5(2) UPR are met (same set of claims) and the request for unitary effect complies with r.6 UPR (time limit, contents), the EPO shall register the unitary effect in the Register for unitary patent protection and communicate the date of this registration to the requester.	1054
r.7(2) UPR	If the requirements under r.5(2) UPR are not met (same set of claims) or the request for unitary effect does not comply with r.6(1) UPR (time limit), the EPO shall reject the request.	
UPG	Before a decision to reject the request is taken, the EPO must give the requester the opportunity to comment (since r.20(1) UPR applies Art. 113 EPC), i.e. by sending a communication according to r.7(3) UPC requesting the correction of a formal defect or sending a communication drawing attention to a fundamental deficiency and inviting comments (see paragraph 70).	
Comment	In the case of a decision to reject the request, an appeal to the Unified Patent Court is possible.	

14.7.8   *Date the decision takes effect*

EU1257 Art. 4(1)	A European patent with unitary effect shall take effect in the participating Member States on the date of publication by the EPO of the mention of the grant of the European patent in the European Patent Bulletin.	1055

14.7.9   *Withdrawal of a request for unitary effect*

UPG	The request may be withdrawn at any time until a decision has been taken under r.7(1) or (2) UPR (see paragraph 68)..	1056

14.7.10   *Provision of a certificate for unitary effect*

UPG	The proprietor will be sent a certificate equivalent to the certificate for a European patent under r.74 EPC once unitary effect has been registered (see paragraph 111). However, there is no separate publication of the unitary patent. The unitary patent is assigned a code "C0" to distinguish it from the rest of the European patent.

14.8   Provision of a translation when requesting unitary effect will only be required for a limited period

1057   EU1260 Art. 6(1)

During a transitional period starting on the date of application of this Regulation a request for unitary effect as referred to in Art. 9 EU1257 shall be submitted together with the following:

(a)   where the language of the proceedings is French or German, a full translation of the specification of the European patent into English; or

(b)   where the language of the proceedings is English, a full translation of the specification of the European patent into any other official language of the Union.

EU1260 Art. 6(3)

Six years after the date of application of this Regulation and every two years thereafter, an independent expert committee shall carry out an objective evaluation of the availability of high quality machine translations of patent applications and specifications into all the official languages of the Union as developed by the EPO. This expert committee shall be established by the participating Member States in the framework of the European Patent Organisation and shall be composed of representatives of the EPO and of the non-governmental organisations representing users of the European patent system invited by the Administrative Council of the European Patent Organisation as observers in accordance with Art. 30(3) of the EPC.

EU1260 Art. 6(4)

On the basis of the first evaluation referred to in Art. 6(3) EU1260 and every two years thereafter on the basis of the subsequent evaluations, the Commission shall present a report to the Council and, if appropriate, make proposals for terminating the transitional period.

EU1260 Art. 6(5)

If the transitional period is not terminated on the basis of a proposal from the Commission, it shall lapse 12 years from the date of the application of this Regulation.

Comment

The translation is for information only (just like the translation of the claims filed in response to a communication under r.71(3) EPC) and has no legal effect.

14.9   Publication of the translation provided when requesting unitary effect

1058   EU1257 Art. 9(1) (d)

The EPO publishes the translation referred to in Art. 6 of Regulation (EU) No EU1260/2012 during the transitional period referred to in that Article.

EU1260 Art. 6(2)

In accordance with Art. 9 EU1257, the participating Member States shall give, within the meaning of Art. 143 EPC, the EPO the task of publishing the translations referred to in Art. 6(1) EU1260 as soon as possible after the date of the submission of a request for unitary effect as referred to in Art. 9 EU1257. The text of such translations shall have no legal effect and shall be for information purposes only.

r.18 UPR

The President of the EPO shall determine the form of the publication of the translations referred to in r.6(2)(d) UPR, and the data to be included.

Comment

Publication is expected to be electronic.

14.10   Requirement to provide a translation of a unitary patent for enforcement

1059   EU1260 Art. 4(1)

In the event of a dispute relating to an alleged infringement of a European patent with unitary effect, the patent proprietor shall provide at the request and the choice of an alleged infringer, a full translation of the European patent with unitary effect into an official language of either the participating Member State in which the alleged infringement took place or the Member State in which the alleged infringer is domiciled.

EU1260 Art. 4(2)

In the event of a dispute relating to a European patent with unitary effect, the patent proprietor shall provide in the course of legal proceedings, at the request of a court competent in the participating Member States for disputes concerning European patents with unitary effect, a full translation of the patent into the language used in the proceedings of that court.

EU1260 Art. 4(3)

The cost of the translations referred to in Art. 4(1) and Art. 4(2) EU1260 shall be borne by the patent proprietor.

EU1260 Art. 4(4)   In the event of a dispute concerning a claim for damages, the court hearing the dispute shall assess and take into consideration, in particular where the alleged infringer is a SME, a natural person or a non-profit organisation, a university or a public research organisation, whether the alleged infringer acted without knowing or without reasonable grounds for knowing, that he was infringing the European patent with unitary effect before having been provided with the translation referred to in Art. 4(1) EU1260.

14.11   Protection conferred by a unitary patent – no double protection

EU1257 Art. 3(2)   A European patent with unitary effect shall have a unitary character. It shall provide uniform protection and shall have equal effect in all participating Member States.
It may only be limited, revoked or lapse in respect of all the participating Member States.   1060

EU1257 Art. 3(3)   The unitary effect of a European patent shall be deemed not to have arisen to the extent that the European patent has been revoked or limited.

EU1257 Art. 5(1)   The European patent with unitary effect shall confer on its proprietor the right to prevent any third party from committing acts against which that patent provides protection throughout the territories of the participating Member States in which it has unitary effect, subject to applicable limitations.

EU1257 Art. 5(2)   The scope of that right and its limitations shall be uniform in all participating Member States in which the patent has unitary effect.

EU1257 Art. 5(3)   The acts against which the patent provides protection referred to in Art. 5(1) and the applicable limitations shall be those defined by the law applied to European patents with unitary effect in the participating Member State whose national law is applicable to the European patent with unitary effect as an object of property in accordance with Art. 7

EU1257 Art. 6   The rights conferred by a European patent with unitary effect shall not extend to acts concerning a product covered by that patent which are carried out within the participating Member States in which that patent has unitary effect after that product has been placed on the market in the Union by, or with the consent of, the patent proprietor, unless there are legitimate grounds for the patent proprietor to oppose further commercialisation of the product.

UPCA Art. 3   The Unified Patent Court has exclusive jurisdiction for European patents with unitary effect.

EU1257 Art. 4(2)   The participating Member States shall take the necessary measures to ensure that, where the unitary effect of a European patent has been registered and extends to their territory, that European patent is deemed not to have taken effect as a national patent in their territory on the date of publication of the mention of grant in the European Patent Bulletin.

14.12   Unitary patent as property – transfer and license

EU1257 Art. 7(1)   A European patent with unitary effect as an object of property shall be treated in its entirety and in all the participating Member States as a national patent of the participating Member State in which that patent has unitary effect and in which, according to the European Patent Register: 1061
(a)   the applicant had his residence or principle place of business on the date of filing of the application for the European patent; or
(b)   where point (a) does not apply, the applicant had a place of business on the date of filing of the application for the European patent.

EU1257 Art. 7(2)   Where two or more persons are entered in the European Patent Register as joint applicants, Art. 7(1)(a) shall apply to the joint applicant indicated first. Where this is not possible, Art. 7(1)(a) shall apply to the next joint applicant indicated in the order of entry. Where Art. 7(1)(a) does not apply to any of the joint applicants, Art. 7(1)(b) shall apply accordingly.

EU1257 Art. 7(3)   Where no applicant had his residence, principle place of business or place of business in a participating Member State in which that patent has unitary effect for the purposes of Art. 7(1) or Art. 7(2), the European patent with unitary effect as an object of property shall be treated in its entirety and in all the participating Member States as a national patent of the State where the European Patent Organisation has its headquarters in accordance with Art. 6(1) of the EPC.

Comment	This is Germany since the European Patent Organisation is headquartered in Munich according to Art. 6(1) EPC.
EU1257 Art. 7(4)	The acquisition of a right may not be dependent on any entry in a national patent register.
EU1257 Art. 3(2)	A European patent with unitary effect may only be transferred in respect of all the participating Member States.
	It may be licensed in respect of the whole or part of the territories of the participating Member States.
r.20(2) UPR	Since r.22 EPC applies, the EPO will record the transfer or license of a unitary patent in the register for unitary patent protection on production of the usual evidence and payment of the administrative fee.
UPRRF Art. 5	The administrative fees provided for in the Rules relating to Unitary Patent Protection and the fees and expenses charged for any services rendered by the EPO other than those specified in the present RRF shall be payable in the amounts laid down by the President of the EPO pursuant to Art. 3 RRF EPC.
UPG	The procedure for registering a transfer or license is the same as that for a European patent application (see paragraphs 112–121)

14.13 Licenses of right may be offered for a unitary patent – reduced renewal fees

1062	EU1257 Art. 8(1)	The proprietor of a European patent with unitary effect may file a statement with the EPO to the effect that the proprietor is prepared to allow any person to use the invention as a licensee in return for appropriate consideration.
	EU1257 Art. 8(2)	A license obtained under this Regulation shall be treated as a contractual license.
	EU1257 Art. 9 (1)(c)	The EPO is responsible for processing and registering statements on licensing referred to in Art. 8, their withdrawal and licensing commitments undertaken by the proprietor of the European patent with unitary effect in international standardisation bodies.
	EU1257 Rec. 10	Compulsory licenses for European patents with unitary effect should be governed by the laws of the participating Member States as regards their respective territories.
	EU1257 Art. 11(3)	Renewal fees which fall due after receipt of the statement referred to in Art. 8(1) (offering licenses of right) shall be reduced.
	r.12(1) UPR	The proprietor of a European patent with unitary effect may file a statement with the EPO that he is prepared to allow any person to use the invention as a licensee in return for appropriate consideration. In that case, the renewal fees for the European patent with unitary effect which fall due after receipt of the statement shall be reduced; the amount of the reduction shall be fixed in the Rules relating to Fees for Unitary Patent Protection. The statement shall be entered in the Register for unitary patent protection.
	UPRRF Art. 3	The reduction is 15 %.
	r.12(2) UPR	The statement referred to in r.12(1) UPR may be withdrawn at any time by a communication to this effect to the EPO. Such withdrawal shall not take effect until the amount by which the renewal fees were reduced is paid to the EPO.
	r.12(3) UPR	The statement referred to in r.12(1) UPR may not be filed as long as an exclusive license is recorded in the Register for unitary patent protection or a request for the recording of such a license is pending before the EPO.
	r.12(4) UPR	No request for recording an exclusive license in the Register for unitary patent protection shall be admissible after the statement referred to in r.12(1) UPR has been filed, unless that statement is withdrawn.
	Comment	The Unified Patent Court has jurisdiction in relation to disputes concerning compensation under licenses of right (Art. 32(1)(h) UPCA).

14.14 Register for unitary patent protection and file inspection

1063	EU1257 Art. 2(e)	'Register for unitary patent protection' means the register constituting part of the European Patent Register in which the unitary effect and any limitation, license, transfer, revocation or lapse of a European patent with unitary effect are registered.
	EU1257 Art. 9(1) (b)	The EPO is responsible for setting up and administering the Register for unitary patent protection.

EU1257 Art. 9(1) (h)

The EPO is responsible for ensuring that unitary effect is indicated in the Register for unitary patent protection, where a request for unitary effect has been filed and, during the transitional period provided for in Art. 6 of Regulation (EU) No EU1260/2012, has been submitted together with the translations referred to in that Article, and that the EPO is informed of any limitations, licenses, transfers or revocations of European patent with unitary effect.

r.15(1) UPR

The Register for unitary patent protection provided for in Art. 9(1)(b), Regulation (EU) No EU1257/2012 is hereby established as a special part of the European Patent Register kept by the EPO under Art. 127 EPC.

r.15(2) UPR

Entries in the Register for unitary patent protection shall be made in the three official languages of the European Patent Office. In case of doubt, the entry in the language of the proceedings shall be authentic.

r.16(1) UPR

The Register for unitary patent protection shall contain the following entries:
(a) date of publication of the mention of the grant of the European patent;
(b) date of filing of the request for unitary effect for the European patent;
(c) particulars of the representative of the proprietor of the European patent as provided for in r.41(2)(d) EPC; in the case of several representatives, only the particulars of the representative first named followed by the words "and others" and, in the case of an association referred to in r.152(11) EPC, only the name and address of the association.
(d) date and purport of the decision on the registration of unitary effect for the European patent;
(e) date of registration of the unitary effect of the European patent;
(f) date of effect of the European patent with unitary effect pursuant to Art. 4(1), Regulation (EU) No EU1257/2012;
(g) Participating Member States in which the European patent with unitary effect has unitary effect pursuant to Art. 18(2), Regulation (EU) No EU1257/2012;
(h) particulars of the proprietor of the European patent with unitary effect as provided for in r.41(2)(c) EPC;
(i) family name, given names and country and place of residence of the inventor designated by the applicant for or proprietor of the patent, unless he has waived his right to be mentioned under r.20(1) EPC;
(j) rights and transfer of such rights relating to the European patent wit unitary effect where the present Rules provide that they shall be recorded at the request of an interested party;
(k) licensing commitments undertaken by the proprietor of the European patent with unitary effect in international standardisation bodies pursuant to Art. 9(1)(c), Regulation (EU) No EU1257/2012, where the proprietor requested their registration;
(l) date of filing and date of withdrawal of the statement provided for in r.12 UPR (licenses of right);
(m) date of lapse of the European patent with unitary effect;
(n) data as to the payment of renewal fees for the European patent with unitary effect, including, where applicable, data on the payment of an additional fee pursuant to r.13(3) UPR;
(o) a record of the information communicated to the EPO concerning proceedings before the Unified Patent Court;
(p) a record of the information communicated to the EPO by the central industrial property offices, courts and other competent authorities of the participating Member States;
(q) date and purport of the decision on the validity of a European patent with unitary effect taken by the Unified Patent Court;
(r) date of receipt of a request for re-establishment of rights;
(s) refusal of a request for re-establishment of rights;
(t) date of re-establishment of rights;
(u) dates of interruption and resumption of proceedings;
(v) date of issuance, date of expiry and date and purport of the decision on the validity of a supplementary protection certificate for a product protected by the European patent with unitary effect as well as the participating Member State issuing it;

(w) information regarding a place of business of the applicant on the date of filing of the application for the European patent pursuant to Art. 7(1)(b), Regulation (EU) No EU1257/2012, which may be provided by the proprietor of the European patent together with the request for unitary effect referred to in r.6 (determining relevant national law applying to the patent as an object of property);

(x) information regarding the residence or principal place of business of the applicant on the date of filing of the application for the European patent pursuant to Art. 71(a), Regulation (EU) No 1257/2012 (determining relevant national law applying to the patent as an object of property).

r.16(2) UPR   The President of the EPO may decide that entries additional to those referred to in r.16(1) UPR shall be made in the Register for unitary patent protection.

OJ   See Decision of the President dated 24 April 2023 ([2023] O.J. Supplementary Publication 3, page 1). A further entry will be made: Date of lapse of the European patent with unitary effect during the opposition period and, where appropriate, pending a final decision on opposition.

r.19 UPR   The EPO shall include a copy of any decision of the Unified Patent Court forwarded to it by the Court and relating to European patents with unitary effect, including those decisions referred to in r.1 UPR (Art. 32(1)(i) UPCA), in the files relating to the European patent with unitary effect, where it shall be open to inspection.

UPG   Inspection of the file for a unitary patent will be available since r.20(2) UPR applies Art. 128(4) and r.144–147 EPC (see paragraph 110).

14.15 Compensation scheme for certain unitary patent proprietors if the patent was filed in an EU language other than English, French or German

1064 EU1257 Art. (1)(f)   9The EPO is responsible for administering the compensation scheme for the reimbursement of translation costs referred to in Art. 5 of Regulation (EU) No EU1260/2012.

EU1260 Art. 5(1)   Given the fact that European patent applications may be filed in any language under Art. 14(2) EPC, the participating Member States shall in accordance with Art. 9 EU1257, give, within the meaning of Art. 143 EPC, the EPO the task of administering a compensation scheme for the reimbursement of all translation costs up to a ceiling, for applicants filing patent applications at the EPO in one of the official languages of the Union that is not an official language of the EPO.

EU1260 Art. 5(2)   The compensation scheme referred to in Art. 5(1) EU1260 shall be funded through the fees referred to in Art. 11 EU1257 (unitary patent renewal fees) and shall be available only for SMEs, natural persons, non-profit organisations, universities and public research organisations having their residence or principle place of business within a Member State.

r.8(1) UPR   Proprietors of European patents with unitary effect for which the European patent application was filed in an official language of the European Union other than English, French or German shall be entitled to compensation for translation costs if their residence or principle place of business is in a Member State of the European Union and they are an entity or natural person referred to in r.8(2) UPR.

UPG   It does not matter whether the EU language is an official language of a participating or non-participating EU member state (see paragraph 76).

r.8(2) UPR   Compensation for translation costs shall be granted, on request, to a patent proprietor falling within one of the following categories:

(a) small and medium-sized enterprises as defined in European Commission recommendation 2003/361/EC dated 06 May 2003;

(b) natural persons; or

(c) non-profit organisations as defined in Art. 2(1)(14) of Regulation (EU) No 1290/2013, universities and public research organisations.

OJ   See Notice from the EPO dated 10 January 2014 ([2014] O.J. A23) for the definition of "non-profit organisation", "university", "public research organisation" and "small and medium-sized enterprise". An enterprise according to r.8(2)(a) UPR must employ less than 250 persons, have an annual turnover not exceeding 50 million Euros and/or an annual balance sheet total not exceeding 43 million Euros and be an enterprise for which no more than 25 % of the capital is held directly or indirectly by another company which is itself not an SME.

r.8(3) UPR	If the patent has multiple proprietors, compensation will be granted only if each proprietor fulfils the conditions referred to in r.8(1) and (2) UPR.
r.8(4) UPR	If the European patent application or the European patent was transferred before a request for unitary effect was filed, compensation will be granted only if both the initial applicant and the proprietor of the patent fulfil the conditions referred to in r.8(1) and (2) UPR.
r.8(5) UPR	The compensation scheme provided for in r.8(1) UPR shall also apply to Euro-PCT applications originally filed at a receiving office in an official language of the European Union other than English, French or German.
Comment	The requirements of r.8(1) UPR are judged at the time the application is filed; the requirements of r.8(4) UPR are judged at the time the compensation is requested.
r.9(1) UPR	The proprietor of a European patent who wishes to benefit from compensation under r.8 UPR shall file a request for it together with the request for unitary effect referred to in r.6 UPR.
r.9(2) UPR	The request for compensation for translation costs shall contain a declaration that the proprietor of the European patent is an entity or a natural person referred to in r.8(2) UPR.
r.10(1) UPR	After the EPO has registered the unitary effect of the European patent in the Register for unitary patent protection and has examined the request for compensation, it shall inform the patent proprietor whether that request has been granted or rejected.
r.10(2) UPR	Once granted, compensation shall not be rescinded, even if, as a result of changed circumstances, the proprietor no longer qualifies for it under r.8 UPR.
r.10(3) UPR	Should the Office have reason to doubt the veracity of the declaration filed under r.9(2) UPR, it shall invite the patent proprietor to provide evidence that he fulfils the requirements of r.8(2) UPR. Article 113(1) and 114 EPC shall apply.
r.10(4) UPR	If the Office finds that the compensation was granted on the basis of a false declaration, it shall invite the patent proprietor to pay, together with the next renewal fee falling due, an additional fee composed of the amount of the compensation paid and an administrative fee as laid down in the Rules relating to Fees for Unitary Patent Protection. If this additional fee is not paid in due time, the European patent with unitary effect shall lapse under r.14 UPR.
UPRRF Art. 4(2)	The administrative fee is 50 % of the lump sum paid under Art. 4(1) UPRRF.
Comment	The invitation to pay an additional fee may be made during the 6 month grace period if the renewal fee has not been paid on time.
Comment	Decisions of the EPO regarding compensation can be appealed to the Unified Patent Court.
r.11 UPR	Reimbursement of translation costs shall be made up to a ceiling and paid in the form of a lump sum, in accordance with the Rules relating to Fees for Unitary Patent Protection. The ceiling shall be fixed on the basis of the average length of a European patent and the average translation cost per page, taking account of the average reduction granted under r.6 EPC.
UPRRF Art. 4(1)	The lump sum amount is 500 Euros.

14.16   Renewal fees for a unitary patent

14.16.1   *Renewal fees for a unitary patent are to be paid to the EPO*

EU1257 Art. 9 (1)(e)	The EPO is responsible for the collection and administration of renewal fees for European patents with unitary effect, in respect of the years following the year in which the mention of the grant is published in the European Patent Bulletin; and for the collection and administration of additional fees for late payment of renewal fees where such late payment is made within six months of the due date, as well as the distribution of part of the collected renewal fees to the participating Member States.	1065
EU1257 Art. 11 (1)	Renewal fees for European patents with unitary effect and additional fees for their late payment shall be paid to the European Patent Organisation by the patent proprietor. Those fees shall be due in respect of the years following the year in which the mention of the grant of the European patent which benefits from unitary effect is published in the European Patent Bulletin.	

| r.13(1) UPR | Renewal fees for European patents with unitary effect and additional fees for their late payment shall be paid to the EPO. Those fees shall be due in respect of the years following the year in which the mention of the grant of the European patent which benefits from unitary effect is published in the European Patent Bulletin. |

14.16.2   Due date for renewal fees

| 1066 | r.13(2) UPR | A renewal fee for the European patent with unitary effect in respect of the coming year shall be due on the last day of the month containing the anniversary of the date of filing of the European patent application which led to the European patent with unitary effect. Renewal fees may not be validly paid more than three months before they fall due. |
| | UPG | Rules relating to the payment of renewal fees for European patent applications will also apply to the payment of renewal fees for unitary patents (see paragraph 93). Thus, if a renewal fee falls due on a day on which the EPO is closed, the due date is not shifted but the fee can still be validly paid without surcharge on the next day on which the EPO is open for business (J4/91). |

14.16.3   Consequences of non-payment – grace period

1067	UPG	As a courtesy, the EPO will inform the proprietor when a renewal fee is not paid by the due date and draw attention to the grace period (see paragraph 90).
	r.13(3) UPR	If a renewal fee is not paid in due time, the fee may still be paid within six months of the due date, provided that an additional fee is also paid within that period.
	UPRRF Art. 2(1) (2)	The additional fee for belated payment of a renewal fee is 50 % of the belated renewal fee.
	UPG	See paragraphs 94–95 – J4/91 applies to the calculation of the 6 month grace period which therefore expires on the last day of the sixth month from the month in which anniversary falls. Since r.131 and r.134 EPC apply to the calculation of time limits (r.20(2)(g) UPR), the end of the six-month period is adjusted to account for days on which the EPO is closed for business.

14.16.4   Payment of renewal fees falling due between grant and the registration of unitary effect or shortly after registration of unitary effect

1068	r.13(5) UPR	A renewal fee for a European patent with unitary effect which would have fallen due under r.13(2) UPR in the period starting on the date of publication of the mention of grant of the European patent in the European patent bulletin up to and including the date of notification of the communication referred to in r.7(1) UPR (communication of the date of registration of unitary effect) shall be due on the latter date. This fee may still be paid within three months of that latter date without the additional fee referred to in r.13(3) UPR.
	r.13(4) UPR	A renewal fee in respect of a European patent with unitary effect falling due under r.13(2) UPR within three months of the notification of the communication referred to in r.7(1) UPR (communication of the date of registration of unitary effect) may still be paid within that period without the additional fee referred to in r.13(3) UPR.
	Comment	This system is more generous than the mandatory 2m period of Art. 141(2) EPC.
	UPG	See paragraphs 97–102 for helpful illustrations of how these periods work.

14.16.5   Consequences of not complying with the grace period

1069	EU1257 Art. 11(2)	A European patent with unitary effect shall lapse if a renewal fee and, where applicable, any additional fee have not been paid in due time.
	r.14(1)(b) UPR	A European patent with unitary effect shall lapse if a renewal fee and, where applicable, any additional fee have not been paid in due time.
	r.14(2) UPR	The lapse of a European patent with unitary effect for failure to pay a renewal fee and any additional fee within the due period shall be deemed to have occurred on the date on which the renewal fee was due.
	r.22(1) UPR	Re-establishment is available

UPG

See paragraphs 91–92 – if the renewal fee is not paid by the end of the 6-month grace period, the patent lapses and a loss of rights pursuant to r.112(1) EPC is sent to the proprietor (r.20(2)(d) UPR). The appropriate remedy is re-establishment or else if the EPO has made a mistake, a decision can be requested under r.112(2) EPC and, if necessary, appealed to the Unified Patent Court.

14.16.6   *Payment in cases where lapse or revocation is reversed*

r.13(6) UPR
Comment

r.51(4) and (5) EPC shall apply mutatis mutandis   1070

r.51(4) EPC will apply when the unitary patent lapses and a request for re-establishment is successful. Any renewal fee that fell due between the lapse of the patent and notification of the decision on re-establishment is considered to have fallen due on that notification date. This fee and any renewal fee due within four months of the due date can be paid within that four-month period without surcharge. Any renewal fee for which the six-month grace period was still running at the point the patent lapsed may be paid with surcharge within six months of the date of notification of the decision on re-establishment. r.51(5) EPC will apply when the patent is revoked and a petition for review under Art. 112a EPC or a rehearing under Art. 81 UPCA is successful. Any renewal fee that fell due between the revocation of the patent and notification of the decision to set aside the revocation is considered to have fallen due on that notification date. This fee and any renewal fee due within four months of the due date can be paid within that four-month period without surcharge. Any renewal fee for which the six-month grace period was still running at the point the patent was revoked may be paid with surcharge within six months of the date of notification of the decision setting aside the revocation.

14.16.7   *Amount of renewal fees*

EU1257 Art. 12(1)

Renewal fees for European patents with unitary effect shall be: 1071
  (a)   progressive throughout the term of the unitary patent protection;
  (b)   sufficient to cover all costs associated with the grant of the European patent and the administration of the unitary patent protection; and
  (c)   sufficient, together with the fees to be paid to the European Patent Organisation during the pre-grant stage, to ensure a balanced budget of the European Patent Organisation.

EU1257 Art. 12(2)

The level of the renewal fees shall be set, taking into account, among others, the situation of specific entities such as small and medium-sized enterprises, with the aim of:
  (a)   facilitating innovation and fostering the competitiveness of European businesses;
  (b)   reflecting the size of the market covered by the patent; and
  (c)   being similar to the level of the national renewal fees for an average European patent taking effect in the participating Member States at the time the level of the renewal fees is first set.

EU1257 Art. 12(3)

In order to attain the objectives set out in this Chapter, the level of renewal fees shall be set at a level that:
  (a)   is equivalent to the level of the renewal fee to be paid for the average geographical coverage of current European patents;
  (b)   reflects the renewal fee rate of current European patents; and
  (c)   reflects the number of requests for unitary effect.

UPRRF Art. 2(1)(1)

Renewal fees for a European Patent with unitary effect, calculated in each case from the date of filing of the application are (in Euros):

Year	Amount	Year	Amount
For the 2nd year	35	For the 12th year	1775
For the 3rd year	105	For the 13th year	2105
For the 4th year	145	For the 14th year	2455
For the 5th year	315	For the 15th year	2830
For the 6th year	475	For the 16th year	3240
For the 7th year	630	For the 17th year	3640

Year	Amount	Year	Amount
For the 8th year	815	For the 18th year	4055
For the 9th year	990	For the 19th year	4455
For the 10th year	1175	For the 20th year	4855
For the 11th year	1460		

14.16.8   Distribution of renewal fees

1072   EU1257 Art. 13(1)   The EPO shall retain 50 % of the renewal fees referred to in Article 11 paid for European patents with unitary effect. The remaining amount shall be distributed to the participating Member States in accordance with the share of distribution of renewal fees set pursuant to Art. 9(2) EU1257.

EU1257 Art. 13(2)   In order to attain the objectives set out in this Chapter, the share of distribution of renewal fees among the participating Member States shall be based on the following fair, equitable and relevant criteria:
(a)   the number of patent applications;
(b)   the size of the market, while ensuring a minimum amount to be distributed to each participating Member State;
(c)   compensation to the participating Member States which have:
    a.   an official language other than one of the official languages of the EPO;
    b.   a disproportionately low level of patenting activity; and/or
    c.   acquired membership of the European Patent Organisation relatively recently.

UPRRF Art. 7(a)   No later than five years from the date of application of Regulation (EU) No EU1257/2012, and every five years thereafter, the EPO shall submit a report to the Select Committee of the Administrative Council assessing the financial impact of the European patent with unitary effect on the budget of the European Patent Organisation and on the renewal fee income of the participating Member States and, where necessary, make an appropriate proposal for adjusting the level of renewal fees.

14.17   Expiry of the patent

1073   r.14(1)(a) UPR   A European patent with unitary effect shall lapse 20 years after the date of filing of the European patent application.

14.18   Common provisions governing procedure

1074   r.20(1) UPR   The following provisions of the EPC, as amended, shall apply mutatis mutandis:
Art. 14(1) EPC – official languages of EPO are English, French and German.
Art. 14(3) EPC – language of proceedings is language of filing/translation.
Art. 14(7) EPC – Bulletin, OJ both published in all 3 official languages
Art. 113(1) EPC – right to be heard
Art. 114 EPC – EPO to examine facts of own motion; may disregard facts submitted late.
Art. 117 EPC – means of taking evidence.
Art. 119 EPC – notification of document by the EPO.
Art. 120 EPC – Time limits
Art. 125 EPC – principles of law generally recognised
Art. 128(4) EPC – inspection of files possible after publication of application
Art. 131 EPC – EPO and courts to cooperate
Art. 133 EPC – general principles of representation – employee representatives possible.
Art. 134(1) EPC – representation only by professional representatives
Art. 134(5) EPC – professional representatives can act in all EPO proceedings
Art. 134(8) EPC – legal practitioners can also act as representatives

Comment   Thus the requirements for representation are the same as for a European patent application and there is no distinction made between non-participating EPC states and participating states.

r.20(2) UPR   The following provisions of the Implementing Regulations to the EPC, as amended, shall apply mutatis mutandis:
r.1 EPC – use of the written form
r.2 EPC – filing of documents and signature thereof

| | r.3(1) EPC, first paragraph, unless otherwise provided – any official language can be used in written proceedings. |
| Comment | A request for unitary effect must be filed in the language of the proceedings (r.6(2) UPR). In practice, the EPO form will be written all three languages. Any other communication may be in any official language. |

r.3(3) EPC – documentary evidence in any language but translation may be required.
r.4 EPC – languages in oral proceedings
r.5 EPC – translations may have to be certified
r.22 EPC – registration of transfers
r.23 EPC – registration of licenses and other rights
r.24 EPC – registration of exclusive and sub-licenses
r.50(2) EPC – documents to be typewritten or printed
r.50(3) EPC – documents to be signed unless annexed
r.111(1) EPC – decisions, oral and in writing, reasoning
r.112 EPC – noting loss of rights and decision thereon
r.113 EPC – authentication of EPO decisions, summonses etc
r.115 EPC – summons to oral proceedings, 2m notice, consequences of not attending
r.116(1) EPC – points to be discussed, date for final submissions
r.117 EPC – taking of evidence
r.118 EPC – summons to give evidence
r.119 EPC – examination of evidence
r.120 EPC – hearing of evidence by a national court
r.121 EPC – appointment of an expert by the EPO
r.122 EPC – costs of taking evidence
r.123 EPC – conservation of evidence
r.124 EPC – minutes or oral proceedings and taking of evidence
r.125 EPC – notification by the EPO
r.126 EPC – notification by postal services
r.127 EPC – notification by electronic means
r.128 EPC – notification by hand
r.129 EPC – public notification
r.130 EPC – representative to be notified when appointed
r.131 EPC – calculation of periods
r.133(1) EPC, subject to the proviso that the document referred to in that provision has been received no later than one month after expiry of the period – late receipt of documents sometimes excused
r.134 EPC – extension of time limits when EPO closed etc
r.139 EPC, first sentence – correction of mistakes in documents
r.140 EPC – correction of errors in decisions
r.142 EPC – interruption of proceedings
r.144 EPC – parts of file excluded from inspection
r.145 EPC – inspection of files
r.146 EPC – communication of information in the files
r.147 EPC – maintenance of files
r.148 EPC – communication between the EPO and authorities of Contracting States
r.149 EPC – inspection of files by courts and national authorities
r.150 EPC – letters rogatory
r.151 EPC – common representative
r.152 EPC – need for authorisation
r.153 EPC – attorney-client evidentiary privilege

| r.20(3) UPR | When applying the provisions referred to in r.20(1) and (2) UPR mutatis mutandis, the term "Contracting States" shall be understood as meaning the Contracting States to the EPC, except in Art. 125 EPC, where it shall be understood as meaning the participating Member States. |
| r.20(4) UPR | Where the present Rules, including the provisions of the EPC applicable mutatis mutandis under the present Rules, refer to "a period to be specified", this period shall be specified by the EPO. Unless otherwise provided, a period specified by the EPO shall be neither less than one month nor more than four months. |

14.19 Oral proceedings

1075 r.21(1) UPR	Oral proceedings shall take place either at the instance of the EPO if it considers this to be expedient or at the request of any party to the proceedings. However, the EPO may reject a request for further oral proceedings where the parties and the subject of the proceedings are the same.
r.21(2) UPR	Nevertheless, in the procedure concerning the request for unitary effect, oral proceedings shall take place before the Unitary Patent Protection Division at the request of the proprietor of the European patent only where the Unitary Patent Protection Division considers this to be expedient.
Comment	Thus oral proceedings will occur only in exceptional cases where the request for unitary effect is concerned. In other cases, such as re-establishment proceedings, the right remains absolute.
r.21(3) UPR	Oral proceedings before the Unitary Patent Protection Division shall not be public.
OJ	Oral proceedings before the Unitary Patent Protection Division are to be held by videoconference unless there are serious reasons against its use (see Decision on the President dated 24 April 2023 ([2023] O.J. Supplementary Publication 3, pages 2–4).

14.20 Re-establishment of rights

1076 r.22(1) UPR	A proprietor of a European patent or of a European patent with unitary effect who, in spite of all due care required by the circumstances having been taken, was unable to observe a time limit vis-à-vis the EPO shall have his rights re-established upon request if the non-observance of this time limit has the direct consequence of causing the European patent with unitary effect to lapse according to r.14(1)(b) UPR (renewal fee), or the loss of any other right or means of redress.
r.22(2) UPR	Any request for re-establishment of rights under r.22(1) UPR shall be filed in writing within two months of the removal of the cause of non-compliance with the period, but at the latest within one year of expiry of the unobserved time limit. However, a request for re-establishment of rights in respect of the period specified in r.6(1) UPR (for filing a request for unitary effect) shall be filed within two months of expiry of that period. The request for re-establishment of rights shall not be deemed to have been filed until the fee prescribed in the Rules relating to Fees for Unitary Patent Protection has been paid.
r.22(3) UPR	The request shall state the grounds on which it is based and shall set out the facts on which it relies. The omitted act shall be completed within the relevant period for filing the request according to r.22(2) UPR.
r.22(4) UPR	The EPO shall grant the request, provided that the conditions laid down in the present Rule are met. Otherwise, it shall reject the request.
r.22(5) UPR	If the request is granted, the legal consequences of the failure to observe the time limit shall be deemed not to have ensued.
r.22(6) UPR	Re-establishment of rights shall be ruled out in respect of the time limit for requesting re-establishment of rights and in respect of the period referred to in r.7(3) UPR (time limit for correcting deficiencies in the request for unitary effect).
r.22(7) UPR	Any person who, in one or several participating Member States, has in good faith used or made effective and serious preparations for using an invention which is the subject of a European patent with unitary effect in the period between the loss of rights referred to in r.22(1) UPR and publication in the Register for unitary patent protection of the mention of re-establishment of those rights, may without payment continue such use in the course of his business or for the needs thereof.
UPRRF Art. 2(2)	The re-establishment fee is the same as that due under the EPC RRF Art. 2(1)(13) which is currently 640 Euros.

14.21 Languages

1077 r.20(1) UPR	Since Art. 14(1) and (3) EPC are applicable, any of the three official languages of the EPO may be used in proceedings before the EPO relating to unitary effect. However, the exception to this is that the initial request for unitary effect must be filed in the language of proceedings of the patent (EU1257 Art. 9(1)(g) and EU1260 Art. 3(2).
UPG	However, since Art. 14(4) EPC is not applied, it will not be possible to use an official language of a Contracting State which is not an EPO language (see paragraph 130).

14.22 Representation and authorisation

r.20(1) UPR

Since Art. 133 EPC, Art. 134(1) EPC, Art. 134(5) EPC and Art. 134(8) EPC apply, the usual rules for representation at the EPO are applicable.

r.20(2) UPR

Since r.152 applies, the usual rules for authorisation are applicable.

UPG

An authorisation to act in respect of a European patent application and patent does not apply to proceedings in respect of a unitary patent for which a separate authorisation is required (see paragraph 133).

1078

14.23 Certain decisions to be reasoned

r.23 UPR

Decisions of the EPO against which actions can be brought before the Unified Patent Court in accordance with Art. 32(1)(i) UPCA shall be reasoned and shall be accompanied by a communication pointing out the possibility of bringing an action before the Unified Patent Court. The parties may not invoke the omission of the communication.

1079

14.24 Filing an appeal at the Unified Patent Court

14.24.1 Jurisdiction of the Unified Patent Court

EU1257 Art. 9(3)

The participating Member States shall ensure effective legal protection before a competent court of one or several participating Member States against the decisions of the EPO in carrying out the tasks referred to in Eu1257 Art. 9(1).

UPCA Art. 32(1)

The Court shall have exclusive competence in respect of:
(i) actions concerning decisions of the European Patent Office in carrying out the tasks referred to in Art. 9 of Regulation (EU) No EU1257/2012.

UPCA Art. 33(9)

Actions referred to in Art. 32(1)(i) UPCA shall be brought before the central division.

UPCA r.86

An action against a decision of the Office shall have suspensive effect.

UPCA r.87

An action against a decision of the Office may be brought on grounds of:
an infringement of Regulation (EU) No EU1257/2012 or of Regulation (EU) No EU1260/2012 or of any rule of law relating to their application;
infringement of any of the implementing rules of the EPO for carrying out the tasks referred to in Art. 9(1) of Regulation (EU) No EU1257/2012;
infringement of an essential procedural requirement;
misuse of power.

1080

14.24.2 Expedited review of a decision to refuse a request for unitary effect

UPCA r.85(2)

This Rule and Rules 88 UPCA (save as expressly provided for in Rule 97.2), 89 UPCA, and 91 to 96 UPCA shall not apply to an expedited action against a decision of the Office pursuant to Rule 97 UPCA (where a request for unitary effect has been rejected).

UPCA r.97(1)

The proprietor of a patent whose request for unitary effect has been rejected by the Office shall lodge an Application at the Registry in accordance with Art. 7(2) of the Agreement and Annex II thereto, to reverse the decision of the Office, in the language in which the patent was granted, within three weeks of service of the decision of the EPO.

UPCA r.97(2)

The Application shall contain particulars in accordance with r.88.2(a), (c), (d) and (f) to (i) UPCA and the proprietor shall pay the fee for the action against the decision of the Office in accordance with Part 6. Rule 15.2 UPCA shall apply mutatis mutandis.

UPCA r.97(3)

If the requirements referred to in paragraph 2 have been complied with, r.90 UPCA shall apply mutatis mutandis.

UPCA r.97(4)

The Registry shall as soon as practicable forward the Application to the standing judge who may invite the President of the EPO to comment on the Application but shall in any event decide the Application within three weeks of the date of receipt of the Application.

1081

UPCA r.97(5)	A Statement of appeal by the proprietor of the patent or the President of the EPO against the decisions of the standing judge pursuant to paragraph 4 may be lodged within three weeks of service of the said decision. The Statement of appeal shall contain the particulars previously lodged pursuant to paragraph 2 and also the reasons for setting aside the contested decision. The appellant shall pay the fee for appeal in accordance with Part 6. Rule 15.2 UPCA shall apply mutatis mutandis. If the requirements of this paragraph 5 have been complied with, the Registry shall record the appeal in accordance with r.230.1 UPCA and shall as soon as practicable assign the appeal to the standing judge of the Court of Appeal [r.345.5 and 345.8 UPCA] who may invite the other party to comment on the appeal but shall in any event decide the appeal within three weeks of receipt by the Registry of the Statement of appeal.
UPCA r.97(6)	The Registry shall as soon as practicable notify the Office of the decision on the Application or on the appeal as the case may be.
Comment	Interlocutory revision by the EPO does not apply.

14.24.3   Review of other decisions of the EPO concerning unitary effect

1082 UPCA r.85(1)	Subject to r.85(2) UPCA, where an action is brought against a decision of the EPO in carrying out the tasks referred to in Art. 9 of Regulation (EU) No EU1257/2012 (hereinafter "decision of the Office"), proceedings before the Court of First Instance shall consist of: (a) a written procedure, which shall include a possibility for interlocutory review by the EPO; (b) an interim procedure, which may include an interim conference; and (c) an oral procedure which, at the request of the claimant or at the instance of the Court, may include an oral hearing
UPCA r.88(1)	The claimant shall lodge an Application at the Registry, in accordance with Art. 7(2) of the Agreement (UPCA) and Annex II thereof, to annul or alter a decision of the Office in the language in which the patent was granted, within two months of service of the decision of the Office.
UPCA r.88(2)	The Application to annul or alter a decision of the Office shall contain: (a) the names of the claimant and, where applicable, of the claimant's representative; (b) where the claimant is not the proprietor of or applicant for the European patent with unitary effect, an explanation and evidence that he is adversely affected by the decision of the Office and entitled to start proceedings (Art. 47(7) of the Agreement); (c) postal and electronic addresses for service of the claimant and the names and addresses of the persons authorised to accept service; (d) a reference to the contested decision of the Office; (e) where applicable, information about any prior or pending proceedings relating to the patent concerned before the Court, EPO or any other court or authority; (f) an indication whether the action shall be heard by a single judge (normally three judges before the central division but parties can agree to have a single judge); (g) the order or the remedy sought by the claimant; (h) one or more grounds for annulling or altering the contested decision, in accordance with r.87 UPCA; (i) the facts, evidence and arguments relied on; and (j) a list of the documents, including any witness statements, referred to in the Application together with any request that all or part of any such document need not be translated and/or any request pursuant to R.262.1 UPCA (confidentiality). Rule 13.2 and 3 UPCA shall apply mutatis mutandis (attach copy of document referred to, immediate decision on translation/confidentiality).
UPCA r.88(3)	The claimant shall pay the fee for the action against a decision of the Office in accordance with Part 6. Rule15.2 UPCA shall apply mutatis mutandis (not deemed filed until fee paid).
UPCA r.88(4)	Rule 8 UPCA shall not apply (representation).
UPCA r.89(1)	The Registry shall, as soon as practicable after an Application to annul or alter a decision of the Office has been lodged, examine whether the requirements of Art. 47(7) and Art. 49(6) of the Agreement and r.88.1 UPCA, r.88.2(a)-(d) UPCA and r.88.3 UPCA have been complied with.
UPCA r.89(2)	If the Registry considers that any of the requirements referred to in r.89(1) UPCA has not been complied with, it shall invite the claimant to:

	(a) correct the deficiencies noted, within 14 days from the date of service of such notification; and
	(b) where applicable, pay the fee for the action against a decision of the Office, within said 14 days.
UPCA r.89(3)	The Registry shall at the same time inform the claimant that if the claimant fails to correct the deficiencies or pay the fee within the time stated, a decision by default may be given in accordance with r.355 UPCA.
UPCA r.89(4)	If the claimant fails to correct the deficiencies noted or pay the fee for the action against a decision of the Office, the Registry shall inform the President of the Court of First Instance who may reject the action as inadmissible by a decision by default. He may give the claimant an opportunity to be heard beforehand.
UPCA r.90	If the requirements referred to in r.89.1 UPCA have been complied with, the Registry shall as soon as practicable:
	(a) record the date of receipt of the Application to annul or alter a decision of the Office and attribute an action number to the file;
	(b) record the file in the register;
	(c) inform the claimant of the action number of the file and the date of receipt; and
	(d) forward the Application to the EPO, with an indication that the Application is admissible.
UPCA r.91(1)	If the EPO considers that the Application to annul or alter a decision of the Office is well founded, it shall within two months of the date of receipt of the Application:
	(a) rectify the contested decision in accordance with the order or remedy sought by the claimant (Rule 88.2(f) UPCA]; and
	(b) inform the Court that the decision has been rectified.
UPCA r.91(2)	Where the Court is informed by the EPO that the contested decision has been rectified, it shall inform the claimant that the action is closed. It may order full or partial reimbursement of the fee for the action against a decision of the Office, in accordance with Part 6.
r.24 UPR	If the EPO is informed by the Unified Patent Court that an application to annul or alter a decision of the EPO is admissible and if the EPO considers that the application is well founded, it shall, within two months of the date of receipt of the application,
	(a) rectify the contested decision in accordance with the order or remedy sought by the claimant and
	(b) inform the Unified Patent Court that the decision has been rectified.
UPCA r.92	Where the action is not closed in accordance with Rule 91.2 UPCA, the action shall, as soon as practicable after the expiry of the period referred to in r.91.1 UPCA, be assigned to a panel of the central division or to a single judge if requested by the claimant (Rule 88.2(f) UPCA) in accordance with Rule 345.3 UPCA. Rule 18 UPCA shall apply.
UPCA r.93(1)	In the examination of the Application to annul or alter a decision of the Office, the judge-rapporteur may invite the claimant to lodge further written pleadings, within a time period to be specified.
UPCA r.93(2)	Where appropriate, the judge-rapporteur may, after consulting the claimant, set a date and time for an interim conference.
UPCA r.93(3)	Rule 35 UPCA shall apply mutatis mutandis.
UPCA r.94	The judge-rapporteur may, on his own initiative or on request by the President of the EPO, invite the President of the EPO to comment in writing on any question arising in the course of the proceedings under this Section. The claimant shall be entitled to submit his observations on the President's comments.
UPCA r.95	During the interim procedure, the judge-rapporteur shall invite the claimant to indicate whether he wishes that an oral hearing be convened. The judge-rapporteur may convene an oral hearing at his own instance.
UPCA r.96(1)	Rules 110.3, 111, 115 and 118.6 UPCA shall apply to the oral hearing and to the decision of the Court.
UPCA r.96(2)	If an oral hearing is not convened, the panel shall decide in accordance with r.117 UPCA.
UPCA r.98	The parties shall bear their own costs in any action pursuant to Rule 85 or 97 UPCA.

14.25 Payment of fees

1083 UPRRF Art. 5   The administrative fees provided for in the Rules relating to Unitary Patent Protection and the fees and expenses charged for any services rendered by the EPO other than those specified in the present RRF shall be payable in the amounts laid down by the President of the EPO pursuant to Art. 3 RRF EPC.

Comment   These fees are, for example, for the registration of a transfer, license or other right and for communication information in the files.

UPRRF Art. 6   The following provisions of the RRF under the EPC shall apply mutatis mutandis:
EPC RRFArt. 4 – due date for fees
EPC RRFArt. 5 – payment of fees
EPC RRFArt. 6 – particulars concerning payment
EPC RRFArt. 7 – date to be considered as the date on which payment is made
EPC RRFArt. 8 – insufficiency of the amount paid
EPC RRFArt. 12 – refund of insignificant amounts
EPC RRFArt. 13 – termination of financial obligations

Comment   It is therefore possible to use the usual means of fee payment available at the EPO including the use of a deposit account

14.26 Application of competition law and the law relating to unfair competition

1084 EU1257 Art. 15   This Regulation shall be without prejudice to the application of competition law and the law relating to unfair competition.

14.27 EPO publications

1085 r.17(1) UPR   The European Patent Bulletin referred to in Art. 129(a) EPC shall contain, as a special part, the particulars the publication of which is prescribed by the present Rules, the Chairperson of the Select Committee of the Administrative Council or the President of the EPO.

r.17(2) UPR   The Official Journal referred to in Art. 129(b) EPC shall contain, as a special part, notices and information of a general character issued by the Select Committee of the Administrative Council or by the President of the EPO, as well as any other information relevant to the implementation of unitary patent protection.

14.28 Entry into force

1086 EU1257 Art. 18(1)   This Regulation shall enter into force on the twentieth day following that of its publication in the Official Journal of the European Union (31.12.2012).

EU1257 Art. 18(2)   It shall apply from 01 January 2014 or the date of entry into force of the Agreement on a Unified Patent Court (the 'Agreement'), whichever is the later.

EU1260 Art. 7(1)   This Regulation shall enter into force on the twentieth day following that of its publication in the Official Journal of the European Union (31.12.2012).

EU1260 Art. 7(2)   It shall apply from 01 January 2014 or the date of entry into force of the Agreement on a Unified Patent Court, whichever is the later.

UPR   These Rules shall enter into force on the date of application of Regulations (EU) No EU1257/2012 and No EU1260/2012 in accordance with Art. 18(2) of Regulation (EU) No EU1257/2012 and Art. 7(2) of Regulation (EU) No EU1260/2012 (Art. 2 of the Decision of 15 December 2015 adopting the Rules relating to Unitary Patent Protection).

UPRRF   These Rules shall enter into force on the date of application of Regulations (EU) No EU1257/2012 and No EU1260/2012 in accordance with Art. 18(2) of Regulation (EU) No EU1257/2012 and Art. 7(2) of Regulation (EU) No EU1260/2012 (Art. 2 of the Decision of 15 December 2015 adopting the Rules relating to fees for Unitary Patent Protection).

14.29 Status of the Rules relating to unitary patent protection

1087 r.1(1) UPR   The participating Member States hereby entrust the EPO with the tasks referred to in Art. 9(1), Regulation (EU) No EU1257/2012. In carrying out these tasks, the EPO shall apply the present Rules and shall be bound by decisions handed down by the Unified Patent Court in actions brought under Art. 32(1)(i), Agreement on a Unified Patent Court.

UCA Art. 32(1)(i)   The Court shall have exclusive competence in respect of actions concerning decision of the EPO in carrying out the tasks referred to in Art. 9 of Regulation (EU) No EU1257/2012.

r.1(2) UPR   In cases of conflict between the provisions of the present Rules and Union law, including Regulation (EU) No EU1257/2012 and Regulation (EU) EU1260/2012, the provisions of Union law shall prevail.

Chapter 15: Opposition Proceedings

15.1 General considerations

1088 OJ
Comment

A guide to opposition procedure has been published by the EPO ([2016] O.J. A42). Opposition proceedings are not a continuation of the examination proceedings that led to the grant of the opposed patent but entirely separate proceedings. Thus, for example, the Opposition Division is not bound by any decision of a Board of Appeal relevant to the grant proceedings in the same way that the Examining Division in those proceedings would have been. The Enlarged Board of Appeal in decisions G9/91 and G10/91 has developed the concept of opposition proceedings as being contentious. This means that the EPO does not take such a proactive role in the opposition proceedings as it would in grant proceedings but, instead, primarily listens impartially to the submissions of each party and decides on the issues raised. The right of EPO departments under Art. 114(1) to examine facts of their own motion is therefore somewhat curtailed in opposition proceedings. Note also that opposition proceedings can only be terminated by a decision of some kind (see G1/90) – usually either that the opposition is inadmissible, that the patent is revoked, that the patent is maintained as granted, or that the patent is maintained in amended form. Occasionally, it is necessary to simply take a decision that opposition proceedings are terminated (e.g. when revocation proceedings under Art. 105a are already in existence when the opposition is filed or when the patent lapses in all states and the opponent does not wish to continue).

15.2 Filing an opposition

15.2.1 Time limit for filing a notice of opposition

1089 Art. 99(1)

Notice of opposition to a granted European patent must be given to the EPO within nine months of the publication of the mention of the grant of the European Patent in the European Patent Bulletin.

T438/87

Any delay in the publication of the patent specification does not affect the opposition period since the publication of the mention of grant is decisive.

T702/89

A would-be opponent is not entitled to re-establishment in respect of the missed nine-month time limit.

Guidelines

See D-X, 7.2. If limitation proceedings have commenced and finished within the nine-month period, a new nine-month period is not initiated by publication of the decision to limit in the European Patent Bulletin.

15.2.2 Where and how should the opposition be filed?

1090 Art. 99(1)
r.2(1)

The opposition must be filed at the EPO.

In proceedings before the EPO, documents may be filed by delivery by hand, by postal services or by means of electronic communication. The President of the EPO lays down the details and conditions and, where appropriate, any special formal or technical requirements for the filing of documents. In particular, he may specify that confirmation must be supplied. If such confirmation is not supplied in due time, the opposition will be deemed not to have been received.

OJ

According to Decision of the President dated 03 January 2017 ([2017] O.J. A11), the filing offices of the EPO are Munich (headquarter and PschorrHofe buildings), the Hague and Berlin. Vienna is not a filing office. An opposition may be filed by fax but not by telegram or teletex (see Decision of the President dated 20.2.2019, [2019] O.J. A18). A confirmation copy may be requested but is not routinely required. If a requested confirmation copy is not filed within the two month period set then the opposition is deemed not to have been filed. Oppositions may also be filed electronically using EPO Online Filing (OLF), Online Filing 2.0 or the EPO Contingency Upload Service (see Decision of the President dated 03 May 2023, [2023] O.J. A48). The web form filing service may not be used and the opposition will be deemed not to have been received if filed in this way. E-mail should not be used as it has no legal force ([1999] O.J. 509; [2000] O.J. 458).

T858/18	Where an opposition filed by fax is received partly before midnight and partly after midnight it is considered to have been received on the later day. It is not possible to give the part of the opposition received before midnight the earlier filing date. This is due to the wording of the President's decision which distinguishes between the filing of patent applications and the receipt of other documents.

15.2.3 Who may file a notice of opposition?

Art. 99(1)	Any person may give notice to the European Patent Office of opposition to a granted European patent. 1091
G9/93	Headnote: A European patent cannot be opposed by its own proprietor.
Comment	The Enlarged Board overruled previous decision G1/84, holding that "any person" must be interpreted in the context of the EPC as a whole and, as determined in G9/91 and G10/91, opposition proceedings are essentially contentious proceedings. In the interests of equity and good faith the decision did not apply to pending self-oppositions.
G3/97	Headnote (1): (a) An opposition is not inadmissible purely because the person named as opponent according to r.55(a) EPC (now r.76(2)(a) EPC2000) is acting on behalf of a third party (i.e. as a strawman). (b) Such an opposition is, however, inadmissible if the involvement of the opponent is to be regarded as circumventing the law by abuse of process. (c) Such a circumvention of the law arises, in particular, if: (i) the opponent is acting on behalf of the patent proprietor; (ii) the opponent is acting on behalf of a client in the context of activities which, taken as a whole, are typically associated with professional representatives, without possessing the relevant qualifications required by Art. 134 EPC. (d) However, a circumvention of the law by abuse of process does not arise purely because (i) a professional representative is acting in his own name on behalf of a client; (ii) an opponent with either a residence or principal place of business in one of the EPC Contracting States is acting on behalf of a third party who does not meet this requirement. Headnote (2): In determining whether the law has been circumvented by abuse of process, the principle of the free evaluation of evidence is to be applied (i.e. on case by case basis, no special rules to be applied). The burden of proof is to be borne by the person alleging that the opposition is inadmissible. The deciding body has to be satisfied on the basis of clear and convincing evidence that the law has been circumvented by abuse of process (i.e. more than on the balance of probabilities).
G4/97	Headnotes (1) and (2): identical to G3/97(1) and (2). Headnote (3): The admissibility of an opposition on grounds relating to the identity of an opponent may be challenged during the course of the appeal, even if no such challenge has been raised before the Opposition Division. The Enlarged Board also decided that the decision should be applied to all pending proceedings since there was no valid legitimate expectation to protect on the basis of past case law.
Comment	In both these cases the Enlarged Board felt that it was allowable for a strawman to file an opposition as long as the "principal" he was acting for would have had the legal right to do so. No special interest is necessary since every member of the public has an interest to the extent that the ability to carry out certain acts is restricted by the patent.
G3/99	Headnote (1): An opposition filed in common by two or more persons, which otherwise meets the requirements of Art. 99 EPC and r.1 (now r.3 EPC2000) and r.55 EPC (now r.76 EPC2000) EPC is admissible on payment of only one opposition fee.
Comment	The situation where several natural or legal persons file an opposition in common is anticipated by r.151(1).
G3/99	Headnote (3): In order to safeguard the rights of the patent proprietor and in the interests of procedural efficiency, it has to be clear throughout the procedure who belongs to the group of common opponents or common appellants. If either a common opponent or appellant (including the common representative) intends to withdraw from the proceedings, the EPO shall be notified accordingly by the common representative or by a new common representative determined under r.100(1) EPC (now r.151(1) EPC2000) in order for the withdrawal to take effect.

G1/13	Headnote (1): Where an opposition is filed by a company which subsequently, under the relevant national law governing the company, for all purposes ceases to exist, but that company is subsequently restored to existence under a provision of that governing national law, by virtue of which the company is deemed to have continued in existence as if it had not ceased to exist, all these events taking place before a decision of the Opposition Division maintaining the opposed patent in amended form becomes final, the European Patent Office must recognise the retroactive effect of that provision of national law and allow the opposition proceedings to be continued by the restored company. Headnote (2): Where, in the factual circumstances underlying Question 1, a valid appeal is filed in due time in the name of the non-existent opponent company against the decision maintaining the European patent in amended form, and the restoration of the company to existence, with retroactive effect as described in Question 1, takes place after the expiry of the time limit for filing the notice of appeal under Article 108 EPC, the Board of Appeal must treat the appeal as admissible.
Comment	The Enlarged Board of Appeal considered that so far as the EPC is concerned, the existence and non-existence of legal entities is exclusively a matter of national law.
T9/00	One legal or natural entity may only file one opposition to a given patent – a second opposition filed will be deemed inadmissible for lack of legitimate interest.
OJ	An exclusive licensee is not barred from opposing the patent under which he is licensed (Decision of Opposition Division, [1992] O.J. 747).
Guidelines	See D-I, 4.

15.2.4   Form and content of the notice of opposition

1092	Art. 99(1)	Notice of opposition must be filed in accordance with the Implementing Regulations.
	r.76(1)	Notice of opposition must be filed in a written reasoned statement.
	r.1	In written proceedings before the EPO, the requirement to use the written form will be satisfied if the content of the documents can be reproduced in a legible form on paper.
	r.76(2)	The notice of opposition must contain: (a) particulars of the opponent as provided for in r.41(2)(c) (requirement for identifying the applicant in the request for grant); (b) the number of the European patent against which opposition is filed, the name of the proprietor of the patent and the title of the invention; (c) a statement of the extent to which the European patent is opposed (e.g. which claims) and of the grounds on which the opposition is based as well as an indication of the facts and evidence presented in support of these grounds; and (d) particulars of any representative appointed by the opponent as provided for in r.41(2)(d) (requirement for identifying a representative in the request for grant).
	Case law	Only an "indication" of the facts and evidence is necessary so that further facts and evidence can in principle be filed later (T204/91), but the opponent's case must be properly understood on an objective basis (T222/85). In the case of a prior use, the substantiation should include specific details of what was made available, where, when, how and by whom (T328/87, T93/89). If the wrong opponent is specified, or there are conflicting indications, this can be corrected under r.139 in order to introduce what was originally intended (T615/14 applying G1/12 by analogy). In particular, evidence of the original intention can be presented after expiry of the opposition period.
	r.76(3)	Part III of the Implementing Regulations (rr.35–54 – provisions governing the application) apply to the notice of opposition.
	Guidelines	In particular, the opposition must be signed pursuant to r.50(3) EPC (D-III, 3.4).
	r.83	Documents referred to in the notice of opposition must be filed along with it. If such documents are neither enclosed nor filed in due time upon invitation by the EPO, it may decide not to take into account any arguments based on them.
	Guidelines	See D-III, 3.1 and 6. A notice of opposition should be typewritten or printed with a left-hand margin of about 2.5 cm. An opponent not requiring representation can specify a further address for correspondence if it is the opponent's own address. See also D-VI, 1 – any ground, fact or evidence filed later than the opposition period is late-filed unless justified by a change in the proceedings.

15.2.5 Grounds for opposition

Art. 100	Opposition may only be filed on the grounds that: (a) the subject matter of the European patent is not patentable under Arts. 52–57; (b) the European patent does not disclose the invention in a manner sufficiently clear and complete for it to be carried out by a person skilled in the art; (c) the subject matter of the European patent extends beyond the content of the application as filed, or, if the patent was granted on a divisional application or on a new application filed under Art. 61, beyond the content of the earlier application as filed.
G1/91	Lack of unity is not a ground of opposition and may not even be raised as an objection against a patent that has been amended in opposition proceedings.
T263/05	Similarly, r.43(2), which limits the circumstances in which more than one independent claim in the same category may be used, is not a ground of opposition and should not be used as the basis for an objection to amended claims in opposition proceedings.
T443/97	Equally, the provisions of r.137(5) first sentence (amendment not to relate to unsearched subject matter which is not unitary) is a pre-grant issue only.
G1/95	A ground is an individual legal basis and Art. 100(a) describes a collection of individual grounds.
Guidelines	See D-III, 5 and D-V, 3–6. Lack of novelty with respect to an earlier national right, non-entitlement to the grant of a patent, lack of support for the claims under Art. 84 and the filing of an incorrect designation of inventor are examples of grounds that may not be invoked.

1093

15.2.6 Payment of the opposition fee

Art. 99(1)	The notice of opposition is not deemed to have been filed until the opposition fee has been paid.
RRFArt. 2(1)(10)	The opposition fee is € 880.
G1/18	By analogy with this decision relating to the appeal fee, the opposition fee should be refunded if the opposition is deemed not filed. See section 15.3.5 below concerning circumstances in which an opposition is deemed not filed.
Guidelines	The opposition fee falls due on the date that the notice of opposition is filed (A-X, 5.2.6). Only one fee is required in the case of joint opponents (D-III, 2 as per G3/99).

1094

15.2.7 Language of the notice of opposition

Art. 14(1)	The notice of opposition must be filed in an official language of the EPO.
Art. 14(4)	Nevertheless, natural or legal persons having their residence or principal place of business within a Contracting State having a language other than English, French or German as an official language, and nationals of that State who are resident abroad may file an opposition in an official language of that State and file a translation into an official language later.
r.6(2)	In the case where an official language of a Contracting State is used, a translation into an official language of the EPO must be filed within a period of one month, or within the opposition period if that expires later. If the time limit is not observed then further processing is not available since it is only available to the applicant in pre-grant proceedings (Art. 121). Furthermore, re-establishment would not be available since it only applies to the proprietor in first instance opposition proceedings (Art. 122).
T149/85	A person who files an opposition in an official language of a Contracting State must possess the necessary nationality/residence demanded by Art. 14(4).
Art. 14(4)	If any document, other than those making up the European patent application, is not filed in the prescribed language, or if any required translation is not filed in due time, the document is deemed not to have been filed.
Guidelines	See A-VII, 5. If filed in the wrong language, the notice of opposition is nevertheless put on file and communicated to the proprietor.

1095

15.2.8 Opposition may be filed even where a patent is surrendered or has lapsed

r.75	An opposition may be filed even if a European patent has been surrendered or has lapsed in all the designated Contracting States.
Comment	An opposition may also be continued in similar circumstances (see section 15.7.6).

1096

15.3   Examination of the opposition for admissibility and circumstances in which it is deemed not filed

15.3.1   An opposition must be admissible to be examined

1097 Art. 101(1)   The opposition must be admissible before it will be examined by the Opposition Division.
      T925/91   No comment is made on the substantive issues if the opposition is deemed inadmissible.
      Guidelines   See D-IV, 4.

15.3.2   A formalities officer can decide on admissibility in certain circumstances

1098 G1/02   Headnote: Points 4 and 6 of the Notice from the Vice-President Directorate-General 2 dated 28 April 1999 ([1999] O.J. 506) do not conflict with provisions of a higher level.

      Comment   This decision overruled T295/01, which had suggested that formalities officers could never decide on the admissibility of an opposition, only the Opposition Division being competent. A formalities officer can decide on admissibility where there are no technical or legal difficulties.

      T295/01   A formalities officer cannot decide on admissibility under r.76(2)(c) due to the complicated legal and technical matters involved.

      OJ   See Decision of the President 12.7.2007 ([2007] O.J. Special Edition No. 3, p. 106).

15.3.3   Deficiencies that must be corrected before the opposition period expires

1099 r.77(1)   If the notice of opposition:
                    (a) does not comply with Art. 99(1) (nine-month period); or
                    (b) does not comply with r.76(2)(c) (extent opposed, grounds of opposition, indication of facts and evidence); or
                    (c) does not sufficiently identify the opposed patent;
                    the Opposition Division will reject the opposition as inadmissible unless the deficiencies are remedied before the expiry of the opposition period.

      T376/90   If there is serious doubt about the extent of the opposition, it must be rejected as inadmissible.

      Case law   Admissibility has nothing to do with the strength of the case – an opposition that would have succeeded can be rejected as inadmissible whilst an opposition doomed to failure might be properly substantiated (T222/85, T2/89). Substantiation by way of just citing certain documents to support the alleged grounds is not enough. The legal and factual reasons (T550/85) must also be stated in order to allow the opponent's case to be understood on an objective basis (T222/85, T2/89). If the facts and evidence supplied cannot support the grounds of opposition as a matter of law then the opposition is inadmissible (e.g. using a prior national right to support an alleged lack of novelty) (T550/88).

      Guidelines   See D-IV, 1.2.2.1 in general. If the opposition does not indicate beyond any doubt the identity of the person filing the opposition then this is a deficiency under r.77(1) that must be corrected before the opposition period expires (see section 15.3.4 below for case law). The EPO should inform an opponent of any deficiency in good time for him to correct it where this is possible. However, such a communication cannot be expected as of right (D-IV, 1.3.3).

15.3.4   Deficiencies that may be corrected after the opposition period expires

1100 r.77(2)   If the Opposition Division notes that the notice of opposition does not comply with provisions other than those listed in r.77(1) it will communicate this to the opponent and invite him to remedy the deficiencies noted within a period to be specified. If the deficiencies are not remedied in due time, the Opposition Division will reject the opposition as inadmissible.

      T25/85   Thus deficiencies concerning the designation of the opponent, such as a missing address, may be remedied under r.77(2). The identify of the opponent, however, according to this decision, must be established within the opposition period for the opposition to be admissible.

T615/14	More recently, this decision (see also T2644/19) has cast some doubt on the principle established in T25/85 that the identity of the opponent must be established within the opposition period. According to this decision, T25/85 has been "superseded" by G1/12 and it is possible to correct a notice of opposition under r.139 in order to indicate the name of the opponent as long as it can be established, with evidence filed after the end of opposition period where necessary, what the true intention of the opponent was when filing the opposition. In both T615/14 and G1/12, however, it was a case of choosing between two different names that had been given rather than adding a name where none was originally indicated. According to the Guidelines (see D-IV, 1.2.2.1), the identity of the opponent must be indicated beyond any doubt by the end of the opposition period.
Guidelines	See D-IV, 1.2.2.2.

15.3.5 Circumstances in which the opposition is deemed not to have been filed

Art. 99(1)	Where no opposition fee is paid before the end of the opposition period, the opposition is deemed not to have been filed.	1101
r.76(3)/r.50(3)	The opposition must be signed. Where such a defect is not remedied following an invitation from the EPO the opposition is deemed not to have been received.	
r.2(1)	If the opposition is filed by facsimile, written confirmation must be supplied if asked for by the EPO (Decision of the EPO dated 20 February 2019, [2019] O.J. A18). If this is not provided within the time limit set, the opposition is deemed not to have been received.	
T665/89	Where a representative is necessary but the notice of opposition is filed by the proprietor and the signature of the proprietor on the request is not corrected then the opposition will be deemed not to have been filed.	
r.152(6)	Where the opposition is filed by a representative who does not present an authorisation when requested then the opposition will be deemed not to have been filed.	
Art. 14(1) and (4)	If the opposition is filed in the wrong language or if it is filed in the official language of a Contracting State and the translation required by Art. 14(4) is not filed in due time, the opposition is deemed not to have been filed.	
G1/18	By analogy with this decision, the opposition fee should be refunded if the opposition is deemed not to have been filed, in particular where either the notice of opposition, or the opposition fee, or both, are received after the expiry of the opposition period. See also T193/87.	
Guidelines	See D-IV, 1.2.1.	

15.3.6 Decision that opposition is inadmissible or deemed not filed is to be communicated to the proprietor

r.77(3)	Any decision to reject an opposition as inadmissible is communicated to the proprietor of the patent, together with a copy of the notice of opposition.	1102
Guidelines	See D-IV, 1.4.1, D-IV, 3, D-IV, 5.1 and D-IV, 5.5. A finding that the notice of opposition is deemed not filed is also communicated. Where the opposition is deemed not to have been filed, the would-be opponent can ask for an appealable decision according to r.112(2). The opposition fee is refunded. Where an opposition is considered inadmissible, the would-be opponent is notified of the relevant deficiency/deficiencies and asked to comment before a decision is taken. In all cases, the purported opposition is kept on file and treated as third party observations.	

15.4 Intervening in an opposition

Art. 105(1)	Any third party may, in accordance with the Implementing Regulations, intervene in opposition proceedings after the opposition period has expired, if the third party proves that: (a) proceedings for infringement of the same patent have been instituted against him (action letter not enough – proceedings must have started – this is a matter of national law); or (b) following a request of the proprietor of the patent to cease alleged infringement, the third party has instituted proceedings for a ruling that he is not infringing the patent.	1103
Art. 105(2)	An admissible intervention will be treated as an opposition.	

r.89(1)	Notice of intervention must be filed within three months of the date on which proceedings referred to in Art. 105 are instituted.
T296/93	The three-month period starts from the first relevant proceedings (e.g. in the case where the proprietor has sued for infringement and the alleged infringe has later applied for a declaration of non-infringement, the date of institution of the first action).
G4/91	Headnote: In a case where, after issue of a final decision by an Opposition Division (date decision handed to internal EPO postal system in the case of written proceedings– T631/94 as per G12/91), no appeal is filed by a party to the proceedings before the Opposition Division, a notice of intervention which is filed during the two-month period for appeal provided by Art. 108 EPC has no legal effect.
Comment	The Enlarged Board decided that an intervention can only be filed if opposition proceedings are in existence. This is not so where a decision of the Opposition Division has been issued, such a decision being final in the sense that the Opposition Division has no power to change it. Such a decision therefore terminates the opposition proceedings regardless of the fact that it takes legal effect only after the period for appeal has expired.
G1/94	Headnote: Intervention of the assumed infringer under Art. 105 EPC is admissible during pending appeal proceedings and may be based on any ground for opposition under Art. 100 EPC.
Comment	The convenience of having centralised revocation being balanced by the complication and delay to the appeal proceedings, the Enlarged Board was most swayed by the travaux préparatoires which indicated that intervention was contemplated during the appeal stage. The Board further considered that the intervener should be given the unfettered right to raise any ground of opposition. However, in view of G10/91, if a fresh ground is raised then the case should be remitted to the first instance unless there are special reasons to decide otherwise, such as the agreement of the patentee.
Comment	It is not yet clear whether an intervener can attack claims that were not attacked in the original opposition.
T2951/18	Not only may an intervener raise new grounds in opposition appeal proceedings, he may also rely on evidence that was filed by an opponent and not admitted by the opposition division.
T694/01	An intervention is dependent on the degree to which opposition/appeal proceedings are still pending. Thus, where the intervention occurs after a Board of Appeal has already decided on the allowable claims, in subsequent appeal proceedings concerning the adaptation of the description to those claims, the allowed claims may not be challenged.
G3/04	Headnote: After withdrawal of the sole appeal, the proceedings may not be continued with a third party who intervened during the appeal proceedings.
Comment	The Enlarged Board had previously decided that intervention during opposition appeal proceedings was possible (G1/94) but there was some doubt about the intervener's procedural status in this situation. This decision has made it clear that the intervener attains the status of an opponent under Art. 105(2) EPC and is a party to the appeal proceedings of right under Art. 107 EPC. The intervener does not, however, have the status of an appellant since he was not adversely affected by the decision taken. No appeal fee therefore needs to be paid. It also follows, from decision G7/91, that withdrawal of a sole appeal will terminate the proceedings, the consent of the intervener not being required.
RPBAArt. 14	RPBAArt. 12 (Basis of proceedings) and RPBAArt. 13 (Amendment to a party's case) apply to an intervention in opposition appeal proceedings mutatis mutandis.
T446/95	It is not possible to intervene based on proceedings initiated in respect of a national patent, even if the opposed European patent claims the priority of the national patent.
T7/07	It is not possible to intervene based on proceedings initiated in a state to which the European patent has been extended.
T1746/15	Proceedings for infringement under Art. 105(1)(a) are proceedings which establish whether or not a third party is commercially active in an area that falls within the patentee's right to exclude and not, for example, separate ex-parte evidentiary proceedings such as BSV proceedings in Germany or "saisie-contrefaçon" proceedings in France. See also T439/17.
T1702/17	It is admissible for an intervener to be part of the same group of companies as the opponent as long as it is a separate legal entity.

r.89(2)	Notice of intervention must be filed in a written reasoned statement. The requirements as to the form and content of an opposition (r.76) and the admissibility of an opposition (r.77) apply to a notice of intervention. It is not deemed to have been filed until the opposition fee has been paid.
RRFArt. 2(1)(10)	The opposition fee is € 880.
Guidelines	See D-I, 5, D-IV, 5.6 and D-VII, 6. Admissibility needs to be considered as for an opposition but only according to Art. 105 and r.89. The intervener is asked whether he wishes to receive copies of documents already filed in the proceedings.

15.5 Opposition to apply to all designated States

Art. 99(2)	An opposition applies to the European patent in all the Contracting States in which that patent has effect.	1104
Guidelines	See D-I, 3. If the opposition is filed in respect of some of the States, it is treated as if it were in respect of all the States.	

15.6 Parties to the opposition and transfer of party status

15.6.1 Proprietor and opponents are parties

Art. 99(2)	An opponent is a party to the opposition proceedings as well as the proprietor of the patent.	1105
Guidelines	See D-I, 6. An intervener also becomes a party to the proceedings. An opponent/intervener ceases to be a party to the proceedings if the opposition/intervention is withdrawn or rejected as inadmissible. Those filing third party observations in opposition proceedings do not become parties to the proceedings.	

15.6.2 Replacement of party status as a result of entitlement proceedings

Art. 99(4)	Where a person provides evidence that in a Contracting State, following a final decision, he has been entered in the patent register of such State instead of the previous proprietor, such person will, at his request, replace the previous proprietor in respect of such State. Notwithstanding Art. 118, the previous proprietor and the person making the request will not be deemed to be joint proprietors unless both so request.	1106
Guidelines	See D-I, 6.	

15.6.3 Transfer of the patent to a new proprietor during opposition proceedings

r.85	Rule 22 (registration of transfers) applies to any transfer of the European patent made during the opposition period or during opposition proceedings.	1107
NatLaw	The transfer must also be recorded in many designated States (see Table IX).	

15.6.4 Transfer of the opposition during opposition proceedings

r.84(2)	An opposition is automatically transferred in the case of universal succession from a deceased opponent to his or her heir.	1108
T425/05	An opposition is also automatically transferred in the case of universal succession when the opponent is a legal person, e.g. by merger or acquisition.	
G4/88	Headnote: An opposition pending before the EPO may be transferred or assigned to a third party as part of the opponent's business assets together with the assets in the interests of which the opposition was filed.	
Comment	The Enlarged Board considered that an opposition, giving rise to legal rights as a party, constitutes as inseparable part of a business's assets and may therefore be transferred with those assets.	
T234/18	However, party status is not automatically transferred along with the transfer of assets – there must be specific transfer of party status as well as a transfer of the assets in the interests of which the opposition was filed for the EPO to register the new opponent.	
G2/04	Headnote (1): (a) The status as an opponent cannot be freely transferred. (b) A legal person who was a subsidiary of the opponent when the opposition was filed and who carries on the business to which the opposed patent relates cannot acquire the status as opponent if all its shares are assigned to another company.	

Comment	This decision confirmed that an opposition cannot be freely assigned but may be transferred as a result of universal succession (e.g. from a deceased opponent to his/her heir (r.60(2) EPC now r.84(2) EPC2000) or in the takeover of a company, or the relevant assets of a company, by another legal entity (G4/88)). Where, however, company A, which has a legally independent subsidiary B, files an opposition relating to a business area in which company B operates, the opposition may not be transferred from A to a company which buys subsidiary B. The opposition would have been transferable if: (a) it had been filed in the name of the subsidiary company; or (b) B had not had its own legal status but had merely been a department of company A. Where a holding company files an opposition on behalf of a legally distinct subsidiary it is thus safer to file the opposition jointly in both names.
Case law	The right to appeal against maintenance of the patent may be transferred in the same way (T563/89) as may an appeal once initiated (T659/92).
Guidelines	See D-I, 4. The EPO should examine the validity of any purported transfer at all stages of the proceedings (as per T1178/04).

15.7   Procedure for examination of the opposition

15.7.1   *Steps taken prior to examination of the opposition*

1109	r.79(1)(2)	The Opposition Division communicates the contents of the opposition to the proprietor and invites him to file his observations and to amend, where appropriate, the description, claims and drawings, within a period to be specified. At the same time, where several notices of opposition have been filed, the Opposition Division will communicate them to the other opponents.
	OJ	See Notice from the EPO dated 09 March 2022 ([2022] O.J. A28) – cited documents and other annexes (other than those that cannot be easily accessed by online file inspection) are no longer routinely sent along with communications under r.79(1) and (2) but are still supplied on special request by a party.
	r.132(1)	'A period to be specified' is one which is specified by the EPO.
	r.132(2)	The time limit set for reply must be from two to six months, usually from two to four months.
	r.132(2)	The time limit may be extended, at the discretion of the EPO, if a request for extension is submitted before its expiry.
	Guidelines	See D-IV, 5.2. A four month time limit is set.
	Guidelines	See E-VIII, 1.6. Any request for an extension of a time limit in opposition proceedings must be reasoned and will only be granted in exceptional circumstances (see also [2016] O.J. A42).
	OJ	In the case where accelerated proceedings have been requested by a party in view of litigation concerning the patent in a Contracting State or at the Unified Patent Court, an extension is particularly hard to obtain ([2023] O.J. Supplementary Publication 3, page 9).
	T663/99	The proprietor's right to be heard is violated if the Opposition Division hands a revocation decision to the internal postal service before this time limit for filing observations has expired.
	r.79(3)	Any observations and/or amendments filed by the proprietor are communicated to the other parties, who are themselves invited, if the Opposition Division considers it expedient, to reply within a period to be specified.
	r.79(4)	These communications are optional in the case of an intervention.
	Guidelines	See D/IV/5.2 and 5.4. See also E/VIII/1.6 – if a response is not filed in due time then there is no loss of rights but the proceedings progress to the next stage in any case which could be a decision under Art. 101(2) or (3).

15.7.2   *Examination as to whether the grounds of opposition prejudice the patent*

1110	Art. 101(1)	If the opposition is admissible, the Opposition Division will examine, in accordance with the Implementing Regulations, whether at least one ground for opposition under Art. 100 prejudices the maintenance of the European patent.

r.81(1)	The Opposition Division will examine those grounds for opposition which are invoked in the opponent's statement under r.76(2)(c). Grounds for opposition not invoked by the opponent may be examined by the Opposition Division of its own motion if they would prejudice the maintenance of the European patent.
Art. 101(1)	While examining the opposition, the Opposition Division will invite the parties, as often as necessary, to file observations on communications from another party or issued by itself.
r.81(2)	Communications under Art. 101(1), and all replies thereto, will be sent to all parties. If the Opposition Division considers it expedient, it will invite the parties to reply within a period to be specified.
r.81(3)	In any communication under Art. 101(1), the proprietor of the European patent shall, where necessary, be given the opportunity to amend, where appropriate, the description, claims and drawings. Where necessary, the communication will contain a reasoned statement covering the grounds against the maintenance of the European patent.
Case law	The Opposition Division has discretion whether or not to treat observations (other than those under r.79(1)) as admissible and in many circumstances no Art. 101(1) invitation will be necessary (e.g. T275/89). However, Art. 113(1) must be respected (e.g. T669/90).
Guidelines	See D-V

15.7.3 Permissible amendments of the patent during opposition

Art. 123(1)	A European patent may be amended in accordance with the Implementing Regulations.	1111
r.80	Without prejudice to r.138 (different text for different States due to prior national rights), the description, claims and drawings may be amended provided that the amendments are occasioned by a ground for opposition under Art. 100, even if that ground has not been invoked by the opponent.	
T295/87	It follows from r.79(1) and r.81(3) that amendments must be "appropriate" and "necessary" in order to be admissible.	
Art. 101(3)	Amendments made must meet all the requirements of the EPC. In particular, the protection should not be extended (Art. 123(3) – see section 21.6).	
Case law	There is a wide power to consider all the requirements of the EPC (T227/88) except unity (G1/91) and r.43(2) (T263/05) but in the case of a lack of clarity, which is not a ground of opposition, only to the extent that objections arise directly from the amendments themselves (G3/14).	
G3/14	Headnote: In considering whether, for the purposes of Article 101(3) EPC, a patent as amended meets the requirements of the EPC, the claims of the patent may be examined for compliance with the requirements of Article 84 EPC only when, and then only to the extent that the amendment introduces non-compliance with Article 84.	
Comment	The Enlarged Board settled the divergence in the case law by deciding that the established jurisprudence should prevail over more recent decisions such as T1459/05. Since lack of clarity is not a ground of opposition, the examination of clarity in opposition proceedings is strictly limited to a lack of clarity arising directly from an amendment made during the opposition proceedings. The simple combination of an independent claim and one of its dependent claims cannot introduce a lack of clarity if both were present in the patent as granted.	
Guidelines	See D-V, 5. No lack of clarity therefore arises from merely: (1) combining an independent claim with a dependent claim of the granted patent; (2) combining an embodiment of a dependent claim with an independent claim in the granted patent; (3) deleting part of a claim of the granted patent to narrow its scope and leaving a pre-existing lack of clarity; or (4) deleting optional features from a claim. However, a lack of clarity may arise if: (1) a feature is taken from the description; or (2) a feature is extracted from a dependent claim in which it was associated with other features.	
T123/85	Where claims are limited during opposition proceedings, this does not imply any surrender of the subject matter of the claims as granted and deleted claims may in principle be reinstated during appeal proceedings.	
Comment	If the number of claims increases as a result of amendments made to the patent then no additional claims fees are payable.	

Guidelines	See H-II, 3.1 and 3.2. Under r.80, for example, a proprietor can submit amendments to address a potential added subject-matter problem even if this ground has not been raised but cannot simply add further claims. However, corrections and clarifications not related to a ground of opposition may also be allowed pursuant to r.139 EPC once an amendment which is occasioned by a ground of opposition has been admitted (see H-VI, 2.1.1).
	See H-III, 3. One or more auxiliary requests may be submitted along with the main request. If the main request is allowable, auxiliary requests are ignored. If the main request is not allowable, on the other hand, the Opposition Division will consider any auxiliary requests in the sequence indicated by the proprietor until an allowable request is encountered. Reasons for the non-allowability of any higher-ranking request must be given. Each auxiliary request is a request for amendment and may be held to be inadmissible.
Guidelines	Amendments must be submitted in a timely manner in order to be admitted into the proceedings. See E-VI, 2.2 referring to H-II, 2.7.1 – late filed requests must be clearly allowable to be admitted. See E-VI, 2.2 and E-III, 8.6 in relation to oral proceedings and the r.116(1) time limit. The behaviour of both parties needs to be taken into account in considering the admissibility of late-filed amendments.

15.7.4   *Requirements relating to documents filed during opposition proceedings*

1112	r.86	Part III of the Implementing Regulations (rr.35–54 – provisions governing the application) apply to documents filed in opposition proceedings.

15.7.5   *Continuation of the opposition by the EPO of its own motion in the event of the withdrawal of an opposition or the death of an opponent*

1113	r.84(2)	Where an opposition is withdrawn or in the event of the death or legal incapacity of an opponent, the opposition proceedings may be continued by the EPO of its own motion, even without the participation of heirs or legal representatives.
	Case law	The opposition should be continued if it has reached the stage where a limitation or revocation is likely without further assistance from the opponent, e.g. in T197/88 where a r.58(4) (now r.82(1) EPC2000) communication had issued. If the Opposition Division does not continue the proceedings, it takes a decision to reject the opposition. Opposition appeal proceedings initiated by the opponent are terminated without a decision if an heir cannot be identified in response to a communication (T1213/13).
	Guidelines	See D-VII, 5.2. Proceedings should also be continued where the proprietor has submitted amendments (citing T560/90).
	G8/93	A Board of Appeal, however, cannot continue opposition appeal proceedings if the opponent is sole appellant and withdraws his appeal or opposition or if the proprietor is the sole appellant and withdraws his appeal.

15.7.6   *Continuation of the opposition where the patent has been surrendered or has lapsed*

1114	r.84(1)	If the European patent has been surrendered in all the designated Contracting States or has lapsed in all those States, the opposition proceedings may be continued at the request of the opponent filed within two months of a communication from the EPO informing him of the surrender or lapse.
	T329/88	The EPO must terminate the opposition proceedings if no reply is received from the opponent.
	T1403/16	The Opposition Division must take a reasoned decision when terminating proceedings.
	Case law	In opposition appeal proceedings, it is the appellant who has the choice whether to continue the proceedings or not, whether the appellant is the opponent or proprietor (see, e.g. T660/13). Where there is more than one appellant any one of them may choose to continue the proceedings.
	Guidelines	See D-VII, 5.1.

15.7.7 Extent to which the Opposition Division may examine the patent beyond the stated extent of and grounds for the opposition

G9/91	Headnote: The power of an Opposition Division or a Board of Appeal to examine and decide on the maintenance of a European patent under Articles 101 and 102 EPC (NB. now Art. 101 EPC2000) depends upon the extent to which the patent is opposed in the notice of opposition pursuant to Rule 55(c) EPC (NB. Now r.76(2)(c) EPC2000). However, subject-matters of claims depending on an independent claim, which falls in opposition or appeal proceedings, may be examined as to their patentability even if they have not been explicitly opposed, provided their validity is prima facie in doubt on the basis of already available information.
Comment	Rule 55(c) EPC1973 (now r.76(2)(c) EPC2000) was interpreted by the Enlarged Board as governing the legal and factual framework within which substantive examination of an opposition must in principle be conducted. Therefore, if the extent of the opposition is only partial (i.e. not all the independent claims are opposed) the Opposition Division has no competence to examine those claims which are not subject to any "opposition" at all. In contrast, where an independent claim is opposed, the Opposition Division may also examine any dependent claims provided that their validity is prima facie in doubt on the basis of the available information.
T809/21	There is no need for the proprietor to file a specific request that the patent be maintained on the basis of non-opposed claims. If any of the proprietor's broader claims are unallowable then the opposition division must commence the procedure to uphold the patent on the basis of the non-opposed claims in any case.
r.81(1)	Regarding new grounds of opposition, the Opposition Division may examine them of its own motion if they prejudice the maintenance of the opposed patent.
Comment	Before new r.81(1) was introduced as part of EPC2000, the right of the Opposition Division to examine new grounds was already apparent from G10/91. The Enlarged Board held that the Opposition Division is not obliged to consider all the grounds for opposition referred to in Art. 100 of its own motion but may nevertheless exceptionally consider grounds not substantiated in the notice of opposition where, prima facie, in whole or in part, they would seem to prejudice the maintenance of the European patent.
Guidelines	See D-V, 2.2 – it seems that the lack of the words "exceptionally" and "prima facie" in r.81(1) as compared with G10/91 is not significant as far as the EPO is concerned.
T736/95	The Opposition Division is obliged to at least consider whether any new ground raised by an opponent should be admitted.
Case law	Where an Opposition Division introduces a new ground it must inform the proprietor of the legal and factual bases supporting the new ground and give him a proper opportunity to comment (T433/93). In terms of citing new documents, the Opposition Division may introduce a document from the European Search Report if it has strong reasons to consider it relevant (T387/89) or a document cited in the patent as important prior art related to the problem solved (T536/88).
Guidelines	See D-V, 2.2 – Prior art acknowledged in the patent which is important for elucidating the technical problem addressed by the claimed invention is always part of the proceedings (citing T536/88).

15.7.8 Acceleration of proceedings

OJ	Opposition proceedings are accelerated at the request of any party when infringement proceedings relating to the patent are pending before the court of a Contracting State or the Unified Patent Court (see Notice from the EPO dated 24 April 2023, [2023] O.J. Supplementary Publication 3, page 9). In an accelerated procedure, the EPO aims to issue actions within a period of three months and will only extend time limits in exceptional and substantiated cases.
Guidelines	See D-VII, 1.2 and E-VIII, 5.

15.7.9 Further searches

Guidelines	See D-VI, 5. The Opposition Division may request the Search Division to carry out an additional European search where one is required. It may also cite new documents itself.

1115

1116

1117

15.7.10   Stay in the case of entitlement proceedings

1118   r.78(1)

If a third party provides evidence, during opposition proceedings or during the opposition period, that he has instituted proceedings against the proprietor of the European patent, seeking a decision within the meaning of Art. 61(1), opposition proceedings will be stayed unless the third party communicates to the EPO in writing his consent to the continuation of such proceedings. Such consent is irrevocable. However, proceedings will not be stayed until the Opposition Division has deemed the opposition admissible. The provisions of r.14(2)–(4) apply mutatis mutandis.

Comment

Note that the Protocol on Recognition does not operate after grant. See also section 21.3 (stay during grant proceedings) for further details, e.g. concerning time limits on resumption. A specific example of the calculation of time limits on resumption is also given in Guidelines D-VII, 4.3.

Guidelines

See D-VII, 4. The Legal Division is responsible for decisions on stay and resumption of proceedings. The EPO may set a date on which it intends to continue the proceedings, taking into account the time it will take for a final judgement of the court to be obtained. Proceedings should be resumed if delaying tactics are being used by the third party, a judgement against the third party has been issued which has been appealed or the patent can in any case be maintained unamended. The patent proprietor is not consulted before a decision to stay proceedings is taken but he can ask for an appealable decision if he disagrees with the stay. Automatic debit orders cease to be effective if a stay is instituted and must be re-filed on resumption of the proceedings.

15.7.11   Different claims for different States when two proprietors are defending the patent

1119   r.78(2)

Where a third party has, in accordance with Art. 99(4), replaced the previous proprietor for one or some of the designated Contracting States, the patent as maintained in opposition proceedings may, for these States, contain claims, a description and drawings different from those for the other designated States.

15.7.12   Revocation where no text is approved or patent is surrendered

1120   Guidelines

See D-VI, 2.2 and D-VII, 5.1. The patent will be revoked where the proprietor no longer approves the text as granted and does not propose another text, asks for revocation or "surrenders" the patent.

15.7.13   Requirement to submit cited documents

1121   r.83

Documents referred to by a party to opposition proceedings must be filed together with the written submissions. If such documents are neither enclosed nor filed in due time upon invitation by the EPO, it may decide not to take into account any arguments based on them.

Guidelines

See D-IV, 1.2.2.1(v). A time limit of two months is usually set.

15.8   Procedure if the opposition succeeds

1122   Art. 101(2)

If the Opposition Division is of the opinion that at least one ground for opposition prejudices the maintenance of the European patent, it will revoke the patent.

Art. 101(3)(b)

If the Opposition Division is of the opinion that, taking into consideration the amendments made by the proprietor of the European patent during the opposition proceedings, the patent and the invention to which it relates do not meet the requirements of the EPC, it will revoke the patent.

Guidelines

See D-VIII, 1.2. The patent is also revoked if the proprietor fails to complete the formalities of maintaining the patent in amended form (r.82(3)) or the proceedings are interrupted and a required new representative is not appointed (r.142(3)(a)).

Art. 68

In the case of revocation, the patent and application giving rise to it will be deemed, from the outset, not to have given rise to any rights.

15.9 Procedure if the opposition fails

Art. 101(2)   If the Opposition Division is of the opinion that none of the grounds for opposition prej-   1123
udices the maintenance of the European patent, it will reject the opposition.

15.10 Procedure if the opposition is partly successful

15.10.1 Interlocutory decision or decisions prior to final decision

Art. 101(3)(a)   If the Opposition Division is of the opinion that, taking into consideration the amend-   1124
ments made by the proprietor of the European patent during the opposition proceedings,
the patent and the invention to which it relates meet the requirements of the EPC, it will
decide to maintain the patent as amended, provided that the conditions laid down in the
Implementing Regulations are fulfilled.

r.82(4)   The decision to maintain the European patent as amended will state which text of the
patent forms the basis for the decision.

Art. 68   In the case where the patent is maintained in amended form, the patent and application
giving rise to it will be deemed, from the outset, not to have given rise to any rights in
respect of deleted subject matter.

Comment   Instead of conducting the formalities of r.82(1) and r.82(2) and taking a decision to maintain the patent directly, the opposition division will take an interlocutory decision that
the patent as amended, and the invention to which it relates, meet the requirements of the
EPC. Such an interlocutory decision is subject to appeal and avoids the proprietor having
to potentially pay translation and printing fees and revalidate the patent twice should the
text of the patent change again on appeal. Such an interlocutory decision is provided for
in principle by Art. 106(2) – one that does not terminate proceedings with respect to one
of the parties – and was recognised by G1/88. It may be that during appeal proceedings
the claims are further amended but the board of appeal remits the matter back to the opposition divison for corresponding amendment of the description. In this case, opposition
proceedings will be reopened before the opposition division for amendment of the description and another interlocutory decision will be issued concerning the final text of the
patent which is also subject to appeal with respect to the description amendments. Only
after all appeal proceedings are terminated and the text of the patent to be maintained is
finally fixed will the opposition division proceed according to r.82(1) and r.82(2) and take
a final decision.

15.10.2 Notification of the text of the amended patent

r.82(1)   Before the Opposition Division decides to maintain the European patent as amended it   1125
will inform the parties of the text in which it intends to maintain the patent, and will invite
them to file their observations within two months if they disapprove of that text.

OJ   The communication under r.82(1) is rarely used now following G1/88 since the parties
will usually be asked to comment on the proposed text during oral proceedings and this
suffices for an interlocutory decision to be issued ([1989] O.J. 393).

Comment   It will, however, be necessary if oral proceedings are not held and the procedure is conducted in writing. This is often the case, for instance, when the description is being amended following agreement on a set of claims in appeal proceedings.

G1/88   Headnote: The fact that an opponent has failed, within the time allowed, to make any
observations on the text in which it is intended to maintain the European patent after being invited to do so under r.58(4) EPC (now r.82(1) EPC2000) does not render his appeal
inadmissible.

Comment   It had become practice that in the event the opponent made no comment his silence was
interpreted as tacit approval and hence he was not "adversely effected" and could not
appeal. This practice was reversed. Rule 82(1) is seen not as a mandatory procedure but
one option for obtaining the proprietor's approval of the text (Art. 113(2)) and giving the
opponent a chance to comment (Art. 113(1)). These objects can also be achieved at oral
proceedings.

r.82(2)   If a party disapproves of the text communicated by the Opposition Division, examination
of the opposition may be continued.

Guidelines	See D-VI, 7.2. The patent proprietor's approval for the text can be inferred where he has filed that text himself. If the patent proprietor objects to the proposed text, proceedings are continued and the patent can be revoked if a new text is not put forward. If the opponent objects to the proposed text then the proceedings are continued if the Opposition Division agrees with any of the objections.

15.10.3 Need for payment of printing fee/filing of claim translations

1126	r.82(2)	If the opposition preoceedings are not to be continued, based on an objection of one of the parties to the text proposed by the opposition division, the Opposition Division will, on expiry of the period under r.82(1), invite the proprietor of the patent to pay the prescribed fee and to file a translation of any amended claims in the official languages of the EPO other than the language of the proceedings, within a period of three months.
	RRFArt. 2(1)(8)	The prescribed fee is € 85.
	Comment	Note that no provision exists for the payment of any claims fees if the number of claims has increased.
	r.82(2)	Where, in oral proceedings, decisions under Art. 106(2) (interlocutory decisions taken by the Opposition Division) or Art. 111(2) (decisions taken by a Board of Appeal to remit the case for further prosecution by the Opposition Division), have been based on documents not complying with the applicable requirements prescribed by the President of the EPO under r.49(2), the proprietor of the patent shall be invited to file the amended text in a form compliant with those requirements within the three month period.
	OJ	The applicable requirements under r.49(2) are those in Art. 2(7) of Decision of the President dated 25 November 2022 ([2022] O.J. A113), as specified in Art. 5 of that decision (documents to be typed or printed etc).
	OJ	See Notice from the EPO dated 09 March 2016 ([2016] O.J. A22). Amendments that do not comply with the requirements prescribed by the President under r.49(2) are only accepted in oral proceedings before the Opposition Division and not in written proceedings. Proprietors will still be encouraged to submit formally compliant documents in oral proceedings and given facilities to support this. The authentic text remains the text submitted and agreed in the oral proceedings.
	r.82(3)	If the acts required under r.82(2) are not performed in due time they may still be validly performed within two months of a communication concerning the failure to observe the time limit, provided that a surcharge is paid within this period.
	Comment	The acts are not performed if (1) no reply is received; (2) no fee is paid; (3) no claim translations are filed; (4) documents submitted to comply with the applicable requirements prescribed by the President under r.49(2) are incomplete; (5) documents submitted to comply with the applicable requirements prescribed by the President under r.49(2) are still formally deficient; or (6) documents submitted to comply with the applicable requirements prescribed by the President under r.49(2) have a different content from the corresponding documents submitted in oral proceedings.
	RRFArt. 2(1)(9)	The surcharge is € 135.
	r.82(3)	If the relevant acts are still not performed on expiry of the two months grace period then the patent is revoked.
	G1/90	Headnote: The revocation of a patent under Art. 102(4) and (5) EPC requires a decision (NB. The relevant provision is now r.82(3) under EPC2000). The Enlarged Board considered that whereas grant proceedings can be terminated by a loss of rights or a decision, the EPC requires that opposition proceedings are terminated by a decision and this literal interpretation of the EPC is in accord with the travaux préparatoires, procedural convenience and legal certainty.
	Art. 122	Re-establishment is available (see Guidelines E-VII, 2.2.3 – further processing is not possible in post-grant proceedings).
	T1934/16	However, an appeal is not a suitable remedy. In this case an appeal was filed following revocation of the patent and the missing claim translations were filed along with the grounds of appeal, the fee and surcharge also both being paid at the same time. The Board of Appeal found the appeal unallowable since the finding of the Opposition Division had been correct.
	Guidelines	See D-VI, 7.2.3 and D-VIII, 1.2.2.

15.10.4   Publication of a new specification where the patent is amended – new patent certificate

Art. 103   If a European patent is maintained as amended under Art. 101(3)(a), the EPO will publish   1127
a new specification of the European patent as soon as possible after the mention of the
opposition decision has been published in the European Patent Bulletin.

r.87   The new specification of the European patent includes the description, claims and drawings as amended. The provisions of r.73(2) (President of the EPO to determine the form
of the publication and the data to be included), r.73(3) (designated States to be included in
the specification) and r.74 (issue of a certificate) apply.

Guidelines   See D-VII, 7.

15.11   Costs

15.11.1   Rules for the apportionment of costs

Art. 104(1)   Each party to the opposition proceedings must bear the costs it has incurred unless the   1128
Opposition Division, for reasons of equity, orders, in accordance with the Implementing
Regulations, a different apportionment of costs.

Case law   Equity may demand a different apportionment where evidence has been late filed (e.g.
T117/86), a request for oral proceedings has been withdrawn at the last minute (e.g.
T556/96) or a party has not attended oral proceedings (e.g. T930/92).

r.88(1)   Apportionment of costs will be dealt with in the decision on the opposition. Such apportionment will only take into consideration the expenses necessary to assure proper
protection of the rights involved. The costs will include the remuneration of the representatives of the parties.

T212/88   A request for a decision on costs must be made before the final decision is taken.

Guidelines   See D-IX and E-IV, 1.9. The decision on costs deals only with the obligation of the party or parties to bear costs and does not consider the amount to be paid (see fixing of
costs below). The Opposition Division may take a decision to apportion costs even if
no application has been made by one of the parties. Costs taken into account may include expenditure associated with witnesses/experts, remuneration of representatives and
travel expenses. Costs may be equitably apportioned, for example, where the proprietor
surrenders the patent just before oral proceedings and it was obvious he had no case to
argue or a party deliberately files a document late leading to the necessity for further oral
proceedings.

15.11.2   Opposition Division to fix amount of costs to be paid

Art. 104(2)   The procedure for fixing costs is laid down in the Implementing Regulations.   1129

r.88(2)   The Opposition Division will, on request, fix the amount of costs to be paid under a final
decision apportioning them. A bill of costs, with supporting evidence, must be attached
to the request. Costs may be fixed once their credibility is established.

Guidelines   See D-IX, 2.1. Once a decision on the apportionment of costs has become final, the Opposition Division fixes the amount to be paid when requested. The parties are then notified of the amounts fixed.

r.88(3)   A request for a decision by the Opposition Division may be filed within one month of the
communication on the fixing of costs under r.88(2). The request must be filed in writing
and state the grounds on which it is based. It will not be deemed to be filed until the prescribed fee has been paid.

Guidelines   See D-IX, 2.2. A party may ask the Opposition Division to review the costs it has fixed
and take a decision on the matter. The decision is then subject to appeal if the amount
fixed in the decision is more than the appeal fee (see below).

RRFArt. 2(1)(16)   The fee for a decision on the fixing of costs under r.88(3) is € 85.

Art. 122   Re-establishment is available for the proprietor if the time-limit is missed (further processing is not available in post-grant proceedings).

r.88(4)   The Opposition Division will decide on the request under r.88(3) without oral proceedings.

15.11.3   Enforcement of decisions on costs in Contracting States

1130   Art. 104(3)

Any final decision of the European Patent Office fixing the amount of costs must be dealt with, for the purpose of enforcement in the Contracting States, in the same way as a final decision given by a civil court of the State in which enforcement is to take place. Verification of such decision must be limited to its authenticity.

Guidelines

See D-IX, 3. A "decision" in this sense refers to either the fixing of costs by the Opposition Division under r.88(2) or a decision on the fixing of costs taken by the Opposition Division under r.88(3).

15.11.4   Restrictions on appealing an award of costs

1131   Art. 106(3)

The right to file an appeal against decisions relating to the apportionment or fixing of costs in opposition proceedings may be restricted in the Implementing Regulations.

r.97(1)

The apportionment of costs of opposition proceedings cannot be the sole subject of an appeal.

r.97(2)

A decision fixing the amount of costs of opposition proceedings cannot be appealed unless the amount exceeds that of the fee for appeal.

RRFArt. 2(1)(11)

The appeal fee is € 2015 or € 2925 depending on the appellant.

15.11.5   Costs in opposition appeal proceedings

1132   RPBAArt. 16(1)

Subject to Art. 104(1) EPC, a Board of Appeal may on request order a party to pay some or all of another party's costs. Without limiting the Board's discretion, such costs include those incurred by any:
(a) amendment pursuant to RPBAArt. 13 to a party's appeal case;
(b) extension of a period;
(c) acts or omissions prejudicing the timely and efficient conduct of oral proceedings;
(d) failure to comply with a direction of the Board;
(e) abuse of procedure.

RPBAArt. 16(2)

The costs ordered to be paid may be all or part of those incurred by the receiving party and may inter alia be expressed as a percentage or as a specific sum. In the latter event, the Board's decision shall be a final decision for the purposes of Art. 104(3) EPC. The costs ordered may include costs charged to a party by its professional representative, costs incurred by a party itself whether or not acting through a professional representative, and the costs of witnesses or experts paid by a party but shall be limited to costs necessarily and reasonably incurred.

Chapter 16: Limitation and Revocation Proceedings

16.1   The right to limit a European patent or have it revoked

Art. 105a(1)	At the request of the proprietor, a European patent may be revoked or limited by an amendment of the claims.
Guidelines	See D-X, 1. The request may be filed at any time after the grant of the patent, even after expiry of the patent since the effects of limitation/revocation are retroactive (Art. 68). See also D-X, 11 – multiple requests for limitation are possible so that the patent may be limited sequentially in a series of steps.
r.90	The subject of limitation or revocation proceedings is the European patent as granted or as amended in opposition proceedings or previous limitation proceedings before the EPO.
Comment	Limitation or revocation proceedings cannot therefore be based on the patent as amended in national proceedings in a Contracting State though limitation proceedings could be used to bring the European patent as a whole into line with such amendments.
Guidelines	See D-X, 4.2 – where more than one post-grant proceeding has already taken place the basis for limitation or revocation is the outcome of the most recent one.
r.91	Decisions on requests for limitation or revocation are taken by the Examining Division, composed according to Art. 18(2).
Art. 105b(3)	The decision to limit or revoke the patent applies in respect of all Contracting States and it is therefore necessary for the requester to be the sole proprietor or to file evidence that he is entitled to act on behalf of any other proprietors (r.92(2)(c)). This is true even if the patent has lapsed in those States in which the requester is not the proprietor in view of the retroactive effect of limitation and revocation (Art. 68).
Guidelines	See D-X, 10.1 – although the decision applies to all states, different claim sets may be maintained for different states pursuant to r.138 if prior national rights exists or, for applications filed under EPC1973, if a prior European right applies to only some states (Art. 54(4), r.23a and r.87 EPC1973). See also D-X, 10.2 – the effect of the limitation may also be different in different states if the claims are already heterogeneous across the designated states.

1133

16.2   Where and how should a request for limitation or revocation be filed?

Art. 105a(1)	The request must be filed with the EPO.
r.2(1)	In proceedings before the EPO, documents may be filed by delivery by hand, by postal services or by means of electronic communication. The President of the EPO lays down the details and conditions and, where appropriate, any special formal or technical requirements for the filing of documents. In particular, he may specify that confirmation must be supplied. If such confirmation is not supplied in due time, documents filed subsequent to the application will be deemed not to have been received.
OJ	According to Decision of the President dated 03 January 2017 ([2017] O.J. A11), the filing offices of the EPO are Munich (headquarter and PschorrHofe buildings), the Hague and Berlin. Vienna is not a filing office. A request for limitation or revocation may be filed by fax but not by telegram or teletex (see Decision of the EPO dated 20.2.2019, [2019] O.J. A18). A confirmation copy may be requested but is not routinely required. If a requested confirmation copy is not filed within the two month period set then the fax is deemed not to have been received. A request for limitation or revocation may also be filed electronically using EPO Online Filing (OLF), Online Filing 2.0 or the EPO Contingency Upload Service (see Decision of the President dated 03 May 2023, [2023] O.J. A48). The web form filing service may not be used – a request filed in this manner is considered not to have been received. E-mail should not be used as it has no legal force ([1999] O.J. 509; [2000] O.J. 458).
Comment	If the request is filed at a different EPO office or at a national office and forwarded to an EPO filing office then it makes little difference since there is no time limit for filing a request for limitation or revocation (except that a request for revocation received before opposition proceedings commence will be processed whereas a request for revocation received after opposition proceedings commence will be deemed not filed – see below).

1134

16.3   What language may a request for limitation or revocation be filed in?

1135   r.92(1)

A request for limitation or revocation can be filed in either an official language of the EPO or an official language of a Contracting State if a translation is filed in one of the official languages of the EPO within the period specified in r.6(2).

Comment

It seems that an official language of a Contracting State can be used by anybody in this case, regardless of nationality or residence, since no reference to Art. 14(4) is made.

Guidelines

See D-X, 2.1.

r.6(2)

A translation, where required, must be filed within one month of filing the request for limitation or revocation.

Art. 14(4)

If the translation is not filed in time then the request is deemed not filed.

Comment

Further processing (Art. 121) is not available in post-grant proceedings. Re-establishment is therefore available if the time limit is missed in spite of all due care having been shown (Art. 122). However, the easier way to proceed would be to simply file the request again.

16.4   What fees are due in respect of a request for limitation or revocation?

1136   Art. 105a(1)

A request for limitation or revocation will not be deemed filed until the limitation or revocation fee has been paid.

RRFArt. 2(1)(10a)

The fee is € 1305 for limitation and € 590 for revocation.

Guidelines

The fee falls due on the day that the request for limitation or revocation is filed (A-X, 5.2.6).

16.5   Content and form of the request for limitation or revocation

1137   Art. 105a(1)

The request for limitation or revocation must be filed in accordance with the Implementing Regulations.

r.92(1)

The request for limitation or revocation must be filed in writing. Part III of the Implementing Regulations (rr.35–54, requirements relating to a European patent application) apply mutatis mutandis to documents filed in limitation or revocation proceedings.

r.1

In written proceedings before the EPO, the requirement to use the written form is satisfied if the contents of the documents can be reproduced in a legible form on paper.

r.92(2)

The request must contain:

(a) particulars of the proprietor of the European patent making the request (the requester) as provided for in r.41(2)(c) (requirements relating to the request for grant) and an indication of the Contracting States for which the requester is the proprietor of the patent;

(b) the number of the patent whose limitation or revocation is requested and a list of the Contracting States in which the patent has taken effect;

(c) where appropriate, the names and addresses of the proprietors of the patent for those Contracting States in which the requester is not the proprietor of the patent, and evidence that the requester is entitled to act on their behalf in the proceedings;

(d) where limitation of the patent is requested, the complete version of the amended claims and, as the case may be, of the amended description and drawings; and

(e) where the requester has appointed a representative, particulars as provided in r.41(2)(d) (requirements relating to the request for grant).

Guidelines

One or more auxiliary requests may be filed along with the main request (H-III, 3.5).

16.6   Opposition proceedings take precedence

1138   Art. 105a(2)

A request for limitation or revocation may not be filed while opposition proceedings in respect of the European patent are ongoing.

r.93(1)

If such a request is filed when opposition proceedings in respect of the patent are pending, the request will be deemed not to have been filed.

r.93(2)

If, at the time of filing an opposition to a European patent, limitation proceedings in respect of that patent are pending, the Examining Division will terminate the limitation proceedings and order reimbursement of the limitation fee. Any fee paid according to r.95(3) first sentence will also be reimbursed.

Guidelines

See D-X, 7 – note that pending revocation proceedings are not terminated by the filing of an opposition. A decision to terminate limitation proceedings is notified to the requester.

16.7 Circumstances in which the request is deemed not to have been filed

Guidelines

See D-X, 2.1. The request is deemed not to have been filed if the fee has not been paid   1139
(Art. 105a(1)), if it is filed while opposition proceedings are pending (r.93(1)), if the request is filed in an inadmissible language or if it is filed in the official language of a Contracting State and a translation is not filed (Art. 14(4)), where a representative is necessary
but it is filed by the proprietor and the signature of the proprietor on the request is not
corrected (T665/89), where it is filed by a representative who does not present an authorisation when requested (r.152(6)), where it is not signed and the defect is not rectified
(r.92(1)/r.50(3), where it is filed by facsimile and a requested confirmation copy is not filed
(Decision of the EPO dated 20 February 2019, [2019] O.J. A18).

16.8 Circumstances in which the request is rejected as inadmissible

r.94

If the Examining Division finds that the request for limitation or revocation fails to com-   1140
ply with the requirements of r.92, it will invite the requester to correct the deficiencies
noted, within a period to be specified. If the deficiencies are not corrected in due time, the
Examining Division will reject the request as inadmissible.

r.132

The period will be specified by the EPO and will likely be from two to four months in
duration. Extension is possible.

Art. 121

Further processing is not available in post-grant proceedings.

Art. 122

Re-establishment would be available but re-filing the request would be more
straightforward.

Guidelines

See D-X, 2.2.

16.9 Decision on a request for revocation

Art. 105b(1)

The EPO will examine whether the requirements laid down in the Implementing Regula-   1141
tions for revoking the European patent have been met.

Art. 105b(2)

If the EPO considers that the request for revocation of the European patent meets the
requirements laid down in the Implementing Regulations, it will decide to revoke the European patent in accordance with the Implementing Regulations. Otherwise it will reject
the request.

r.95(1)

If a request for revocation is admissible, the Examining Division will revoke the patent
and communicate this to the requester.

Art. 105b(3)

The decision to revoke the European patent applies to the European patent in all the Contracting States in respect of which it has been granted. It takes effect on the date on which
the mention of the decision is published in the European Patent Bulletin.

Art. 68

The effect of revocation is retrospective so that the application and patent are deemed
never to have bestowed any rights.

Guidelines

See D-X, 3. If a request for revocation is admissible then the patent is revoked without
any further examination.

16.10 Decision on a request for limitation

Art. 105b(1)

The EPO will examine whether the requirements laid down in the Implementing Regula-   1142
tions for limiting the European patent have been met.

r.95(2)

If a request for limitation is admissible, the Examining Division will examine whether
the amended claims constitute a limitation vis-à-vis the claims as granted or amended in
opposition or limitation proceedings and comply with Art. 84 (clarity, conciseness, support), Art. 123(2) (added matter) and Art. 123(3) (extension of protection). If the request
does not comply with these requirements, the Examining Division will give the requester
one opportunity to correct any deficiencies noted, and to amend the claims and, where
appropriate, the description and drawings, within a period to be specified.

r.132(2)

A period to be specified by the EPO is usually between two and four months and in certain cases up to six months and may be extended on request if such a request is presented
before expiry of the original period set.

r.95(4)

If the requester does not respond in due time to the communication issued under r.95(2),
the Examining Division will reject the request.

Comment	Further processing is not available in post-grant proceedings but reestablishment would be available if the time limit was missed in spite of all due care having been taken. Alternatively, the request for limitation can simply be re-filed.
Guidelines	See D-X, 4.3–4.5. A "limitation" according to the EPO is a reduction in the extent of protection conferred by one of the claims. Mere clarifications are not allowable. Nor is the introduction of a new dependent claim possible. It is allowable, however, to limit the scope of a dependent claim without limiting any independent claim. The patentability of the amended claims is not examined (unless the limitation results in a prima facie non-compliance, e.g. when a generic claim to plants is limited to a particular variety – see H-IV, 5.4.3). If a limitation has been made, then correction of transcription and obvious mistakes can be corrected under r.139. Oral proceedings must be granted if requested. Third-party observations under Art. 115 are possible while limitation proceedings are pending. Different claim sets in respect of different States are possible where relevant national rights exist or where the application was filed under EPC1973 and a prior European right exists only in respect of some States.
Art. 105b(2)	If the EPO considers that the request for limitation of the European patent meets the requirements laid down in the Implementing Regulations, it will decide to limit the European patent in accordance with the Implementing Regulations. Otherwise, it will reject the request.
r.95(4)	If the request for limitation is not allowable, the Examining Division will reject the request.
Art. 106(1)	A decision to reject the request can be appealed.
r.95(3)	If a request for limitation is allowable under r.95(2), the Examining Division will communicate this to the requester and invite him to pay the prescribed fee and to file a translation of the amended claims in the official languages of the EPO other than the language of the proceedings within a period of three months.
Guidelines	See D-X, 5. See also H-III, 3.5. If there are auxiliary requests and the main request allowable, a communication pursuant to r.95(3) based on the main request is sent. If the main request is unallowable, however, the Examining Division will inform the proprietor in a communication pursuant to r.95(2) and invite him to abandon the higher ranking request(s) in favour of an allowable auxiliary request – or else the request will be rejected. The Examining Division may not propose amendments itself with the r.95(3) communication since the proprietor would not have a chance to comment on them contrary to Art. 113(1).
RRFArt. 2(1)(8)	The prescribed fee is € 85.
r.95(3)/r.82(3)	If the acts under r.95(3) are not performed in due time, they may still be performed within two months of a communication concerning the failure to observe the time limit, provided that a surcharge is paid within this period.
RRFArt. 2(1)(9)	The surcharge is € 135.
r.95(3)	If the requester performs the acts in due time, the Examining Division will limit the patent.
r.95(4)	If the requester fails to perform the acts required under r.95(3) in due time, the Examining Division will reject the request.
Comment	Further processing is not available in post-grant proceedings. Reestablishment would be available if a time limit was missed in spite of all due care having been taken. Alternatively, the request for limitation can simply be re-filed.
Art. 105b(3)	The decision to limit the European patent applies to the European patent in all the Contracting States in respect of which it has been granted. It takes effect on the date on which the mention of the decision is published in the European Patent Bulletin.

16.11 Publication of an amended specification if the patent is limited

1143 Art. 105c	If the European patent is limited under Art. 105b(2), the EPO will publish the amended specification of the European patent as soon as possible after the mention of the limitation has been published in the European Patent Bulletin.
r.96	The amended European patent specification will include the description, claims and drawings as amended. The following provisions apply: r.73(2) (President to determine the form of the publication), r.73(3) (designated States to be indicated) and r.74 (certificate to be issued).

Chapter 17: Appeal Proceedings

17.1 The nature of appeal proceedings

G9/91	An appeal is a judicial procedure and the Boards of Appeal act as courts.	1144
T34/90	An appeal is a review of the decision under appeal on its merits and not a re-examination.	
RPBAArt. 12(2)	In view of the primary object of the appeal proceedings to review the decision under appeal in a judicial manner, a party's appeal case shall be directed to the requests, facts, objections and evidence on which the decision under appeal was based.	
G9/92	The initial request on appeal determines the extent of the proceedings in accordance with the principle of party disposition.	
RPBA	Note that in appeal proceedings, the provisions of Art. 106–Art. 111 and rr.97–103 are supplemented by the Rules of Procedure of the Boards of Appeal. A knowledge of the Rules of Procedure of the Boards of Appeal is therefore important for the EQE. See Supplementary Publication 1 of OJ 2022 for the most recent version.	

17.2 Decisions which may be appealed

Art. 106(1)	An appeal lies from decisions of the Receiving Section, Examining Divisions, Opposition Divisions and the Legal Division (NB. not the Search Division).	1145
J8/81, J2/93	A decision decides one or more issues and should be distinguished from a notification (of some event) and a communication (which usually requires a reply). Whether a document issued is a decision is a matter of substance, not a matter of form.	
J29/92	Where no decision has been issued, an appeal is inadmissible. However, the appeal fee is not refunded (J37/97).	
r.98	An appeal may be filed against the decision of an Opposition Division even if the European patent has been surrendered in all the designated Contracting States or has lapsed in all those States.	
Art. 106(2)	A decision which does not terminate proceedings as regards one of the parties can only be appealed together with the final decision, unless the decision allows separate appeal (interlocutory decision – see Guidelines E-X, 3).	
Art. 106(3)	The right to appeal a decision relating to the apportionment or fixing of costs in opposition proceedings is restricted in accordance with the Implementing Regulations.	
r.97(1)	The apportionment of costs of opposition proceedings cannot be the sole subject of an appeal.	
r.97(2)	A decision fixing the amount of costs of opposition proceedings cannot be appealed unless the amount exceeds that of the fee for appeal.	
G5/91	Headnote (2): There is no legal basis under the EPC for any separate appeal against an order of a director of a department of the first instance such as an Opposition Division rejecting an objection to a member of the division on the ground of suspected partiality. However, the composition of the Opposition Division may be challenged on such a ground of appeal against the final decision of the division or against an interlocutory decision under Art. 106(3) EPC allowing separate appeal.	
Comment	Here it was seen that Examining and Opposition Divisions have a duty to be impartial even though the EPC does not expressly provide for objections to their composition.	

17.3 Suspensive effect of an appeal on the decision appealed

Art. 106(1)	An appeal has suspensive effect.	1146
G2/19	If a third party within the meaning of Art. 115 EPC files an appeal against a decision to grant a European patent, the appeal does not have suspensive effect.	

Case law

The suspensive effect deprives the contested decision of all legal effect until the appeal is decided (J28/94). Such suspensive effect does not depend on the admissibility of the appeal (J8/98). But note that in J23/13 it was decided that if a decision to refuse an application was appealed and no grounds were filed so that the appeal was inevitably inadmissible, a divisional application could only be filed until the deadline for filing the grounds of appeal. The suspensive effect does not cancel the decision, it merely "freezes" the usual consequences of the decision until the appeal has been decided (J28/03). In this decision of the Legal Board of Appeal it was decided that a divisional application could validly be filed following the appeal of a decision to refuse but where a decision to grant was appealed a subsequently filed divisional would only be validly filed if the appeal was upheld (assuming the mention of grant had already taken place).

Guidelines

See E-XII, 1.

17.4   Who may appeal and who is a party to the appeal?

1147   Art. 107

Any party to proceedings adversely affected by a decision may appeal. Any other parties to the proceedings are parties to the appeal proceedings as of right.

J12/85

A party is adversely affected when what is decided is contrary to what was requested, including the granting of a patent with a text not approved by the applicant (J12/83). In contrast, if an opponent has indicated that he would not object to a patent amended in a certain way, he cannot be adversely affected by a decision maintaining the patent in that form (T156/90).

T611/90

There is no right of appeal when a party is only adversely affected to the extent that it disagrees with the reasoning or the grounds of a decision in its favour (see also T73/88).

G3/99

This case concerns the filing of an appeal by several opponents acting in common.
Headnote (2): If the opposing party consists of a plurality of persons, an appeal must be filed by the common representative under r.100 EPC (now r.151 EPC2000). Where the appeal is filed by a non-entitled person, the Board of Appeal will consider it not to be duly signed and consequently invite the common representative to sign it within a given time limit. The non-entitled person who filed the appeal will be informed of this invitation. If the previous common representative is no longer participating in the proceedings, a new common representative will be determined pursuant to r.100 EPC (now r.151 EPC2000).
Headnote (3): In order to safeguard the rights of the patent proprietor and in the interests of procedural efficiency, it has to be clear throughout the procedure who belongs to the group of common opponents or common appellants. If either a common opponent or appellant (including the common representative) intends to withdraw from the proceedings, the EPO shall be notified accordingly by the common representative or by a new common representative determined under r.100(1) EPC (now r.151 EPC2000) in order for the withdrawal to take effect.

T656/98

The party that appeals must be the same party that was adversely affected. If the company name has changed in the meantime (other than by a universal succession of rights), the transfer must be recorded at the EPO pursuant to r.22 before the expiry of the period for appeal under Art. 108. Later recordal does not retroactively validate the appeal.

T425/05

In the case of a universal succession of rights (i.e. where the opponent ceases to exist as a legal entity due to take-over or merger or where the opponent dies), the universal successor automatically acquires the right to appeal and no transfer needs to be recorded. See also T15/01.

G2/04

Headnote (2): If, when filing an appeal, there is a justifiable legal uncertainty as to how the law is to be interpreted in respect of the question of who the correct party to the proceedings is, it is legitimate that the appeal is filed in the name of the person whom the person acting considers, according to his interpretation, to be the correct party, and at the same time, as an auxiliary request, in the name of a different person who might, according to another possible interpretation, also be considered to be the correct party to the proceedings.

Comment

The questions answered by this decision of the Enlarged Board arose in opposition proceedings where the opposition had been filed by a holding company on behalf of its subsidiary which had been sold during the opposition proceedings. It was not clear whether the holding company or the new owner of the subsidiary was the correct appellant – the decision clarified that it was the holding company that had the right to appeal.

| G2/19 | An appeal filed by a third party within the meaning of Art. 115 EPC is inadmissible and the third party does not have the right to be heard orally. |

17.5 Notice of appeal

17.5.1 Time limit for filing a notice of appeal

Art. 108	A notice of appeal must be filed within two months of notification of the decision appealed.	1148
T390/86	The appeal period starts from notification in writing even if the decision has been announced orally after oral proceedings.	
T389/86	A notice of appeal may nevertheless be validly filed between oral pronouncement of a decision and written notification (see also T1354/18).	
Art. 121(4)	Further processing is not possible in respect of the time limit for filing a notice of appeal.	
Art. 122	Re-establishment is possible for an applicant or proprietor who has missed the deadline despite all due care required by the circumstances having been taken.	
G1/86	However, an opponent may not apply for re-establishment.	

17.5.2 Where and how may a notice of appeal be filed?

Art. 108	A notice of appeal must be filed directly at the EPO.	1149
r.2(1)	In proceedings before the EPO, documents may be filed by delivery by hand, by postal services or by means of electronic communication. The President of the EPO lays down the details and conditions and, where appropriate, any special formal or technical requirements for the filing of documents. In particular, he may specify that confirmation must be supplied. If such confirmation is not supplied in due time, an appeal will be deemed not to have been received.	
OJ	According to Decision of the President dated 03 January 2017 ([2017] O.J. A11), the filing offices of the EPO are Munich (headquarter and PschorrHofe buildings), the Hague and Berlin. Vienna is not a filing office. An appeal may be filed by fax but not by telegram or teletex (see Decision of the EPO dated 20.2.2019, [2019] O.J. A18). A confirmation copy may be requested but is not routinely required. If a requested confirmation copy is not filed within the two month period set then the notice of appeal is deemed not to have been filed. Appeals may also be filed electronically using EPO Online Filing (OLF), Online Filing 2.0 or the EPO Contingency Upload Service (see Decision of the President dated 03 May 2023, [2023] O.J. A48). The web form filing service may not be used – an appeal filed in this manner is deemed not received. E-mail should not be used as it has no legal force ([1999] O.J. 509; [2000] O.J. 458).	

17.5.3 Content and form of the notice of appeal

Art. 108	A notice of appeal must be filed in accordance with the Implementing Regulations.	1150
r.99(1)	The notice of appeal must contain: (a) the name and address of the appellant in accordance with r.41(2)(c) (requirements of the request); (b) an indication of the decision impugned; and (c) a request defining the subject of the appeal.	
Case law	Simply paying the appeal fee is not sufficient; the notice must contain an unequivocal statement of definite intent to contest the decision (T460/95) so that, e.g. an appeal as a subsidiary request is not good enough (T371/92).	
G9/92	The initial request defines the legal framework of the appeal proceedings according to the principle of party disposition (ne ultra petita).	
r.99(3)	Part III of the Implementing Regulations (rr.35–54, requirements for the European patent application) apply mutatis mutandis to the notice of appeal.	

17.5.4 Appeal fee

Art. 108	The notice of appeal is not deemed to have been filed until the appeal fee has been paid.	1151
RRFArt. 2(1)(11)	The appeal fee is € 2015 if the appeal is filed by a natural person or an entity referred to in r.6(4) and (5) EPC and € 2925 if filed by any other entity.	
Comment	Note that the reduction does not depend on the residence or nationality of the appellant or the language in which the appeal is filed.	

OJ

The appellant must make a declaration that it is an appropriate person or entity in the notice of appeal or a separate letter ([2018] O.J. A5). Where there are joint appellants, each one must be a natural person or an entity defined by r.6(4) EPC. The status of the appellant at the time the notice of appeal is filed is relevant and subsequent changes have no effect. Evidence may be request by the EPO in cases of doubt. If the appellant pays the reduced fee but does not have the correct status then the fee may be deemed not to have been paid which will have the consequence that the appeal is deemed not to have been filed (see G1/18 below).

T1060/19

If the declaration is not made when the fee is paid, this deficiency may be remedied at any time until the two-month time limit for filing the notice of appeal expires.

G2/97

Headnote: The principle of good faith does not impose any obligations on the Boards of Appeal to notify an appellant that an appeal fee is missing when the notice of appeal is filed so early that the appellant could react and pay the fee in time, if there is no indication – either in the notice of appeal or in any other document filed in relation to the appeal – from which it could be inferred that the appellant would, without such notification, inadvertently miss the time limit for payment of the appeal fee.

G1/18

Headnote (1): "An appeal is deemed not to have been filed in the following cases:
(a) where notice of appeal was filed within the two-month time limit prescribed in Art. 108, first sentence, EPC and the appeal fee was paid after expiry of that two-month time limit;
(b) where notice of appeal was filed after expiry of the two-month time limit presecribed in Art. 108, first sentence, EPC and the appeal fee was paid after expiry of that two-month time limit;
(c) where the appeal fee was paid within the two-month time limit prescribed in Art. 108, first sentence, EPC, for filing notice of appeal and notice of appeal was filed after expiry of that two-month time limit."
Headnote (2): "In the cases referred to in answers 1(a) to (c), reimbursement of the appeal fee is to be ordered ex officio."
Headnote (3): "Where the appeal fee was paid within or after the two-month time limit prescribed in Art. 108, first sentence, EPC for filing notice of appeal and no notice of appeal was filed at all, the appeal fee is to be reimbursed."

Case law

When an appellant pays the reduced amount of the appeal fee but is not entitled to the reduction, the case law concerning whether a remedy is available or whether the underpayment can be excused is inconsistent. See T1474/19 which reviews the case law in detail. In that case the appellant specified that the reduced fee should be paid by direct debit from an EPO account but a relevant declaration as to its status was not filed. The Board found that it is for the EPO to establish the amount of the appeal fee which should be debited based on all the information available to it and that the full amount should have been debited in spite of the applicant's indication to the contrary.

17.5.5   Refund of the appeal fee

r.103(1)

The appeal fee is reimbursed in full:
(a) in the event of interlocutory revision or where the Board of Appeal deems an appeal to be allowable, if such reimbursement is equitable by reason of a substantial procedural violation; or
(b) if the appeal is withdrawn before the filing of the statement of grounds of appeal and before the period for filing that statement has expired.

r.103(2)

The appeal fee is reimbursed at 75 % if, in response to a communication from the Board of Appeal indicating its intention to start substantive examination of the appeal, the appeal is withdrawn within two months of notification of that communication.

r.103(3)

The appeal fee is reimbursed at 50 % if the appeal is withdrawn after expiry of the period under r.103(1)(b), provided withdrawal occurs:
(a) if a date for oral proceedings has been set, within one month of notification of a communication issued by the Board of Appeal in preparation for these oral proceedings;
(b) if no date for oral proceedings has been set, and the Board of Appeal has issued a communication inviting the appellant to file observations, before expiry of the period set by the Board for filing observations;
(c) in all other cases, before the decision is issued.

r.103(4)

The appeal fee is reimbursed at 25 %:

(a) if the appeal is withdrawn after expiry of the period under r.103(3)(a) but before the decision is announced at oral proceedings;

(b) if the appeal is withdrawn after expiry of the period under r.103(3)(b) but before the decision is sent;

(c) if any request for oral proceedings is withdrawn within one month of notification of the communication issued by the Board of Appeal in preparation for the oral proceedings, and no oral proceedings take place.

r.103(5)	The appeal fee will be reimbursed under only one of the provisions of r.103(1)–(4). Where more than one rate of reimbursement applies, reimbursement will be at the higher rate.
r.103(6)	The department whose decision is impugned orders the reimbursement if it revises its decision and considers reimbursement equitable by reason of a substantial procedural violation. In all other cases, matters of reimbursement are decided by the Board of Appeal.
Comment	Current r.103 with new sections (2) to (5) entered into force on 01 April 2020 and applies both to appeals pending at that date and appeals filed later.
G3/03	The first instance can decide to refund the appeal fee under r.103(1)(a) but does not have the power to decide not to refund it – that decision lies with a Board of Appeal.
T5/81	If the procedural violation does not affect the ratio decidendi then it cannot be substantial (in repsect of r.103(1(a)).
Case law	Examples of substantial procedural violations include ignoring a request for oral proceedings (e.g. T283/88), not giving a party the right to be heard (e.g. J 14/82) and issuing an unreasoned decision (e.g. T493/88). A refund is usually considered "equitable" if the relevant procedural violation made the filing of the appeal necessary.
T853/16	The 75 % refund under r.103(2) is contingent on the board sending a relevant communication before it starts substantive examination of the appeal and such a communication is not mandatory. If no such communication is sent then the 75 % refund is not possible.
T1402/13	The "withdrawal" referred to in r.103(3) (which was numbered as r.103(2) at the time of this decision) is a procedural declaration of withdrawal on the part of the appellant and does not include a deemed withdrawal of the appeal as the result of a deemed withdrawal of the application in grant proceedings.
T1548/15	If a party agrees to terminate appeal proceedings due to the lapse of the patent in all states (r.84(1) EPC) then this is equivalent to the withdrawal of the appeal and a refund is possible.
T2361/18	If an appeal is withdrawn after a date for oral proceedings has been set but before the notification of a communication issued in preparation for the oral proceedings, the withdrawal occurs "within one month of notification" for the purpose of r.103(3)(a).
T265/14	The possibility of a refund under r.103(3)(b) (which was numbered as r.103(2)(b) at the time of this decision) applies to each and every communication sent by the Board.
T1730/16	It is also irrelevant under r.103(4)(c) whether the request for oral proceedings is withdrawn following the first or second communication in preparation for oral proceedings and whether the communication concerned addresses substantive issues or not.
Case law	There is disagreement in the case law as to whether a refund under r.103(4)(c) is possible for a party when a different party withdraws a request for oral proceedings and the oral proceedings then do not take place. Decisions T488/18 (appellant had not filed any request for oral proceedings) and T 598/19 (appellant's request for oral proceedings already withdrawn before the Board's communication) decided that reimbursement was possible in these circumstances. Decisions T795/19 and T777/15, however, consider that only a party that has requested oral proceedings and then actually withdraws its request within the terms of r.103(4)(c) can benefit from a refund. According to T2698/17 and T73/17, the withdrawal of the request for oral proceedings needs to be explicit and a simple statement that a party will not attend the oral proceedings is not sufficient, whereas T517/17 finds the opposite.
Guidelines	The fee falls due on the date that the notice of appeal is filed (A-X, 5.2.6).

17.5.6 Language of the notice of appeal

r.3(1)	Any official language of the EPO may be used.	1152

Art. 14(4)	An official language of one of the Contracting States may also be used by natural or legal persons having their residence or principle place of business within a Contracting State having an official language other than English, French or German, and nationals of such a state who are resident abroad. In this case, a translation into an official language of the EPO is required.
T149/85	It is the residence/nationality of the applicant, proprietor or opponent that is important, not that of the representative.
r.6(2)	A translation required under Art. 14(4) must be filed within one month of the filing of the notice of appeal, or within the deadline for filing the notice of appeal, whichever expires later.
Art. 14(4)	Where a translation is not filed in time, the notice of appeal is deemed not to have been filed.
Art. 121	Further processing is available to the applicant in pre-grant proceedings.
RRFArt. 2(1)(12)	The further processing fee is € 290 in this case.
Art. 122	Re-establishment is available to the proprietor in post-grant proceedings if all due care has been shown. Based on the reasoning of G1/86 it is probably not available to an opponent in this situation since the appeal is deemed not to have been filed, hence appeal proceedings are not yet pending.
r.6(3)	For appeals filed before 01 April 2014, a 20 % reduction in the appeal fee was available to an applicant, proprietor or opponent who availed himself of the Art. 14(4) option. The reduction was available regardless of the commercial status of the appellant. In order to take advantage of the reduction, the notice of appeal had to be filed in an official language of a Contracting State – the language of the grounds of appeal was irrelevant (G6/91).

17.6 Grounds of appeal

17.6.1 Time limit

1153	Art. 108	Within four months of notification of the decision, a statement setting out the grounds of appeal must be filed.
	T390/86	The appeal period starts from notification in writing even if the decision has been announced orally after oral proceedings.
	Art. 121(4)	Further processing is not possible in respect of the time limit for filing grounds of appeal.
	Art. 122	Re-establishment is possible for an applicant or proprietor who has missed the deadline despite all due care required by the circumstances having been taken.
	G1/86	Headnote: Art. 122 is not to be interpreted as being applicable only to the applicant and patent proprietor. An appellant as opponent may have his rights re-established under Art. 122 if he has failed to observe the time limit for filing the statement of grounds of appeal.
	Comment	An opponent may therefore apply for re-establishment where he has validly filed a notice of appeal but missed the time limit for filing the grounds. This is justified on the basis that a Board of Appeal is akin to a court and that the Contracting States all recognise the principle that parties before a court must be accorded the same procedural rights. Thus, once an appeal has been started, by filing a notice of appeal, the parties must be given equal procedural rights.

17.6.2 Where and how may grounds of appeal be filed?

1154	OJ	The filing offices of the EPO are Munich, the Hague and Berlin (Decision of the President dated 03 January 2017 – [2017] O.J. A11). Vienna is not a filing office. If grounds of appeal are filed at the Vienna office or a national office they will not receive a filing date until forwarded to and received by a filing office.
	r.2(1)	In proceedings before the EPO, documents may be filed by delivery by hand, by postal services or by means of electronic communication. The President of the EPO lays down the details and conditions and, where appropriate, any special formal or technical requirements for the filing of documents. In particular, he may specify that confirmation must be supplied. If such confirmation is not supplied in due time, documents filed subsequent to the application will be deemed not to have been received.
	OJ	See section 17.5.2 (notice of appeal) – the relevant decisions of the President apply in the same way.

Art. 14/r.6(2)	Grounds of appeal can either be filed in an official language of the EPO or in an official language of a Contracting State in the case of a person defined by Art. 14(4) EPC. In the latter case, a translation into an official language of the EPO must be filed within a one month period, or within the period for filing the grounds of appeal if it expires later.

17.6.3   Content of the grounds of appeal

Art. 108 r.99(2)	The grounds must be filed in accordance with the Implementing Regulations In the statement of grounds of appeal the appellant must indicate the reasons for setting aside the decision impugned, or the extent to which it is to be amended, and the facts and evidence on which the appeal is based.	1155
RPBA Art. 12(3)	The statement of grounds of appeal shall contain a party's complete case. Accordingly, it must set out clearly and concisely the reasons why it is requested that the decision under appeal be reversed, amended or upheld, and should specify expressly all the facts, arguments and evidence relied on. All documents referred to shall be: (a) attached as annexes insofar as they have not already been filed in the course of the grant, opposition or appeal proceedings or produced by the Office in said proceedings; (b) filed in any event to the extent that the Board so directs in a particular case.	
Case law	The statement of grounds must include a concise statement of the reasons why the appeal should be allowed and the contested decision set aside (J22/86, T145/88). The notice must address the actual grounds of the decision and not just add new material (T213/85) unless the situation has changed, e.g. new claims have been filed (T105/87) or the patentee has requested revocation in the meantime (T459/88). It is a legitimate ground for appeal that an opposition was itself inadmissible.	

17.7   Examination of the appeal for admissibility

Art. 110 RPBA Art. 4(1) r.101(1)	The appeal must be admissible for it to be examined. A specific member of the Board of Appeal is designated to consider admissibility. If the appeal does not comply with Art. 106 to Art. 108 (appealable decision, person entitled to appeal, time limit and form of appeal), r.97 (restrictions on appealing decision relating to costs), r.99(1)(b) (notice to contain an indication of the decision impugned), r.99(1)(c) (notice to contain a request defining the subject of the appeal) or r.99(2) (grounds to indicate reasons, facts and evidence, etc.) the Board of Appeal will reject it as inadmissible unless any deficiency has been rectified before the relevant period under Art. 108 (two or four months) has expired.	1156
r.101(2)	If the Board of Appeal notes that the appeal does not comply with r.99(1)(a) (name and address of appellant) it will communicate this to the appellant and invite him to remedy the deficiencies noted within a period to be specified. If the deficiencies are not remedied in due time the Board of Appeal will reject the appeal as inadmissible.	
G1/12	Headnote (1): The answer to reformulated question (1) – namely whether when a notice of appeal, in compliance with Rule 99(1)(a) EPC, contains the name and address of the appellant as provided in Rule 41(2)(c) EPC and it is alleged that the identification is wrong due to an error, the true intention having been to file on behalf of the legal person which should have filed the appeal, is it possible to correct this error under Rule 101(2) EPC by a request for substitution by the name of the true appellant – is yes, provided the requirements of Rule 101(1) EPC have been met. Headnote (2): Proceedings before the EPO are conducted in accordance with the principle of free evaluation of evidence. This also applies to the problems under consideration in the present referral. Headnote (3): In cases of an error in the appellant's name, the general procedure for correcting errors under Rule 139, first sentence, EPC is available under the conditions established by the case law of the boards of appeal.	
Comment	The Enlarged Board approved of the principles established by T97/98 in this decision and held that the applicant's name can be corrected if such correction does not reflect a change of mind but only expresses what was originally intended. Evidence of that true intention can be brought forward after the expiry of the period for filing a notice of appeal.	
G1/13	For admissibility when a company is dissolved and later restored, see section 15.2.3.	

Comment	In certain cases, an appeal will be deemed not filed. This is the case, for example, if the appeal fee has not been paid in time (Art. 108, G1/18), if the notice of appeal is filed in an inadmissible language or if it is filed in the official language of a Contracting State and a translation is not filed (Art. 14(1) and (4)), where a representative is necessary but the notice of appeal is filed by the applicant/proprietor/opponent and the signature is not corrected (T665/89), where the notice of appeal is filed by a representative who does not present an authorisation when requested (r.152(6)), where the notice of appeal is not signed and the defect is not rectified (r.92(1)/r.50(3) and where the notice of appeal is filed by facsimile and a requested confirmation copy is not filed (see section 17.5.2).

17.8   Interlocutory revision

1157 Art. 109(1)	If the department whose decision is contested considers the appeal to be admissible and well founded, it will rectify its decision. This does not apply where the appellant is opposed by another party to the proceedings.
Comment	This means that interlocutory revision is only possuble during grant proceedings or where all opponents have withdrawn their oppositions.
T139/87	An appeal is "well founded" where the first instance changes its mind or where amendments submitted meet the objection on which the decision was based, even where other objections still exist.
T898/96	Where an application is refused because no text for grant has been approved and the applicant files an appeal, approving the previously proposed text, interlocutory revision should be allowed but the appeal fee should not be refunded.
T219/93	Where amendments are proposed that meet the objections in the decision but raise new issues not yet discussed, interlocutory revision must be allowed since the applicant is entitled to consideration by two instances.
T919/95	Where an application has been refused and the applicant files an appeal maintaining, as a main request, a request considered unallowable by the Examining Division and also filing, as an auxiliary request, a request considered allowable by the Examining Division, no interlocutory revision on the basis of the auxiliary request is possible. See also Guidelines E-XII, 7.4.3.
r.103(1)(a)	In the event of interlocutory revision, the appeal fee is reimbursed if such reimbursement is equitable by reason of a substantial procedural violation (see section 17.5.5 for case law).
r.103(6)	Reimbursement of the appeal fee is ordered by the department whose decision is impugned if it sees fit – in all other cases, matters of reimbursement are decided by the Board of Appeal.
Art. 109(2)	If the appeal is not allowed within three months of receipt of the statement of grounds, it must be remitted to the Board of Appeal without delay, and without comment as to its merit.
Guidelines	See E-XII, 7.4.1 and 7.4.2. Interlocutory revision should be granted if the applicant draws attention to a substantial procedural violation that took place during first instance proceedings (e.g. a violation of the right to be heard or the right to oral proceedings) regardless of the first instance division's opinion on the substantive merits of the requests put forward on appeal. It should generally be allowed if amendments have been made which overcome the grounds for refusal, even if further new objections arise, but not if the amendments are clearly unallowable under Art. 123(2) EPC.

17.9   Examination of the appeal

17.9.1   General procedure to be used

1158 Art. 110	If the appeal is admissible, the Board of Appeal will examine whether the appeal is allowable. The examination of the appeal is conducted in accordance with the Implementing Regulations.
r.100(2)	In the examination of the appeal, the Board of Appeal invites the parties, as often as necessary, to file observations, within a period to be specified, on communications issued by itself or observations submitted by another party.

RPBAArt. 5	A member of the Board, the 'rapporteur', is designated to conduct a preliminary study of the appeal, assess the priority of the appeal, prepare communications, make preparations for meetings of the Board and oral proceedings and draft decisions. Where warranted, the Chairman may also designate an additional rapporteur. These activities are carried out under the direction of the Chair.
RPBAArt. 12(1)	Appeal proceedings are based on (a) the decision under appeal and minutes of any oral proceedings before the department having issued that decision; (b) the notice of appeal and statement of grounds of appeal filed pursuant to Art. 108 EPC; (c) in cases where there is more than one party, any written reply of the other party or parties to be filed within four months of notification of the grounds of appeal; (d) any communications sent by the Board and any answer thereto filed pursuant to the directions of the Board; and (e) minutes of any video or telephone conference with the party or parties sent by the Board.
RPBAArt. 12(3)	The statement of grounds of appeal and the reply must contain a party's complete case. Accordingly they shall set out clearly and concisely the reasons why it is requested that the decision under appeal be reversed, amended or upheld, and should specify expressly all the requests, facts, objections, arguments and evidence relied on. All documents referred to must be: (a) attached as annexes insofar as they have not already been filed in the course of the grant, opposition or appeal proceedings or produced by the Office in said proceedings; (b) filed in any event to the extent that the Board so directs in a particular case.
RPBAArt. 12(4)	Any part of a party's appeal case that does not meet the requirements of RPBAArt. 12(2) (i.e. which goes beyond the requests, facts, objections, arguments and evidence on which the decision under appeal was based) is to be regarded as an amendment, unless the party demonstrates that this part was admissibly raised and maintained in the proceedings leading to the decision under appeal. Any such amendment may be admitted only at the discretion of the Board. The party shall clearly identify each amendment and provide reasons for submitting it in the appeal proceedings. In the case of an amendment to a patent application or patent, the party shall also indicate the basis for the amendment in the application as filed and provide reasons why the amendment overcomes the objections raised. The Board shall exercise its discretion in view of, inter alia, the complexity of the amendment, the suitability of the amendment to address the issues which led to the decision under appeal, and the need for procedural economy.
RPBAArt. 12(5)	The Board has discretion not to admit any part of a submission by a party which does not meet the requirements in RPBAArt. 12(3) (i.e. not contained in the grounds of appeal).
RPBAArt. 12(6)	The Board shall not admit requests, facts, objections or evidence which were not admitted in the proceedings leading to the decision under appeal, unless the decision not to admit them suffered from an error in the use of discretion or unless the circumstances of the appeal case justify their admittance. The Board shall not admit requests, facts, objections or evidence which should have been submitted, or which were no longer maintained, in the proceedings leading to the decision under appeal, unless the circumstances of the appeal case justify their admittance.
RPBAArt. 12(7)	Periods specified by the Board may exceptionally be extended at the Board's discretion upon a written and reasoned request, presented before the expiry of such period. The same applies mutatis mutandis to the period referred to in RPBAArt. 12(1)(c) (response of other parties to grounds of appeal); however, this period may only be extended up to a maximum of six months.
RPBAArt. 12(8)	Subject to Art. 113 and Art. 116 EPC, the Board may decide the case at any time after filing of the statement of grounds of appeal or, in the cases where there is more than one party, after expiry of the period referred to in RPBAArt. 12(1)(c) (response of other parties to grounds of appeal).
r.100(3)	In pre-grant appeal proceedings, if the applicant fails to reply in due time to an invitation under r.100(2), the European patent application is deemed to be withdrawn, unless the decision impugned was taken by the Legal Division.
Art. 121	Further processing is possible in this situation.
RRFArt. 2(1)(12)	The further processing fee is € 290 in this case.

Art. 122	Re-establishment is possible in respect of the Art. 121 time limit.
r.100(1)	Unless otherwise provided, the provisions relating to proceedings before the department which took the decision impugned apply to appeal proceedings.
r.99(3)	Part III of the Implementing Regulations (rr.35–54, requirements for the European patent application) apply mutatis mutandis to documents filed in appeal proceedings.
RPBAArt. 17(1)	In the written phase of proceedings, replies to requests and directions on matters of procedure shall be given by means of communications.
RPBAArt. 17(2)	If a Board deems it expedient to communicate with the parties regarding a possible appreciation of substantive or legal matters, such communication shall be made in such a way as not to imply that the Board is in any way bound by it.

17.9.2   Extent to which the Board of Appeal in opposition proceedings may introduce new grounds or examine new claims

1159 G9/91	Headnote: The power of an Opposition Division or a Board of Appeal to examine and decide on the maintenance of a European patent under Articles 101 and 102 EPC (NB. now Art. 101 EPC2000) depends upon the extent to which the patent is opposed in the notice of opposition pursuant to Rule 55(c) EPC (NB. Now r.76(2)(c) EPC2000). However, subject-matters of claims depending on an independent claim, which falls in opposition or appeal proceedings, may be examined as to their patentability even if they have not been explicitly opposed, provided their validity is prima facie in doubt on the basis of already available information.
Comment	This case, along with G10/91, concerns the extent to which an Opposition Division or Board of Appeal is allowed to or obliged to examine a patent beyond the stated extent of and grounds for an opposition. Rule 76(2)(c) was interpreted by the Enlarged Board as governing the legal and factual framework within which substantive examination of an opposition must in principle be conducted. Therefore, if the extent of the opposition is only partial (i.e. not all the independent claims are opposed) the Board of Appeal has no competence to examine non-opposed claims, such claims not being subject to any "opposition" at all. In contrast, where an independent claim is opposed, the Board of Appeal may also examine any dependent claims provided that their validity is prima facie in doubt on the basis of the available information.
G10/91	As regards grounds of opposition, a Board of Appeal is not obliged to consider all grounds of opposition referred to in Art. 100 and indeed may in principle not introduce new grounds of opposition at the appeal stage. The only exception is where the patentee consents to the introduction of such grounds. This more restricted approach (as compared with the Opposition Division) is justified by the less administrative, more judicial nature of appeal proceedings.
G1/95	Headnote: In a case where a patent has been opposed on the grounds set out in Art. 100(a) EPC, but the opposition has only been substantiated on the grounds of lack of novelty and lack of inventive step, the ground of unpatentable subject matter based on Art. 52(1) and (2) EPC (i.e. non-invention) is a fresh ground for opposition and accordingly may not be introduced into the appeal proceedings without the agreement of the patentee.
G7/95	Headnote: In a case where a patent has been opposed under Art. 100(a) EPC, on the ground that the claims lack an inventive step in view of documents cited in the notice of opposition, the ground of lack of novelty based on Art. 52(1) and Art. 54 EPC is a fresh ground for opposition and accordingly may not be introduced into the appeal proceedings without the agreement of the patentee. However, the allegation that the claims lack novelty in view of the closest prior art document (i.e. only this document which is an integral part of the inventive step determination) may be considered in the context of deciding upon the ground of lack of inventive step.
Comment	Thus, if the ground of novelty is new but the claims lack novelty over the closest prior art then the patent can be revoked for lack of inventive step since there is no difference between the invention and the closest prior art on the basis of which to formulate an objective technical problem. This does not mean that the ground of lack of novelty has been introduced into the proceedings.

In consolidated cases G1/95 and G7/95 "grounds for opposition" under Art. 100(a) were interpreted as individual legal bases for objection, i.e. "invention", "novelty", "inventive step" and "industrial application". In the context of G10/91, a fresh ground was seen as one which was neither raised and substantiated in the notice of opposition nor introduced into the proceedings by the Opposition Division under Art. 114(1).

T443/96   Similarly, a ground of added matter under Art. 123(2)/Art. 100(c) cannot be raised during appeal proceedings without the consent of the patentee if not raised during the opposition proceedings.

T131/01   Where a notice of opposition has raised the grounds of lack of novelty and lack of inventive step over a particular document but only the lack of novelty has been substantiated, it would be inconsistent to argue for lack of inventive step at the same time (there being no "step" between the prior art and the invention). In these circumstances, the Board of Appeal may consider a lack of inventive step attack without the permission of the patentee. Note that in this case the ground "lack of inventive step" had been formally entered by ticking the appropriate box on the notice of opposition form and was properly substantiated in view of the substantiation of the "lack of novelty" ground. In this context, the Board of Appeal was not technically introducing a new ground of opposition into the proceedings.

T184/17   Building on T131/01, the Board found in this case that even when the ground of inventive step is neither raised nor substantiated in the notice of opposition nor discussed during opposition proceedings, an objection of lack of inventive step can exceptionally be examined in appeal proceedings without the agreement of the patentee if it stays within the same factual and evidentiary framework of a novelty objection properly raised and substantiated in the notice of opposition.

T274/95   It is possible to introduce a ground substantiated in the notice of opposition even if it is not part of the decision appealed and was not relied on by the opponent before the first instance.

17.9.3 Extent to which the Board of Appeal in examination proceedings may introduce new grounds or examine new claims

G10/93   Headnote: In an appeal from a decision of an Examining Division in which a European   1160
             patent application was refused, the Board of Appeal has the power to examine whether
             the application or the invention to which it relates meets the requirements of the EPC.
             The same is true for requirements which the Examining Division did not take into consid-
             eration in the examination proceedings or which it regarded as having been met. If there
             is reason to believe that such a requirement has not been met, the board shall include this
             ground in the proceedings.

Comment   The Enlarged Board contrasted ex parte examination appeals where the grounds for re-
             fusal under Art. 97(2) are comprehensive and the appeal can only improve the position
             of the applicant whose application has been refused with inter partes opposition appeals
             where the grounds for opposition are limited and in the event of the patent being upheld
             in amended form the applicant could have his position improved or made worse. Whether
             an additional matter should be ruled on by the Board or remitted to the first instance for
             examination is a matter of judgement depending on the facts of each case.

17.9.4 Reformatio in peius

Comment   "The prohibition of reformatio in peius" refers to the principle that when somebody ap-   1161
             peals a legal decision as the sole appellant, they should not end up in a worse position than
             if they had not appealed. Note that the doctrine only applies where a patent is maintained
             in amended form in opposition proceedings, leaving both parties adversely affected, and
             only one of the parties is an appellant.

G9/92   This case examines the situation where a patent is maintained in amended form during op-
             position proceedings and only one of the parties appeals. The principle of the prohibition
             of reformatio in peius applies such that the non-appealing party may not make requests
             more favourable to itself than the decision of the Opposition Division.

Headnote (1): If the patent proprietor is the sole appellant against an interlocutory decision maintaining a patent in amended form, neither the Board of Appeal or the non-appealing opponent as a party to the proceedings as of right under Art. 107 EPC may challenge the maintenance of the patent as amended in accordance with the interlocutory decision.

Headnote (2): If the opponent is the sole appellant against an interlocutory decision maintaining a patent in amended form, the patent proprietor is primarily restricted during appeal proceedings to defending the patent in the form in which it was maintained by the Opposition Division in its interlocutory decision. Amendments proposed by the patent proprietor as a party to the proceedings as of right under Art. 107 may be rejected as inadmissible by the Board of Appeal if they are neither appropriate nor necessary.

Comment The Enlarged Board (by majority) felt that the subject matter of proceedings is the appeal itself and not a general re-examination. Further, it would be unfair if one party did not comply with the time limit for appeal but was still allowed, effectively, to appeal the decision.

G1/99 This decision considered in more detail the position in Headnote (2) of G9/92 where the opponent is sole appellant and in particular the meaning of "neither appropriate nor necessary".

Headnote: In principle, an amended claim, which would put the opponent and sole appellant in a worse situation than if it had not appealed, must be rejected. However, an exception to this principle may be made in order to meet an objection put forward by the opponent/appellant or the Board during the appeal proceedings, in circumstances where the patent as maintained in amended form would otherwise have to be revoked as a direct consequence of an inadmissible amendment held allowable by the Opposition Division in its interlocutory decision. In such circumstances, in order to overcome the deficiency, the patent proprietor/respondent may be allowed to file requests, as follows: (i) in the first place, for an amendment introducing one or more originally disclosed features which limit the scope of the patent as maintained; (ii) if such a limitation is not possible, for an amendment introducing one or more originally disclosed features which extend the scope of the patent as maintained, but within the limits of Art. 123(3) EPC; (iii) finally, if such amendments are not possible, for deletion of the inadmissible amendment but within the limits of Art. 123(3) EPC.

Comment In the view of the Enlarged Board, equity demands that the proprietor should not lose his patent where he has not appealed against a decision taken by the Opposition Division to maintain a patent in a form considered by the Board of Appeal to be invalid, the invalidity only being curable by increasing the scope of protection vis-à-vis the interlocutory decision. In particular, the opponent always has another chance to contest validity at the national level.

Case law If the factual situation changes on appeal then this may justify an exception to the principle of the prohibition of reformation in peius since the decision of the proprietor not to appeal is based on the facts of the first instance proceedings. This may occur, for example, if a lack of clarity objection is made against the limiting amendment (T974/10) or a new document is introduced whose prior art effect makes the validity of the priority claim important, the right to priority having been compromised by the limiting amendment (T1843/09).

17.9.5 *Intervention of an assumed infringer is possible in appeal proceedings*

1162 **G1/94** See section 15.4.

17.9.6 *Discretion to hear accompanying persons*

1163 **G4/95, G2/94** See section 25.11.6.

17.9.7 *Amendment of case during appeal proceedings*

1164 **r.100(1)** Unless otherwise provided, the provisions relating to proceedings before the department which has taken the decision impugned shall apply to appeal proceedings.

RPBA Art. 13(1) Any amendment to a party's appeal case after it has filed its grounds of appeal or reply is subject to the party's justification for its amendment and may be admitted only at the discretion of the Board.

RPBAArt. 12(4)–(6) shall apply mutatis mutandis (see section 17.9.1 above).

The party shall provide reasons for submitting the amendment at this stage of the proceedings.

The Board shall exercise its discretion in view of, inter alia, the current state of the proceedings, the suitability of the amendment to resolve the issues which were admissibly raised by another party in the appeal proceedings or which were raised by the Board, whether the amendment is detrimental to procedural economy, and, in the case of an amendment to a patent application or patent, whether the party has demonstrated that any such amendment, prima, facie, overcomes the issues raised by another party in the appeal proceedings or by the Board and does not give rise to new objections.

RPBAArt. 13(2) Any amendment to a party's appeal case made after the expiry of a period specified by the Board in a communication under r.100(2) EPC (asking for observations to be filed within a specified period) or, where such a communication is not issued, after notification of a summons to oral proceedings shall, in principle, not be taken into account unless there are exceptional circumstances, which have been justified with cogent reasons by the party concerned.

RPBAArt. 13(3) Other parties shall be entitled to submit their observations on any amendment not held inadmissible by the Board ex officio.

17.9.8 Accelerated procedure

OJ Appeal proceedings may be accelerated where a legitimate interest exists, e.g. where infringement proceedings have been brought or are envisaged, where a licensing deal is contingent on the result of the appeal or where an opposition subject to accelerated processing is involved (see Notice from the vice-President of DG3 dated 17 March 2008, [2008] O.J. 220). See also Guidelines E-VIII, 6. 1165

RPBAArt. 10(3) On request by a party, the Board may accelerate the appeal proceedings. The request shall contain reasons justifying the acceleration and shall, where appropriate, be supported by documentary evidence. The Board shall inform the parties whether the request has been granted.

RPBAArt. 10(4) If a court or other competent authority in a Contracting State requests acceleration of the appeal proceedings, the Board shall inform the court or authority and the parties whether the request has been granted and when oral proceedings, if foreseen, are likely to take place.

RPBAArt. 10(5) The Board may accelerate the appeal proceedings of its own motion.

RPBAArt. 10(6) If the Board accelerates the appeal proceedings, it shall give the appeal priority over other appeals. The Board may adopt a strict framework for the proceedings.

17.9.9 Consolidation of proceedings

RPBAArt. 10(1) If several appeals are filed from a decision, these appeals shall be dealt with in the same proceedings. 1166

RPBAArt. 10(2) If appeals are filed from separate decisions but are clearly connected to each other and if they are to be examined by a Board in the same composition, that Board shall endeavour to deal with them one immediately after another. The Board may, after having heard the parties, also deal with such appeals in consolidated proceedings.

17.9.10 EPO President's right to comment

RPBAArt. 18 The Board may, of its own motion or at the written, reasoned request of the President of the EPO, invite the President to comment in writing or orally on questions of general interest which arise in the course of proceedings pending before it. The parties shall be entitled to submit their observations on the President's comments. 1167

17.9.11 Oral proceedings before the Board of Appeal

Comment See section 25.11 1168

17.10 Decision on the appeal

17.10.1 Taking a decision – discretion of the Board to remit proceedings to the first instance

1169	Art. 111(1)	Following the examination as to the allowability of the appeal, the Board of Appeal decides on the appeal. The Board of Appeal may either exercise any power within the competence of the department which was responsible for the decision appealed or remit the case to that department for further prosecution.
	RPBAArt. 12(8)	Subject to Art. 113 and Art. 116 EPC, the Board may decide the case at any time after filing of the statement of grounds of appeal or, in the cases where there is more than one party, after expiry of the period referred to in RPBAArt. 12(1)(c) (response of other parties to grounds of appeal).
	RPBAArt. 19(1)	If the members of a Board are not all of the same opinion, the Board shall meet to deliberate regarding the decision to be taken. Only members of the Board shall participate in the deliberations; the Chair in the particular appeal may, however, authorise other officers to attend. Deliberations shall be secret.
	RPBAArt. 19(2)	During the deliberations of the Board, the opinion of the rapporteur shall be heard first, followed by that of the additional rapporteur if one has been appointed and, if the rapporteur is not the Chair, by that of the Chair last.
	RPBAArt. 19(3)	If voting is necessary, votes shall be taken in the same sequence, except that the Chair, even when rapporteur, shall vote last. Abstentions shall not be permitted.
	r.111(1)	The decision is either issued in writing or orally, at the end of oral proceedings, with written confirmation.
	RPBAArt. 11	The Board shall not remit a case to the department whose decision was appealed for further prosecution, unless special reasons present themselves for doing so. As a rule, fundamental deficiencies which are apparent in the proceedings before that department constitute such special reasons.
	Case law	The overriding reason for remitting to the first instance is to allow examination of all issues by two instances. The Board is unlikely to examine issues which go beyond the decision taken in view of RPBAArt. 12(2). Remittal for adaptation of the description to a set of allowed claims is also routine. Remittal is more likely: where a relevant document is admitted into the proceedings (e.g. T28/81); where major amendments are proposed (T63/86); where a substantial procedural violation has occurred (e.g. T125/91).

17.10.2 The binding effect of a decision on remittal

1170	Art. 111(2)	If the Board of Appeal remits the case for further prosecution to the department whose decision was appealed, that department is bound by the ratio decidendi of the Board of Appeal, in so far as the facts are the same. If the decision under appeal was taken by the Receiving Section, the Examining Division is also bound by the ratio decidendi of the Board of Appeal (see Guidelines E-X, 9).
	Case law	Decisions of the Boards of Appeal are final and cannot be contested even by another Board of Appeal in subsequent proceedings after remission to the first instance (T79/89). However, a decision on appeal before the Examining Division has no binding effect on either instance during opposition (T167/93).
	T308/14	The binding effect of a decision extends to the reasoning by which the decision was reached. Hence a decision finding that a feature is clear and that the claims comply with Art. 84 EPC prevents a further objection that the patent lacks sufficiency from succeeding where the alleged lack of sufficiency arises from the ambiguity of that same feature.
	RPBAArt. 20(1)	Should a Board consider it necessary to deviate from an interpretation or explanation of the Convention given in an earlier decision of any Board, the grounds for this deviation shall be given, unless such grounds are in accordance with an earlier opinion or decision of the Enlarged Board of Appeal according to Art. 112(1) EPC. The President of the EPO shall be informed of the Board's decision.

17.10.3 Form and content of the decision

1171	r.102	The decision must be authenticated by the Chairman of the Board of Appeal and by the competent employee of the registry of the Board of Appeal, either by their signature or by any other appropriate means.

The decision must contain:
(a) a statement that it was delivered by the Board of Appeal;
(b) the date when the decision was taken;
(c) the names of the chairman and of the other members of the Board of Appeal taking part;
(d) the names of the parties and their representatives;
(e) the requests of the parties;
(f) a summary of the facts;
(g) the reasons; and
(h) the order of the Board of Appeal, including, where appropriate, a decision on costs.

r.2(2)   Where the EPC provides that a document must be signed, the authenticity of the document may be confirmed by handwritten signature or other appropriate means the use of which has been permitted by the President of the EPO. A document authenticated by such other means will be deemed to meet the legal requirements of signature in the same way as a document bearing a handwritten signature which has been filed in paper form.

OJ   See [2012] O.J. 14. Decisions are now usually authenticated by electronic means rather than by signature.

Comment   See also section 24.8

17.11 Withdrawal of the appeal and the effect of deemed withdrawal of an application

G7/91   Headnote: In so far as the substantive issues settled by the contested decision at first instance are concerned, a Board of Appeal may not continue opposition appeal proceedings after the sole appellant, who was the opponent in the first instance, has withdrawn his appeal. See also G8/91.   1172

Comment   This is to be contrasted with opposition proceedings where under r.84(2) an opposition can be continued. The reasoning of the Enlarged Board was that appeal proceedings should be conducted in accordance with the principle of party disposition whereby a court should not continue proceedings if the procedural act giving rise to the proceedings has been retracted.

G8/93   Headnote: The filing by an opponent, who is sole appellant, of a statement withdrawing his opposition immediately and automatically terminates the appeal proceedings, irrespective of whether the patent proprietor agrees to termination of those proceedings and even if in the Board of Appeal's view the requirements under the EPC for maintaining the patent are not satisfied.

Comment   It was the opinion of the Enlarged Board that withdrawal of the opposition by the opponent and sole appellant could only mean he wished to withdraw the appeal which was examining whether any ground of opposition might prejudice maintenance of the patent. The rest follows from G7/91 and G8/91 (see above). Proceedings are terminated even if the patent clearly requires amendment – if the patentee wants to amend the only possible avenue is limitation under Art. 105a EPC.

G2/91   Headnote (1): A person who is entitled to appeal but does not do so and instead confines himself to being a party to the appeal proceedings under Art. 107 second sentence has no independent right to continue the proceedings if the appellant withdraws the appeal.

G3/04   When the sole appellant withdraws, the appeal may not even be continued for an intervener who intervened at the appeal stage.

T629/90   Where the patentee has appealed against revocation by the Opposition Division and the opponent withdraws his opposition, the proceedings continue.

Case law   Once an appeal is withdrawn it cannot be reinstated. The suspensive effect finishes immediately and, in the case of a single appeal, the decision of the first instance becomes final. Where there are multiple appellants the withdrawing party remains a party to the proceedings and the extent of the appeal is limited to the initial requests of the remaining parties. Auxiliary procedural issues can still be decided after withdrawal, including apportionment of costs (T117/86) and refund of the appeal fee (J12/86).

T1008/19   Withdrawal of an appeal by the sole appellant after a decision is announced in oral proceedings has no effect since the appeal proceedings are then terminated. In particular, the Board will still notify the decision in writing along with reasons.

r.100(3)   If the applicant fails to reply to a communication from the Board of Appeal under r.100(2) EPC, the application will be deemed withdrawn.

Art. 86(2)   If a renewal fee is not paid in due time, a European patent application will be deemed withdrawn.

T1402/13   Deemed withdrawal of the application leads to termination of the appeal proceedings without a decision on substantive matters, though ancillary matters such as refund of the appeal fee can still be decided. However, deemed withdrawal does not have the effect of a voluntary withdrawal under r.103(2) EPC.

Chapter 18: Proceedings before the Enlarged Board of Appeal

18.1 Interpretation of the law by the Enlarged Board of Appeal

Art. 22(1)	The Enlarged Board of Appeal is responsible for deciding points of law referred to it by Boards of Appeal under Art. 112 and giving opinions on points of law referred to it by the President of the EPO under Art. 112.
Art. 112(1)(a)	In order to ensure uniform application of the law, or if a point of law of fundamental importance arises the Board of Appeal will, during proceedings on a case and either of its own motion or following a request from a party to the appeal, refer any question to the Enlarged Board of Appeal if it considers that a decision is required for the above purposes. If the Board of Appeal rejects the request, it must give the reasons in its final decision.
Art. 112(1)(b)	The President of the EPO may also refer a point of law to the Enlarged Board of Appeal where two Boards of Appeal have given different decisions on that question.
Art. 112(2)	In the cases covered by Art. 112(1)(a) the parties to the appeal proceedings are parties to the proceedings before the Enlarged Board of Appeal.
Art. 112(3)	The decision of the Enlarged Board of Appeal referred to in Art. 112(1)(a) is binding on the Board of Appeal in respect of the appeal in question.
RPBA Art. 21	Furthermore, where a Board considers it necessary to deviate from an interpretation or explanation of the EPC contained in an earlier opinion or decision of the Enlarged Board it must refer the question back to the Enlarged Board.
RPBA Art. 22(1)	If a point is to be referred to the Enlarged Board of Appeal, a decision to this effect shall be taken by the Board concerned.
RPBA Art. 22(2)	The decision shall contain the items specified in r.102, sub-paragraphs (a), (b), (c), (d) and (f), EPC and the question which the Board refers to the Enlarged Board of Appeal. The context in which the point originated shall also be stated.
RPBA Art. 22(3)	The decision shall be communicated to the parties.
Guidelines	See E-VII, 3. Proceedings may be stayed by an Examining Division or an Opposition Division if the decision to be taken in those proceedings depends entirely on the outcome of a referral. Parties are informed of an intention to stay the proceedings and asked to comment. If no party objects within the time limit set then proceedings are stayed and the parties are informed. If one or more parties object then the Examining Division or Opposition Division will take a decision to stay proceedings if it maintains its opinion. A request for accelerated proceedings by a party during such a stay has no effect until proceedings are resumed.

1173

18.2 Petition for review by the Enlarged Board of Appeal

18.2.1 Petition for review

Comment	The review procedure only applies to decisions of the Boards of Appeal taken after the entry into force of EPC2000 (Art. 1(4) of the Decision of the Administrative Council of 28 June 2001 on the transitional provisions under Article 7 of the Act revising the European Patent Convention of 29 November 2000).
Art. 22(1)(c)	The Enlarged Board of Appeal is responsible for deciding on petitions for review of decisions of the Boards of Appeal under Art. 112a.
Art. 112a(1)	Any party to appeal proceedings adversely affected by the decision of the Board of Appeal may file a petition for review of the decision by the Enlarged Board of Appeal.

1174

18.2.2 Grounds on which a petition may be filed

Art. 112a(2)	The petition may only be filed on the grounds that: (a) a member of the Board of Appeal took part in the decision in breach of Art. 24(1) (partiality) or despite being excluded pursuant to a decision under Art. 24(4); (b) the Board of Appeal included a person not appointed as a member of the Boards of Appeal; (c) a fundamental violation of Art. 113 occurred (right to be heard and approve text); (d) any other fundamental procedural defect defined in the Implementing Regulations occurred in the appeal proceedings; or

1175

(e) a criminal act established under the conditions laid down in the Implementing Regulations may have had an impact on the decision.

r.104   A fundamental procedural defect under Art. 112a(2)(d) may have occurred where the Board of Appeal:

(a) contrary to Art. 116, failed to arrange for the holding of oral proceedings requested by the petitioner; or

(b) decided on the appeal without deciding on a request relevant to that decision.

r.105   A petition for review may be based on Art. 112a(2)(e), if a competent court or authority has finally established that the criminal act occurred; a conviction is not necessary.

Comment   Note that the right to review is restricted to cases where the decision has been adversely affected by a procedural defect or a criminal act. There is no possibility of review in the case where the Board of Appeal has simply applied the law wrongly. Most petitions have been based on the alleged violation of Art. 113 but in reality the petitioner has been complaining about how the law or the Board of Appeal's discretion has been exercised – such petitions are unlikely to be successful. Petitions have been successful, for example, where, (1) due to a misunderstanding, a decision was taken to revoke a patent for lack of inventive step during oral proceedings and the patentee had only commented on novelty (Art. 112a(2)(c), R3/10); (2) grounds of appeal were never notified to the patentee who therefore had no chance to comment on them before the Board of Appeal took a decision to revoke the patent in written proceedings (Art. 112a(2)(c), R7/09); and (3) a Board of Appeal failed to decide on a request to admit an expert report into the proceedings (r.104(b), R21/11).

18.2.3   Obligation to raise objections

1176   r.106   A petition under Art. 112a(2)(a)–(d) is only admissible where an objection in respect of the procedural defect was raised during the appeal proceedings and dismissed by the Board of Appeal, except where such objection could not be raised during the appeal proceedings.

18.2.4   A petition does not have suspensive effect

1177   Art. 112a(3)   The petition for review does not have suspensive effect.

18.2.5   Filing a petition for review

1178   Art. 112a(4)   The petition for review must be filed in a reasoned statement, in accordance with the Implementing Regulations.

r.2(1)   In proceedings before the EPO, documents may be filed by delivery by hand, by postal services or by means of electronic communication. The President of the EPO lays down the details and conditions and, where appropriate, any special formal or technical requirements for the filing of documents. In particular, he may specify that confirmation must be supplied. If such confirmation is not supplied in due time, a petition for review will be deemed not to have been received.

OJ   According to Decision of the President dated 03 January 2017 ([2017] O.J. A11), the filing offices of the EPO are Munich (headquarter and PschorrHofe buildings), the Hague and Berlin. Vienna is not a filing office. A petition may be filed by fax but not by telegram or teletex (see Decision of the EPO dated 20.2.2019, [2019] O.J. A18). A confirmation copy may be requested but is not routinely required. If a requested confirmation copy is not filed within the two month period set then the petition is deemed not to have been filed. A petition may also be filed electronically using EPO Online Filing (OLF), Online Filing 2.0 or the EPO Contingency Upload Service (see Decision of the President dated 03 May 2023, [2023] O.J. A48). The web form filing service may not be used – a petition filed in this manner is deemed not received. E-mail should not be used as it has no legal force ([1999] O.J. 509; [2000] O.J. 458).

r.107(1)   The petition must contain:
(a) the name and address of the petitioner as provided in r.41(2)(c) (requirements of the request);
(b) an indication of the decision to be reviewed.

r.107(2)   The petition must indicate the reasons for setting aside the decision of the Board of Appeal, and the facts and evidence on which the petition is based.

r.107(3)	Part III of the Implementing Regulations (rr.35–54, requirements relating to the application) apply mutatis mutandis to the petition for review and the documents filed in the proceedings.
Art. 112a(4)	If based on Art. 112a(2)(a)–(d), the petition must be filed within two months of notification of the decision of the Board of Appeal. If based on Art. 112a(2)(e), the petition must be filed within two months of the date on which the criminal act has been established and in any event no later than five years from notification of the decision of the Board of Appeal.
Art. 112a(4)	The petition will not be deemed to have been filed until after the prescribed fee has been paid.
RRFArt. 2(1)(11a)	The fee is € 3270.
Art. 121(4)	Further processing is not available for the Art. 112a(4) time limit.
Art. 122	Re-establishment is available for the applicant or proprietor but must be filed within two months of the expiry of the normal period (r.136(1)). Based on the reasoning of G1/86 it may be available to an opponent as well.
Comment	The petition is deemed not to have been filed if the fee has not been paid (Art. 112a(4)), if the petition is filed in an inadmissible language or if it is filed in the official language of a Contracting State and a translation is not filed (Art. 14(1) and (4)), where a representative is necessary but the petition is filed by the applicant/proprietor/opponent and the signature is not corrected (T665/89), where the petition is filed by a representative who does not present an authorisation when requested (r.152(6)), where the petition is not signed and the defect is not rectified (r.92(1)/r.50(3)) and where the petition is filed by facsimile and a requested confirmation copy is not filed (see above).
r.3(1)	Any official language of the EPO may be used.
Art. 14(4)	An official language of one of the Contracting States may also be used by natural or legal persons having their residence or principle place of business within a Contracting State having an official language other than English, French or German, and nationals of such a state who are resident abroad. In this case, a translation into an official language of the EPO is required.
T149/85	It is the residence/nationality of the applicant, proprietor or opponent that is important, not that of the representative.
r.6(2)	A translation required under Art. 14(4) must be filed within one month of the filing of petition, or within the deadline for filing the petition, whichever expires later.
Art. 14(4)	Where a translation is not filed in time, the petition is deemed not to have been filed.
Art. 121	Further processing is available to the applicant in pre-grant proceedings.
RRFArt. 2(1)(12)	The further processing fee is € 290 in this case.
Art. 122	Re-establishment is available to the proprietor in post-grant proceedings if all due care has been shown. Based on the reasoning of G1/86 it may be available to an opponent as well.
r.6(3)	For petitions filed before 01 April 2014, a 20 % reduction in the fee was available to a petitioner who fulfilled the residence or nationality requirement of Art. 14(4) and filed the petition for review in an appropriate language. This was the case regardless of the commercial status of the petitioner. The item referred to in r.107(2) had to be filed in the official language of a Contracting State in order to benefit from the fee reduction (as per G6/91).

18.2.6   Communication to the parties

RPEBAArt. 11(a)	All parties are informed when a petition for review is received and receive a copy of the petition.	1179

18.2.7   Examination of the petition for review

Art. 112a(5)	The Enlarged Board of Appeal will examine the petition for review in accordance with the Implementing Regulations.	1180
r.109(1)	In proceedings under Art. 112a, the provisions relating to proceedings before the Boards of Appeal apply unless otherwise provided. The following do not apply: (a) r.115(1) second sentence (at least two months notice of summons to oral proceedings to be given); (b) r.118(2) first sentence (at least two months notice of summons to testify to be given); and	

(c) r.132(2) a period to be set to be two to four months unless otherwise specified, up to six months in certain circumstances, extensible on request.

The Enlarged Board of Appeal may also specify a period deviating from r.4(1) first sentence (time limit for indicating an EPO language other than the language of proceedings to be used at oral proceedings).

r.108(1)   If the petition does not comply with:
(a) Art. 112a(1) (party adversely affected);
(b) Art. 112a(2) (grounds);
(c) Art. 112a(4) (written reasoned statement, time limit, fee);
(d) r.106 (obligation to raise objections);
(e) r.107(1)(b) (indication of the decision to be reviewed); or
(f) r.107(2) (reasons, facts, evidence);
the Enlarged Board of Appeal will reject it as inadmissible, unless any defect has been remedied before the relevant period under Art. 112a(4) expires.

r.108(2)   If the Enlarged Board of Appeal notes that the petition does not comply with r.107(1)(a) (name and address of the petitioner), it will communicate this to the petitioner and invite him to remedy the deficiencies noted within a period to be specified. If the deficiencies are not remedied in due time, the Enlarged Board of Appeal will reject the petition as inadmissible.

G1/12   See section 17.7 for this decision which by analogy should apply to a correction when the wrong petitioner is named.

r.109(2)(a)   The Enlarged Board of Appeal consisting of two legally qualified members and one technically qualified member will examine all petitions for review and will reject those which are clearly inadmissible or unallowable; such decision will require unanimity.

r.109(3)   The Enlarged Board of Appeal composed according to r.109(2)(a) will decide without the involvement of other parties and on the basis of the petition.

Comment   Thus, in inter partes proceedings (typically opposition proceedings), only the petitioner and the 3-membered panel of the Enlarged Board of Appeal will be involved at this stage. Typically, the petitioner will request oral proceedings and a decision under r.109(3) will be taken after the petitioner has been heard orally.

RPEBAArt. 11(b)   Parties are informed if a petition has been rejected as clearly inadmissible or clearly unallowable.

RPEBAArt. 17   If no unanimity can be reached the case is forwarded on to the next stage of examination without comment.

r.109(2)(b)   The Enlarged Board of Appeal consisting of four legally qualified members and one technically qualified member will decide on any petition not rejected under r.109(2)(a).

Comment   At this stage, all parties to the Board of Appeal proceedings which are the subject of the petition will be involved. If requested, oral proceedings will be appointed.

RPEBAArt. 11(c)   Parties are also informed if a petition is forwarded for examination under r.109(2)(b).

Art. 112a(5)   If the petition is allowable, the Enlarged Board of Appeal will set aside the decision and reopen proceedings before the Boards of Appeal in accordance with the Implementing Regulations.

r.108(3)   If the petition is allowable, the Enlarged Board of Appeal will set aside the decision of the Board of Appeal and order the reopening of the proceedings before the Board of Appeal responsible under r.12(4) (allocation of duties by the presidium). The Enlarged Board of Appeal may order that members of the Board of Appeal who participated in taking the decision set aside will be replaced.

r.110   The Enlarged Board of Appeal will order the reimbursement of the fee for a petition for review if the proceedings before the Boards of Appeal are reopened.

18.2.8   Third-party rights

1181   Art. 112a(6)   Any person who, in a designated Contracting State, has in good faith used or made effective and serious preparation for using an invention which is the subject of a published European patent application or a European patent in the period between the decision of the Board of Appeal and publication in the European Patent Bulletin of the mention of the decision of the Enlarged Board of Appeal on the petition, may without payment continue such use in the course of his business or for the needs thereof.

18.3 Procedure before the Enlarged Board of Appeal

Art. 23(4) The procedure before the Enlarged Board of Appeal is governed by The Rules of Proce- 1182
dure of the Enlarged Board of Appeal which were adopted on December 10, 1982, and approved on December 10, 1982 ([1983] O.J. 3). Subsequent amendments have been made.
For the current version, updated in view of EPC2000, see decision of the Administrative
Council dated 07 December 2006, [2007] O.J. 303.

Chapter 19: The Application and Patent in the Contracting States

19.1 The effect of a European patent application having a filing date

1183	Art. 66	A European patent application which has been accorded a date of filing is, in the designated Contracting States, equivalent to a regular national filing, where appropriate with the priority claimed for the European patent application.
	Art. 140	The European application is also, where appropriate, equivalent to a national application in respect of a utility model or utility certificate.
	OJ	Under the extension agreements, a European patent application is also equivalent to a regular national application in the extension states when it is accorded a date of filing.
	OJ	See [2016] O.J. A5 for information on the validation agreement with Morocco. A European patent application for which a validation fee has been paid is equivalent to a regular national application in the validation state.

19.2 The effect of a published European patent application

1184	Art. 67(1)	A European patent application provisionally confers upon the applicant, from the date of its publication, the protection provided for by Art. 64 (rights conferred by a European patent), in the Contracting States designated in the application.
	Art. 67(2)	Any Contracting State may prescribe that a European patent application will not confer such protection as is conferred by Art. 64. However, the protection attached to the publication of the European patent application may not be less than that which the laws of the State concerned attach to the compulsory publication of unexamined national patent applications. In any event, each State must ensure at least that, from the date of publication of a European patent application, the applicant can claim compensation reasonable in the circumstances from any person who has used the invention in that said State in circumstances where that person would be liable under national law for infringement of a national patent.
	Art. 67(3)	Any Contracting State which does not have as an official language the language of the proceedings, may prescribe that provisional protection in accordance with Art. 67(1) and (2) will not be effective until such time as a translation of the claims in one of its official languages at the option of the applicant or, where that State has prescribed the use of one specific official language, in that language: (a) has been made available to the public in the manner prescribed by national law, or (b) has been communicated to the person using the invention in the said State.
	Art. 67(4)	A European patent application will be deemed never to have had the effects set out in Art. 67(1) and (2) if it is withdrawn, deemed to be withdrawn, or finally refused. The same applies in respect of the effects of a European patent application in a Contracting State the designation of which is withdrawn or deemed to be withdrawn.
	NatLaw	See Table III for national provisions relating to provisional protection under Art. 67.
	OJ	Under the extension agreements, a published European patent application provisionally confers the same protection as is conferred by a national application from the date on which a translation of the claims of the published application into an official language of the extension state has been communicated to a person using the invention in the extension state.
	OJ	See [2016] O.J. A5 for information on the validation agreement with Morocco. A published European patent application for which a validation fee has been paid confers provisional protection provided the applicant files the claims with the Moroccan authority OMPIC in Arabic or French.

19.3 The effect of a granted European patent

1185	Art. 2(2)	The European patent, in each of the Contracting States for which it is granted, has the effect of and is subject to the same conditions as a national patent granted by that State, unless otherwise provided for by the EPC.

Art. 64(1)	Subject to Art. 64(2), a European patent confers on its proprietor, from the date on which the mention of its grant is published in the European Patent Bulletin, in each Contracting State in respect of which it is granted, the same rights as would be conferred by a national patent granted in that State.
Art. 64(2)	If the subject matter of the European patent is a process, the protection conferred by the patent shall extent to the products directly obtained by such process.
Art. 64(3)	Any infringement of a European patent is to be dealt with by national law.
OJ	Under the extension agreements, an extended European patent confers from the date of the publication of the mention of its grant the same rights as would be conferred by a national patent granted under the law of the extension state.
OJ	See [2016] O.J. A5 for information on the validation agreement with Morocco. A European patent whose mention of grant has been published and for which a validation fee has been paid has the same effects as a national patent in Morocco.

19.4 Effect of a granted European patent may be dependent on the filing of a translation

Art. 65(1)	Any Contracting State may prescribe that, if the European patent as granted, amended or limited by the EPO is not drawn up in one of its official languages, the proprietor of the patent must supply to its central industrial property office a translation of the patent as granted, amended or limited in one of its official languages at his option or, where that State has prescribed the use of one specific official language, in that language.	1186
	The period for supplying the translation ends three months after the date on which the mention of the grant, maintenance in amended form or limitation of the European patent is published in the European Patent Bulletin, unless the State concerned prescribes a longer period.	
Art. 65(2)	Any Contracting State which has adopted provisions pursuant to Art. 65(1) may prescribe that the proprietor of the patent must pay all or part of the costs of publication of such translation within a period laid down by that State.	
Art. 65(3)	Any Contracting State may prescribe that in the event of failure to observe the provisions adopted in accordance with Art. 65(1) and (2), the European patent will be deemed to be void ab initio in that State.	
NatLaw	See Table IV for national requirements relating to the filing of a translation, the payment of a fee, requirements for representation and other related matters.	
OJ	Similar provisions to Art. 65 exist under the extension and validation agreements and can be found in Table IV of NatLaw. For Morocco, for example, the proprietor has three months to file an Arabic or French translation of the claims with OMPIC and pay the prescribed fee ([2016] O.J. A5).	

19.5 The London Agreement

Comment	A group of Contracting States concluded an agreement in London in the year 2000 with the intention of reducing the need to translate a granted European patent.	1187
	The agreement provides that any country that has an official language of the EPO (i.e. English, French or German) as one of its official languages will no longer require any translation of a European patent. Thus, for example, European patents granted in French and German are automatically in force in the UK without the filing of any translation. The safeguard for the public is that during the grant phase of a European patent application, the claims have to be provided in all three official languages of the EPO so at least the claims will be available in a comprehensible language. Furthermore, in the case of litigation, the proprietor will have to provide a full translation of the patent to a defendant in a country in which the language of the patent is not an official language.	
	The agreement further provides that countries not having an official language chosen from English, French and German will not require a full translation of the patent if it is in a preferred language selected by that State from among the three official languages. Many countries have chosen English as their preferred language and only require full translation of the patent if it is in German or French. Other countries accept any of the three official EPO languages. These countries may, however, demand translation of the claims whatever the language of the patent.	

The London Agreement first came into force on May 1, 2008 and applies to all European patents for which the grant is mentioned after its entry into force.

EPC Contracting State	Date London Agreement entered into force	Effect
Albania	01.09.2013	No translation requirements under Art. 65(1) EPC
Belgium	01.09.2019	No translation requirements under Art. 65(1) EPC
Croatia	01.05.2008	Claims must be translated in Croatian No translation of the description needed if in English
Denmark	01.05.2008	Claims must be translated into Danish No translation of the description needed if in English
Finland	01.11.2011	Claims must be translated into Finnish No translation of the description needed if in English
France	01.05.2008	No translation requirements under Art. 65(1) EPC
Germany	01.05.2008	No translation requirements under Art. 65(1) EPC
Hungary	01.01.2011	Claims must be translated into Hungarian No translation of the description needed if in English
Iceland	01.05.2008	Claims must be translated into Icelandic No translation of the description needed if in English
Ireland	01.03.2014	No translation requirements under Art. 65(1) EPC
Latvia	01.05.2008	Claims must be translated into Latvian No translation of the description required
Liechtenstein	01.05.2008	No translation requirements under Art. 65(1) EPC
Lithuania	01.05.2009	Claims must be translated into Lithuanian No translation of the description required
Luxembourg	01.05.2008	No translation requirements under Art. 65(1) EPC
North Macedonia	01.02.2012	Claims must be translated into Macedonian No translation of the description required
Monaco	01.05.2008	No translation requirements under Art. 65(1) EPC
Netherlands	01.05.2008	Claims must be translated into Dutch No translation of the description needed if in English
Norway	01.01.2015	Claims must be translated into Norwegian No translation of the description needed if in English
Slovenia	01.05.2008	Claims must be translated into Slovenian No translation of the description required
Sweden	01.05.2008	Claims must be translated into Swedish No translation of the description needed if in English

EPC Contracting State	Date London Agreement entered into force	Effect
Switzerland	01.05.2008	No translation requirements under Art. 65(1) EPC
United Kingdom	01.05.2008	No translation requirements under Art. 65(1) EPC

19.6   Effect of revocation during opposition on rights pre- and post-grant

Art. 68

A European patent application and the resulting patent will be deemed not to have had, from the outset, the effects specified in Art. 64 and Art. 67, to the extent that the patent is revoked or limited in opposition, limitation or revocation proceedings.   1188

OJ

The same applies to extension and validation states under the relevant agreements.

19.7   Extent of protection of a European application or patent

Art. 69(1)

The extent of the protection conferred by a European patent or a European patent application is to be determined by the claims. Nevertheless, the description and drawings are to be used to interpret the claims.   1189

Art. 164(1)

The Protocol on the Interpretation of Art. 69 is an integral part of the EPC.

Protocol Art. 1

Article 69 should not be interpreted as meaning that the extent of the protection conferred by a European patent is to be understood as that defined by the strict, literal meaning of the wording used in the claims, the description and drawings being employed only for the purpose of resolving an ambiguity found in the claims. Neither should it be taken to mean that the claims serve only as a guideline and that the actual protection conferred may extend to what, from a consideration of the description and drawings by a person skilled in the art, the patent proprietor has contemplated. On the contrary, it is to be interpreted as defining a position between these extremes which combines a fair protection for the patent proprietor with a reasonable degree of legal certainty for third parties.

Protocol Art. 2

For the purpose of determining the extent of protection conferred by a European patent, due account must be taken of any element which is equivalent to an element specified in the claims.

r.43(7)

Any reference signs in the claims to the drawings are not to be construed as limiting the claims.

Art. 69(2)

For the period up to grant of a European patent, the extent of the protection conferred by the European patent application is determined by the claims contained in the application as published. However, the European patent as granted or as amended in opposition, limitation or revocation proceedings determines retroactively the protection conferred by the application, insofar as such protection is not thereby extended.

Art. 64(2)

If the subject matter of the European patent is a process, the protection conferred by the patent extends to the products directly obtained by such process.

G2/88

Article 64(2) relates to processes for the manufacture of a product and does not relate to processes to achieve an effect (i.e. use or method claims).

19.8   The term of a European patent

Art. 63(1)

The term of a European patent is 20 years from the date of filing of the application.   1190

Art. 63(2)

However, this does not limit the right of a Contracting State to extend the term of a European patent, or to grant corresponding protection which follows immediately on expiry of the term of the patent, under the same conditions as those applying to national patents:
(a) in order to take account of a state of war or similar emergency conditions affecting that State;
(b) if the subject matter of the European patent is a product or a process for manufacturing a product or a use of a product which has to undergo an administrative authorisation procedure required by law before it can be put on the market in that State.

Art. 63(3)

Article 63(2) applies mutatis mutandis to European patents granted jointly for a group of Contracting States in accordance with Art. 142.

Art. 63(4)   A Contracting State which makes provision for extension of the term or corresponding protection under Art. 63(2)(b) may, in accordance with an agreement concluded with the Organisation, entrust to the EPO tasks associated with implementation of the relevant provisions.

Comment   Regulation (EC) No 469/2009 concerning supplementary protection for medicinal products is an example of corresponding protection under Art. 63(2) granted by EPC Contracting States which are members of the EEA.

19.9 Conversion of a European patent application into a national patent application

19.9.1 Circumstances in which conversion is possible

1191 Art. 135(1)   The central industrial property office of a designated Contracting State will at the request of the applicant for or proprietor of a European patent, apply the procedure for the grant of a national patent in the following circumstances:
(a) where the European patent application is deemed to be withdrawn under Art. 77(3) (not forwarded in time to the EPO by a national office);
(b) in such other cases as are provided for by the national law, in which the European patent application is refused or withdrawn or deemed to be withdrawn, or the European patent is revoked under the EPC.

NatLaw   See Table VII for national laws relating to Art. 135(1)(b).
Guidelines   See A-IV, 6.
Art. 140   A European patent application can, where appropriate, be converted into a national application for a utility model or utility certificate.

19.9.2 Time limit for requesting conversion

1192 r.155(1)   The request for conversion referred to in Art. 135(1)(a) and (b) must be filed within three months of the withdrawal of the European patent application, or of the communication that the application is deemed to be withdrawn, or of the decision refusing the application or revoking the European patent.

Art. 135(4)   The effect of the European patent application under Art. 66 will lapse if the request is not filed in due time (this is echoed by r.155(1)).

19.9.3 Submission and transmission of the request

1193 Art. 135(2)   In the case referred to in Art. 135(1)(a) (national security requirements), the request for conversion must be filed with the central industrial property office with which the European patent application has been filed. That office will, subject to the provisions governing national security, transmit the request directly to the central industrial property offices of the Contracting States specified therein.

Art. 135(3)   In the cases referred to in Art. 135(1)(b) (refusal, withdrawal, etc.), the request for conversion must be submitted to the EPO in accordance with the Implementing Regulations. It will not be deemed to have been filed until the conversion fee has been paid. The EPO will transmit the request to the central industrial property offices of the Contracting States specified therein.

RRFArt. 2(1)(14)   The conversion fee is € 85.
r.155(2)   When transmitting the request for conversion to the central industrial property offices of the Contracting States specified in the request, the central industrial property office concerned or the EPO will attach to the request a copy of the file relating to the European patent application or European patent.

r.155(3)   Article 135(4) applies if the request for conversion referred to in Art. 135(1)(a) and (2) is not transmitted before expiry of a period of 20 months from the date of filing or, if priority has been claimed, the date of priority, i.e. the effect of the European patent application under Art. 66 (equivalence of European patent application having a filing date with regular national filing) will lapse.

19.9.4   Formal requirements for conversion

Art. 137(1)   A European patent application transmitted in accordance with Art. 135(2) or (3) may not   1194
be subjected to formal requirements of national law which are different from or additional
to those provided for in the EPC.

Art. 137(2)   Any central industrial property office to which the European patent application is transmitted may require that the applicant must, within a period of not less than two months:
(a) pay the national application fee; and
(b) file a translation of the original text of the European patent application in an official
language of the State in question and, where appropriate, of the text as amended during
proceedings before the EPO which the applicant wishes to use as the basis for the national
procedure.

19.9.5   Information available to the public in the event of conversion

r.156(1)   The documents accompanying the request for conversion under r.155(2) will be made   1195
available to the public by the central industrial property office under the same conditions
and to the same extent as documents relating to national proceedings.

r.156(2)   The printed specification of any national patent resulting from the conversion of a European patent application must mention that application.

19.10   Revocation of a European patent in Contracting States

19.10.1   Grounds for revocation

Art. 138(1)   Subject to Art. 139 (collision with national applications and patents), a European patent   1196
can be revoked with effect for a Contracting State, only on the grounds that:
(a) the subject matter of the European patent is not patentable under Arts 52–57;
(b) the European patent does not disclose the invention in a manner sufficiently clear and
complete for it to be carried out by a person skilled in the art;
(c) the subject matter of the European patent extends beyond the content of the application as filed or, if the patent was granted on a divisional application or on a new application filed under Art. 61, beyond the content of the earlier application as filed;
(d) the protection conferred by the European patent has been extended; or
(e) the proprietor of the European patent is not entitled under Art. 60(1).

19.10.2   Partial revocation – right to amend

Art. 138(2)   If the grounds for revocation affect the European patent only in part, the patent will be   1197
limited by a corresponding limitation of the claims and revoked in part.

Art. 138(3)   In proceedings before the competent court or authority relating to the validity of the European patent, the proprietor of the patent has the right to limit the patent by amending
the claims. The patent as thus limited forms the basis for proceedings.

19.11   Collision of European and national patents and patent applications

Art. 139(1)   In any designated Contracting State a European patent application and a European patent   1198
have with regard to a national patent application and a national patent the same prior right
effect as a national patent application and a national patent.

Art. 139(2)   A national patent application and a national patent in a Contracting State have with regard
to a European patent designating that Contracting State the same prior right effect as if the
European patent were a national patent.

r.138   If the EPO is informed of the existence of a prior right under Art. 139(2), the European
patent application or European patent may, for such State or States, contain claims and,
where appropriate, a description and drawings which are different from those for the
other designated States.

Art. 139(3)   Any Contracting State may prescribe whether and on what terms an invention disclosed
in both a European patent application or patent and a national application or patent having the same date of filing or, where priority is claimed, the same date of priority, may be
protected simultaneously by both applications or patents.

Guidelines   See G-IV, 6 and H-III, 4.

NatLaw	See Table X for national provisions relating to Art. 139(3).	
Art. 140	These provisions also apply, where appropriate, to utility models and utility certificates and applications for the same.	

19.12   National renewal fees for European patents

1199	Art. 141(1)	Renewal fees for a European patent may only be imposed for the years which follow that referred to in Art. 86(2) (year in which the mention of grant is published).
	Art. 141(2)	Any renewal fees falling due within two months of the publication in the European Patent Bulletin of the mention of the grant of the European patent are deemed to have been validly paid if they are paid within that period. Any additional fee provided for under national law cannot be charged.
	NatLaw	See Table VI for national provisions relating to the payment of renewal fees.

19.13   Provisions which apply to national utility models and utility certificates

1200	Art. 140	Art. 66 (equivalence of European filing and national filing), Art. 124 (supply of information by applicant/proprietor regarding national applications), Art. 135 and Art. 137 (conversion) and Art. 139 (collision of European and national rights) apply to utility models and utility certificates and to applications for utility models and utility certificates registered or deposited in the Contracting States whose laws make provision for such models or certificates.

19.14   Authentic text in national proceedings

1201	Art. 70	See section 25.13.

19.15   Request by a national court for a technical opinion from an Examining Division

1202	Art. 25	At the request of the competent national court hearing an infringement or revocation action, the EPO is obliged, on payment of an appropriate fee, to give a technical opinion concerning the European patent which is the subject of the action. The Examining Division is responsible for issuing such opinions.
	RRFArt. 2(1)(20)	The fee for a technical opinion is € 4385.
	RRFArt. 10	However, 75 % of the fee will be refunded where the request is withdrawn at a time when the EPO has not yet begun to draw up the technical opinion.
	RRFArt. 4(1)(2)	The due date is the date of receipt of the request. However, the President of the EPO may decide that such services may be carried out without advance payment.
	Guidelines	See E-XIII. The Examining Division does not specifically comment on whether a patent is valid or infringed but gives an answer to any questions of a technical nature that are posed.

Chapter 20: Time Limits and Procedural Safeguards

20.1 Time limits

20.1.1 What is a "time limit"?

Guidelines	See E-VIII, 1.1. A time limit is a specific period of time within which an act vis-à-vis the EPO must be carried out. This has important consequences for the various provisions below under which time limits can be extended or the under which missing a time limit can be excused. Single points in time, such as the dates of oral proceedings, renewal fee due dates, grant dates are not time limits. Note that the Articles of the EPC refer in general to "time limit" whereas the rules refer in general to "period".
J18/04	According to this decision, which explores the concept of a time limit in some detail, a time limit has two conceptual elements, a period of time determined in years, months or days and a relevant date which specifies the starting point of the time limit. The condition that a divisional application can only be filed in respect of a pending parent application is not a time limit in this sense.

1203

20.1.2 Computation of time limits

Art. 120(a)	Time limits to be observed in proceedings before the EPO which are not fixed in the EPC itself are specified in the Implementing Regulations.
Art. 120(b)	The Implementing Regulations specify the manner of computation of time limits.
Guidelines	See E-VIII, 1.1. Most time limits are now laid down in the Implementing Regulations. Notable exceptions are the priority year (Art. 87), the opposition period (Art. 99) and the time limit for filing an appeal (Art. 108).

1204

20.1.3 Units of time used

r.131(1)	Periods are laid down in terms of full years, months, weeks or days.

1205

20.1.4 Day on which computation of time limit is to start

r.131(2)	Computation starts on the day following the day on which the relevant event occurred, the event being either a procedural step or the expiry of another period. Where the procedural step is a notification, the relevant event is the deemed receipt of the document notified, unless otherwise provided.
J14/86	This does not mean that a day must be added to time limits fixed in years, months or weeks.
r.126(2)	Where notification is effected in accordance with r.126(1), the document shall be deemed to be delivered to the addressee on the date it bears, unless it has failed to reach the addressee. In the event of any dispute concerning the delivery of the document, it shall be incumbent on the EPO to establish that the document has reached its destination and to establish the date on which the document was delivered to the addressee.
r.127(2)	Where notification is effected by means of electronic communication, the electronic document shall be deemed to be delivered to the addressee on the date it bears, unless it has failed to reach its destination. In the event of any dispute concerning the delivery of the electronic document, it shall be incumbent on the EPO to establish that the document has reached its destination and to establish the date on which it reached its destination.
Comment	For documents notified before 01 November 2023, a 10 day deemed notification period applied.
Comment	Note that deemed notification does not apply in relation to the removal of the cause of non-compliance (Art. 122) if this is the result of receiving a notification – the actual date of receipt is determinative.
OJ	See Notice from the EPO dated 06 March 2023 ([2023] O.J. A29). The term "document" covers decisions, summonses, notices and communications and has been used to indicate that the notification date is the date printed on the document itself and not, for example, any date stamped on an accompanying envelope. In case of dispute, the EPO bears the burden of proof. If the EPO is unable to prove a document has been delivered then notification has not occurred and the document concerned with be reissued.

1206

20.1.5   *Expiry of time limits – years, months and weeks*

1207   r.131(3)   When a period is expressed as one year or a certain number of years, it will expire in the relevant subsequent year, in the month having the same name and on the day having the same number as the month and the day on which the said event occurred (see r.131(2) – procedural step or expiry of other period); if the relevant subsequent month has no day with the same number, the period will expire on the last day of that month.

r.131(4)   When a period is expressed as one month or a certain number of months, it will expire in the relevant subsequent month on the day which has the same number as the day on which the said event occurred (see r.131(2) – procedural step or expiry of other period); if the relevant subsequent month has no day with the same number, the period will expire on the last day of that month.

r.131(5)   When a period is expressed as one week or a certain number of weeks, it will expire in the relevant subsequent week on the day having the same name as the day on which the said event occurred (see r.131(2) – procedural step or expiry of other period).

20.1.6   *Duration of time limits that are to be determined by the EPO*

1208   r.132(1)   Where the EPC or Implementing Regulations refer to "a period to be specified", this period is specified by the EPO.

Art. 120(c)   The Implementing Regulations specify the minima and maxima for time limits to be determined by the EPO.

r.132(2)   Unless otherwise provided, a period specified by the EPO must be neither less than two months nor more than four months; in certain special circumstances it may be up to six months.

Guidelines   See E-VIII, 1.2. The length of the period set should correspond to the amount of work which must be carried out. The EPO sets a two-month period for minor or formal matters and for responses to communications from the Legal Division and a four-month period for substantive matters. A six-month time limit is set in cases of exceptional complexity (but as standard in the case of r.70(2)).

20.1.7   *Extension of time limits determined by the EPO*

1209   Comment   Note that time limits specified in the EPC and Implementing Regulations may not be extended.

Art. 120(b)   The Implementing Regulations specify the conditions under which time limits may be extended.

r.132(2)   A period specified by the EPO may be extended in special cases if the request for extension is presented before the expiry of the period.

Guidelines   See E-VIII, 1.6. Before the Examining Division, Legal Division or Receiving Section, a four month time limit in the case of a substantive matter and a two month time limit in the case of a minor or formal matter are each usually extended by two months without any reasons being necessary. However, the extension of a six month time limit in the case of a substantive matter or a second extension will usually only be granted if good reasons are presented. Good reasons may include serious illness or the need to conduct tests. Pressure of work and holiday arrangements, however, do not constitute good reasons. The acceleration of grant proceedings will cease if the applicant requests the extension of a time limit. Before the Opposition Division, on the other hand, an extension of any kind is only granted in exceptional, duly substantiated cases. An extension in opposition proceedings may be requested by any party, regardless of which party was invited to file a response, and, if granted, applies equally to all parties.

Comment   The extension is not a separate time limit running from the expiry of the original time limit (i.e. not an aggregate time limit) but an extension of the original period set which must therefore be recalculated.

OJ   Extensions of periods set by the EPO in the course of opposition proceedings which are subject to a request for accelerated prosecution are particularly difficult to obtain ([1008] O.J. 221).

RPBAArt. 12(7)   Note that in appeal proceedings, a time limit set by the EPO may also be extended but under Art. 120(b) and RPBAArt. 12(7). According to this provision, no extension is possible unless a written, **reasoned** request is filed.

20.2 Circumstances in which a missed time limit is excused where a document is sent in good time

r.133(1)	Where a document (does not apply to fees – see RRFArt. 7(3) for the complementary provision) is received late at the EPO it will nevertheless be deemed to have been received in good time if it was delivered to a recognised postal service provider in due time before the expiry of the period in accordance with the conditions laid down by the President of the EPO, unless the document was received later than three months after expiry of the period.
r.133(2)	This provision also applies mutatis mutandis to any period where transactions are carried out with the competent authority in accordance with Art. 75(1)(b) or Art. 75(2)(b) (application filed with the competent central industrial property office of a Contracting State).
OJ	See Decision of the President dated 11 March 2015, [2015] O.J. A29. The President has decided that the document must have been delivered to a specified postal service provider at least five days prior to the expiry of the time limit. The specified postal service providers generally recognised for the purposes of r.133 are the designated operators within the meaning of Article 1 of the Universal Postal Convention, Chronopost, DHL, Federal Express, Flexpress, TNT, Skynet, UPS and Transworld. Furthermore, the document, must have been sent by registered letter or the equivalent thereof and, if posted outside Europe, sent by airmail.
Comment	The failure to meet any time limit can be excused under r.133 if the relevant conditions are met. This includes, for example, the priority year if a priority-claiming European patent application is received late at the EPO. In this case, the filing date remains the date on which the application is actually received at the EPO but the application is deemed to have met the requirements of Art. 87(1). However, only the failure to meet a time limit, within the meaning that term has under the EPC, can be excused. Thus r.133 is not applicable to any condition which must be met at a certain point in time such as the requirement under r.36(1) for a divisional to be filed before the grant of the parent application. Note also that the "three months" of r.133(1) is not a time limit but a condition that must be met.
Guidelines	See E-VIII, 1.7. The five days specified in the decision of the president are calendar days rather than working days.

1210

20.3 Extension of time limits in the case of late notification or where the EPO or a national office is not open for business

Art. 120(b)	The Implementing Regulations specify the conditions under which time limits may be extended.
r.126(2)	If the EPO establishes that a document notified by postal services was delivered to the addressee more than seven days after the date it bears, a period for which the deemed receipt of that document is the relevant event under r.131(2) shall expire later by the number of days by which the seven days were exceeded.
r.127(2)	If the EPO establishes that a document notified by means of electronic communication has reached its destination more than seven days after the date it bears, a period for which the deemed receipt of that document is the relevant event under r.131(2) shall expire later by the number of days by which the seven days were exceeded.
Comment	For documents notified before 01 November 2023, this 7-day rule did not apply. Instead, documents were deemed notified 10 days following the date they were sent in order to take into account delays in delivery.
Oj	See Notice from the EPO dated 06 March 2023 ([2023] O.J. A29). The EPO bears the burden of proof in establishing the date of delivery. As an example, if a document is received 12 days after the date it bears, any period calculated on the basis of the document's notification will be extended by five days. These additional days are to be added before any adjustment of the time limit under r.134 (see below).
r.134(1)	If a period expires on a day on which one of the filing offices of the EPO under r.35(1) (i.e. Munich, The Hague or Berlin) is not open for receipt of documents or on which, for reasons other than those referred to in r.134(2) (general dislocation in the delivery or transmission of mail), mail is not delivered there, the period will extend to the first day thereafter on which all the filing offices are open for receipt of documents and on which mail is delivered. This applies mutatis mutandis if documents filed by one of the means of electronic communication permitted by the President of the EPO under r.2(1) cannot be received.

1211

Comment	Note that the time limit is extended regardless of the EPO filing office with which the document is to be filed.
OJ	See Notice from the EPO dated 22 October 2020 ([2020] O.J. A120). "Means of electronic communication" includes all available means for filing documents including online filing (OLF), Web-Form Filing, New Online Filing (also known as case management system, CMS), ePCT and fax. Where there is a general outage for at least one of these means of commnunication on the last date of a period, the period is extended under r.134(1) EPC until the first working day on which all means of electronic communication are available (regardless of the means actually used to file the document). This is the case for all documents including those that could not have been filed using the suspended service (e.g. the time limit for filing a notice of opposition is extended even if it is only the web-form filing service which is unavailable). In some cases the outage will be planned and announced in advance by the EPO and in other cases will be unplanned and announced as soon as brought to light. In cases where a means of electronic communication is unavailable unexpectedly for a particular party the safeguard of r.134(1) also applies but the party concerned bears the burden of proof. Note that there is no extension under r.134(1) EPC if the outage is not attributable to the EPO. Where a means of electronic filing is unavailable for less than four hours and the outage has been published at least two days in advance then periods will not be extended under r.134(1) EPC since in this case users are expected to plan accordingly.
OJ	All periods are extended where one of the conditions of r.134(1) applies (filing office shut for receipt of documents, mail not delivered, a means of electronically filing documents not available), including periods for the payment of fees. According to the Notice from the EPO dated 22 October 2020 ([2020] O.J. A120), if the payment of a fee expires on a day on which one of the accepted means specifically provided for the payment of fees is not available then the fee may also be validly paid on the first working day on which all such means for making payments are available. Therefore, if there is an outage relating to the Online Fee Payment Tool or the EPO credit card payment service or bank transfers, payment periods are extended to the first working day thereafter on which all accepted means for making a payment are available. This applies even if the outage only affects one means of payment. However, where a means of payment is unavailable for less than four hours and the outage has been published at least two days in advance then periods will not be extended since in this case users are expected to plan accordingly. Note that an outage relating to the Online Fee Payment Tool or the EPO credit card payment service or bank transfers does not lead to a general extension of time limits under r.131(4) EPC but to a specific extension of time limits for the payment of fees.
r.134(3)	This provision applies mutatis mutandis where acts are performed with the competent authority in accordance with Art. 75(1)(b) and Art. 75(2)(b) (application filed with the central industrial property office of a Contracting State).
Comment	Note that in this case, the time limit is only extended in respect of the relevant national office concerned.
Comment	All time limits are extended under r.134(1) and (3) including the priority period. If the last day of the priority period is a day on which one of the EPO filing offices is shut then the priority period is extended under r.134(1) to the next day on which all the EPO filing offices are open, regardless of the EPO filing office with which the application is actually filed.
OJ	Information is published each year in the Official Journal specifying days on which the EPO is shut for the receipt of documents. See also the Notice from the EPO dated 22 October 2020 (cited above) – the priority period may be extended under r.134(3) EPC where there is an outage preventing the online filing of a European patent application with the office of an EPC Contracting State and the applicant can provide evidence.
Guidelines	See E-VIII, 1.6.2.3. Any extension under r.134 applies to all periods under the EPC including time limits for the filing of submissions and the payment of fees, the priority period and the time limit for a national office to forward a European patent application under r.37(2) EPC. It does not, however, affect situations in which a period is not involved such as the pendency of an application for the purposes of r.36(1) EPC, renewal fee due dates and the date on which examination starts.

20.4 Extension of time limits where there is a general interruption in mail delivery in a Contracting State

Art. 120(b)	The Implementing Regulations specify the conditions under which time limits may be extended.	1212
r.134(2)	If a period expires on a day on which there is a general dislocation in the delivery or transmission of mail in a Contracting State, the period will extend to the first day following the end of the interval of dislocation for parties which are resident in the State concerned or have appointed representatives with a place of business in that State. Where the State concerned is the State in which the EPO is located, this provision applies to all parties and their representatives. This provision applies mutatis mutandis to the period referred to in r.37(2) (forwarding of a European application by a national authority).	
r.134(4)	The date of commencement and the end of any dislocation under r.134(2) is published by the EPO.	
r.134(3)	This provision applies mutatis mutandis where acts are performed with the competent authority in accordance with Art. 75(1)(b) and Art. 75(2)(b) (filing of an application with the central industrial property offices of a Contracting State).	
OJ	The EPO considered the restrictions to public life in Germany in view of the 2020 Covid-19 pandemic to constitute a dislocation under r.134(2) and all periods expiring on or after 15 March 2020 were extended for European and international applications until 02 June 2020 (see [2020] O.J. A29 and subsequent updates). Decision J10/20 doubts whether r.134(2) was really applicable but nevertheless recognises that the EPO notices could be relied on bearing in mind the protection of legitimate expectations (see section 20.9).	
J1/93	Loss of a single postbag is not enough; an area of some magnitude must be affected for the interruption to be "general".	

20.5 Extension of time limits where there is a war, revolution or similar event affecting the applicant or his representative

Art. 120(b)	The Implementing Regulations specify the conditions under which time limits may be extended.	1213
r.134(5)	Without prejudice to r.134(1)–(4), where evidence is produced by a party that on any of the 10 days preceding the day of expiry of a period, the delivery or transmission of mail was dislocated due to an exceptional occurrence such as a natural disaster, war, civil disorder, a general breakdown in any of the means of electronic communication permitted by the President of the EPO under r.2(1), or other like reasons, affecting the locality where the party or his representative resides or has his place of business and the evidence produced satisfies the EPO, a document received late will be deemed to have been received in due time provided that the mailing or the transmission was effected at the latest on the fifth day after the end of the dislocation.	
OJ	As an example of this see the Notice of the President of August 1, 2005, concerning the events of July 7, 2005 in London.	

20.6 Further processing

Art. 121(1)	If an applicant fails to observe a time limit vis-à-vis the EPO, he may request further processing of the European patent application.	1214
Art. 1221(2)	The EPO will grant the request for further processing provided that the requirements laid down in the Implementing Regulations are met. Otherwise, it will reject the request.	
r.135(1)	Further processing is requested simply by paying the required fee within two months of the communication concerning either the failure to observe a time limit or a loss of rights. The omitted act must also be completed within this period.	
Comment	For further processing to apply there must be a loss of rights and a communication from the EPO relating to that loss of rights from which the time limit can be calculated. Since further processing is requested by paying the fee, it is no longer necessary to file a formal written request. In the case where the relevant application is subject to the automatic debiting procedure, the further processing fee is automatically debited when the omitted procedural act is carried out.	

RRFArt. 2(1)(12)	The fee is 50 % of the relevant fee in the event of late payment of a fee, € 290 in the case where one or more of the acts required by r.71(3) is/are not performed in time and € 290 in other cases.
J16/92	Where the omitted act is a response to an Art. 94(3) communication, it is not completed by asking for an extension of the original time limit.
Guidelines	Neither would the omitted act be completed by any other purely procedural request, such as a request for oral proceedings, when a deadline for filing a substantive response has expired (E-VIII, 2).
Art. 121(4)	Further processing is not available for the r.135(1) time limit!
Art. 122	Re-establishment is, however, available for the r.135(1) time limit.
r.135(3)	The department competent to decide on the omitted act decides on the request for further processing.
Art. 121(3)	If the request is granted, the legal consequences of the failure to observe the time limit will be deemed not to have ensued.
Art. 121(4)	Further processing is ruled out in respect of the following time limits: (a) Art. 87(1) (priority year); (b) Art. 108 (two-month period for filing notice of appeal and four-month period for filing grounds of appeal); (c) Art. 112a(4) (time limits for filing a petition for review by the Enlarged Board of Appeal); (d) the time limit for requesting further processing (r.135(1)); (e) the time limit for requesting re-establishment of rights (r.136(1)); and (f) other time limits ruled out in the Implementing Regulations.
r.135(2)	Further processing is ruled out in respect of the periods referred to in Art. 121(4) (see above) and the periods under the following Rules: (a) r.6(1) (two-month period for filing a translation of the application in an official language of the EPO); (b) r.16(1)(a) (three-month period for taking advantage of remedies after successful entitlement proceedings); (c) r.31(2) (time limit for details relating to a deposit of biological material); (d) r.36(2) (time limit for filing a required translation of a divisional application); (e) r.40(3) (two-month period for filing a copy of a previous application referred to in order to establish a filing date or translation thereof); (f) r.51(2)–(5) (time limits for paying renewal fees); (g) r.52(2) and (3) (time limits for making or correcting a declaration of priority); (h) r.55 (two-month period for remedying deficiencies preventing the allocation of a filing date); (i) r.56 (time limits for filing missing parts of the description and drawings); (j) r.58 (two-month period for correcting deficiencies in the application documents); (k) r.59 (period for correcting deficiencies in a priority claim); (l) r.62a (period for indicating to the Search Division claims which comply with r.43(2)); (m) r.63 (period for indicating to the Search Division subject-matter complying with the EPC to a sufficient extent to allow a meaningful search to be carried out; (n) r.64 (period for responding to a lack of unity objection); (o) r.112(2) (two-month period for requesting a decision following a loss of rights) and (p) r.164(1) and (2) (two-month periods for paying additional search fees on entry into the regional phase with a Euro-PCT application).
Guidelines	See E-VIII, 2. A fee must be paid in respect of each omitted act (other than under r.71(3)). Where these acts have the same legal basis (e.g. request for examination and payment of the examination fee) it is considered that a single further processing fee is due comprising one or two elements as appropriate. Where the acts have different legal basis then it is considered that two separate further processing fees are due. This has implications for the number of re-establishment fees that may be due if the further processing period is not observed (see E-VIII, 3.1.3). There is no need to wait for a loss of rights communication – a request for further processing can be validly filed at any time following the failure to observe a relevant time limit. See also E-VIII, 1.6 – where further processing is necessary following the unreasonable refusal of the EPO to extend a time limit, the applicant can ask for a refund of the further processing fee. A decision to refuse the refund is open to appeal (J37/89).

20.7   Re-establishment of rights

20.7.1   Conditions necessary for re-establishment

Art. 122(1)	The applicant for or proprietor of a European patent who, in spite of all due care required 1215 by the circumstances having been taken, was unable to observe a time limit vis-à-vis the EPO will have his rights re-established upon request if the non-observance of this time limit has the direct consequence of causing the refusal of the European patent application, or of a request, or the deeming of the application to have been withdrawn, or the revocation of the European patent, or the loss of any other right or means of redress.
Comment	Re-establishment, unlike further processing, is therefore possible both before and after grant.
J3/80	The time limit must be one that the applicant or proprietor has to observe and therefore re-establishment is not applicable to the Art. 77(3) time limit regarding forwarding of an application to the EPO by a national patent office.
J24/03	Where an application is no longer pending under r.36(1) because it has been granted, re-establishment cannot be applied in order to file a divisional application.
T26/95	Where several time limits have been missed a separate application and fee is necessary in respect of each of them.
J7/16	However, in this case it was deemed sufficient that one fee had been paid even though both the two month time limit for filing a notice of appeal and the four month time limit for filing grounds of appeal had been missed.
Case law	Usually, in relation to showing all due care, the mistake must be shown to be an isolated mistake in an otherwise satisfactory system (J2/86, J3/86) or else exceptional circumstances must apply. Such exceptional circumstances include major health problems (J7/16), a complex transfer of company ownership (T469/93), an unexpected breakdown in takeover negotiations (J13/90) and internal reorganisation (T14/89). Financial difficulties can also justify re-establishment (J22/88) where all due care has been taken in attempting to gain financial support.
Guidelines	See E-VIII, 3. A separate re-establishment fee is required for each independent procedural act which has given rise to a loss of rights. For a unitary procedural act having a single legal basis, a single fee is due. In the case where re-establishment of the further processing time limit is requested, a separate re-establishment fee is due for each further processing fee that was not paid – this could require multiple payments, e.g. in the case that no action was taken on entry into the regional phase.

20.7.2   Which parties to EPO proceedings can use re-establishment?

Art. 122(1)	An applicant or a proprietor is entitled to apply for re-establishment. 1216
G1/86	An opponent who has filed a notice of appeal but missed the time limit for filing the grounds of appeal may also apply for re-establishment. According to the logic of this decision an opponent should be able to use re-establishment throughout the pendency of appeal proceedings.
T210/89	However, an opponent is not entitled to re-establishment for missing the time limit for filing a notice of appeal.
T702/89	Neither is a would-be opponent entitled to re-establishment having missed the nine-month time limit for filing an opposition.
T555/02	If a party requests re-establishment in opposition proceedings, other parties to the opposition proceedings are also party to the re-establishment proceedings (see also T1561/05).
Guidelines	See E-VIII, 3.1.2.

20.7.3   Grant or refusal – the effect of an allowable request

Art. 122(2)	The EPO will grant the request for re-establishment provided that the conditions of 1217 Art. 122(1) and any other requirements laid down in the Implementing Regulations are met. Otherwise it will reject the request.
Art. 122(3)	If the request is granted, the legal consequences of the failure to observe the time limit will be deemed not to have ensued.

20.7.4   Exclusion of certain time limits from re-establishment

1218	Art. 122(4)	Re-establishment of rights is ruled out in respect of the time limit for requesting re-establishment of rights. The Implementing Regulations may rule out re-establishment for other time limits.
	r.136(3)	Re-establishment of rights is ruled out in respect of any period for which further processing under Art. 121 is available and in respect of the period for requesting re-establishment of rights.
	Guidelines	See E-VIII, 3.1.1. Note that re-establishment is nevertheless possible in respect of the further processing time limit of r.135(1) if this is not observed. It is also possible in respect of the priority period.

20.7.5   Procedure for applying for re-establishment – time limits

1219	Art. 122(2)	The EPO will only grant the request for re-establishment if the conditions of Art. 122(1) and any other requirements laid down in the Implementing Regulations are met.
	r.136(1)	Any request for re-establishment of rights under Art. 122(1) must be filed in writing within two months from the removal of the cause of non-compliance with the period but at the latest within one year of expiry of the unobserved time limit. However, a request for re-establishment of rights in respect of either of the periods specified in Art. 87(1) (priority year) and Art. 112a(4) (petition for review) must be filed within two months of expiry of that period.
	Case law	The cause of non-compliance is removed, for example, on the actual date of receipt by the responsible person (the person responsible to take decision on applying for re-establishment, such as the applicant or agent, T191/82, J27/88) of notification from the EPO that a loss of rights has occurred (J7/82) or the date on which the responsible person otherwise realises the mistake (J17/89).
	T428/98	Where the removal of the cause for compliance is an EPO notification, the removal of the cause of non-compliance is the actual date on which the notification was received by the relevant person and not the date deemed to be the date of notification under r.126(2). Note that this decision was taken before 01 November 2023 at which time a 10 day notification period applied.
	J16/86	The two-month and one-year time limits can be interrupted under r.142 but are otherwise absolute in the interests of legal certainty.
	Art. 121(4)	Further processing is ruled out in respect of the r.136(1) time limits.
	Art. 122(4)	Re-establishment is not available either! (See also r.136(3)).
	Guidelines	See E-VIII, 3.1.3.

20.7.6   Grounds must be filed and fee paid

1220	Art. 122(2)	The EPO will only grant the request for re-establishment if the conditions of Art. 122(1) and any other requirements laid down in the Implementing Regulations are met.
	r.136(1)	The request for re-establishment of rights will not be deemed to have been filed until the prescribed fee has been paid.
	RRFArt. 2(1)(13)	The fee is € 720.
	r.136(2)	The request must state the grounds on which it is based and set out the facts on which it relies. The omitted act must be completed within the relevant period for filing the request according to r.136(1).
	T167/97	The completed omitted act must meet the requirements of the EPC, e.g. be admissible.
	J6/90	Where the request is filed in due time, the grounds may be filed after the one-year time limit.
	T324/90	Evidence may be supplied later than the two-month time limit.
	J14/89	Where an appeal is mistakenly filed instead of an application for re-establishment, it can be accepted as the latter where the contents are sufficient to cover the grounds that must be filed and sufficient funds to cover the fee have been paid (see also T522/88). In this case the EPO has a duty to request the re-establishment fee if sufficient time remains.
	Guidelines	See E-VIII, 3.1.3 and 3.1.4.

20.7.7   Department qualified to decide on the application for re-establishment

r.136(4) | The department competent to decide on the omitted act decides on the request for re-es- | 1221
tablishment of rights.

Case law | Where a non-competent department decides, the decision is void (J10/93). Where the two-month and four-month periods for filing an appeal are concerned, the Board of Appeal takes the decision (T473/91).

Guidelines | See E-VIII, 3.3.

20.7.8   Third-party rights may be awarded

Art. 122(5) | Any person who, in a designated Contracting State, has in good faith used or made effec- | 1222
tive and serious preparations for using an invention which is the subject of a published European patent application or a European patent in the period between the loss of rights referred to in Art. 122(1) and publication in the European Patent Bulletin of the mention of re-establishment of those rights, may without payment continue such use in the course of his business or for the needs thereof.

J5/79 | Third-party rights are only relevant when a restored application has been published.

20.7.9   Contracting States may grant re-establishment for the EPC time limits that they have to administer

Art. 122(6) | Nothing in Art. 122 limits the right of a Contracting State to grant re-establishment of | 1223
rights in respect of time limits provided for in the EPC and to be observed vis-à-vis the authorities of such State.

20.8   Interruption of proceedings

20.8.1   Circumstances under which proceedings may be interrupted

r.142(1) | Proceedings before the EPO are interrupted: | 1224
(a) in the event of the death or legal incapacity of the applicant for or proprietor of a European patent or of the person authorised by national law to act on his behalf. To the extent that the above events do not affect the authorisation of a representative appointed under Art. 134, proceedings are interrupted only on application by such a representative;
(b) in the event of the applicant for or proprietor of a patent, as a result of some action taken against his property, being prevented by legal reasons from continuing the proceedings; or
(c) in the event of the death or legal incapacity of the representative of an applicant for or proprietor of a patent, or of his being prevented for legal reasons resulting from action taken against his property from continuing the proceedings.

J23/88 | A "representative" within the meaning of r.142(1)(c) is a professional representative within the meaning of Art. 134 other than for the purposes of filing a European patent application or performing the acts necessary for entry of a Euro-PCT application into the regional phase.

J26/95 | The crucial question under (b) is whether the action taken makes it impossible for the applicant to continue the proceedings.

Case law | The EPO must apply this rule of its own motion when it becomes aware of relevant circumstances. Legal incapacity is defined by reference to national law for the applicant and proprietor but according to a uniform standard for representatives (J900/85) and is typically characterised by mental illness of some kind.

T54/17 | If a patentee is aware that the proceedings have been interrupted, but continues to be actively involved in the proceedings, then it is not possible for him to invoke interruption at a later stage since this would be contrary to the principle of good faith.

Guidelines | See E-VII.

20.8.2   *Resumption of the proceedings*

1225   r.142(2)

Where, in the cases referred to in r.142(1)(a) or (b), the EPO has been informed of the identity of the person authorised to continue the proceedings, it will notify such person and, where applicable, any third party, that the proceedings will be resumed as from a specified date. If, three years after the publication of the date of interruption in the European Patent Bulletin, the EPO has not been informed of the identity of the person authorized to continue the proceedings, it may set a date on which it intends to resume the proceedings of its own motion.

OJ

Thus, according to the last sentence of r.142(2), the EPO may resume proceedings ex officio with the applicant or proprietor registered in the European Patent Register and the consequent failure to pay a fee or carry out a procedural act may lead to a loss of rights (see Notice from the EPO dated 29 May 2020, [2020] O.J. A76). This is to increase legal certainty for third parties. Where there is a succession of title, the proposed resumption date may be postponed if a reasoned and substantiated request is made.

r.142(3)

In the case referred to in r.142(1)(c), the proceedings will be resumed when the EPO has been informed of the appointment of a new representative of the applicant or when the EPO has informed the other parties of the appointment of a new representative of the proprietor of the patent. If, three months after the beginning of the interruption of the proceedings, the EPO has not been informed of the appointment of a new representative, it will communicate to the applicant for or proprietor of the patent:

(a) where Art. 133(2) is applicable (natural or legal persons not having residence/principal place of business within a Contracting State), that the European patent application will be deemed withdrawn or the European patent will be revoked if the information is not submitted within two months of the communication; or

(b) otherwise, that the proceedings will be resumed with the applicant for or proprietor of the patent as from the notification of the communication.

J12/19

Where opposition proceedings are interrupted as a result of the proprietor being unable to continue the proceedings, the opponent is a party to the interruption proceedings before the Legal Division and has the right to comment and make relevant requests concerning resumption.

20.8.3   *Time limits on resumption*

1226   r.142(4)

Any periods, other than those for requesting examination and paying renewal fees, in force at the date of interruption of the proceedings, shall begin again as from the day on which the proceedings are resumed. If such date is less than two months before the end of the period within which the request for examination must be filed, such a request may be filed within two months of such date.

Case law

Thus, on resumption, all time limits start again for their full term except for the period for requesting examination where only the remaining time resumes, subject to a minimum of two months (J7/83) and the period for paying renewal fees. Where the due date for a renewal fee has fallen due during the period of incapacity it becomes due on the date of resumption (J902/87, also known as J./87, [1988] O.J. 323). The six-month grace period for paying a renewal fee late with a surcharge is interrupted but only the time remaining at the point of interruption is available on resumption.

Guidelines

See E-VII, 1.4 and 1.5. Any communication or decision which has been notified by the EPO during the period of interruption is regarded as null and void and must be notified anew following resumption. The Guidelines do not indicate how the remaining time in respect of an interrupted period for requesting examination or an interrupted grace period for paying a renewal fee is to be calculated but the information relating to the calculation of periods following a stay of proceedings under r.14 may be applicable (see A-IV, 2.2.4 and section 21.3.3 below).

20.8.4   *Department responsible for questions concerning interruption*

1227   OJ

See Decision of the President dated 12 July 2007 ([2007] O.J. Special Edition No. 3 G1) and Guidelines E/VII/1.2. The Legal Division has responsibility.

T54/17

However, in appeal proceedings the Legal Division does not have jurisdiction to interrupt proceedings. The Board of Appeal is responsible.

20.9   Principle of good faith – protection of legitimate expectations

Case law

This is a doctrine which has no direct basis in the EPC but is a principle generally rec-   1228
ognised in the Contracting States to the EPC which has been applied by the Boards of
Appeal consistently and by the Enlarged Board in, for example, G5/88, G7/88 and G8/88
(regarding President's agreement with German Patent Office) and G2/97 (see below). The
principle establishes that the EPO must not violate the reasonable expectations of parties.

G2/97

This decision contains a useful summary of previous case law relating to the protection of
legitimate expectations and sets out the main principles. The protection of the legitimate
expectations of users of the European patent system requires that such a user must not
suffer a disadvantage as a result of having relied on erroneous information received from
the EPO (e.g. J2/87) or on a misleading communication (e.g. J3/87). The protection of
legitimate expectations also requires the EPO to warn the applicant of any loss of rights
or easily remediable deficiencies if such a warning can be expected in all good faith. This
presupposes that the deficiency can be readily identified by the EPO within the framework of the normal handling of the case at the relevant stage of the proceedings and that
the user is in a position to correct it within the time limit.

Case law

When the law changes fundamentally as a result of a new interpretation established by the
Boards of Appeal (particularly the Enlarged Board of Appeal), the principle of protecting
legitimate expectations acts to protect those who have relied on the law as it was. See for
instance G9/93 where proprietors who had already opposed their patents were allowed to
continue and G5/93 where applicants for re-establishment following a failure to pay the
national fee for regional phase entry were allowed to continue under Art. 122.

Chapter 21: Amendment and Correction

21.1 Circumstances in which amendment is allowed

1229   Art. 123(1)

A European patent application or European patent may be amended in proceedings before the EPO in accordance with the Implementing Regulations. In any event, the applicant must be given at least one opportunity to amend the application of his own volition.

21.1.1   Amendment before receipt of the search report (direct filed European application)

1230   r.137(1)

Before receiving the European Search Report, the applicant may not amend the description, claims or drawings of a European patent application, unless otherwise provided.

Guidelines

See H-III, 3.2 – no auxiliary requests are therefore admissible at this stage. See A-V, 2.1–2.2 – amendments which are made in response to objections made during the formalities examination are of course allowable if they remedy the relevant deficiencies. Additional material meeting the requirements of r.56 is also allowable.

21.1.2   Single chance for voluntary amendment (direct filed European application)

1231   r.137(2)

Together with any comments, corrections or amendments made in response to communications by the EPO under r.70a(1) or (2), the applicant may amend the description, claims and drawings of his own volition.

Guidelines

See H-II, 2.2. Although it does not follow from the wording of r.137(2), if no search opinion is issued, voluntary amendments may be submitted in response to the first communication from the Examining Division. This may be the case, for example, if the applicant has requested examination before transmittal of the search report and also dispensed with the invitation to indicate whether he wishes to proceed with examination or not.

21.1.3   Further amendments require the consent of the Examining Division

1232   r.137(3)

Following the single chance to amend under r.137(2) EPC, no further amendment may be made without the consent of the Examining Division.

T946/96

If the Examining Division is not going to allow such a discretionary amendment then it must communicate its decision in a reasoned way to the applicant to satisfy Art. 113(1) (applicant has the chance to comment) prior to refusal of the application.

T798/95

The handing over to the EPO postal service of the decision to grant is the point at which no further amendment under r.137(3) is possible in written proceedings. See also G7/93.

Guidelines

See H-II, 2.3. Amendments which clearly remedy a deficiency raised by the Examining Division without giving rise to a new deficiency, further limit an allowable claim or add clarity should generally be allowed automatically. Otherwise, the EPO must balance the right of the applicant to obtain a valid patent against the need for an efficient procedure. The Examining Division cannot refuse to admit amendments without having first considered their admissibility (citing T1105/96 and T246/08).

21.1.4   Amendment during opposition and appeal

1233   r.79, r.80, r.81

There are important restrictions on amendment during opposition proceedings – see section 15.7.3.

RPBA

The Rules of Procedure of the Boards of Appeal apply in appeal proceedings and limit the opportunities for filing amendments (RPBA Art. 12 and RPBA Art. 13) – see section 17.9.7.

21.2 Requirement to identify amendments and the basis for them

1234   r.137(4)

Where amendments are made, they must be identified along with their basis in the application as filed. Where these requirements are not met, the Examining Division sends a communication setting a time limit of one month for remedying the deficiency.

Art. 94(4)   If the applicant fails to reply in good time then the application is deemed withdrawn.

Art. 121   Further processing is possible.

RRF Art. 2(1)(12)   The further processing fee is € 290 in this case.

Art. 122	Re-establishment would be possible if the further processing time limit was missed in spite of all due care having been shown.
Guidelines	See H-III, 2.1. In the case of an application filed in a language other than an official language of the EPO, basis in the translation should be indicated. The requirement to indicate basis also applies to auxiliary requests though in this case the Examining Division has the alternative option of deeming them inadmissible where no basis is given. Where new amendments are filed in response to the r.137(4) communication, the basis for these amendments must be indicated within that period to avoid the application being deemed withdrawn. The basis for amendments filed in preparation for or during oral proceedings should be indicated orally during those proceedings – or else they may be rejected as inadmissible.

21.3   Language and form of amendments

r.3(2)	Amendments to a European patent application or a European patent must be filed in the language of the proceedings.	1235
r.49(2)	See section 25.2.2 for the general requirements applying to documents filed subsequent to a European patent application and the need for retyped pages.	

21.4   Amendment must not add subject matter

Art. 123(2)	A European patent application or European patent may not be amended in such a way that it contains subject matter which extends beyond the content of the application as filed.	1236
Art. 70(2)	If a European patent application has been filed in a language which is not an official language of the EPO, that text (and not the translation) is the application as filed within the meaning of the EPC.	
T605/93	In the case of an international application which is filed in a non-EPO language and translated on entry into the regional phase the original text in the non-EPO language is the application as filed.	
r.7	Unless evidence is provided to the contrary, the EPO will assume, for the purposes of determining whether the subject matter of a European patent application or European patent extends beyond the content of the application as filed, that the translation referred to in Art. 14(2) or r.40(3) is in conformity with the original text of the application.	
Case law	The basic test for assessing whether an amendment adds subject matter or not is whether the amended text can be directly and unambiguously derived by the skilled person from the application as filed at the filing date, using his common general knowledge (G2/10). This test is referred to in G2/10 as the "gold" standard for assessing compliance of an amendment with Art. 123(2). Both the explicit and implicit content of the application as filed may be used as basis (T860/00). The content of the application as filed is the description, claims and drawings (G11/91) but not the abstract (T246/86) nor the priority document (T260/85). Cross-referenced documents are prima facie not part of the application as filed (T689/90) but can sometimes be used under strict conditions (T689/90, T6/84 – see also Guidelines H-IV, 2.3.1). An addition of a reference to the prior art does not contravene Art. 123(2) (T11/82, T51/87, T450/97, Guidelines F-II, 4.3). Equally, amendments to the claim preamble in view of the closest prior art changing (T13/84) or changing the position of a feature from the preamble to the characterising portion (T16/86) are both allowed. It is not usually permissible to take a feature from an embodiment and combine it with the general disclosure (intermediate generalisation) – this is only exceptionally allowable if the feature is not inextricably linked with other features of the embodiment (e.g. T151/13, T714/00).	
Guidelines	See H-IV, 2.	

G1/93	Headnote (2): A feature which has not been disclosed in the application as filed but which has been added to the application during examination and which, without providing a technical contribution to the subject-matter of the claimed invention, merely limits the protection conferred by the patent as granted by excluding protection for part of the subject-matter of the claimed invention as covered by the application as filed, is not to be considered as subject-matter which extends beyond the content of the application as filed within the meaning of Art. 123(2) EPC. The ground for opposition under Art. 100(c) EPC therefore does not prejudice the maintenance of a European patent which includes such a feature.
Comment	This decision provides a very specific exception to the usual strict application of Art. 123(2) in a situation in which a patentee is caught in an "inescapable trap" in opposition proceedings (see below under section 20.6). The exception sits somewhat uncomfortably with the logic of later decisions G2/98 and G2/10 (see below) but an undisclosed disclaimer that meets the conditions set out in G1/03 (see below) would certainly be an example of such an amendment (see T768/20 which comes to the conclusion that an undisclosed disclaimer is the only kind of amendment that would be allowable under G1/93, deadnote 2).
G1/03, G2/03	Headnote (1): An amendment to a claim by the introduction of a disclaimer may not be refused under Art. 123(2) EPC for the sole reason that neither the disclaimer nor the subject-matter excluded by it from the scope of the claim have a basis in the application as filed.
	Headnote (2): The following criteria are to be applied for assessing the allowability of a disclaimer which is not disclosed in the application as filed.
	2.1 A disclaimer may be allowable in order to:
	(a) restore novelty by delimiting a claim against state of the art under Art. 54(3) and (4) EPC (NB. now just Art. 54(3) under EPC2000);
	(b) restore novelty by delimiting a claim against an accidental anticipation under Art. 54(2) EPC; an anticipation is accidental if it is so unrelated to and remote from the claimed invention that the person skilled in the art would never have taken it into consideration when making the invention; and
	(c) disclaim subject-matter which, under Arts 52 to 57 EPC, is excluded from patentability for non-technical reasons.
	2.2 A disclaimer should not remove more than is necessary either to restore novelty or to disclaim subject-matter excluded from patentability for non-technical reasons.
	2.3 A disclaimer which is or becomes relevant for the assessment of inventive step or sufficiency of disclosure adds subject-matter contrary to Art. 123(2) EPC.
	2.4 A claim containing a disclaimer must meet the requirements of clarity and conciseness of Art. 84 EPC.
G2/10	Headnote (1): An amendment to a claim by the introduction of a disclaimer disclaiming from it subject matter disclosed in the application as filed infringes Art. 123(2) EPC if the subject-matter remaining in the claim after the introduction of the disclaimer is not, be it explicitly or implicitly, directly and unambiguously disclosed to the skilled person using common general knowledge, in the application as filed.
	Headnote (2): Determining whether or not that is the case requires a technical assessment of the overall technical circumstances of the individual case under consideration, taking into account the nature and extent of the disclosure in the application as filed, the nature and extent of the disclaimed subject matter and its relationship with the subject-matter remaining in the claim after amendment.
G1/16	In this case the Enlarged Board decided that G2/10 only applies to the assessment of amendments in which a disclosed disclaimer is introduced and not to cases in which an undisclosed disclaimer is involved. The compliance of an undisclosed disclaimer with Art. 123(2) EPC is to be assessed solely according to the criteria established by G1/03.
Guidelines	See H/V/4.2
20.5	Circumstances in which amended claims may not to relate to unsearched

21.5   Circumstances in which amended claims may not to relate to unsearched subject matter

r.137(5)	Amended claims may not relate to unsearched subject matter which does not combine with the originally claimed invention or group of inventions to form a single general inventive concept.	1237
T708/00	Amended claims may only be refused on the basis of r.137(5) first sentence if the subject matter of the claims filed originally and that of the amended claims is such that, had all the claims originally been filed together, a further search fee would have been payable in respect of the amended claims, these claims relating to a different invention within the meaning of r.64(1).	
r.137(5)	Amended claims may not relate to subject-matter which has not been searched in accordance with r.62a (plurality of independent claims) or r.63 (non-compliance with the EPC so that no meaningful search is possible).	
Guidelines	See H-IV, 4.	

21.6   Amendment must not extend the protection conferred by a patent

Art. 123(3)	A European patent may not be amended in such a way as to extend the protection it confers.	1238
G2/88	Headnote (1): A change of category of granted claims in opposition proceedings is not open to objection under Art. 123(3) EPC, if it does not result in extension of the protection conferred by the claims as a whole, when they are interpreted in accordance with Art. 69 EPC and its protocol. In this context, the national laws of the Contracting States relating to infringement should not be considered.	
	Headnote (2): An amendment of granted claims directed to a compound and to a composition including such compound, so that the amended claims are directed to the use of that compound in a composition for a particular purpose is not open to objection under Art. 123(3) EPC.	
Comment	The reasoning is that the protection conferred is to be decided under the EPC whereas the rights conferred (infringing acts, etc.) are a matter for national law. Here, the compound/composition claims conferred absolute protection in respect of all uses and hence the change to a use claim necessarily narrowed the extent of protection.	
T54/90	A product claim may be amended to a claim relating to a process for making the product without contravening Art. 123(3).	
T423/89	A product-by-process claim may be amended to a process claim without contravening Art. 123(3).	
T20/94	A process claim may not be amended to a product-by-process claim since the latter claim is construed as relating to the product per se.	
T1635/09	A use claim (here use of a compound as a contraceptive) may not be amended to a Swiss-style second medical use claim without contravening Art. 123(3) since the latter is a process for manufacture whose scope is extended by Art. 64(2) to the direct product of the process (when made for the claimed use), such direct product not being covered by a use claim.	
T1149/97	It is possible for Art. 123(3) to be contravened by amendments to the description. For compliance with Art. 123(3), nothing should infringe the patent as amended which did not infringe the patent as granted.	
Guidelines	See H-IV, 3. Any amended claims are compared with the patent in the form in which it exists, i.e. as first granted or as maintained in previous opposition or limitation proceedings.	
Guidelines	If an application is filed in a language other than English, French or German, a translation is necessary and the translation can usually be brought into conformity with the original text according to Art. 14(2). The exception to this rule is that no amendment may be made in post-grant proceedings which extends the protection of the patent contrary to Art. 123(3) (A-VII, 7).	
G1/93	This decision confirmed that an inescapable trap lurks for the unwary applicant who makes a limiting amendment during grant proceedings which adds subject matter.	

Headnote (1): If a European patent as granted contains subject matter which extends be-yond the content of the application as filed within the meaning of Art. 123(2) EPC and which also limits the scope of protection conferred by the patent, such a patent cannot be maintained in opposition proceedings unamended, because the ground for opposition under Art. 100(c) EPC prejudices the maintenance of the patent. Nor can it be amended by deleting such limiting subject-matter from the claims, because such amendment would extend the protection conferred, which is prohibited by Art. 123(3) EPC. Such a patent can, therefore, only be maintained if there is a basis in the application as filed for replacing such subject-matter without violating Art. 123(3) EPC.

The second headnote provides an potential escape from the trap under certain circum-stances (see section 21.4).

T82/93   Where a claim includes method steps not allowable pursuant to Art. 52(4) EPC, the claim cannot be maintained since to take out these features would extend the protection.

21.7   Correction of errors in documents

21.7.1   *What corrections are allowable?*

1239   r.139   Linguistic errors, errors of transcription and mistakes in any document filed with the EPO may be corrected on request.

However, if the request for such correction concerns the description, claims or drawings, the correction must be obvious in the sense that it is immediately evident that nothing else would have been intended other than what is offered as the correction.

G1/12   According to this decision, r.139 is applies generally. The correction, if allowed, has retro-spective effect. The following general principles are to be taken into account (see Reasons 37):

(a) The correction must introduce what was originally intended; it is not possble to use r.139 to give effect to a change of mind or a development of plans; it is the party's actual rather than ostensible intention which must be considered (J8/80);

(b) Where the original intention is ot immediately apparent, the requester bears the bur-den of proof, which must be a heavy one (J8/80);

(c) The error to be remedied may be an incorrect statement or an omission;

(d) The request for correction must be filed without delay.

T824/00   A correction under r.139 is not normally allowable if the result of the correction would be to breach a principle relating to the fundamental value of legal procedural certainty. Such principles include the ability of the EPO to take a decision under Art. 113(2) based on the final requests of the parties and that a party is not adversely affected by and hence cannot appeal a decision which grants his final request. A party statement relied on in a formal juridical act cannot therefore be corrected under r.139.

T309/03   Rule 139 cannot be used to correct a document in which an appeal has been filed such that no appeal is subsequently deemed to have been filed when a representative has filed the appeal against the wishes of his client.

Guidelines   See H-VI, 2. Although the incorporation of a missing part under r.56 can be based on the disclosure of the priority document, a correction under r.139 can only be based on the disclosure of the application as filed, which does not include the priority application (H-VI, 2.2.2).

21.7.2   *Corrections to the description, claims and drawings are governed by Art. 123(2) EPC*

1240   G3/89   Headnote (1): The parts of a European patent application or of a European patent relating to the disclosure (the description, claims and drawings) may be corrected under r.88 (now r.139 EPC2000), second sentence, EPC only within the limits of what a skilled person would derive directly and unambiguously, using common general knowledge, and seen objectively and relative to the date of filing, from the whole of these documents (therefore not including priority document/abstract) as filed. Such a correction is of a strictly declar-atory nature and thus does not infringe the prohibition of extension under Art. 123(2) EPC.

Headnote (2): Evidence of what was common general knowledge on the date of filing may be furnished in connection with an admissible request for correction in any suitable form.

Comment	The Enlarged Board considered that Art. 123(2) applies equally to amendments which are and which are not corrections. Further, the requirements of r.139 imply that the skilled person is able to recognise that certain information in the disclosure is incorrect as well as what the correct version should be. Hence, the correction is declaratory in the sense of the corrected version merely expressing what the skilled person would already understand. The only relevant evidence is that contained in documents shedding light on the common general knowledge of the skilled man at the filing date. These proceedings were joined with G11/91.

21.7.3   *Examples of allowable and non-allowable corrections*

G2/95	Headnote: The complete documents forming a European patent application, that is the description, claims and drawings, cannot be replaced by way of a correction under r.88 EPC (now r.139 EPC2000) by other documents which the applicants had intended to file with their request for grant. This decision follows very straightforwardly from G3/89 and G11/91 in that the subject matter that may not be extended under Art. 123(2) is that contained in the claims, description and drawings accorded a filing date under Art. 80.	1241
G1/12	Headnote (3): In cases of an error in the appellant's name, the general procedure for correcting errors under Rule 139, first sentence, EPC is available under the conditions established by the case law of the boards of appeal. This decision establishes that the incorrect designation of the appellant in a notice of appeal can be corrected under either r.101(2) or r.139 under certain conditions (see section 17.7).	
J21/94 Case law	Correction of the request is possible when the wrong request is filed with an application. Many corrections are contingent on the public not being adversely affected or misled. Correction of an omitted designation (J21/84, J7/90), correction of the withdrawal of a designation (J10/87) and correction of the withdrawal of an application (J10/87) fall into this category. An inaccurate or missing priority claim may be corrected (e.g. J4/82, J14/82, J9/91) but only if received in time for a warning to be included in the publication of the application (as recalculated if necessary) or otherwise in exceptional circumstances (e.g. J12/80, EPO partly to blame; J6/91, correction of an obvious discrepancy).	
Comment	Priority claims can now also be added and corrected under the provisions of r.52, including cases in which the applicant simply changes his mind.	
R3/22	Correction of the mistaken withdrawal of an appeal is possible.	
T1678/21	It is possible to correct a notice of appeal in order to pay the full amount of the appeal fee when the reduced amount was accidentally indicated.	
Guidelines	See H-VI, 2.2 and 2.3 for examples of allowable and non-allowable corrections. The correction of grammatical errors is usually allowed.	

21.7.4   *Correction is only possible where proceedings are pending*

J42/92 Guidelines	Correction under r.139 is only possible while proceedings are pending before the EPO. See A-V, 3 and H-VI, 2.1. Requests for correction can only be considered in grant proceedings until a decision to grant has been taken, i.e. handed to the EPO internal postal service (during written proceedings) or announced (in oral proceedings). Requests for correction can also be considered if opposition or limitation proceedings are initiated (H-II, 3.2, D-X, 4.3).	1242

21.7.5   *Competent body to decide on correction*

Guidelines	See H-VI, 2. Requests for correction under r.139 are dealt with by the department responsible for the relevant proceedings. A formality officer may decide on a request for correction unless the correction concerns the description, claims or drawings.	1243
J4/85	A request for correction of the description, claims or drawings in grant proceedings must be decided on by the Examining Division when it has assumed responsibility and not the Receiving Section.	

21.8   Correction of errors in decisions

1244   r.140

In decisions of the EPO, only linguistic errors, errors of transcription and obvious mistakes may be corrected.

T212/88

The correction has retrospective effect to the date of the decision and does not affect the time limits under Art. 108 for filing a notice and grounds of appeal.

G1/10

Headnote (1): Since Rule 140 EPC is not available to correct the text of a patent, a patent proprietor's request for such a correction is inadmissible whenever made, including after the initiation of opposition proceedings.

Comment

The Enlarged Board decided that although the text of a patent (description, claims and drawings) is an integral part of the decision to grant, it cannot be corrected under r.140 EPC once the decision has been taken since this would prejudice legal certainty for third parties. It is therefore important for applicants to thoroughly check the text proposed for grant according to r.71(3) EPC and to correct any obvious mistakes under r.139 EPC before grant. If the text granted does not correspond to that approved by the applicant then an appeal is possible.

Guidelines

See H-VI, 3. Whereas r.139 is available to correct mistakes in documents submitted by the applicant or proprietor, r.140 is only available for the correction of mistakes in decisions taken by the EPO. Correction of a decision is only possible when the text of the decision is manifestly other than what was intended by the department concerned. The Opposition Division cannot correct errors in the decision to grant since the Examining Division has exclusive competency in respect of its own decisions. The Opposition Division can only correct a decision which it has issued itself. Claim translations filed in response to a r.71(3) communication cannot be corrected under r.140 since they are not part of the decision to grant.

Chapter 22: Inventorship, Ownership and Suspension of Proceedings

22.1 Right of the inventor to be mentioned

22.1.1 Right of the inventor to be mentioned

Art. 62   The inventor has the right, vis-à-vis the applicant for or proprietor of a European patent, to be mentioned as such before the EPO.   1245

22.1.2 Designation of the inventor

Art. 81, r.19   See section 6.9.   1246

22.1.3 Rectification of the designation of the inventor

r.21(1)   An incorrect designation of an inventor may be rectified upon request, but only with the consent of the wrongly designated person and, where such a request is filed by a third party, the consent of the applicant for or proprietor of the patent. The provisions of r.19 (designation of the inventor) apply mutatis mutandis.   1247

r.21(2)   Where an incorrect designation of the inventor has been recorded in the European Patent Register or published in the European Patent Bulletin, its rectification or cancellation will also be recorded or published therein.

Guidelines   See A-III, 5.5. Designation of an additional inventor does not require the permission of the existing inventors. Correction of the designation of an inventor is possible even after grant of the patent. Rectification falls under the responsibility of the Legal Division.

22.1.4 Publication of mention of the inventor

r.20(1)   The designated inventor will be mentioned in the published European patent application and the European patent specification, unless he informs the EPO in writing that he has waived his right to be thus mentioned.   1248

r.20(2)   The provisions of r.20(1) apply where a third party files with the EPO a final decision determining that the applicant for or proprietor of a European patent is required to designate him as an inventor.

22.2 Right to a European patent

Art. 60(1)   The right to a European patent belongs to the inventor or his successor in title. If the inventor is an employee the right to a European patent is determined in accordance with the law of the State in which the employee is mainly employed; if the State in which the employee is mainly employed cannot be determined, the law to be applied is that of the State in which the employer has the place of business to which the employee is attached.   1249

Art. 60(2)   If two or more persons have made an invention independently of each other, the right to the European patent belongs to the person whose European patent application has the earliest date of filing, provided that this first application has been published.

Art. 89   The right of priority has the effect that the date of priority counts as the date of filing of the European patent application for the purposes of Art. 60(2).

Art. 60(3)   In proceedings before the EPO, the applicant is deemed to be entitled to exercise the right to a European patent.

J18/93   The EPO does not need to investigate the existence of entitlement.

22.3 Procedure where the applicant does not have the right to a European patent

22.3.1 Jurisdiction of the Contracting States

PonRArt. 1(1)   The courts of the Contracting States have, in accordance with Arts 2–6 of the Protocol of Recognition, jurisdiction to decide claims, against the applicant, to the right to the grant of a European patent in respect of one or more of the Contracting States designated in the European patent application.   1250

Comment   Note that the Protocol on Recognition only applies pre-grant.

PonRArt. 5   If the parties agree on the courts of a particular EPC State, that court applies, as long as, in the case of an employee/employer dispute, the agreement conforms to national law governing the contract of employment.

PonRArt. 4   If the parties do not have an agreement and the invention has been made by an employee and the right to be granted a patent is determined by the law of a Contracting State pursuant to Art. 60(1) second sentence, the court of that Contracting State applies.

PonRArt. 2   Where neither PonRArt. 4 nor PonRArt. 5 applies, the court of the EPC State where the applicant has his residence or principle place of business is competent.

PonRArt. 3   Where neither PonRArt. 4 nor PonRArt. 5 applies, and the applicant does not have his residence or principle place of business in an EPC State, the court of the EPC State in which the person raising the entitlement question has his residence or principle place of business is competent.

PonRArt. 6   Where none of the above apply, the default court is the German court.

22.3.2   Stay of proceedings during examination

1251   r.14(1)   If a third party provides evidence that he has instituted proceedings against the applicant seeking a decision within the meaning of Art. 61(1) (i.e. that he is entitled to the grant of the European patent), the proceedings for grant (i.e. only applies up until mention of grant in Bulletin, not possible if application refused or deemed withdrawn) will be stayed unless the third party communicates to the EPO in writing his consent to the continuation of such proceedings. Such consent is irrevocable. However, proceedings for grant are not stayed before publication of the European patent application.

r.14(2)   Where evidence is provided that a final decision within the meaning of Art. 61(1) (i.e. that a person other than the applicant is entitled to the grant of the European patent) has been taken, the EPO will inform the applicant and any other party that the proceedings for grant will be resumed as from the date stated in the communication, unless a new European patent application under Art. 61(1)(b) has been filed for all the designated Contracting States. If the decision is in favour of the third party, the proceedings may not be resumed earlier than three months after the decision has become final, unless the third party requests the resumption.

r.14(3)   Upon staying the proceedings for grant, or thereafter, the EPO may set a date on which it intends to resume the proceedings for grant, regardless of the stage reached in the national proceedings instituted under r.14(1). It will communicate this date to the third party, the applicant and any other party. If no evidence has been provided by that date that a final decision has been taken, the EPO may resume proceedings.

Case law   If proceedings are instituted before the court of a Contracting State then proceedings must be stayed whether that court has jurisdiction under the Protocol on Recognition or not (J36/97, J10/02). However, according to J6/03, proceedings before a non-EPC State court (here Canada) cannot be used to stay proceedings before the EPO. If the stay is refused, the third party can appeal. If granted, the applicant can challenge the decision and then appeal if the stay is maintained. If the stay is removed after challenge from the applicant the third party can appeal. The applicant is party to any appeal proceedings initiated by the third party (J28/94). An appeal by a third party has suspensive effect so that the application cannot proceed to grant (J7/96, J28/94). If necessary, the EPO must publish a cancellation of the mention of grant. A stay can be granted even after a decision to grant has been taken if the grant has not yet taken effect (J36/97). A divisional application may not be filed while proceedings are stayed (J20/05, J9/12).

Guidelines   See A-IV, 2.2. Proceedings should be stayed for a sufficient time to allow the court considering the matter to issue a judgement. Proceedings will be resumed if the third party is using delaying tactics or a decision has been given in favour of the applicant which is being appealed. For a Euro-PCT application, no stay is possible until the application has entered the regional phase. Any automatic debit order ceases to be valid when proceedings are stayed and must be re-filed on resumption. Proceedings are not resumed if a replacement application pursuant to Art. 61(1)(b) EPC is filed.

22.3.3   *Calculation of time limits when proceedings are resumed*

r.14(4)

All periods other than those for the payment of renewal fees, running at the date of the   1252
stay of proceedings, are interrupted by such stay. The time which has not yet elapsed
begins to run from the date on which proceedings are resumed. However, the time still to
run after such resumption is a minimum of two months.

Comment

Therefore, the rightful owner of the invention needs to monitor renewal fee payments and
pay them himself if necessary.

Guidelines

See A-IV, 2.2.4. An Example is given regarding the manner in which interrupted time
limits are to be calculated on resumption. For a period involving a number of months, it
appears that the remaining time is calculated on the basis of the number of whole months
remaining and the basis of the number of days remaining in the month that has partially
elapsed. The day before the day on which proceedings have been stayed is the last day to
have elapsed. The day of resumption is included as the first day of the period remaining.

22.3.4   *No withdrawal during stay of proceedings*

r.15

From the date on which a third party provides evidence that he has instituted national   1253
proceedings under r.14(1), and up to the date on which the proceedings for grant are resumed, neither the European patent application nor the designation of any Contracting
State may be withdrawn.

22.3.5   *Remedies following a final decision*

Art. 61(1)

If by a final decision it is adjudged that a person other than the applicant is entitled to   1254
the grant of a European patent, that person may, in accordance with the Implementing
Regulations:
(a) prosecute the European patent application as his own application in place of the
applicant;
(b) file a new European patent application in respect of the same invention; or
(c) request that the European patent application be refused.

r.16(1)

A person entitled to the grant of a European patent may only avail himself of the remedies
under Art. 61(1) if:
(a) he does so no later than three months after the decision recognising his entitlement has
become final, and
(b) the European patent has not yet been granted.

r.135(2)

Further processing is not available if the r.16(1)(a) time limit is missed.

Art. 122

Re-establishment is, however, available if all due care has been shown.

r.16(2)

The remedies under Art. 61(1) shall only apply in respect of Contracting States designated
in the European patent application in which the decision has been taken or recognised, or
must be recognised on the basis of the Protocol on Recognition.

G3/92

This case split the Enlarged Board of Appeal. The majority decided that:
"When it has been adjudged by a final decision of a national court that a person other than
the applicant is entitled to the grant of a European patent, and that person, in compliance
with the specific requirements of Art. 61(1) EPC, files a new European patent application
in respect of the same invention under Art. 61(1)(b) EPC, it is not a pre-condition for the
application to be accepted that the earlier original usurping application is still pending
before the EPO at the time the new application is filed."
The Enlarged Board felt that the potential risk to legal certainty in respect of parties commencing commercial activities on the basis that the application was dead were outweighed
by the damaging consequences of parties stealing an invention and withdrawing their
application shortly after publication (they felt that national courts could take into account
particular circumstances of this kind). Nothing in the language of the EPC was seen to
prevent this interpretation and in particular the provision governing divisional applications that a pending parent application must be in existence was seen not to apply. The
Enlarged Board felt that exercise of the remedies provided by Art. 61(1)(a) and (c) did
require a pending application.

Art. 61(2)

Art. 76(1) applies mutatis mutandis to a new European patent application filed under
Art. 61(1).

Art. 76(1)	A replacement application must therefore be filed directly with the EPO in accordance with the Implementing Regulations. It may only be filed in respect of subject matter which does not extend beyond the content of the earlier application as filed; insofar as this requirement is complied with, the replacement application will be deemed to have been filed on the date of filing of the earlier application and will enjoy any right of priority.
r.17(1)	Where the person adjudged by a final decision to be entitled to the grant of the European patent files a new European patent application under Art. 61(1)(b), the original application will be deemed to be withdrawn on the date of filing of the new application for the Contracting States designated therein in which the decision has been taken or recognised on the basis of the Protocol on Recognition.
Guidelines	See A-IV, 2.5–2.7 and C-IX, 2.

22.3.6   *Partial transfer of right by virtue of a final decision*

1255	r.18(1)	If a final decision determines that a third party is entitled to the grant of a European patent in respect of only part of the subject matter disclosed in the original European patent application, Art. 61, r.16 and r.17 apply to such part.
	r.18(2)	Where appropriate, the original European patent application may contain, for the designated Contracting States in which the decision was taken or recognised, or must be recognised on the basis of the Protocol on Recognition, claims, a description and drawings which are different from those for the other designated Contracting States.
	Guidelines	See A-IV, 2 and C-IX, 2.4.

22.3.7   *EPO division responsible*

1256	OJ	The Legal Division is responsible for decisions relating to the suspension and resumption of proceedings. See Decision of the President dated 12 July 2007, [2007] O.J. Special Edition No. 3 G1).

22.3.8   *Stay in opposition proceedings*

1257	Comment	See section 15.7.10.

Chapter 23: Representation

23.1 Kinds of representation available

23.1.1 Choice of representation for a person having a residence or principal place of business within a Contracting State

Art. 133(1)(2)	A natural or legal person having either a residence or principal place of business in a Contracting State is not compelled to be represented by a professional representative and may therefore represent itself.	1258
Comment	A legal person may represent itself through an officer of a corporation or a director.	
Art. 133(3)	Natural or legal persons having their residence or principal place of business in a Contracting State may also be represented in proceedings established by the EPC by an employee, who need not be a professional representative but who must be authorised in accordance with the Implementing Regulations. The Implementing Regulations may provide whether and under what conditions an employee of such a legal person may also represent other legal persons which have their principal place of business in a Contracting State and which have economic connections with the first legal person.	
Comment	No such provision concerning businesses with economic connections has been made in the Regulations.	
Art. 134(1)(5)(8)	Natural or legal persons having their residence or principal place of business within the territory of one of the Contracting States may also be represented professionally, either by a professional representative on the EPO list or by a qualified legal practitioner (see below).	
Guidelines	See A-VIII, 1.1–1.3.	

23.1.2 Choice of representation for a person not having a residence or principal place of business within a Contracting State

Art. 133(2)	Natural or legal persons not having their residence or principal place of business in a Contracting State must be represented by a professional representative and act through him in all proceedings established by the EPC, other than in filing a European patent application (in view of Art. 58 – see also J11/93); the Implementing Regulations may permit other exceptions.	1259
Comment	No other exceptions have been specified in the Implementing Regulations.	
Guidelines	See A-VIII, 1.1. The equivalent for a Euro-PCT application is entry into the regional phase which may also be performed by the applicant regardless of residence/place of business. All acts leading up to the assignment of a filing date or initiating the regional phase within the applicable time limit are covered. It is also possible for any person to pay a fee (A-X, 1).	
Art. 134(1)(5)(8)	Professional representation may be provided by either a professional representative on the EPO list or by a qualified legal practitioner (see below).	
r.152(3)	Where the requirements of Art. 133(2) have not been satisfied, the same period will be specified for the appointment of a representative and for the filing of an authorisation.	
Case law	Acts performed by a non-qualified person, apart from the filing of a European patent application, are normally invalid (e.g. the filing of a request for examination – J28/86). However, the deficiency is usually seen as a signing error and the document can be resubmitted with the signature of a person entitled to act and retain its original date (T665/89, as confirmed by G3/99).	
Guidelines	See A-VIII, 1.1–1.2.	

23.1.3 Common representative for parties acting in common

Art. 133(4)	The Implementing Regulations may lay down special provisions concerning the common representation of parties acting in common.	1260

r.151(1)   If there is more than one applicant and the request for grant of a European patent does not name a common representative, the applicant first named in the request will be deemed to be the common representative. However, if one of the applicants is obliged to appoint a professional representative, this representative will be deemed to be the common representative, unless the applicant first named has appointed a professional representative. The same applies to third parties acting in common in filing a notice of opposition or intervention and to joint proprietors of a European patent.

r.151(2)   If the European patent application is transferred to more than one person, and such persons have not appointed a common representative, r.151(1) applies mutatis mutandis. If it is not possible to apply these rules, the EPO will invite such persons to appoint a common representative within a period to be specified. If this invitation is not complied with, the EPO will appoint the common representative.

Guidelines   See A-VIII, 1.4. See also A-VIII, 3.4 – where there are joint applicants, the designation by the EPO of a deemed common representative does not negate the requirement for the request to be signed by all of the applicants. All other documents thereafter need only be signed by the common representative.

23.2   Professional representation

23.2.1   *Those who can act as a professional representative*

1261   Art. 134(1)(5)(8)   Representation of natural or legal persons in proceedings established by the EPC may only be undertaken by:
(a) professional representatives whose names appear on a list maintained for this purpose by the EPO; or
(b) a legal practitioner qualified in a Contracting State and having his place of business in that State, to the extent that he is entitled, in that State, to act as a professional representative in patent matters.

Comment   Whilst legal practitioners can "act as" professional representatives they do not become professional representatives.

J19/89   A "legal practitioner" is a lawyer – patent attorneys are not legal practitioners for the purposes of Art. 134(8).

23.2.2   *Right of a person acting as a professional representative to set up in business*

1262   Art. 134(6)   For the purpose of acting as a professional representative, any person whose name appears on the list of professional representatives (or who is a relevant legal practitioner) is entitled to establish a place of business in any Contracting State in which proceedings established by the EPC may be conducted, having regard to the Protocol on Centralisation annexed to the EPC. The authorities of such State may remove that entitlement in individual cases only in application of legal provisions adopted for the purpose of protecting public security and law and order. Before such action is taken, the President of the EPO must be consulted.

23.2.3   *Procedure for being entered on the list of professional representatives*

1263   Art. 134(2)   Any natural person who:
(a) is a national of a Contracting State;
(b) has his place of business or employment in a Contracting State; and
(c) has passed the European Qualifying Examination;
may be entered on the list of professional representatives.

Art. 134(3)   During a period of one year from the date on which the accession of a State to this Convention takes effect, entry on that list may also be requested by any natural person who:
(a) is a national of a Contracting State;
(b) has his place of business or employment in the State having acceded to the EPC; and
(c) is entitled to represent natural or legal persons in patent matters before the central industrial property office of that State. Where such entitlement is not conditional upon the requirement of special professional qualifications, the person must have regularly so acted in that State for at least five years.

Art. 134(4)   Entry is effected upon request, accompanied by certificates indicating that the conditions laid down in Art. 134(2) or Art. 134(3) are fulfilled.

Art. 134(7)	The President of the EPO may grant exemption from: (a) the requirement of Art. 134(2)(a) or Art. 134(3)(a) in special circumstances; (b) the requirement of Art. 134(3)(c), second sentence, if the applicant furnishes proof that he has acquired the requisite qualification in another way.
OJ	See Decision of the President dated 01 December 2011 ([2012] O.J. 13). The President has delegated his powers under Art. 134(7) to the Vice-President of DG5 pursuant to Art. 10(2)(i) EPC.
OJ	The Legal Division has sole responsibility for entries and deletions in the Register of Representatives (Decision of the President dated 12 July 2007, [2007] O.J. Special Edition No. 3 G1).

23.2.4   The European Qualifying Exam

| Art. 134a(1)(b) | The Administrative Council is competent to adopt and amend provisions governing the qualifications and training required of a person for admission to the European Qualifying Examination and the conduct of such examination. | 1264 |
| OJ | A regulation on the EQE for professional representatives has been drawn up by the Administrative Council and the current version can be found at [2009] O.J. 9 and applies from the 2010 exam onwards. Further, Implementing Regulations for this regulation have been drawn up by the Examination Board (see [2009] O.J. 347). | |

23.2.5   Institute of Professional Representatives before the EPO

Art. 134a(1)(a)	The Administrative Council is competent to adopt and amend provisions governing the Institute of Professional Representative before the EPO, hereinafter referred to as the Institute.	1265
OJ	The Administrative Council has indeed set up an institute of professional representatives called the European Patent Institute (EPI) ([1997] O.J. 350; [2002] O.J. 429; [2004] O.J. 361; [2007] O.J. 12). A code of conduct for EPI members has been drawn up ([2003] O.J. 523).	
Art. 134a(2)	Any person entered on the list of professional representatives referred to in Art. 134(1) is a member of the Institute.	
Art. 134a(1)(c)	The Administrative Council is competent to adopt and amend provisions governing the disciplinary power exercised by the Institute or the EPO in respect of professional representatives.	
OJ	A code of conduct has been drawn up by the Administrative Council ([1978] O.J. 91; [2008] O.J. 14). Under this code a disciplinary committee of EPI is set up with its own rules of procedure ([1980] O.J. 177; [2007] O.J. 552–553). Further, the code also allows for a Disciplinary Board of the EPO ([1980] O.J. 183; [2007] O.J. 552 and 555) and a Disciplinary Board of Appeal ([1980] O.J. 188; [2007] O.J. 548) which each have their own rules of procedure.	
Art. 134a(1)(d)	The Administrative Council is competent to adopt and amend provisions governing the obligation of confidentiality on the professional representative.	

23.2.6   Circumstances in which a representative may be deleted from the list

| r.154(1) | The entry of a professional representative will be deleted from the list of professional representatives if he so requests or if, despite a reminder, he fails to pay the applicable annual subscription to the Institute within five months from either:
(a) 01 January for members on the list at that date; or
(b) the date of entry for members entered on the list after 01 January of the year for which the subscription is due. | 1266 |
| r.154(2) | Without prejudice to any disciplinary measures to be taken under Art. 134a(1)(c), the entry of a professional representative may be deleted ex officio only:
(a) in the event of his death or legal incapacity;
(b) where he is no longer a national of one of the Contracting States, unless he was granted an exemption under Art. 134(7)(a); or
(c) where he no longer has his place of business or employment within one of the Contracting States. | |

OJ	The Legal Division has sole responsibility for entries and deletions in the Register of Representatives (Decision of the President dated 12 July 2007, [2007] O.J. Special Edition No. 3 G1).

23.2.7   *Re-entry on the list following deletion*

1267 r.154(3)	Any person entered on the list of professional representatives under Art. 134(2) or (3) whose entry has been deleted will, upon request, be re-entered on that list if the conditions for deletion no longer exist.

23.2.8   *Attorney-client evidentiary privilege*

1268 Art. 134a(1)(d)	The Administrative Council is competent to adopt and amend provisions governing the privilege from disclosure in proceedings before the EPO in respect of communications between a professional representative and his client or any other person.
r.153(1)	Where advice is sought from a professional representative in his capacity as such, all communications between the professional representative and his client or any other person, relating to that purpose and falling under Art. 2 of the Regulations on discipline for professional representatives, are permanently privileged from disclosure in proceedings before the EPO, unless such privilege is expressly waived by the client.
r.153(2)	Such privilege from disclosure applies, in particular, to any communication or document relating to: (a) the assessment of the patentability of an invention; (b) the preparation or prosecution of a European patent application; (c) any opinion relating to the validity, scope of protection or infringement of a European patent or a European patent application.
Comment	This provision was introduced in EPC2000. The EPO has never had, in any case, any rights of disclosure vis-à-vis a European patent applicant or proprietor (except the limited right relating to the disclosure of equivalent applications under Art. 124, now extended to prior art under EPC2000). The provision was introduced, in fact, in order to try and protect documents relating to European applications and patents from disclosure in US court proceedings. The US will generally recognise attorney-client privilege in respect of documents created in foreign jurisdictions only to the extent that the law in those jurisdictions also provides for such privilege.

23.3   Authorisation

23.3.1   *Requirement to file an authorisation*

1269 Comment	Authorisation is giving an agent the power to act as opposed to appointment, which is a matter of telling the EPO who the representative is going to be. If authorised, it is possible for a professional representative to appoint himself. According to J17/98, filing a general authorisation does not on its own imply appointment with respect to any specific case. According to current EPO practice, an appointed representative can withdraw from representation but cannot himself directly appoint a new representative. The new representative must himself confirm he is taking over representation or else the EPO will ask the applicant to appoint a new representative.
r.152(1)	The President of the EPO determines the cases in which a signed authorisation must be filed by representatives acting before the EPO.

OJ	See Decision of the President dated 12.7.2007, [2007] O.J. Special Edition No. 3 L1). The President has decided that professional representatives appearing on the list only need to present a signed authorisation when there is a change of representation and the previous representative does not terminate his representation or in specific cases where there is some doubt about the representative's entitlement to act. Legal practitioners and employee representatives, however, always need to file a signed authorisation or a reference to general authorisation already on file. Where there is a change of professional representative, an invitation sent to the new representative to file an authorisation can be ignored if the previous representative informs the EPO that his authorisation is terminated before expiry of the period set by the EPO (Art. 1(2) of the decision). The original document is required (Art. 1(2) of the decision) which means that fax filing is not possible (as explicitly stated by Decision of the President dated 20.2.2019, [2019] O.J. A18 concerning fax filing). Curiously, however, in spite of the apparent need for an original, the EPO allows the filing of authorisations electronically using either EPO Online Filing (OLF), Online Filing 2.0 or the EPO Contingency Upload Service (Decision of the President dated 03 May 2023, [2023] O.J. A48). The web form filing service may not be used – an authorisation filed by these means is considered not received. In the case of telephone consultations and during interviews and oral proceedings held by videoconference (Decision of the President dated 13 May 2020, [2020] O.J. A71), authorisations must be filed exceptionally by e-mail.
r.152(2)	Where a representative fails to file an authorisation which is required, the EPO will invite him to do so within a period to be specified.
r.152(2)	Where the requirements of Art. 133(2) have not been satisfied, (natural or legal persons not having a residence or principle place of business in a Contracting State must be represented professionally) the same period will be specified for the appointment of a representative and for the filing of an authorisation.
OJ	See Decision of the President dated 12 July 2007 ([2007] O.J. Special Edition No. 3 F2). The examination of appointments and authorisations and invitations under r.152(2) are entrusted to a formalities officer.
Guidelines	See A-VIII, 1.6–1.8. An authorisation remains in force until its termination is communicated to the EPO. A separate authorisation is required for a divisional application unless the original authorisation specifically empowers the filing of a divisional application (A-IV, 1.6).

23.3.2   Form and content of an authorisation

r.152(2)	An authorisation may cover one or more European patent applications or European patents and must be filed in the corresponding number of copies.	1270
r.152(4)	A general authorisation may be filed enabling a representative to act in respect of all the patent transactions of a party. A single copy is sufficient.	
r.152(5)	The President of the EPO may determine the form and content of: (a) an authorisation relating to the representation of persons under Art. 133(2) (natural or legal persons not having their residence or principle place of business in a Contracting State); (b) a general authorisation.	
OJ	Form 1004.1 is recommended for general authorisation ([2007] O.J. 27).	
Guidelines	See A-VIII, 1.7. The filing of a general authorisation does not negate the need to appoint a representative for each matter he is to deal with. See also J17/98.	

23.3.3   Consequences of not filing an authorisation when requested

r.152(6)	If a required authorisation is not filed in due time, any procedural steps taken by the representative, other than the filing of a European patent application, will be deemed not to have been taken, without prejudice to any other legal consequences provided for by the EPC.	1271
Art. 121	Further processing is available.	

23.3.4   *Withdrawal/termination of an authorisation*

1272   r.152(7)   Rule 152(2) and r.152(4) apply mutatis mutandis to a document withdrawing an authorisation (may withdraw authorisation for one or more applications/patents and should be filed in a corresponding number of copies; can be a general withdrawal in which case one copy is sufficient).

r.152(8)   A representative will be deemed to be authorised until the termination of his authorisation has been communicated to the EPO.

r.152(9)   Unless it expressly provides otherwise, an authorisation will not terminate vis-à-vis the EPO upon the death of the person who gave it.

23.3.5   *Where several representatives are appointed*

1273   r.152(10)   If a party appoints several representatives, they may act either jointly or singly, notwithstanding any provision to the contrary in the communication of their appointment or in the authorisation.

OJ   See Notice from the EPO dated 28 August 2013 ([2013] O.J. 535). Only the first named representative in the Request for Grant form is published in the register, Bulletin and application and all correspondence is sent to this representative's business address.

23.3.6   *The authorisation of an association*

1274   r.152(11)   The authorisation of an association of representatives will be deemed to be authorisation of any representative who can provide evidence that he practises within that association.

J16/96   It is not necessary to be in private practice to be an "association".

OJ   See Notice from the EPO dated 28 August 2013 ([2013] O.J. 535). The Legal Division considers requests for the registration of an association. Associations may only comprise professional representatives (and not legal practitioners acting as such). They may be practicing in private practice or industry.

Chapter 24: Languages

24.1 Languages of the EPC – authentic text

Art. 177(1)
The EPC, drawn up in a single original, in the English, French and German languages, 1275 is deposited in the archives of the Government of the Federal Republic of Germany, the three texts being equally authentic.

Art. 177(2)
The texts of the EPC drawn up in official languages of Contracting States other than those specified in Art. 177(1) will, if they have been approved by the Administrative Council, be considered as official texts. In the event of disagreement on the interpretation of the various texts, the texts referred to in Art. 177(1) are authentic.

24.2 Official languages of the EPO

Art. 14(1)
The official languages of the EPO are English, French and German. 1276

24.3 Language in which an application can be filed

Art. 14(2)
A European patent application can be filed in any language but, if not filed in an official 1277 language of the EPO, must be translated into an official language (see section 6.10).

24.4 Language of filing determines the language of proceedings and the authentic text

Art. 14(3)
The official language of the EPO in which a European patent application is filed, or into 1278 which it is translated, is used as the language of the proceedings.

J7/80
The language of the description and claims is determinative (now just the description under EPC2000 since claims are no longer required for a filing date).

Art. 70(1)
The text of a European patent application or a European patent in the language of the proceedings is the authentic text in all proceedings before the EPO and in any Contracting State.

Guidelines
See A-VII, 2.

24.5 Language of the proceedings to be used in all proceedings except where exceptions are provided for

Art. 14(3)
The language of the proceedings must be used in all proceedings before the EPO unless 1279 the Implementing Regulations provide otherwise.

24.6 Language to be used in written procedures – exceptions to the use of the language of the proceedings

r.3(1)(2)
In written proceedings before the EPO, any party may use any official language of the 1280 EPO. Amendments to a European patent application or European patent, however, must be filed in the language of the proceedings.

T706/91
References to the application during opposition proceedings must be in the language of proceedings even if the opposition is drafted in another official language.

G4/08
Headnote (2): In written proceedings on a European patent application or on an international application in the regional phase, EPO departments cannot use an EPO official language other than the language of the proceedings used for the application pursuant to Article 14(3) EPC.

Art. 14(4)
Natural or legal persons having their residence or principal place of business within a Contracting State having a language other than English, French or German as an official language, and nationals of that State who are resident abroad, may file documents which have to be filed within a time limit in an official language of that State. They must however, file a translation in an official language of the EPO in accordance with the Implementing Regulations.

r.3(1)(2)
The translation referred to in Art. 14(4) may be filed in any official language of the EPO, except for amendments to a European patent application or European patent which must be in the language of the proceedings.

r.6(2)	A translation under Art. 14(4) must be filed within one month of filing the document. This also applies to requests under Art. 105a (request for limitation or revocation). Where the document is a notice of opposition or an appeal, or a statement of grounds of appeal, or a petition for review, the translation may be filed within the period for filing such a notice or statement or petition, if that period expires later.
Art. 121/122	Further processing is available to the applicant if the time limit is not observed in pre-grant proceedings. Re-establishment is available in post-grant proceedings.
r.6(3)–(7)	Where a person who is a natural or legal person having a residence or principle place of business within a Contracting State having an official language other than English, French or German, or a national of such a State resident abroad files a European patent application or a request for examination in an official language of that State, the filing fee or examination fee is reduced in accordance with the Rules relating to Fees. However, the reduction only applies if the applicant is a small or medium-sized company (the definition of which is found in Commission recommendation 2003/361/EC of 6 May 2003, see Official Journal of the EU, L/124/p36 of 20 May 2003), a natural person, or a non-profit organisation, university or public research organisation. The applicant must declare himself to be such a person or entity and provide evidence if required by the EPO. In the case of multiple applicants, each one must be a qualifying person or entity.
Comment	New r.6(3)–(7) entered into force on 01 April 2014 and apply to direct European patent applications filed on or after that date and Euro-PCT applications entering the European phase on or after that date. Under the previous version of the rule, a reduction of 20 % applied to all applicants having the necessary residency/nationality regardless of their commercial status. Furthermore, under the previous version of the rule, the fee reduction also applied to the opposition fee, appeal fee, fee for petition for review, limitation fee and revocation fee.
RRFArt. 14(1)	The reduction is 30 %.
G6/91	Headnote (1): The persons referred to in Art. 14(2) EPC (NB. now Art. 14(4) according to EPC2000) are entitled to the fee reduction under r.6(3) EPC if they file the essential item of the first act in filing, examination or appeal proceedings in an official language of the State concerned other than English, French or German, and supply the necessary translation no earlier than simultaneously.
T149/85	The nationality/residency of the applicant is determinative, not that of the representative.
J4/18	In the case of joint applicants, each one must be a natural person or entity within the meaning of r.6(4) EPC, as specified in r.6(7) EPC, but only one of them needs to be a person defined by Art. 14(4) for the fee reduction to apply.
Guidelines	See A-X, 9.2. A small or medium-sized enterprise (SME) is one that employs fewer than 250 persons, that has an annual turnover not exceeding 50 million Euros and/or an annual balance sheet total not exceeding 43 million Euros and for which no more than 25 % of the capital is held directly or indirectly by another company that is not an SME. If the status of the applicant changes after the fee has been paid then this does not retroactively invalidate the reduction. If the reduction is claimed by a party not entitled to it at the time the fee is paid, however, and that fact comes to the attention of the EPO at a later date, the application will be deemed to be withdrawn and further processing will be necessary.
r.3(3)	Documentary evidence and, in particular, publications may be filed in any language. The EPO may, however, require that a translation in one of its official languages be filed within a period to be specified.

24.7   Consequence of not using an admissible language or not filing a required translation in written proceedings

1281 Art. 14(1)	The official languages of the EPO are English, French and German.
Comment	The implication of Art. 14(1) EPC is that all documents must be filed in one of these languages unless a specific exception is made in the EPC.

Guidelines	See A-VII, 5. If a document, other than the application, is filed in a non-admissible language, it is deemed not to have been filed. Likewise, if a required translation is not filed in time then the original document is deemed not to have been filed. The person who has filed the document is notified of this by the EPO. The document concerned is nevertheless added to the public file. Accompanying documents which are of relevance to the procedure, however (e.g. priority document) are put on file if the application number can be established and are considered properly filed. Third party observations and notices of opposition are communicated to the applicant or proprietor, even if deemed not filed.
Art. 14(4)	Where a document, other than the application itself, is filed in a language which the party concerned is not entitled to use under this provision, or else the required translation is not filed in time, the document is deemed not to have been filed.
r.3(3)	If a required translation of a piece of evidence is not filed in due time, the EPO may disregard the document in question.

24.8 Language to be used in oral proceedings – exceptions to the use of the language of the proceedings

r.4(4)	If the parties and the EPO agree, any language may be used in oral proceedings.	1282
r.4(1)	Any party to oral proceedings before the EPO may use an official language of the EPO other than the language of the proceedings if such party gives notice to the EPO at least one month before the date of such oral proceedings or provides for interpretation into the language of the proceedings.	
r.4(1)	Any party may likewise use an official language of a Contracting State, if he provides for interpretation into the language of the proceedings.	
r.4(1)	The EPO may permit derogations from the provisions of r.4(1).	
OJ	A separate request must be made before an appeal hearing where a request has already been made in first instance proceedings (communication dated 16.7.2007, [2007] O.J. Special Edition No. 3 H3).	
r.4(2)	In the course of oral proceedings, employees of the EPO may use an official language of the EPO other than the language of the proceedings.	
r.4(3)	Where evidence is taken, any party, witness or expert to be heard who is unable to express himself adequately in an official language of the EPO or of a Contracting State may use another language. Where evidence is taken upon request of a party, parties, witnesses or experts expressing themselves in a language other than an official language of the EPO may be heard only if that party provides for interpretation into the language of the proceedings. The EPO may, however, permit interpretation into one of its other official languages.	
r.4(5)	The EPO will, if necessary, provide at its own expense interpretation into the language of the proceedings, or, where appropriate, into its other official languages, unless such interpretation is the responsibility of one of the parties.	
r.4(6)	Statements made by employees of the EPO, parties, witnesses or experts, made in an official language of the EPO, will be entered in the minutes in that language. Statements made in any other language are entered in the official language into which they are translated. Amendments to a European patent application or European patent are entered in the minutes in the language of the proceedings.	
T2696/16	A party which elects to use the language of the proceedings (here German) cannot request the EPO to provide translation (here into English) for the benefit of one of its own accompanying persons (here an employee).	
Guidelines	See E-V, 1–6.	

24.9 Certification of translated documents

r.5	Where the translation of a document is required, the EPO may require that a certificate that the translation corresponds to the original text be filed within a period to be specified. If the certificate is not filed in due time, such document will be deemed not to have been filed unless otherwise provided.	1283
r.132(2)	A period specified by the EPO is usually from two to four months or in rare cases up to six months and may be extended upon request presented before the expiry of the period.	

Guidelines   See A-VII, 7. A certificate is only required when there are serious doubts as to the accuracy of the translation. If the certificate is not filed in time, further processing would be available to the applicant in grant proceedings and re-establishment would be available to the proprietor in opposition or limitation proceedings.

24.10 Language of publication of applications, patents, the Bulletin, the Official Journal and entries in the Register

1284   Art. 14(5)   European patent applications are published in the language of the proceedings.

Art. 14(6)   The specifications of European patents are published in the language of the proceedings and include a translation of the claims in the two other official languages of the EPO.

Art. 14(7)   The following are published in the three official languages of the EPO:
(a) the European Patent Bulletin;
(b) the Official Journal of the EPO.

Art. 14(8)   Entries in the European Patent Register are made in the three official languages of the EPO. In cases of doubt, the entry in the language of the proceedings is authentic.

24.11 Languages of the Administrative Council

1285   Art. 31(1)   The languages used in the deliberations of the Administrative Council are English, French and German.

Art. 31(2)   Documents submitted to the Administrative Council, and the minutes of its deliberations, are drawn up in the three languages mentioned in Art. 31(1).

Chapter 25: Miscellaneous Common Provisions

25.1 Principles of interpretation relevant to the EPC

G5/83   The Enlarged Board has indicated that the Vienna Convention should be used to help interpret the EPC even though it did not apply when the EPC was concluded. The relevant principles of Arts 31 and 32 of the Vienna Convention are: 1286
(a) the EPC should be interpreted in good faith;
(b) unless it is established that the Contracting States intended a particular meaning should be given to a term, the terms of the EPC should be given their ordinary meaning in their context and in light of the object and purpose of the EPC;
(c) that context is the text of the EPC (including preamble, Regulations and Protocols);
(d) also to be taken into account are any subsequent agreement between the parties regarding the interpretation or application of the provisions, any subsequent practice which establishes the agreement of the parties regarding interpretation and any relevant rules of public international law;
(e) the preparatory documents and the circumstances of the conclusion of the EPC may be taken into consideration in order to confirm the meaning resulting from the application of the previous rules or to determine the meaning when applying those rules either leaves the meaning ambiguous/obscure or leads to a manifestly absurd or unreasonable result.

Art. 164(1)   The Implementing Regulations, the Protocol on Recognition, the Protocol on Privileges and Immunities, the Protocol on Centralisation, the Protocol on Interpretation of Art. 69 and the Protocol on Staff Complement are integral parts of the EPC.

Art. 164(2)   In case of conflict between the provisions of the EPC and those of the Implementing Regulations, the provisions of the EPC prevail.

25.2 Rules relating to documents filed subsequently to the filing of the application

25.2.1   Where and how to file subsequent documents

r.2(1)   In proceedings before the EPO, documents may be filed by delivery by hand, by postal   1287
services or by means of electronic communication. The President of the EPO lays down the details and conditions and, where appropriate, any special formal or technical requirements for the filing of documents. In particular, he may specify that confirmation must be supplied. If such confirmation is not supplied in due time, documents filed subsequent to the application will be deemed not to have been received.

OJ   According to Decision of the President dated 03 January 2017 ([2017] O.J. A11), the filing offices of the EPO are Munich (headquarter and PschorrHofe buildings), the Hague and Berlin. Vienna is not a filing office. Subsequent documents, except authorisations and priority documents, may be filed by fax but not by telegram or teletex (see Decision of the EPO dated 20.2.2019, [2019] O.J. A18). A confirmation copy may be requested but is not routinely required. If a requested confirmation copy is not filed within the two month period set then the document is deemed not to have been received. Subsequent documents may also be filed electronically using EPO Online Filing (OLF), Online Filing 2.0, the web-form filing service or the EPO Contingency Upload Service (see Decision of the President dated 03 May 2023, [2023] O.J. A48) except that priority documents may only be filed electronically if they have been digitally signed by the issuing authority in a manner acceptable to the EPO and may not in any case be filed by web-form filing or the EPO Contingency Upload Service. Many other exceptions exist for web-form filing (can't be used to file authorizations or any documents in opposition, limitation, revocation, appeal or review proceedings). E-mail should not generally be used as it has no legal force (see [1999] O.J. 509; [2000] O.J. 458). The exception is that e-mail is acceptable and indeed must be used during telephone consultations and during interviews and oral proceedings held by videoconference to file all documents including authorisations (Decision of the President dated 13 May 2020, [2020] O.J. A71).

OJ	According to the Decision of the President dated 03 May 2023 ([2023] O.J. A49), applicants may use a service called "MyEPO Portfolio" in order to file a response to a r.71(3) communication (with or without further processing), to reply to communications from the examining division in respect of requests for correction or amendment of the bibliographic data set out in a r.71(3) communication or possible inconsistencies in the claim translations submitted in response to a r.71(3) communication, to reply to a communication under Art. 94(3) (with or without further processing), to respond to an extended European search report under r.70a (with or without further processing) or to reply to an invitation to indicate the subject matter to be searched under r.62a or r.63. The facility is an online web-based service requiring the use of a smart card and accessible to professional representatives and legal practitioners entitled to act according to Art. 134(8) EPC and parties who have a residence or place of business in an EPC contracting state.
T858/18	Where a document other than a patent application (e.g. an opposition) is filed by fax and is received partly before midnight and partly after midnight it is considered to have been received on the later day. It is not possible to give the part of the document received before midnight the earlier filing date. This is due to the wording of the President's decision which distinguishes between the filing of patent applications and the receipt of other documents.
Guidelines	See A-VIII, 2.5.

25.2.2   *Rules relating to content and form*

r.1	In written proceedings before the EPO, the requirement to use the written form is satisfied if the content of the documents can be reproduced in a legible form on paper.
r.50(1)	The following rules apply to documents replacing documents making up the European patent application: r.42 (content of the description); r.43 (form and content of the claims); r.47 (form and content of the abstract); r.48 (prohibited matter), and; r.49 (general provisions governing the presentation of the application documents).
r.50(1)	Rule 49(2) (President of the EPO to determine provisions governing the presentation of the application documents) applies to the translation of the claims referred to in r.71 (translation of the allowed claims).
r.50(2)	The President of the EPO determines the presentation requirements of all documents other than those making up the application.
OJ	See Art. 3 of Decision of the President dated 25 November 2022 ([2022] O.J. A113). All documents other than those making up the application should generally be typewritten or printed. There must be a margin of about 2.5 cm on the left-hand side of each page.
OJ	See Notice from the EPO dated 08 November 2013 ([2013] O.J. 603). As of 01 January 2014, the EPO has been requiring that any document replacing part of a European patent application is typed or printed. Handwritten amendments are no longer accepted. This is in line with r.50(1) in combination with r.49(2) EPC.
Guidelines	See E-III, 8.7. In oral proceedings before the Examining Division the applicant must also submit amended pages in retyped format and facilities are provided to facilitate this. If for some reason the applicant is unable to provide retyped pages on which a decision can be taken: (a) if the application is to be refused, the decision will be taken on the basis of the formally deficient documents; (b) if agreement as been reached on an allowable text, the Examining Division will take a decision that a certain text meets the requirements of the EPC and continue the procedure in writing; the applicant should be set a two month time limit for filing formally correct documents when the written procedure is resumed.
T1635/10	Before the Boards of Appeal, decisions can still be taken in oral proceedings on the basis of formally deficient documents and such deficiencies can be dealt with on remittal.
r.82	In oral proceedings before the Opposition Division, or in opposition appeal oral proceedings, when the patent is maintained in amended form, a decision may be taken on the basis of formally deficient documents and the applicant must submit retyped pages during the three month time limit set for filing new translations of the claims and paying the corresponding fee.
OJ	See Notice from the EPO dated 09 March 2016 ([2016] O.J. A22). The r.82 procedure only applies in oral proceedings and not in written opposition proceedings. See also Guidelines E-III, 8.7.1 and 8.7.3.

1288

25.2.3 *Need for a signature*

r.50(3) Documents filed after filing the application must be signed, with the exception of annexed   1289
documents. If a document has not been signed, the EPO will invite the party concerned
to do so within a time limit to be specified. If signed in due time, the document will retain
its original date of receipt; otherwise it will be deemed not to have been filed.

r.132(2) A period to be specified by the EPO shall be neither less than two months nor more than
four months; in certain circumstances it may be up to six months. In certain circumstances
it may be extended upon request, presented before the expiry of such period.

r.2(2) Where the EPC provides that a document must be signed, the authenticity of the document may be confirmed by handwritten signature or other appropriate means the use of
which has been permitted by the President of the EPO. A document authenticated by
such other means will be deemed to meet the legal requirements of signature in the same
way as a document bearing a handwritten signature which has been filed in paper form.

Guidelines See A-VIII, 3. Subsequent documents must be signed by the applicant or representative
(with the exception of an authorisation which may only be signed by the applicant). Ini-
tials or other abbreviated form of signature are not acceptable. The entitlement of a person
signing on behalf of a legal person is not verified. Once a common representative has been
appointed, only he needs to sign subsequent documents.

25.3 Withdrawal of applications, patents, designations, extensions, priority claims, oppositions, requests for limitation/revocation and appeals

25.3.1 *Withdrawal of an application*

Case law An application may be withdrawn any time before grant but the withdrawal must be   1290
unambiguous and unqualified (J11/87, J11/80). The withdrawal is binding in the interests
of legal certainty and no further processing or retraction is possible though a withdrawal,
if mistaken, may be corrected under r.139 in certain circumstances (see J4/97). Generally
speaking, once the withdrawal has been notified to the public, through publication in the
European Patent Bulletin or via the Register of European patents, correction is no longer
possible (J4/97, J25/03, J3/22).

r.143(n) Withdrawal is recorded in the Register and published in the Bulletin under Art. 129(a).

Art. 67(4) When an application is withdrawn it is deemed that no protection existed under Art. 67(1)
and (2).

r.15 Applications may not, however, be withdrawn during a stay of proceedings following
entitlement action.

r.67(2) The application will not be published if it is withdrawn before the termination of the
technical preparations for publication.

Guidelines See E-VIII, 8.1 and C-V, 11.

25.3.2 *Withdrawal of part of the subject matter of an application*

Case law Claims may be seen to be irrevocably abandoned if they are deleted and no phrase such   1291
as "without prejudice to the filing of a divisional application" is used (J15/85). This applies to any subject matter abandoned (T61/85), e.g. by deletion before grant (T1149/97).
However, according to T123/85, when a request is made in opposition proceedings to
maintain the patent in amended form, this does not represent abandonment of any of the
subject matter of the claims as granted.

Guidelines See C-IX, 1.3 and H-III, 2.5.

25.3.3 *Withdrawal of a designation*

Art. 79(3) The designation of a Contracting State may be withdrawn at any time up to the grant of   1292
the European patent (i.e. the date grant takes effect).

r.15 Designations may not, however, be withdrawn during a stay of proceedings following
entitlement action.

r.39(2) If the designation fee is not paid in time, or if all designations are withdrawn, then the
European patent application is deemed withdrawn.

Guidelines See A-III, 11 and E-VIII, 8.1. Designation fees are not refunded.

25.3.4   *Withdrawal of a request for extension or validation*

1293   Guidelines   See A-III, 12.3. A request for extension or validation of a European patent may be withdrawn at any time and is deemed withdrawn if a European patent application is finally refused, withdrawn or deemed withdrawn. No separate communication is sent to the applicant. Extension and validation fees are not refunded.

25.3.5   *Withdrawal of a priority claim*

1294   Guidelines   See F-VI, 3.5 and E-VIII, 8.2. Priority claims may be withdrawn at any time and publication will be delayed in appropriate circumstances.

25.3.6   *Withdrawal of an opposition*

1295   See section 15.7.5.

25.3.7   *Withdrawal of an appeal*

1296   See section 17.11.

25.3.8   *Withdrawal of a patent*

1297   Case law   A patent will be revoked if the proprietor no longer approves the text as granted in opposition proceedings and does not propose any other text for maintenance of the patent (e.g. T73/84). Alternatively, the proprietor can simply request revocation (T92/88).

       Guidelines   See E-VIII, 8.4. Surrender of a patent (with no retrospective effect) is a matter for national proceedings.

25.3.9   *Withdrawal of a request for limitation/revocation*

1298   Guidelines   See D-X, 9. Withdrawal is possible if proceedings are pending but the revocation/limitation fee is not refunded.

25.4   Renewal fees

25.4.1   *Requirement to pay renewal fees*

1299   Art. 86(1)   Renewal fees are due in respect of the third year and each subsequent year, calculated from the date of filing of the application.

       RRFArt. 2(1)(4)   Renewal fees are € 530 for the third year, € 660 for the fourth year, € 925 for the fifth year, € 1180 for the sixth year, € 1305 for the seventh year, € 1440 for the eighth year, € 1570 for the ninth year and € 1775 for the tenth and each subsequent year.

       Art. 86(2)   The obligation to pay renewal fees terminates with the payment of the renewal fee due in respect of the year in which the mention of the grant of the European patent is published in the European Patent Bulletin.

       Art. 86(1)   Renewal fees for a European patent application are paid to the EPO in accordance with the Implementing Regulations.

       r.51(1)   A renewal fee for a European patent application in respect of the coming year is due on the last day of the month containing the anniversary of date of filing of the European patent application. The renewal fee in respect of the third year may not be validly paid more than six months before it falls due. All other renewal fees may not be validly paid more than three months before they fall due.

       J4/91   If the due date falls on day on which one of the filing offices of the EPO is closed then it may still be paid without surcharge on the next day on which they are all open (by analogy with r.134(1) – note that the due date is not a time limit so r.134(1) does not apply directly).

Guidelines	See A-X, 5.2.4. The earliest day for payment is the last day of the third month previous to the month in which the anniversary falls, or the sixth month in the case of the first renewal fee. A renewal fee paid too early is refunded. In deciding which is the last fee due to the EPO, it is not the due date which is significant (usually falling at the end of the month) but the anniversary of the filing date. If the mention of grant is to be published after the next anniversary of the filing date, the renewal fee for the next year is due to the EPO. If the mention of the grant is published before or on the anniversary of the filing date, the renewal fee for the next year is due to national offices.
r.51(2)	If a renewal fee is not paid on the due date there is no loss of rights since it can still be paid with surcharge during a six-month grace period (see below).

25.4.2   *Consequences of non-payment – grace period*

r.51(2)	If a renewal fee is not paid on the due date, the fee may still be paid within six months of the due date, provided that an additional fee is also paid within that period.	1300
RRFArt. 2(1)(5)	The additional fee is 50 % of the belated renewal fee.	
J4/91	In the case of a standard renewal fee falling due on the last day of a month containing an anniversary of the filing date, the six-month period ends on the last day of the sixth month from the month in which the renewal fee fell due (and is subject to any extension under r.134(1)). It is NOT calculated as an aggregate time limit.	
J12/84	The applicant is informed of the period for late payment with surcharge but may not invoke the lack of such a communication (see also J1/89).	
r.135(2)	Further processing is not available in respect of the r.51(2) time limit.	
Art. 122	Re-establishment of rights is, however, available if all due care was shown.	
Art. 86(1), r.51(2)	If a renewal fee is not paid in due time (i.e. within the six month grace period with surcharge) the European patent application is deemed to be withdrawn.	
OJ	The additional fee was waived in view of the COVID-19 pandemic from 01 June 2020 to 31 August 2020, for any renewal fee with a due date on or after 15 March 2020 which was not paid on the due date (see [2020] O.J. A70). Hence, any renewal fee falling due on or after 15 March 2020 could be validly paid by 31 August 2020 with no additional fee.	

25.4.3   *Provisions in respect of divisional applications*

r.51(3)	Renewal fees already due in respect of an earlier application at the date on which a divisional application is filed must also be paid for the divisional application and are due on its filing. These fees and any renewal fee falling due within four months of filing the divisional application may be paid within that period without an additional fee. Rule 51(2) applies, i.e. if payment is not made by the end of the four-month period, the renewal fees may still be validly paid within six months of their due date provided that an additional fee is paid at the same time (the due date here could be the date of filing of the divisional for renewal fees already due on filing or the actual due date for later fees).	1301
r.135(2)	Further processing is not available in respect of the r.51(3) time limits.	
Art. 122	Re-establishment of rights would, however, be available if the six month grace period was missed in spite of all due care having been taken.	
Guidelines	See A-IV, 1.4.3.	

25.4.4   *Provisions in respect of applications which have been refused or deemed withdrawn*

r.51(4)	If a European patent application has been refused or deemed to be withdrawn as a result of non-observance of a time limit, and if the applicant's rights are re-established under Art. 122, a renewal fee: (a) which would have fallen due under r.51(1) in the period starting on the date on which the loss of rights occurred, up to and including the date of the notification of the decision re-establishing the rights is due on that latter date. This fee and any renewal due within four months from that latter date may still be paid within four months of that latter date without an additional fee. Rule 51(2) applies (i.e. six-month grace period for paying the renewal fee late with an additional fee also runs in parallel);	1302

(b) which, on the date on which the loss of rights has occurred, was already due but the period provided for in r.51(2) has not yet expired, may still be paid within six months from the date of the notification of the decision re-establishing the rights, provided that the additional fee pursuant to r.51(2) is also paid within that period.

r.135(2)   Further processing is not available in respect of the r.51(4) time limits.
Art. 122   Re-establishment of rights is, however, would be available if the six month grace period was missed in spite of all due care having been taken.

25.4.5   *Renewal fees when the Enlarged Board of Appeal reopens proceedings before the Board of Appeal*

1303   r.51(5)   If the Enlarged Board of Appeal reopens proceedings before the Board of Appeal under Art. 112a(5) second sentence, a renewal fee:
(a) which would have fallen due under r.51(1) in the period starting on the date when the decision of the Board of Appeal subject to the petition for review was taken, up to and including the date of the notification of the decision of the Enlarged Board of Appeal re-opening proceedings before the Board of Appeal shall be due on that latter date. This fee and any renewal fee due within four months from that latter date may still be paid within four months of that latter date without an additional fee. Rule 51(2) applies (i.e. six-month grace period for paying the renewal fee late with an additional fee also runs in parallel);
(b) which, on the date on which the decision of the Board of Appeal was taken, was already due but the period provided for in r.51(2) has not yet expired, may still be paid within six months from the date of the notification of the decision of the Enlarged Board of Appeal reopening proceedings before the Board of Appeal, provided that the additional fee pursuant to r.51(2) is also paid within that period.

r.135(2)   Further processing is not available in respect of the r.51(5) time limits.
Art. 122   Re-establishment of rights is, however, would be available if the six month grace period was missed in spite of all due care having been taken.

25.4.6   *Provisions in respect of replacement applications*

1304   r.51(3)   A renewal fee is not payable for a new European patent application filed under Art. 61(1) (b) in respect of the year in which it was filed and any preceding year.

25.4.7   *Refund of a renewal fee*

1305   Guidelines   A renewal fee will be refunded if the application is withdrawn before the due date (see A-X, 10.1.1).

25.5   Assignment, licensing and other property transactions

25.5.1   *Transfer and constitution of rights*

1306   Art. 71   A European patent application may be transferred or give rise to rights for one or more of the designated Contracting States.

Guidelines   See E-XIV.

25.5.2   *Assignment*

1307   Art. 72   An assignment of a European patent application must be made in writing and requires the signatures of the parties to the contract.

25.5.3   *Contractual licensing*

1308   Art. 73   A European patent application may be licensed in whole or in part for the whole or part of the territories of the designated Contracting States.

25.5.4   *Law applicable*

1309   Art. 74   Unless the EPC provides otherwise, a European patent application as an object of property is, in each designated Contracting State and with effect for such State, subject to the law applicable in that State to national patent applications.

25.5.5   *Registration of a transfer of an application or a patent*

r.22(1)	The transfer of a European patent application (or patent during opposition proceedings or the opposition period – see r.85) will be recorded in the European Patent Register at the request of an interested party, upon production of documents providing evidence of such transfer.
Art. 127	No entry is made in the register prior to publication of the application.
r.22(2)	The request will not be deemed to have been filed until an administrative fee has been paid. It may be rejected only if r.22(1) has not been complied with.
RRFArt. 3(1)	The amount of the administrative fee is fixed by the President of the EPO.
OJ	The amount is € 115 (see decision of the President dated 17 January 2023, [2023] O.J. A3).
r.22(3)	A transfer has effect vis-à-vis the EPO only at the date when and to the extent that the documents referred to in r.22(1) have been produced.
Guidelines	See E-XIV, 3 and 4. Any suitable written evidence is admissible. In view of Art. 72, any document submitted as evidence must be signed by the parties. Evidence may also be necessary to show that a person signing on behalf of a legal entity has the authority to do so. A separate fee must be paid for each application transferred.
OJ	See [2021] O.J. A86. Evidence supporting requests for the registration of a transfer of rights must contain the handwritten signature of the party concerned or, where filed electronically, a qualified electronic signature fulfilling certain specified criteria. For these purposes, the President's general decision on electronic filing does not apply.

1310

25.5.6   *Registration of the grant or transfer of a licence and other transactions relating to a patent application*

r.23(1)	Rule 22(1) and (2) (registration of a transfer) apply mutatis mutandis to the registration of the grant or transfer of a licence, the establishment or transfer of a right in rem (e.g. a security right) in respect of a European patent application and any legal means of execution of such an application.
Comment	Note that r.85 only applies to the **transfer** of a patent so this provision does not apply to patents, only applications.
r.23(2)	A registration under r.23(1) will be cancelled upon request, supported by documents providing evidence that the right has lapsed, or by the written consent of the proprietor of the right to the cancellation of the registration. Rule 22(2) applies mutatis mutandis – the request will not be deemed to have been filed until an administrative fee has been paid and it may be rejected only if the foregoing provisions have not been complied with.
RRFArt. 3(1)	The amount of the administrative fee is fixed by the President of the EPO.
OJ	The amount is € 115 (see decision of the President dated 17 January 2023, [2023] O.J. A3).
r.24	A licence in respect of a European patent application will be recorded: (a) as an exclusive licence if the applicant and the licensee so request; (b) as a sub-licence where it is granted by a licensee whose licence is recorded in the European Patent Register.

1311

25.5.7   *EPO department responsible*

Art. 20	The Legal Division is responsible for decisions in respect of entries in the Register of European Patents.
OJ	See Decision of the President dated 12 July 2007 ([2007] O.J. Special Edition No. 3 G1). The Legal Division is responsible for registration and cancellation of licenses and other rights pursuant to Art. 71, 73 and 74 and rr.23 and 24 EPC).

1312

25.6   Observations by third parties

Art. 115	In proceedings before the EPO, following the publication of the European patent application, any third party may, in accordance with the Implementing Regulations, present observations concerning the patentability of the invention to which the application or patent relates. That person does not become a party to the proceedings.
Guidelines	See E-VI, 3 – a party to the proceedings is not a third party and is not entitled to file third party observations.
r.114(1)	Any observations by a third party must be filed in writing in an official language of the EPO and state the grounds on which they are based. Rule 3(3) applies.

1313

Guidelines	See A-VII, 3.5 and E-VI, 3. Third party observations in any other language are deemed not to have been received but are put on file nevertheless.
OJ	See [2017] O.J. A86. If not filed in an EPO language, the EPO will ask the third party (where possible) to file a translation.
r.3(3)	Documentary evidence and, in particular, publications may be filed in any language. The EPO may, however, require that a translation in one of its official languages be filed, within a period to be specified. If a required translation is not filed in due time, the EPO may disregard the document in question.
Case law	The case law concerning anonymous third party observations is not consistent. According to T1336/09, anonymous third party observations are admissible in ex parte proceedings and the requirement that documents be signed according to r.50(3) EPC only applies to parties to the proceedings and not third parties. According to decision T146/07, however, the requirement for third party observations to be in writing does imply that they have to be signed according to r.50(3) EPC and this is particularly important in inter partes proceedings so that the EPO can ensure the observations are indeed filed by a third party and not a party to the proceedings (e.g. so that an appropriate award of costs can be made when documents are late filed by a party to the proceedings). Unsigned third party observations are therefore deemed not filed according to this decision (at least in inter partes proceedings). On the other hand, in decision T735/04, a document cited in anonymous third party observations was introduced into inter partes proceedings by the Board of Appeal on the basis of its relevance and the fact that it was known to the patentee. Hence, even if, according to T146/07, unsigned third party observations are inadmissible per se in inter partes proceedings, they can be adopted by a party to the proceedings or the EPO itself and introduced in this way.
r.2(1)	In EPO proceedings, documents may be filed by delivery by hand, by postal services or by means of electronic communication according to the conditions laid down by the President of the EPO.
Guidelines	See E-VI, 3. Third party observations may be filed in writing by post, fax or electronically (see section 25.2) or via a specific interface provided by the EPO on its website (see Decision of the President dated 10 May 2011, [2011] O.J. 418). They may concern novelty, inventive step, clarity, sufficiency of disclosure, exceptions to patentability under Art. 52(2), Art. 53 or Art. 57 and the allowability of amendments under Art. 123(2) and Art. 123(3). No signature is required and the third party does not have to be identified. Observations filed whilst proceedings are pending will be put on the public part of the file and commented on by the EPO in the next office action. Observations filed after a decision has been taken are included in the file but not taken into account. Observations filed when proceedings are no longer pending are neither taken into account nor added to the public file.
OJ	See [2017] O.J. A86. If the third party observations are not anonymous and are properly substantiated then the EPO will make every effort to issue the next office action within three months of their receipt. Any third party observations filed in the international phase will be considered on EPO regional phase entry and, if the third party has so requested, and the observations are in an EPO language, substantiated and not anonymous, the EPO will make every effort to issue a first office action within three months of the expiry of the period under r.161.
r.114(2)	The observations are communicated to the applicant for or proprietor of the patent who may comment on them.
OJ	See Notice from the EPO dated 09 March 2022 ([2022] O.J. A28) – cited documents and other annexes (other than those that cannot be easily accessed by online file inspection) are no longer routinely sent along with communications under r.114(2) but are still supplied on special request by a party.

25.7   Notification by the EPO

25.7.1   Subject matter of notifications

1314	Art. 119	Decisions, summonses, notices and communications must be notified by the EPO of its own motion in accordance with the Implementing Regulations.

25.7.2   Form of notification

r.125(1)   In proceedings before the EPO, any notification to be made must take the form of the   1315
original document, a copy thereof certified by or bearing the seal of the EPO, a computer
printout bearing such seal or an electronic document containing such seal or otherwise
certified. Copies of documents emanating from the parties themselves do not require such
certification.

25.7.3   Person to whom notification is made

OJ   Where no representative is appointed, the notification will be made to the applicant who   1316
may specify an address for service different from the address recorded in the register and
the published application (see Notice from the EPO dated 04 September 2014, [2014] O.J.
A99). Use of such an address for correspondence is only possible, for a direct European
application or a Euro-PCT application in the regional phase, where (1) it is the applicant's
own address; (2) the address is in an EPC Contracting State; and (3) the applicant explicitly informs the EPO that it is to be used (see also Guidelines A-III, 4.2.1). When the EPO
is acting as an international authority, on the other hand, it will accept an address for
correspondence which is the address of any person in any country.

r.130(1)   If a representative has been appointed, notification will be addressed to the representative.

T703/92   Thus, where a representative has been appointed and notification is made to the applicant,
notification only occurs when the representative receives the relevant document.

r.130(2)   If several such representatives have been appointed for a single party, notification to any
one of them is sufficient.

r.130(3)   If several parties have a common representative, notification to the common representative is sufficient.

Guidelines   See E-II, 2.5.

25.7.4   Notification by postal services – deemed notification on the date of posting –
possible extension of time limit

r.125(2)(a)   Notification may be made by postal services in accordance with r.126.   1317

r.126(1)   All notifications by postal services must be by registered letter.

Comment   The current wording of r.126(1) applies as of 01 November 2019. Before this date, certain
decisions and summonses were notified by registered letter with advice of delivery.

r.126(2)   Where notification is effected in accordance with r.126(1), the document shall be deemed
to be delivered to the addressee on the date it bears, unless it has failed to reach the addressee. In the event of any dispute concerning the delivery of the document, it shall be
incumbent on the EPO to establish that the document has reached its destination and
to establish the date on which the document was delivered to the addressee. If the EPO
establishes that the document was delivered to the addressee more than seven days after
the date it bears, a period for which the deemed receipt of that document is the relevant
event under r.131(2) shall expire later by the number of days by which the seven days were
exceeded.

Comment   For documents notified before 01 November 2023, a 10 day deemed notification period
applied.

r.126(3)   Notification in accordance with r.126(1), will be deemed to have been effected even if
acceptance of the letter has been refused.

r.126(4)   To the extent that notification by postal services is not covered by r.126(1)–(3), the law of
the State in which the notification is made will apply.

OJ   See Notice from the EPO dated 16 June 2019 ([2019] O.J. A57). Decisions incurring a
period for appeal or a petition for review and summonses are notified by registered letter.
An acknowledgement of receipt is enclosed which the addressee is requested to sign, date
and return, preferably via online electronic filing (Form 1038). The same applies to certain
decisions, summonses and communications from the Board of Appeal which should be
acknowledged using Form 3936.

Guidelines   See E-II, 2.3.

25.7.5   *Notification by delivery by hand*

1318 r.125(2)(c)	Notification may be made by delivery on the premises of the EPO in accordance with r.128.
r.128	Notification may be effected on the premises of the EPO by delivery by hand of the document to the addressee who must acknowledge receipt on delivery. Notification will be deemed to have been effected even if the addressee refuses to accept the document or acknowledge receipt thereof.

25.7.6   *Notification by public notice*

1319 Art. 125(2)(d) r.129(1)	Notification may be made by public notice in accordance with r.129. If the address of the addressee cannot be established or if notification in accordance with r.126(1) (by post) has proved to be impossible, even after a second attempt, notification may be effected by public notice.
r.129(2)	The President of the EPO determines how the public notice is to be given and the beginning of the period of one month on the expiry of which the document will be deemed to have been notified.
OJ	The President has decided that public notification should occur via the Bulletin, indicating various particulars and where the relevant document can be inspected (Decision of the President dated 14.7.2007, [2007] O.J. Special Edition No. 3 K1). The document is deemed notified one month after the date of publication in the Bulletin.

25.7.7   *Notification by technical means of communication – deemed notification on the date of sending – possible extension of time limit*

1320 r.125(2)(b)	Notification may be made by means of electronic communication in accordance with r.127.
r.127(1)	Notification may be effected by means of electronic communication as determined by the President of the EPO and under the conditions laid down by him.
r.127(2)	Where notification is effected by means of electronic communication, the electronic document shall be deemed to be delivered to the addressee on the date it bears, unless it has failed to reach its destination. In the event of any dispute concerning the delivery of the electronic document, it shall be incumbent on the EPO to establish that the document has reached its destination and to establish the date on which it reached its destination. If the EPO establishes that the electronic document has reached its destination more than seven days after the date it bears, a period for which the deemed receipt of that document is the relevant event under r.131(2) shall expire later by the number of days by which the seven days were exceeded.
Comment	For documents notified before 01 November 2023, a 10 day deemed notification period applied.
OJ	See Decision of the President dated 11 March 2015 ([2015] O.J. A28). The EPO has started notifying various documents electronically as part of a pilot programme. Notification is being made to professional representatives holding an EPO smart card and having an activated Mailbox. Transmission of a document in accordance with r.127(2) EPC is deemed to have occurred on the date of the document, provided that the document has been made available in the Mailbox by that date.
OJ	See Notice of the EPO dated 30 March 2015 ([2015] O.J. A36). If a document bears a date which is later than the date on which it is available in the representative's Mailbox, the date of transmission is the date of the document. If a document bears the same date as the date on which it is available in the representative's Mailbox, the date of transmission is the date of the document. If a document bears a date which is earlier than the date on which it is available in the representative's Mailbox then the date of transmission is the date on which it is available in the Mailbox (the EPO bearing the proof of showing which date it was made available in the Mailbox).

25.7.8   *Notification through the central industrial property office of a Contracting State*

1321 Art. 119	Notifications may, where exceptional circumstances so require, be effected through the intermediary of the central industrial property offices of the Contracting States.

r.125(3)	Notification through the central industrial property office of a Contracting State is made in accordance with the law applicable to that office in national proceedings.

25.7.9   *Irregularities in notifications*

r.125(4)	Where a document has reached the addressee, if the EPO is unable to prove that it has been duly notified, or if provisions relating to its notification have not been observed, the document will be deemed to have been notified on the date established by the EPO as the date of receipt.	1322
Guidelines	See E-II, 2.6.	

25.7.10   *Notification of loss of rights*

r.112(1)	If the EPO notes that a loss of rights has occurred, without any decision concerning the refusal of the European patent application or the grant, revocation or maintenance of the European patent, or the taking of evidence, it will communicate this to the party concerned.	1323
Guidelines	See E-VIII, 1.9.	
OJ	See Decision of the President dated 12 July 2007 ([2007] O.J. Special Edition No. 3 F2). Communications under r.112(1) are entrusted to a formalities officer.	

25.7.11   *Communications and notices to be signed and identify author*

r.113(1)	Any decisions, summonses, notices and communications from the EPO must be signed by, and state the name of, the employee responsible.	1324
r.113(2)	Where a document referred to in r.113(1) is produced by the employee responsible using a computer, a seal may replace the signature. Where the document is produced automatically by a computer, the employee's name may also be dispensed with. The same applies to pre-printed notices and communications.	
r.2(2)	Where the EPC provides that a document must be signed, the authenticity of the document may be confirmed by handwritten signature or other appropriate means the use of which has been permitted by the President of the EPO. A document authenticated by such other means will be deemed to meet the legal requirements of signature in the same way as a document bearing a handwritten signature which has been filed in paper form.	
Guidelines	See E-II, 1.3.	

25.8   Decisions

25.8.1   *Decisions only to be based on grounds/evidence on which the parties have had an opportunity to comment*

Art. 113(1)	The decisions of the EPO may only be based on grounds or evidence on which the parties concerned have had an opportunity to present their comments.	1325
Case law	The principle of Art. 113(1) is often referred to as the "right to be heard" and ensures every party to the proceedings has had a fair chance to present its case. A violation of Art. 113(1) is a substantial procedural violation (J7/82).	
G4/92	Headnote (1): A decision against a party who has been duly summoned but who fails to appear at oral proceedings may not be based on facts put forward for the first time during those oral proceedings.	
	Headnote (2): Similarly, new evidence may not be considered unless it has been previously notified and it merely supports the assertions of the party who submits it, whereas new arguments may in principle be used to support the reasons for the decision.	
Comment	As the reasons make clear, this decision only applies to inter partes proceedings. Furthermore, according to T706/00, it no longer applies to the Boards of Appeal whose rules of procedure were later amended to specifically state that a decision in oral proceedings does not have to be delayed by virtue of the non-attendance of a party (RPBA Art. 15(3) – see O.J. [2007] 536).	
RPBA Art. 15(3)	The Board is not obliged to delay any step in the proceedings, including its decision, by reason only of the absence at the oral proceedings of any party duly summoned who may then be treated as relying only on its written case.	

Guidelines	See E-III,8.3.3.2. The decision should still apply, however, to an opposition division which, if it introduces a new document in oral proceedings, should continue the proceedings in writing for a non-attending proprietor to be able to comment before a decision based on that document is taken. The submission of new claims by the proprietor in the absence of the opponent is not a new "fact" within the meaning of G4/92 and nor is the examination of claims for formal deficiencies in the absence of the proprietor a new "fact" of this kind. A decision may also be taken based on new facts which are introduced in the absence of the opponent but are in the opponent's favour.
T892/94	By deciding to take no further part in proceedings a party forfeits his right under Art. 113(1).
OJ	If the applicant chooses not to attend oral proceedings before the Examining Division then he is deemed to have forfeited his right under Art. 113(1) and a decision may be taken at those oral proceedings on the basis of any objection which arises against the claims on file, whether previously notified to the applicant or not – see Notice from the EPO, [2008] O.J. 471.

25.8.2   *Applicant or proprietor to submit or agree text decided on – auxiliary requests*

1326	Art. 113(2)	The EPO can examine and decide upon a European patent application or a European patent only in the text submitted to it, or agreed, by the applicant or the proprietor of the patent.
	Guidelines	Where a proprietor withdraws his approval of the text and does not submit an amended text the patent will be revoked (D-VI, 2). See also T73/84.
	Guidelines	See H-III, 3. The applicant or proprietor is entitled to submit a main request in EPO proceedings and, if desired, one or more auxiliary requests in case the main request is unallowable. If the main request is allowable, auxiliary requests are ignored. If the main request is not allowable, on the other hand, the Examining Division will consider any auxiliary requests in the sequence indicated by the applicant until an allowable request is encountered. Reasons for the non-allowability of any higher-ranking request must be given. Each auxiliary request is a request for amendment whose admissibility needs to be considered.
	Case law	The EPO is bound by auxiliary requests and their order such that when granting an auxiliary request, reasons must be given for the rejection of all preceding requests (T234/86). This applies equally where an auxiliary request forms the basis for a r.71(3) communication – the communication must give reasons for the non-allowance of the main and any higher-ranking auxiliary request (T1255/04).

25.8.3   *Form of decisions*

1327	r.111(1)	Where oral proceedings are held before the EPO, the decision may be given orally. The decision will subsequently be put in writing and notified to the parties.
	T390/86	The appeal period starts from the notification in writing.
	T666/90	A disparity between the oral and written decision represents a substantial procedural violation. See also T425/97.
	RPBA Art. 15(5)	When a case is ready for decision during oral proceedings, the Chair shall state the final requests of the parties and declare the debate closed. No submissions may be made by the parties after the closure of the debate unless the Board decides to reopen the debate.
	RPBA Art. 15(6)	The Board shall ensure that each case is ready for decision at the conclusion of the oral proceedings, unless there are special reasons to the contrary. Before the oral proceedings are closed, the decision may be announced orally by the Chair.
	RPBA Art, 15(7)	Where the decision on the appeal has been announced orally in accordance with RPBA Art. 15(6), the reasons for the decision, or parts thereof, may, with the explicit consent of the parties, be put in writing in abridged form. However, where it has been indicated to the Board that a third party or a court has, in the particular case, a legitimate interest in the reasons for the decision not being in abridged form, they shall not be abridged. Where appropriate, the reasons for the decision in abridged form may already be included in the minutes for the oral proceedings.
	RPBA Art. 15(8)	If the Board agrees with the finding of the department which issued the decision under appeal, on one or more issues, and with the reasons given for it in the decision under appeal, the Board may put the reasons for its decision in abridged form in respect of that issue.

RPBAArt. 15(9)	The Board shall issue the decision on the appeal in a timely manner.

(a) Where the Chair announces the decision on the appeal orally in accordance with RP-BAArt. 15(6), the Board shall put the decision in writing and dispatch it within three months of the date of the oral proceedings. If the Board is unable to do so, it shall inform the parties when the decision is to be dispatched. The President of the Boards of Appeal shall be informed thereof.

(b) When a case is ready for decision at the conclusion of the oral proceedings but the Chair does not announce the decision on the appeal orally in accordance with RP-BAArt. 15(6), the Chair shall indicate the date on which the decision on the appeal is to be dispatched, which shall not be later than three months after the closure of the oral proceedings. If the Board is unable to dispatch the decision on the appeal by that date, it shall inform the parties of a new date or, in exceptional circumstances, shall issue a communication specifying the further procedural steps that will be taken.

r.111(2)	Decisions of the EPO which are open to appeal must be reasoned and must be accompanied by a communication pointing out the possibility of appeal and drawing the attention of the parties to Arts 106–108, the text of which must be attached. However, the parties may not invoke the omission of the communication (i.e. omission does not on its own invalidate the decision).
Comment	Decisions pronounced orally do not have to be reasoned but the written confirmation must be.
J8/81	Whether a document is a decision or a communication is a matter of substance rather than form. See also T42/84.
T278/00	A lack of proper reasoning in a decision, which is, for instance, inconsistent, amounts to a substantial procedural violation.
Art. 111, r.102	See also section 16.10 for decisions of the Boards of Appeal.
Guidelines	See E-III, 9 (decision at oral proceedings), E-X, 1.3 (written decision) and E-X, 1.3.3 (decision to be reasoned). A decision must be drafted in the language of the proceedings (E-X,2.3).

25.8.4   The finality of a decision

T390/86	Once a decision is taken it is final and binding and can only be changed by the filing of an appeal or correction under r.140 (see also G4/91 and T212/88).	1328
Comment	Under EPC2000, decisions of the Boards of Appeal can be challenged according to Art. 112a (petition for review).	
G12/91	Headnote: The decision-making process following written proceedings is completed on the date the decision to be notified is handed over to the EPO postal service by the decision-taking department's formalities section. On this date the Examining or Opposition Division no longer has the power to change its mind. It corresponds to the moment in oral proceedings where debate is closed and the parties may no longer submit anything further. Further amendments or comments will therefore not be taken into account after this date.	
T713/02	A decision during the grant procedure which does not terminate it (e.g. a decision to allow the correction of a priority claim) does not become final until the final decision to grant or refuse is taken.	

25.8.5   Obtaining a decision after the EPO has notified a loss of rights

r.112(2)	Following the communication of a loss of rights, if the party concerned considers that the finding of the EPO is inaccurate, it may, within two months of the communication under r.112(1), apply for a decision on the matter. The EPO will take such decision only if it does not share the opinion of the party requesting it; otherwise it will inform that party.	1329
Comment	This provision exists so that the EPO may review the facts according to which an alleged loss of rights has occurred and either withdraw the loss of rights in the case that an error has been made or take a decision that the loss of rights did indeed occur. In the latter case, the decision may be appealed so that a second review of the facts can be carried out by a Board of Appeal.	
G1/90	The loss of rights becomes final if the time limit is missed.	
r.135(2)	No further processing is available if the r.112(2) time limit is missed.	

Art. 122	Re-establishment, however, is available if the time limit is missed in spite of all due care having been shown.
OJ	See Decision of the President dated 12 July 2007 ([2007] O.J. Special Edition No. 3 F2). Decisions under r.112(2) are entrusted to a formalities officer.
Guidelines	See E-VIII, 1.9.3. It is possible to ask for a decision under r.112(2), arguing that the loss of rights did not occur, and to ask for an appropriate remedy such as further processing or re-establishment as an auxiliary request.

25.8.6   Decisions to be signed and identify author

1330	r.113(2)	Any decisions from the EPO must be signed by, and state the name of, the employee responsible.
	r.113(2)	Where the decision is produced by the employee responsible using a computer, a seal may replace the signature. Where the document is produced automatically by a computer, the employee's name may also be dispensed with.
	r.2(2)	Where the EPC provides that a document must be signed, the authenticity of the document may be confirmed by handwritten signature or other appropriate means the use of which has been permitted by the President of the EPO. A document authenticated by such other means will be deemed to meet the legal requirements of signature in the same way as a document bearing a handwritten signature which has been filed in paper form.
	RPBAArt. 8(3)	A member who is unable to act after the Board has already reached a decision on the appeal shall not be replaced. If the Chair in a particular case is unable to act, the member of the Board having the longer or longest service on the Boards of Appeal, or in the case where members have the same length of service, the elder or eldest member, shall sign the decision on behalf of the Chair.
	T862/98	Where the composition of an Opposition Division changes after oral proceedings, so that the decision cannot be signed by the original members of the division, new oral proceedings should generally be appointed.
	T714/92	A decision was set aside as null and void where it was not clear from the public part of the file that a member of the Examining Division had signed or at least approved the decision before leaving the Division.
	T243/87	However, if, following oral proceedings, a member of a division is prevented from signing the written decision by incapacity, another member can sign on his behalf.
	Guidelines	See E-X, 1.3.

25.8.7   Notification of decisions

1331	Art. 119	Decisions must be notified by the EPO of its own motion in accordance with the Implementing Regulations (see section 25.7).

25.8.8   Correction of errors in decisions

1332	r.140	See section 21.8.

25.8.9   Interlocutory decisions

1333	Art. 106(2)	See sections 15.10 and 17.2.

25.9   Examination by the EPO of its own motion

1334	Art. 114(1)	In proceedings before it, the EPO can examine the facts of its own motion; it is not restricted in this examination to the facts, evidence and arguments provided by the parties and the relief sought.
	Case law	See sections 15.7.7 and 17.9.2 for the limits of this principle in opposition and opposition appeal proceedings.
	Guidelines	See E-VI, 1.

25.10   Facts and evidence submitted late may be ignored

1335	Art. 114(2)	The EPO may disregard facts or evidence which are not submitted in due time by the parties concerned.

r.116	See section 25.11.4 for written submissions prior to oral proceedings.
RPBAArt. 12(6)	A Board of Appeal may hold inadmissible requests, facts, objections or evidence which should have been submitted in the proceedings leading to the decision under appeal unless the circumstances of the appeal case justify their admittance.
RPBAArt. 13(1)	Any amendment to a party's appeal case after it has filed its grounds of appeal or reply is subject to the party's justification for its amendment and may be admitted only at the discretion of the Board.
RPBAArt. 13(2)	Any amendment to a party's case made after the expiry of a period specified by the Board in a communication under r.100(2) EPC or, where such a communication is not issued, after notification of a summons to oral proceedings shall, in principle, not be taken into account unless there are expectional circumstances, which have been justified with cogent reasons by the party concerned.
Guidelines	See E-VI, 2.

25.11   Oral proceedings

25.11.1   *Extent of the right to oral proceedings*

Art. 116(1)	Oral proceedings will take place either at the instance of the EPO if it considers this to be expedient or at the request of any party to the proceedings. However, the EPO may reject a request for further oral proceedings before the same department where the parties and the subject of the proceedings are the same.	1336
Art. 116(2)	Nevertheless, oral proceedings will take place before the Receiving Section at the request of the applicant only where the Receiving Section considers this to be expedient or where it intends to refuse the European patent application.	
OJ	Such refusal must be pursuant to Art. 90(5), a decision under r.69(2) (now r.112(2) EPC2000) following the loss of rights not counting according to [1985] O.J. 159.	
T299/86	A request for oral proceedings must be unambiguous. Reserving the right to oral proceedings is not sufficient.	
T555/95	A request for oral proceedings must be honoured at any time while proceedings are pending, i.e. up to the decision to grant or refuse.	
T34/90	A fresh request is necessary in all new proceedings, e.g. at the appeal stage.	
Guidelines	See E-III, 2–4.	

25.11.2   *Summons to oral proceedings*

r.115(1)	Parties are summoned to oral proceedings under Art. 116, drawing their attention to r.115(2) (proceedings may be conducted in the absence of a summoned party who does not turn up). At least two months' notice of the summons must be given unless the parties agree to a shorter period.	1337
r.109(1)	In proceedings under Art. 112a (petition for review), r.115(1) second sentence (at least two months' notice) does not apply.	
J14/91	If the subject of the oral proceedings would be irrelevant (e.g. in view of an impending publication) after a two-month delay then a shorter period may be set in the summons.	
RPBAArt. 15(1)	Without prejudice to r.115(1) EPC, the Board shall, if oral proceedings are to take place, endeavour to give at least four months' notice of the summons. In cases where there is more than one party, the Board shall endeavour to issue the summons no earlier than two months after receipt of the written reply or replies referred to in RPBAArt. 12(1)(c). A single date is fixed for the oral proceedings.	
Guidelines	See E-III, 6. Any period of notice is acceptable if the parties agree to it. Otherwise, notice of at least four months is usually given in examination proceedings (six months where the summons is the first office action) and notice of at least six months is usually given in opposition proceedings.	
RPBAArt. 15(2)	A request of a party for a change of the date fixed for oral proceedings may be allowed if the party has put forward serious reasons which justify the fixing of a new date. If the party is represented, the serious reasons must relate to the representative.	

(a) The request shall be filed in writing, reasoned and, where appropriate, supported by documentary evidence. The request shall be filed as soon as possible after the summons to oral proceedings has been notified and the serious reasons in question have arisen. The request should include a list of dates on which the requesting party is not available for oral proceedings.

(b) Reasons which may justify a change of th date for oral proceedings include: (i) notification of a summons to oral proceedings in other proceedings before the EPO or a national court received before notification of the summons to oral proceedings before the Board; (ii) serious illness; (iii) a death within the family; (iv) marriage or formation of a similar recognised partnership; (v) military service or other obligatory performance of civic duties; (vi) holidays or business trips which have been firmly booked before notification of the summons to oral proceedings.

(c) Reasons which, as a rule, do not justify a change of the date for oral proceedings include: (i) filing of new requests, facts, objections, arguments or evidence; (ii) excessive work pressure; (iii) unavailability of a duly represented party; (iv) unavailability of an accompanying person; (v) appointment of a new professional representative.

OJ

In first instance oral proceedings, a single date is selected which may only be changed in exceptional circumstances and if serious reasons are involved (see Notice from the EPO dated 18 December 2008, [2009] O.J. 68 and Guidelines E-III, 7) such as previously notified conflicting oral proceedings before the EPO, the UPC or a national court, serious illness, previously booked holidays or business travel, bereavement, marriage or military service. Excessive work pressure is not generally an acceptable reason. Such reasons must apply to a participant in the oral proceedings whose presence is essential, e.g. a representative or witness. The approach taken is particularly strict in opposition proceedings with multiple opponents. The approach is broadly the same in appeal proceedings (see [2007] O.J. Special Edition No. 3 H1) – the request should include an explanation of why another representative cannot be substituted.

T1012/03

Oral proceedings will take place wherever the relevant Division or Board is based. The applicant does not have the right to request that oral proceedings take place at a different location that is more convenient to him.

Guidelines

See D-VI, 3.2 (re. opposition) and E-III, 6–7.

25.11.3   Consequence of summoned party not turning up

1338   r.115(2)

If a party duly summoned to oral proceedings before the EPO does not appear as summoned, the proceedings may continue without that party.

RPBAArt. 15(3)

The Board shall not be obliged to delay any step in the proceedings, including its decision, by reason only of the absence at the oral proceedings of a party duly summoned who may then be treated as relying on its written case.

T3/90

Where a party says that they will not turn up this is interpreted as a withdrawal of a request for oral proceedings.

T930/92

A late decision not to attend may lead to an award of costs in opposition proceedings (see also T338/90).

G4/92

See section 25.8.1. A decision in oral proceedings before the Opposition Division may not be based on new facts or evidence when one party does not appear.

T986/00

A proprietor who chooses not to be present at oral proceedings should ensure that he has filed all amendments that he wishes to be considered. Here, the main request was seen to lack inventive step and all auxiliary requests to lack clarity. In the absence of the proprietor to agree an acceptable text under Art. 113(2) EPC the patent was revoked.

OJ

See Notice from the EPO dated 10 November 2020, [2020] O.J. A124. If an applicant decides not to attend oral proceedings before the Examining Division it should inform the EPO as early as possible and unambiguously withdraw its request for oral proceedings. A request for a decision according to the state of the file is interpreted as a withdrawal of any request for oral proceedings (citing T2704/16). If the applicant announces he will not attend oral proceedings then this is also usually interpreted as a withdrawal of the request for oral proceedings and the Examining Division is not bound by any request that the oral proceedings occur in their absence.

| Guidelines | See E-III, 7.2.2. The relevant division decides whether oral proceedings should go ahead when a party withdraws its request (either explicitly or by indicating it will not attend). If the oral proceedings go ahead this means that there are outstanding objections to the requests on file and a decision may be given orally as long as the applicant or propietor will not be taken by surprise based on the written proceedings up to that point. | |

25.11.4   *Preparation for oral proceedings by the parties*

r.116(1)	When issuing a summons to oral proceedings, the EPO will draw attention to the points which in its opinion need to be discussed for the purposes of the decision to be taken. At the same time, a final date for making written submissions in preparation for the oral proceedings will be fixed. Rule 132 does not apply. New facts and evidence presented after that date need not be considered, unless admitted on the grounds that the subject of the proceedings has changed.	1339
RPBAArt. 15(1)	In order to help concentrate on essentials during the oral proceedings, the Board shall issue a communication drawing attention to matters that seem to be of particular significance for the decision to be taken. The Board may also provide a preliminary opinion. The Board shall endeavour to issue the communication at least four months in advance of the date of the oral proceedings.	
G6/95	Headnote: Rule 71a(1) EPC (NB. now r.116(1) EPC2000) does not apply to the Boards of Appeal.	
T1183/02	Where a response is filed to the summons to oral proceedings including good faith responsive amendments and arguments, the summons is not suspended and the oral proceedings will, in principle, go ahead. The Examining Division is not under a duty to confirm that the summons remains valid.	
Guidelines	See E-III, 8.6. New facts and evidence may be admitted later than the expiry of the period under r.116(1) if justified by a change in the proceedings, e.g. amendments filed by the proprietor.	
r.116(2)	If the applicant or patent proprietor has been notified of the grounds prejudicing the grant or maintenance of the patent, he may be invited to submit, by the date specified in r.116(1) second sentence, documents which meet the requirements of the EPC. Rule 116(1) third and fourth sentences shall apply mutatis mutandis.	
T951/97	Clearly allowable amendments overcoming the outstanding objections should always be admitted. The subject of the proceedings may change, e.g. where the Examining Division has introduced a new document during oral proceedings.	
T755/96	If amended claims are not admitted then reasons must be given.	
Guidelines	See H-II, 2.7.1 for grant proceedings. Late-filed requests will not be admitted unless they are clearly allowable or filed in response to a change in the course of the proceedings (e.g. the admission of a new prior art document). See also E-VI, 2 for opposition proceedings – discretion is exercised by the opposition division based on the relevance of late filed facts or evidence or the prima facie allowability of new amended claims. Procedural expediency (e.g. the need to adjourn oral proceedings) and possible abuse of the procedure are also taken into account.	

25.11.5   *Extent to which oral proceedings are open to the public*

Art. 116(3)	Oral proceedings before the Receiving Section, the Examining Divisions and the Legal Division are not public.	1340
Art. 116(4)	Oral proceedings, including delivery of the decision, are public as regards the Boards of Appeal and the Enlarged Board of Appeal, after publication of the European patent application, and also before the Opposition Divisions, in so far as the department before which the proceedings are taking place does not decide otherwise in cases where the admission of the public could have serious and unjustified disadvantages, in particular for a party to the proceedings.	
Guidelines	See E-III, 8.1.	

25.11.6   Procedure in oral proceedings

1341 OJ	Oral proceedings before examining divisions, opposition divisions, the Legal Division and the Receiving Section will take place by videoconference unless there are serious reasons preventing the use of videoconference (see Decision of the President dated 22 November 2022, [2022] O.J. A103). If a request to hold oral proceedings on the premises of the EPO is refused, the parties are informed of the reasons but the decision is not separately appealable. See also Notice from the EPO dated 22 November 2022 ([2022] O.J. A106) for further details. Serious reasons usually relate to the ability of a participant to take part in a videoconference (e.g. because of visual impairment) or the need for a demonstration or inspection of an object where haptic features are essential. As an exception to the general rule, during oral proceedings held by videoconference, documents, including authorisations, can and must be filed by e-mail (Decision of the President dated 13 May 2020, [2020] O.J. A71).
OJ	Oral proceedings before the Unitary Patent Protection Division are also to be held by videoconference unless there are serious reasons against its use (see Decision on the President dated 24 April 2023 ([2023] O.J. Supplementary Publication 3, pages 2–4).
Guidelines	See E-III,1.2–1.4.
RPBA Art. 15a(1)	The Board may decide to hold oral proceedings pursuant to Art. 116 EPC by videoconference if the Board considers it appropriate to do so, either upon request by a party or of its own motion.
RPBA Art. 15a(2)	Where oral proceedings are scheduled to be held on the premises of the European Patent Office, a party, representative or accompanying person may, upon request, be allowed to attend by videoconference.
RPBA Art. 15a(3)	The Chair in the particular appeal and, with the agreement of that Chair, any other member of the Board in the particular appeal may participate in the oral proceedings by videoconference.
G1/21	Headnote: "During a general emergency impairing the parties' possibilities to attend in-person oral proceedings at the EPO premises, the conduct of oral proceedings before the boards of appeal in the form of a videoconference is compatible with the EPC even if not all of the parties to the proceedings have given their consent to the conduct of oral proceedings in the form of a videoconference." In answering the question posed, the Enlarged Board restricted itself to considering oral proceedings before the Boards of Appeal in the context of a pandemic infectious disease. It found that the holding of oral proceedings by videoconference was compatible with the EPC but that such proceedings were not as satisfactory as an in-person hearing. As a result, oral proceedings by videoconference should only be imposed on a party who prefers an in-person hearing if there are good reasons for doing so – an in-person hearing should be the default option.
OJ	In oral proceedings before the Boards of Appeal held by videoconference, as an exception to the general rule, documents, including authorisations, can and must be filed by e-mail (Decision of the President dated 13 May 2020, [2020] O.J. A71)
RPBA Art. 15(4)	In oral proceedings before the Board of Appeal, the Chair presides over the oral proceedings and ensures their fair, orderly and efficient conduct.
OJ	The use of recording devices is not allowed before the Board of Appeal (Notice dated 16.7.2007, [2007] O.J. Special Edition No. 3 H2) but the use of electronic devices such as laptop computers is permitted provided their use does not create any nuisance or disturbance.
G4/95	Headnote (1): During oral proceedings under Art. 116 EPC in the context of opposition or opposition appeal proceedings, a person accompanying the professional representative of a party may be allowed to make oral submissions on specific legal or technical issues (including facts, evidence or argument) on behalf of that party, otherwise than under Art. 117 EPC, in addition to the complete presentation of the party's case by the professional representative.

Headnote (2): (a) Such oral submissions cannot be made as a matter of right, but only with the permission of and under the discretion of the EPO. (b) The following main criteria should be considered by the EPO when exercising its discretion to allow the making of oral submissions by an accompanying person in opposition or opposition appeal proceedings: (i) The professional representative should request permission for such oral submissions to be made. The request should state the name and qualifications of the accompanying person, and should specify the subject-matter of the proposed oral submissions. (ii) The request should be made sufficiently in advance of the oral proceedings so that all opposing parties are able properly to prepare themselves in relation to the proposed oral submissions. (iii) A request which is made shortly before or at the oral proceedings should in the absence of exceptional circumstances be refused, unless each opposing party agrees to the making of the oral submissions requested. (iv) The EPO should be satisfied that oral submissions by an accompanying person are made under the continuing responsibility and control of the professional representative. (c) No special criteria apply to the making of oral submissions by qualified patent lawyers of countries which are not Contracting States to the EPC.

G2/94 | Headnote (1): A Board of Appeal has a discretion to allow an accompanying person (who is not entitled under Art. 134(1) or (7) EPC to represent parties in proceedings before the EPO) to make submissions during oral proceedings in ex parte proceedings, in addition to the complete presentation of a party's case by the professional representative.

Headnote (2): (a) In ex parte proceedings a professional representative should request permission for the making of such oral submissions in advance of the day appointed for oral proceedings. The request should state the name and qualifications of the person for whom permission is requested, and should specify the subject matter of the proposed oral submissions. The Board of Appeal should exercise its discretion in accordance with the circumstances of each individual case. The main criterion to be considered is that the Board should be fully informed of all relevant matters before deciding the case. The Board should be satisfied that the oral submissions are made by the accompanying person under the continuing responsibility and control of the professional representative. (b) During either ex parte or inter partes proceedings, a Board of Appeal should refuse permission for a former member of the Boards of Appeal to make oral submissions during oral proceedings before it, unless it is completely satisfied that a sufficient period of time has elapsed following termination of such former member's appointment to the Boards of Appeal, so that the Board of Appeal could not reasonably be suspected of partiality in deciding the case if it allowed such oral submissions to be made. A Board of Appeal should normally refuse permission for a former member of the Boards of Appeal to make oral submissions during oral proceedings before it, until at least three years have elapsed following termination of the former member's appointment to the Boards of Appeal. After three years have elapsed, permission should be granted except in very special circumstances.

RPBA Art. 15(5) | When a case is ready for decision during oral proceedings, the Chair shall state the final requests of the parties and declare the debate closed. No submissions may be made by the parties after the closure of the debate unless the Board decides to reopen the debate.

RPBA Art. 15(6) | The Board shall ensure that each case is ready for decision at the conclusion of the oral proceedings, unless there are special reasons to the contrary. Before the oral proceedings are closed, the decision may be announced orally by the Chair.

T1122/01 | Oral proceedings are generally restricted to the presentation of a case using the spoken word and powerpoint presentations or other visual aids are not encouraged.

Guidelines | See E-III, 8 and 9.

OJ | See [2014] O.J. A32. Paralegals may now provide administrative support to Examining and Opposition Divisions during oral proceedings though they do not become part of the division or participate in any decision-making process.

Comment | See section 25.2.2 concerning the need for amendments made during oral proceedings before the Examining Division to be submitted in a formally correct manner.

25.11.7 *Minutes of oral proceedings*

r.124(1) | The minutes of oral proceedings are drawn up containing the essentials of the oral proceedings, the relevant statements made by the parties and the testimony of the parties, witnesses or experts. | 1342

r.124(2)	The minutes of the testimony of a witness, expert or party must be read out, submitted to him so that he may examine them or, where they are recorded by technical means, played back to him, unless he waives this right. It is noted in the minutes that this formality has been carried out and that the person who gave the testimony approved the minutes. If his approval is not given, his objections are noted. It is not necessary to play back the minutes or to obtain approval of them if the testimony has been recorded verbatim and directly using technical means.
r.124(3)	The minutes are authenticated by the employee responsible for drawing them up and by the employee who conducted the oral proceedings, either by their signature or by any other appropriate means.
r.2(2)	Where the EPC provides that a document must be signed, the authenticity of the document may be confirmed by handwritten signature or other appropriate means the use of which has been permitted by the President of the EPO. A document authenticated by such other means will be deemed to meet the legal requirements of signature in the same way as a document bearing a handwritten signature which has been filed in paper form.
r.124(4)	The parties are provided with a copy of the minutes.
Guidelines	See E-III, 10.

25.11.8   *Fresh oral proceedings if the composition of a Board of Appeal changes*

1343	RPBA Art. 8(1)	If the composition of a Board is changed after oral proceedings, the parties shall be informed that, at the request of any party, fresh oral proceedings shall be held before the Board in its new composition. Fresh oral proceedings shall also be held if so requested by the new member and if the other members of the Board in the particular appeal have given their agreement.

25.12 Taking of evidence

25.12.1   *Forms of evidence available to the EPO*

1344	Art. 117(1)	In proceedings before the EPO the means of giving or obtaining evidence include the following: (a) hearing the parties; (b) requests for information; (c) the production of documents; (d) hearing the witnesses; (e) opinions by experts; (f) inspection; (g) sworn statements in writing.
	T798/93	All these means of gathering evidence are entirely at the discretion of the EPO and cannot be ordered by a party to proceedings.
	Guidelines	See E-IV, 1.2.

25.12.2   *Principles to be applied when evaluating evidence*

1345	T482/89	Free evaluation of evidence applies to the department taking a decision. Any kind of document is therefore admissible as evidence but the amount of weight given to it will depend on the circumstances of the case.
	T182/89	The standard of proof to be applied in most cases, with notable exceptions (e.g. the allegation of public use by an opponent who holds all the evidence – T472/92, T97/94), is the balance of probabilities.
	T219/83	The burden of proof is always on the party asserting a particular fact. In opposition proceedings where there are contrary assertions and the truth cannot easily be established by the EPO, the proprietor has the benefit of the doubt.
	T474/04	If assertions made in an unsworn witness declaration remain contested, as a rule a request from a party to hear the witness must be granted before these assertions are made the basis of a decision against the contesting party.
	Guidelines	See E-IV, 4 for general comments on the evaluation of evidence.

25.12.3   *Decision to take evidence*

Art. 117(2) r.117	The procedure for taking evidence is laid down in the Implementing Regulations. When the EPO considers it necessary to hear a party, witness or expert, or to carry out an inspection, it will take a decision to that end, setting out the investigation which it intends to carry out, relevant facts to be proved, the date, time and place of the investigation and whether it will be conducted by videoconference. If the hearing of a witness or expert is requested by a party, the decision will specify the period within which the requester must make known the name and address of any witness or expert concerned.
OJ	See Notice from the EPO dated 17 December 2020 ([2020[O.J. A135) on the use of video-conference to take evidence by the examining and opposition divisions. Where evidence is to be taken during oral proceedings held by videoconference then the evidence will also be taken by videoconference. Videoconference may also be used to take evidence during oral proceedings that are held on the premises of the EPO.

1346

25.12.4   *Summons to give evidence before the EPO*

Art. 117(2) r.118(1)	The procedure for taking evidence is laid down in the Implementing Regulations. A summons to give evidence before the EPO will be issued to the parties, witnesses or experts concerned.
r.118(2)	At least two months' notice of a summons issued to a party, witness or expert to testify will be given, unless they agree to a shorter period. The summons will contain: (a) an extract from the decision under r.117, indicating the date, time and place of the investigation ordered, specifying whether it will be conducted by videoconference and stating the facts in respect of which parties, witnesses or experts are to be heard; (b) the names of the parties and particulars of the rights which the witnesses or experts may invoke under r.122(2)–(4) (reimbursement of expenses); (c) an indication that a party, witness or expert who has been summoned to appear before the EPO on its premises may, at his request, be heard by videoconference; (d) an indication that the party, witness or expert may request to be heard by a competent court in his country of residence under r.120, and an invitation to inform the EPO, within a period to be specified, whether he is prepared to appear before it.
r.120(1)	A party, witness or expert who is summoned before the EPO may request the latter to allow him to be heard by a competent court in his country of residence. If this is request-ed, or if no reply is received within the period specified in the summons, the EPO in the summons, the EPO may, in accordance with Art. 131(2), request the competent court to hear the person concerned.
r.120(2)	If a party, witness or expert has been heard by the EPO, the latter may, if it considers it advisable for the testimony to be given under oath or in an equally binding form, issue a request under Art. 131(2) to the competent court in the country of residence of the person concerned to re-examine his testimony under such conditions.
Guidelines	See E-IV, 1.5–1.6.

1347

25.12.5   *Hearing of evidence before a competent court*

Art. 131(2)	At the request of the EPO, the courts or other competent authorities of Contracting States must undertake, on behalf of the office and within the limits of their jurisdiction, any necessary enquiries or other legal measures.
r.120(3)	When the EPO requests a competent court to take evidence, it may request the court to take the evidence under oath or in an equally binding form and to permit a member of the department concerned to attend the hearing and question the party, witness or expert, either through the intermediary of the court or directly.
r.150 Guidelines	Special provisions apply to the sending of letters rogatory by the EPO. See E-IV, 3.

1348

25.12.6   *Examination of evidence before the EPO*

Art. 117(2) r.119(1)	The procedure for taking evidence is laid down in the Implementing Regulations. The Examining Division, Opposition Division or Board of Appeal may commission one of its members to examine the evidence adduced.

1349

| r.119(2) | Before a party, witness or expert may be heard, he must be informed that the EPO may request the competent court in the country of residence of the person concerned to re-examine his testimony under oath or in an equally binding form. |
| r.119(3) | The parties may attend an investigation and may put relevant questions to the testifying party, witness or expert. |

25.12.7 *The opinion of experts*

1350	r.121(1)	The EPO decides in what form the opinion of an expert whom it appoints should be submitted.
	r.121(2)	The terms of reference of the expert must include: (a) a precise description of his task; (b) the period specified for the submission of his opinion; (c) the names of the parties to the proceedings; and (d) particulars of the rights which he may invoke under rr.122(2)–(4) (reimbursement of expenses).
	r.121(3)	A copy of any written opinion is submitted to the parties.
	r.121(4)	The parties may object to an expert. The department of the EPO concerned will decide on any objection.
	Guidelines	See E-IV, 1.8.

25.12.8 *Costs of taking evidence*

1351	r.122(1)	The taking of evidence by the EPO may be made conditional upon deposit with it, by the party requesting the evidence be taken, of an amount fixed by reference to an estimate of the costs.
	r.122(2)	Witnesses and experts who are summoned by and appear before the EPO are entitled to appropriate reimbursement of expenses for travel and subsistence. An advance for these expenses may be granted to them. This also applies to persons who appear before the EPO without being summoned by it and are heard as witnesses or experts.
	r.122(3)	Witnesses entitled to reimbursement under r.122(2) are also entitled to appropriate compensation for loss of earnings and experts to fees for their work. These payments are made to the witnesses and experts after they have fulfilled their duties or tasks.
	r.122(4)	The Administrative Council lays down details implementing r.122(2) and (3). Any amounts due under these provisions are paid by the EPO.
	OJ	See [1983] O.J. 100 ("Compensation and fees payable to witnesses and experts") – to secure payment of costs for the taking of evidence, the EPO may make the taking of evidence conditional upon deposit with it, by the party who requested the evidence to be taken, of a sum the amount of which shall be fixed by reference to an estimate of the costs. The Administrative Council have adopted a Regulation of 21 October 1977 ([1983] O.J. 102) specifying the rates of compensation that will be paid.
	Guidelines	See E-IV, 1.9–1.10.

25.12.9 *Conservation of evidence*

1352	r.123(1)	On request, the EPO may, without delay, take measures to conserve evidence of facts liable to affect a decision which it may be called upon to take with regard to a European patent application or a European patent, where there is reason to fear that it might subsequently become more difficult or even impossible to take evidence. The date on which the measures are to be taken will be communicated to the applicant for or proprietor of the patent in sufficient time to allow him to attend. He may ask relevant questions.
	r.123(2)	The request must contain: (a) particulars of the requester as provided in r.41(2)(c) (as for the request); (b) sufficient identification of the European patent application or European patent in question; (c) an indication of the facts in respect of which evidence is to be taken; (d) particulars of the means of giving or obtaining evidence; and (e) a statement establishing a prima facie case for fearing that it might subsequently become more difficult or impossible to take evidence.
	r.123(3)	The request will not be deemed to have been filed until the prescribed fee has been paid.

RRFArt. 2(1)(17)	The fee for the conservation of evidence is € 85.
r.123(4)	The decision on the request and any resulting taking of evidence will be incumbent on the department of the EPO which would have to take the decision liable to be affected by the facts to be established. The provisions with regard to the taking of evidence in proceedings before the EPO apply.
Guidelines	See E-IV, 2.

25.12.10   Minutes of taking of evidence/inspection

r.124(1)	The minutes of the taking of evidence must be drawn up containing the essentials of the taking of evidence, the relevant statements made by the parties, the testimony of the parties, witnesses or experts and the result of any inspection.	1353
r.124(2)	The minutes of the testimony of a witness, expert or party must be read out, submitted to him, so that he may examine them or, where they are recorded by technical means, played back to him, unless he waives this right. It will be noted in the minutes that this formality has been carried out and that the person who gave the testimony approved the minutes. If his approval is not given, his objections will be noted. It is not necessary to play back the minutes or to obtain approval of them if the testimony has been recorded verbatim and directly using technical means.	
r.124(3)	The minutes must be authenticated by the employee responsible for drawing them up and by the employee who conducted the taking of evidence, either by their signature or by any other appropriate means.	
r.2(2)	Where the EPC provides that a document must be signed, the authenticity of the document may be confirmed by handwritten signature or other appropriate means the use of which has been permitted by the President of the EPO. A document authenticated by such other means will be deemed to meet the legal requirements of signature in the same way as a document bearing a handwritten signature which has been filed in paper form.	
r.124(4)	The parties will be provided with a copy of the minutes.	
Guidelines	See E-IV, 1.7.	

25.13   Authentic text of a European patent or application

Art. 70(1)	The text of a European patent application or a European patent in the language of the proceedings is the authentic text in any proceedings before the EPO and in any Contracting State.	1354
Art. 70(2)	If, however, the European patent application has been filed in a language which is not an official language of the EPO, that text represents the application as filed within the meaning of the EPC.	
Art. 70(3)	Any Contracting State may provide that a translation into one of its official languages, as prescribed by it according to the EPC (see, for example, Art. 65), will in that State be regarded as authentic, except for revocation proceedings, in the event of the European patent application or European patent in the language of the translation conferring protection which is narrower than that conferred by it in the language of the proceedings.	
Art. 70(4)	Any Contracting State which adopts a provision under Art. 70(3): (a) must allow the applicant for or proprietor of the patent to file a corrected translation of the European patent application or European patent. Such corrected translation does not have any legal effect until any conditions established by the Contracting State under Art. 65(2) (fee may be required for publication of translation of patent), and Art. 67(3) (translation of the claims of application in official language of state concerned must be made available to the public or communicated to an alleged infringer), have been complied with; (b) may prescribe that any person who, in that State, in good faith has used or has made effective and serious preparations for using an invention the use of which would not constitute infringement of the application or patent in the original translation may, after the corrected translation takes effect, continue such use in the course of his business or for the needs thereof without payment.	
Guidelines	See A-VII, 8.	
NatLaw	See Table V for national provisions relating to the authentic text. Similar provisions concerning the authentic text exist in respect of extension states and validation states under the terms of the relevant agreements.	

25.14 Unity of a European patent application or European Patent

1355   Art. 118   Where the applicants for or proprietors of a European patent are not the same in respect of different designated Contracting States, they are regarded as joint applicants or proprietors for the purposes of proceedings before the EPO. The unity of the application or patent in these proceedings are not affected; in particular the text of the application or patent must be uniform for all designated Contracting States unless the EPC provides otherwise.

r.138   If the EPO is informed of the existence of a prior right under Art. 139(2), the European patent application or European patent may, for such State or States, contain claims and, where appropriate, a description and drawings which are different from those for the other designated States.

r.18(2)   Where appropriate, a European patent application may contain, for the designated Contracting States in which a decision that a third party is entitled to the grant of a European was taken or recognised or must be recognised on the basis of the Protocol on Recognition, claims, a description and drawings which are different from those for the other designated Contracting States.

r.78(2)   Where a third party has, in accordance with Art. 99(4), replaced the previous proprietor for one or some of the designated Contracting States, the patent as maintained in opposition proceedings may, for these States, contain claims, a description and drawings different from those for the other designated States.

r.87 EPC1973   For an application filed before the coming into force of EPC2000, where an Art. 54(3) document exists in respect of only some designated States, the application and corresponding patent may have different claims and, if the EPO agrees, a different description and drawings for different States, as an exception to the unity requirement of Art. 118.

Guidelines   See H-III, 4 and A-III, 12.1 – r.138 does not apply to extension and validation states since the relevant agreements do not apply this provision. However, where the application or patent contains different claims for different Contracting States, the applicant or proprietor may decide which text applies to any extension of validation states.

25.15 Request for information concerning prior art

1356   Art. 124(1)   The EPO may, in accordance with the Implementing Regulations, invite the applicant to provide information on prior art taken into consideration in national or regional patent proceedings and concerning an invention to which the European patent application relates.

r.141(1)   An applicant claiming priority within the meaning of Art. 87 shall file a copy of the results of any search carried out by the authority with which the previous application was filed together with the European patent application, in the case of a Euro-PCT application on entry into the European phase, or without delay after such results have been made available to him.

OJ   See Notice from the EPO dated 28 July 2010 ([2010] O.J. 410). Where multiple priorities are claimed, search results are required in respect of each previous application. The applicant's obligation extends to search results in any format, e.g. citations in a search report or examination report. Copies of original search reports are required rather than a list of citations drawn up by the applicant. No translation, however, is required, and copies of cited documents do not have to be filed. No search results need to be filed for a divisional application if they have already been filed in respect of the parent.

r.141(2)   The copy referred to in r.141(1) shall be deemed to be duly filed if it is available to the EPO and to be included in the file of the European patent application under the conditions determined by the President of the EPO.

OJ   See Decision of the President dated 05 October 2010 ([2010] O.J. 600). Where the search report drawn up in respect of the priority application was drawn up by the EPO and was a European search report (Art. 92 EPC), an international search report (Art. 15(1) PCT), an international-type search report (Art. 15(5) PCT) or a search report made on behalf of a national office on a national application, no copy needs to be filed by the applicant. According to Guidelines A-III, 6.12, countries currently falling in the latter category are Belgium, Cyprus, France, Greece, Italy, Latvia, Lithuania, Luxembourg, Malta, Monaco, Netherlands, San Marino and United Kingdom.

OJ   Further exemptions from the need to file a copy of search results pursuant to r.141(2) EPC have been granted in respect of priority applications filed in the following countries:

Country	Decision of the President
Austria	19 September 2012 ([2012] O.J. 540)
China	08 April 2021 ([2021] O.J. A38)
Czech Republic	11 July 2022 ([2022] O.J. A79)
Denmark	10 December 2014 ([2015] O.J. A2)
Japan	19 September 2012 ([2012] O.J. 540)
Republic of Korea	27 February 2013 ([2013] O.J. 216)
Spain	10 February 2016 ([2016] O.J. A18)
Sweden	14 May 2021 ([2021] O.J. A39)
Switzerland	04 June 2019 ([2019] O.J. A55)
United Kingdom	19 September 2012 ([2012] O.J. 540)
United States of America	19 September 2012 ([2012] O.J. 540)

r.141(3)	Without prejudice to r.141(1) and r.141(2), the EPO may invite the applicant to provide, within a period of two months, information on prior art within the meaning of Art. 124(1).
OJ	See Notice from the EPO dated 28 July 2010 ([2010] O.J. 410). The EPO may therefore also ask for information on prior art cited in respect of applications other than those whose priority is claimed but which relate to the same invention. It may also, under r.141(3), ask for the copy referred to in r.141(1) and r.70b(1) at any stage of the proceedings if not available at the start of examination. Invitations under r.141(3) are only issued during the examination phase of grant proceedings and only in individual cases.
Art. 124(2)	If the applicant fails to reply in due time to an invitation under Art. 124(1), the European patent application will be deemed to be withdrawn.
Art. 140	Such an invitation may also relate, where appropriate, to utility models, utility certificates and applications for the same.
r.70b(1)	Where the EPO notes, at the time the Examining Division assumes responsibility, that a copy referred to in r.141(1) has not been filed by the applicant and is not deemed to be duly filed under r.141(2), it shall invite the applicant to file, within a period of two months, the copy or a statement that the results of the search referred to in r.141(1) are not available to him.
OJ	See Notice from the EPO dated 28 July 2010 ([2010] O.J. 410). For a divisional application, no response to the invitation is required where all relevant search results have been filed in respect of the parent application. However, if a statement of non-availability has been filed in respect of the parent application, the applicant needs to also file such a statement in respect of the divisional or, if appropriate, file the results which have become available in the meantime.
r.70b(2)	If the applicant fails to reply in due time to the invitation under r.70b(1), the European patent application shall be deemed withdrawn.
Art. 121	Further processing is available for the time limits of r.141(3) and r.70b(1).
RRFArt. 2(1)(12)	The further processing fee is € 290 in this case.
Art. 122	Re-establishment would be available if the further processing time limit was missed in spite of all due care having been shown.
Guidelines	See A-III, 6.12. The requirement of r.141(1) applies even where the priority claim has been withdrawn or has lapsed. It applies to all European and Euro-PCT applications filed on or after 01 January 2011 (for a divisional application, the actual filing date of the divisional is the relevant date). See also C-II, 5.

25.16 Reference to the procedural law of the Contracting States

Art. 125	In the absence of procedural provisions in the EPC, the EPO takes into account the principles of procedural law generally recognised in the Contracting States.	1357

Chapter 26: Information Made Available by the EPO

26.1 The Register of European patents

26.1.1 Content of the register

1358 Art. 127   The EPO keeps a European Patent Register, in which the particulars specified in the Implementing Regulations are recorded.

r.143   The European Patent Register has the following entries:

(a) the number of the European patent application;

(b) the date of filing of the application;

(c) the title of the invention;

(d) classification symbols assigned to the application;

(e) the Contracting States designated;

(f) particulars of the applicant for or proprietor the patent as provided for in r.41(2)(c);

(g) the family name, given names and country and place of residence of the inventor designated by the applicant for or the proprietor of the patent, unless he has waived his right to be mentioned under r.20(1);

(h) particulars of the representative of the applicant for or proprietor of the patent as provided for in r.41(2)(d); in the case of several representatives, only the particulars of the representative first named, followed by the words "and others" and, in the case of an association referred to in r.152(11), only the name and address of the association;

(i) priority data (date, State and file number of the previous application);

(j) in the event of a division of an application, the numbers of all the divisional applications;

(k) in the case of a divisional application or a new application under Art. 61(1)(b), the information referred to in r.143(1)(a), (b) and (i) with regard to the earlier application;

(l) date of publication of the application and, where appropriate, date of the separate publication of the European Search Report;

(m) date of filing of the request for examination;

(n) date on which the application is refused, withdrawn or deemed to be withdrawn;

(o) date of publication of the mention of the grant of the European patent;

(p) date of lapse of the European patent in a Contracting State during the opposition period and, where appropriate, pending a final decision on the opposition;

(q) date of filing opposition;

(r) date and purport of a decision on opposition;

(s) dates of stay and resumption of proceedings in the cases referred to in rr.14 and 78;

(t) dates of interruption and resumption of proceedings in the case referred to in r.142;

(u) date of re-establishment of rights provided that an entry has been made under r.143(1) (n) or (r);

(v) the filing of a request for conversion under Art. 135(3);

(w) rights and transfer of such rights relating to an application or a European patent where these Implementing Regulations provide that they will be recorded;

(x) date and purport of the decision on the request for limitation or revocation of the European patent;

(y) date and purport of the decision of the Enlarged Board of Appeal on the petition for review.

r.143(2)   The President of the EPO may decide that entries other than those referred to in r.143(1) will be made in the European Patent Register.

OJ   See Decision of the President dated 15 July 2014, [2014] O.J. A86 for the list of additional entries: no opposition filed; patent specification corrected on [date]; date of dispatch of supplementary European search report; date of dispatch of first examination communication; date of receipt of request for re-establishment of rights; refusal of request for re-establishment of rights; opponent's name, address and country of residence/principle place of business; name and business address of opponent's representative; new documents coming to light after drawing up of the European search report; international filing number, publication number and publication date; date of request for limitation or revocation; requester's name, address and country of residence/principle place of business; date of petition for review; petitioner's name, address and country of residence/principle place of business; file number of a petition for review; date of refusal, withdrawal or deemed withdrawal of a divisional if it gives rise to its non-publication; date of dispatch of the examining division's first communication in respect of the earliest application for which such communication has been issued (for communications issued before 01 April 2014); date of dispatch of a communication from the examining division to which search results under r.164(2) EPC are annexed.

OJ   See also Decision of the President dated 24 April 2023 ([2023] O.J. Supplementary Publication 3, page 1). A further entry will be made: Date of lapse of the European patent with unitary effect during the opposition period and, where appropriate, pending a final decision on opposition.

26.1.2   *No entry in the register prior to publication of the application*

Art. 127   No entry may be made in the European Patent Register before the publication of a European patent application.   1359

26.1.3   *Register to be open to the public*

Art. 127   The European Patent Register is open to public inspection.   1360
OJ   See Notice from the EPO dated 15 August 2006 ([2006] O.J. 535). The register can only now be inspected online from the EPO website.
Guidelines   See A-XI, 4. Register data may also be obtained by telephoning the EPO. In exceptional, substantiated cases, an extract from the register on paper may be provided – no fee is payable.

26.1.4   *Language of the register*

Art. 14(8)   Entries are made in all three EPO official languages.   1361

26.2   Inspection of files relating to applications

26.2.1   *No inspection of files relating to unpublished application except where rights have been invoked*

Art. 128(1)   Files relating to European patent applications which have not yet been published are not made available for inspection without the consent of the applicant.   1362
Art. 128(2)   Any person who can prove that the applicant has invoked the rights under the European patent application against him may obtain inspection of the files before the publication of that application and without the consent of the applicant.
J14/91   Inspection will be allowed where the European application has been invoked against somebody or a national application has been invoked and the European application has been mentioned.
Guidelines   According to A-XI, 2.5, the applicant is notified of the identity of the person making a request under Art. 128(2). The applicant is entitled to be heard on the matter and an appealable decision is issued in due course.
Art. 128(3)   Where a European divisional application or a new European patent application filed under Art. 61(1), is published, any person may obtain inspection of the files of the earlier application before the publication of that application and without the consent of the applicant.
Art. 128(5)   Even before the publication of the European patent application, the EPO may communicate to third parties or publish the particulars specified in the Implementing Regulations.
Guidelines   According to A-XI, 2.6, no communication or publication under Art. 128(5) takes place.

26.2.2   Inspection of files after publication of the application

1363 Art. 128(4)	After the publication of the European patent application, the files relating to the application and the resulting European patent may be inspected on request, subject to the restrictions laid down in the Implementing Regulations.
r.144	The parts of the file excluded from inspection under Art. 128(4) are: (a) the documents relating to the exclusion of or objections to members of the Boards of Appeal or of the Enlarged Board of Appeal; (b) draft decisions and notices, and all other documents, used for the preparation of decisions and notices, which are not communicated to the parties; (c) the designation of the inventor, if he has waived his right to be mentioned under r.20(1); and (d) any other document excluded from inspection by the President of the EPO on the ground that such inspection would not serve the purpose of informing the public about the European patent application or the resulting patent.
T516/89	A party can ask for evidence submitted to be confidential and a decision is taken by the President. If the answer is no then the evidence is returned unexamined. See also Guidelines A-XI, 2.3.
T760/89	Documents filed in breach of confidentiality may also be returned.
OJ	The President has specified those documents that will be excluded under r.144(d) (Decision of the President dated 12 July 2007–[2007] O.J. Special Edition No. 3 J3). These include medical certificates, documents relating to the issue of priority documents, file inspection proceedings or the communication of information from the files, requests for exclusion from inspection and requests for accelerated procedure if made on a separate sheet.
T2893/18	Regardless of whether a document would prejudice the legitimate personal or economic interests of a patry, its exclusion from file inspection is only possible if it would not serve the purpose of informing the public about the application or patent in suit. A document relevant to a decision to be taken, for example, cannot be excluded. In opposition proceedings, documents will be communicated to other parties even when a request for their exclusion from the file has been made and is being considered.
Guidelines	See A-XI, 2.4. Requests for inspection are themselves confidential and the applicant is not informed. See also D-II, 4.3 – as the public must be informed of the grounds prejudicing or supporting the maintenance of a patent, excluded documents (or excluded parts thereof) may not be used as evidence to prove or refute a ground for opposition.

26.2.3   Procedure for the inspection of files and communication of information in the files

1364 r.145(1)	Inspection of the files of European patent applications and patents will either be of the original document, or of copies thereof, or of technical means of storage if the files are stored in this way.
r.145(2)	The President of the EPO determines all file inspection arrangements, including the circumstances in which an administrative fee is payable.
RRFArt. 3(1)	The amount of the administrative fee is fixed by the President of the EPO.
OJ	See Decision of the President dated 20 February 2019 ([2019] O.J. A16) for manner of inspection. See decision of the President dated 17 January 2023 ([2023] O.J. A3 for current fees. Files are now available for inspection online free of charge. The EPO also provides computers for online file inspection on its premises. File inspection by means of uncertified paper copies is only available in exceptional cases (see Guidelines below). Certified copies of documents are available on payment of a fee of € 115.
RRFArt. 4(1)	The fee is due on the date of the request for inspection.
r.149(1)	Rule 145 does not apply to inspection by courts or other authorities in the Contracting States – originals or copies are inspected in these cases.
r.146	Subject to the restrictions laid down in Art. 128(1)–(4) and r.144, the EPO may, upon request, communicate information concerning any file relating to a European patent application or European patent, subject to the payment of an administrative fee. However, the EPO may refer to the option of file inspection where it deems this to be appropriate in view of the amount of information to be supplied.
OJ	See decision of the President dated 17 January 2023, [2023] O.J. A3. The fee is € 115.

RRFArt. 4(1)	The fee is due on the date of the request for information.
Guidelines	See A-XI, 2.2 and 3. See also A-XI, 5 – the EPO will issue certified copies of a European patent application, a European patent or any other document in the file which is open to inspection (on payment of a fee). However, file inspection by the issuance of uncertified paper copies of documents in the file will only be allowed in exceptional circumstances and only if the request is duly substantiated. No fee is now payable for file inspection in this manner.

26.2.4   Maintenance of the files

r.147(1)	The EPO shall constitute, maintain and preserve files relating to all European patent applications and patents in electronic form.	1365
r.147(2)	The President of the EPO shall determine all necessary technical and administrative arrangements relating to the management of electronic files according to r.147(1).	
OJ	See Decision of the President dated 12 July 2007, [2007] O.J. Special Edition No. 3 J1 specifying the use of the electronic file system PHOENIX.	
r.147(3)	Documents incorporated in an electronic file shall be considered to be originals. The initial paper version of such documents shall only be destroyed after expiry of at least five years. This preservation period starts at the end of the year in which the document was incorporated in the electronic file.	
Comment	This version of r.147(1)–(3) entered into force on 01 November 2016, specifying that files will be now be maintained in electronic form, and applied to all European patent applications and patents with the proviso that the period mentioned in r.147(3) cannot expire before 31 December 2018.	
OJ	See [2017] O.J. A90. The five year period applies only to paper versions of documents stored electronically and does not apply to initial versions of documents submitted in an admissible electronic form. Neither does it apply to record copies of international applications filed with the EPO on paper and kept by the EPO on behalf of the IB.	
r.147(4)	Any files shall be preserved for at least five years from the end of the year in which: (a) the application is refused or withdrawn or is deemed to be withdrawn; (b) the patent is revoked by the EPO; or (c) the patent or the corresponding protection under Art. 63(2) (protection going beyond the usual 20 year term) lapses in the last of the designated States.	
r.147(5)	Without prejudice to r.147(4), files relating to applications which have given rise to divisional applications under Art. 76 or new applications under Art. 61(1))(b), shall be preserved for at least the same period as the files relating to any one of these last applications. The same shall apply to files relating to any resulting European patents.	

26.3   The Official Journal

Art. 129(b)	The EPO periodically publishes an Official Journal, containing notices and information of a general character issued by the President of the EPO, as well as any other information relevant to the EPC or its implementation.	1366
Art. 14(7)	The Official Journal is published in all three official EPO languages.	

26.4   The Bulletin

Art. 129(a)	The EPO periodically publishes a European Patent Bulletin containing the particulars the publication of which is prescribed by the EPC, the Implementing Regulations or the President of the EPO.	1367
Comment	See, for example, the mention of the publication of the European Search Report (r.70(1)), the mention of grant (Art. 64(1), Art. 65(1), Art. 86(2), Art. 97(3), Art. 98, Art. 99(1), Art. 141(2)), the mention of maintenance of a patent in amended form (Art. 65(1), Art. 103), the mention of limitation of a patent (Art. 65(1), Art. 105b(3), Art. 105c), the mention of revocation of a patent (Art. 103), Art. 105b(3)), the mention of rejection of an opposition (Art. 103), the mention of the decision of the Enlarged Board of Appeal on a petition for review (Art. 112bis(6)), the mention of re-establishment of rights (Art. 122(5)) and the mention of the international publication of a Euro-PCT application in an EPO official language (Art. 153(3)).	

OJ	Details of designation fees paid are published in the Bulletin ([1997] O.J. 479). Details of extension of a European patent to other States are also published in the Bulletin ([1997] O.J. 115). See also under Art. 129 for modifications made to the content of the Bulletin ([1983] O.J. 459; [1986] O.J. 63; [1988] O.J. 37).
Art. 14(7)	The Bulletin is published in all three official EPO languages.

26.5 Exchanges of information between the EPO and national authorities/courts

1368	Art. 130(1)	Unless the EPC or national laws provide otherwise, the EPO and the central industrial property office of any Contracting State will, on request, communicate to each other any useful information regarding European or national patent applications and patents and regarding any proceedings concerning them.
	Art. 130(2)	Art. 130(1) applies to the communication of information by virtue of working agreements between the EPO and: (a) the central industrial property office of other States; (b) any intergovernmental organisation entrusted with the task of granting patents; (c) any other organisation.
	Art. 130(3)	The communications under Art. 130(1) and Art. 130(2)(a) and (b) are not subject to the restrictions laid down in Art. 128. The Administrative Council may decide that communications under Art. 130(2)(c) are not be subject to such restrictions, provided that the organisation concerned treats the information communicated as confidential until the European patent application has been published.
	r.148(1)	Communications between the EPO and the central industrial property offices of the Contracting States which arise out of the application of the EPC are effected directly between these authorities. Communication between the EPO and the courts or other authorities of the Contracting States may be effected through the intermediary of the said central industrial property offices.
	r.148(2)	Expenditure in respect of communications under r.148(1) will be borne by the authority making the communications, which will be exempt from fees.
	Art. 131(1)	Unless the EPC or national laws provide otherwise, the EPO and the courts or authorities of Contracting States will on request give assistance to each other by communicating information or opening files for inspection. Where the EPO makes files available for inspection by courts, Public Prosecutors' Offices or central industrial property offices, the inspection is not subject to the restrictions laid down in Art. 128.
	r.149(2)	Courts or Public Prosecutors' offices of the Contracting States may, in the course of their proceedings, communicate to third parties files or copies thereof transmitted to them by the EPO. Such communications are effected in accordance with Art. 128 and are not subject to any fee.
	r.149(3)	The EPO will, when transmitting the files, draw attention to the restrictions which may, under Art. 128(1) and (4), apply to file inspections by third parties.
	Art. 131(2)	At the request of the EPO, the courts or other competent authorities of Contracting States must undertake, on behalf of the EPO and within the limits of their jurisdiction, any necessary enquiries or other legal measures.
	r.150	Special provisions apply to the sending of letters rogatory by the EPO.
	Art. 132(1)	The EPO and the central industrial property offices of the Contracting States despatch to each other on request and for their own use one or more copies of their respective publications free of charge.
	Art. 132(2)	The EPO may conclude agreements relating to the exchange or supply of publications.

Chapter 27: Special Agreements under the EPC

27.1 Unitary patents

27.1.1 Grant of a unitary patent by the EPO

Art. 142(1)	Any group of Contracting States, which has provided by a special agreement that a European patent granted for those States has a unitary character throughout their territories, may provide that a European patent may only be granted jointly in respect of all those States.	1369
Art. 142(2)	Where any group of Contracting States has availed itself of the authorisation given in Art. 142(1), the provisions of this Part apply (Arts. 142–149a).	

27.1.1.1 Switzerland/Liechtenstein unitary patent

OJ	Such an agreement has been drawn up between Switzerland and Liechtenstein (Treaty between the Swiss Confederation and the Principality of Liechtenstein on Patent Protection of 22 December 1978, [1980] O.J. 407). A European patent application may only jointly designate Switzerland and Liechtenstein and a European patent may only be jointly granted for these two states.	1370

27.1.1.2 EU unitary patent

Comment	See Chapter 14 for European patent with unitary effect.	1371

27.1.2 Special department of the EPO

Art. 143(1)	The group of Contracting States may give additional tasks to the EPO.	1372
Art. 143(2)	Special departments common to the Contracting States in the group may be set up within the EPO in order to carry out the additional tasks. The President of the EPO will direct such special departments; Art. 10, paras 2 and 3 apply mutatis mutandis (President's powers and functions).	
OJ	See decision of the Select Committee of the Administrative Council of 15 December 2015 adopting the Rules relating to Unitary Patent Protection ([2016] O.J. A39). A Unitary Patent Protection Division is to be established within the EPO to carry out tasks associated with EU unitary patents (r.4 UPR). Decisions of the division are taken by one legally qualified member, assisted by formalities staff.	

27.1.3 Representation before special departments

Art. 144	The group of Contracting States may lay down special provisions to govern representation of the parties before the departments referred to in Art. 143(2).	1373

27.1.4 Select Committee of the Administrative Council

Art. 145(1)	The group of Contracting States may set up a Select Committee of the Administrative Council for the purpose of supervising the activities of the special departments set up under Art. 143(2); the EPO will place at its disposal such staff, premises and equipment as may be necessary for the performance of its duties. The President of the EPO will be responsible for the activities of the special departments to the select committee of the Administrative Council.	1374
Art. 145(2)	The composition, powers and functions of the select committee are determined by the group of Contracting States.	
OJ	See decision of the Select Committee of the Administrative Council of 15 December 2015 adopting the Rules relating to Unitary Patent Protection ([2016] O.J. A39). A Select Committee of the Administrative Council is established to supervise the activities of the EPO associated with administration of the EU Unitary Patent (r.2 UPR).	

27.1.5   *Cover for expenditure for carrying out special tasks*

1375   Art. 146   Where additional tasks have been given to the EPO under Art. 143, the group of Contracting States bears the expenses incurred by the Organisation in carrying out these tasks. Where special departments have been set up in the EPO to carry out these additional tasks, the group must bear the expenditure on staff, premises and equipment chargeable in respect of these departments. Art. 39(3) and (4), Art. 41 and Art. 47 apply mutatis mutandis.

27.1.6   *Payments in respect of renewal fees for unitary patents*

1376   Art. 147   If the group of Contracting States has fixed a common scale of renewal fees in respect of European patents, the proportion referred to in Art. 39(1) will be calculated on the basis of the common scale; the minimum amount referred to in Art. 39(1) will apply to the unitary patent. Art. 39(3) and (4) apply mutatis mutandis.

27.1.7   *The European patent application as an object of property*

1377   Art. 148(1)   Art. 74 applies unless the group of Contracting States has specified otherwise (law applicable to an object of property).

Art. 148(2)   The group of Contracting States may provide that a European patent application for which these Contracting States are designated may only be transferred, mortgaged or subjected to any legal means of execution in respect of all the Contracting States of the group and in accordance with the provisions of the special agreement.

27.1.8   *Joint designation*

1378   Art. 149(1)   The group of Contracting States may provide that these States may only be designated jointly, and that the designation of one or some only of such States will be deemed to constitute the designation of all the States of the group.

Art. 149(2)   Where the EPO acts as a designated office under Art. 153(1), Art. 149(1) applies if the applicant has indicated in the international application that he wishes to obtain a European patent for one or more of the designated States of the group. The same applies if the applicant designates in the international application one of the Contracting States in the group, whose national law provides that the designation of that State has the effect of the application being for a European patent.

OJ   See [1980] O.J. 407. Switzerland and Liechtenstein may only be jointly designated.

27.2   Other agreements between the Contracting States

1379   Art. 149a(1)   Nothing in the EPC should be construed as limiting the right of some or all of the Contracting States to conclude special agreements on any matters concerning European patent applications or European patents which under the EPC are subject to and governed by national law, such as, in particular:
(a) an agreement establishing a European Patent Court common to the Contracting States party to it;
(b) an agreement establishing an entity common to the Contracting States party to it to deliver, at the request of national courts or quasi-judicial authorities, opinions on issues of European or harmonised national patent law;
(c) an agreement under which the Contracting States party to it dispense fully or in part with translations of European patents under Art. 65;
(d) an agreement under which the Contracting States party to it provide that translations of European patents as required under Art. 65 may be filed with, and published by, the EPO.

OJ   For the Agreement on a Unified Patent Court under Art. 149a(1)(a), see section 27.1. For the London Agreement under Art. 149a(1)(c), see section 19.5.

Art. 149a(2)   The Administrative Council is competent to decide that:
(a) the members of the Boards of Appeal or the Enlarged Board of Appeal may serve on a European Patent Court or a common entity and take part in proceedings before that court or entity in accordance with such an agreement;

(b) the EPO will provide a common entity with such support staff, premises and equipment as may be necessary for the performance of its duties, and the expenses incurred by that entity will be borne fully or in part by the Organisation.

Chapter 28: Rules Relating to Fees

28.1 The Administrative Council adopts the rules relating to fees

1380   Art. 33(2)(d)   The Administrative Council is competent to adopt the rules relating to fees.
OJ   See O.J. supplement 3/2019 for the latest version (last amended by decision of the Administrative Council dated 12 December 2018).

28.2 Purpose of the rules relating to fees

1381   Art. 51(1)   The EPO may levy fees for any official task or procedure carried out under the EPC.
Art. 51(3)   The Rules relating to Fees determine, in particular, the amounts of the fees and the ways in which they are to be paid.
RRFArt. 1   The following are levied in accordance with the provisions contained in these Rules:
(a) fees due to be paid to EPO as provided for in the EPC and in the Implementing Regulations and the fees and expenses which the President of the EPO lays down under RRFArt. 3(1);
(b) fees and expenses pursuant to the PCT the amounts of which may be fixed by the EPO.

28.3 Fees, costs and prices laid down by the President

1382   RRFArt. 3(1)   The President lays down the amount of the administrative fees provided for in the Implementing Regulations and, where appropriate, the amount of the fees and expenses for any services rendered by the EPO other than those specified in RRFArt. 2.
RRFArt. 3(2)   The President also lays down the prices of the publications referred to in Art. 93, Art. 98, Art. 103 and Art. 129.

28.4 Amounts of fees to be published

1383   RRFArt. 3(3)   The amounts of the fees laid down in RRFArt. 2 and of the expenses laid down in accordance with RRFArt. 3(1) are published in the O.J. and on the website of the EPO.

28.5 Due date for fees where not specified

1384   RRFArt. 4(1)(2)   Fees in respect of which the due date is not specified in the provisions of the EPC or of the PCT or of the Implementing Regulations thereto fall due on the date of receipt of the request for the service incurring the fee concerned. However, the President of the EPO may decide not to make services of this kind dependent on the advance payment of the corresponding fee.

28.6 Currency to be used

1385   RRFArt. 5(1)   All fees must be paid in Euros.

28.7 Payment or transfer to an EPO bank account

1386   RRFArt. 5(1)   Fees due to the EPO may be paid by payment or transfer to an EPO bank account.
RRFArt. 7(1)   Payment will be considered to have been made on the date on which the amount of the payment or transfer is actually entered into the EPO bank account.
OJ   See [2020] O.J. A130 for practical information concerning payment by bank transfer.
Guidelines   See A-X, 2 and 4.1.

28.8 Payment by other methods – deposit accounts and credit cards

1387   RRFArt. 5(2)   The President of the EPO may allow other methods of paying fees than those set out in RRFArt. 5(1).
RRFArt. 7(2)   In these cases the President decides when payments are considered to have been made.
OJ   Payment by cheque has not been possible since April 1, 2008 (see [2007] O.J. 626).

OJ

As from 01 December 2017, payment of fees by credit card is possible (see Decision of the President dated 22 August 2017, [2017] O.J. A72 and Notice from the EPO dated 16 February 2022, [2022] O.J. A18). Payments must be made in euros using a credit card accepted by the EPO (American Express, Mastercard or Visa). Payment is made through the EPO website – a user name and password must be established but no smart card is required. Payment is deemed to have been made on the date on which the transaction is approved, this date being indicated in the transaction confirmation made available to the payer. If a transaction fails before it is approved, the fee payment is considered not to have been made, even if the failure in the transaction process was not attributable to the payer. Where, due to a failure in the transaction process, the payment of a fee is not considered to have been made until after expiry of the period in which it should have been made, it will be considered that the period was observed if evidence is provided to the EPO that, within the period, the payer received a confirmation that the transaction was approved. The time zone for determining the date of payment is Central European Time. There is a daily limit of € 10,000 per payer.

OJ

Payment may be made by means of a deposit account (see Decision of the President dated 19 July 2022, [2022] O.J. supplementary publication 3 and Decision of the President dated 24 April 2023, [2023] O.J. supplementary publication 3, pages 10–19).

A deposit account may be set up by any natural or legal person. The account is kept in Euros and is replenished by payment into an EPO account. Debiting may only be carried out online on the basis of a signed electronic debit order using one of the EPO's approved systems. Debit orders submitted on paper, by fax or in any other way are invalid and will not be processed. The other option is automatic direct debiting of the account by the EPO (see below for more detail).

Debit orders are processed immediately upon receipt (automatic debiting takes place at the end of the day onw which payment is made). Debit orders in respect of multiple applications are booked in ascending order of application number, PCT before EP/Euro-PCT before unitary patent. Individual fees for the same application are processed in the order of priority: (a) appeal fee; (b) opposition fee; (c) other fees in ascending order of their fee codes.

Where a debit order is used, the date of payment is the date that the debit order is received by the EPO, assuming there are sufficient funds in the deposit account. A payment cannot be considered to have been made on the date the debit order was received if insufficient funds exist and it is not possible to retrospectively top up the account by paying an administrative fee – payment is considered to have been made on the date that the account is actually topped up. However, late payment is excused if evidence is provided that (a) a Single European Payment Area Credit transfer resulting in adequate replenishment was ordered at least one day before expiry of the period for paying the fee; or (b) a Single European Payment Area Instant Credit Transfer resulting in adequate replenishment was ordered at the latest on the last day of the period for paying the fee; or (c) any other type of order resulting in adequate replenishment was given to a banking establshment located in an EPC contracting state not participating in the Single European Payment Area at least three days before expiry of the period for paying the fee. The use of further processing and other similar remedies provided for under the EPC and Unitary Patent Rules is necessary if none of these excuses applies. If a payment period expires on a day on which any of the accepted means of electronic filing of debit orders for a particular application is not available then the payment period is extended until the first day on which they are all available (see also r.134(5) EPC and r.82*quater*.1 PCT).

Where a European patent application or a PCT application for which the EPO acts as receiving Office is filed via a national authority (Art. 75(1)(b) or Art. 151/Art. 75(2)(b) EPC), a debit order for fees due on filing may be filed electronically in the usual way. If the application is filed on paper then it may be accompanied with the debit order on form 1020. If the debit order is only received by the EPO after a deadline for fee payment has expired then the fee is deemed paid in time if evidence can be offered showing that the debit order was filed with the application and the relevant account contained sufficient funds on the last day of the deadline.

The automatic debiting procedure may be applied by the applicant or proprietor to any proceedings before the EPO involving a European patent application or an international patent application other than when the EPO acts as Supplementary International Searching Authority. Proceedings relating to unitary patents are also covered. An automatic debit order must be filed in electronic format. It may not be restricted to specific types of fees or to a specific period of time.

A new automatic debit order must be filed after grant in order to cover limitation or revocation proceedings and any subsequent appeal or review proceedings and to cover any proceedings relating to a unitary patent. A new automatic debit order is also required when a Euro-PCT application enters the regional phase. However, an automatic debit order active in grant proceedings remains active for any subsequent opposition proceedings. When an automatic debit order is validly filed, it is the EPO's responsibility to debit from the deposit account most fees which fall due. Excluded are the conversion fee (Art. 135(3), r.140); the fee for the awarding of costs (r.88(3)); the fee for the conservation of evidence (r.123(3)); the fee for a technical opinion (r.25); the fee for a supplementary international search (r.45*bis*.3(a) PCT); the review fee relating to a supplementary international search (r.45*bis*.6(c) PCT); the supplementary search handling fee (r.45*bis*.2 PCT); the late payment fee relating to supplementary international search (r.45*bis*.4(c) PCT); the additional search fee in the event of correction of an erronous filing (r.40*bis* PCT/r.20.5*bis* PCT); the further search fee for a European search pursuant to r.56a(8) and any further processing fee due in the event of the late payment of that fee; and some of the fees laid down by the President of the EPO under Art. 3 RRF.

Fees that are to be paid within a specific period are usually debited on the last day of the relevant period. There are, however, several exceptions. When early processing of a Euro-PCT application is requested, fees are debited on the date of receipt of the request for early processing as long as the EPO has received a copy of the international application and international search report. The examination fee is debited on the date that a waiver of the right to an invitation under r.70(2) is received or on the date a request for accelerated examination is received. The fees for re-establishment of rights, limitation, revocation, appeal, petition for review, restoration of priority (r.26*bis*.3(d) PCT) and international preliminary examination (r.57 and r.58 PCT and r.158(2) EPC) and administrative fees which are eligible for automatic debiting are debited on the day the relevant request is received. The fee for grant and publishing is debited on the date on which claim translations are filed. Claims fees payable under r.71(4) are also debited on the date on which translations of the relevant claims are filed. The fee for publishing a new European patent specification is debited on the date of receipt of claim translations. Renewal fees are debited on the date they fall due. The further processing fee is debited on the last day of the further processing period when the omitted act was the non-payment of a fee (along with the non-paid fee) or on the date of completion of the omitted act when the omitted act was something else. Specific provisions exist to cover situations in which an automatic debit order is filed while proceedings are ongoing. For example, if an automatic debit order is filed during the period for requesting re-establishment, the re-establishment fee is debited on the later of the date of the request for re-establishment and the date on which the automatic debit order is filed. In this situation, any fees which consitute the omitted act are not debited automatically and must be paid by filing a specific debit order or in some other way.

Even when an automatic debit order is active, the applicant or proprietor can always pay any fees that fall due by other means and, in this case, the fee will not be automatically debited if payment is received at least two days before the automatic debit date.

Automatic debit orders cease to be effective in a number of situations such as when an application is withdrawn, finally refused or finally deemed withdrawn. When a patent grants, the automatic debit order ceases to be effective unless an opposition is filed in which case it becomes effective again. However, it does not become effective again in the case that limitation or revocation proceedings are initiated – a new automatic debit order is necessary for each proceeding of this kind. It also ceases to be effective if either proceedings are stayed under r.14 or proceedings are interrupted under r.142.

Guidelines

See A-X, 2, 4.2 and 4.3. Apart from payment or transfer to a bank account, the use of a credit card or the debiting of a deposit account the only other way of paying a fee is by requesting reallocation of a refund.

T1146/20 Although a deposit account can only be debited if instructions are provided in electronically processable format, the Board of Appeal in this case allowed an opponent to use r.139 to correct the forms used to file an opposition in order to retrospectively include proper electronic instructions to pay the opposition fee. The original forms simply included a statement in the notice of opposition that the EPO should debit the fee from the opponent's deposit account.

28.9 Extension of deadlines when a means of payment is not available

OJ All periods are extended where one of the conditions of r.134(1) applies (filing office shut for receipt of documents, mail not delivered, a means of electronically filing documents not available), including periods for the payment of fees. According to the Notice from the EPO dated 22 October 2020 ([2020] O.J. A120), if the payment of a fee expires on a day on which one of the accepted means specifically provided for the payment of fees is not available then the fee may also be validly paid on the first working day on which all such means for making payments are available. Therefore, if there is an outage relating to the Online Fee Payment Tool or the EPO credit card payment service or bank transfers, payment periods are extended to the first working day thereafter on which all accepted means for making a payment are available. This applies even if the outage only affects one means of payment. However, where a means of payment is unavailable for less than four hours and the outage has been published at least two days in advance then periods will not be extended since in this case users are expected to plan accordingly. Note that an outage relating to the Online Fee Payment Tool or the EPO credit card payment service or bank transfers does not lead to a general extension of time limits under r.131(4) EPC (e.g. for the filing of documents) but to a specific extension of time limits for the payment of fees.

28.10 Safeguard in cases where payment is deemed not to have been made in time

RRFArt. 7(3) Where under the provisions of RRFArt. 7(1) and (2), payment of a fee is not considered   1388
to have been made until after the expiry of the period in which it should have been made, it shall be considered that this period has been observed if evidence is provided to the EPO that the person who made the payment fulfilled one of the following conditions in a Contracting State within the period within which the payment should have been made:
(i) he effected the payment through a banking establishment;
(ii) he duly gave an order to a banking establishment to transfer the amount of the payment.

RRFArt. 7(4) The EPO may request the person who made the payment to produce evidence as to the date on which a condition according to RRFArt. 7(3) was fulfilled within a period specified by it. If he fails to comply with this request or if the evidence is insufficient, the period for payment shall be considered not to have been observed.

J20/00 RRFArt. 7(3) applies to the payment of a renewal fee even though the renewal fee due date is not a time limit.

Guidelines See A-X, 6.2. This safeguard also applies to payments made to replenish a deposit account. If a loss of rights pursuant to r.112(1) EPC is received then the applicant should submit evidence showing that RRFArt. 7(3) was complied with and request a decision under r.112(2) EPC.

28.11 The EPO must be able to establish what a payment is for

RRFArt. 6(1) Every payment must indicate the name of person making the payment and must contain   1389
the necessary particulars to enable the EPO to establish immediately the purpose of the payment.

RRFArt. 6(2) If the purpose of the payment cannot be immediately established, the EPO will require the person making the payment to notify it in writing of this purpose within such period as it may specify. If he does not comply with this request in due time, the payment will be considered not to have been made.

Guidelines See A-X, 7.

28.12 Who may make payments? To whom will refunds be paid?

1390 Guidelines   Fees may validly be paid by anyone (A-X, 1) and refunds are made to the party or to a representative authorised to receive payments (A-X, 10.4).

28.13 Procedure where the amount paid is insufficient

1391 RRFArt. 8   A time limit for payment shall in principle be deemed to have been observed only if the full amount of the fee has been paid in due time. If the fee is not paid in full, the amount which has been paid will be refunded after the period for payment has expired. The EPO may, however, insofar as this is possible within the time remaining before the end of the period, give the person making the payment the opportunity to pay the amount lacking. It may also, where this is considered justified, overlook any small amounts lacking, without prejudice to the rights of the person making the payment.

T637/21   According to this decision, a small amount lacking is so small that its absence is overlooked by the EPO and any shortfall does not need to be made up. It should be of the same order as the amount considered under RRFArt. 12 to be too insignificant for the EPO to refund automatically.

T2035/14   If a party's intention is clear (here the intention was to pay the appeal fee and this was clear from filed form 1010) then the EPO must debit the correct amount even if the wrong amount is specified on the form. See also T152/82, cited in the decision and Guidelines A-X, 4.2.3. If the EPO debits the wrong amount then the fee is still considered to have been paid.

OJ   A transitional arrangement is always provided during the six months from the date on which the amount of a fee is increased. If, during this period, the amount due before the fee increase is paid, the fee will nevertheless be deemed to have been paid in full if the deficit is made good within two months of an invitation to that effect from the EPO (see, for example, Art. 4(3) of the Decision of the Administrative Council dated 14 December 2022, [2023] O.J. A2).

28.14 Refund of insignificant amounts

1392 RRFArt. 12   Where too large a sum is paid to cover a fee, the excess will not be refunded if the amount is insignificant and the party concerned has not expressly requested a refund. The President of the EPO decides what constitutes an insignificant amount.

OJ   See Decision of the President dated 07 March 2023 ([2023] OJ A27). Any amount up to € 17 is considered insignificant.

Guidelines   See A-X, 10.1.3.

28.15 Refund in other cases

1393 Guidelines   See A-X, 10. Fees are refunded if they are paid without legal basis (e.g. the application for which the fee has been paid does not exist or is no longer pending). Fees paid before the relevant due date are also refunded unless otherwise specified. A fee paid after the expiry of a time limit in which the fee should have been paid is not valid and is refunded unless further processing applies and is requested. Refunds are credited to an EPO deposit account or else made by cheque or, at the request of the relevant party, reallocated.

OJ   See Notice from the EPO dated 20 August 2019 ([2019] OJ A82). The EPO will make a refund to any deposit account nominated by the relevant party to the proceedings (whether it belongs to that party or not). Where no deposit account is available, a party will be able to claim a refund via the EPO website by nominating a bank account into which the refund should be paid.

PART C - THE PCT

Chapter 29: Institutional Aspects and Definitions

29.1 Establishment of a Union

Art. 1(1)   The States party to the PCT constitute a union for co-operation in the filing, searching   1394
and examination of applications for the protection of inventions and for rendering special
technical services. The union is known as the International Patent Co-operation Union.

Art. 62(1)   Any State member of the International Union for the Protection of Industrial Property
may become party to the PCT by (i) signature followed by deposit of an instrument of
ratification, or (ii) deposit of an instrument of ratification.

PC Art. 19   The countries of the Union (as established by the Paris Convention) have the right to
make separately between themselves special agreements for the protection of industrial property, as long as these agreements do not contravene the provisions of the Paris
Convention.

Art. 1(2)   No provision of the PCT is to be interpreted as diminishing the rights under the Paris
Convention of any national or resident of any country party to that Convention.

Art. 3(1)   Applications for the protection of inventions in any of the Contracting States may be filed
as international applications under the PCT.

29.2 Parts of the Union

29.2.1 The Assembly

Art. 53(1)   The Assembly consists essentially of the Contracting States, each government being rep-   1395
resented by one delegate.

29.2.2 The International Bureau

Art. 55(1)–(3)   The International Bureau performs the administrative tasks of the Union and provides the   1396
Secretariat of the various organs of the Union, the chief executive of which is the Director
General.

29.3 Regulations and Administrative Instructions

29.3.1 Regulations under the PCT

Art. 58(1)   Regulations are annexed to the PCT and provide rules concerning: 1397
(a) matters in respect of which the PCT expressly refers to the Regulations or provides
that they are or will be prescribed;
(b) any administrative requirements, matters or procedures; and
(c) any details useful in the implementation of the provisions of the PCT.

Art. 58(5)   In the case of conflict between the provisions of the PCT and those of the Regulations, the
provisions of the PCT prevail.

29.3.2 Administrative Instructions

Art. 58(4)   The Regulations provide for the establishment, under the control of the Assembly, of   1398
Administrative Instructions by the Director General.

r.89.1(a)   The Administrative Instructions contain provisions concerning:
(i) matters in respect of which the Regulations expressly refer; and
(ii) any details in respect of the application of the Regulations.

29.4 The Gazette

Art. 55(4)   The International Bureau publishes a Gazette.   1399
Comment   The Gazette is now only available in electronic form.
r.86.1   The Gazette contains:
(i) for each published application, data as specified in the Administrative Instructions tak-
en from the front page of the publication, any drawing on the front page and the abstract;

(ii) the schedule of all fees payable to the receiving Offices, the International Bureau and the International Preliminary Examining and Searching Authorities;

(iii) notices the publication of which is required under the PCT and its Regulations;

(iv) information concerning events at the designated and elected Offices notified to the International Bureau under r.95.1 in relation to published international applications; and

(v) any other useful information, provided that access to such information is not prohibited under the PCT or its Regulations.

r.48.6(a)   If a notification under r.29.1(ii), that the receiving Office considers the international application to be withdrawn, reaches the International Bureau too late to prevent international publication of the application, the International Bureau will promptly publish a notice in the Gazette reproducing the essence of such a notification.

r.48.6(c)   If the application, the designation of a State or a priority claim is withdrawn by the applicant under r.90bis after the technical preparations for publication have been completed, notice of the withdrawal will be published in the Gazette.

29.5   Definitions/Interpretations

1400 **r.2.2**   **Agent**: an agent appointed under r.90.1, unless the contrary clearly follows from the wording of the nature of the provision, or the context in which the word is used.

r.2.1   **Applicant**: includes the agent or other representative of the applicant, except where the contrary clearly follows from the wording or the nature of the provision, or the context in which the word is used, such as, in particular, where the provision refers to the residence or nationality of the applicant.

Art. 2(i)   **Application**: an application for the protection of an invention including an application for a patent for invention, an inventors' certificate, a utility certificate, utility models, a patent or certificates of addition, an inventors' certificate of addition and a utility certificate of addition.

Art. 2(viii) **Application**: references to an application shall be construed as references to international applications and national applications.

Art. 2(xvii) **Assembly**: the Assembly of the Union.

r.2.2bis   **Common Representative**: an applicant appointed as, or considered to be, the common representative under r.90.2.

Art. 1(1)   **Contracting States**: states party to the PCT.

Art. 2(xiii) **Designated Office**: the national office of or acting for a State designated by the applicant under Chapter I of the PCT.

Art. 4(1)(ii) **Designated States**: those Contracting States in which protection for the invention is required on the basis of the international application and which are designated in the request.

Art. 2(xx)   **Director General**: the Director General of the Organisation and, as long as the United International Bureaux for the Protection of Intellectual Property (BIRPI) subsists, the Director of the BIRPI.

Art. 2(xiv) **Elected Office**: the national office of or acting for a State elected by the applicant under Chapter II of the PCT.

Art. 2(vii) **International Application**: an application filed under the PCT.

Art. 2(xix) **International Bureau**: the International Bureau of the Organisation and, as long as it subsists, the United International Bureaux for the Protection of Intellectual Property (BIRPI).

Art. 2(vi)   **National Application**: an application for a national or a regional patent other than an application filed under the PCT.

Art. 2 (x)   **National Law**: the national law of a Contracting State or, where a regional application or a regional patent is involved, the law of the treaty providing for the filing of regional applications or the granting of regional patents.

Art. 2(xii) **National Office**: the government authority of a Contracting State entrusted with the granting of patents or any intergovernmental authority which several States have entrusted with the task of granting regional patents, provided that at least one of those States is a Contracting State and provided that the said States have authorised that authority to assume the obligations and exercise the powers which the PCT and its Regulations provide for in respect of national Offices.

Art. 2(iii)   **National Patent**: a patent granted by a national authority.

Art. 2(xviii) **Organisation**: the World Intellectual Property Organisation.

Art. 2(ii)	**Patent**: a patent for invention, an inventors' certificate, a utility certificate, a utility model, a patent or certificate of addition, an inventors' certificate of addition or a utility certificate of addition.
Art. 2(ix)	**Patent**: references to a patent shall be construed as references to national patents and regional patents.
Art. 2(xi)	**Priority Date**: the priority date is: (a) where the international application contains a priority claim under Art. 8, the filing date of the application whose priority is so claimed; (b) where the international application contains several priority claims under Art. 8, the filing date of the earliest application whose priority is so claimed; or (c) where the international application does not contain any priority claim under Art. 8, the international filing date of such application.
r.2.4	**Priority Period**: whenever the term "priority period" is used in relation to a priority claim, it should be construed as meaning the period of 12 months from the filing date of the earlier application whose priority is claimed. The day of filing of the earlier application is not to be included in that period. Rule 80.5 applies mutatis mutandis to the priority period (there will be extension of this period where an Office is shut on the last day of the period).
Art. 2(xv)	**Receiving Office**: the national Office or intergovernmental organisation with which the international application has been filed.
Art. 2(v)	**Regional Application**: an application for a regional patent.
Art. 2(iv)	**Regional Patent**: a patent granted by a national or an intergovernmental authority having the power to grant patents effective in more than one State.
r.2.3	**Signature**: if the national law applied by the receiving Office or the competent International Searching or Preliminary Examining Authority requires the use of a seal instead of a signature, the word for the purposes of that Office or Authority, means seal.
r.1.1(a)	**Treaty**: the Patent Co-operation Treaty (PCT).
Art. 2(xvi)	**Union**: the International Patent Co-operation Union.

Chapter 30: The Application

30.1 Elements of the application

1401 Art. 3(2)   An international application must contain, as specified in the PCT and the Regulations, a request, a description, one or more claims, one or more drawings (where required), and an abstract.

AdminInst   See s.207(a) – the application should be arranged in the order: request, description, claim(s), abstract, drawings. See s.207(b) – sheets should be numbered in a first series comprising the request, a second series comprising the description, claims and abstract and, where applicable, a third series comprising the drawings and, where applicable, a fourth series comprising the sequence listing part of the description.

30.2 General and physical requirements of the application

30.2.1 Prohibited matter

1402 r.9.1   The international application must not contain:
(i) expressions or drawings contrary to morality;
(ii) expressions or drawings contrary to public order;
(iii) statements disparaging the products or processes of those other than the applicant, or to the validity of such a person's application(s) or patent(s) (mere comparisons with the prior art, however, not being considered disparaging per se); or
(iv) statements or other matter obviously irrelevant or unnecessary.

r.9.2   The receiving Office, the International Searching Authority, the Authority specified for supplementary search and the International Bureau may note lack of compliance with the prescriptions of Rule 9.1 and may suggest to the applicant that he voluntarily corrects his international application accordingly, in which case the receiving Office, the competent International Searching Authority, the competent Authority specified for supplementary search and the International Bureau, as applicable, shall be informed of the suggestion.

Art. 21(6)   The International Bureau may omit offending material on publication (see section 36.6).

30.2.2 Number of copies to be filed

1403 r.11.1   The application and documents referred to in the checklist (r.3.3 (a)(ii)) should normally be filed in one copy. However, the receiving Office may demand they be filed in two or three copies (except for the receipt for fees paid or the check for the payment of fees). In the case that multiple copies are required, the receiving Office must check their identity.

r.21.1   See r.21.1 (section 31.2.2) for the consequences of not submitting enough copies.

EPC r.157(2)   The President of the EPO may determine that the international application and any related item must be filed in more than one copy.

OJ   Only one copy is required by the EPO ([2006] O.J. 439). See also AppGuide, Annex C (EP).

30.2.3 Terminology and signs

1404 r.10   Requirements relating to terminology and signs are listed.

30.2.4 Physical requirements

1405 Art. 3(4)(ii)   An international application must comply with the prescribed physical requirements.
r.11.2–11.13   Detailed physical requirements are laid down.

30.3 Requirements relating to the request

1406 Art. 3(2)   An international application must contain a request.

30.3.1 Use of a specified form

1407 r.3.1/3.4   The request must be made on a printed form or presented as a computer printout. Particulars are given in the Administrative Instructions (see s.102(h)).

r.3.2	Copies of the printed form are furnished free of charge by the receiving Offices and the International Bureau.
AdminInst	See s.102(a)(i) for the request form PCT/RO/101.

30.3.2   *Petition*

Art. 4(1)(i)	The request must contain a petition asking that the application be processed according to the PCT (see also r.4.1(a)(i)).	1408
r.4.2	The petition is preferably worded: "The undersigned requests that the present international application be processed according to the PCT" and must at least be worded to the same effect.	

30.3.3   *Title*

Art. 4(1)(iv)	The request must contain the title of the invention (see also r.4.1(a)(ii)).	1409
r.4.3	The title should be short (preferably 2–7 words when in English or translated into English) and precise.	

30.3.4   *Details of the applicant*

Art. 4(1)(iii)	The request must contain the name of and other prescribed data concerning the applicant (see also r.4.1(a)(iii)).	1410
r.4.5(a)–(e)	Apart from the name, the request must indicate the address, nationality and residence of the applicant or applicants, the nationality and residence being indicated by the name of the appropriate State. Names and addresses must be indicated in accordance with r.4.4 (see below). There may be different applicants in respect of different designated States. Any number or other indication under which the applicant is registered with the receiving Office may be indicated.	
Comment	Note that before 16 September 2012 it was necessary to name the inventors as applicants in respect of the US designation of a PCT application but this is no longer the case in view of the changes to US law enacted through the America Invents Act.	

30.3.5   *Details of the inventor*

Art. 4(1)(v)	The request must contain the name of and other prescribed data concerning the inventor, when the national law of at least one designated State requires this information to be disclosed on filing a national application. Otherwise, this information can either be supplied in the request or communicated to designated Offices separately (where their national law requires the furnishing of such information but allows it to be furnished at a time later than the filing of a national application). See also r.4.1(a)(iv).	1411
Art. 4(4)	Failure to indicate in the request the name and other prescribed data concerning the inventor will have no consequence in any designated State whose national law requires the furnishing of the said indications but allows that they be furnished at a time later than the filing of a national application. Failure to furnish the said indications in a separate notice shall have no consequence in any designated State whose national law does not require the furnishing of the said indications.	
r.4.1(c)(i)	The request may contain indications concerning the inventor even where the national law of none of the designated States requires the name of the inventor to be furnished on filing.	
r.4.6(a)–(c)	Apart from the name, the address of the inventor or inventors should be indicated. Alternatively a statement that the applicant is the inventor may be included. Due to differences in national law, different inventors may be indicated for different States. Names and addresses must be indicated in accordance with r.4.4 (see below).	
r.4.17(ii)	The request may optionally contain a declaration stating the applicant's entitlement to apply for and be granted a patent as referred to in r.51*bis*.1(a)(ii).	

30.3.6   *Details of any agent*

Art. 4(1)(iii)	The request must contain the name of and other prescribed data concerning any appointed agent (see also r.4.1(a)(iii)).	1412

r.4.7

Apart from the name, the request must indicate an address of any appointed agent. The name and address must be indicated in accordance with r.4.4 (see below). Any number or other indication under which the agent is registered with the receiving Office may be indicated.

30.3.7   Details of any common representative

1413   r.4.8

Where a common representative is appointed, the request must so indicate.

30.3.8   Requirements for providing names and addresses

1414   r.4.4

The names of natural persons must be indicated by the person's family name (first) and given names (last). The names of legal entities must be indicated by their full, official designations. Addresses must be detailed enough to satisfy prompt postal delivery, indicating relevant administrative units up to and including the house number, if any (failure to indicate a house number will only have negative consequences in designated States whose national law so provides). It is recommended that other means of communication (phone, facsimile, teleprinter) are also indicated.

r.4.16

Where any name or address is written in characters other than those of the Latin alphabet the same must be indicated in characters of the Latin alphabet either through transliteration or translation into English. The name of any country written in characters other than those of the Latin alphabet must also be indicated in English.

30.3.9   Address for correspondence

1415   r.4.4(d)

Whilst, in general, only one address may be indicated for each applicant, inventor and agent, where no agent is appointed the applicant or common representative may indicate a further address for correspondence.

OJ

See Notice from the EPO dated 04 September 2014 ([2014] O.J. A99). If the EPO is acting as a receiving Office, an International Searching Authority, a Supplementary International Searching Authority or an International Preliminary Examining Authority, the applicant may provide an address for correspondence which is that of any person in any country and it will be accepted by the EPO regardless of whether the applicant is a natural or legal person, whether the address is the applicant's own or that of another person, and whether the address is in an EPC contracting state.

30.3.10   Designation of Contracting States

1416   Art. 4(1)(ii)

The request must contain the designation of those Contracting States in which protection is desired. If a regional patent rather than a national patent for a particular designated State is desired then this must be indicated.

Art. 43

In respect of any designated State whose law provides for the grant of inventors' certificates, utility certificates, utility models, patents or certificates of addition, inventor's certificates of addition, or utility certificates of addition, the applicant may indicate, as prescribed in the Regulations, that his international application is for the grant, as far as that State is concerned, of an inventors' certificate, a utility certificate or a utility model rather than a patent, or that it is for the grant of a patent or certificate of addition, an inventor's certificate of addition, or a utility certificate of addition, and the ensuing effect shall be governed by the applicant's choice. For the purposes of this Article and any Rule thereunder, Art. 2(ii) (the term "patent" includes other forms of protection) shall not apply.

Art. 44

In respect of any designated State whose law permits an application, while being for the grant of a patent or one of the other kinds of protection referred to in Art. 43, to be also for the grant of another of the said kinds of protection, the applicant may indicate, as prescribed in the Regulations, the two kinds of protection he is seeking, and the ensuing effect will be governed by the applicant's indications. For the purposes of this Article, Art. 2(ii) (the term "patent" includes other forms of protection) shall not apply.

Art. 45(1)	Any regional patent treaty which gives to all persons entitled to file international applications (under Art. 9) the right to file applications for a regional patent under such a treaty may provide that international applications designating a State party to both that regional patent treaty and the PCT may be filed as applications for such patents.
r.4.9	The filing of a request is now taken to constitute the designation of all Contracting States for which the PCT is in force on the filing date, in respect of every kind of protection available in those States (Art. 43 and 44) and in respect of both a national and regional patent where a choice is available (Art. 45). The request may, however, specifically exclude the designation of a State in which the filing of an international application claiming priority from a national application in that country has the effect of the automatic withdrawal of that national application if the priority of an application filed in that State is actually claimed. Such States must have informed the International Bureau accordingly by January 5, 2006.
WIPO	These States are Germany, the Republic of Korea and Japan.
r.90*bis*.2(a)	Designations can be withdrawn during the international phase.
Art. 45(2)	The national law of a designated State which is party to a regional patent treaty may provide that the designation of that State has the effect of an indication of the wish to obtain a regional patent under the regional patent treaty.
Art. 4(1)(ii)	The PCT allows national law to specify that designation of that State will have the effect of the designation of a relevant regional patent organisation. Thus, for example, Belgium, Cyprus, France, Greece, Ireland, Italy, Latvia, Lithuania, Malta, Monaco, Netherlands, San Marino and Slovenia provide that their designation via the PCT indicates the wish to obtain a European patent from the EPO. Further, the PCT allows that where a regional patent treaty specifies that the applicant cannot limit his application to certain States then designation of one of those States for a regional patent will be treated as designation of all the States to the treaty.
Art. 8(2)(b)	An international application may designate a State in which a prior application whose priority it claims was filed (see section 30.8.13).

30.3.11   *Designation of the EPO*

EPC Art. 153(1)	The EPO will act as a designated Office for those EPC Contracting States in respect of which the PCT has entered into force, which are designated in the international application and for which the applicant wishes to obtain a European patent.	1417
Comment	Extension states and validation states must be separately designated for a national patent. All states are now automatically designated by the filing of a request (r.4.9).	

30.3.12   *Kind of protection sought*

Art. 4(3)	The designation of a State means its designation in respect of obtaining a patent (the Art. 2(ii) definition does not apply here) unless the applicant asks for any other kind of protection referred to in Art. 43.	1418
r.4.9	However, filing the request now amounts to the designation of all States in respect of all kinds of protection (see above).	

30.3.13   *Priority claim*

Art. 8	The request may contain a declaration claiming the priority of an earlier application or applications (see also r.4.1(b)(i)).	1419
r.4.10	The declaration must state the date on which the earlier application was filed, its number and the Paris Convention country or World Trade Organisation Country (for national applications), regional authority (for regional applications) or receiving Office (for international applications) in/with which it was filed. When claiming the priority of an international or regional application, one or more countries party to the Paris Convention for which the application was filed may be indicated. In the case of a regional application where at least one of the Contracting States is neither a member of the Paris Convention nor the World Trade Organisation, at least one Contracting State which is a member of the Paris Convention or the World Trade Organisation must be indicated. The definition of "national patent" given in Art. 2(vi) does not apply for the purpose of r.4.10.	
r.26*bis*.1	Under the PCT, claims to priority may also be made after filing the request – see below.	

30.3.14   Restoration of the right of priority

1420   r.4.1(c)(v)   The request may contain a request for the restoration of the right of priority.

30.3.15   Transmittal of certified copy

1421   r.4.1(c)(ii)   The request may contain a request to the receiving Office to prepare and transmit the priority document to the International Bureau where the application whose priority is claimed was filed with the national office or intergovernmental authority which is the receiving Office.

30.3.16   Statement of incorporation by reference

1422   r.4.1(c)(iv)   The request may contain a statement as provided by r.4.18.
       r.4.18   Where the international application, on the date on which one or more elements referred to in Art. 11(1)(iii) were first received by the receiving Office, claims the priority of an earlier application, the request may contain a statement that, where an element of the international application referred to in Art. 11(1)(iii)(d) or (e), or a part of the description, claims or drawings referred to in r.20.5(a), or an element or part of the description, claims or drawings referred to in r.20.5bis(a) is not otherwise contained in the international application but is completely contained in the earlier application, that element or part is, subject to confirmation under r.20.6, incorporated by reference in the international application for the purposes of r.20.6. Such a statement, if not contained in the request on that date, may be added to the request if, and only if, it was otherwise contained in, or submitted with, the international application on that date.
       Comment   Such a statement is contained in PCT Request Form PCT/RO/101.

30.3.17   Choice of international searching authority

1423   r.4.14*bis*   The applicant must indicate his choice of International Searching Authority if two or more are competent (see also r.4.1(b)(iv)).
       AppGuide   See Annex C (EP). When the EPO acts as receiving Office, the EPO is the only competent International Searching Authority.

30.3.18   Use of the results of earlier search or search opinion

1424   r.4.1(b)(ii)   The request must contain, where applicable, indications relating to an earlier search as provided for in r.4.12(i) and r.12*bis*.1(b) and (d).
       r.4.1(c)(vi)   The request may also contain a statement as provided for in r.4.12(ii).
       r.4.12   If the applicant wishes the International Searching Authority to take into account, in carrying out the international search, the results of an earlier international, international-type or national search carried out by the same or another International Searching Authority or by a national office ("earlier search"):
                      (i) the request must so indicate and specify the Authority or Office concerned and the application in respect of which the earlier search was carried out;
                      (ii) the request may, where applicable, contain a statement to the effect that the international application is the same, or substantially the same, as the application in respect of which the earlier search was carried out, or that the international application is the same, or substantially the same, as that earlier application except that it is filed in a different language.
       r.12*bis*.1(a) Where the applicant has, under r.4.12, requested that the International Searching Authority takes into account the results of an earlier search carried out by the same or another International Searching Authority or by a national Office, the applicant shall, subject to r.12*bis*.1(b) to (d), submit to the receiving Office, together with the international application, a copy of the results of the earlier search, in whatever form (for example, in the form of a search report, a listing of cited prior art or an examination report) they are presented by the Authority or Office concerned.

r.12*bis*.1(b)	Where the earlier search was carried out by the same Office as that which is acting as the receiving Office, the applicant may, instead of submitting the copy referred to in r.12*bis*.1(a), indicate the wish that the receiving Office prepare and transmit it to the International Searching Authority. Such request shall be made in the request and may be subjected by the receiving Office to the payment to it, for its own benefit, of a fee.
r.12*bis*.1(c)	Where the earlier search was carried out by the same International Searching Authority, or by the same Office as that which is acting as the International Searching Authority, no copy referred to in r.12*bis*.1(a) shall be required to be submitted under that paragraph.
r.12*bis*.1(d)	Where a copy referred to in r.12*bis*.1(a) is available to the receiving Office or the International Searching Authority in a form and manner acceptable to it, for example, from a digital library, and the applicant so indicates in the request, no copy shall be required to be submitted under that paragraph.
OJ	See Notice from the EPO dated 22 June 2015 ([2015] O.J. A51). The EPO has implemented a "PCT Direct" service according to which the EPO acting International Searching Authority will take into account certain comments filed with the international application. The service may be used by an applicant who has had an earlier application (national application or European application) searched by the EPO and who is filing an international application claiming priority from that earlier application. The applicant can file informal comments with the international application explaining why any objections made by the EPO in the search opinion drawn up for the earlier application have been overcome in respect of the international application. The comments do not form part of the international application as filed but are nevertheless transmitted to the EPO as International Searching Authority and to the International Bureau (and are hence publicly available on WIPO's PATENTSCOPE). The comments are then taken into account by the EPO acting as International Searching Authority when drawing up the international search report and written opinion. As of 01 April 2017, the written opinion may explicitly acknowledge that such comments have been taken into account by referring to the PCT Direct letter and its content (notice from the EPO dated 08 March 2017, [2017] O.J. A21). The service may be used regardless of which Receiving Office the international application is filed with, as long as the EPO is acting as International Searching Authority.

30.3.19 Standardised declarations

r.4.17	One or more declarations may be included in the request for the purposes of the national law applicable to one or more designated States (see also r.4.1(c)(iii)). The relevant wording is prescribed by the Administrative Instructions (see ss.211 to 215). These declarations are: (i) a declaration as to the identity of the inventor as referred to in r.51*bis*.1(a)(i); (ii) a declaration as to the applicant's entitlement, as at the international filing date, to apply for and be granted a patent as referred to in r.51*bis*.1(a)(ii); (iii) a declaration as to the applicant's entitlement, as at the international filing date, to claim the priority of the earlier application as referred to in r.51*bis*.1(a)(iii); (iv) a declaration of inventorship as referred to in r.51*bis*.1(a)(iv) and signed as indicated in the Administrative Instructions; and (v) a declaration as to non-prejudicial disclosures or exceptions to lack of novelty as referred to in r.51*bis*.1(a)(v).	1425
r.26*ter*.1	The applicant may correct or add any of these declarations up until 16 months from the priority date by writing to the International Bureau. Any such addition or correction received late but before the technical preparations for publication are complete will be considered as received in time.	
r.26*ter*.2(b)	Where a declaration or correction is received after the expiration of the time limit specified in r.26*ter*.1 (i.e. later than 16 months from the priority date and after the technical preparations for publication have been completed), the International Bureau will notify the applicant and proceed as set out in the Administrative Instructions.	
AdminInst	See s.214(a) – any declaration of inventorship (r.4.17(iv)) must be signed and dated by the inventors.	

30.3.20   Check list

1426	r.3.3(a)

r.3.3(a)   The request must contain a list indicating:
(i) the number of sheets comprising: (a) the request; (b) the description (separately indicating the number of sheets of any sequence listing part of the description); (c) the claims; (d) the drawings; (e) the abstract; and (f) the international application as a whole;
(ii) that the application is accompanied, where applicable, by: (a) a power of attorney, (i.e. a document appointing an agent or a common representative); (b) a copy of a general power of attorney; (c) a priority document; (d) a sequence listing in electronic form; (e) a document relating to the payment of fees; or (f) any other document (to be specified in the checklist); and
(iii) the number of the figure of the drawings which the applicant suggests should accompany the abstract on publication (in exceptional cases, more than one may be nominated).

r.3.3(b)   If the applicant does not complete the list, it will be completed by the receiving Office except for item (iii) above.

30.3.21   Signature of the applicant

1427 r.4.1(d)   The request must be signed.

r.4.15   The signature must be that of the applicant or, if there is more than one, all of them,

r.2.3   In respect of some Offices, a seal is required rather than a signature (e.g. Korea). See AppGuide, International Phase, paragraph 5.091.

r.90.3   Once properly appointed, an agent can sign the request on the applicant's behalf.

r.92.4(b)   A signature appearing on a document transmitted by facsimile is recognised for the purposes of the PCT and its Regulations as a proper signature.

r.26.2*bis*(a)   Note that in the case of multiple applicants, the receiving Office will not object if the request is signed by at least one of them, despite the requirements of r.4.15.

AppGuide   See International Phase, paragraph 5.088 – a full set of signatures may be required by any designated or elected state in the national phase (r.51*bis*.1(a)(vi)).

30.3.22   Reference to a parent application or patent

1428 r.4.1(b)(iii)   The request may contain a reference to a parent application or parent patent.

r.4.11(a)   The request must indicate the relevant parent application or parent patent or other parent grant if:
(i) the applicant intends to make an indication under r.49*bis*.1(a) or (b) of the wish that the international application be treated, in any designated State, as an application for a patent of addition, certificate of addition, inventor's certificate of addition or utility certificate of addition; or
(ii) the applicant intends to make an indication under r.49*bis*.1(d) of the wish that the international application be treated, in any designated State, as an application for a continuation or a continuation-in-part of an earlier application.

r.4.11(b)   The inclusion in the request of an indication under r.4.11(a) shall have no effect on the operation of r.4.9 (designation of States, kinds of protection, national and regional patents).

r.26*quater*.1   The applicant may correct or add to the request any indication referred to in r.4.11 by a notice submitted to the International Bureau within a time limit of 16 months from the priority date, provided that any notice which is received by the International Bureau after the expiration of that time limit shall be considered to have been received on the last day of that time limit if the notice reaches the International Bureau before the technical preparations for international publication have been completed.

r.26*quater*.2   Where any correction or addition of an indication referred to in r.4.11 is not timely received under r.26quater.1, the International Bureau shall notify the applicant accordingly and shall proceed as provided for in the Administrative Instructions.

Comment   New r.26*quater* entered into force on 01 July 2020 and applies to any international application with an international filing date on or after that date.

30.3.23 No further content of the request is allowed

r.4.19 | The request may only contain those matters specified in rr.4.1 to 4.18 and any other matter specified by the Administrative Instructions. Any additional matter will be deleted by the receiving Office *ex officio*. Any additional matter specified in the Administrative Instructions is purely optional. | 1429

AdminInst | See s.109 – inclusion of the applicant's reference is encouraged.

30.4 Requirements Relating to the Description

Art. 3(2) | An international application must contain a description. | 1430

30.4.1 Need for a sufficient disclosure

Art. 5 | The description must disclose the invention in a sufficiently clear and complete manner for the invention to be carried out by a person skilled in the art. | 1431

30.4.2 Content of the description

r.5.1(a) | The description must: | 1432
(a) state the title as it appears in the request;
(b) specify the technical field to which the invention relates;
(c) indicate the background art which, as far as the applicant knows, is useful for the understanding, searching and examination of the invention and preferably cite documents reflecting such art;
(d) disclose the invention, as claimed, in such a way that the technical problem (even if not expressly stated as such) and its solution can be understood and state the advantageous effects, if any, of the invention with reference to the background art;
(e) briefly describe the figures in the drawings, if any;
(f) in respect of any designated States that so require, set forth at least the best mode contemplated by the applicant for carrying out the invention claimed in terms of examples, where appropriate, and with reference to the drawings; and
(g) indicate explicitly, when it is not obvious from the description or nature of the invention, the way in which the invention is capable of exploitation in industry and the way in which it can be made and used, or, if it can only be used, the way in which it can be used. "Industry" is to have a broad meaning as defined in the Paris Convention.

30.4.3 Order of presentation of the content of the description

r.5.1(b)(c) | The order and manner of presentation described in r.5.1 above should be followed unless, due to the nature of the invention, a different order or manner would facilitate understanding or lead to a more economical presentation and each of (b) to (g) above should preferably be preceded by an appropriate heading as suggested in the Administrative Instructions. | 1433

AdminInst | See s.204. The headings are "Technical Field", "Background Art", "Disclosure of Invention", "Brief Description of Drawings", "Best Mode for Carrying Out the Invention", "Industrial Applicability", "Sequence Listing" and "Sequence Listing Free Text".

30.5 Requirements relating to the claims

Art. 3(2) | An international application must contain one or more claims. | 1434

30.5.1 Requirement for clarity, conciseness and support

Art. 6 | The claims must be clear and concise and fully supported by the description. | 1435

30.5.2 Claims to define matter the applicant seeks to protect

Art. 6 | The claims must define the matter for which protection is sought. | 1436
r.6.3(a) | Such definition must be in terms of the technical features of the invention.

30.5.3   *Situations in which two-part form is required*

1437   r.6.3(b)   Wherever appropriate a claim should contain:
(i) a statement indicating those technical features of the invention which are necessary for the definition of the claimed subject matter but which, in combination, are part of the prior art; and
(ii) a characterising part (preceded by the words "characterised in that"/"characterised by"/"wherein the improvement compromises" or other such phrase) stating concisely the technical features which, in combination with the features stated in (i), it is desired to protect;

r.6.3(c)   However, in countries where the national law does not require this manner of claiming, failure to use it has no effect in that State.

30.5.4   *Number and type of claims allowed*

1438   r.6.1   The number of claims must be reasonable in consideration of the nature of the invention claimed.

r.13.4   Subject to the requirement for unity of invention, a reasonable number of dependent claims, claiming specific forms of the invention claimed in an independent claim, are allowed, even where the features of such a dependent claim could be considered as constituting an invention in themselves.

r.6.4(a)   Any dependent claim (i.e. a claim which includes all the features of one or more other claim(s)) should refer to the other claim or claims, if possible at the beginning, and then state the additional feature claimed.

r.6.4(a)   A multiple dependent claim (i.e. one referring to more than one other claim) must do so in the alternative and must not serve as a basis for any other multiple dependent claim.

r.6.4(a)   Where the national law of a national Office acting as an International Searching Authority stipulates that multiple dependent claims must be drafted as indicated above, failure to comply may result in an indication under Art. 17(2)(b) (no search report established in respect of these claims) but will have no effect in a designated State which allows the actual manner of claiming used.

r.6.4(b)   Any dependent claim will be construed as including all the limitations contained in the claim to which it refers or, if the claim is a multiple dependent claim, all the limitations contained in the particular claim in relation to which it is considered.

r.6.4(c)   All dependent claims referring back to a single previous claim or several previous claims must be grouped together to the extent and in the most practicable way possible.

30.5.5   *Numbering of the claims*

1439   r.6.1   The claims must be numbered consecutively in arabic numerals. The Administrative Instructions indicate how claims should be numbered in the case of amendment.

AdminInst   See s.205. Claims do not have to be renumbered where one is deleted but, if they are, they must be renumbered consecutively.

30.5.6   *Omnibus claims generally not allowed*

1440   r.6.2(a)   Except where absolutely necessary, the claims may not rely, in respect of technical features of the invention, on references to the description or drawings such as, "as described in part … of the description" or, "as illustrated in figure … of the drawings".

30.5.7   *References in claims to reference signs in figures*

1441   r.6.2(b)   Where the international application contains drawings, the technical features mentioned in the claims should preferably be followed by the reference signs relating to such features (preferably placed between parentheses) unless this would not particularly facilitate quicker understanding of the claim. Such reference signs may be removed by designated Offices for the purposes of publication.

30.5.8   Manner of claiming in respect of an application for a utility model

r.6.5 | Any designated State in which the grant of a utility model is sought on the basis of an international application may substitute for rr.6.1–6.4 (relating to the claims) the provisions of its national law concerning utility models once national processing of the application has begun. The applicant must be allowed at least two months from the expiration of the Art. 22 time limit to adapt his application to the requirements of these provisions of national law.   1442

30.5.9   Unity of invention

Art. 3(4)(iii) | An international application must comply with the prescribed requirement of unity of invention.   1443

r.13.1 | This means that the international application must relate to one invention only or to a group of inventions so linked as to form a single general inventive concept.

r.13.2 | Such a general inventive concept is taken to unite a group of inventions claimed in the same application when there is a technical relationship among them involving one or more of the same or corresponding special technical features, i.e. those technical features that define a contribution which each of the claimed inventions, considered as a whole, makes over the prior art.

r.13.3 | This will be determined in the same way whether the inventions are claimed in separate claims or as alternatives within a single claim.

AdminInst | See s.206. The determination of unity by an International Searching or Preliminary Examining Authority must be made in line with the instructions in Annex B of the Administrative Instructions.

r.13.5 | Any State in which the grant of a utility model is sought on the basis of an international application may, instead of the above, apply the provisions of its national law concerning utility models once the processing of the application has started in that State, provided that the applicant must be allowed at least two months from the expiry of the time limit applicable under Art. 22 to adapt his application to those provisions.

30.6   Requirements relating to the abstract

Art. 3(2) | An international application must contain an abstract.   1444

Art. 3(3) | The abstract merely serves as a source of technical information and must not be used to interpret the scope of protection or for any other purpose.

r.8.3 | The abstract must be drafted so that it can efficiently serve the scientist, engineer or researcher as a scanning tool for the purposes of searching in the particular art and formulating an opinion as to whether the international application itself needs to be consulted.

r.8.1(a) | The abstract must contain a summary of the disclosure as contained in the description, the claims and any drawings, indicating the technical field to which the invention pertains and allowing a clear understanding of the technical problem, the gist of the solution of that problem through the invention and the principal use or uses of the invention. The abstract should also, where applicable, contain the chemical formula which, among all the formulae contained in the international application, best characterises the invention.

r.8.1(b)–(d) | The abstract must be as concise as possible (preferably 50 to 150 words in English or when translated into English) and avoid statements as to the alleged merits or value of the claimed invention or on its speculative application. Each main technical feature mentioned in the abstract and illustrated by a drawing in the international application must be followed by a reference sign, placed between parentheses.

r.8.2 | If the applicant fails to include in the request the number of the figure or figures of the drawings which he suggests should accompany the abstract on publication (r.3.3(a)(iii) – should be in checklist part of Request) or if the International Searching Authority finds a different figure or different figures would be more appropriate, the International Bureau will publish the abstract accompanied by the choice of figure indicated by the International Searching Authority. If the International Searching Authority finds that none of the figures are useful for the understanding of the abstract it will notify the International Bureau accordingly and no figure will be included on publication (even if the applicant has suggested one or more).

30.7   Requirements relating to the drawings

1445 Art. 3(2)	An international application must, where required, contain one or more drawings.
Art. 7(1)	One or more drawings must be included in the application where necessary for the understanding of the invention.
Art. 7(2)(i)	Where drawings are not necessary for the understanding of the invention but the invention admits of illustration by drawings, the applicant may include them on filing.
Art. 7(2)(ii)	Where drawings are not necessary for the understanding of the invention but the invention admits of illustration by drawings, any designated Office may require that they are filed within a prescribed time limit.
r.7.2	This time limit must be reasonable under the circumstances of the case and in any case not shorter than two months from the date of the written invitation to provide drawings.
r.7.1	Flow sheets and diagrams are considered to be drawings.
r.11.13	This rule sets out the detailed physical requirements for the presentation of drawings.
AppGuide	See International Phase, paragraph 5.159 – photographs may be included as drawings if they are in black and white format and reproducible.

30.8   Requirements relating to any priority claim

30.8.1   *Relevance of the Paris Convention*

1446 Art. 8(2)(a)	The conditions for and effect of any priority claim follow Art. 4 of the Stockholm Act of the Paris Convention.
Comment	The PCT directly applies the provisions of the Paris Convention, unlike the EPC which sets out its own priority code which is in conformity with the provisions of the Paris Convention.

30.8.2   *Who may make a claim to priority?*

1447 PCArt. 4(A)(1)	Any person who has duly filed a certain kind of application, or his successor in title, enjoys a right of priority.

30.8.3   *Length of the priority period*

1448 PCArt. 4(C)(1)	The priority period in respect of a patent is 12 months.
PCArt. 4(C)(2)	The period starts from the filing date of the first application and does not include the day of filing.
PCArt. 4(C)(3)	The priority year is extended where the last day in any relevant Office is a closed day until the next day when that Office is open for business.

30.8.4   *Restoration of a right to priority by the receiving Office where the time limit is missed*

1449 r.26*bis*.3(a)	Where an international application has an international filing date which is later than the date on which the priority period expired but within the period of two months from that date, the receiving Office will, on the request of the applicant, and subject to r.26*bis*.3(b)–(g), restore the right of priority if it finds that a criterion applied by it ("criterion for restoration") is satisfied, namely, that the failure to file the international application within the priority period: (i) occurred in spite of due care required by the circumstances having been taken; or (ii) was unintentional.
r.26*bis*.3(a)	Each receiving Office must apply at least one of those criteria and may apply both of them (unless it has declared its incompatibility – see below).
OJ	The EPO applies the due care criterion only (see [2007] O.J. 692). See also AppGuide, Annex C (EP).
r.26*bis*.3(b)	A request under r.26*bis*.3(a) must: (i) be filed with the receiving Office within the time limit applicable under r.26*bis*.3(e); (ii) state the reasons for the failure to file the international application within the priority period; and (iii) preferably be accompanied by any declaration or other evidence required under r.26*bis*.3(f).

r.26*bis*.3(c)	Where a priority claim in respect of the earlier application is not contained in the international application, the applicant must submit, within the time limit applicable under r.26*bis*.3(e), a notice under r.26*bis*.1(a) adding the priority claim.
r.26*bis*.3(d)	The submission of a request under r.26*bis*.3(a) may be subjected by the receiving Office to the payment to it, for its own benefit, of a fee for requesting restoration, payable within the time limit applicable under r.26*bis*.3(e). The amount of that fee, if any, shall be fixed by the receiving Office. The time limit for payment of the fee may be extended, at the option of the receiving Office, for a period of up to two months from the expiration of the time limit applicable under r.26*bis*.3(e).
RRFArt. 2(1)(13)	The EPO fee for requesting restoration under r.26*bis*.3(d) is € 720.
r.26*bis*.3(e)	The time limit referred to in r.26*bis*.3(b)(i), (c) and (d) is two months from the date on which the priority period expired, provided that, where the applicant makes a request for early publication under Art. 21(2)(b), any request under r.26*bis*.3(a) or any notice referred to in r.26*bis*.3(c) submitted, or any fee referred to in r.26*bis*.3(d) paid, after the technical preparations for international publication have been completed shall be considered as not having been submitted or paid in time.
r.26*bis*.3(f)	The receiving Office may require that a declaration or other evidence in support of the statement of reasons referred to in r.26*bis*.3(b)(ii) be filed with it within a time limit which must be reasonable under the circumstances.
r.26*bis*.3(g)	The receiving Office cannot refuse, totally or in part, a request under r.26*bis*.3(a) without giving the applicant the opportunity to make observations on the intended refusal within a time limit which must be reasonable under the circumstances. Such notice of intended refusal by the receiving Office may be sent to the applicant together with any invitation to file a declaration or other evidence under r.26*bis*.3(f).
r.26*bis*.3(h)	The receiving Office will promptly: (i) notify the International Bureau of the receipt of a request under r.26*bis*.3(a); (ii) make a decision upon the request; (iii) notify the applicant and the International Bureau of its decision and the criterion for restoration upon which the decision was based. (iv) subject to r.26*bis*.3(h-*bis*), transmit to the International Bureau all documents received from the applicant relating to the request under r.26*bis*.3(a) (including a copy of the request itself, any statement of reasons referred to in r.26*bis*.3(b)(ii) and any declaration or other evidence referred to in r.26*bis*.3(f)).
r.26*bis*.3(h-bis)	The receiving Office will, upon a reasoned request by the applicant or on its own decision, not transmit documents or parts thereof received in relation to the request under r.26*bis*.3(a), if it finds that: (i) this document or part thereof does not obviously serve the purpose of informing the public about the international application; (ii) publication or public access to any such document or part thereof would clearly prejudice the personal or economic interests of any person; and (iii) there is no prevailing public interest to have access to that document or part thereof. Where the receiving Office decides not to transmit documents or parts thereof to the International Bureau, it shall notify the International Bureau accordingly.
Comment	Sections (h) and (h-bis) apply to international applications with a filing date on or after 01 July 2016. For earlier applications, the applicant was responsible for submitting any such documents to the International Bureau himself.
r.26*bis*.3(i)	Each receiving Office will inform the International Bureau of which of the criteria for restoration it applies and of any subsequent changes in that respect. The International Bureau will promptly publish such information in the Gazette.
r.26*bis*.3(j)	If, on October 5, 2005, r.26*bis*.3(a) to (i) are not compatible with the national law applied by a receiving Office, those paragraphs will not apply in respect of that Office for as long as they continue not to be compatible with that law, provided that the Office informs the International Bureau accordingly by April 5, 2006. The information received will be promptly published by the International Bureau in the Gazette.
WIPO	Incompatibility with r.26*bis*.3(a)-(i) has been registered and is still maintained by the receiving Offices of the following countries and organisations: Algeria, Brazil, Columbia, Cuba, Czech Republic, Germany, Greece, India, Indonesia, Korea, Philippines.

| Guidelines | See Guidelines for Search and Examination at the EPO as a PCT Authority, A-VI, 1.5. To satisfy the due care requirement when the EPO acts as receiving Office the applicant must show that the late filing of the international application was the result of exceptional circumstances or an isolated mistake in a normally satisfactory system. Case law of the Boards of Appeal under Art. 122 EPC is followed. |

30.8.5   *The whole content of the previous application can support a priority right*

| 1450 | PCArt. 4(H) | Priority may not be refused on the ground that certain elements of the invention for which priority is claimed do not appear among the claims formulated in the application in the country of origin, provided that the application documents as a whole specifically disclosed such elements. |

30.8.6   *What kind of application may be used as a basis for claiming priority?*

1451	PCArt. 4(A)(1)	Priority may be claimed from an application for a patent, or for the registration of a utility model.
	PCArt. 4(I)(1)	Applications for inventors' certificates also give rise to a right of priority.
	Art. 8(1), Art. 2(i)	The international application may claim the priority of an earlier application or applications, "application" in this context being an application for the protection of an invention, including applications for patents for invention, inventors' certificates, utility certificates, utility models, patents or certificates of addition, inventors' certificates of addition and utility certificates of addition.
	PCArt. 4(A)(2)	Any filing that is equivalent to a regular national filing under the domestic legislation of any country of the Union or under bilateral or multilateral treaties concluded between countries of the Union is recognised as giving rise to the right of priority.
	PCArt. 4(A)(3)	By regular national filing is meant any filing that is adequate to establish the date on which the application was filed in the country concerned, whatever may be the subsequent fate of the application.
	Art. 8(1), r.4.10	Under the PCT, the earlier application must have been filed in or for any country party to the Paris Convention for the Protection of Industrial Property or in or for any Member of the World Trade Organisation that is not party to the Paris Convention.
	PCArt. 4(C)(4)	A subsequent application concerning the same subject as a previous first application within the meaning of PCArt. 4(C)(2) filed in the same country of the Union, will be considered as the first application, of which the filing date will be the starting point of the period of priority, if, at the time of filing the subsequent application, the said previous application has been withdrawn, abandoned or refused, without having been laid open to public inspection and without leaving any rights outstanding, and if it has not yet served as a basis for claiming a right of priority. The previous application may not thereafter serve as a basis for claiming a right of priority.

30.8.7   *Priority claims originating in World Trade Organisation countries do not apply in respect of the EPO if the priority-claiming application was filed before the coming into force of EPC2000*

| 1452 | WIPO | The EPO filed reservations under r.4.10 PCT so that priority claims originating in WTO countries that were not Paris Convention counties were not recognised before the coming into force of EPC2000. |
| | G2/02 | The Enlarged Board confirmed that priority rights originating in a non-Paris Convention WTO country were not recognised under the EPC for applications filed before the coming into force of EPC2000. |

30.8.8   *Procedure for claiming priority – declaration*

1453	PCArt. 4(D)(1)	Any person desiring to take advantage of the priority of a previous filing is required to make a declaration indicating the date of such filing and the country in which it was made. Each country determines the latest date on which such declaration must be made.
	PCArt. 4(D)(5)	Any person who avails himself of the priority of a previous application will be required to specify the number of that application.
	Art. 8(1)	The international application must contain the declaration as prescribed in the Regulations.

r.4.10(a)	A declaration of priority must be made in the request (see also r.4.1(b)).
r.4.10(a)(b)(c)	The request must state the date on which the earlier application was filed, its number and the Convention country or World Trade Organisation Country (for national applications), regional authority (for regional applications) or receiving Office (for international applications) in/with which it was filed. When claiming the priority of an international or regional application, one or more countries party to the Paris Convention for which the application was filed may be indicated. In the case of a regional application where at least one of the Contracting States is neither a member of the Paris Convention or the World Trade Organisation, at least one Contracting State which is a member of the Paris Convention or World Trade Organisation must be indicated. The definition of "national patent" given in Art. 2(vi) does not apply for the purpose of r.4.10.
r.26*bis*.1(a)(b)	A priority claim may be corrected or added if the applicant submits a notice to the receiving Office or the International Bureau within the later of (a) four months from the international filing date or (b) the earlier of 16 months from the priority date and 16 months from the corrected/added priority date if this is different. The correction may include the addition of any indication referred to in r.4.10 (date, number, filing country/authority/receiving Office). Such notice, if received after the applicant has made a request for early publication (Art. 21(2)(b)) will be considered not submitted unless the request for early publication is withdrawn before the technical preparations for publication are complete.
Comment	The applicant thus always has four months from the filing date to correct a priority claim regardless of whether the originally quoted priority date was too early or too late. This is important since otherwise the earlier of P + 16 (original date) and P + 16 (corrected date) could already have expired on the filing date of the application if an erroneously early priority date was quoted on filing.
r.26*bis*.1(c)	Where a priority date is changed, any outstanding time limit that has not yet expired is recomputed from the new date.

30.8.9   *Procedure for claiming priority – certified copy*

PCArt. 4(D)(3)	The countries of the Union may require any person making a declaration of priority to produce a copy of the application previously filed. The copy, certified as correct by the authority which received it, does not require any authentication, and may in any case be filed, without fee, any time within three months of the filing of the subsequent application.
r.17.1(a)(b)	A copy of the earlier application, certified by the authority with which it was filed (the priority document) must be submitted to the International Bureau or the receiving Office no later than 16 months from the priority date (it will be taken to have arrived on the last day of that period if received by the International Bureau before the date of publication) unless: (a) it was filed at the receiving Office with the application itself; or (b) the priority document is to be issued by the receiving Office in which case the applicant may request that the receiving Office (who may levy a fee) transmit it to the International Bureau directly as long as the request is made no later than 16 months from the priority date.
r.21.2	A receiving Office will provide a certified copy of any international application filed with it against payment of a fee.
RRFArt. 3(1)	The amount of the administrative fee for providing a certified copy of an international patent application is fixed by the President of the EPO and is currently € 115 (see decision of the President dated 17 January 2023, [2023] O.J. A3).
r.4.1(c)(ii)	Such a request for the receiving Office to transmit a copy of the priority document to the International Bureau under r.17 may be made on filing the application in the request.
r.17.1(b-bis)	Where the priority document is, in accordance with the Administrative Instructions, made available to the International Bureau from a digital library prior to the date of international publication of the international application, the applicant may, instead of submitting the priority document, request the International Bureau, prior to the date of international publication, to obtain the priority document from such digital library.

1454

r.17.1(c)(d)   Where no priority document is submitted, as outlined above, any designated State may, in principle, disregard the priority claim, but it must first give the applicant a further chance to submit the priority document within a reasonable time limit. In any case, it may not disregard the priority claim if the priority document was filed with it in its capacity as a national Office or if the priority document is, in accordance with the Administrative Instructions, available to it from a digital library.

Guidelines   See Guidelines for Search and Examination at the EPO as a PCT Authority, A-III, 4.4 – the EPO will provide a certified copy of any previous European or international application filed with it. A copy will not, however, be included in the file free of charge.

30.8.10   Procedure for claiming priority – translation

1455   PCArt. 4(D)(3)   A translation of the priority document may also be required by any country of the Union.
r.20.6(a)(iii)   A translation of the priority document must be filed if an element of the international application is incorporated by reference and the priority document is not in the same language as the international application.

r.66.7(b)   A translation of the priority document may also be required by the International Preliminary Examining Authority in certain circumstances.

30.8.11   Can one application claim more than one priority?

1456   PCArt. 4(F)   No country of the Union may refuse a priority or a patent application on the ground that the applicant claims multiple priorities, even if they originate in different countries.

30.8.12   Effect of the claim to priority in the international phase

1457   Art. 2   For the purposes of the PCT a priority date means: (a) where the international application contains a priority claim under Art. 8, the filing date of the application whose priority is so claimed; (b) where the international application contains several priority claims under Art. 8, the filing date of the earliest application whose priority is so claimed; or (c) where the international application does not contain any priority claim under Art. 8, the international filing date of such an application.

30.8.13   Effect of designating a State in which the priority application was filed

1458   Art. 8(2)(b)   The international application may designate a State in which or for which a priority application was filed. In such a case, or where the priority of an international application only designating one State is claimed, the national law of such a State governs the conditions for and the effect of the priority claim in that State.

30.9   Language requirements of the application

30.9.1   Acceptable languages of filing

1459   Art. 3(4)(i)   The international application must be in a prescribed language.
r.12.1(a)(c)(d)   The international application may be filed in any language that is accepted by the receiving Office with the proviso that:
(i) the request must be in a language selected from Arabic, Chinese, English, French, German, Japanese, Korean, Portuguese, Russian or Spanish (i.e. a language of publication – r.48.3) accepted by the receiving Office; and
(ii) any language-dependent free text contained in the sequence listing part of the description must be filed in a language which the receiving Office accepts for that purpose. Any language accepted under this r.12.1(d) but not accepted under r.12.1(a) shall meet the requirements of r.12.1(b). The receiving Office may permit but shall not require the language-dependent free text to be filed in more than one language in accordance with the Administrative Instructions.

EPC r.157(2)   The EPO as receiving Office accepts international applications in English, French and German.

Guidelines   See Guidelines for Search and Examination at the EPO as a PCT Authority, A-VII, 1.2.2. The request may be in a different EPO official language than the description, claims and drawings.

30.9.2 *Languages the receiving Office must accept*

r.12.1(b) Each receiving Office must accept applications in at least one language selected from Arabic, Chinese, English, French, German, Japanese, Korean, Portuguese, Russian or Spanish (i.e. a language of publication) that is also accepted by at least one of the International Searching Authorities competent for searching international applications filed with that Office. 1460

30.9.3 *Circumstances in which the applicant must provide a translation for international search*

r.12.3(a)(b) Where the language in which the international application is filed is not accepted by the International Searching Authority that is to carry out the international search, the applicant must, within one month of the date of receipt of the application by the receiving Office, provide the receiving Office with a translation of the application (except the request) into a language of publication which is accepted by the Searching Authority and, unless the filing language was a language of publication, accepted by the receiving Office. 1461

r.12.3(a-*bis*) For any sequence listing part of the description, such a translation is only required in respect of language-dependent free text; any translation of the language-dependent free text shall be provided in accordance with the Administrative Instructions

r.12.3(c)(i)(ii) Where such a translation has not been supplied before the receiving Office sends the applicant notification of the application number and filing date under r.20.2(c), the Office will (preferably with that notification) invite the applicant to (i) furnish the translation within the one-month deadline and, (ii) in the event the one-month deadline expires without the translation being furnished, to furnish it within one month of the invitation or two months from the date of receipt of the application by the receiving Office (whichever is later) along with a late furnishing fee (if the receiving Office chooses to levy one).

r.12.3(e) The late furnishing fee is for the benefit of the receiving Office and is 25 % of the international filing fee, not taking into account any fee for each sheet in excess of 30.

r.12.3(d) Where such an invitation is ignored by the applicant and the translation is not furnished within the time limit set under r.20.2(c)(ii), or the late furnishing fee, where required, is not paid within that time limit, the application will be considered to be withdrawn and the receiving Office will so declare. However, any translation and/or fee received by the receiving Office before such a declaration is made and before the expiry of 15 months from the priority date is considered to have been received before the expiry of the time limit.

AppGuide See Annex D (EP). For the EPO as International Searching Authority, the application must be in English, French or German (or Dutch if the receiving Office was the Netherlands Office). Otherwise, a translation into English, French or German is required. See also Art. 3(1) and Annex A to the agreement between the EPO and the International Bureau ([2017] O.J. A115 and [2018] O.J. A24).

AdminInst See s.305*bis* – if copies need to be made, the receiving Office is responsible and may charge the applicant a fee.

30.9.4 *Circumstances in which the applicant must provide a translation for international publication*

r.12.4(a) Where the language in which the international application is filed is not a language of publication (i.e. Arabic, Chinese, English, French, German, Japanese, Korean, Portuguese, Russian or Spanish) and no translation is required for international search under r.12.3(a), the applicant must provide the receiving Office with a translation of the application into any of the languages of publication accepted by the receiving Office for this purpose. The translation must be provided within 14 months from the priority date. 1462

r.12.4(b) This requirement does not, however, apply to the request

r.12.4(a-*bis*) Furthermore, for any sequence listing part of the description, the requirement for a translation only applies to the language-dependent free text; any translation of the language-dependent free text shall be provided in accordance with the Administrative Instructions.

r.12.4(c)	Where no translation is provided within the 14 month time limit, the receiving Office will invite the applicant to file such a translation and, at the discretion of the receiving Office, pay a late furnishing fee within 16 months from the priority date. However, any translation received before the invitation is sent is considered received within the 14 month time limit.
r.12.4(e)	The late furnishing fee is for the benefit of the receiving Office and is 25 % of the international filing fee, not taking into account any fee for each sheet in excess of 30.
r.12.4(d)	Where no translation is submitted or, where applicable, the late furnishing fee is not submitted within the 16 month time limit, the application will be considered withdrawn and the receiving Office will so declare. However, any translation or payment received before the receiving Office so declares, and before 17 months from the priority date, is considered received within the 16-month period.
AdminInst	See s.305*bis* – if copies need to be made, the receiving Office is responsible and may charge the applicant a fee.

30.9.5   *Procedure where the request is not in a language of publication accepted by the receiving Office*

1463 r.26.3*ter*(c)	Where the request is not in a language of publication accepted by the receiving Office (contrary to r.12.1(c)) the receiving Office will invite the applicant to file a translation. Rules 3 (form of request), 26.1(a) (timing of invitation to correct formal deficiency), 26.2 (time limit for correction), 26.5 and 29.1 (procedure when time limit missed) apply to the submission of such a translation mutatis mutandis.

30.9.6   *Procedure where language of filing is not accepted by the receiving Office*

1464 r.19.4(a)(ii)	In this circumstance, the application is deemed to have been received by the relevant Office on behalf of the International Bureau (which accepts applications in any language).
r.19.4(b)(c)	The national Office concerned will, subject to any national security provisions, transmit the application promptly to the International Bureau and may charge a fee equal to the transmittal fee for the service. The international application is considered to have been received by the International Bureau as receiving Office on the original date of filing with the national office except that the actual date of receipt by the International Bureau counts as the date of receipt for the purposes of r.14.1(c) (time limit for paying the transmittal fee), r.15.3 (time limit for paying the international filing fee) and r.16.1(f) (time limit for paying the search fee).
Guidelines	See Guidelines for Search and Examination at the EPO as a PCT Authority, A-II, 2. The EPO does not charge a fee for forwarding the application to the IB.

30.10   Requirements relating to biotechnological inventions

30.10.1   *Sequence listings*

1465 r.5.2(a)	Where the international application contains disclosure of nucleotide and/or amino acid sequences that, pursuant to the Administrative Instructions, are required to be included in a sequence listing, the description shall include a sequence listing part of the description complying with the standard provided for in the Administrative Instructions.
r.5.2(b)	Language-dependent free text included in the sequence listing part of the description shall not be required to be included in the main body of the description.
r.13*ter*.1(e)	Any sequence listing not contained in the international application as filed does not form part of the application but this does not prevent the applicant from amending the application in relation to a sequence listing under Art. 34(2)(b).
r.13*ter*	For procedure where an International Searching or Preliminary Examining Authority or a designated Office finds that the sequence listing is not supplied or is supplied in the wrong form see under the appropriate Chapter below.
AdminInst	See s.208 and Annex C for the required format for a sequence listing. The current standard is ST.26.

AppGuide | See International Phase, paragraph 5.100 – a sequence listing should be filed in electronic form (XML format). See also paragraph 5.101 – if filed in the correct format, no page fees are payable for the sequence listing. See also paragraph 5.103 – if a receiving Office does not accept the filing of sequence listings in XML format, the application will be forwarded to the IB to act as receiving Office.

OJ | See [2022] O.J. A60. Where the EPO acts as receiving Office, an electonically filed sequence listing complying with ST.26 will not be taken into account for the calculation of the filing fee. If an electronic sequence listing is filed in any other format, however, it will be reformatted as part of the description and the applicant will be asked to indicate whether the reformatted listing is to be part of the description (in which case the pages will count towards the calculation of the filing fee) or not.

30.10.2 Deposit of biological material

r.13*bis*.2 | Any reference to a deposit of biological material must be made in accordance with r.13*bis* | 1466
and, if so made, will be taken to satisfy the requirements of the national law of each designated State.

r.13*bis*.3(b) | Failure to include a reference to a deposit in an application or failure to include any indication under r.13*bis*.3(a) has no effect in a State which does not require such a reference or indication.

r.12.1*ter* | There are certain language requirements relating to indications in relation to deposited biological material.

OJ | See Notice from the EPO dated 07 July 2010 ([2010] O.J. 498).

Chapter 31: Filing an International Patent Application

31.1 Who is entitled to file an international patent application?

1467 Art. 9(1)	Any resident or national of a PCT Contracting State may file an international application.
Art. 9(2)	In addition, the Assembly may decide to extend this right to residents and nationals of non-PCT countries party to the Paris Convention.
Comment	No decision under Art. 9(2) has been taken by the Assembly.
Art. 9(3)	The concepts of residence and nationality and the application of these concepts in cases where there are several applicants or where the applicants are not the same for all the designated States are defined in the Regulations.
r.18.1(a)(b)	Questions of residency and nationality are decided by the receiving Office under the national law of the appropriate Contracting State but in any case: (a) possession of a real and effective industrial or commercial establishment in a Contracting State is considered to be residence there; and (b) a legal entity constituted according to the national law of a Contracting State is considered a national of that State.
r.18.1(c)	Where the International Bureau is the receiving Office it asks (in the circumstances specified in the Administrative Instructions) the national Office of, or acting for, the Contracting State concerned to decide any question of residency or nationality and informs the applicant that it is doing so. The applicant has the right to submit arguments to the national Office directly and the national Office must decide the question promptly.
r.4.5(d)	Different applicants may be indicated for different States in respect of the same application.
AppGuide	But different applicants may not be indicated for different kinds of protection in respect of the same State – see International Phase, paragraph 5.022.
AdminInst	See s.203. Different applicants may be indicated for different States within the designation of a regional patent but where the same State has been indicated for both a national and regional patent, the applicants for each must be the same.
r.18.3	If there are two or more applicants at least one of them must be entitled to file an international application.
r.18.4	The International Bureau periodically publishes information on the various national laws in respect of who is qualified to file a national application (e.g. the inventor, his successor in title, the owner of the invention) accompanied by a warning that the effect of the international application in any designated State may depend on whether the person designated as applicant for that State is qualified, under the law of that State, to file a national application.
Art. 27(3)	In particular, the international application may be rejected in the US national phase if the applicant is not the inventor under US law in force before 16 September 2012. As a result of the America Invents Act the applicant can now be the assignee rather than the inventor.
Art. 27(8)	In the interests of its national security or general economic interests, a State may limit the right of its residents or nationals to file international applications.

31.2 Where may an international patent application be filed?

1468 Art. 10	An international patent application must be filed with a prescribed receiving Office which will check and process it according to the PCT and its Regulations.
r.19.1(a)(b)	The competent receiving Offices are:
	(a) the International Bureau, in all cases;
	(b) a national Office of, or acting for, the Contracting State of which the applicant is a resident or a national;
	(c) the national Office of another State or an intergovernmental organisation where a relevant agreement has been implemented between the State of which the applicant is a national or resident and that other State. Even so, the national Office of the state for which the applicant is a resident or national is considered the competent Office for the purposes of Art. 15(5) (whether national law permits the carrying out of an international-type search on a national application).
r.19.3	The delegating State making an agreement under (c) must promptly inform the International Bureau of such an agreement which will then be promptly published in the Gazette.

r.19.1(c)	Where residents or nationals of a country party to the Paris Convention but not the PCT are allowed to file international applications under Art. 9(2), the Assembly appoints the national Office or intergovernmental organisation (with its consent) which will act as receiving Office in respect of that country.
r.19.2	Where there are two or more applicants, the application must be filed at the national Office of, or acting for, a Contracting State of which at least one of the applicants is a national or resident or at the International Bureau (as long as one of the applicants is a resident or national of a Contracting State).
Art. 27(8)	Nothing in the PCT or its Regulations limits the freedom of each Contracting State to apply measures deemed necessary for the preservation of its national security or to limit, for the protection of the general economic interests of that State, the right of its own residents or nationals to file international applications.
OJ	The Belgian Patent Office will not act as a PCT receiving Office and Belgian nationals and residents must use the EPO or IB as receiving Office instead ([2018] O.J. A17).
OJ	The Monaco Patent Office will not act as a PCT receiving Office and Monaco nationals and residents must use the EPO or IB as receiving Office instead ([2018] O.J. A105).
OJ	The San Marino Patent Office will not act as a receiving Office and nationals and residents must use the EPO or IB as receiving Office instead ([2019] O.J. A96).
OJ	The Montenegro Patent Office will not act as a receiving Office and nationals and residents must use the EPO or IB as receiving Office instead ([2022] O.J. A82).

31.3 Procedure when the application is filed in the wrong place

r.19.4(a)(b)(c)	When the international application is filed with a national Office that acts as a receiving Office under the PCT but: (i) that national Office is not competent to act as a receiving Office under r.19.1 (applicant must be a resident or national) or r.19.2 (one of joint applicants must be a resident or national), or (ii) the international application is not in a language accepted under r.12.1(a) or the language dependent free text contained within the sequence listing part of the description is not in a language accepted under r.12.1(d) by that national Office but is in a language accepted under that Rule by the International Bureau as receiving Office, or (ii-bis) all or part of the international application is filed in electronic form in a format not accepted by that national Office, or (iii) the national Office and the International Bureau agree for any other reason (with the authorisation of the applicant) that the procedure under r.19.4 should apply): the international application is considered to have been received by the national Office on behalf of the International Bureau as receiving Office under r.19.1(a)(iii), and is promptly transmitted to the International Bureau unless prescriptions concerning national security apply. A fee equal to the transmittal fee charged under r.14 may be levied by the national Office for such transmittal. The application is considered to have been received by the International Bureau on the date that it was received by the national Office except that the date of receipt for the purposes of r.14.1(c), r.15.3 and r.16.1(f) (deadlines for paying the transmittal fee, international filing fee and search fee) is the actual date of receipt by the International Bureau.
Guidelines	See Guidelines for Search and Examination at the EPO as a PCT Authority, A-II, 2. The EPO does not charge a fee for forwarding the application to the IB.

1469

31.4 The receiving Office can apply national law relating to representation

Art. 27(7)	Any receiving Office may apply national law in so far as it relates to any requirement that the applicant be represented by an agent having the right to represent applicants before that Office.
Comment	Where the EPO is receiving Office, Art. 133 and Art. 134 EPC determine the requirements for representation. An applicant having neither residency nor a principle place of business in an EPC Contracting State requires representation other than for filing the PCT application.

1470

31.5   Those entitled to use the EPO as a receiving Office

1471	EPC Art. 151	The EPO is competent to act as receiving Office within the meaning of the PCT in accordance with the Implementing Regulations.
	EPC r.157(1)	The EPO is competent if the applicant is a resident or national of a Contracting State to both the EPC and the PCT.

31.6   Filing an international application with the EPO

1472	EPC Art. 151	The EPO's competence as a receiving Office is subject to any national security requirements of the EPC Contracting States (as required by Art. 27(8) PCT).
	EPC r.157(1)	An international application for which the EPO is to act as a receiving Office must be filed directly at the EPO unless national security provisions apply.
	Comment	Thus, international applications must, in principle, be filed with the EPO directly. An application filed via a national office will only be accorded a date of filing when it arrives at the EPO. However, this does not apply to applications subject to national security provisions – such applications that must be filed at a national office according to national law will be entitled to their original filing date when forwarded to the EPO as receiving Office.
	EPC r.157(3)	Where an international application for which the EPO is to act as a receiving Office is filed with the patent Office of an EPC Contracting State, that State must ensure that the international application reaches the EPO no later than two weeks before the end of the 13th month after the filing date/priority date.
	EPC Art. 151	The EPO will act as receiving Office in accordance with the Implementing Regulations.
	EPC r.157(2)	Where the EPO acts as receiving Office, the application must be filed in English, French or German. The President of the EPO decides how many copies are to be filed.
	OJ	Only one copy is required by the EPO ([2006] O.J. 439). See also AppGuide, Annex C (EP).
	OJ	See Notice from the EPO dated 20 February 2019 ([2019] O.J. A19). The EPO acknowledges receipt of an international application filed on paper or by fax using an automatically generated form 1031. Electronic filings are acknowledged immediately within the submission session.
	OJ	Applications may be filed directly with the EPO at any of the filing offices (see decision of the President dated 03.01.2017, [2017] O.J. A11). The Berlin office, being a sub-office of The Hague, is such a filing office. However, the Vienna sub-office is not a filing office. Applications may be filed in Munich at the EPO Pschorrhofe building or at the Isar building.

31.7   Manner of filing the application

31.7.1   *The use of paper*

1473	r.89*bis*.1(a)	All receiving Offices must permit the filing of international applications on paper.
	r.89*ter*.1	Any Office or intergovernmental organisation may provide that, where an international application is filed on paper, a copy thereof in electronic form, in accordance with the Administrative Instructions, may be furnished by the applicant.

31.7.2   *The use of telegraph, teleprinter, or facsimile*

1474	r.92.4(a)(h)	A document making up the international application may be transmitted, if feasible, by telegraph, teleprinter, facsimile or other like means of communication resulting in the filing of a printed or written document but no national Office or intergovernmental organisation is obliged to receive a document submitted in this way unless it has notified the International Bureau to the effect that it will and such information has been published in the Gazette.
	r.92.4(c)	Where such means are used to transmit the application and part or all of it is not received or is illegible on receipt, the application is treated as not received to the extent that it is not received or illegible. The relevant national Office or intergovernmental organisation will promptly inform the applicant accordingly.

r.92.4(d)	Where such means are used to transmit the application, any national Office or intergovernmental organisation may require that the original and an accompanying letter identifying the earlier transmission is forwarded within 14 days of such transmission, provided that such a requirement has been notified to the International Bureau and published in the Gazette.
r.92.4(e)	Where the original is not so forwarded, the relevant Office or organisation may, depending on the kind of document involved, and having regard to r.11 (physical requirements) and r.26.3 (checking of physical requirements): (i) waive the requirement; or (ii) invite the applicant to forward the original within a reasonable time limit fixed in the invitation; or where the document transmitted contains defects or shows that the original contains defects warranting an invitation to correct, issue such an invitation instead of or in addition to (i) or (ii).
r.92.4(f)	If the forwarding of an original is not required under r.92.4(d), but the relevant Office or organisation nevertheless considers it necessary to receive the original, it may invite the applicant to forward the original in accordance with r.92.4(e)(ii).
r.92.4(g)(i)	Where the applicant fails to comply with an invitation under r.92.4(e)(ii) or r.92.4(f), the application will be considered to be withdrawn and the receiving Office will so declare.
r.92.4(b)	A signature appearing on a document transmitted by facsimile is recognised for the purposes of the PCT and its Regulations as a proper signature.
OJ	The EPO will accept filings by fax but not by telegram, teletex or similar means. Confirmation is still required, in contrast to the procedure for European applications where it is no longer routinely required. See Decision of the President dated 20.2.2019, [2019] A18.

31.7.3   Filing in electronic form

r.89*bis*.1(a)	International applications may be filed in electronic form or by electronic means (in accordance with the Administrative Instructions).	1475
r.89*bis*.1(b)(c)	The PCT Regulations apply equally to applications filed electronically, subject to any special provisions of the Administrative Instructions which set out the requirements for the filing and processing of applications filed wholly or partly in electronic form.	
r.89*bis*.1(d)(e)	No national Office or intergovernmental organisation is required to receive international applications filed in electronic form or by electronic means unless it has notified the International Bureau that it is prepared to do so according to the provisions of the Administrative Instructions. Such notification is published by the International Bureau in the Gazette. Having issued such a notification, a receiving Office may not refuse to process international applications filed in electronic form or by electronic means which comply with the requirements of the Administrative Instructions.	
AdminInst	See Part 7 and Annex F.	
OJ	The EPO allows electronic filing (see Decision of the President dated 03 May 2023, [2023] O.J. A48) using EPO Online Filing (OLF), Online Filing 2.0, the web form filing service or the EPO Contingency Upload Service.	

31.8   Payment of Fees

Art. 3(4)(iv)	An international application is subject to the payment of fees.	1476

31.8.1   Transmittal fee

r.14.1(a)(b)	Any receiving Office may charge the applicant a transmittal fee for receiving and transmitting the international application and other associated tasks. The amount is fixed by the receiving Office.	1477
r.14.1(c)	The transmittal fee must be paid within one month of the date of receipt of the application by the receiving Office (except where the application is received on behalf of the International Bureau – see r.19.4(c)). The amount payable is the amount applicable on the date of receipt of the application by the receiving Office.	

31.8.2   Transmittal fee where the EPO is the receiving Office

EPC Art. 151	The EPO acts as receiving Office in accordance with the Implementing Regulations.	1478

r.157(4)	Where the EPO is acting as the receiving Office for an international application, a transmittal fee is due within one month of the filing of the application.
RRF Art. 2(1)(18)	The fee is not payable if the PCT request and international application are filed with the EPO as receiving Office online in character-coded format but is € 145 in all other cases.
RRF Art. 2(3)	The President of the EPO decides the conditions under which a document is deemed to have been filed online in character-coded format.
RRF Art. 2(4)	Fee levels which relate to a means of electronic communication or a format referred to in RRF Art. 2(1) or Art. 2(2) shall not apply until a date set by the President of the Office.
OJ	See Decision of the President dated 12 December 2018 ([2019] O.J. A3) and Notice from the EPO dated 24 January 2019 ([2019] O.J. A6). New RRF Art. 2(4) applies as of 01 April 2019 to item (i) of RRF Art. 2(1)(1) and as a consequence a transmittal fee of € 145 continues to be payable in all cases for the time being.

31.8.3   *International filing fee*

1479	r.15.1	An international filing fee must be paid to the receiving Office for the benefit of the International Bureau.
	r.15.2	The amount is specified in the Schedule of Fees. The receiving Office decides which currency the fee is to be paid in. Rules are given for determining the amount to be paid in currencies other than the Swiss franc. Transfer is made according to r.96.2.
	SoF	The international filing fee is currently 1,330 Swiss francs plus 15 Swiss francs for each sheet of the application in excess of 30. It is reduced by 100, 200 or 300 francs where the application is filed in electronic form, depending on the format used. It is also/further reduced by 90 % when the applicant (or all the applicants where there are 2 or more) is/are from certain low per capita income countries or a UN least developed country.
	r.15.3	The international filing fee must be paid within one month of the date of receipt of the application by the receiving Office (except where the application is received on behalf of the International Bureau – see r.19.4(c)). The amount payable is the amount applicable on the date of receipt of the application by the receiving Office.
	r.15.4	The international fee is refunded if either: (i) the determination under Art. 11(1) (whether to accord a filing date) is negative; (ii) the application is withdrawn or considered so before transmittal of the record copy to the International Bureau; or (iii) the international application is not treated as such due to prescriptions concerning national security.
	Art. 4(2)	Every designation is subject to the payment of a prescribed fee but this designation fee is now included in the international filing fee (see r.27.1(b)).

31.8.4   *Search fee*

1480	r.16.1(a)(b)	A search fee, collected by the receiving Office, may be charged by the International Searching Authority for its own benefit for carrying out the international search and its other duties under the PCT.
	RRF Art. 2(1)(2)	The fee is € 1,775 where the EPO is International Searching Authority.
	r.16.1(f)	The search fee must be paid within one month from the date of receipt of the international application by the receiving Office (except where the application is received on behalf of the International Bureau – see r.19.4(c)) and the amount payable is the amount due on that date of receipt.
	r.16.1(b)–(e)	The receiving Office decides which currency the fee is to be paid in. Rules are given for determining the amount of the fee in currencies other than the one in which the fee is set by the International Searching Authority. Transfer is made according to r.96.2.
	r.16.2	The search fee is refunded to the applicant by the receiving Office if: (i) the determination under Art. 11(1) (according a filing date to the application) is negative; (ii) before transmittal of the application to the International Searching Authority, the application is withdrawn or considered to be withdrawn; or (iii) the international application is not treated as such due to prescriptions concerning national security.

OJ	See Art. 5(2)(ii) and Annex D of the agreement between the EPO and the International Bureau ([2017] O.J. A115). Where the international application is withdrawn or considered withdrawn under Art. 14(1), (3) or (4) before the start of the international search, the search fee is fully refunded.
r.16.3	Where the International Searching Authority takes into account, under r.41.1, the results of an earlier search in carrying out the international search, that Authority shall refund the search fee paid in connection with the international application to the extent and under the conditions provided for in the agreement under Art. 16(3)(b).
OJ	See Art. 5(2)(i) and Annex D of the agreement between the EPO and the International Bureau ([2017] O.J. A115) and Decision of the President dated 17 January 2023 ([2023] O.J. A5) for the amount refunded which varies from 17.5 % to 100 % depending on the nature of the previous search and the use made of it (full or partial).
OJ	Where the EPO acts as International Searching Authority for an applicant who is (a) a natural person, who is a national and resident of a state which is not an EPC contracting state, and which, on the date on which the international application is filed, is classified by the World Bank as a low-income or lower-middle-income economy; or (b) a natural or legal person who, within the meaning of r.18 PCT, is a national and resident of a state in which a validation agreement with the European Patent Organisation is in force; then the international search fee is reduced by 75 % (Decision of the Administrative Council dated 12 December 2019, [2020] O.J. A4; Art. 5 and Annex D of the agreement between the EPO and the International Bureau, [2020] O.J. A35). If there are several applicants then each must satisfy the relevant criterion. For the list of qualifying low-income and lower-middle-income countries see [2022] O.J. A72.

31.8.5   Late payment of fees

r.16*bis*.1(a)(d)	If the transmittal fee, the international filing fee or the search fee, is not paid in time or is underpaid, the receiving Office will invite the applicant to correct the deficiency and, if the receiving Office so desires, pay a late payment fee, within one month of the invitation. However, if payment is received before the invitation is sent, it will be considered to have been received before the expiry of the appropriate time limit.	1481
AppGuide	See International Phase, paragraph 6.037 – the time limit may not be extended.	
r.16*bis*.2	The amount of the late payment fee is (a) 50 % of the unpaid fees or (b) the transmittal fee, whichever is higher, but is capped at 50 % of the international filing fee specified in item 1 of the Schedule of Fees, not taking into account the fee for any sheet in excess of 30.	
OJ	The EPO late payment fee is 50 % of the unpaid fees as specified in r.16*bis*.2 PCT ([1992] O.J. 383).	
r.16*bis*.1(c)(e)	Where such an invitation is not complied with the receiving Office will make a declaration under Art. 14(3) (application considered withdrawn) and proceed as provided for in r.29, though if payment is received before the Art. 14(3) declaration is made it will be considered to have been received before the end of the one-month deadline.	

31.8.6   Consequences of not paying fees

Art. 14(3)(a)(b)	If any prescribed fees have not been paid (Art. 3(4)(iv) and Art. 4(2)) the international application will be considered withdrawn and the receiving Office will so declare.	1482
r.27	The relevant prescribed fees under Art. 3(4)(iv) are the transmittal fee (r.14), the international filing fee (r.15.1), the search fee (r.16) and, where required, the late payment fee (r.16*bis*.2). The designation fees provided for by Art. 4(2) are now part of the international filing fee.	
Art. 25	If the application is considered withdrawn, the applicant can, within a prescribed two-month time limit (r.51.1), get the International Bureau to forward copies of any document in the file to any designated Office and, within the same time limit, enter the national phase in such a State, requesting review of the decision under Art. 14(3) that the application is considered withdrawn.	

Chapter 32: Procedure of the Receiving Office

32.1 Examination as to whether a filing date can be accorded

1483   r.20.1(a)

Promptly after receipt of the papers purporting to be an international application, the receiving Office will determine whether the papers fulfil the requirements for awarding a filing date under Art. 11(1).

32.1.1   *Incorporation of the description and claims by reference – reservations*

1484   Comment

Article 11(1)(iii) expressly requires that the papers filed with a receiving Office and purporting to be an international application contain a description and claim in order to be awarded a filing date (see below). For applications filed before April 1, 2007, an international application missing one of these elements would not have been accorded a filing date – instead, an invitation to correct under Art. 11(2)(a) would have been issued and if the invitation was complied with the date on which the missing element was filed would have become the filing date. However, for applications filed on or after April 1, 2007, amended r.20 provides that an international application missing a description and/or a claim can retain its original filing date if (a) the application claims priority from any earlier filing in the originally filed papers, (b) an indication is present in the originally filed papers that certain elements of the priority filing will be incorporated by reference (r.4.18), and (c) if the applicant later confirms such incorporation by reference by filing certain documents (r.20.6(a)). Missing parts of the description, claims and drawings can also be added without changing the filing date under similar conditions.

Comment

New r.20.5*bis*, allowing the correction of an erroneously filed element or part, entered into force on 01 July 2020 and applies to any international application in respect of which one or more elements referred to in Art. 11(1)(iii) (elements required for a filing date) were first received by the receiving Office on or after that date. An erroneously filed part may also be corrected without changing the filing date under the same conditions that apply to adding a missing element or part by reference to the priority application.

r.20.8(a)(b)

This possibility to incorporate missing elements and parts by reference to the priority application, however, does not apply to any receiving Office or designated Office whose national law is incompatible on October 5, 2005, for as long as it continues to be incompatible, provided that the Office informs the IB accordingly by April 5, 2006. Relevant information is published in the Gazette.

r.20.8(a-*bis*)(b-*bis*)

Furthermore, the ability to incorporate by reference in the case of erroneously filed elements and parts (r.20.5*bis*) does not apply to any receiving Office or designated Office whose law is incompatible on 09 October 2019 if it informs the IB accordingly by 09 April 2020. Relevant information is published in the Gazette.

WIPO

The receiving Offices of the following countries and organisations have notified and still maintain their incompatibility under r.20.8(a) in respect of r.20.3(a)(ii), r.20.3(b)(ii), r.20.5(a)(ii), r.20.5(d) and r.20.6: Cuba, Czech Republic, Germany, Indonesia, Korea, Mexico. Reservations previously filed by the EPO were lifted with the coming into force of EPC2000. The EPO will allow incorporation by reference as a receiving Office in respect of any international application filed on or after December 13, 2007 ([2007] O.J. 692).

r.19.4(a)(iii)

If the receiving Office will not allow incorporation by reference and the applicant wants to use it, he can ask for the application to be transferred so that the International Bureau acts as receiving Office instead.

WIPO

The following designated Offices have notified and still maintain their incompatibility under r.20.8(b) in respect of r.20.3(a)(ii), r.20.3(b)(ii), r.20.5(a)(ii), r.20.5(d) and r.20.6: China, Cuba, Czech Republic, Germany, Indonesia, Korea, Mexico, Turkey. Reservations previously filed by the EPO were lifted with the coming into force of EPC2000. The EPO will allow incorporation by reference as a designated office in respect of any Euro-PCT application entering the regional phase on or after December 13, 2007 ([2007] O.J. 692).

WIPO

The following receiving Offices have notified and still maintain their incompatibility under r.20.8(a-*bis*) in respect of r.20.5*bis*(a)(ii) and (d): Chile, Cuba, Czech Republic, Germany, Spain, France, Indonesia, Korea, Mexico. Reservations originally notified by the EPO were lifted for applications filed on or after 01 November 2022.

WIPO

The following designated Offices have notified and still maintain their incompatibility under r.20.8(b-*bis*) in respect of r.20.5*bis*(a)(ii) and (d): Chile, China, Cuba, Czech Republic, Germany, Spain, Indonesia, Korea, Mexico, Turkey. Reservations originally notified by the EPO were lifted for applications filed on or after 01 November 2022.

r.20.8(a-*ter*)

Where the receiving Office has notified its incompatibility, and incorporation by reference is requested by the applicant, the receiving Office proceeds under r.20.3(b)(i), r.20.5(b), r.20.5(c), r.20.5*bis*(b) or r.20.5*bis*(c), as appropriate (allocation of later filing date corresponding to date on which all requirements have been met). Where the receiving Office proceeds as provided for in r.20.5(c) or r.20.5*bis*(c), the applicant may proceed as provided for in r.20.5(e) or r.20.5*bis*(e), as the case may be (request that the missing or corrected part or element is disregarded in order to maintain an earlier date).

r.20.8(c)

Where an element (all of the description, or all of the claims) or part (part of the description, part of the claims or part or all of the drawings) is considered to have been incorporated by reference in the international application by virtue of a finding of the receiving Office under r.20.6(b) but that incorporation by reference does not apply to the international application for the purposes of the procedure before a designated Office because of the operation of r.20.8(b) or r.20.8(b-*bis*), the designated Office may treat the application as if the international filing date had been accorded under r.20.3(b)(i), r.20.5(b) or r.20.5*bis*(b), or corrected under r.20.5(c) or r.20.5*bis*(c), as the case may be (award of a later filing date when all requirements were met) provided that r.82*ter*.1(c) and (d) apply mutatis mutandis (right to submit comments and/or disregard part of the application in order to retain the original date).

Guidelines

See Guidelines for Search and Examination at the EPO as a PCT Authority, H-II, 2.2.2.2 – if a receiving Office awards a filing date on the basis that an element or part was completely contained in the priority document, the filing date accorded to the application is valid during the international phase regardless of whether the ISA or IPEA agrees with the determination made. It can only be challenged by individual designated or elected states in the national/regional phase (r.82*ter*.1(b) PCT). However, the ISR may cite documents that would become relevant should redating of the application take place.

OJ

Incompatibility was originally declared by the EPO under r.20.8(a-bis) and r.20.8(b-bis) for the situation where a correct part or element is filed to replace a wrongly filed part or element and the correct part or element is incorporated by reference in order to avoid changing the filing date. See Notice from the EPO dated 14 June 2020, [2020] O.J. A81. This incompatibility no longer exists for applications filed on or after 01 November 2022 (see Notice from the EPO dated 23 June 2022 ([2022] O.J. A71). Where the correct element or part is filed on or before the date accorded as international filing date there has never been any incompatibility. During the period of incompatibility, when the EPO is acted as receiving Office, the application could be sent to the International Bureau under r.19.4(b) PCT and the International Bureau acted as receiving Office instead. However, the incompatibility when the EPO acted as designated or elected office meant that either the filing date had to be changed to the date on which the correct part was actually filed or else the correct part had to be ignored for the EPO procedure.

Guidelines

See Guidelines for Search and Examination at the EPO as a PCT Authority, A-II, 6. During the period of incompatibility, the EPO did not charge a fee for forwarding the application to the IB. If the applicant did not agree to the IB acting as receiving Office then the EPO as receiving Office proceeded according to r.20.5*bis*(b) or (c), as the case may be.

Guidelines

See C-III, 1.3. During the period of incompatibility, when the application entered the EPO regional phase, the EPO sent a communication pursuant to r.20.8(c) and 82*ter*.1(c) and (d) PCT with a 2 month time limit explaining that it intended to take into account the corrected application documents but change the filing date. If the applicant asked for the corrected documents to be disregarded, the EPO accorded as filing date the original date accorded by the receiving Office, disregard the corrected application documents and issued an interlocutory decision to this effect. If the applicant filed obervations then these were taken into account and an interlocutory decision taken accordingly. Otherwise, the EPO confirmed its findings and proceeded accordingly without issuing any decision. The applicant could avoid this procedure by stating its preferred way of proceeding on entry into the regional phase.

32.1.2   Requirements for a filing date

1485 Art. 11(1)(iii)	In order for an international application to be awarded a filing date, it must contain the following elements: (a) an indication that it is intended as an international application; (b) the designation of at least one Contracting State; (c) the name of the applicant, as prescribed; (d) a part which on the face of it appears to be a description; (e) a part which on the face of it appears to be a claim or claims.
r.4.9(1)	The filing of a request now automatically constitutes the designation of all Contracting States.
AppGuide	See International Phase, paragraph 5.052 – the official request form PCT/RO/101 does not have to be used.
r.20.1(b)	For the purposes of Art. 11(1)(iii)(c), it is sufficient to indicate the name of the applicant in a way which allows the identity of the applicant to be established even if the name is misspelled, the given names are not fully indicated, or, in the case of legal entities, the indication of the name is abbreviated or incomplete.
r.4.18	Where the international application claims the priority of an earlier application on the date the application is filed, it may incorporate by reference parts of that earlier application in lieu of a description or claim. Such a statement must be included in the request and is subject to confirmation under r.20.6. Such a statement, if not contained in the request on that date, may be added to the request if, and only if, it was otherwise contained in, or submitted with, the international application on that date.
r.4.10	In order to claim priority, it is necessary to state the date, number and filing office of the earlier application.
Art. 11(1)(i)(ii)	The award of a filing date is also, in principle, dependent on the applicant having the right to file an international application with the receiving Office by virtue of his residence or nationality and the application being in a prescribed language.
r.20.1(c)(d)	For the purposes of Art. 11(1)(ii) (language requirement), it is sufficient that the part which appears to be a description (other than any sequence listing part thereof) and the part which appears to be a claim or claims is in a language accepted by the receiving Office under r.12.1(a). If, however, this provision, on October 1, 1997, is not compatible with the national law applied by a receiving Office, it will not apply to that receiving Office for as long as the incompatibility continues, provided that the Office informs the International Bureau accordingly by December 31, 1997. The information received is promptly published by the International Bureau in the Gazette.
WIPO	Incompatibility has only been declared by the USPTO.
r.19.4(a)	In any case, the fact that the applicant lacks the right to use the receiving Office, or the fact that the application is not in a language accepted by the receiving Office, is not fatal to the award of a filing date since the application is forwarded to the IB, which acts as receiving Office instead, and the application retains its initial date of filing – see sections above under receiving Office (r.19.4(a)(i)) and languages (r.19.4(a)(ii)) respectively.
AdminInst	See s.329 – if the applicant lacks the right to use the receiving Office with which the international application was filed, the receiving Office may first issue an invitation to correct under Art. 11(2)(a) and if a request is made to change details concerning the applicant (e.g. because the wrong residence or nationality has been specified) the receiving Office will treat this as a correction under Art. 14(1)(a)(ii) and award a filing date where possible. However, the USPTO will not apply this procedure (see AppGuide, International Phase, paragraph 6.036).

32.1.3   Procedure where a filing date can be accorded

1486 r.20.2(a)	If the receiving Office determines that, at the time of receipt of the papers purporting to be an international application, the requirements of Art. 11(1) were fulfilled, the receiving Office will accord as the international filing date the date of receipt of the international application.
r.20.2(b)	The receiving Office will stamp the request of the international application which it has accorded an international filing date as prescribed by the Administrative Instructions. The copy whose request has been so stamped is the record copy of the international application.

Art. 12(2)	The record copy is considered to be the true copy of the international application.
r.20.2(c)	The receiving Office promptly notifies the applicant of the international application number and the international filing date. At the same time, it sends to the International Bureau a copy of the notification sent to the applicant, except where it has already sent, or is sending at the same time, the record copy to the International Bureau under r.22.1(a).

32.1.4 *Procedure where a filing date cannot be accorded*

r.19.4(a)	For the procedure followed where the applicant lacks the required nationality or residence or the application is filed in a language which is not accepted by the receiving Office, see sections above under receiving Office (r.19.4(a)(i)) and languages (r.19.4(a)(ii)) respectively.	1487
Art. 11(2)(a)	Where a filing date cannot be accorded, the applicant is invited to file any necessary correction.	
r.20.3(a)	Where, in determining whether the papers purporting to be an international application fulfil the requirements of Art. 11(1), the receiving Office finds that any of the requirements of Art. 11(1) are not, or appear not to be, fulfilled, it will promptly invite the applicant, at the applicant's option:	

(i) to furnish the required correction under Art. 11(2); or

(ii) where the requirements concerned are those relating to an element referred to in Art. 11(1)(iii)(d) or (e) (description or claim missing), to confirm in accordance with r.20.6(a) that the element is incorporated by reference under r.4.18;

and to make observations, if any, within the applicable time limit under r.20.7. If that time limit expires after the expiration of 12 months from the filing date of any application whose priority is claimed, the receiving Office will call that circumstance to the attention of the applicant.

r.20.7(a)(b)	The time limit is two months from the date of the invitation but will in any case be considered to have been met if a correction under Art. 11(2) or confirmation of incorporation by reference under r.20.6(a) is received before the receiving Office sends a notification to the applicant under r.20.4(i) (no filing date to be awarded – see below).
AppGuide	See International Phase, paragraph 6.037 – no extension of the time limit is possible.
r.20.6(a)	The applicant may submit to the receiving Office, within the applicable time limit under r.20.7, a written notice confirming that an element is incorporated by reference in the international application under r.4.18, accompanied by:

(i) a sheet or sheets embodying the entire element as contained in the earlier application;

(ii) where the applicant has not already complied with r.17.1(a), (b) or (b-*bis*) in relation to the priority document, a copy of the earlier application as filed; and

(iii) where the earlier application is not in the language in which the international application is filed, a translation of the earlier application into that language or, where a translation of the international application is required under r.12.3(a) (for international search) or r.12.4(a) (for international publication), a translation of the earlier application into both the language in which the international application is filed and the language of that translation.

r.12.1*bis*	An element furnished under r.20.6(a) must be in the language of the international application as filed or, where a translation is necessary under r.12.3(a) or r.12.4(a), in both the language of the application as filed and the language of the translation.
Art. 11(2)(b)	If the applicant complies with the invitation, the receiving Office will accord as the date of filing the date on which the corrections were received.
r.20.3(b)	Where, following an invitation under r.20.3(a) or otherwise:

(i) the applicant furnishes to the receiving Office the required correction under Art. 11(2) after the date of receipt of the purported international application but on a later date falling within the applicable time limit under r.20.7, the receiving Office will accord that later date as the international filing date and proceed as provided in r.20.2(b) and (c) (procedure in the case of a positive determination);

(ii) an element referred to in Art. 11(1)(iii)(d) or (e) is, under r.20.6(b), considered to have been contained in the international application on the date on which one or more elements referred to in Art. 11(1)(iii) were first received by the receiving Office, the receiving Office will accord as the international filing date the date on which all of the requirements of Art. 11(1) are fulfilled and proceed as provided in r.20.2(b) and (c).

r.20.7(a)(b)   The time limit is two months from the date of the invitation, if one is sent, or two months from the date on which one or more elements referred to in Art. 11(1)(iii) were first received in other cases, but will in any case be considered to have been met if a correction under Art. 11(2) or confirmation of incorporation by reference under r.20.6(a) is received before the receiving Office sends a notification to the applicant under r.20.4(i) (no filing date to be awarded – see below).

AppGuide   See International Phase, paragraph 6.037 – no extension of the time limit is possible.

r.12.1*bis*   The element referred to in Art. 11(iii)(d) or (e) must be in the language of the international application as filed or, where a translation is necessary under r.12.3(a) or r.12.4(a), in both the language of the application as filed and the language of the translation.

r.20.6(b)   Where the receiving Office finds that the requirements of r.4.18 (statement of incorporation by reference in the request) and r.20.6(a) (confirmation of incorporation by reference) have been complied with and that the element referred to in r.20.6(a) is completely contained in the earlier application concerned, that element will be considered to have been contained in the purported international application on the date on which one or more elements referred to in Art. 11(1)(iii) were first received by the receiving Office.

r.20.6(c)   Where the receiving Office finds that a requirement under r.4.18 (statement of incorporation by reference in the request) or r.20.6(a) (confirmation of incorporation by reference) has not been complied with or that the element referred to in r.20.6(a) is not completely contained in the earlier application concerned, the receiving Office will proceed as provided for in r.20.3(b)(i), 20.5(b), 20.5(c), 20.5*bis*(b) or 20.5*bis*(c), as the case may be (allocation of a later filing date).

r.20.3(c)   If the receiving Office later discovers, or on the basis of the applicant's reply realises, that it has erred in issuing an invitation under r.20.3(a) since the requirements of Art. 11(1) were fulfilled when the papers were received, it shall proceed as provided in r.20.2 (to award a filing date).

r.20.4   If the receiving Office does not receive, within the applicable time limit under r.20.7 (see above), a correction or confirmation referred to in r.20.3(a), or if a correction or confirmation has been received but the application still does not fulfil the requirements of Art. 11(1), the receiving Office will:
(i) promptly notify the applicant that the application is not and will not be treated as an international application and indicate the reasons therefor;
(ii) notify the International Bureau that the number it has marked on the papers will not be used as an international application number;
(iii) keep the papers constituting the purported international application and any correspondence relating thereto as provided in r.93.1; and
(iv) send a copy of the said papers to the International Bureau where, pursuant to a request by the applicant under Art. 25(1) (review by designated Offices), the International Bureau needs such a copy and specially asks for it.

32.1.5   *Procedure where a part of the application is missing*

1488   Art. 14(2)   If the international application refers to drawings which are missing, the receiving Office will notify the applicant, giving him a chance to supply them within the prescribed time limit. If the drawings are supplied in time the international filing date will be the date of receipt of the drawings. Otherwise, references to the drawings in the application will be considered non-existent.

r.20.5(a)   Where, in determining whether the papers purporting to be an international application fulfil the requirements of Art. 11(1), the receiving Office finds that a part of the description, claims or drawings is or appears to be missing, including the case where all of the drawings are or appear to be missing (missing part) but not including the case where an entire element referred to in Art. 11(1)(iii)(d) or (e) (description and claims) is or appears to be missing and not including the case referred to in r.20.5*bis*(a) (erroneously filed elements and parts), it will promptly invite the applicant, at the applicant's option:
(i) to complete the purported international application by furnishing the missing part; or
(ii) to confirm, in accordance with r.20.6(a), that the part was incorporated by reference under r.4.18 (see above for the requirements of r.20.6(a));

and to make observations, if any, within the applicable time limit under r.20.7. If that time limit expires after the expiration of 12 months from the filing date of any application whose priority is claimed, the receiving Office must call that circumstance to the attention of the applicant.

r.20.7(a)   The applicable time limit is two months from the date of the invitation.

AppGuide   See International Phase, paragraph 6.037 – no extension of the time limit is possible.

r.20.6(a)   The applicant may submit to the receiving Office, within the applicable time limit under r.20.7, a written notice confirming that a part is incorporated by reference in the international application under r.4.18, accompanied by:

(i) a sheet or sheets embodying the part concerned;

(ii) where the applicant has not already complied with r.17.1(a), (b) or (b-*bis*) in relation to the priority document, a copy of the earlier application as filed;

(iii) where the earlier application is not in the language in which the international application is filed, a translation of the earlier application into that language or, where a translation of the international application is required under r.12.3(a) (for international search) or r.12.4(a) (for international publication), a translation of the earlier application into both the language in which the international application is filed and the language of that translation; and

(iv) an indication as to where that part is contained in the earlier application and, where applicable, in any translation referred to in r.20.6(a)(iii).

r.20.5(b)   Where, following an invitation under r.20.5(a) or otherwise, the applicant furnishes to the receiving Office, on or before the date on which all of the requirements of Art. 11(1) are fulfilled but within the applicable time limit under r.20.7, a missing part referred to in r.20.5(a) so as to complete the purported international application, that part will be included in the application and the receiving Office will accord as the international filing date the date on which all of the requirements of Art. 11(1) are fulfilled and proceed as provided in r.20.2(b) and (c) (positive determination for a filing date).

r.20.7(a)   The applicable time limit is two months from the date of any invitation sent under r.20.5(a) or, where no such invitation has been sent, two months from the date on which one or more elements referred to in Art. 11(1)(iii) (requirements of a filing date) were first received by the receiving Office.

r.20.5(c)   Where, following an invitation under r.20.5(a) or otherwise, the applicant furnishes to the receiving Office, after the date on which all of the requirements of Art. 11(1) were fulfilled but within the applicable time limit under r.20.7, a missing part referred to in r.20.5(a) so as to complete the international application, that part will be included in the application, and the receiving Office will correct the international filing date to the date on which the receiving Office received that part, notify the applicant accordingly and proceed as provided for in the Administrative Instructions.

r.20.7(a)   The applicable time limit is two months from the date of any invitation sent under r.20.5(a) or, where no such invitation has been sent, two months from the date on which one or more elements referred to in Art. 11(1)(iii) (requirements of a filing date) were first received by the receiving Office.

r.20.5(d)   Where, following an invitation under r.20.5(a) or otherwise, a part referred to in r.20.5(a) is, under r.20.6(b), considered to have been contained in the purported international application on the date on which one or more elements referred to in Art. 11(1)(iii) were first received by the receiving Office (i.e. if the requirements of r.4.18 relating to the request and the requirements of r.20.6(a) relating to confirmation of incorporation by reference are met), the receiving Office will accord as the international filing date the date on which all of the requirements of Art. 11(1) are fulfilled and proceed as provided in r.20.2(b) and (c) (positive determination for a filing date).

r.20.5(e)   Where the international filing date has been corrected under r.20.5(c), the applicant may, in a notice submitted to the receiving Office within one month from the date of the notification under r.20.5(c), request that the missing part concerned be disregarded, in which case the missing part will be considered not to have been furnished and the correction of the international filing date under that paragraph will be considered not to have been made, and the receiving Office will proceed as provided for in the Administrative Instructions.

r.12.1*bis*   The missing part must be in the language of the international application as filed or, where a translation is necessary under r.12.3(a) or r.12.4(a), in both the language of the application as filed and the language of the translation.

32.1.6   *Procedure where a part or element of the application is erroneously filed*

1489 r.20.5*bis*(a)	Where, in determining whether the papers purporting to be an international application fulfill the requirements of Art. 11(1), the receiving Office finds that an entire element referred to in Art. 11(1)(iii)(d) or (e) has or appears to have been erroneously filed, or that a part of the description, claims or drawings has or appears to have been erroneously filed, including the case where all drawings have or appear to have been erroneously filed ("erroneously filed element or part"), it shall promptly invite the applicant, at the applicant's option:

(i)   to correct the purported international application by furnishing the correct element or part; or

(ii)   to confirm, in accordance with r.20.6(a), that the correct element or part was incorporated by reference under Rule 4.18;

and to make observations, if any, within the applicable time limit under r.20.7. If that time limit expires after the expiration of 12 months from the filing date of any application whose priority is claimed, the receiving Office shall call that circumstance to the attention of the applicant.

r.20.7(a)	The applicable time limit is two months from the date of the invitation.
AppGuide	See International Phase, paragraph 6.037 – no extension of the time limit is possible.
r.20.6(a)	The applicant may submit to the receiving Office, within the applicable time limit under r.20.7, a written notice confirming that an element or part is incorporated by reference in the international application under r.4.18, accompanied by:

(i) a sheet or sheets embodying the part concerned;

(ii) where the applicant has not already complied with r.17.1(a), (b) or (b-*bis*) in relation to the priority document, a copy of the earlier application as filed;

(iii) where the earlier application is not in the language in which the international application is filed, a translation of the earlier application into that language or, where a translation of the international application is required under r.12.3(a) (for international search) or r.12.4(a) (for international publication), a translation of the earlier application into both the language in which the international application is filed and the language of that translation; and

(iv) an indication as to where that part is contained in the earlier application and, where applicable, in any translation referred to in r.20.6(a)(iii).

r.20.5*bis*(b)	Where, following an invitation under r.20.5 *bis* (a) or otherwise, the applicant furnishes to the receiving Office, on or before the date on which all of the requirements of Art. 11(1) are fulfilled but within the applicable time limit under r.20.7, a correct element or part so as to correct the purported international application, that correct element or part shall be included in the application, the erroneously filed element or part concerned shall be removed from the application and the receiving Office shall accord as the international filing date the date on which all of the requirements of Art. 11(1) are fulfilled and proceed as provided in r.20.2(b) and (c) and as provided for in the Administrative Instructions.
r.20.7(a)	The applicable time limit is two months from the date of any invitation sent under r.20.5*bis*(a) or, where no such invitation has been sent, two months from the date on which one or more elements referred to in Art. 11(1)(iii) (elements required for a filing date) were first received by the receiving Office.
r.20.5*bis*(c)	Where, following an invitation under r.20.5 *bis* (a) or otherwise, the applicant furnishes to the receiving Office, after the date on which all of the requirements of Art. 11(1) were fulfilled but within the applicable time limit under r.20.7, a correct element or part so as to correct the international application, that correct element or part shall be included in the application, the erroneously filed element or part concerned shall be removed from the application, and the receiving Office shall correct the international filing date to the date on which the receiving Office received that correct element or part, notify the applicant accordingly and proceed as provided for in the Administrative Instructions.
r.20.7(a)	The applicable time limit is two months from the date of any invitation sent under r.20.5*bis*(a) or, where no such invitation has been sent, two months from the date on which one or more elements referred to in Art. 11(1)(iii) (requirements of a filing date) were first received by the receiving Office.

r.20.5*bis*(d)	Where, following an invitation under r.20.5 *bis* (a) or otherwise, a correct element or part is, under r.20.6(b), considered to have been contained in the purported international application on the date on which one or more elements referred to in Art. 11(1)(iii) were first received by the receiving Office, the erroneously filed element or part concerned shall remain in the application, and the receiving Office shall accord as the international filing date the date on which all of the requirements of Art. 11(1) are fulfilled and proceed as provided in r.20.2(b) and (c) and as provided for in the Administrative Instructions.
r.20.5*bis*(e)	Where the international filing date has been corrected under r.20.5 *bis* (c), the applicant may, in a notice submitted to the receiving Office within one month from the date of the notification under r.20.5bis(c), request that the correct element or part be disregarded, in which case the correct element or part shall be considered not to have been furnished, the erroneously filed element or part concerned shall be considered not to have been removed from the application and the correction of the international filing date under r.20.5 *bis* (c) shall be considered not to have been made, and the receiving Office shall proceed as provided for in the Administrative Instructions.
r.12.1*bis*	The corrected element or part must be in the language of the international application as filed or, where a translation is necessary under r.12.3(a) or r.12.4(a), in both the language of the application as filed and the language of the translation.

32.1.7   Review of the decision to award a filing date

Art. 14(4), r.30	If the receiving Office finds within four months of the international filing date that, despite the award of an international filing date, the requirements of Art. 11(1)(i)–(iii) were not complied with at that date, the application will be considered withdrawn and the receiving Office will so declare.	1490
r.29.4(a)	However, before the receiving Office issues any declaration under Art. 14(4), it must notify the applicant of its intent to issue such declaration and the reasons therefor. The applicant may, if he disagrees with the tentative finding of the receiving Office, submit arguments to that effect within two months from the date of the notification.	
r.29.4(b)	Where the receiving Office intends to issue a declaration under Art. 14(4) in respect of an element mentioned in Art. 11(1)(iii)(d) (requirement for a description) or Art. 11(1)(iii) (e) (requirement for a claim), the receiving Office must, in the notification referred to in r.29.4(a), invite the applicant to confirm in accordance with r.20.6(a) that the element is incorporated by reference under r.4.18. For the purposes of r.20.7(a)(i), the invitation sent to the applicant under this paragraph will be considered to be an invitation under r.20.3(a) (ii).	
r.29.4(c)	Rule 29.4(b) does not apply where the receiving Office has informed the International Bureau in accordance with r.20.8(a) of the incompatibility of r.20.3(a)(ii) and r.20.3(b)(ii) and r.20.6 with the national law applied by that office.	
WIPO	Reservations have been made and are still in force in respect of Cuba, Czech Republic, Germany, Indonesia, Italy, Korea, Mexico.	
Art. 25	If the application is considered withdrawn, the applicant can, within a prescribed two-month time limit (r.51.1), get the International Bureau to forward copies of any document in the file to any designated Office and, within the same time limit, enter the national phase in such a State, requesting review of the decision.	

32.1.8   Supply to the applicant of certified copies of the application as filed

r.21.2	On request and the payment of a fee, the receiving Office must supply the applicant with certified copies of the international application as filed and any corrections made thereto.	1491

32.2   Copying and transmittal of the international application by the receiving Office

32.2.1   National security provisions

Art. 27(8), r.22.1	National security restrictions are allowed under the PCT and may prevent the receiving Office from transmitting the application.	1492

32.2.2 *Number of copies of the application required – responsibility for their provision*

1493 Art. 12(1)	Three copies of the international application are necessary, a home copy, a record copy and a search copy.
r.11.1	Only one copy of the international application must be filed by the applicant unless the receiving Office prescribes the filing of two or three copies.
r.21.1(a)(b)	Where the receiving Office requires the filing of only one copy, this copy becomes the record copy (see r.20.2(b)) and the receiving Office is responsible for preparing the other two copies. In the case where the receiving Office requires the filing of two copies, the receiving Office is responsible for preparing the home copy.
r.21.1(c)	Where less than the prescribed number of copies are filed by the applicant, the receiving Office must still prepare the other copies but may charge the applicant a fee for doing so.
OJ	Only one copy is required by the EPO ([2006] O.J. 439). See also AppGuide, Annex C (EP).

32.2.3 *Retention of the home copy by the receiving Office*

1494 Art. 12(1)	The home copy is kept by the receiving Office.

32.2.4 *Transmittal by the receiving Office of the record copy to the International Bureau*

1495 Art. 12(1)	The record copy is transmitted by the receiving Office to the International Bureau.
r.22.1(a)	Where a filing date has been accorded (Art. 11(1)), the record copy is sent immediately by the receiving Office to the International Bureau unless any national security provisions prevent such transmission. It must be sent in time to reach the International Bureau by the expiration of the 13th month from the priority date (five days must be allowed if transmitted by mail).
Art. 12(2)	The record copy is considered the true copy of the international application.

32.2.5 *An international application is considered withdrawn if the International Bureau does not receive the record copy in time*

1496 r.22.1(b)	When the International Bureau has received a notification under r.20.2(c) (that an application number and filing date have been accorded to a new international application) but is not in possession of the record copy by 13 months from the priority date, it reminds the receiving Office to transmit it promptly.
r.22.1(c)	When the International Bureau has received a notification under r.20.2(c) but is not in possession of the record copy by 14 months from the priority date it notifies the applicant and receiving Office accordingly.
Art. 12(3), r.22.3	If the record copy is not received by the International Bureau within three months of the notification sent to the applicant and receiving Office under r.22.1(c), the international application is considered withdrawn.
r.22.1(d)(e)	After expiration of 14 months from the priority date the applicant may request the receiving Office to certify a copy of the application as being identical to the application as filed (free of charge) and transmit it himself to the International Bureau. The request may only be refused if (i) the copy is not identical to the application as filed; or (ii) national security provisions apply; or (iii) the receiving Office has already transmitted the record copy and the International Bureau has acknowledged receipt to the receiving Office.
r.22.1(f)	In these circumstances, the certified copy will be considered by the International Bureau to be the record copy unless or until it receives the genuine record copy.
r.22.1(g)	If, by the expiration of the time limit under Art. 22 (usually 30 months) the applicant has discharged his duties under that Article (i.e. entered the national or regional phase) but the designated Office has not been informed by the International Bureau that it has received the record copy, the designated Office informs the International Bureau who promptly informs the applicant and the receiving Office unless it is in possession of the record copy or it has already notified them at the 14-month stage under r.22.1(c). This rule also applies to national phase entry under Chapter II by virtue of r.76.5.

Art. 12(3), r.22.3	If the record copy is not received by the International Bureau within three months of the notification sent to the applicant and receiving Office under r.22.1(g), the international application is considered withdrawn.
r.24.2(c)	If the record copy is received by the International Bureau after the expiration of the time limit under r.22.3 (usually three months from notification at the 14-month stage) it notifies the applicant, receiving Office and International Searching Authority accordingly.
Art. 25	The applicant can, within a prescribed two-month time limit (r.51.1), ask the International Bureau to forward copies of any document in the file to any designated Office and, within the same time limit, enter the national phase in such a State, requesting review of the decision under Art. 12(3) that the application is considered withdrawn.

32.2.6   Procedure where the International Bureau receives the record copy in time – notification of receipt

r.24.2	(a)(b) On receiving the record copy, the International Bureau promptly notifies the applicant, the receiving Office and the International Searching Authority (unless it has declared it does not wish to be informed) of the fact and the date of the receipt, identifying the number of the application, the international filing date, the name of the applicant and the filing date of any priority document. The notification sent to the applicant also includes a list of designated States and, in the case of regional patent Offices, the States designated for such a regional patent.	1497

32.2.7   Transmittal by the receiving Office of a translation of the international application to the International Bureau

r.22.1(h)	Where the international application is to be published in the language of a translation provided for under r.12.3 (for the purposes of international search) or r.12.4 (filing language not a language of publication), that translation must be transmitted by the receiving Office to the International Bureau together with the record copy or, if the record copy has already been transmitted, promptly after receipt of the translation.	1498

32.2.8   Transmittal by the receiving Office of the search copy and any sequence listing in electronic form to the International Searching Authority

Art. 12(1)	The search copy is transmitted by the receiving Office to the International Search Authority.	1499
r.23.1(a)	If no translation is required under r.12.3(a) (for international search), and the search fee has been paid, the receiving Office will transmit the search copy to the International Searching Authority at the latest on the same day that the record copy is transmitted to the International Bureau. Where the search fee has not been paid, it will be transmitted promptly after the payment of that fee.	
r.23.1(b)	Where a translation is provided under r.12.3(a) (for international search), and the search fee has been paid, a copy of the translation and the request, together considered as the search copy, are transmitted to the International Searching Authority by the receiving Office. Where the search fee has not been paid, they are transmitted promptly after the payment of that fee.	
r.23.1(c)	Any sequence listing in electronic form submitted to the receiving Office rather than the International Searching Authority is forwarded by the receiving Office.	

32.2.9   Procedure of the International Searching Authority on receipt of the search copy

r.25	The International Searching Authority promptly notifies the International Bureau, the applicant and the receiving Office (unless it is itself the receiving Office) of the fact and the date of receipt of the search copy.	1500

32.2.10   Transmittal of documents relating to earlier search or classification

r.23*bis*.1(a)	The receiving Office shall transmit to the International Searching Authority, together with the search copy, any copy referred to in r.12*bis*.1(a) related to an earlier search in respect of which the applicant has made a request under r.4.12, provided that any such copy:	1501

(i) has been submitted by the applicant to the receiving Office together with the international application;

(ii) has been requested by the applicant to be prepared and transmitted by the receiving Office to that Authority; or

(iii) is available to the receiving Office in a form and manner acceptable to it, for example, from a digital library, in accordance with r.12*bis*.1(d).

r.23*bis*.1(b)   If it is not included in the copy of the results of the earlier search referred to in r.12*bis*.1(a), the receiving Office shall also transmit to the International Searching Authority, together with the search copy, a copy of the results of any earlier classification effected by that Office, if already available.

r.23*bis*.2(a)   For the purposes of r.41.2, where the international application claims the priority of one or more earlier applications filed with the same Office as that which is acting as the receiving Office and that Office has carried out an earlier search in respect of such an earlier application or has classified such earlier application, the receiving Office shall, subject to Art. 30(2)(a) as applicable by virtue of Art. 30(3) and r.23*bis*.2(b), (d) and (e), transmit to the International Searching Authority, together with the search copy, a copy of the results of any such earlier search, in whatever form (for example, in the form of a search report, a listing of cited prior art or an examination report) they are available to the Office, and a copy of the results of any such earlier classification effected by the Office, if already available. The receiving Office may, subject to Art. 30(2)(a) as applicable by virtue of Art. 30(3), also transmit to the International Searching Authority any further documents relating to such an earlier search which it considers useful to that Authority for the purposes of carrying out the international search.

r.23*bis*.2(b)   Notwithstanding r.23*bis*.2(a), a receiving Office may notify the International Bureau by April 14, 2016 that it may, on request of the applicant submitted together with the international application, decide not to transmit the results of an earlier search to the International Searching Authority. The International Bureau shall publish any notification under this provision in the Gazette.

WIPO   The relevant countries are Germany, Finland and Sweden.

r.23*bis*.2(c)   At the option of the receiving Office, r.23*bis*.2(a) shall apply *mutatis mutandis* where the international application claims the priority of one or more earlier applications filed with an Office different from the one which is acting as the receiving Office and that Office has carried out an earlier search in respect of such an earlier application or has classified such earlier application, and the results of any such earlier search or classification are available to the receiving Office in a form and manner acceptable to it, for example, from a digital library.

r.23*bis*.2(d)   r.23*bis*.2(a) and (c) shall not apply where the earlier search was carried out by the same International Searching Authority or by the same Office as that which is acting as the International Searching Authority, or where the receiving Office is aware that a copy of the earlier search or classification results is available to the International Searching Authority in a form and manner acceptable to it, for example, from a digital library.

r.23*bis*.2(e)   To the extent that, on October 14, 2015, the transmission of the copies referred to in r.23*bis*.2(a), or the transmission of such copies in a particular form, such as those referred to in r.23*bis*.2(a), without the authorization by the applicant is not compatible with the national law applied by the receiving Office, that paragraph shall not apply to the transmission of such copies, or to the transmission of such copies in the particular form concerned, in respect of any international application filed with that receiving Office for as long as such transmission without the authorization by the applicant continues not to be compatible with that law, provided that the said Office informs the International Bureau accordingly by April 14, 2016. The information received shall be promptly published by the International Bureau in the Gazette.

WIPO   The relevant countries are Australia, Czech Republic, Finland, Hungary, Israel, Japan, Norway, Singapore, Sweden and the US.

32.3   Examination of formal requirements under Art. 14(1)(a)

32.3.1   *Was the application signed properly?*

1502   Art. 14(1)(a)(i)   The receiving Office will check whether the application is signed as provided for in the Regulations (see r.4.15).

r.26.2*bis*(a)	Where there is more than one applicant, it is sufficient for the purposes of this check that it is signed by one of them.
Art. 14(1)(b)	Where there is a defect, see below for the procedure to be followed.

32.3.2   Are the correct indications concerning the applicant present?

Art. 14(1)(a)(ii)	The receiving Office will check whether the prescribed indications concerning the applicant are contained in the application (see r.4.4 and r.4.5).	1503
r.26.2*bis*(b)	Where there is more than one applicant, it is sufficient for the purposes of this check that indications required under r.4.5(a)(ii) (address) and (iii) (nationality and residence) are supplied in respect of one applicant who is entitled under r.19.1 to file an international application with the receiving Office.	
Art. 14(1)(b)	Where there is a defect, see below for the procedure to be followed.	

32.3.3   Does the application contain a title?

Art. 14(1)(a)(iii)	The receiving Office will check whether the application contains a title (see r.4.1(a)(ii)).	1504
Art. 14(1)(b)	Where there is a defect, see below for the procedure to be followed.	

32.3.4   Does the application contain an abstract?

Art. 14(1)(a)(iv)	The receiving Office will check whether the application contains an abstract (see Art. 3(2) and r.8).	1505
Art. 14(1)(b)	Where there is a defect, see below for the procedure to be followed.	

32.3.5   Are certain of the physical requirements met?

Art. 14(1)(a)(v)	The receiving Office will check whether the application meets the prescribed physical requirements, provided in the Regulations.	1506
r.26.3(a)	Where the application is filed in a language of publication, the receiving Office will check: (i) that the requirements of r.11 (physical requirements) have been met only to the extent that compliance is necessary for the purpose of reasonably uniform international publication; and (ii) that any translation filed under r.12.3 (for international search) complies with r.11 to the extent that compliance is necessary for the purpose of satisfactory reproduction.	
r.26.3(b)	Where the application is filed in a language which is not a language of publication, the receiving Office will check: (i) that the requirements of r.11 (physical requirements) have been met only to the extent that compliance is necessary for the purpose of satisfactory reproduction; and (ii) that any translation filed under r.12.3 (for international search) or 12.4 (for publication) and the drawings comply with r.11 to the extent that compliance is necessary for the purposes of uniform international publication.	
Art. 14(1)(b)	Where there is a defect, see below for the procedure to be followed.	

32.3.6   Invitation to correct defects where formal requirements of Art. 14(1)(a) are not met

Art. 14(1)(b)	If the receiving Office finds any of the defects listed in Art. 14(1)(a) it will invite the applicant to correct the application within the prescribed time limit.	1507
r.26.1	Such an invitation to correct must be issued by the receiving Office as soon as possible and preferably within one month of receiving the international application. In the invitation, the receiving Office will invite the applicant to furnish the required correction and give the applicant the opportunity to make observations within the time limit under r.26.2.	
r.26.2	The time limit referred to in r.26.1 is two months from the date of the invitation to correct. It can be extended by the receiving Office at any time before a decision is taken.	
r.12.2(c)	Any correction of a defect in the application submitted by the applicant under r.26 must be in the language in which the application is filed. Any correction under r.26 of a defect in a translation of the international application furnished under r.12.3 (for international search) or r.12.4 (for international publication) or any correction of a defect in a translation of the request furnished under r.26.3*ter*(c) must be in the language of the translation.	

r.26.3*bis*	The receiving Office is not required to issue an invitation to correct under Art. 14(1)(b) where the defect relates to physical requirements prescribed by r.11 and the application meets the minimum physical requirements specified in r.26.3(a) and (b).
Art. 14(1)(b)	If the applicant does not correct the application within the time limit set, the application will be considered withdrawn and the receiving Office will so declare.
r.26.5	The receiving Office decides whether any correction is submitted in due time and whether it is sufficient to avoid the application being considered withdrawn. However, no application should be considered withdrawn because the physical requirements (r.11) are not met to any extent other than to ensure reasonably uniform international publication.
Art. 25	If the application is considered withdrawn, the applicant can, within a prescribed two-month time limit (r.51.1), get the International Bureau to forward copies of any document in the file to any designated Office and, within the same time limit, enter the national phase in such a State, requesting review of the decision under Art. 14(1)(b) that the application is considered withdrawn.

32.3.7   *Format of any correction offered to the receiving Office*

1508 r.26.4	A correction of the request offered to the receiving Office may be stated in a letter addressed to that Office if the correction is of such a nature that it can be transferred from the letter to the request without adversely affecting the clarity and the direct reproducibility of the sheet onto which the correction is to be transferred; otherwise, and in the case of a correction of any other element of the international application, the applicant must submit a replacement sheet embodying the correction and the letter accompanying the replacement sheet must draw attention to the differences between the replacement sheet and the replaced sheet.

32.4   Examination of other formal requirements

32.4.1   *Are the abstract, request and text matter of the drawings in the correct language?*

1509 r.26.3*ter*(a)	Where the abstract or any text matter of the drawings is filed in a language which is different from the language of the description and the claims, the receiving Office will invite the applicant to furnish a translation of these sections into the language in which the application is to be published, unless: (a) a translation of the application is required under r.12.3(a) (for international search); or (b) the alternative language used is the language in which the application is to be published.
r.26.3*ter*(a)	The following rules apply mutandis mutatis: r.26.1 (issue of invitation to correct to be timely), r.26.2 (time limit for reply), r.26.3 (requirement for compliance with physical requirements is limited), r.26.3*bis* (only some objections to physical requirements possible), r.26.5 (receiving Office to decide whether time limit complied with and whether application to be considered withdrawn) and r.29.1 (actions of the receiving Office if the application is considered withdrawn).
r.26.3*ter*(c)	Where the request does not comply with r.12.1(c) (must be in a language of publication which is accepted by the receiving Office) the receiving Office will invite the applicant to supply a translation that does.
r.26.3*ter*(c)	The following rules apply mutandis mutatis: r.3 (regulations governing the form of the request), r.26.1 (issue of invitation to correct to be timely), r.26.2 (time limit for reply), r.26.5 (receiving Office to decide whether time limit complied with and whether application to be considered withdrawn) and r.29.1 (actions of the receiving Office if the application is considered withdrawn).
r.26.3*ter*(b)(d)	If on October 1, 1997, either of the above two paragraphs 26.3*ter*(a) and (c) is not compatible with the law applied by any receiving Office, it will not apply to that Office for as long as it is incompatible provided the Office informed the International Bureau by December 31, 1997. Such information is promptly published in the Gazette.
WIPO	Only the US has filed such reservations.
Art. 25	If the application is considered withdrawn, the applicant can, within a prescribed two-month time limit (r.51.1), get the International Bureau to forward copies of any document in the file to any designated Office and, within the same time limit, enter the national phase in such a State, requesting review of the decision.

32.4.2   Has any priority claim been made correctly?

r.26*bis*.2(a)
Where the receiving Office or, if the receiving Office fails to do so, the International Bureau, finds in relation to a priority claim: 1510
(i) that the international application has an international filing date which is later than the date on which the priority period expired and that a request for restoration of the right of priority under r.26*bis*.3 has not been submitted (see section 30.8.4);
(ii) that the priority claim does not comply with the requirements of r.4.10; or
(iii) that any indication in the priority claim is inconsistent with the corresponding indication appearing in the priority document;
the receiving Office or the International Bureau, as the case may be, will invite the applicant to correct the priority claim.
In the case referred to in r.26*bis*.2(a)(i), where the international filing date is within two months from the date on which the priority period expired, the receiving Office or the International Bureau, as the case may be, will also notify the applicant of the possibility of submitting a request for the restoration of the right of priority in accordance with r.26*bis*.3 (see section 30.8.4), unless the receiving Office has notified the International Bureau under r.26*bis*.3(j) of the incompatibility of r.26*bis*.3(a) to (i) with the national law applied by that Office.

r.26*bis*.2(b)
If the applicant does not, before the expiration of the time limit under r.26*bis*.1(a), submit a notice correcting the priority claim, that priority claim shall, subject to r.26*bis*.2(c), for the purposes of the procedure under the PCT, be considered not to have been made ("considered void") and the receiving Office or the International Bureau, as the case may be, will so declare and will inform the applicant accordingly. Any notice correcting the priority claim which is received before the receiving Office or the International Bureau, as the case may be, so declares and not later than one month after the expiration of that time limit is considered to have been received before the expiration of that time limit.

Comment
Time limits based on the priority date will be recalculated if the priority claim is considered void.

r.26*bis*.1(a)
The relevant time limit is the later of (a) four months from the international filing date; and (b) 16 months from the priority date or, where the correction or addition of a priority claim causes a change in the priority date, 16 months from the priority date as so changes, whichever expires first.

r.26*bis*.2(c)
However, a priority claim will not be considered void only because:
(i) the indication of the number of the earlier application referred to in r.4.10(a)(ii) is missing;
(ii) an indication in the priority claim is inconsistent with the corresponding indication appearing in the priority document; or
(iii) the international application has an international filing date which is later than the date on which the priority period expired, provided that the international filing date is within the period of two months from that date.

r.26*bis*.2(d)
Where the receiving Office or the International Bureau has made a declaration under r.26*bis*.2(b) or where the priority claim has not been considered void only because r.26*bis*.2(c) applies, the International Bureau will publish, together with the international application, information concerning the priority claim as prescribed by the Administrative Instructions, as well as any information submitted by the applicant concerning such priority claim which is received by the International Bureau prior to the completion of the technical preparations for international publication. Such information will be included in the communication under Art. 20 (to designated Offices) where the international application is not published by virtue of Art. 64(3) (only States not requiring publication are designated).

r.26*bis*.2(e)
Where the applicant wishes to correct or add a priority claim but the time limit under r.26*bis*.1 has expired, the applicant may, prior to the expiration of 30 months from the priority date and subject to the payment of a special fee whose amount shall be fixed in the Administrative Instructions, request the International Bureau to publish information concerning the matter, and the International Bureau will promptly publish such information.

AdminInst
See s.113(c). The fee is 50 Swiss francs plus 12 Swiss francs for each page in excess of one.

32.4.3   Is any declaration under r.4.17 correctly made?

1511 r.26*ter*.2(a)	If the receiving Office or International Bureau finds that one of the r.4.17 declarations is not worded properly or the declaration of inventorship referred to in r.4.17(iv) is not signed properly it will invite the applicant to correct the deficiency within 16 months from the priority date.
r.26*ter*.2(b)	Where a correction is received after the expiration of the time limit specified in r.26*ter*.1 (i.e. later than 16 months from the priority date and after the technical preparations for publication have been completed), the International Bureau will notify the applicant and proceed as set out in the Administrative Instructions.
AdminInst	See s.419(c) – the applicant is informed that he must make the correction in each designated State.
AppGuide	See International Phase, paragraph 6.049 – the declaration is published in the corrected form if received in time or otherwise in the uncorrected form.

32.4.4   Requirements relating to the submission of a translation

1512	See sections 30.9.3 and 30.9.4.

32.4.5   The role of the International Bureau and International Searching Authority in identifying defects

1513 r.28.1	If the International Bureau is of the opinion that the application contains a defect mentioned in Art. 14(1)(a)(i) (not signed), Art. 14(1)(a)(ii) (absence of information concerning the applicant) or Art. 14(1)(a)(v) (non-compliance with physical requirements) it will inform the receiving Office which will, unless in disagreement with the International Bureau, proceed under Art. 14(1)(b) and r.26 (invitation to correct).
r.29.3	If the International Bureau or the Searching Authority considers that the receiving Office should make a declaration under Art. 14(4) (application considered withdrawn due to defects found at a later stage which mean a filing date should not have been accorded) it will call the relevant facts to the attention of the receiving Office.

32.4.6   Procedure when the receiving Office declares that the application is considered withdrawn

1514 r.29.1	If the receiving Office declares that an international application is considered withdrawn because: (a) the applicant failed to correct certain defects (Art. 14(1)(b) and r.26.5); (b) the applicant failed to pay prescribed fees according to r.27.1(a) (Art. 14(3)(a)); (c) there is a later finding of non-compliance with Art. 11(1)(i)–(iii) (Art. 14(4)); (d) the applicant failed to furnish a translation required for search (r.12.3(d)) or publication (r.12.4(d)) or, where applicable, to pay a late furnishing fee; (e) the applicant failed to furnish the original of a document (r.92.4(g)(i)); the following consequences will ensue: (i) the receiving Office will transmit the record copy (unless already transmitted) and any corrections offered by the applicant to the International Bureau; (ii) (ii) the receiving Office will promptly notify the applicant and the International Bureau of the declaration and the International Bureau will subsequently notify all the designated Offices that have already been notified of their designation; (iii) the receiving Office will not transmit the search copy under r.23 or, if it has already done so, will inform the International Searching Authority of the declaration; (iv) the International Bureau is not required to notify the applicant of the receipt of the record copy; (v) no international publication of the international application will be effected if the notification of the said declaration transmitted by the receiving Office reaches the International Bureau before the technical preparations for international publication have been completed.
Art. 25	In these circumstances, the applicant can, within a prescribed two-month time limit (r.51.1), get the International Bureau to forward copies of any documents in the file to any designated Office and, within the same time limit, enter the national phase in such a State, requesting review of the decision.

Chapter 33: Drawing up the International Search Report

33.1 Authorities competent to carry out international search

33.1.1 What is an International Searching Authority?

Art. 16(1) The international search is carried out by an International Searching Authority which is a national Office or intergovernmental organisation set up to establish documentary search reports on prior art with respect to inventions which are the subject of applications.   1515

33.1.2 Requirements that must be met by an International Searching Authority

Art. 16(3)(c) Any prospective International Searching Authority must satisfy certain minimum requirements, particularly as to manpower and documentation, in order to be appointed and to remain appointed. They are prescribed by the Regulations.   1516

r.36 It must have access to the minimum documentation listed in r.34 in searchable form and at least 100 full-time employees technically qualified to carry out searches in the required technical fields and having the language facilities to understand at least those languages in which the minimum documentation is written or translated. It must also be appointed as an International Preliminary Examining Authority. It must also have in place a quality management system and internal review arrangements, in accordance with the common rules on international search.

33.1.3 Appointment of International Searching Authorities

Art. 16(3)(a)(b) A national Office or intergovernmental organisation satisfying the minimum requirements of Art. 16(3)(c) may be appointed as an International Searching Authorities by the Assembly. Such appointment is conditional on the consent of the national Office or intergovernmental organisation concerned and the conclusion of an agreement with the International Bureau, specifying rights and obligations, which is approved by the Assembly.   1517

OJ See [2017] O.J. A115 for details of the EPO agreement with the International Bureau.

Art. 16(3)(d) Each appointment is for a fixed (and extendable) period.

Art. 16(3)(e) Before deciding to appoint a new Authority, extend an appointment or allow an appointment to lapse, the Assembly must hear the relevant Office or organisation and seek advice from the Committee for Technical Co-operation (see Art. 56).

33.1.4 Receiving Offices specify the competent International Searching Authority or Authorities

Art. 16(2) In the case where more than one International Searching Authority has been appointed by the International Bureau, each receiving Office must state which International Searching Authority or Authorities are competent to search applications filed with it, in accordance with the provisions of the applicable agreements between the International Bureau and the International Searching Authorities under Art. 16(3)(b).   1518

r.35.1, r.35.2 The International Bureau publishes this information. In the case where more than one Searching Authority is competent, the receiving Office may leave the choice of which one to select with the applicant or may declare that one or more of them are competent for specific types of applications. In any event, where more than one Searching Authority is competent for a particular application, the applicant is allowed to choose which one to use.

r.35.3(a)(b) When the International Bureau acts as the receiving Office, any International Searching Authority is competent if it would have been competent had the application been filed with a receiving Office itself competent under r.19.1(a)(i) and (ii), (b) or (c) or r.19.2(i) (rules specifying which receiving Offices are competent for a particular national or resident). The applicant can choose where two or more are competent. The provisions r.35.1 and r.35.2 do not apply to the International Bureau as receiving Office.

AppGuide See Annex C (EP). When the EPO acts as receiving Office, the EPO is the only competent International Searching Authority.

AppGuide   See Annex C. Apart from the Contracting States to the EPC (see Protocol on Centralisation), some non-European receiving Offices have also given the EPO competence as an International Searching Authority, including Japan and the US.

33.1.5   *Limitations set by the EPO on its competence as International Searching Authority*

1519 EPC Art. 152   The EPO will act as an International Searching Authority in accordance with an agreement between the European Patent Organisation and the IB for applicants who are residents or nationals of an EPC Contracting State. The agreement may also provide that the EPO will also act for other applicants.

OJ   The EPO has, in principle, agreed to act as International Searching Authority for applications filed with any receiving Office that specifies it for this purpose according to Art. 3(1) and Annex A of the agreement between the EPO and the International Bureau (see [2017] O.J. A115).

33.2   The nature of an international search

33.2.1   *The purpose of an international search*

1520 Art. 15(1)(2)(4)   An international search is conducted on every international application in order to discover relevant prior art. The International Searching Authority must attempt to discover as much prior art as possible, consulting at least the documentation specified in the Regulations.

33.2.2   *Basis of the international search*

1521 Art. 15(3)   An international search is made on the basis of the claims, with due regard to the description and drawings (if any).

r.33.3   There is a particular emphasis on the inventive concept towards which the claims are directed. In so far as possible and reasonable, an international search should cover the entire subject matter to which the claims are directed or to which they might reasonably be expected to be directed after they have been amended.

Comment   The search is carried out on the basis of the search copy of the international application or translation thereof. There is no chance to amend the application before receipt of the International Search Report (though errors can be corrected under r.91.1). The first chance to amend is under Art. 19.

33.2.3   *Definition of relevant prior art*

1522 r.33.1(a)   Relevant prior art (within the meaning of Art. 15(2)) consists of everything which has been made available to the public, prior to the international filing date, anywhere in the world, by means of written disclosure (including drawings and other illustrations) and which is capable of being of assistance in determining whether the claimed invention is new and non-obvious.

r.33.1(b)   When a written disclosure (made available to the public on the same day as or later than the international filing date) refers to an oral disclosure, use, exhibition or other means whereby the contents of the written disclosure were made available to the public on a date before the filing date, that fact and the earlier date are separately mentioned in the search report.

r.33.1(c)   Any application or patent published on the same day or later than the international filing date having an earlier filing/priority date which would constitute relevant prior art had it been published before the international filing date is also mentioned in the search report.

33.2.4   *Fields to be covered*

1523 r.33.2(a)–(c)   The international search must cover all technical fields that may contain material pertinent to the invention, including arts analogous to the art in which the invention is classifiable (analogy being judged by what appears to be the necessary essential function or use of the invention as well as functions expressly indicated in the application).

r.33.2(d)	The international search should embrace all subject matter that is generally recognised as equivalent to the subject matter of the claimed invention for all or certain of its features.

33.2.5   *Minimum documentation*

r.34	This rule specifies the minimum documentation that must be consulted when drawing up the International Search Report.

1524

33.3   **The nature of an international-type search**

Art. 15(5)(a)	If the national law of a Contracting State so permits, an applicant who files a national application with the national Office of (or acting for) such a State may, subject to the conditions provided for in such law, request that an international-type search (a search similar to an international search) be carried out on that application.
Art. 15(5)(b)	If the national law of a Contracting State so permits, a national Office of or acting for such State may decide to subject a national application filed with it to an international-type search.
r.19.1(b)	Where the national Office of one State is acting as the competent receiving Office for nationals and residents of another State, the law of the latter State is relevant for the purposes of Art. 15(5).
Art. 15(5)(c)	Such an international-type search is carried out by a competent International Searching Authority appointed under Art. 16 which would have been competent for carrying out international search had the national application been an international application. The applicant must prepare a translation of the national application where necessary in a language prescribed for international applications which is acceptable to the International Searching Authority chosen. The national application (and translation when required) must be presented in the form prescribed for international applications.
OJ	According to Art. 8 and Annex G of the agreement between the EPO and the International Bureau ([2017] O.J. A115), the EPO will carry out international-type searches on behalf of certain national offices. See also Guidelines B-II, 4.5.
OJ	The fee for an international type search is € 1360 for first filings and € 2125 for all other cases (see decision of the President dated 17 January 2023, [2023] O.J. A3).

1525

33.4   **Procedure for conducting the search**

33.4.1   *General aspects*

Art. 17(1)	Procedure before the International Searching Authority is governed by the PCT, its Regulations and the appropriate agreement between the International Searching Authority and the International Bureau.

1526

33.4.2   *Check that title and abstract are present and appropriate*

r.37.1, r.38.1	If the international application does not contain a title (Art. 14(1)(a)(iii)) or an abstract (Art. 14(1)(a)(iv)) and the receiving Office has notified the International Searching Authority that it has invited the applicant to correct such a defect, the Searching Authority will proceed with its search unless, and until, it receives notification that the application is considered withdrawn.
r.37.2, r.38.2	If there is no title or there is no abstract and the International Searching Authority has not received such notification, or if the title does not comply with r.4.3 (short and precise) or the abstract does not comply with r.8, the International Searching Authority will establish a title or abstract (as appropriate) for itself in the language in which the application is to be published or, if a translation was transmitted by the receiving Office under r.23.1(b) (translation for the purposes of international search) and the International Searching Authority so wishes, in the language of that translation.
r.38.3	The applicant may, until the expiration of one month from the date of mailing of the International Search Report, submit to the International Searching Authority: (i) proposed modifications of the abstract; or

1527

(ii) where the abstract has been established by the Authority, proposed modifications of, or comments on, that abstract, or both modifications and comments; and the Authority will decide whether to modify the abstract accordingly. Where the Authority modifies the abstract, it will notify the modification to the International Bureau.

r.8.2

The best Figure to accompany the abstract is also chosen.

33.4.3   Check whether sequence listings have been provided properly

1528   r.13*ter*.1(a)

Where the international application contains disclosure of nucleotide and/or amino acid sequences that, pursuant to the Administrative Instructions, are required to be included in a sequence listing, the International Searching Authority may invite the applicant to furnish a sequence listing complying with the standard provided for in the Administrative Instructions unless such a listing is already available to it in a form, language and manner acceptable to it. A late furnishing fee may be charged by the International Searching Authority.

r.13*ter*.1(c)

The late-furnishing fee under r.13*ter*.1(a) is for the benefit of and fixed by the International Searching Authority but may not exceed 25 % of the international filing fee (excluding the fee for each sheet in excess of 30).

r.13*ter*.1(d)

If the required listing under r.13*ter*.1(a) is not furnished, or a required late-furnishing fee is not paid, the search only has to be carried out to the extent it is meaningfully possible without the sequence listing.

OJ

See Decision of the President dated 28 April 2011 ([2011] O.J. 372) for applications filed before 01 July 2022 and Decision of the President dated 09 December 2021 ([2021] O.J. A96) for applications filed on or after 01 July 2022. The EPO as International Searching Authority will ask for the provision of a sequence listing in electronic form complying with WIPO Standard ST.25 (or ST.26 for applications filed on or after 01 July 2022) if one is not available. A non-extendable time limit of one month is set. The EPO also charges a late-furnishing fee which is currently € 255 (see decision of the President dated 17 January 2023, [2023] O.J. A3).

r.13*ter*.1(e)

Any sequence listing submitted under r.13*ter*.1(a) or otherwise and not contained in the application as filed is not part of the application but the applicant may still amend the description in relation to a sequence listing pursuant to Art. 34(2)(b).

AppGuide

See International Phase, paragraph 7.011 – any sequence listing submitted by the applicant is made available by the International Bureau on publication of the application.

33.4.4   Determination as to whether a search is possible

1529   Art. 17(2)(a)(i)

If the International Searching Authority considers either:
(a) that the international application concerns subject matter which it is not required to search, that is:

r.39.1

(i) scientific and mathematical theories,
(ii) plant or animal varieties or essentially biological processes for the production of plants and animals, other than microbiological processes and the products thereof,
(iii) schemes, rules or methods of doing business, performing purely mental acts or playing games,
(iv) methods of treatment of the human or animal body by surgery or therapy, as well as diagnostic methods,
(v) mere presentations of information, or
(vi) computer programs (to the extent that the Authority is not equipped to search prior art concerning such programs)
and it decides therefore not to search it; or

Art. 17(2)(a)(ii)

(b) that the description, claims or drawings fail to comply with the prescribed requirements (see Art. 5 to Art. 7) to such an extent that a meaningful search cannot be carried out;
the International Searching Authority will so declare and notify the applicant and the International Bureau that no International Search Report will be established.

Art. 17(2)(b)

If this situation applies only to certain claims, the international search report will so indicate in respect of such claims but be established in the usual manner under Art. 18 for other claims.

OJ	See Art. 4 and Annex C of the agreement between the EPO and the International Bureau ([2017] O.J. A115). All subject matter specified in r.39.1 PCT is excluded to the extent that it would not be searched by the EPO Search Division in grant proceedings concerning a direct-filed European patent application.
OJ	See Notice from the EPO dated 01 March 2011 ([2011] O.J. 327). The EPO will now seek informal clarification from the applicant where the description, claims or drawings fail to comply with the prescribed requirements (e.g. claims lacking clarity and/or support) that a meaningful search cannot be carried for all or some of the claims. A two week time limit is set. There is no sanction for not responding. It is not possible to file amended claims at this stage of the procedure.
Guidelines	See Guidelines fort Search and Examination at the EPO acting as PCT Authority, B-VI-II – a meaningful search may not be possible, for instance, where the claims are broad and speculative compared to the disclosure.
AppGuide	See International Phase, paragraphs 7.013 and 7.014 – the lack of an International Search Report has no effect on the validity or continued processing of the international application.

33.4.5   Check for unity of invention

AdminInst	See s.206. The determination of unity by the International Searching Authority must be made in line with the instructions in Annex B of the Administrative Instructions.
Art. 17(3)(a)	If the International Searching Authority considers the international application lacks unity (see section 30.5.9), the applicant will be invited to pay additional fees.
r.40.1(i)(ii)	The invitation will specify the reasons why the application lacks unity and the amount of additional fees to be paid and specify a time limit of one month for payment.
AppGuide	See International Phase, paragraph 7.017 – the International Searching Authority may optionally annex to the invitation the preliminary search results for the first invention mentioned in the claims.
r.40.2(a)(b)	The amount of the additional fees is determined by the International Searching Authority and is payable direct to that Authority.
r.40.1(iii)	The invitation must also invite the payment of a protest fee (r.40.2(e)), where one is due (see below), within one month of the date of the invitation and indicate the amount to be paid.
r.40.2(c)(d)	The applicant may pay the additional fees under protest, i.e. accompanied by a statement explaining why the application complies with the requirement of unity or why the fees are excessive. The protest will be examined by a review body of the Searching Authority, which may include but may not be limited to the person responsible for the decision under protest. To the extent that the protest is found justified, the total or partial reimbursement of the additional fees will be ordered. If the applicant so requests, the text of the protest and subsequent decision will be notified to the designated Offices together with the search report. The applicant must submit any translation thereof with the furnishing of any translation of the international application required under Art. 22.
r.40.2(e)	The examination of such a protest may be made conditional by the International Searching Authority on the payment of a protest fee. Where the applicant has not furnished the protest fee within the one-month time limit of r.40.1(iii) the protest will be considered not to have been made and the International Searching Authority will so declare. The protest fee will be refunded if examination of the protest reveals that it was entirely justified.
Art. 17(3)(a)	The International Searching Authority will establish the International Search Report on those parts of the application which relate to the invention first mentioned in the claims (the main invention) and, in the case where additional fees have been paid within the prescribed time limit, on those parts of the application which relate to inventions for which fees have been paid.
Art. 17(3)(b)	Where additional fees are not paid, there are potential consequences in the national phase – see section 40.3.5.

1530

33.4.6   *Lack of unity where the EPO is the International Searching Authority*

1531 OJ	See [2017] O.J. A20. As from 01 April 2017 the EPO will send the applicant a copy of the partial search results and a copy of the partial written opinion concerning the first invention mentioned in the claims along with the invitation to pay additional search fees. The partial written opinion is for information only and no response is required or taken into account. See also Guidelines for Search and Examination by the EPO as a PCT authority, B-VII, 2).
EPC r.158(1)	An additional fee, equal to the international search fee, is payable in respect of each additional invention.
RRFArt. 2(1)(2)	The fee is € 1,775.
EPC r.158(3)	Where an additional fee has been paid under protest, the EPO will examine the protest in accordance with r.40.2(c) to (e) PCT, subject to payment of the prescribed protest fee. Further details concerning the procedure are determined by the President of the EPO.
OJ	See Decision of the President dated 09 June 2015 ([2015] O.J. A59). The protest is examined by a review panel consisting of three examiners, one of whom will chair the panel and another of whom will be the examiner who was responsible for issuing the invitation to pay additional fees.
RRFArt. 2(1)(21)	The protest fee is € 980.
G1/89	Headnote: "The agreement between the EPO and WIPO dated October 7, 1987, including the obligation under its Art. 2 for the EPO to be guided by the PCT guidelines for international search, is binding on the EPO when acting as an International Searching Authority and upon the Boards of Appeal of the EPO when deciding on protests against the charging of additional search fees under the provisions of Art. 17(3)(a) PCT. Consequently, as foreseen in these guidelines, an international application may, under Art. 17(3)(a) PCT, be considered not to comply with the requirement of unity of invention, not only a priori but also a posteriori, i.e. after taking prior art into consideration. However, such consideration has only the procedural effect of initiating the special procedure laid down in Art. 17 and r.40 PCT and is, therefore, not a 'substantive examination' in the normal sense of the term."
G2/89	Headnote: "The EPO in its function as an International Searching Authority may, pursuant to Art. 17(3)(a) PCT, request a further search fee where the international application is considered to lack unity a posteriori."
Guidelines	See Guidelines for Search and Examination at the EPO as a PCT Authority, B-VII, 7. The protest is first checked for admissibility by a formalities officer (protest fee paid, reasoned statement). The review panel will become the Examinig Division on regional phase entry.

33.4.7   *Taking into account results of an earlier search or search opinion*

1532 r.41.1	Where the applicant has, under r.4.12, requested the International Searching Authority to take into account the results of an earlier search and has complied with r.12*bis*.1 and: (i) the earlier search was carried out by the same International Searching Authority, or by the same office as that which is acting as the International Searching Authority, the International Searching Authority shall, to the extent possible, take those results into account in carrying out the international search; (ii) the earlier search was carried out by another International Searching Authority, or by an office other than that which is acting as the International Searching Authority, the International Searching Authority may take those results into account in carrying out the international search.
r.12*bis*.1(a)	See section 30.3.18 for what should to be submitted with the application.
r.23*bis*.1(a)	See section 32.2.10 for the duty of the receiving Office in forwarding documents submitted with the application.
r.12*bis*.2(a)	The International Searching Authority may, subject to r.12*bis*.2(b) and (c), invite the applicant to furnish to it, within a time limit which shall be reasonable under the circumstances: (i) a copy of the earlier application concerned; (ii) where the earlier application is in a language which is not accepted by the International Searching Authority, a translation of the earlier application into a language which is accepted by that Authority;

(iii) where the results of the earlier search are in a language which is not accepted by the International Searching Authority, a translation of those results into a language which is accepted by that Authority;

(iv) a copy of any document cited in the results of the earlier search.

r.12*bis*.2(b) Where the earlier search was carried out by the same International Searching Authority, or by the same Office as that which is acting as the International Searching Authority, or where a copy or translation referred to in r.12*bis*.2(a) is available to the International Searching Authority in a form and manner acceptable to it, for example, from a digital library, or in the form of the priority document, no copy or translation referred to in r.12*bis*.2(a) shall be required to be submitted under that paragraph.

r.12*bis*.2(c) Where the request contains a statement under Rule 4.12(ii) to the effect that the international application is the same, or substantially the same, as the application in respect of which the earlier search was carried out, or that the international application is the same, or substantially the same, as that earlier application except that it is filed in a different language, no copy or translation referred to in r.12*bis*.2(a)(i) and (ii) shall be required to be submitted under those paragraphs.

OJ See the Decision of the President of the EPO dated 21 February 2014 ([2014] O.J. A30). The EPO refunds part of the international search fee if it can base the international search on an earlier application from which priority is claimed and which was searched by the EPO. The amount refunded depends on whether full or partial use is made of the previous search report, and whether the previous search is accompanied by a written opinion or not.

r.41.2(a) Where the international application claims the priority of one or more earlier applications in respect of which an earlier search has been carried out by the same International Searching Authority, or by the same Office as that which is acting as the International Searching Authority, the International Searching Authority shall, to the extent possible, take the results of any such earlier search into account in carrying out the international search.

r.42.2(b) Where the receiving Office has transmitted to the International Searching Authority a copy of the results of any earlier search or of any earlier classification under r.23*bis*.2(a) or (c), or where such a copy is available to the International Searching Authority in a form and manner acceptable to it, for example, from a digital library, the International Searching Authority may take those results into account in carrying out the international search.

OJ For applicants using the "PCT Direct" service, the EPO acting as International Searching Authority may take into account informal comments made by the applicant regarding objections made by the EPO when drawing up a written opinion for an application from which the international application claims priority. See section 30.3.18.

33.4.8 *Taking into account the rectifications of obvious mistakes*

r.43.6*bis* The International Searching Authority will take into account the rectification of an ob-   1533
vious mistake that is authorized under r.91.1 for the purposes of the international search unless it is authorised or notified after work has started on drawing up the International Search Report.

33.4.9 *Taking into account the the late filing of missing parts or the late correction of erroneously filed elements or parts*

r.40*bis*.1 The International Searching Authority may invite the applicant to pay additional fees   1534
where the fact that a missing part or a correct element or part:

(i) is included in the international application under r.20.5(c) or r.20.5*bis*(c), respectively; or

(ii) is considered, under r.20.5(d) or r.20.5*bis*(d), respectively, to have been contained in the international application on the date on which one or more elements referred to in Art. 11(1) were first received by the receiving Office;

is notified to that Authority only after it has begun to draw up the international search report. The invitation shall invite the applicant to pay the additional fees within one month from the date of the invitation and indicate the amount of those fees to be paid. The amount of the additional fees shall be determined by the International Searching Authority but shall not exceed the search fee; the additional fees shall be payable directly to that Authority. Provided any such additional fees have been paid within the prescribed time limit, the International Searching Authority shall establish the international search report on the international application including any such missing part or any such correct element or part.

Comment   In adopting new r.20.5*bis* (corretion of erroneously filed elements and parts, July 2020), the Assembly agreed that, in the case of incorporation by reference of a correct element or part under r.20.5*bis*(d), the International Searching Authority would only be required to carry out the international search on the basis of the international application ('the claims, with due regard to the description and the drawings, if any') including the correct element or part incorporated by reference, and would not need to take into account any erroneously filed element or part which, pursuant to r.20.5*bis*(d), remained in the application. The Assembly further agreed that, in the case referred to in r.40*bis*.1, where no additional fees were paid within the prescribed time limit, the International Searching Authority would only be required to carry out the international search on the basis of the international application ('the claims, with due regard to the description and the drawings, if any') including the erroneously filed element or part, and would not need to take into account any correct element or part included in the application under r.20.5*bis*(c) or incorporated by reference under r.20.5*bis*(d).

Guidelines   See Guidelines for Search and Examination at the EPO as a PCT Authority, A-III, 5.1 and B-III, 2.3.3. The EPO acting as ISA only requires the payment of an additional search fee in the case of the late correction of an erroneously filed part and not in the case where a missing part is added. Note that the EPO notification of incompatibility in respect of corrected parts/elements filed using incorporation by reference does not apply when it acts as International Searching Authority. The extra fee charged by the EPO if it has already started to draw up the International Search Report is equal to the international search fee. In this case, the EPO also completes the search report it had started on the basis of the uncorrected application which is just for the information of the applicant.

33.5 The International Search Report, the written opinion and the International Preliminary Report on Patentability

33.5.1 *Time limit for establishing the search report*

1535   Art. 18(1), r.42   The search report (or the declaration under Art. 17(2)(a) – inability to establish a search report) must be established within a prescribed time limit, which is the later of three months from the receipt of the search copy by the International Searching Authority or nine months from the priority date.

33.5.2 *Form of the search report*

1536   Art. 18(1)   The search report must be established in the prescribed form.

r.43.1   It must indicate the name of the International Searching Authority, the international application number, the name of the applicant and the international filing date.

r.43.2   It must be dated and also indicate the date on which the international search report was actually completed and the filing date of any earlier application whose priority is claimed (or the earliest in the case where there is more than one).

r.43.3   It must contain the classification of the subject matter, at least according to the International Patent Classification (as determined by the International Searching Authority).

OJ   See Art. 6 of the agreement between the EPO and the International Bureau ([2017] O.J. A115). The EPO indicates solely the International Patent Classification.

r.43.4   Every International Search Report and any declaration made under Art. 17(2)(a) must be in the language in which the international application to which it relates is to be published, provided that:

(i) if a translation of the international application into another language was transmitted under r.23.1(b) (for the purposes of international search) and the International Searching Authority so wishes, the International Search Report and any declaration made under Art. 17(2)(a) may be in the language of that translation; or

(ii) if the international application is to be published in the language of a translation furnished under r.12.4 (for international publication), which is not accepted by the International Searching Authority, and that Authority so wishes, the International Search Report and any declaration made under Art. 17(2)(a) may be in a language which is both a language accepted by that Authority and a language of publication referred to in r.48.3(a).

r.43.5	It must cite the documents considered to be relevant in the form regulated by the Administrative Instructions and specially indicate citations of particular relevance. Citations which are not relevant to all the claims should be cited in relation to the claim or claims to which they are relevant. Where only certain passages of a document are relevant, or particularly relevant, they should be identified where practicable (e.g. by page, column or line numbers).
AdminInst	See s.505. The indication "X" is used where a document prejudices the novelty or inventive step of a claim on its own and "Y" where it prejudices the novelty or inventive step of a claim in combination with another document in the same category, the combination being obvious to the skilled person. See s.507 for the meaning of other indications used.
r.43.6	It must list the classification identification of the fields searched. The International Searching Authority must publish the name of the classification used if it is other than the International Patent Classification. If the international search extended to patents, inventors' certificates, utility certificates, utility models, patents or certificates of addition, inventors' certificates of addition, utility certificates of addition, or published applications for any of these (definitions in Art. 2(ii) do not apply here) which relate to a State, period or language outside the scope of the minimum documentation (see r.34), the search report must, where practicable, identify the kinds of documents, States, periods and languages to which it is extended. If an electronic database was used for any part of the search, the search report may indicate its name and, where considered useful to others and practicable, the search terms used.
r.43.6*bis*	The International Search Report will indicate whether the rectification of an obvious mistake has been taken into account or where appropriate, indicate that authorisation or notification was received too late. If, in the latter case (notification received too late), it is not possible to include such comments in the International Search Report, the International Searching Authority will notify the International Bureau accordingly and the International Bureau will proceed as provided for in the Administrative Instructions.
r.43.7	It must, where appropriate, indicate the fact that the applicant has paid additional fees in response to a unity objection. Where only part of the application has been searched (see Art. 17(3)(a)), the search report must indicate that part.
r.43.8	It must indicate the name of the responsible Officer who drew up the report.
r.43.9	It must not contain any matter other than that specified in rr.33.1(b) (written account of an oral disclosure or prior use), 33.1(c) (intervening publication), 43.1, 43.2, 43.3, 43.5, 43.6, 43.7, 43.8, 44.2 (approval of the title and abstract) and Art. 17(2)(b) (claims not searchable) and any matter specified by the Administrative Instructions. No expressions of opinion, reasoning, arguments or explanations may be included, by permission of the Administrative Instructions or otherwise.
r.43.10	It must conform to the physical requirements indicated in the Administrative Instructions.
r.44.2	It must state that the title and abstract as submitted by the applicant are approved or be accompanied by the text of the title and/or abstract as established by the International Searching Authority (see r.37 and r.38 above).

33.5.3   Written opinion of the International Searching Authority

1537 r.43*bis*.1(a)	The International Searching Authority will, subject to r.69.1(b-*bis*) (search and preliminary examination to start at the same time), at the same time that it establishes the search report (or declaration that no search report is possible under Art. 17(2)(a)), establish a written opinion as to whether the claimed invention appears to be novel, to involve an inventive step (be non-obvious) and to be industrially applicable and whether the international application complies with the requirements of the PCT and its Regulations in so far as checked. The written opinion may be accompanied by other observations provided for in the Regulations.
r.69.1(b-bis)	However, where the International Searching and Preliminary Examining Authorities are part of the same Office/organisation, and that Office/organisation wants to start international preliminary examination at the same time as carrying out the international search and the conditions set out in Art. 34(2)(c)(i)–(iii) are met (the invention is novel, inventive and industrially applicable, the application complies with the provisions of the PCT and Regulations checked and no supplementary observations are to be made) no written opinion according to r.43*bis*.1 is necessary.
r.43*bis*.1(b)	When establishing the written opinion Art. 33(2)–(6), Art. 35(2) and Art. 35(3) and rr.43.4, 43.6*bis*, 64, 65, 66.1(e), 66.7, 67, 70.2(b) and (d), 70.3, 70.4(ii), 70.5(a), 70.6 to 70.10, 70.12, 70.14 and 70.15(a) apply mutatis mutandis (these Articles and rules establish the procedure for carrying out international preliminary examination).
r.43*bis*.1(c)	The written opinion must contain a notification informing the applicant that, if a demand for international preliminary examination is made, the written opinion will, under r.66.1*bis*(a), but subject to r.66.1*bis*(b), be considered to be a written opinion of the International Preliminary Examining Authority for the purposes of r.66.2(a), in which case the applicant is invited to submit to that Authority, before the expiration of the r.54*bis*.1(a) time limit (time limit for making a demand), a written reply together, where appropriate, with amendments.
r.66.1*bis*(a)(b)	The written opinion of the International Searching Authority is considered to be a written opinion of the International Preliminary Examining Authority unless, where the two Authorities are different, the International Preliminary Examining Authority notifies the International Bureau otherwise, in respect of one or more International Searching Authorities.
WIPO	The EPO has filed reservations. It only considers the written opinion of the ISA to be a written opinion of the IPEA when it acted as ISA.
AppGuide	See International Phase, paragraph 7.030. When the International Searching Authority notifies the International Search Report and the written opinion to the applicant (form PCT/ISA/220) it invites the applicant to send informal comments on the written opinion to the International Bureau and indicates they will be sent by the IB to the designated Offices unless International Preliminary Examination is to be conducted. Such comments are also made available by the International Bureau as part of the application file on international publication. The written opinion itself (form PCT/ISA/237) invites the applicant to file a response to the written opinion with the International Preliminary Examining Authority, if the written opinion is to be considered as the first written opinion of the IPEA, within the time limit for filing a demand.

33.5.4   Transmittal of the search report and written opinion to the applicant and the International Bureau

1538 Art. 18(2), r.44.1	The search report (or the declaration that some or all the claims were unsearched under Art. 17(2)(a)) and written opinion must be submitted by the International Searching Authority immediately, and on the same day, to both the applicant and the International Bureau.

33.5.5   Preparation by the International Bureau of an International Preliminary Report on Patentability (IPRP) and transmission to the applicant

r.44*bis*.1 — Unless an International Preliminary Examination Report has been or is to be established, i.e. unless a demand has been filed, the International Bureau will issue a report on behalf of the International Searching Authority having the same contents as the written opinion established under r.43*bis*.1. The report will be called "International Preliminary Report on Patentability" and will contain an indication that it is issued under r.44*bis* by the International Bureau on behalf of the International Searching Authority. A copy will promptly be transmitted to the applicant by the International Bureau.   **1539**

33.5.6   Translation of the search report by the International Bureau

Art. 18(3), r.45 — The International Search Report (or the declaration that some or all the claims were unsearched under Art. 17(2)(a)) is translated by (or under the responsibility of) the International Bureau into English when in another language.   **1540**

33.5.7   Translation of the written opinion or Preliminary Report on Patentability by the International Bureau and communication of the report and its translation to designated Offices

r.44*bis*.2 — Where an International Preliminary Report on Patentability has been issued by the International Bureau under r.44*bis*.1, the International Bureau will communicate it to each designated Office in accordance with r.93*bis*.1 (on request and at the requested time) but not before the expiration of 30 months from the priority date. However, a copy of the written opinion of the International Searching Authority may be communicated earlier at the request of the applicant or a designated Office where the applicant has requested early national processing under Art. 23(2).   **1541**

AppGuide — See International Phase, paragraph 7.031 – informal comments on the written opinion filed by the applicant are also communicated to the designated Offices along with the IPRP.

r.44*bis*.3(a) — Any designated State may, where an International Preliminary Report on Patentability has been issued by the International Bureau under r.44*bis*.1 in a language other than the official language, or one of the official languages, of its national Office, require a translation of the report into English. Any such requirement must be notified to the International Bureau, and will be promptly published in the Gazette.

r.44*bis*.3(b)(c) — Such a translation is prepared by or under the responsibility of the International Bureau and will be transmitted to the applicant and any interested designated Office at the same time as it communicates the International Preliminary Report on Patentability.

r.44*bis*.3(d) — In the case referred to in r.44*bis*.2(b) (supply of a copy of the written opinion of the International Searching Authority on early national processing), the written opinion will, upon request of the designated Office concerned, be translated by or under the responsibility of the International Bureau into English. Such a translation will be transmitted within two months of the request for translation, simultaneously to the interested designated Office and to the applicant.

r.44*bis*.4 — The applicant may make written observations as to the correctness of the translations referred to in r.44*bis*.3(b) and (d) and must send a copy of such observations to each of the interested designated Offices and to the International Bureau.

r.62*bis* — The International Bureau will also translate the written opinion of the International Searching Authority into English when requested to do so by the International Preliminary Examining Authority. Copies of the translation will be sent to the applicant and the relevant Authority at the same time and within two months of the receipt of the request for translation. The applicant may make written observations on the correctness of the translation and must send a copy of such observations to the International Bureau and International Preliminary Examining Authority.

33.5.8   *Requests by a receiving Office or the applicant for copies of cited documents*

1542   Art. 20(3), r.44.3   The International Searching Authority will supply copies of documents cited in an International Search Report when so requested by a designated Office or the applicant at any time during seven years from the international filing date of the corresponding application. A fee for preparing and mailing the copies may be requested, the amount of which is fixed in the agreement under Art. 16(3)(b) between the International Searching Authority and the International Bureau. The Searching Authority may use an agency to perform this *function* if it wishes.

33.5.9   *Publication of the search report*

1543   Art. 21(3)   The international search report or the declaration referred to in Art. 17(2)(a) (no international search report to be established) is published as described in the Regulations. See section 36.5.5.

33.5.10   *Public availability of the written opinion*

1544   r.44*ter*   See section 45.2.

Chapter 34: Supplementary International Searches

34.1 Filing a request for a supplementary international search

34.1.1 Time limit

r.45*bis*.1(a)   A request for a supplementary international search must be filed prior to the expiration   1545
of 22 months from the priority date.

34.1.2 Where must the request be filed and what language should be used?

r.45*bis*.1(b)
r.92.2(d)

The request must be filed with the International Bureau.   1546
Before 01 July 2016, correspondence with the International Bureau had to be in English
or French but may now also be in any other language permitted by the Administrative
Instructions.

AdminInst

See s.104. If the language of the application is English or French then that language should
be used for any letter – otherwise the applicant may choose either of the two languages.
Communications sent using ePCT may be in any of English, French or the language of
publication or any other language permitted by the Director General.

34.1.3 Can more than one request be filed?

r.45*bis*.1(a)   Requests may be made in respect of one or more competent International Searching   1547
Authorities.

34.1.4 Competent International Searching Authority

r.45*bis*.9(a)(b)

Any International Searching Authority which has stated its willingness to conduct sup-   1548
plementary international searches in its agreement with the International Bureau pursuant
to Art. 16(3)(b) is competent, subject to any limitations and conditions set out in that
agreement. The Authority carrying out the international search pursuant to Art. 16(1),
however, is not competent to carry out a supplementary international search.

r.45*bis*.9(c)

Limitations on its competency imposed by an International Searching Authority under
r.45*bis*.9(a) may, for example, include limitations as to the subject matter for which supplementary international searches will be carried out, other than limitations under Art. 17(2)
as applicable by virtue of r.45*bis*.5(c), limitations as to the total number of supplementary
international searches which will be carried out in a given period and limitations to the
effect that the supplementary international searches will not extend to any claim beyond
a certain number of claims.

OJ

See Art. 3(4) and Annex B of the agreement between the EPO and the International Bureau ([2017] O.J. A115). The EPO requires that the application is in English, French or
German or that a translation into one of these languages is provided.

34.1.5 Content of the request

r.45*bis*.1(b)(i)(ii)

The supplementary search request must indicate: 1549
(1) the name and address of the applicant;
(2) the name and address of any agent;
(3) the title of the invention;
(4) the international filing date;
(5) the international application number; and
(6) the International Searching Authority that is to carry out the supplementary search.

AppGuide

See International Phase, paragraph 8.016 – in the case of multiple applicants, only one of
them needs to be indicated.

r.45*bis*.1(b)(iii)

Where the international application was filed in a language which is not accepted the
International Searching Authority which is to carry out the supplementary search the
request must indicate whether any translation furnished to the receiving Office under
r.12.3 or r.12.4 is to form the basis of the supplementary international search.

r.45*bis*.1(c)(i)	If neither the language in which the international application was filed, nor the language of any translation submitted pursuant to r.12.3 or r.12.4 is accepted by the International Searching Authority which is to carry out the supplementary search, the request must be accompanied by a translation of the international application into a language which is accepted by that Authority.
OJ	See Art. 3(4) and Annex B of the agreement between the EPO and WIPO ([2017] O.J. A115). The EPO will only accept applications filed in or translated into English, French or German.
r.45*bis*.1(c)(ii)	If the International Searching Authority which is to carry out the supplementary search requires a copy of a sequence listing in electronic form complying with the standard provided for in the Administrative Instructions, it should preferably be filed with the request.
r.45*bis*.1(d)	Where the International Searching Authority has found that the international application does not comply with the requirement of unity of invention, the supplementary search request may contain an indication of the wish of the applicant to limit the supplementary international search to one of the inventions as identified by the International Searching Authority other than the main invention referred to in Art. 17(3)(a).
r.92.1	As with all documents submitted in respect of an international patent application, the request must be signed by the applicant (or agent, r.90.3(a)).

34.1.6 Requirement to pay fees

1550 r.45*bis*.3(a)	A supplementary search fee may be charged for the benefit of the International Searching Authority that is carrying out the supplementary international search.
r.45*bis*.2(a)	A supplementary search handling fee must be paid for the benefit of the International Bureau.
r.45*bis*.3(b)	The supplementary search fee is collected by the International Bureau and r.16.1(b) to (e) (collection of the search fee by the receiving Office) apply mutatis mutandis.
r.45*bis*.2(b)	The supplementary search handling fee must be paid in the currency specified in the Schedule of Fees, in the amount specified there, or else in any other currency accepted by the International Bureau.
SoF	The supplementary search handling fee is currently 200 Swiss francs. It is reduced by 90 % when the applicant (or all the applicants where there are 2 or more) is/are from certain low per capita income countries or a UN least developed country.
AppGuide	See International Phase, paragraph 8.031 – both fees must be paid in Swiss francs.
r.45*bis*.2(c)	The supplementary search handling fee must be paid to the International Bureau within one month from the date of receipt of the supplementary search request. The amount payable is the amount applicable on the date of payment.
r.45*bis*.3(c)	The supplementary search fee must also be paid to the International Bureau within one month from the date of receipt of the supplementary search request. The amount payable is the amount applicable on the date of payment.
r.45*bis*.2(d)	The International Bureau will refund the supplementary search handling fee to the applicant if, before the documents referred to in r.45*bis*.4(e)(i) to (iv) are transmitted to the Authority specified for supplementary search, the international application is withdrawn or considered withdrawn, or the supplementary search request is withdrawn or considered not to have been submitted under r.45*bis*.1(e).
r.45*bis*.3(d)	The International Bureau will refund the supplementary search fee to the applicant if, before the documents referred to in r.45*bis*.4(e)(i) to (iv) are transmitted to the Authority specified for supplementary search, the international application is withdrawn or considered withdrawn, or the supplementary search request is withdrawn or considered not to have been submitted under r.45*bis*.1(e) or r.45*bis*.4(d).
r.45*bis*.3(e)	The Authority specified for supplementary search shall, to the extent and under the conditions provided for in the applicable agreement under Art. 16(3)(b), refund the supplementary search fee if, before it has started the supplementary international search in accordance with r.45*bis*.5(a), the supplementary search request is considered not to have been submitted under r.45*bis*.5(g).
RRFArt. 2(1)(2)	The supplementary search fee is € 1,775 when the EPO conducts the supplementary international search.

OJ	See Art. 5 and Annex D of the agreement between the EPO and the International Bureau ([2017] O.J. A115). The supplementary search fee is refunded in full if the supplementary search request is considered not to have been submitted under r.45*bis*.5(g) (search entirely excluded and supplementary search request deemed not filed) before the search has started. The fee is also refunded in full if, after receipt of the documents specified in r.45*bis*.4(e)(i)–(iv) (documents transmitted by the International Bureau) but before it has started the supplementary international search in accordance with r.45*bis*.5(a), the EPO is notified of the withdrawal of the international application or the supplementary search request.
OJ	Where the EPO acts as Supplementary International Searching Authority for an applicant who is (a) a natural person, who is a national and resident of a country which is not an EPC contracting state, and which, on the date on which the supplementary international search fee is paid, is classified by the World Bank as a low-income or lower-middle-income economy; or (b) a natural or legal person who, within the meaning of r.18 PCT, is a national and resident of a state in which a validation agreement with the European Patent Organisation is in force; then the supplementary international search fee is reduced by 75 % (Decision of the Administrative Council dated 12 December 2019, [2020] O.J. A4; Annex D of the agreement between the EPO and the International Bureau, [2020] O.J. A35). If there are several applicants then each must satisfy the relevant criterion. See [2022] O.J. A72 for the current list of low-income and lower-middle-income countries.

34.1.7   *Situations under which the request is considered not to have been submitted*

r.45*bis*.1(e)	The supplementary search request shall be considered not to have been submitted, and the International Bureau shall so declare: (i) if it is received after the expiration of the time limit referred to in r.45*bis*.1(a); or (ii) if the Authority specified for supplementary search has not stated, in the applicable agreement under Art. 16(3)(b), its preparedness to carry out such searches or is not competent to do so under r.45*bis*.9(b).	1551

34.2   Processing of the request for supplementary international search by the International Bureau

34.2.1   *Checking of the supplementary search request*

r.45*bis*.4(a)	Promptly after receipt of a supplementary search request, the International Bureau will check whether it complies with the requirements of: (i) r.45*bis*.1(b) (mandatory content of the request); (ii) r.45*bis*.1(c)(i) (translation, where necessary).	1552

34.2.2   *Correction of defects and late payment of fees*

r.45*bis*.4(a)	If the International Bureau notes a defect in the request for supplementary search, it will invite the applicant to correct it within a time limit of one month from the date of the invitation.	1553
r.45*bis*.4(b)(c)	Where, by the time they are due under r.45*bis*.2(c) and r.45*bis*.3(c), the International Bureau finds that the supplementary search handling fee and the supplementary search fee have not been paid in full, it will invite the applicant to pay to it the amount required to cover those fees, together with a late payment fee, within a time limit of one month from the date of the invitation. The late payment fee, which is for the benefit of the International Bureau, is 50 % of the supplementary search handling fee.	
r.45*bis*.4(d)	If the applicant does not furnish the required correction or does not pay the full amount of the fees due, including the late payment fee, before the expiration of the time limit applicable under r.45*bis*.4(a) or r.45*bis*.4(b), respectively, the supplementary search request will be considered not to have been submitted and the International Bureau will so declare and inform the applicant accordingly.	

34.2.3   Transmittal to International Searching Authority

1554   r.45*bis*.4(e)   If the International Bureau finds that the requirements of r.45*bis*.1(b) (mandatory content of the request), r.45*bis*.1(c)(i) (translation where necessary), r.45*bis*.2(c) (payment of the supplementary search handling fee) and r.45*bis*.3(c) (payment of the supplementary search fee) have been complied with, the International Bureau will promptly, but not before the date of receipt by it of the International Search Report or the expiration of 17 months from the priority date, whichever occurs first, transmit to the Authority specified for supplementary search a copy of each of the following:
(i) the supplementary search request;
(ii) the international application;
(iii) any sequence listing furnished under r.45*bis*.1(c)(ii); and
(iv) any translation furnished under r.12.3, r.12.4 or r.45*bis*.1(c)(i) which is to be used as the basis of the supplementary international search;
and, at the same time, or promptly after their later receipt by the International Bureau:
(v) the International Search Report and the written opinion established under r.43*bis*.1;
(vi) any invitation by the International Searching Authority to pay additional fees referred to in Art. 17(3)(a); and
(vii) any protest by the applicant under r.40.2(c) and the decision thereon by the review body constituted in the framework of the International Searching Authority.

   r.45*bis*.4(f)   Upon request of the Authority specified for supplementary search, the written opinion referred to in r.45*bis*(e)(v) will, when not in English or in a language accepted by that Authority, be translated into English by or under the responsibility of the International Bureau. The International Bureau will transmit a copy of the translation to that Authority within two months from the date of receipt of the request for translation, and shall at the same time transmit a copy to the applicant.

34.3   Procedure for carrying out the supplementary international search

34.3.1   Start date for the search

1555   r.45*bis*.5(a)   The Authority specified for supplementary search will start the supplementary international search promptly after receipt of the documents transmitted by the International Bureau pursuant to r.45*bis*.4(e)(i) to (iv), although it may optionally delay the start of the search until it has also received the documents specified in r.45*bis*.4(e)(v) (International Search Report and written opinion) or until the expiration of 22 months from the priority date, whichever occurs first.

   OJ   See Annex B of the agreement between the EPO and the International Bureau ([2017] O.J. A115). The EPO will only start the search, where applicable, if a copy of a sequence listing in electronic form complying with the standard provided for in the Administrative Instructions is furnished under r.45*bis*.1(c)(ii) and transmitted to it under r.45*bis*.4(e)(iii).

34.3.2   Basis for the search

1556   r.45*bis*.5(b)   The supplementary international search is carried out on the basis of the international application as filed, or of a translation referred to in r.45*bis*.1(b)(iii) or r.45*bis*.1(c)(i), taking due account of the International Search Report and the written opinion established under r.43*bis*.1 where they are available to the Authority specified for supplementary search before it starts the search. Where the supplementary search request contains an indication under r.45*bis*.1(d) (limitation to one invention in the case of a lack of unity), the supplementary international search may be limited to the invention specified by the applicant under r.45*bis*.1(d) and those parts of the international application which relate to that invention.

   Guidelines   Note that no amendments made under Art. 19 or Art. 34 are taken into account (Guidelines for Search and Examination at the EPO as PCT Authority, B-XII,3).

34.3.3   General procedure

1557   r.45*bis*.5(c)   For the purposes of the supplementary international search, Art. 17(2)/r.39 (cases in which an international search does not have to be carried out), r.13*ter*.1 (sequence listings) and r.33 (relevant prior art) apply mutatis mutandis. See Chapter 33 for further details.

Guidelines	See Guidelines for Search and Examination at the EPO as PCT Authority, B-XII, 5. The EPO applies the same criteria that it applies as International Searching Authority.
r.45*bis*.5(d)	Where the International Search Report is available to the Authority specified for supplementary search before it starts the search, that Authority may exclude from the supplementary search any claims which were not the subject of the international search.
r.45*bis*.5(e)	Where the International Searching Authority has made the declaration referred to in Art. 17(2)(a) (that no international search report will be established) and that declaration is available to the Authority specified for supplementary search before it starts the search, that Authority may decide not to establish a supplementary International Search Report, in which case it shall so declare and promptly notify the applicant and the International Bureau accordingly.
Guidelines	See Guidelines for Search and Examination at the EPO as PCT Authority, B-XII, 5. The EPO will not limit the search automatically on these grounds but will make a case-by-case assessment based on EPO practice.
r.45*bis*.5(f)	The supplementary international search must cover at least the documentation indicated for that purpose in the applicable agreement under Art. 16(3)(b).
r.45*bis*.5(g)	If the Authority specified for supplementary search finds that carrying out the search is excluded by a limitation or condition referred to in r.45*bis*.9(a) (in its agreement with the International Bureau), other than a limitation under Art. 17(2) as applicable by virtue of r.45*bis*.5(c), the supplementary search request shall be considered not to have been submitted, and the Authority shall so declare and shall promptly notify the applicant and the International Bureau accordingly.
r.45*bis*.5(h)	The Authority specified for supplementary search may, in accordance with a limitation or condition referred to in r.45*bis*.9(a) (in its agreement with the International Bureau), decide to restrict the search to certain claims only, in which case the supplementary international search report shall so indicate.

34.3.4   *Procedure in the case of a lack of unity*

r.45*bis*.6(a)	If the Authority specified for supplementary search finds that the international application does not comply with the requirement of unity of invention, it will: (i) establish the supplementary International Search Report on those parts of the international application which relate to the invention first mentioned in the claims ("main invention"); (ii) notify the applicant of its opinion that the international application does not comply with the requirement of unity of invention and specify the reasons for that opinion; and (iii) inform the applicant of the possibility of requesting, within the time limit referred to in r.45*bis*.6(c), a review of the opinion.
r.45*bis*.1(d)	However, where the International Searching Authority has already found a lack of unity, the applicant may specifically designate one of the inventions other than the invention first mentioned in the claims for the supplementary search.
r.45*bis*.6(b)	In considering whether the international application complies with the requirement of unity of invention, the Authority must take due account of any documents received by it under r.45*bis*.4(e)(vi) and (vii) (unity determination by the International Searching Authority and protest decision) before it starts the supplementary international search.
r.45*bis*.6(c)	The applicant may, within one month from the date of the notification of a lack of unity under r.45*bis*.6(a)(ii), request the Authority to review its opinion. The request for review may be subjected by the Authority to the payment to it, for its own benefit, of a review fee, the amount of which it is free to decide.
r.45*bis*.6(d)	If the applicant requests such a review in a timely fashion and pays any required review fee, the opinion will be reviewed by the Authority. The review must not be carried out only by the person who made the decision which is the subject of the review. Where the Authority: (i) finds that the opinion was entirely justified, it will notify the applicant accordingly; (ii) finds that the opinion was partially unjustified but still considers that the international application does not comply with the requirement of unity of invention, it will notify the applicant accordingly and, where necessary, proceed as provided for in r.45*bis*.6(a)(i) (supplementary search report to relate to main invention only);

1558

(iii) finds that the opinion was entirely unjustified, it shall notify the applicant accordingly, establish the supplementary International Search Report on all parts of the international application and refund the review fee to the applicant.

r.45*bis*.6(e)   On the request of the applicant, the text of both the request for review and the decision thereon shall be communicated to the designated offices together with the supplementary International Search Report. The applicant must submit any translation thereof with the furnishing of the translation of the international application required under Art. 22.

r.45*bis*.6(f)   The above procedure of r.45*bis*.6(a) to (e) applies mutatis mutandis where the Authority specified for supplementary search decides to limit the supplementary international search in accordance with the second sentence of r.45*bis*.5(b) or with r.45*bis*.5(h), provided that any reference in the said paragraphs to the "international application" shall be construed as a reference to those parts of the international application which relate to the invention specified by the applicant under r.45*bis*.1(d) or which relate to the claims and those parts of the international application for which the Authority will carry out a supplementary international search, respectively.

OJ   See Decision of the President dated 09 June 2015 ([2015] O.J. A59). The review is examined by a three-member review panel consisting of three examiners, one of whom will chair the panel and another of whom will be the examiner who was responsible for issuing the supplementary international search report containing the notification under r.45*bis*.6(a)(ii) PCT.

OJ   See also Part III of the Decision of the President dated 24 March 2010 ([2010] O.J. 322. The EPO acting as Supplementary International Searching Authority establishes the supplementary international search report on the invention first mentioned in the claims, taking into account any information provided by the applicant under r.45*bis*.1(d). On receipt of the supplementary international search report, containing a reasoned explanation for the lack of unity, the applicant may file a request for review within a one month period and pay the review fee in order to take advantage of the review procedure under r.45*bis*.6(d).

RRFArt. 2(1)(22)   The review fee when the EPO acts as supplementary International Searching Authority is € 980.

34.4   The supplementary International Search Report

34.4.1   *Drawing up the supplementary International Search Report*

1559   r.45*bis*.7(a)   The Authority specified for supplementary search shall, within 28 months from the priority date, establish the supplementary International Search Report, or make the declaration referred to in Art. 17(2)(a) as applicable by virtue of r.45*bis*.5(c) that no supplementary International Search Report will be established.

r.45*bis*.7(b)   Every supplementary International Search Report, any declaration referred to in Art. 17(2)(a) as applicable by virtue of r.45*bis*.5(c) and any declaration under r.45*bis*.5(e) shall be in a language of publication.

r.45*bis*.7(c)   For the purposes of establishing the supplementary International Search Report, r.43.1, r.43.2, r.43.5, r.43.6, r.43.6*bis*, r.43.8 and r.43.10 will, subject to r.45*bis*.7(d) and r.45*bis*.7(e) below, apply mutatis mutandis. These rules apply to the drawing up of the International Search Report. Furthermore, r.43.9 (content of the International Search Report) applies mutatis mutandis, except that the references therein to r.43.3, r.43.7 and r.44.2 shall be considered nonexistent. In addition, Art. 20(3) and r.44.3 (requirement to supply copies of documents) apply mutatis mutandis.

r.45*bis*.7(d)   The supplementary International Search Report need not contain the citation of any document cited in the International Search Report, except where the document needs to be cited in conjunction with other documents that were not cited in the International Search Report.

r.45*bis*.7(e)   The supplementary International Search Report may contain explanations:
(i) with regard to the citations of the documents considered to be relevant;
(ii) with regard to the scope of the supplementary international search.

| Guidelines | The EPO will provide explanations similar to the comments it makes in a written opinion when acting as supplementary International Searching Authority. If no priority document is available then the right to priority is assumed to be valid. See sections B-XII, 7 and B-XII, 8, respectively, of the Guidelines for Search and Examination at the EPO as a PCT Authority. |

34.4.2   Transmittal and effect of the supplementary International Search Report

r.45*bis*.8(a)	The Authority specified for supplementary search will, on the same day, transmit one copy of the supplementary International Search Report or the declaration that no supplementary International Search Report shall be established, as applicable, to the International Bureau and one copy to the applicant.	1560
r.45*bis*.8(b)	Subject to r.45*bis*.8(c) below, the following apply as if the supplementary International Search Report was part of the International Search Report: Art. 20(1) (i.e. the supplementary International Search Report is communicated to designated states by the International Bureau); r.45.1 (i.e. the supplementary International Search Report is translated into English by the International Bureau if it is drawn up in any other language); r.47.1(d) (i.e. each designated Office is entitled to receive a copy of any translation of the supplementary International Search Report into English); and r.70.7(a) (i.e. the International Preliminary Examining Authority will cite documents it considers to be relevant whether or not they were cited in the supplementary International Search Report or not and will only cite those documents in the supplementary International Search Report that it considers to be relevant.	
r.45*bis*.8(c)	A supplementary International Search Report need not be taken into account by the International Preliminary Examining Authority for the purposes of a written opinion or the International Preliminary Examination Report if it is received by that Authority after it has begun to draw up that opinion or report.	
AppGuide	See International Phase, paragraph 8.050 – some supplementary International Searching Authorities transmit copies of cited documents for free along with the report, others charge a fee. The EPO provides cited documents for free ([2010] O.J. 316).	

34.4.3   Public availability of the supplementary International Search Report

| AppGuide | See International Phase, paragraph 8.053. The supplementary International Search Report is not published but is made available by the International Bureau as part of the application file as soon as it is available if international publication has taken place. | 1561 |

Chapter 35: Amendment of the Application under Article 19

35.1 Amendment of claims before the International Bureau

35.1.1 When can the applicant amend the claims?

1562	Art. 19(1)	Having received the International Search Report, the applicant is entitled to one chance to amend the claims of his international application before the International Bureau within a prescribed time limit.
	r.46.1	The prescribed time limit is the later of: (a) 16 months from the priority date; and (b) two months from the date of transmittal of the International Search Report to the International Bureau and the applicant by the International Searching Authority; provided that if the amendment is received later but before the technical preparations for international publication have been completed it will be considered to have been received on the last day of the time limit.
	AppGuide	See International Phase, paragraph 9.004 – it follows that if the International Searching Authority declares that no International Search Report is to be drawn up, no amendment under Art. 19 is possible.

35.1.2 Where should any amendments be filed?

1563	r.46.2	Any such amendment should be filed directly with the International Bureau.

35.1.3 Language of the amendments

1564	r.12.2(a)	Any amendment of the international application, subject to r.46.3 and r.55.3 must be in the language in which the international application was filed.
	r.46.3	However, if the language of publication is different from the language of filing any Art. 19 amendment must be in the language of publication.

35.1.4 Form of any amendments

1565	r.46.5(a)	The applicant, when making amendments under Art. 19, is required to submit a replacement sheet or sheets containing a complete set of claims in replacement of all the claims originally filed.
	r.46.5(b)	The replacement sheet or sheets must be accompanied by a letter which: (i) identifies the claims which, on account of the amendments, differ from the claims originally filed, and draws attention to the differences between the claims originally filed and the claims as amended; (ii) identifies the claims originally filed which, on account of the amendments, are cancelled; and (iii) indicates the basis for the amendments in the application as filed.
	r.11.14	The amendments must comply with all the requirements of r.10 (terminology and signs) and r.11.1 to r.11.13 (physical requirements).
	r.92.2(d)	The letter may be in English or French or, as from 01 July 2016, in any other language of publication permitted by the Administrative Instructions.
	AdminInst	See s.104. If the language of the application is English or French then that language should be used for any letter – otherwise the applicant may choose either of the two languages. Communications sent using ePCT may be in any of English, French or the language of publication or any other language permitted by the Director General.
	AppGuide	See International Phase, paragraph 9.009A – the absence of a letter only has adverse consequences in the international phase if international preliminary examination is requested in which case the amendments need not be taken into account during that examination (r.70.2(c-*bis*)).

35.1.5 *Statement accompanying the amendments*

Art. 19(1), r.46.4

The applicant may also file a brief statement explaining the amendments and their possible impact on the description and drawings, identified as such by a heading, preferably "Statement under Article 19(1)". The statement must be in the language of publication of the application and should not exceed 500 words in English or if translated into English. It must not contain any disparaging comments on the International Search Report or the relevance of the citations given therein. Reference to a citation, relevant to a given claim and contained in the International Search Report, may be made only in connection with an amendment of that claim.

1566

r.48.2(a)(vi)

The statement will be published with the application if in the correct form

35.1.6 *Prohibition on added subject matter*

Art. 19(2)(3)

Any amendments under Art. 19 may not go beyond the disclosure of the international application as filed but such a transgression will have no consequences in designated States that allow such added subject matter.

1567

35.2 Notification of amendments to the International Preliminary Examining Authority when a demand has been filed

r.62.1

When the International Bureau receives a demand or receives a copy of the demand from the International Preliminary Examining Authority, it will promptly transmit to that Authority any amendments filed under Art. 19, any statement filed under Art. 19 explaining such amendments and the letter required under r.46.5(b) (details of amendments made), unless International Preliminary Examining Authority has indicated that it has already received such a copy.

1568

r.62.2

If a demand has already been submitted when the applicant files amendments under Art. 19, the applicant should preferably file simultaneously with the International Preliminary Examining Authority a copy of such amendments, a copy of any accompanying statement under Art. 19 and a copy of the letter required under r.46.5(b) (details of amendments made). In any case, the International Bureau will promptly transmit a copy of such documents to the International Preliminary Examining Authority.

Chapter 36: Publication of the Application and the Search Report

36.1 Responsibility for international publication

1569	Art. 21(1)

The International Bureau is responsible for the publication of international applications.

36.2 Timing of international publication

1570   Art. 21(2)(a)   The International Bureau publishes an international application promptly after the expiration of 18 months from the priority date.

Art. 21(2)(b)   However, it may be published earlier at the request of the applicant.

r.48.4(b)   Where the applicant has made a request for early publication under Art. 21(2)(b), the International Bureau will proceed to publication promptly after it has received the request and any extra fee due concerning the search report under r.48.4(a) (special publication fee where the search report is not yet available).

AdminInst   See s.113(a) – the fee is 200 Swiss francs.

r.90*bis*.3(d)(e)   Where the withdrawal of a priority claim changes the priority date, time limits starting on the priority date which have not already expired may be recalculated from the new priority date with the proviso that the International Bureau may nevertheless publish the application 18 months from original priority under Art. 21(2)(a) if the withdrawal is received by the International Bureau after the technical preparations for publication are complete.

AdminInst   See s.406 – publication takes place on a given day of the week.

AppGuide   See International Phase, paragraph 9.013 – publication usually takes place on a Thursday.

Comment   See section 36.3 below for the date on which the technical preparations for publication are complete.

36.3 Circumstances where no publication takes place

1571   Art. 64(3)(a)   Any State may declare that it does not require international publication.

Art. 64(3)(b)   Where the application contains only the designation of such States at the expiration of 18 months from the priority date, no publication under Art. 21(2) will occur unless:

Art. 64(3)(c)(i)   (1) the applicant specifically requests it; or

Art. 64(3)(c)(ii)   (2) a national application or patent based on the international application is published by or on behalf of a national Office of any designated State that has made a declaration under Art. 64(3)(a) (in which case publication under Art. 21(2) will follow shortly after such national publication but not before the expiration of 18 months from the priority date).

r.48.4(b)   Where the applicant has made a request for publication under Art. 64(3)(c)(i), the International Bureau will proceed to publication promptly after it has received the request and any extra fee due concerning the search report under r.48.4(a) (special publication fee where the search report is not yet available).

AdminInst   See s.113(a) – the fee is 200 Swiss francs.

r.48.5   Where the publication of the international application by the International Bureau is governed by Art. 64(3)(c)(ii), the national Office concerned will, promptly after effecting the national publication referred to in the said provision, notify the International Bureau of the fact of such national publication.

WIPO   Only the US has made such a declaration.

Art. 21(5)   No publication takes place if the international application is withdrawn or considered withdrawn before the technical preparations for publication have been completed (see r.90*bis* for withdrawal procedure).

AppGuide   Such preparations are complete 15 days prior to the date of publication (see International Phase, paragraph 9.014). So any letter withdrawing the application must reach the International Bureau at least 16 days before the date of publication to be taken into account (i.e. by midnight on a Tuesday two weeks earlier if publication is on a Thursday).

36.4 Language and form of the publication

36.4.1 *Where the language of filing is used*

1572   Art. 21(4)   The language of the international publication is governed by the Regulations.

r.48.3(a)	If the international application is filed in Arabic, Chinese, English, French, German, Japanese, Korean, Portuguese, Russian or Spanish (a language of publication), it will be published in the language in which it was filed.

36.4.2   *Where the language of a translation is used*

Art. 21(4) r.48.3(b)	The language of the international publication is governed by the Regulations. If the international application was not filed in a language of publication but a translation into a language of publication has been furnished under r.12.3 (for international search) or r.12.4 (for publication) then the application will be published in the language of that translation.

1573

36.4.3   *Translation of parts of the pamphlet into English where English is not the language of publication*

Art. 21(4) r.48.3(c)	The language of the international publication is governed by the Regulations. If the international application is published in a language other than English, then the following documents will also be published in an English translation prepared by the International Bureau (if not furnished by the applicant under r.12.3 for the purposes of international search): (a) the International Search Report, to the extent that it is published under r.48.2(a)(v), or the Art. 17(2)(a) declaration; (b) the title of the invention; and (c) the abstract and any text matter pertaining to the figure(s) accompanying the abstract.

1574

36.4.4   *Form of the publication*

Art. 21(4) r.48.1 AdminInst AppGuide	The form of international publication is governed by the Regulations. The form in which and the means by which international applications are published are governed by the Administrative Instructions. See s.406(b) – international publication can be in paper form or electronic form. See International Phase, paragraph 9.015 – international publication takes place solely in electronic form. Published applications can be downloaded free from the internet. The applicant is only provided with a paper copy of the publication if one is specifically requested.

1575

36.5   Contents of the publication

r.48.2	The pamphlet prepared for international publication must contain the following elements.

1576

36.5.1   *A standardised front page (r.48.2(a)(i))*

r.48.2(b)(d)(e)	The standardised front page must include: (i) data from the request sheet and other data prescribed by the Administrative Instructions (see s.406 – Director General decides); (ii) a figure, or figures where the application contains drawings (unless r.8.2(b) applies– International Searching authority considers none of the drawings suitable). The figure is chosen according to r.8.2 (the International Searching Authority having the final say) and may be reduced; (iii) the abstract. If the abstract is both in English and another language, the English version will appear first. If the abstract (or translation thereof under r.48.3 (c)) is too long, it may be continued on the back of the front page; (iv) where applicable, an indication that the request contains one of the declarations referred to in r.4.17 received before the appropriate time limit (r.26*ter*.1); (v) where the international filing date has been accorded by the receiving Office under r.20.3(b)(ii), r.20.5(d) or r.20.5bis(d) on the basis of the incorporation by reference under r.4.18 and r.20.6 of an element or part, an indication to that effect, together with an indication as to whether the applicant, for the purposes of r.20.6(a)(ii), relied on compliance with r.17.1(a),(b) or (b-*bis*) in relation to the priority document (provision of certified copy), or on a separately submitted copy of the earlier application concerned;

1577

(vi) where applicable, an indication that the published application contains information under r.26*bis*.2(d) (regarding a priority claim that is considered void or that has defects);

(vii) where applicable, an indication that the published international application contains information concerning a request under r.26*bis*.3 for restoration of the right of priority and the decision of the receiving Office upon such request;

(viii) where applicable, an indication that an erroneously filed element or part has been removed from the international application in accordance with r.20.5*bis*(b) or (c)

r.48.2(c) However, where the search report could not be established (Art. 17(2)(a)), this will be conspicuously noted on the front page and the abstract and any figure may be omitted.

r.90*bis*.2(e) Where a designation is withdrawn, that designation will not be included in the international publication if the notice of withdrawal reaches the International Bureau (from the applicant or via the receiving Office or International Preliminary Examining Authority) before the technical preparations for publication have been completed.

J26/87 There are no consequences for the applicant if the International Bureau does not publish a designation that was validly made.

36.5.2   *The description (r.48.2(a)(ii))*

1578 The international publication must include the description.

36.5.3   *The claims (r.48.2(a)(iii))*

1579 r.48.2(f) If the claims have been amended under Art. 19, the publication will contain the full text of the claims as filed and as amended. The date of receipt of the amended claims will also be indicated.

r.48.2(h) If, when the technical preparations for international publication are complete, the time limit for amending the claims under Art. 19 has not expired, the front page will say so and indicate that, should the claims be amended under Art. 19 within the time limit, the full text of the amended claims will be published later along with a revised front page. Any Art. 19(1) statement will also be published unless the International Bureau finds it does not comply with r.46.4.

36.5.4   *Any drawings (r.48.2(a)(iv))*

1580 The international publication must contain the drawings, if any.

36.5.5   *The International Search Report or Art. 17(2)(a) declaration (r.48.2(a)(v))*

1581 Art. 21(3) The international search report or the declaration referred to in Art. 17(2)(a) (no international search report to be established) is published as described in the Regulations.

r.48.2(a)(v) The International Search Report or Art. 17(2)(a) declaration will be published.

r.48.2(g) If, however, when the technical preparations for international publication are complete, the search report is not ready, the front page will explain that this is the case and the search report will be separately published when available together with a revised front page.

36.5.6   *Any statement filed under Art. 19(1) (r.48.2(a)(vi))*

1582 r.48.2(a)(vi) The publication contains any statement filed under Art. 19(1) (explaining amendments made) unless the International Bureau finds that the statement does not comply with r.46.4.

r.48.2(f) Confirms that the Art. 19(1) statement is included if it complies with r.46.4.

36.5.7   *Any request for rectification (r.48.2(i))*

1583 r.48.2(i) If the authorisation of a rectification of an obvious mistake in the international application referred under r.91.1 is received by, or where applicable, given by the International Bureau after completion of the technical preparations for international publication, a statement reflecting all the rectifications shall be published, together with the sheets containing the rectifications or the replacement sheets and the letter furnished under r.91.2, as the case may be, and the front page shall be republished.

r.48.2(a)(vii)	The international publication will include any refused request for rectification of an obvious mistake, any reasons and any comments referred to in r.91.3(d) as long as the request for publication under r.91.3(d) is received by the IB before the completion of the technical preparations for international publication.
r.48.2(k)	If a request for publication under r.91.3(d) was received by the International Bureau after the completion of the technical preparations for international publication, the request for rectification, any reasons and any comments referred to in that rule shall be promptly published after the receipt of such request for publication, and the front page shall be republished.

36.5.8   *Indications relating to biological material (r.48.2(viii))*

r.48.2(viii)	The relevant data from any indications in relation to deposited biological material furnished under r.13*bis* will be published separately from the description, together with an indication of the date on which the International Bureau received such indications.	1584

36.5.9   *Information concerning a priority claim (r.48.2(ix))*

r.48.2(ix)	Any information concerning a priority claim referred to in r.26*bis*.2(d) (invitation to correct defects not satisfied).	1585

36.5.10   *Any declaration (r.48.2(x))*

r.48.2(x)	Any declaration referred to in r.4.17 and any correction of such a declaration under r.26*ter*.1 received within the r.26*ter*.1 time limit will be published.	1586

36.5.11   *Request for restoration of the priority right (r.48.2(xi))*

r.48.2(a)(xi)	The publication will contain any information concerning a request under r.26*bis*.3 for restoration of the right of priority and the decision of the receiving Office upon such request, including information as to the criterion for restoration upon which the decision was based.	1587
r.48.2(j)	If, at the time of completion of the technical preparations for international publication, a request made under r.26*bis*.3 for restoration of the right of priority is still pending, the published international application shall contain, in place of the decision of the receiving Office upon that request, an indication to the effect that such decision was not available and that the decision, when it becomes available, will be separately published.	

36.6   Matter excluded from the publication

Art. 21(6)	If, in the opinion of the International Bureau, the international application contains expressions or drawings which are contrary to morality or public order, or disparaging statements, it may omit them on publication, indicating the place and the number of words or drawings omitted. Individual copies of the omitted passages will be provided on request.	1588
r.9.3	In this context, "disparaging statements" are statements disparaging the products or processes of those other than the applicant, or to the validity of such a person's application(s) or patent(s) (mere comparisons with the prior art, however, not being considered disparaging per se).	
r.48.2(l)	The International Bureau will, upon a reasoned request by the applicant received by the International Bureau prior to the completion of the technical preparations for international publication, omit from publication any information, if it finds that: (i) this information does not obviously serve the purpose of informing the public about the international application; (ii) publication of such information would clearly prejudice the personal or economic interests of any person; and (iii) there is no prevailing public interest to have access to that information. r.26.4 (manner of presenting a correction before the receiving Office) applies *mutatis mutandis* as to the manner in which the applicant must present the information which is the subject of a request made under r.48.2(l).	

r.48.2(m)	Where the receiving Office, the International Searching Authority, the Authority specified for supplementary search or the International Bureau notes any information meeting the criteria set out under r.48.2(l), that Office, Authority or Bureau may suggest to the applicant to request the omission from international publication in accordance with r.48.2(l).
r.48.2(n)	Where the International Bureau has omitted information from international publication in accordance with r.48.2(l) and that information is also contained in the file of the international application held by the receiving Office, the International Searching Authority, the Authority specified for supplementary search or the International Preliminary Examining Authority, the International Bureau will promptly notify that Office and Authority accordingly.
Comment	rr.48.2(l)-(n) apply to international applications filed on or after 01 July 2016. The new rules may apply in particular to any documents submitted to the receiving Office by the applicant in support of a request for the restoration of a priority right (see r.26*bis*.3(h-*bis*).

36.7   Notice of publication in the Gazette

1589	r.86.1(i)	Certain information, specified in the Administrative Instructions, taken from the front of the pamphlet, is published in the Gazette (see Annex D of the Administrative Instructions) as well as the abstract and any accompanying figure. This information will be published in both English and French (r.86.2(a)) and any translations are prepared by the International Bureau).
	AppGuide	See International Phase, paragraph 9.020 – The International Bureau also publishes, in English and French, the bibliographic data, title, abstract and accompanying Figure on the WIPO website.

36.8   Publication of a notice that the application is considered withdrawn where withdrawal is received too late to stop publication

1590	r.48.6(a)	If a notification under r.29.1(ii), that the receiving Office considers the international application to be withdrawn, reaches the International Bureau too late to prevent international publication of the application, the International Bureau will promptly publish a notice in the Gazette reproducing the essence of such a notification.
	r.48.6(c)	If the application, the designation of a State or a priority claim is withdrawn by the applicant under r.90*bis* after the technical preparations for publication have been completed, notice of the withdrawal will be published in the Gazette.

Chapter 37: Communications to National and Regional offices

37.1 Communication of the application (Art. 20) to designated States by the International Bureau

37.1.1 *In what circumstances does the communication occur?*

Art. 20(1)(a)   The communication occurs to all designated Offices unless a particular designated Office   1591
waives the requirement in full or in part.

r.93*bis*.1   Designated and elected Offices now have to specifically request that the communication take place.

37.1.2 *Normal timing of the communication and procedure where early national processing has been requested*

r.47.1(a)(b)   The Art. 20 communication is effected by the International Bureau in accordance with   1592
r.93*bis*.1. It may not, subject to r.47.4, be effected before international publication. Any
Art. 19 amendments received by the International Bureau within the time limit of r.46.1 but
which were not included in the Art. 20 communication must be separately communicated.

r.93*bis*.1   Designated and elected Offices that specifically request that the communication takes
place specify the timing of the communication.

r.47.4   The Art. 20 communication can be made earlier than publication where the applicant
has requested that a designated Office proceed to examination earlier than the end of the
international phase (Art. 23(2)) and the applicant or the designated Office so requests.

r.61.2(d)   The Art. 20 communication may also be made earlier where the applicant has requested
that an elected Office (under Chapter II) proceed to examination earlier than the end of
the international phase (Art. 40(2)) and the applicant or the elected Office so requests.

r.76.5   Rule 47.1 applies whether national phase entry is under Chapter I or Chapter II.

37.1.3 *Content of the communication*

The communication includes: 1593

Art. 20(1)(a)   (a) the international application;

Art. 20(1)(b)   (b) the search report (including any declaration that no search will be carried out (Art. 17(2)
(a)) or indication that some claims have not been searched (Art. 17(2)(b));

Art. 20(1)(b)   (c) any prescribed translations of the search report or the Art. 17(2)(a) declaration (see
r.45.1 for possible translation into English);

Art. 20(2)   (d) any Art. 19 amendments that have been made, either by including the claims as filed
and as amended or the claims as filed and an indication of the amendments; and

Art. 20(2)   (e) any statement under Art. 19(1) accompanying Art. 19 amendments.

37.1.4 *Responsibility for making copies*

r.47.2   The International Bureau is responsible for preparing the necessary copies for the com-   1594
munication. Further details are provided in the Administrative Instructions.

37.1.5 *Language of the communication*

r.47.3(a)(b)   The international application is communicated in the language in which it is published   1595
but, where the language of publication is different from the language of filing, the International Bureau will furnish, on request by a designated State, a copy of the application
in the language of filing.

37.1.6 *Notification of the Art. 20 communication to the applicant*

r.47.1(c)   The International Bureau sends a notice to the applicant, promptly after the expiration   1596
of 28 months from the priority date, indicating which designated Offices have asked to
receive the Art. 20 communication pursuant to r.93*bis*.1, which Offices have not asked to
receive the Art. 20 communication pursuant to r.93*bis*.1 and the date of the communication of the application to the former Offices.

However, such a notice must be sent promptly after the expiration of 19 months from the priority date in respect of any designated Office which has an outstanding reservation relating to the Art. 22(1) time limit.

WIPO

Luxembourg and United Republic of Tanzania have such reservations in force.

37.1.7   *Designated Offices must accept the r.47.1(c) notification as evidence that the Art. 20 communication has occurred or is not necessary*

1597   r.47.1(c-*bis*)

The notice sent to the applicant under r.47.1(c) must be accepted by the designated Offices as conclusive evidence that the Art. 20 communication has duly taken place on the date specified in the notice (in the case of designated Offices that have requested the Art. 20 communication) or that the Art. 20 communication is not required (in the case of designated States that have not requested the Art. 20 communication).

37.2   Other information that is communicated to designated States by the International Bureau on request

37.2.1   *Fact and date of receipt of the record copy and priority document*

1598   r.47.1(a-*bis*)

If requested to do so by a designated State under r.93*bis*.1, the International Bureau will notify a designated Office of the fact and date of receipt of (i) the record copy and (ii) any priority document.

37.2.2   *Transmission of the application to a designated Office other than the Art. 20 communication*

1599   Art. 13(1), r.31.1

If asked by a designated Office, the International Bureau will transmit to it a copy of: (a) all; (b) some kinds of; or (c) individual international applications before the Art. 20 communication and as soon as possible after one year from the priority date. Requests for all or some kinds of applications must be renewed each year before November 30 of the preceding year.

Art. 13(2), r.31.1

The applicant may himself, or by asking the International Bureau so to do, transmit a copy of his international application to any designated Office at any time but the International Bureau will not do this in respect of any national Office that has notified it that it does not wish to receive copies in this way. For its services in this regard, the International Bureau may charge the applicant a fee.

r.31.2

The preparation of copies required for any transmission under Art. 13 and r.31.1 is the responsibility of the International Bureau.

Chapter 38: Entry into the National~Regional Phase

38.1 Overview

Art. 22(1)

In order to continue the prosecution of an international application in designated States, the applicant must enter the national/regional phase by supplying a copy of the international application (unless one has already been supplied under Art. 20), supplying a translation of the international application where prescribed and paying a national fee. Where indications concerning the inventor are due and may be supplied later than the filing date then this information should also be supplied on national/regional phase entry.

1600

38.2 Timing of national phase entry under Art. 22

38.2.1 Standard 30 month time limit

Art. 22(1)–(3)

The relevant acts must be carried out no later than 30 months from the priority date or, where national law so allows, a later date, regardless of whether the international searching authority has declared that no International Search Report will be established under Art. 17(2)(a) or not.

1601

Comment

The time limit used to be 20 months but changed to 30 months as of April 1, 2002. However, if on October 3, 2001 this change was incompatible with the law of any designated Office, it will not apply to that Office for as long as such incompatibility exists provided that the Office notified the International Bureau of the incompatibility by January 31, 2002. Such a notification is published in the Gazette. Where a notification is subsequently withdrawn by a designated Office by notification sent to the International Bureau, such notification is also to be published and the change enters into force two months after the date of such publication or on an earlier or later date indicated in the notice.

WIPO

The new time limit does not apply to Luxembourg and United Republic of Tanzania. These reservations only apply to the entry of a PCT application directly into the national phase, they do not apply where protection is to be obtained via a relevant regional patent convention. So, for instance, a Euro-PCT application designating Luxembourg can still validly enter the EPO regional phase at 31 months.

r.49.6(a)

Where the Art. 22 time limit is missed, a designated Office must, upon request of the applicant, reinstate the rights of the applicant if it finds that any delay in meeting that time limit was unintentional or, at the option of the designated Office, that the failure to meet the time limit occurred in spite of due care required by the circumstances having been taken. See section 41.12 for more details – some states have filed reservations.

r.26*bis*.1(c)

Where a priority date is changed, any outstanding time limit that has not yet expired is recomputed from the new date.

r.32.2

When the effect of an international application has been extended to a successor State, the time limit under Art. 22 for national phase entry in that State may be later.

38.2.2 Specification of a later time limit than 30 months by a designated Office

Art. 22(3)
r.50.1(a)–(d)

Any national law may specify an Art. 22 time limit later than 30 months.

If so, the State must notify the International Bureau of the later time limit and the fact will be promptly published by the International Bureau in the Gazette. Where a previously fixed time limit is shortened it will become effective in relation to applications filed after three months from the date of publication of the notification. Where a previously fixed time limit is lengthened it will become effective in relation to applications pending at the time of or filed after the date of publication of the notification or at a later date if the Contracting State so stipulates.

1602

Comment

Most countries, including Germany, Japan, the USA and Canada have specified 30 months from the priority date as the relevant time limit under Art. 22. Others, however, such as the UK, the EPO and Australia have specified a later time limit of 31 months.

38.3 Supply of a copy of the international application

1603   Art. 22(1)

The applicant must supply to each designated Office a copy of the international application within the Art. 22(1) time limit, unless the Art. 20 communication has already taken place.

r.49.1(a-*bis*)

Nor is any copy of the application required if the designated Office has informed the International Bureau that it does not require the applicant to furnish a copy even if the communication of a copy by the International Bureau under r.47 has not taken place by the expiry of the Art. 22 time limit (in which case the International Bureau will publish such information promptly in the Gazette – r.49.1(b)).

r.47.1(e)

Where any designated Office has not, before the expiration of 28 months from the priority date, requested the International Bureau to effect the Art. 20 communication, the Contracting State for which that Office acts as designated Office is considered to have notified the International Bureau under r.49.1(a-*bis*), that it does not require furnishing, under Art. 22, by the applicant of a copy of the international application.

WIPO

However, the relevant time is 19 months from the priority date in respect of any designated Office which has an outstanding reservation relating to the Art. 22(1) time limit (Luxembourg and United Republic of Tanzania).

r.49.3

For these purposes, any Art. 19(1) statement (regarding amendments) and any r.13*bis*.4 indication (regarding biological material) are considered part of the international application.

r.47.1(c-*bis*)

The notice sent to the applicant under r.47.1 must be accepted by the designated Offices as conclusive evidence that the Art. 20 communication has duly taken place (see section 37.1).

AppGuide

See National Chapter (EP) – The EPO has indicated pursuant to r.49.1(a-bis) that it does not require a copy of the application (see PCT Gazette 14/1986, 2367). This is the case even if early processing is requested and the EPO has not yet received a copy of the application from the IB (Guidelines E-IX, 2.1.2).

r.49.1(a-*ter*)

Any designated Contracting State which maintains pursuant to Art. 24(2) that the application will have the effect of a regular national filing as of the international filing date (Art. 11(3)), even if a copy of the international application is not furnished by the Art. 22 time limit, must notify the International Bureau accordingly (and the fact will be promptly published in the Gazette – r.49.1(b)).

38.4 Supply of a translation of the international application

38.4.1   *Requirements of the translation*

1604   Art. 22(1)

The applicant must supply to each designated Office, where prescribed, a translation of the international application within the Art. 22(1) time limit.

r.49.1(a)(i), (b)

The languages from which and into which the translation must occur must be notified by each designated Office to the International Bureau and are promptly published in the Gazette.

r.49.2

The language into which translation is required must be an official language of the designated Office. Where several official languages exist: (i) the designated Office may not require translation where the application is already in one of them and (ii) the applicant may choose any of them for the translation unless one particular official language is prescribed for use by foreigners by that Office.

r.49.3

For these purposes, any Art. 19(1) statement (regarding amendments) and any r.13*bis*.4 indication (regarding biological material) are considered part of the international application.

r.49.5(a)

A translation under Art. 22 must contain:

(1) the description (except that no designated Office may requires the applicant to furnish to it a translation of any text matter contained in the sequence listing part of the description if such a sequence listing part of the description complies with r.12.1(d) (language requirements on filing) and includes the language-dependent free text in a language which the designated Office accepts for the purpose, save that a designated Office which supplies published sequence listings to database providers may require a translation of the sequence listing part of the description into English, in accordance with the Administrative Instructions, where the language-dependent free text is not included in English – r.49.5(a-*bis*));

(2) the claims;

(3) any text matter of the drawings – furnished either in the form of a drawing executed anew or a copy of the drawing with the translation pasted on the original text matter (r.49.5(d)) – the expression "Fig." does not require translation (r.49.5(f)); and
(4) the abstract.
In addition, if required by any designated Office (such requirements will be published by the International Bureau in the Gazette – r.49.5(i))) the translation must:
(5) contain the request. In this case, the designated Office must furnish to the applicant, free of charge, copies of the request form in the language of translation, the use of which is optional (r.49.5(b)). The translated form may not ask for any additional information that is not in the request as filed and must have the same form and contents specified in r.3 and r.4 (r.49.5(b));
(6) contain both claims as filed and as amended if amendment under Art. 19 has taken place (the claims as amended being furnished in the form of a translation of the complete set of claims furnished under r.46.5(a) in replacement of all the claims originally filed);
(7) be accompanied by a copy of the drawings.

r.49.5(j)	No designated Office may require that the translation of the international application comply with any physical requirements other than those prescribed for the application as filed.
r.49.5(k)	Where a title has been established by the International Searching Authority under r.37.2 (no title in application or title not complying with r.4.3), the translation must contain the title as established by that Authority.
r.49.5(l)	This rule (49.5(k)) does not apply where there is conflict with national law and the IB was notified by December 31, 1991.
WIPO	Only the US has notified the IB of conflict.
r.51*bis*.1(d)	National law may require that the translation submitted by the applicant is verified or certified – see below under national phase aspects.

38.4.2 Consequences of certain defects in the translation

r.49.5(h)	Where the translation of the abstract or any indication under r.13*bis*.4 (to deposited biological material) is not furnished and the designated Office deems it to be necessary, it will invite the applicant to correct this defect within a reasonable time limit fixed in the invitation.	1605
r.49.5(c)	If there is no translation of a statement regarding amendments made under Art. 19(1), any designated Office may disregard such a statement.	
r.49.5(c-*bis*)	Where the claims have been amended under Art. 19, and a designated Office requires translations of the claims both as filed and amended and a translation of only one of these is provided, such a designated Office may disregard the untranslated claims or invite the applicant to provide a translation thereof within a reasonable time limit that it sets in the invitation. Where the terms of such an invitation are not met the designated Office may either disregard the untranslated claims or consider the application withdrawn.	
r.49.5(l)	This rule (49.5(c-*bis*)) does not apply where there is conflict with national law and the IB was notified by December 31, 1991.	
WIPO	Only Brazil and the US have notified the IB of conflict.	
r.49.5(e)	When a copy of the drawings is required and is not furnished within the Art. 22 time limit, the designated Office will invite the applicant to correct this defect within a reasonable time limit fixed in the invitation.	
r.49.5(g)	When a copy of the drawings or drawings executed anew furnished according to r.49.5(d) or (e) does not comply with the physical requirements of r.11, the designated Office may invite the applicant to correct this defect within a reasonable time limit fixed in the invitation.	

38.4.3 Where requirements regarding the translation change

r.49.1(c)	Any changes regarding the translation must be notified by the relevant Contracting State to the International Bureau who will promptly publish the new details in the Gazette. If the change involves translation into a language not previously required the change will only apply to international applications filed later than two months from the date of publication in the Gazette. In other cases, the Contracting State determines the effective date.	1606

38.5   Payment of the national fee

1607 Art. 22(1)
      r.49.1(a)(ii), (b)

The applicant must pay any necessary national fee within the Art. 22(1) time limit.
The amount of any fee must be notified by each designated Office to the International Bureau and is promptly published in the Gazette.

      r.49.1(c)

Any changes regarding the fee must be notified by the relevant Contracting State to the International Bureau who will promptly publish the new details in the Gazette. The effective date of the change is determined by the Contracting State.

38.6   Supply of indications concerning the inventor

1608 Art. 22(1)

The applicant must supply to the national Office of or acting for each designated Office the name of and any other prescribed data concerning the inventor, within the Art. 22(1) time limit, where national law requires such indications but allows them to be provided at a time later than the filing of a national application and they were not included in the request.

38.7   Use of a national form

1609 r.49.4

The use of a national form cannot be required for the Art. 22 procedure.

38.8   Procedure where applicant has performed the Art. 22 acts and the designated Office has not been informed that the International Bureau has received the record copy

1610 r.22.1(g)

If, by the expiration of the time limit under Art. 22 (usually 30 months) the applicant has discharged his duties under that Article but the designated Office has not been informed by the International Bureau that it has received the record copy, the designated Office will inform the International Bureau who will promptly inform the applicant and the receiving Office unless it is in possession of the record copy or it has already notified them at the 14-month stage (see under procedure of the receiving Office).

38.9   Indications as to protection sought for the purposes of national processing

1611 r.49*bis*.1(a)(c)

If the applicant wishes the international application to be treated, in a designated State in respect of which Art. 43 applies (kinds of protection other than patent protection available), as an application not for the grant of a patent but for the grant of another kind of protection referred to in Art. 43, the applicant, when performing the acts referred to in Art. 22, must so indicate to the designated Office and, in the case of a patent of addition, certificate of addition, inventor's certificate of addition or utility certificate of addition, indicate the parent patent or other parent grant.

      r.49*bis*.1(e)

Where the amount of the national fee paid under Art. 22 corresponds to a particular kind of protection, payment of that amount is considered to be an indication that the applicant wishes the application to be considered as an application for that kind of protection, even when no express indication to that effect is made. The designated Office will inform the applicant accordingly.

      r.49*bis*.1(b)

The applicant must also indicate at the same time if he wishes to obtain protection of more than one kind, as allowed by Art. 44, and, if necessary, which kind of protection is sought primarily and which is sought secondarily.

      r.49*bis*.1(d)

If the applicant wishes the international application to be treated, in a designated State, as an application for a continuation or a continuation-in-part of an earlier application, the applicant, when performing the acts referred to in Art. 22, must so indicate to the designated Office, identifying the relevant parent application.

      r.49*bis*.2(a)

No designated Office may require that the applicant furnish an indication referred to in r.49*bis*.1, or an indication as to whether the applicant seeks the grant of a national or regional patent, before performing the acts referred to in Art. 22.

      r.49*bis*.2(b)

Furthermore, the applicant may, if so permitted by national law, furnish such an indication or convert one kind of protection to another, at any later time.

      r.76.5

Rule 49*bis* applies whether national phase entry is under Chapter I or Chapter II.

38.10 Consequences of not performing the Art. 22 acts

Art. 24(1)(iii)
The effect of an international application provided for in Art. 11(3) (international applica-   1612
tion to have same effect as a regular national application in each designated State as of the
filing date) will cease in any designated State, with the same consequences as withdrawal
of any national application in that State, if the applicant fails to perform the acts referred
to in Art. 22 within the applicable time limit.

r.49.6
For the chance to reinstate rights in this situation, see under time limits and procedural
safeguards below (section 40.12).

38.11 National and regional phase entry under Art. 39

38.11.1   Effect of election prior to 19 months on the application of Art. 22

Art. 39(1)(a)
If the election of a Contracting State has been effected prior to the expiration of the nine-   1613
teenth month from the priority date, Art. 22 ceases to apply in respect of that State and
Art. 39 applies instead.

Art. 64(2)(a)(i)
Any State, though not having declared it is not bound by Chapter II under Art. 64(1)(a)
may nevertheless declare that it is not bound by Art. 39(1) with respect to the furnishing
of a copy of the international application and a translation thereof (as prescribed).

Art. 64(2)(b)
Such states making a declaration under Art. 64(2)(a)(i) will be bound accordingly.

WIPO
No reservations under Art. 64(2)(a)(i) have been filed.

Comment
A demand filed after the expiry of 19 months from the priority date but within the
r.54*bis*.1(a) time limit for submitting a demand is valid but does not have the effect of delaying entry into the regional/national phase in States where the Art. 22 and Art. 39 time
limits are different.

*38.11.2   Necessary acts to enter the national phase under Art. 39 and the relevant time
limit*

Art. 39(1)(a)
Under Art. 39, the applicant must supply to each elected Office a copy of application (un-   1614
less the Art. 20 communication has already occurred), any prescribed translation thereof
and any necessary fee before the expiration of 30 months from the priority date.

Art. 39(1)(b)
Any Contracting State may specify a later time limit if it wishes

r.77.1(a)–(d)
If it chooses to specify a later time limit, a Contracting State must inform the International
Bureau who will promptly publish such information in the Gazette. If the time limit is
lengthened, such a change applies from the date of publication to demands pending at the
time or submitted later, or, if the relevant State fixes some later date, as from that later
date. If such a time limit is shortened, the shortened time limit only applies to demands
submitted after the period of three months from the date of such publication.

Comment
Most States now have the same time limit under Art. 39 as under Art. 22. For instance,
Germany, Japan, the USA and Canada have specified 30 months from the priority date
and the UK, the EPO and Australia have specified 31 months.

r.32.2
When the effect of an international application has been extended to a successor State, the
time limit under Art. 39(1) for national phase entry in that State may be later.

38.11.3   Consequences of missing the Art. 39 time limit

Art. 39(2)(3)
The effect under Art. 11(3) (international application to have same effect as a regular na-   1615
tional application in each designated State as of the filing date) ceases in an elected State
with the same consequences as the withdrawal of a national application in that State if
the applicant fails to perform the necessary acts referred to in Art. 39(1)(a) within the
Art. 39(1) time limit, unless the national Office wishes to maintain this effect.

38.11.4   Application of certain rules to national phase entry under Art. 39

1616   r.76.5

The following rules apply to national phase entry under Art. 39: r.13*ter*.3 (limitation of requests for sequence listing by designated Office), r.20.8(c) (non-recognition of incorporation by reference), r.22.1(g) (procedure where designated Office has not been informed by the International Bureau of receipt of the record copy by the time the applicant enters the national phase),), r.47.1 (communication to designated Office by the IB), r.49 (details of entering the national phase – see above under Art. 22 procedure), r.49*bis* (indications as to protection sought for national processing), r.49*ter* (restoration of priority right) and r.51*bis* (national requirements that are allowed; except that:

(1) "designated Office" or "designated State" should be replaced with "elected Office" or "elected State" respectively, Art. 22, Art. 23(2) or Art. 24(2) should be replaced with Art. 39(1), Art. 40(2) or Art. 39(3) respectively, "international applications filed" in r.49.1(c) should be replaced with "a demand submitted" and the reference to r.47.4 in r.47.1(a) should be construed as a reference to r.61.2(d); and

(2) a translation of any Art. 19 amendment is only necessary where it is annexed to the International Preliminary Examination Report.

38.11.5   Time limit for supplying a translation of the priority document to an elected State

1617   r.76.4

The applicant is not required to furnish a translation of the priority document to any elected Office before the expiration of the Art. 39 time limit.

38.12   Procedure before the EPO as a designated or elected Office

38.12.1   Entry into the EPO regional phase

1618   Comment

An international application has entered the regional phase and is pending before the EPO when the EPO can and will process it. Two conditions must be fulfilled. First of all, the EPO must be legally capable of processing the application, i.e. either 31 months must have elapsed from the priority date (Art. 23(1) PCT) or the applicant must have specifically asked the EPO to process the application at an earlier date (Art. 23(2) PCT). Secondly, the EPO must be willing to process the application since, at the relevant time, the applicant has performed as many of the essential acts specified by r.159 EPC as are due at that point. If one of these essential acts remains unperformed then the application will not enter the regional phase at all but will instead be deemed withdrawn either on expiry of the 31 month time limit (r.160(1)) or, in the case of an unpaid renewal fee, on expiry of the six-month grace period (Art. 86(1) and r.51(2) EPC).

OJ

See Notice from the EPO dated 21 February 2013 ([2013] O.J. 156) and Guidelines E-IX, 2.8. According to the EPO, the processing of a Euro-PCT application does not start until the expiry of the 31 month time limit unless a valid request for early processing has been made. Such a request for early processing may be made at any time prior to the expiry of the 31 month deadline but, to be effective, any requirements under r.159(1) that are due on the date the request is made must be satisfied. This will always involve payment of the filing fee, the filing of any required translation, the specification of the documents on which examination is to be based and the payment of a supplementary search fee, if required. It may also involve, depending on the timing, payment of the designation fee, payment of a renewal fee, payment of the examination fee and the filing of a request for examination. Note that if the application becomes pending at the EPO before the second anniversary of the filing date then the first renewal fee becomes due in the normal way and not at the 31 month date.

Comment

The procedure on regional phase entry (assuming standard entry at around 31 months from the filing/priority date) is heavily influenced by whether a supplementary European search report is to be drawn up or not (such a search report is required if the EPO did not act as International Searching Authority or a Supplementary International Searching Authority).

If no supplementary European search report is to be drawn up then the applicant can nevertheless, under r.164(2) as in force from 01 November 2014, propose any subject matter for prosecution in the regional phase, regardless of whether it was searched by the EPO in the international phase or not. A communication pursuant to r.161(1) EPC will be issued requiring comment on the written opinion of the ISA or IPER where necessary and giving the applicant his one chance to amend the application as of right (r.137(2) EPC). Substantive examination will then commence, the Examining Division already being responsible for the application (r.10 EPC). If the claims proposed for prosecution in the regional phase contain unsearched subject matter, in whole or in part, the applicant is asked to pay an additional search fee (or fees if unity is lacking, r.164(2)) and the Examining Division conducts any additional searching for which fees have been paid before issuing a first communication including the results of this search.

If a supplementary search report is to be drawn up then the applicant is first given the chance to amend the application under r.161(2) EPC. The claims proposed for search do not have to have been searched in the international phase. Under r.164(1) as in force from 01 November 2014, the applicant has the choice, if unity is lacking in the set of claims proposed for prosecution in the regional phase, to pay further search fees at this point. After notification of the supplementary search report and opinion, the applicant will have the chance to specify whether he wishes to proceed further within a six month time limit according to r.70(2) EPC and will be required to comment on the contents of the opinion under r.70a(2) EPC and file any voluntary amendments under r.137(2) EPC within this period. Substantive examination will then commence, with the Examining Division assuming responsibility when a positive response to the r.70(2) communication is received or, if the r.70(2) communication has been waived, on transmittal of the supplementary European search report (r.10 EPC).

38.12.2   *Supply of a translation*

EPC r.159(1)(a)	The applicant must supply, where applicable, the translation of the international application required under Art. 153(4) EPC within 31 months from the date of filing of the application or, if priority has been claimed, from the priority date.	1619
EPC Art. 153(4)	A translation into one of the official languages of the EPO is required if the Euro-PCT application is published in another language.	
EPC Art. 14(1)	The official languages of the EPO are English, French and German.	
EPC r.160(1)	If a required translation is not filed in due time, the European patent application will be deemed to be withdrawn.	
EPC r.160(3)	If the EPO notes that the application is deemed withdrawn it will communicate this to the applicant. Rule 112(2) of the EPC applies mutatis mutandis (there is a two-month period for requesting a decision on the matter).	
EPC Art. 121	Further processing is available in these circumstances.	
EPC Art. 122	Re-establishment of rights under Art. 122 of the EPC is available if the further processing time limit is missed.	
r.49.6(a)	Reinstatement of rights under the PCT is also possible if the translation is not filed in time.	
G4/08	Headnote (1): If an international patent application has been filed and published under the PCT in one official language of the EPO, it is not possible, on entry into the European phase, to file a translation of the application into one of the other two EPO official languages.	
	In this case a Euro-PCT application in the French language was to be prosecuted in the regional phase by a English-speaking European patent attorney who filed a translation into English when entering the regional phase. It was confirmed in the decision that the language of the proceedings cannot be changed in this way when the Euro-PCT is filed in an official language of the EPO and that the EPO must use the language of the proceedings in communicating with the applicant in writing.	
Guidelines	See E-IX, 2.1.3. In the case where the receiving Office has corrected an erroneously filed element or part pursuant to r.20.5bis(d) PCT, the translation must include both the erroneously filed element or part as well as the correct element or part. See also E-IX, 2.1.2 – no copy of the international application itself is required since the EPO obtains a copy from the IB. See E-IX, 2.5.1 for publication of the translation.	

38.12.3   *Specification of documents on which the grant procedure is to be based*

1620	EPC r.159(1)(b)	The applicant must specify the application documents, as originally filed or as amended, on which the European grant procedure is to be based within 31 months from the date of filing of the application or, if priority has been claimed, from the priority date.
	Comment	As of 01 November 2014, in view of the amendments to r.164 coming into force on that date, applicants can now choose to pursue any subject matter on regional phase entry regardless of whether that subject matter has been searched by the EPO in the international phase or not. Before this date, only applicants requiring a supplementary European search had the choice of pursing such unsearched subject matter under previous r.164.
	Guidelines	See E-IX, 2.1.1. If the applicant does not specify which documents are to form the basis of the procedure, the EPO will proceed on the basis of the international application as published, also taking into account any amendments made in the international phase. The number of pages used to calculate the filing fee will include the application as published supplemented by any pages of amendments that have not been specified as replacing pages of the published application.

38.12.4   *Filing fee*

1621	EPC r.159(1)(c)	The applicant must pay the filing fee provided for in Art. 78(2) of the EPC within 31 months from the date of filing of the application or, if priority has been claimed, from the priority date.
	EPC r.38(2)	For Euro-PCT applications entering the regional phase on or after April 1, 2009 the filing fee is supplemented by an additional fee for the 36th and each subsequent page (r.38(2) in force as of April 1, 2009). This replaces the similar fee which was previously part of the fee for grant and printing and levied according to the length of the application as granted rather than the length of the application as filed (RRFArt. 2(7) as in force before April 1, 2009).
	RRFArt. 2(1)(1)	The filing fee is € 105 if, within the 31 month period of r.159(1) EPC, the form for entry into the regional phase (EPO form 1200) and the international application or, if required, its translation, and any amendments for processing in the European phase, are all filed online in character-coded format; € 135 if all these documents are filed online but any one of them is filed in a format other than character-coded format; and € 285 in other cases.
	RRFArt. 2(3)	The President of the EPO determines the conditions under which a document is deemed to have been filed online in character-coded format.
	RRF Art. 2(4)	Fee levels which relate to a means of electronic communication or a format referred to in RRF Art. 2(1) or Art. 2(2) shall not apply until a date set by the President of the Office.
	OJ	See Decision of the President dated 12 December 2018 ([2019] O.J. A3) and Notice from te EPO dated 24 Jauary 2019 ([2019] O.J. A6). New RRF Art. 2(4) applies as of 01 April 2019 to item (i) of RRF Art. 2(1)(1) and the € 105 filing fee will not apply for the time being.
	RRFArt. 2(1)(1a)	The additional fee for the 36th and each subsequent page is € 17 per page.
	OJ	See [2009] O.J. 118 for the manner in which the number of pages in the application is to be calculated. Pages of the request do not count. Neither do pages of any sequence listing which complies with WIPO Standard ST.25 and which is presented as a separate part of the description.
	Guidelines	See A-III, 13.2. The page fee is calculated on the basis of the international application as published, any amendments under Art. 19 and allowing one page for the abstract. If the regional procedure is to be based on amended claims filed under Art. 34 PCT or on regional phase entry it is important to indicate the pages of the international publication they replace or else the amendments may be counted as additional pages.
	EPC r.160(1)	If the filing fee is not paid in due time, the European patent application will be deemed to be withdrawn.
	EPC r.160(3)	If the EPO notes that the application is to be deemed withdrawn, it will communicate this to the applicant. Rule 112(2) of the EPC applies mutatis mutandis (there is two-month period for requesting a decision on the matter).
	EPC Art. 121	Further processing is available in these circumstances.
	EPC Art. 122	Re-establishment of rights under Art. 122 of the EPC is available if the further processing period is missed.
	r.49.6(a)	Reinstatement of rights under the PCT is also possible if the filing fee is not paid in time.

Comment	Note that the filing fee paid on regional phase entry is not reduced pursuant to r.6(3) since r.6(3) refers specifically to the filing of a European patent application.

38.12.5   *Designation fee*

EPC Art. 79(2)	The designation of a Contracting State is subject to the payment of a designation fee.	1622
RRFArt. 2(1)(3)	The designation fee is € 660 for international applications entering the regional phase on or after 01 April 2009.	
RRFArt. 2(2)(3)	The designation fee is € 115 per state (7 fees being deemed sufficient to designate all states) for international applications entering the regional phase before 01 April 2009.	
RRFArt. 2(2)(3a)	The designation fee for the joint designation of Switzerland and Liechtenstein is also € 115 for international applications entering the regional phase before 01 April 2009.	
EPC r.159(1)(d)	The designation fee must be paid within 31 months from the date of filing of the application or, if priority has been claimed, from the priority date, if the period under r.39 of the EPC has expired earlier.	
EPC r.39(1)	The designation fee must be paid within six months of the date on which the European Patent Bulletin mentions the publication of the European Search Report.	
EPC Art. 153(6)	The international publication of the International Search Report drawn up in respect of a Euro-PCT application, or the declaration replacing it, takes the place of the mention of the publication of the European Search Report in the European Patent Bulletin.	
EPC r.160(1)	The non-payment of the designation fee leads to the European patent application being deemed withdrawn.	
EPC r.160(3)	If the EPO notes that the application (or, before April 1, 2009, a designation) is deemed to be withdrawn it will communicate this to the applicant. Since r.112(1) applies mutatis mutandis, there is the possibility of requesting an appealable decision if the EPO's finding is incorrect.	
EPC Art. 121	Further processing is available in these circumstances.	
EPC Art. 122	Re-establishment of rights under Art. 122 of the EPC is available if the further processing period is missed.	
EPC r.39(3)	No refund of designation fees is made.	
Guidelines	See A-III, 11.2.5, A-III, 11.3.9, E-IX, 2.1.4 and E-IX, 2.3.11.	

38.12.6   *Extension fees*

OJ	A European patent may be extended to Bosnia and Herzegovina ([2004] O.J. 619) and Montenegro ([2010] O.J. 10). See section 7.8. All legal basis in relation to the extension of the European patent to these countries is found in the relevant agreement rather than in the EPC. The deadline for paying the extension fees is the same as that for paying the designation fee under the EPC – see section 38.12.5 above.	1623
OJ	The extension fee is currently € 102 per extension state.	
OJ	If an extension fee is not paid in due time, then according to the extension agreements the request for extension concerned is deemed withdrawn.	
OJ	If the extension fees are not paid, the extension agreements provide that the grace period of r.85a(2) EPC1973 applies, i.e. they may be paid within two months from the expiry of the normal time limit along with a surcharge of 50 %. The continuing validity of this provision has been recognised by the EPO ([2009] O.J. 603).	
Comment	This is an aggregate time limit.	
Guidelines	See A-III, 12.2. Where the designation fee is not paid in time and further processing is used to remedy the consequent loss of rights, further processing may also be used to pay any missing extension fees. Further processing cannot be used, however, if the designation fee is paid in due time and only the extension fees are missing. No loss of rights is notified if an extension fee is not paid in time (though non-payment will be noted in any loss of rights communication concerning the non-payment of the designation fee) and no other EPC remedies such as re-establishment may be invoked.	
RRFArt. 2(1)(12)	The further processing fee in this case will be the usual 50 % of the unpaid extension fees.	
Guidelines	See A-III, 12.3. An extension may be withdrawn at any time but a validly paid extension fee is not refunded.	

38.12.7   Validation fees

<table>
<tr><td>1624</td><td>OJ</td><td>A European patent may be validated in Morocco ([2015] O.J. A20 and [2016] O.J. A5), Moldova ([2015] O.J. A85), Tunisia ([2017] O.J. A85) and Cambodia ([2018] O.J. A15 and A16). See section 7.9. All legal basis in relation to the validation of the European patent in these countries is found in the relevant agreement and under national law rather than in the EPC. The deadline for paying the validation fees is the same as that for paying the designation fee under the EPC (see section 38.12.5 above).</td></tr>
<tr><td></td><td>OJ</td><td>The validation fee is currently € 240 for Morocco, € 200 for Moldova and € 180 for Tunisia and Cambodia.</td></tr>
<tr><td></td><td>OJ</td><td>If a validation fee is not paid in due time, then according to the validation agreements the request for validation concerned is deemed withdrawn.</td></tr>
<tr><td></td><td>OJ</td><td>If a validation fee is not paid, the validation agreements provide that a grace period applies, i.e. it may be paid within two months from the expiry of the normal time limit along with a surcharge of 50 %.</td></tr>
<tr><td></td><td>Comment</td><td>This is an aggregate time limit.</td></tr>
<tr><td></td><td>Guidelines</td><td>See Guidelines A-III, 12.2. Where the designation fee is not paid in time and further processing is used to remedy the consequent loss of rights, further processing may also be used to pay any missing validation fees. Further processing cannot be used, however, if the designation fee is paid in due time and only the validation fees are missing. No loss of rights is notified if a validation fee is not paid in time (though non-payment will be noted in any loss of rights communication concerning the designation fee) and no other EPC remedies such as re-establishment may be invoked.</td></tr>
<tr><td></td><td>RRFArt. 2(1)(12)
Guidelines</td><td>The further processing fee in this case will be the usual 50 % of the unpaid validation fees. See A-III, 12.3. A validation may be withdrawn at any time but a validly paid validation fee is not refunded.</td></tr>
</table>

38.12.8   Supplementary European search and fee

<table>
<tr><td>1625</td><td>EPC Art. 153(7)</td><td>A supplementary European Search Report is drawn up in respect of any Euro-PCT application if it is treated as a European patent application by virtue of Art. 153(5), except for the cases in which the Administrative Council has decided that such a supplementary search is unnecessary. The Administrative Council can also decide to reduce the search fee in certain cases.</td></tr>
<tr><td></td><td>OJ</td><td>No supplementary search is necessary if the international search report or a supplementary international search report was drawn up by the EPO (see Decision of the Administrative Council dated 28 October 2009, [2009] O.J. 594). Nor is a supplementary search report drawn up for international applications filed before 01 July 2005 for which the Austrian Patent Office, the Spanish Patent and Trademark Office or the Swedish Patent and Registration Office was the International Searching Authority (see [1995] O.J. 511). In all other cases, a supplementary search is required.</td></tr>
<tr><td></td><td>EPC r.159(1)(e)</td><td>The applicant must pay the search fee, where a supplementary European Search Report has to be drawn up, within 31 months from the date of filing of the application or, if priority has been claimed, from the priority date.</td></tr>
<tr><td></td><td>RRFArt. 2(1)(2)</td><td>The search fee is € 1460 for international applications filed on or after 01 July 2005 and € 1000 for international applications filed before 01 July 2005.</td></tr>
<tr><td></td><td>OJ</td><td>Until 01 April 2018, the supplementary search fee was reduced by € 190 if an International Searching Authority selected from Australia, China, Japan, Korea, Russia and the US carried out the international search and the international application was filed on or after 01 July 2005 (see decision of the Administrative Council dated 27 October 2005, [2005] O.J. 548). For applications filed before 01 July 2005, the reduction was 20 % (see decisions of the Administrative Council dated 14 September 1979 ([1979] O.J. 368), 11 December 1980 ([1981] O.J. 5), 09 December 1993 ([1994] O.J. 6) and 08 June 2000 ([2000] O.J. 321)). However, this reduction ceased to apply on 01 April 2018 ([2018] O.J A3) – if a fee was paid in the reduced amount within six months of that date then it was deemed to have been validly paid if the deficit was made good within two months of an invitation from the EPO.</td></tr>
</table>

OJ	The supplementary European search fee is reduced by € 1245 if the international search or a supplementary international search was carried out by the Austrian Patent Office or, in accordance with the Protocol on Centralisation, by the Finnish Patent and Registration Office, the Spanish Patent and Trademark Office, the Swedish Patent and Registration Office, the Turkish Patent and Trademark office, the Nordic Patent Institute or the Visegrad Patent Institute (see Art. 2 of the Decision of the Administrative Council dated 14 December 2022, [2023] O.J. A2). The maximum amount of the reduction is equal to the reduction granted on the basis of a single international search report or supplementary international search report drawn up by one of the relevant authorities. The reduction applies to international applications filed up to and including 31 March 2024 for which the fee for supplementary European search is paid on or after 01 April 2023.
RRFArt. 9(1)	The search fee paid for supplementary European search will be fully refunded if the European patent application is withdrawn or refused or deemed to be withdrawn at a time when the office has not yet begun to draw up the search report.
OJ	See Notice from the EPO dated 29 January 2013 – the date on which searching activity starts is now stored electronically in the application file and clearly indicated in the European Patent Register.
RRFArt. 9(2)	Where the European Search Report is based on an earlier search report prepared by the EPO on an application whose priority is claimed or an earlier application within the meaning of Art. 76 or r.17 the EPO will refund the applicant, in accordance with a Decision of the President, an amount which depends on the type of the earlier search and the extent to which the EPO benefits from the earlier search report when carrying out the subsequent search.
OJ	See Decision of the President dated 17 January 2023 ([2023] O.J. A4) which makes it clear that RRFArt. 9(2) also applies to supplementary European searches. The refund varies between 17.5 % and 100 % depending on the kind of search relied on, the availability of a written opinion and the extent to which it is of benefit (full or partial).
EPC r.160(1)	If the search fee is not paid in due time, the European patent application will be deemed to be withdrawn.
EPC r.160(3)	If the EPO notes that the application is deemed withdrawn it will communicate this to the applicant. Rule 112(2) of the EPC applies mutatis mutandis (there is a two-month period for requesting a decision on the matter).
EPC Art. 121	Further processing is available in these circumstances.
EPC Art. 122	Re-establishment of rights is available if the further processing time limit is missed.
EPC r.161(2)	Where the EPO draws up a supplementary European search report on a Euro-PCT application, the application may be amended once within a period of six months from a communication informing the applicant accordingly. The application as amended serves as the basis for the supplementary European search report.
Comment	Any claims may be proposed as the basis for the supplementary search report regardless of whether they have been searched in the international phase or not. Equally, only subject matter covered by the supplementary search report may be pursued before the Examining Division.
EPC r.164(1)	If the EPO considers that the application documents which are to serve as the basis for the supplementary European search do not comply with the requirement of unity of invention, it shall: (a) draw up a partial supplementary search report on those parts of the application which relate to the invention, or the group of inventions within the meaning of Art. 82, first mentioned in the claims; (b) inform the applicant that, for the supplementary European search report to cover the other inventions, a further search fee must be paid, in respect of each invention involved, within a period of two months; and (c) draw up the supplementary European search report for the parts of the application relating to inventions in respect of which search fees have been paid.
r.164(5)	Any fee paid under r.164(1) shall be refunded if the applicant requests a refund and the Examining Division finds that the communication under r.164(1)(b) was not justified.

Comment	The present version of r.164(1) came into force on 01 November 2014 and applied to any application for which the supplementary European search report had not been drawn up at that date. Under the previous version of this rule, the EPO drew up a supplementary search report relating to the invention or unified group of inventions first mentioned in the claims and no request for additional search fees was made.
OJ	See Notice from the EPO dated 10 June 2014 ([2014] O.J. A70). The reduction of the supplementary European search fee provided for in Art. 153(7) EPC does not apply to any further search fees paid pursuant to r.164(1)(b) EPC. Any search carried out under r.164(1) is applicable when considering whether a refund is available under RRFArt. 9(2) in respect of a later-filed divisional application.
OJ	See Notice from the EPO dated 03 March 2017 ([2017] O.J. A20). As of 01 April 2017 the EPO will provide a written opinion on the patentability of the invention first mentioned in the claims along with the partial search results and invitation to pay additional fees under to r.164(1). The applicant will be fully informed of the reasons for the non-unity finding. The preliminary written opinion will be for information only and no response is required or taken into account at this stage.
Guidelines	See A-X, 9.3.1.
r.135(2)	Further processing is not available for the time limit of r.164(1) but re-establishment would be possible if the time limit was missed in spite of all due care having been taken.
OJ	See Notice from the EPO dated 02 August 2016 ([2016] O.J. A66). If an enquiry concerning the progress of the application is filed by the applicant on form 1012, the EPO will try and issue the supplementary European search report (or partial search report in the case of a lack of unity) (a) within one month of the receipt of the enquiry, if it has not been issued within six months of the expiry of the r.161(2) period, for applications filed or or after 01 June 2014; or (b) within six months of the receipt of the enquiry for applications filed before 01 June 2014 which do not claim priority.
J8/83	Where a supplementary search is necessary, and the examination fee has already been paid, an EPC r.70(2) communication is sent to the applicant asking whether he wishes to proceed with examination. See also Guidelines E-IX, 2.5.3.
r.62(1)	A supplementary European search report is accompanied by a search opinion in the same way as a regular European search report – see Guidelines B-II, 4.3.2.
r.70a	A response to the written opinion accompanying the supplementary European search report will be required unless a communication under r.71 can be issued directly – the procedure is the same as for regular European patent applications (see Guidelines E-IX, 2.5.3 and C-II, 3.1).
Guidelines	See B-II, 4.3 which deals with supplementary European Searches.

38.12.9 Request for examination

1626	EPC r.159(1)(f)	The applicant must file the request for examination provided for in Art. 94 of the EPC within 31 months from the date of filing of the application or, if priority has been claimed, from the priority date, if the period under r.70(1) has expired earlier.
	EPC r.70(1)	The applicant may request examination up to six months after the date on which the European Patent Bulletin mentions the publication of the European Search Report.
	EPC Art. 153(6)	The international publication of the international search report drawn up in respect of a Euro-PCT application, or the declaration replacing it, takes the place of the mention of the publication of the European Search Report in the European Patent Bulletin.
	EPC Art. 94(1)	A request for examination is not deemed to be filed until the examination fee has been paid.
	RRFArt. 2(1)(6)	The examination fee is € 2055 for an application filed before July 1, 2005, € 1840 for an application filed on or after July 1, 2005 or € 2055 for an international application filed on or after July 1, 2005 for which no supplementary European Search Report is drawn up.
	RRFArt. 14(2)	Where the EPO has drawn up an International Preliminary Examination Report, the examination fee is reduced by 75 %. If the report was established on certain parts of the international application in accordance with Art. 34(3)(c) of the PCT, the fee will not be reduced if subject matter not covered by the report is also to be examined.
	EPC r.160(1)	If the request for examination is not filed in due time, the European patent application will be deemed to be withdrawn.

EPC r.160(3)	If the EPO notes that the application is deemed withdrawn it will communicate this to the applicant. Rule 112(2) of the EPC applies mutatis mutandis (there is two-month period for requesting a decision on the matter).
EPC Art. 121	Further processing is available in these circumstances.
Guidelines	See E-VIII, 2. In principle there may be two missing acts for which a further processing fee must be paid, a missing request for examination and a missing examination fee. Since both acts have the same legal basis, however, it is considered that a single further processing fee is paid comprising one or two components as appropriate.
EPC Art. 122	Re-establishment of rights under Art. 122 of the EPC is available if the further processing time limit is missed. A single re-establishment fee would be due regardless of the amount of the further processing fee (Guidelines E-VIII, 3.1.3).
Guidelines	See C-II, 1.2. See also A-X, 9.3.2 – the examination fee can benefit from a 75 % reduction pursuant to RRFArt. 14(2) and then a further 30 % reduction pursuant to r.6 EPC, if the relevant criteria are met. The fee reduction according to RRFArt. 14(2) only applies to the Euro-PCT application itself and not to any divisionals filed from it.

38.12.10 Renewal fee

EPC r.159(1)(g)	The applicant must pay the renewal fee in respect of the third year provided for in Art. 86(1) of the EPC within 31 months from the date of filing of the application or, if priority has been claimed, from the priority date, if the fee has fallen due earlier under r.51(1) of the EPC.	1627
RRFArt. 2(1)(4)	The fee for the third year is € 530.	
Comment	The fee falls due under r.51(1) EPC on the last day of the month containing the second anniversary of the filing date and is therefore only usually payable on regional phase entry if no priority is claimed or only partial use of the priority year is made. Where the fee is due on regional phase entry, the six-month grace period provided for in r.51(2) of the EPC is an aggregate time limit running from the 31-month regional phase entry date.	
Guidelines	See A-X, 5.2.4.	

38.12.11 Certificate of exhibition

EPC r.159(1)(h)	The applicant must file, where applicable, the certificate of exhibition referred to in Art. 55(2) and r.25 of the EPC within 31 months from the date of filing of the application or, if priority has been claimed, from the priority date.	1628
Guidelines	See E-IX, 2.4.3. The Receiving Section will issue a notification under r.112(1) if the certificate is not furnished in the time allowed (assuming that r.51*bis*.1(a)(v) was complied with on filing the PCT application) and further processing is available in respect of the loss of rights.	

38.12.12 Amendment of the application and invitation to correct deficiencies where no supplementary European search is to be carried out

Art. 28, Art. 41	The applicant must be given the chance to amend the application on entry into the national/regional phase whether before a designated Office (Art. 28, r.52) or an elected Office (Art. 41, r.78).	1629
Comment	The EPO gives the applicant the chance to amend under Art. 28 and Art. 41, as demanded by the PCT, in response to a communication under r.161(1) EPC.	
EPC r.161(1)	If the EPO has acted as International Searching Authority and, where a demand under Art. 31 PCT was filed, also as International Preliminary Examining Authority for a Euro-PCT application, it gives the applicant the opportunity to comment on the written opinion of the International Searching Authority or the International Preliminary Examination Report and, where appropriate, invites him to correct any deficiencies noted in the written opinion or in the International Preliminary Examination Report and to amend the description, claims and drawings within a period of six months from the respective communication. If the EPO has drawn up a supplementary international search report, an invitation in accordance with the first sentence will be issued in respect of the explanations given in accordance with r.45*bis*.7(e) PCT. If the applicant does not comply with or comment on an invitation in accordance with the first or second sentence, the application shall be deemed to be withdrawn.	

EPC r.137(2)	Where no supplementary European search report is to be drawn up, the applicant's chance to file voluntary amendments must be exercised in response to the r.161(1) communication. Thereafter, all amendments are subject to the consent of the Examining Division under r.137(3) EPC. See Guidelines C-III, 2.2.
OJ	See Notice from the EPO dated 15 October 2009 [2009] O.J. 533 and Guidelines E-IX, 3.3.1. No response to the r.161(1) communication is required if amendments or comments are filed in entry into the regional phase or amendments not considered by the EPO in the international phase are maintained on entry into the regional phase.
Guidelines	See E-IX, 3.3.2. Neither is any response required where the conclusions of the WO-ISA or IPER, as the case may be, were entirely positive. Even if no response is required, the applicant is still given the chance to comment and file amendments.
OJ	See Notice from the EPO dated 05 April 2011 and Guidelines E-IX, 3.2. No communication under r.161 and r.162 will be issued if the applicant has waived the right to such a communication (e.g. in section 6.4 of form 1200) and the other provisions of r.161 (submission of a response where necessary) and r.162 (payment of claims fees) have been complied with. In this case the application progresses immediately to supplementary European search or examination.
EPC Art. 121	In the case of deemed withdrawal, further processing may be requested.
EPC Art. 122	If the further processing time limit is missed in spite of all due care having been taken then re-establishment would be possible.
Guidelines	See E-IX, 3.2. The r.161 communication is combined with a communication under r.162 EPC concerning claims fees (see below).

38.12.13 Claims fees

1630	EPC r.162(1)	If the application documents on which the European grant procedure is to be based comprise more than fifteen claims, a claims fee must be paid for the 16th and each subsequent claim within the period under r.159(1) of the EPC (31 months from the date of filing of the application or, if priority has been claimed, from the priority date).
	EPC r.162(2)	If the claims fees are not paid in due time, they may still be paid within the period under r.161(1) or r.161(2), as the case may be (six month period for amendment). If within this period amended claims are filed, the claims fees due shall be computed on the basis of such amended claims and shall be paid within this period.
	EPC r.162(3)	Any claims fees paid within the period under r.162(1) EPC and in excess of those due under the second sentence of r.162(2) EPC will be refunded.
	EPC r.162(4)	Where a claims fee is not paid in due time, the claim concerned will be deemed to be abandoned.
	RRFArt. 2(1)(15)	Claims fees are € 265 for each claim in the range 16–50 and € 660 for the 51st and each subsequent claim for international applications entering the regional phase on or after 01 April 2009.
	RRFArt. 2(2)(15)	Claims fees are € 265 for the sixteenth and each subsequent claim for international applications entering the regional phase before 01 April 2009.
	OJ	Further processing is available if a claim is deemed abandoned (see Notice from the EPO dated 16 December 2016, [2016] O.J. A103).
	Guidelines	See A-III, 9 and E-IX, 2.3.8. If the fees paid are insufficient the EPO will, where necessary, ask the applicant to indicate for which claims fees have been paid. Features of claims which have been deemed abandoned for failure to pay claims fees may not be reintroduced into the application (i.e. as a later claim amendment) if they are not also present in the description (J15/88).

38.12.14 Designation of the inventor

1631	EPC r.163(1)	Where the designation of the inventor under r.19(1) of the EPC has not yet been made within the period under r.159(1) EPC (31 months from the date of filing of the application or, if priority has been claimed, from the priority date), the EPO will invite the applicant to make the designation within two months.
	EPC r.163(6)	If the designation of the inventor is not made within the two-month period then the European application will be refused.
	EPC Art. 121	Further processing is available in these circumstances.

EPC Art. 122	Re-establishment of rights under Art. 122 EPC is available if the further processing time limit is missed.
J18/08	It should also be possible to appeal the decision and file the designation when filing the grounds.

38.12.15 Requirements relating to a priority claim

EPC r.163(2)	Where the priority of an earlier application is claimed, and the file number of the previous application or the copy thereof provided for in r.52(1) EPC and r.53 EPC have not been submitted within the period under r.159(1) EPC (31 months from the priority date), the EPO will invite the applicant to furnish that number or copy within two months. Rule 53(2) applies.	1632
EPC r.53(2)	The copy will be deemed to be duly filed if a copy of that application available to the EPO is to be included in the file of the European patent application under the conditions determined by the President of the EPO.	
OJ	See section 6.8.7. If a copy cannot be included in the file for any reason, it will not be deemed to have been filed and the EPO will invite the applicant to file a copy pursuant to r.163(2) EPC.	
OJ	A priority document is one of the few documents which cannot be filed by fax (see Decision of the President dated 20 February 2019, [2019] O.J. A18). A priority document may be filed electronically using online filing or the case management system if it has been digitally signed by the issuing authority in a manner acceptable to the EPO (see Decision of the President dated 09 May 2018, [2018] O.J. A45 and Decision of the President dated 15 November 2018, [2018] O.J. A93). A priority document may not, however, be filed using the web-form filing system. If a priority document is filed by an invalid means then it is deemed not to have been received.	
Guidelines	See A-III, 6.7 and F-VI, 3.3.	
J11/95	The priority document must be sent to the correct file to have been received in time.	
EPC r.163(6)	If the file number or copy of the previous application is not supplied within the two-month period then the right of priority will be lost for the application.	
EPC Art. 121	Further processing is available in these circumstances.	
EPC Art. 122	Re-establishment of rights under Art. 122 of the EPC is available if the further processing time limit is missed.	

38.12.16 Provision of a sequence listing

r.13*ter*.3	No designated Office may require the applicant to submit a sequence listing to it other than one which complies with the Administrative Instructions.	1633
r.76.5	r.13*ter*.3 applies whether national phase entry is under Chapter I or Chapter II.	
EPC r.163(3)	Where, at the expiry of the period under r.159(1) of the EPC (31 months from the date of filing of the application or, if priority has been claimed, from the priority date), a sequence listing complying with the standard provided for in the Administrative Instructions under the PCT is not available to the EPO, the applicant will be invited to file a sequence listing complying with the rules laid down by the President of the EPO within two months. Rule 30(2) and (3) of the EPC apply mutatis mutandis.	
OJ	See Decision of the President dated 28 April 2011 ([2011] O.J. 372) for applications filed before 01 July 2022 and Decision of the President dated 09 December 2021 ([2021] O.J. A96) for applications filed on or after 01 July 2022. The EPO will ask for the provision of a sequence listing in electronic form complying with WIPO Standard ST.25 (or ST.26 after the 2022 change) if one is not available.	
Guidelines	See E-IX, 2.4.2. A sequence listing will be available to the EPO if it was part of the international application as filed or else supplied to the EPO acting as ISA or IPEA under r.13*ter* PCT.	
EPC r.30(3)	A late furnishing fee is also due.	
RRFArt. 2(1)(14a)	The late furnishing fee is € 255.	
EPC r.30(3)	If the required sequence listing is not filed or the late furnishing fee is not paid, the application is refused.	

EPC Art. 121	Further processing is possible. Two fees may be due since two omitted acts may be involved; a fee of € 290 will be due if the sequence listing has not been furnished in time and 50 % of the late furnishing fee will be due if this fee has not been paid in time (RR-FArt. 2(1)(12)).
EPC Art. 122	Re-establishment would be possible if the further processing time limit was missed in spite of all due care being shown.
J18/08	It should also be possible to appeal the decision and provide the sequence listing and/or late furnishing fee when filing the grounds.
r.30(2)	A sequence listing filed after the date of filing does not form part of the description.

38.12.17 Details relating to the applicant

1634	EPC r.163(4)	Where, at the expiry of the period under r.159(1) of the EPC (31 months from the date of filing of the application or, if priority has been claimed, from the priority date), any applicant's address, nationality or State of residence/principle place of business is is missing, the EPO will invite the applicant to furnish these indications within two months.
	EPC r.163(6)	If any missing details are not supplied within the two-month period then the European application will be refused.
	EPC Art. 121	Further processing is available in these circumstances.
	EPC Art. 122	Re-establishment of rights under Art. 122 of the EPC is available if the further processing time limit is missed.
	J18/08	It should also be possible to appeal the decision and provide the missing details when filing the grounds.

38.12.18 Representation

1635	Art. 27(8)	See section 43.2 for the relevant PCT provisions.
	EPC r.163(5)	Where, at the expiry of the period under r.159(1) of the EPC (31 months from the date of filing of the application or, if priority has been claimed, from the priority date), the requirements of Art. 133(2) of the EPC have not been satisfied (an applicant not having residence or a principle place of business in an EPC Contracting State must appoint a professional representative), the EPO will invite the applicant to appoint a professional representative within two months.
	EPC Art. 133(2)	Note that the applicant can carry out the acts necessary to timely enter the regional phase himself regardless of whether professional representation is required (see Guidelines A-VIII, 1.1).
	EPC r.163(6)	If a professional representative is not appointed within the two-month period then the European application will be refused.
	EPC Art. 121	Further processing is available in these circumstances.
	EPC Art. 122	Re-establishment of rights under Art. 122 of the EPC is available if the further processing time limit is missed.
	J18/08	It should also be possible to appeal the decision and appoint a representative when filing the grounds.

38.12.19 Circumstances in which international publication takes the place of European publication

| 1636 | EPC Art. 153(3) | Publication of an international application for which the EPO is a designated Office under Art. 21 PCT will usually take the place of publication of a European patent application and will be mentioned in the European Patent Bulletin. |
| | EPC Art. 153(4) | However, where international publication is not in an EPO official language, the EPO will publish the application in the translation supplied for entry into the regional phase. |

38.12.20 Opportunity to have a search report drawn up in repect of an invention not searched by the EPO in the international phase when no supplementary European search is necessary

r.164(2)	If the supplementary European search report is dispensed with and the Examining Division considers that in the application documents which are to serve as the basis for examination an invention, or a group of inventions within the meanding of Article 82, is claimed which was not searched by the European Patent Office in its capacity as International Searching Authority or Authority specified for supplementary international search, the Examining Division shall:

(a) inform the applicant that a search will be performed in respect of any such invention for which a search fee is paid within a period of two months;

(b) issue the results of any search performed in accordance with paragraph (a) together with:

– a communication under Art. 94(3) and r.71(1) and (2), in which it shall give the applicant the opportunity to comment on these results and to amend the description, claims and drawings, or

– a communication under r.71(3), and

(c) where appropriate, in the communication issued under paragraph (b), invite the applicant to limit the application to one invention, or group of inventions within the meaning of Article 82, for which a search report was drawn up by the European Patent Office in its capacity as International Searching Authority or as Authority specified for supplementary international search or for which a search was performed in accordance with the procedure under paragraph (a).

RRFArt. 2(1)(2)	The search fee is € 1460.
r.164(3)	In the procedure under r.164(2)(a), r.62a (applications containing a plurality of independent claims) and r.63 (incomplete search) shall apply mutatis mutandis.
r.164(4)	r.62 (extended European search report) and r.70(2) (invitation to indicate whether to proceed to examination) do not apply to the results of any search performed in accordance with r.164(2).
r.164(5)	Any fee paid under r.164(2) shall be refunded if the applicant requests a refund and the Examining Division finds that the communication under r.164(2)(a) was not justified.
r.135(2)	Further processing is not available for the time limit of r.164(2) but re-establishment would be possible if the time limit was missed in spite of all due care having been taken.
Comment	New r.164(2) entered into force on 01 November 2014 and applies to any application for which the first communication under Art. 94(3) and r.71(1) and (2) EPC or under r.71(3) EPC had not been drawn up at that date. Before the new rule came into force, it was not possible to have any search carried out on entry into the regional phase if a supplementary European search was not necessary and applicants were restricted to pursuing an invention which had been searched by the EPO in the international phase. Now any subject matter can be pursued in the regional phase regardless of whether it has been searched or not in the international phase.
OJ	See Notice from the EPO dated 10 June 2014 ([2014] O.J. A70). Any search carried out under r.164(2) is applicable when considering whether a refund is available under RRFArt. 9(2) in respect of a later-filed divisional application.
Guidelines	See C-III, 3.1. The relevant documents on which the assessment under r.164(2) is carried out are those on file at the end of the six month period specified in r.161(1). It is irrelevant whether the unsearched subject matter was present in the claims of the application during the international phase or not or whether the claims lack unity or not. If the claims on file are so unclear that it is not possible to identify whether an invention has been searched or not, an Art. 94(3) commnication is issued and the chance to have additional inventions searched is lost. Only the main request is considered for the r.164(2) procedure, auxiliary requests being ignored. Only one r.164(2) communication may be issued. If no response is received to a communication under r.164(2) then the first communication from the examiner will require deletion of non-searched subject matter. When the results of an additional search are annexed to the first communication under Art. 94(3), any amendments filed in response under r.164(2)(b) are of the applicant's own volition and the consent of the Examining Division is not required (see also Guidelines H-II, 2.3).

1637

Chapter 39: International Preliminary Examination

39.1 Which designated States does Chapter II apply to?

1638 Art. 64(1)(a)(b)	Any State may declare that it is not bound by the provisions of Chapter II and this has the effect that such a State is not bound by the provisions of Chapter II and the corresponding provisions of the Regulations.
Comment	At present, all Contracting States are bound by Chapter II.

39.2 Who may apply for international preliminary examination and which States may be elected

1639	The following people may demand international preliminary examination:
Art. 31(2)(a)	any applicant who is a resident or national of a Contracting State bound by Chapter II and whose international application has been filed with the receiving Office of or acting for such a State; and
Art. 31(2)(b)	if the Assembly so decides, persons who are entitled to file international applications (Art. 9(2)) even if they are not residents or nationals of a State party to the PCT or bound by Chapter (II).
r.54.3	Where the receiving Office is the International Bureau (r.19.1(a)(iii)), it will be considered to be acting for the Contracting State of which the applicant is a resident or national for the purposes of Art. 31(2)(a).
r.54.2	Where there are joint applicants, it will suffice that one of them qualifies under Art. 31(2)(a).
Art. 31(4)(a)	Only States designated under Art. 4 may be elected.
Art. 31(4)(b)	Applicants falling under Art. 31(2)(a) may elect any Contracting State bound by Chapter II (currently all of them) whereas applicants falling under Art. 31(2)(b) may only elect those States bound by Chapter II that have declared they are willing to be so elected.
r.54.1(a)	Questions of residency and nationality for the purposes of Art. 31(2) are decided according to r.18.1(a) and (b) (see section 31.1).
r.54.1(b)	The International Preliminary Examining Authority will, in circumstances specified in the Administrative Instructions, ask the receiving Office (or, where the International Bureau is the receiving Office, the national Office of, or acting for, the State concerned) to decide any question of residency or nationality and will inform the applicant that it is doing so. The applicant will have an opportunity to submit arguments to the Office concerned directly and that Office will decide the question promptly.
r.54.4	Where the applicant does not have the right to make a demand (or in the case of joint applicants (r.54.2), none of them has) the demand is considered not to have been submitted.

39.3 Authority competent to conduct international preliminary examination

39.3.1 Receiving Offices specify the competent International Preliminary Examining Authority or Authorities

1640 Art. 32(1)	International preliminary examination is carried out by an International Preliminary Examining Authority.
Art. 32(2)	In the case of demands referred to in Art. 31(2)(a), the receiving Office, and, in the case of demands referred to in Art. 31(2)(b), the Assembly, specify, in accordance with the applicable agreement between the interested International preliminary Examining Authority or Authorities and the International Bureau, the International Preliminary Examining Authority or Authorities competent for the preliminary examination.
r.59.1(a)	For demands filed under Art. 31(2)(a), each receiving Office of or acting for a Contracting State bound by the provisions of Chapter II specifies, in accordance with the agreement under Art. 32(2) or (3) between the International Preliminary Authority and the International Bureau, which International Preliminary Examining Authority or Authorities is/are competent in respect of applications filed with it. The International Bureau publishes this information. In the case where more than one International Preliminary Examining Authority is competent, r.35.2 applies mutatis mutandis (Competent International Searching Authority – see section 33.1.4).

r.59.1(b)	When an application is filed with the International Bureau as receiving Office under r.19.1(a)(iii), the above does not apply. Instead, r.35.3(a) and (b) applies mutatis mutandis (competent International Searching Authority when the International Bureau acts as receiving Office – see section 33.1.4).
AppGuide	See Annex C (EP). When the EPO acts as receiving Office, the EPO is the only competent International Preliminary Examining Authority. However, many other receiving Offices give applicants a choice and, for example, the EPO may be selected as International Preliminary Examining Authority for applications filed with the US and Japanese offices.
r.59.2	In the case of applicants who are making a demand under Art. 31(2)(b) (residents or nationals of States not party to the PCT or not bound by Chapter II), the Assembly chooses which Authority is competent. Preference is given to the national Office with which the application is filed if it is an International Preliminary Examining Authority, or, if it is not, preference is given to the Authority which it recommends.
Art. 32(3)	The provisions of Art. 16(3) (appointment of International Searching Authorities by the Assembly) applies mutatis mutandis in respect of International Preliminary Examining Authorities.
r.63	The minimum requirements that such an Authority must comply with are: (i) it must have at least 100 full-time employees with sufficient technical qualifications to carry out examinations; (ii) it must have at its disposal the minimum documentation referred to in r.34 for International search, properly arranged for examination purposes; and (iii) it must have a staff capable of examining in the required technical fields and possessing the language facilities to understand at least those languages in which the minimum documentation of (ii) above is written or translated; (iv) it must have in place a quality management system and internal review arrangements in accordance with the common rules of international preliminary examination; and (v) it must be an International Searching Authority.
OJ	See [2017] O.J. A115 for details of the EPO agreement with the International Bureau according to which it will act as an International Preliminary Examining Authority.

39.3.2 Limitations set by the EPO on its competence as International Preliminary Examining Authority

EPC Art. 152	The EPO will act as an International Preliminary Examining Authority in accordance with an agreement between the European Patent Organisation and the IB for applicants who are residents or nationals of an EPC Contracting State. This agreement may provide that the EPO will also act for other applicants.	1641
OJ	The EPO has, in principle, agreed to act as International Preliminary Examining Authority for applications filed with any receiving Office that specifies it for this purpose, according to Art. 3(2) and Annex A to the agreement between the EPO and the International Bureau (see [2017] O.J. A115). However, the EPO may only be selected as International Preliminary Examining Authority if the International Searching Authority was the EPO itself or the industrial property office of an EPC Contracting State (the Austrian, Finnish, Spanish, Swedish or Turkish patent office, the Nordic Patent Institute or the Visegrad Patent Institute) (see also Guidelines E-IX, 1, Guidelines for Search and Examination at the EPO as PCT Authority C-II, 2 and AppGuide, Annex E [EP]).	

39.4 How to apply for international preliminary examination – the demand

39.4.1 Demand

Art. 31(1)	On the demand of the applicant, his international application will be the subject of an international preliminary examination.	1642
Art. 31(3)	The applicant must demand examination separately from the international application. The demand must contain certain particulars and be in the prescribed form and in the prescribed language.	

39.4.2   Time limit

1643   r.54*bis*.1(a)   A demand may be made at any time prior to the later of (i) three months from the date of transmittal to the applicant of the International Search Report or the declaration referred to in Art. 17(2)(a) (no search report to be established) and of the written opinion established under r.43*bis*.1, and (ii) 22 months from the priority date.

r.54*bis*.1(b)   Any demand made late is considered as if it had not been submitted and the International Preliminary Examining Authority so declares.

39.4.3   Where to apply

1644   Art. 31(6)(a)   The demand must be submitted to the competent International Preliminary Examining Authority referred to in Art. 32.

r.59.3(a)(f)   Where the demand is submitted to:
(i) a receiving Office;
(ii) an International Searching Authority; or
(iii) an International Preliminary Examining Authority which is not competent;
that Office or Authority will mark the date of receipt on it and transmit it promptly to the International Bureau or directly to the competent International Examining Authority.

r.59(b)   Where the demand is submitted to the International Bureau, it will mark the date of receipt on it.

r.59.3(c)(d)(f)   Where the International Bureau receives a demand from a receiving Office, International Searching Authority or non-competent International Preliminary Examining Authority under r.59.3(a) or from the applicant under r.59.3(b), or where the receiving Office, International Searching Authority or non-competent International Preliminary Examining Authority decides to submit the demand directly to the competent International Preliminary Examining Authority under r.59.3(f), the International Bureau or Authority concerned will promptly:
(a) transmit the demand to the competent International Preliminary Examining Authority, where only one is competent, and inform the applicant; or
(b) invite the applicant to indicate, by the later of 15 days from the date of the invitation or the r.54*bis*.1(a) time limit (time limit for making a demand), the International Preliminary Examining Authority that the demand is to be sent to, where more than one is competent. It will transmit the demand in accordance with any indication received from by applicant within the time limit – otherwise the demand will be considered not to have been submitted and the International Bureau/Office/Authority will so declare.

r.59.3(e)(f)   Where the competent International Examining Authority receives the demand indirectly under r.59.3(c) from the International Bureau or relevant Office/Authority, it will be considered to have been received by the competent International Examining Authority on the date marked on it under r.59.3(a) or (b).

Guidelines   See Guidelines for Search and Examination at the EPO as PCT Authority, C-II, 1 – the demand must be filed at an EPO filing office (Munich, Berlin, The Hague) when the EPO acts as IPEA, either by hand, by post, by fax or electronically.

39.4.4   Use of a form

1645   r.53.1(a)(b)   The demand must be made on a printed form or a computer printout, the details of which are specified in the Administrative Instructions. Copies of the form are available free of charge from the receiving Office and the International Preliminary Examining Authority.

39.4.5   Content of the demand

1646   The demand must contain:
r.53.2(a)(i)   (1) a petition;
r.53.3   the petition must be to the effect of, and preferably worded as: "Demand under Article 31 of the PCT: The undersigned requests that the international application specified below be the subject of international preliminary examination according to the PCT."
r.53.2(a)(ii)   (2) indications concerning the applicant and any agent appointed;

r.53.4, r.53.5	indications concerning the applicant and any agent must comply with r.4.4 and r.4.16 (concerning the content of the request – see section 30.3.8). Furthermore, r.4.5 applies mutatis mutandis to indications concerning the applicant and r.4.7 applies mutatis mutandis to indications concerning any agent.
AppGuide	See International Phase, paragraph 10.018 – the registered applicant should be indicated, even if a change of applicant has been requested pursuant to r.92*bis*.1.
r.53.5	(3) the appointment of any common representative, complying with r.4.4 and r.4.16, r.4.7 applying mutatis mutandis.
r.53.2(a)(iii)	(4) indications concerning the international application to which it relates;
r.53.6	the international application must be identified by the name and address of the applicant, the title of the invention, the international filing date (where known) and the international application number or, if such number is not known to the applicant, the name of the receiving Office with which the application was filed.
r.53.2(a)(iv)	(5) where applicable, a statement concerning amendments;
r.53.9(a)–(c)	where amendments under Art. 19 have been made, the statement must indicate whether the applicant wishes those amendments (i) to be taken into account for international preliminary examination (in which case a copy of the amendments and of the letter required under r.46.5(b) should preferably be submitted with the demand) or (ii) to be considered as reversed by an amendment made under Art. 34. Where no Art. 19 amendments have been made but the time limit for making them has not expired the statement may indicate that, if the examining authority wishes to start preliminary examination and search at the same time (as per r.69.1(b)), the applicant wishes the start of preliminary examination to be postponed (as per r.69.1(d)) until the expiration of the applicable time limit (set by r.46.1)). If any amendments under Art. 34 are submitted with the demand, the statement must so indicate.
AppGuide	See International Phase, paragraph 10.025 – if no statement concerning amendments is made, international preliminary examination is carried out on the basis of the application as filed.
r.53.2(b)	(6) a signature;
r.53.8	the demand must be signed by the applicant or, where there is more than one, by all those applicants making the demand.
r.60.1(a-*ter*)	If there are two or more applicants, it is sufficient that the demand is signed by one of them.
r.2.3	A seal is sometimes required rather than a signature (e.g. Korea).
AppGuide	See International Phase, paragraph 10.031 – an agent may sign on behalf of the applicant or applicants who appointed him. The demand may also be signed on behalf of several applicants by an appointed common representative or common agent or a deemed common representative (r.90.2(b)).

39.4.6   Filing the demand constitutes the election of all eligible States

Art. 31(4)(a)	The demand must indicate the Contracting State or States in which the applicant intends to use the results of the international preliminary examination ("elected states"). Additional Contracting States may be elected later.	1647
r.53.7	The filing of a demand constitutes the election of all Contracting States which have been designated and are bound by Chapter II of the PCT.	

39.4.7   The EPO as an elected Office

EPC Art. 153(1)(b)	The EPO will be an elected Office if the applicant has elected an EPC State which was designated for obtaining a European patent (Art. 153(1)(a) EPC).	1648

39.4.8   Fees due

Art. 31(5)	The demand for international preliminary examination is subject to the payment of certain prescribed fees within prescribed time limits.	1649
r.57.1	A handling fee, paid for the benefit of the International Bureau, is collected by the International Preliminary Examining Authority to which the demand is submitted.	

r.57.2(a)–(d)	The amount is set out in the Schedule of Fees and is payable in one or more currencies prescribed by the International Preliminary Examining Authority. Transfer is made according to r.96.2.
SoF	The handling fee is currently 200 Swiss francs. It is reduced by 90 % when the applicant (or all the applicants where there are 2 or more) is/are from certain low per capita income countries or a UN least developed country.
r.58.1(a)–(c)	In addition, each International Preliminary Examining Authority may require a preliminary examination fee, for its own benefit which is paid directly to that Authority. The amount is fixed by that Authority. Where the International Preliminary Examining Authority is a national Office, the preliminary examination fee is payable in the currency prescribed by that Office and where such Authority is an intergovernmental organisation, it is payable in the currency of the State in which the intergovernmental organisation is located or in any other currency which is freely convertible into the currency of the said State.
r.57.3, r.58.1(b)	Both fees must be paid within the later of: (a) one month from the date when the demand was submitted; or (b) 22 months from the priority date; except that where the demand is transmitted to the International Preliminary Examining Authority indirectly under r.59.3, the relevant date under (a) is one month from the date of receipt by that Authority and where, under r.69.1(b), international preliminary examination and international search are to start at the same time, that Authority will invite the applicant to pay the fees within one month of the date of the invitation. The amount due in respect of each fee is the amount applicable on the date of payment.
r.58*bis*.1(a)–(d)	Where the fees are not paid by the time limit or the amount paid is insufficient, the International Preliminary Examining Authority will invite the applicant to pay the outstanding amount (together, optionally, with any late payment fee – see below) within one month of the invitation, except that if the fees are received before such an invitation is sent, they are considered to have been received within the time limit of r.57.3/r.58.1(b). Where the invitation is not fully complied with, the demand will be considered as if it had not been submitted and the International Preliminary Examining Authority will so declare except that if payment is received before such a declaration is made it will be considered to have been received before the expiration of the one month time limit of r.58*bis*.1(a).
AppGuide	See International Phase, paragraph 10.047 – no extension of the period is possible.
r.58*bis*.2(a)–(b)	Where an invitation is submitted because fees have not been paid by the time limit or they are insufficient, the International Preliminary Examining Authority may charge a late payment fee for its own benefit (see above). The amount of such a fee is 50 % of the amount of unpaid fees or, if that amount is less than the handling fee, an amount equal to the handling fee, up to a maximum of twice the amount of the handling fee.
OJ	Before the EPO, the surcharge is 50 % of the unpaid fees ([1998] O.J. 282).
RRFArt. 2(1)(19)	The preliminary examination fee is € 1840 where the EPO is International Preliminary Examining Authority.
OJ	Where the EPO acts as International Preliminary Examining Authority for an applicant who is (a) a natural person, who is a national and resident of a country which is not an EPC contracting state, and which, on the date on which the international preliminary examination fee is paid, is classified by the World Bank as a low-income or lower-middle-income economy; or (b) a natural or legal person who, within the meaning of r.18 PCT, is a national and resident of a state in which a validation agreement with the European Patent Organisation is in force; then the international preliminary examination fee is reduced by 75 % (Decision of the Administrative Council dated 12 December 2019, [2020] O.J. A4; Art. 5 and Annex D of the agreement between the EPO and the International Bureau, [2020] O.J. A35). If there are several applicants then each must satisfy the relevant criterion. For the list of qualifying low-income and lower-middle-income countries see [2022] O.J. A72.
r.57.4	The International Preliminary examining Authority will refund the handling fee to the applicant: (i) if the demand is withdrawn before the demand has been sent by that Authority to the International Bureau; or (ii) if the demand is considered, under r.54.4 (applicant not having the right to make a demand) or r.54*bis*.1(b) (demand made too late), not to have been submitted.

r.58.3

The International Preliminary Examining Authorities inform the International Bureau of the extent, if any, to which, and the conditions, if any, under which they will refund any amount paid as a preliminary examination fee where the demand is considered as if it had not been submitted and the International Bureau promptly publishes such information.

OJ

See the Art. 5(3) and Annex D of the agreement between the EPO and the International Bureau ([2017] O.J. A115). The EPO refunds the examination fee in full where the international application or the demand is withdrawn before examination has started or where the demand is deemed not to have been filed.

39.4.9   *Acceptable languages of the demand*

r.55.1

Where a translation of the international application is required under r.55.2 (see below),   1650
the demand must be in the language of the translation. Otherwise, it must be in either:
(1) the language of the international application as filed; or
(2) the language of publication, if it is different.

39.4.10   *Acceptable languages of the application*

r.55.2(a)(b)

Where neither the language of the international application as filed, nor the language of   1651
publication is accepted by the International Preliminary Examining Authority, the applicant must furnish with the demand a translation of the international application into a language which is both:
(a) accepted by that Authority; and
(b) a language of publication;
unless such a translation has already been transmitted to the International Searching Authority under r.23.1(b) for the purposes of the international search and the International Preliminary Examining Authority is part of the same national Office or intergovernmental organisation. In this case, unless such a translation is nevertheless transmitted, examination will be carried out on the basis of the r.23.1(b) translation.

r.55.2(a-*bis*)

Any translation submitted according to r.55.2(a) must include any element referred to in Art. 11(1)(iii)(d) or (e) (description and claims) furnished by the applicant under r.20.3(b), r.20.5*bis*(b), r.20.5*bis*(c) or r.20.6(a) and any part of the description, claims or drawings furnished by the applicant under r.20.5(b), r.20.5(c), r.20.5*bis*(b), r.20.5*bis*(c) or r.20.6(a) which is considered to have been contained in the international application under r.20.6(b) (incorporation of elements or parts by reference).

r.55.2(a-*ter*)

The International Preliminary Examining Authority will check any translation furnished under r.55.2(a) for compliance with the physical requirements referred to in r.11 to the extent that compliance therewith is necessary for the purposes of the international preliminary examination.

r.55.2(c)(d)

Where a required translation is not submitted, or the submitted translation does not comply with r.55.2(a-*bis*) or r.55.2(a-*ter*), the International Preliminary Examining Authority will invite the applicant, within a reasonable time limit (not shorter than a month), which may be extended at that Authority's discretion at any time before a decision is taken, to correct the deficiency. Where the invitation is not complied with, the demand will be considered never to have been submitted and the International Preliminary Examining Authority will so declare.

r.12.2(c)

Any correction, under r.55.2(c), of a defect in a translation furnished under r.55.2(a) for preliminary examination must be in the language of the translation.

39.4.11   *Acceptable languages of amendments*

Art. 34(2)(b)

The applicant has the right to amend the description, claims and drawings – see   1652
section 39.9.5

r.12.2(a)

Any amendment of the international application, subject to r.55.3, must be in the language in which the international application was filed.

r.55.3(a)

Subject to r.55.3(b), if the international application has been filed in a language other than the language in which it is published, any amendment under Art. 34, as well as any letter referred to in r.66.8(a), r.66.8(b) and r.46.5(b) (explaining the basis for and reasons for amendment) as applicable by virtue of r.66.8(c), shall be submitted in the language of publication.

r.55.3(b)	Where translation of the international application is required under r.55.2:

r.55.3(b)

Where translation of the international application is required under r.55.2:
(i) any amendment and any letter referred to in r.55.3(a); and
(ii) any amendment under Art. 19 which is to be taken into account under r.66.1(c) or (d) and any letter referred to in r.46.5(b);
shall be in the language of that translation. Where such amendments or letters have been or are submitted in another language, a translation shall also be submitted.

r.55.3(c)

If an amendment or letter is not submitted in a language as required under r.55.3(a) or (b), the International Preliminary Examining Authority shall invite the applicant to submit the amendment or letter in the required language within a time limit which shall be reasonable under the circumstances. That time limit shall not be less than one month from the date of the invitation. It may be extended by the International Preliminary Examining Authority at any time before a decision is taken.

r.55.3(d)

If the applicant fails to comply, within the time limit under r.55.3(c), with the invitation to furnish an amendment in the required language, the amendment shall not be taken into account for the purposes of the international preliminary examination. If the applicant fails to comply, within the time limit under r.55.3(c), with the invitation to furnish a letter referred to in r.55.3(a) in the required language, the amendment concerned need not be taken into account for the purposes of the international preliminary examination.

39.4.12   *Languages before the EPO*

1653 OJ

See Art. 3(2) and Annex A to the agreement between the EPO and the International Bureau ([2017] O.J. A115 and [2018] O.J. A24). The languages accepted by the EPO for international preliminary examination are English, French and German or, where the receiving Office was the Netherlands office, Dutch.

39.5   Later election of States

1654 Art. 31(4)(a)
Art. 31(6)(b)

Additional Contracting States not elected in the demand may be elected later.
States may be elected subsequent to submission of the demand. Such election should be submitted to the International Bureau.

r.53.7

This provision has been rendered obsolete since the filing of a demand now has the effect of electing all eligible States.

39.6   Procedure where there are defects in the demand

39.6.1   *Applicant not entitled to make a demand*

1655 r.54.4

Where the applicant does not have the right to make a demand within the meaning of r.54.2 (or, in the case of joint applicants, none of them has) the demand is considered not to have been submitted.

r.61.1(b)
AdminInst

The applicant and International Bureau are informed of the decision.
See s.614 – such a finding can be reversed if the applicant offers evidence that the demand contains an error concerning the applicant's residence or nationality. In such a case the demand is corrected and keeps its original date of filing. See also AppGuide, International Phase, paragraph 10.046.

39.6.2   *Invitation by the International Preliminary Examining Authority to correct formal defects*

1656 r.60.1

(a) Where the demand:(1) has not been made on a printed form or presented as a computer printout complying with the Administrative Instructions (r.53.1);
(2) does not contain a petition (r.53.2(a)(i)) complying with r.53.3, indications concerning the applicant (r.53.2(a)(ii)) complying with r.53.4, indications concerning any appointed agent (r.53.2(a)(ii)) complying with r.53.5 or indications concerning the relevant international application (r.53.2(a)(iii)) complying with r.53.6;
(3) is not signed in the manner indicated by r.53.8 (r.53.2(b)); or
(4) is not in the appropriate language (r.55.1);

	the International Preliminary Examining Authority will invite the applicant to correct the deficiency within a reasonable time limit which may not be less than one month from the date of the invitation and can be extended by that Authority at any time before a decision is taken.
r.60.1(a-*bis*)	However, where there are two or more applicants, it is sufficient that the indications referred to in r.4.5(a)(ii) (address) and (iii) (nationality and residence) are provided in respect of one of them who has the right according to r.54.2 to file a demand.
r.60.1(a-*ter*)	Furthermore, where there are two or more applicants, it is sufficient for the purposes of r.53.8, that the demand is signed by one of them.
r.60.1(b)	If the applicant complies with the invitation within the time limit then the corrected demand will either: (1) be considered as received on its actual filing date if the demand as submitted permitted the international application to be identified, or else (2) be considered as received on the date when the correction was received.
r.60.1(c)	If the applicant does not comply with the invitation within the time limit then the demand will be considered as if it had never been submitted and the International Preliminary Examining Authority will so declare.
r.58*bis*.1	See also above under fees for the procedure where insufficient fees are paid.

39.6.3   *Procedure where a statement concerning amendments is omitted or is misleading*

r.60.1(g)	Where a statement concerning amendments in the demand indicates that amendments under Art. 34 are submitted, as per r.53.9(c), but no such amendments are, in fact, submitted, the International Preliminary Examining Authority will invite the applicant to supply the amendments within a fixed time limit and proceed as provided by r.69.1(e) (start of examination will be delayed until the amendments are received or the time limit in the invitation is exceeded).	1657
r.60.1(f)	Where a statement concerning amendments is omitted, the International Preliminary Examining Authority will proceed in its absence under r.69.1(a) or (b) (regarding when to start examination) and r.66.1 (which amendments are to be taken into account).	

39.6.4   *Defects noticed by the International Bureau*

r.60.1(e)	If the International Bureau notices a defect in the demand it will bring it to the attention of the International Preliminary Examining Authority which will proceed as if it had noticed the defect itself under r.60.1(a) to (c).	1658

39.7   Procedural steps taken by the international authorities on receipt of the demand

39.7.1   *Procedure of the International Preliminary Examining Authority on receipt of the demand – notification to the International Bureau and the applicant*

r.61.1(a)(b)	On receiving a demand, the International Preliminary Examining Authority will: (i) indicate on the demand the date of receipt (or the date of receipt of a correction that leads to a later date under r.60.1(b)); (ii) send a copy of the demand to the International Bureau and keep the original in its files or vice versa; (iii) promptly notify the applicant of the date of receipt of the demand; and (iv) where the demand has been considered as if it had not been submitted under r.54.4 (applicant not entitled to make a demand), r.55.2(d) (translation not furnished), r.58*bis*.1(b) (fees not paid) or r.60.1(c) (defects in the demand not corrected), notify the International Bureau and the applicant accordingly.	1659

39.7.2   *Notification to elected States of their election by the International Bureau and other related actions*

Art. 31(7)	Each elected Office is notified of its election.	1660
r.61.2(a)	This notification is effected by the International Bureau.	

r.61.2(c)	The notification will be sent together with the Art. 20 communication (of the international application to designated Offices), if the elections are made in time, or else promptly if they are made later.
r.61.2(b)	The notification will indicate: (i) the number and filing date of the international application; (ii) the name of the applicant; (iii) the filing date of any application whose priority is claimed, where appropriate; and (iv) the date the demand was received by the International Preliminary Examining Authority.
r.61.3	The International Bureau informs the applicant in writing that the notification under r.61.2 has taken place, stating which elected Offices have been notified.
r.61.4	The International Bureau publishes in the Gazette, promptly after the filing of the demand but not before international publication, information on the demand and the elected States concerned, as provided in the Administrative Instructions.

39.7.3   *Notification of the written opinion and any Art. 19 amendments to the International Preliminary Examining Authority by the International Bureau*

1661	r.62.1	When the International Bureau receives the demand or a copy of the demand from the International Preliminary Examining Authority, it will promptly transmit to the International Preliminary Examining Authority: (a) a copy of the written opinion established under r.43*bis*.1, unless the International Searching Authority and International Preliminary Examination Authority are the same Office or organisation; and (b) a copy of any amendments filed under Art. 19, a copy of any statement filed under Art. 19 explaining such amendments and a copy of the letter required under r.46.5(b) identifying the amendments and their basis (unless the International Preliminary Examining Authority has indicated that it has already received such a copy).
	r.62.2	If a demand has already been submitted when the applicant files amendments under Art. 19 with the International Bureau, the applicant should simultaneously file a copy of such amendments, a copy of any accompanying statement under Art. 19 and a copy of the letter required under r.46.5(b) with the International Preliminary Examining Authority. In any case, the International Bureau will promptly transmit a copy of such documents to the International Preliminary Examining Authority.

39.8   The objective of international preliminary examination

39.8.1   *Aspects of patentability examined*

1662	Art. 33(1)(5)	The objective of the examination is not to decide whether the claimed invention is patentable in the Contracting States but to formulate a preliminary and non-binding opinion as to whether the claimed invention appears to be novel, to involve an inventive step (to be non-obvious) and to be industrially applicable, as defined by the PCT.

39.8.2   *Definitions of novelty, inventive step and industrial applicability*

1663	Art. 33(2)	For the purpose of international preliminary examination, a claimed invention is novel if it is not anticipated by the prior art as defined in the Regulations.
	Art. 33(3), r.65.1	For the purpose international preliminary examination, a claimed invention is taken to involve an inventive step if, at the prescribed relevant date, it is not to be obvious to a person skilled in the art having regard to the prior art as defined in the Regulations and taking into account the relation of a claim to the prior at as a whole, that is individual documents of the prior art (or parts thereof) taken separately and combinations of such documents (or parts) where the combination would have been obvious to a person skilled in the art.
	r.65.2	Inventive step is to be judged at the relevant date as defined in r.64.1 (see below under the definition of prior art).
	Art. 33(4)	For the purpose of international preliminary examination, a claimed invention is taken to be industrially applicable if it can be made or used (in the technological sense) in any kind of industry (understood in its broadest sense as in the Paris Convention).

39.8.3 Definition of prior art

r.64.1(a)(b) For the purposes of Art. 33(2) (novelty) and Art. 33(3) (inventive step), prior art is defined 1664
as everything made available to the public anywhere in the world by means of written
disclosure (including drawings and other illustrations) prior to the filing date of the international application, or where priority is validly claimed, the filing date of the priority
document ("the relevant date"). The priority claim is not to be considered invalid only
because the international application was filed after the end of the priority period if it was
filed within two months from that date.

r.64.2, r.64.3 The prior art does not therefore include:
(1) anything made available to the public by oral disclosure, use, exhibition or other
non-written means before the relevant date (r.64.1(b)) even if the date of such non-written
disclosure is indicated in a written disclosure whose date is the same as or after the relevant date; or
(2) patents and patent applications filed earlier than, or having an priority date earlier
than, the relevant date but published on or later than the relevant date.

r.64.2, r.64.3 Nevertheless, the International Preliminary Examination Report will call attention to
such non-written disclosures, patents and patent applications as indicated in r.70.9 (by indicating the kind of disclosure and dates of written and non-written forms made available
to the public) and r.70.10 (by indicating the filing/priority date, publication date, whether
priority validly claimed).

39.8.4 Documents to be taken into consideration

Art. 33(6) The examination will take into consideration all the documents cited in the International 1665
Search Report and any others considered to be relevant.

39.9 Procedure before the International Preliminary Examining Authority

39.9.1 When international preliminary examination starts and finishes

r.69.1(a) The International Preliminary Examining Authority will start international preliminary 1666
examination when it is in possession of: (a) the demand; (b) all fees that are due (handling
fee, preliminary examination fee, r.58*bis*.2 late payment fee where appropriate); (c) either
the International Search Report or the Art. 17(2)(a) declaration that no search report will
be established; and (d) the written opinion established under r.43*bis*.1; except that:

r.69(1)(a) (1) the applicant may expressly request that the start of international preliminary examination be postponed until the expiration of the time limit under r.54*bis*.1(a);

r.69.1(c) (2) where the statement concerning amendments states that amendments made under
Art. 19 are to be taken into account (r.53.9(a)(i)) preliminary examination may not start
until the International Preliminary Examining Authority has received a copy of such
amendments;

r.69.1(d) (3) where the statement concerning amendments states that preliminary examination is
to be postponed (r.53.9(b)), preliminary examination may not start until either the International Preliminary Examining Authority has received a copy of any amendments made
under Art. 19, or the International Preliminary Examining Authority has received a notice
from the applicant that no Art. 19 amendments are to be made or the r.46.1 time limit (for
amending under Art. 19) has expired; and

r.69.1(e) (4) where the statement concerning amendments indicates that amendments made under Art. 34 are submitted with the demand and none are actually submitted, preliminary
examination may not start until the amendments are received or the r.60.1(g) time limit
has expired (time limit set in an invitation from the International Preliminary Examining
Authority).

r.69.1(b) However, where the competent International Searching and Preliminary Examining Authorities are part of the same national Office or intergovernmental organisation and the
International Preliminary Examining Authority so wishes, international preliminary examination may start at the same time as international search, except that:

r.69.1(d)	(1) where the statement concerning amendments states that preliminary examination is to be postponed (r.53.9(b)), preliminary examination may not start until either the International Preliminary Examining Authority has received a copy of any amendments made under Art. 19, or the International Preliminary Examining Authority has received a notice from the applicant that no Art. 19 amendments are to be made or the r.46.1 time limit (for amending under Art. 19) has expired; and
r.69.1(e)	(2) where the statement concerning amendments indicates that amendments made under Art. 34 are submitted with the demand and none are actually submitted, preliminary examination may not start until the amendments are received or the r.60.1(g) time limit has expired (time limit set in an invitation from the International Preliminary Examining Authority).
r.69.2	The International Preliminary Examining Authority must finish the examination (i.e. establish the International Preliminary Examination Report) by the later of: (a) 28 months from the priority date; (b) six months from the r.69.1 time limit for the start of international preliminary examination; and (c) six months from the date of receipt by the International Preliminary Examining Authority of a translation which is necessary under r.55.2.

39.9.2   General provisions governing procedure

1667	Art. 34(1)	Procedure before the International Preliminary Examining Authority is governed by the provisions of the PCT, its Regulations and the Agreement between the International Bureau and the International Preliminary Examining Authority.

39.9.3   Right of the applicant to communicate with the International Preliminary Examining Authority

1668	Art. 34(2)(a)	The applicant has the right to communicate orally and in writing with the International Preliminary Examining Authority.
	r.66.6	The International Preliminary Examining Authority may communicate informally (by telephone, personal interview or in writing) with the applicant at any time. It will decide, at its discretion, whether to grant more than one personal interview (if so requested by the applicant) or whether it wishes to reply to any informal written communication from the applicant.
	Guidelines	The EPO, acting as International Preliminary Examining Authority, will grant a telephone interview but not a personal interview (see Guidelines for Search and Examination at the EPO as a PCT Authority, C-VII, 1).

39.9.4   Documents on which the examination is based

1669	r.66.1(a)(c)	The international preliminary examination is based on the application as filed, taking into account any amendment made under Art. 19 before the demand is filed unless superseded or considered reversed by an amendment under Art. 34.
	r.66.1(d)	Any amendment made under Art. 19 after the demand is filed and any amendment under Art. 34 must also be taken into account with the proviso that such an amendment does not need to be taken into account for the purposes of a written opinion or the international preliminary examination report if received by the International Preliminary Examining Authority after it has begun to draw up that opinion or report (r.66.4*bis*).
	r.66.1(d-*bis*)	A rectification of an obvious mistake that is authorised under r.91.1 must also taken into account by the International Preliminary Examining Authority for the purposes of the international preliminary examination with the proviso that such a rectification does not need to be taken into account for the purposes of a written opinion or the international preliminary examination report if authorised by or notified to the International Preliminary Examining Authority after it has begun to draw up that opinion or report.
	r.66.1(e)	However, any claim relating to an invention in respect of which no International Search Report has been established need not be the subject of international preliminary examination.

39.9.5 *Applicant's right to amend*

Art. 34(2)(b)

The applicant has the right to amend the claims, description and drawings in the pre- 1670
scribed manner and within the prescribed time limit. Amendment must not go beyond the
disclosure in the international application as filed – see r.70.2(c) for the consequences for
drafting of the International Preliminary Examination Report where subject matter has
been added by an amendment.

r.66.1(b)

The applicant may submit amendments under Art. 34 when filing the demand or at any
time until the International Preliminary Examination Report is established, subject to
r.66.4*bis* (amendments, arguments and rectifications of obvious mistakes need not be tak-
en into account by the International Examining Authority for the purposes of a written
opinion or the International Preliminary Examination Report if they are received by,
authorised by or notified to that authority, as applicable, after it has begun to draw up
that opinion or report).

r.66.5

An amendment is defined as any change other than the rectification of an obvious mistake
in the claims, description or drawings, including the cancellation of claims, omission of
passages in the description and omission of certain drawings.

r.66.8(a)

Subject to r.66.8(b), when amending the description or the drawings, the applicant must
submit a replacement sheet for every sheet of the international application which, on account of an amendment, differs from the sheet previously filed. The replacement sheet
or sheets must be accompanied by a letter drawing attention to the differences between
the replaced sheets and the replacement sheets, indicating the basis for the amendment
in the application as filed and preferably also explaining the reasons for the amendment.
See r.70.2(c-*bis*) for the consequences of not providing a letter explaining the basis for the
amended claims.

r.66.8(b)

Where the amendment consists in the deletion of passages or in minor alterations or additions, the replacement sheet referred to in r.66.8(a) may be a copy of the relevant sheet
of the international application containing the alterations or additions, provided that the
clarity and direct reproducibility of that sheet are not adversely affected. To the extent
that any amendment results in the cancellation of an entire sheet, that amendment must be
communicated in a letter which preferably also explains the reasons for the amendment.

r.66.8(c)

When amending the claims, r.46.5 (form of amendments to the claims under Art. 19) applies mutatis mutandis. The set of claims submitted under r.46.5 as applicable by virtue of this paragraph replaces all the claims originally filed or previously amended under
Art. 19 or Art. 34, as the case may be.

r.11.14

The amendments must comply with all the requirements of r.10 (terminology and signs)
and r.11.1 to r.11.13 (physical requirements).

Comment

See section 39.4.11 for the language in which amendments must be presented.

AppGuide

See International Phase, paragraph 10.028 – Art. 34 amendments should preferably be submitted with the demand since, most frequently, the written opinion of the International
Searching Authority will be considered to be the first written opinion of the International
Preliminary Examining Authority and the International Preliminary Examination Report
may be drawn up at any time following expiry of the period under r.54*bis*.1(a).

Guidelines

See Guidelines for Search and Examination at the EPO as PCT Authority, H-I, 3 – if
the applicant indicates in the demand that he is filing amendments but none are actually
submitted, the EPO will invite the applicant to submit them within a time limit. Amendments should be filed with the demand but if the applicant has asked for preliminary examination to commence only at the expiry of the r.54*bis*.1(a) period then any amendments
filed before then will be taken into account. See also C-IX, 2 – auxiliary requests are not
allowed.

39.9.6 *Situations where the International Preliminary Examining Authority is not*
obliged to examine part of or the whole of an application

Art. 34(4)(a)(i)

If the International Preliminary Examining Authority considers that the subject matter of 1671
the international application relates to:

r.67.1

(i) a scientific or mathematical theory;
(ii) a plant or animal variety or an essentially biological process for the production of
plants or animals, other than a microbiological process or the product of such a process;

(iii) a scheme, rule or method of doing business, performing a purely mental act or playing a game;

(iv) a method of treatment of the human or animal body by surgery or therapy, or a diagnostic method;

(v) a mere presentation of information; or

(vi) a computer program (to the extent that the Examining Authority is not equipped to carry out an international preliminary examination concerning such programs);

that Authority may decide not to examine the application and will inform the applicant of its opinion and the reasons therefore (in the written opinion (r.66.2(a)(i)) and in the International Preliminary Examination Report (r.70.12(iii)).

OJ   See Art. 4 and Annex C of the agreement between the EPO and the International Bureau ([2017] O.J. A115). Before the EPO, those matters listed by r.67 are excluded, with the exception of any particular subject matter than would be examined by the EPO in grant proceedings for a direct-filed European patent application.

Art. 34(4)(a)(ii)   If the Examining Authority considers that the description, claims or drawings are so unclear or the claims are so inadequately supported by the description that no meaningful opinion can be formed on the novelty, inventive step (non-obviousness) or industrial applicability of the claimed invention then it will not carry out a preliminary examination and will inform the applicant of its decision and the reasons therefore (in the written opinion (r.66.2(a)(i)) and the International Preliminary Examination Report (r.70.12(iii)).

Art. 34(4)(b)   If any of these circumstances (Art. 34(4)(a)(i) and (ii)) relate only to certain claims, then the non-examination will likewise apply only to those claims.

r.66.1(e)   Claims relating to inventions in respect of which no International Search Report has been established need not be the subject of international preliminary examination (the applicant being notified in the written opinion (r.66.2(a)(vi)) and the International Preliminary Examination Report (r.70.2(d)).

r.66.2   Where multiple dependent claims have been drafted in a manner incompatible with r.6.4(a), second and third sentences (they must refer to the other claims in the alternative only and not serve as the basis for any other multiply-dependent claim) and the national law of a national Office acting as International Preliminary Examining Authority does not so allow, that Authority will apply Art. 34(4)(b) (that claim will not be examined) and notify the applicant accordingly in writing (in the written opinion (r.66.2)).

r.70.2(c)   Amended claims do not have to be examined if the International Preliminary Examining Authority considers that the amendments go beyond the disclosure in the international application as filed.

r.70.2(c-*bis*)   Amended claims do not have to be examined if amended sheets are not accompanied by a letter required pursuant to r.46.5(b)(iii) (applicable by virtue of r.66.8(c) or r.66.8(a)) indicating the basis for the amendments in the application as filed.

39.9.7   *The written opinion of the International Preliminary Examining Authority and responses thereto*

1672   Art. 34(2)(c)   The International Preliminary Examining Authority must send the applicant at least one written opinion unless it considers that:

(i) the invention satisfies the requirements of Art. 33(1), i.e. is novel, involves and inventive step and is industrially applicable; and

(ii) the international application complies with the requirements of the PCT in so far as checked by the International Preliminary Examining Authority; and

(iii) no observations under Art. 35(2), last sentence, are intended to be made (any other observations on the application provided for in the Regulations).

r.66.1*bis*   However, in certain cases, the written opinion of the International Search Authority is considered to be the written opinion of the International Preliminary Examining Authority (see below).

r.66.4   In addition, the International Preliminary examining Authority may issue one or more additional written opinions using the same rules outlined below (r.66.2 and r.66.3) and if the applicant so requests, that Authority may give him one or more additional opportunities to submit amendments or arguments.

OJ	See Notice from the EPO dated 31 August 2011 ([2011] O.J. 532). The EPO now generally undertakes to issue one additional written opinion before issuing a negative international preliminary examination report if the applicant has filed a substantive response to the first written opinion.
Guidelines	See Guidelines for Search and Examination at the EPO as PCT Authority, C-IV, 2.2 – If the applicant has filed a substantive response to the WO-ISA in good time then he will be given a further chance to comment before issuance of a negative IPER in the form of a further written opinion or the minutes of any telephone consultation.
r.66.2(a)	When drawing up a first written opinion, the International Preliminary Examining Authority must notify the applicant if it:

(i) considers that one of the situations referred to in Art. 34(4) exists (the application relates to subject matter not requiring examination or the description/claims/drawings are so unclear or the claims so lack support that examination is not possible);

(ii) considers that any claim describes an invention which does not appear to be novel, appears to be obvious or does not appear to be industrially applicable;

(iii) notices that there is some defect in the form or contents of the international application under the PCT and its Regulations;

(iv) considers that any amendment goes beyond the disclosure of the application as filed;

(v) wishes to accompany the International Preliminary Examination Report with observations on the clarity of the claims, description or drawings or wishes to question whether the claims are fully supported by the description;

(vi) considers that a claim relates to an invention in respect of which no International Search Report has been established and has decided not to examine that claim;

(vii) considers that a nucleotide and/or amino acid sequence listing is not available to it in such a form that a meaningful examination can be carried out; or

(viii) decides not to examine certain claims that are multiply-dependent in a manner different from that provided for by r.6.4(a) due to provisions of national law.

r.66.2(b)	The first written opinion must state the reasons underlying the opinion of the International Preliminary Examining Authority.
r.66.2(c)(d)(e)	In its notification, the International Preliminary Examining Authority will invite the applicant to submit a written reply (together, where appropriate, with amendments) and will fix a reasonable time limit for reply which is between one and three months from the date of notification (usually two months) and at least two months if the written opinion is submitted with the International Search Report. It may be extended if the applicant so requests before its expiry.
Art. 34(2)(d)	The applicant may respond to the written opinion.
r.66.3(a)(b)	The response should be submitted directly to the International Preliminary Examining Authority and may include arguments and/or amendments as appropriate.
Guidelines	See Guidelines for Search and Examination at the EPO as PCT Authority, C-VI, 3 – if the WO-ISA is considered the first opinion of the IPEA, a one month extension will be granted by the EPO if requested before expiry of the normal time limit under r.54*bis* (time limit for filing a demand) and if the time limit so extended does not expire later than 25 months from the (earliest) priority date. A further extension will not be allowed. If the first written opinion of the IPEA is not the WO-ISA then an extension will be granted if requested before expiry of the time limit set and the extended time limit does not expire later than 27 months from the (earliest) priority date.

39.9.8   Circumstances in which the written opinion established by the International Searching Authority is considered to be a written opinion of the International Preliminary Examining Authority

1673   r.66.1*bis*(a)(b)   The written opinion established by the International Searching Authority pursuant to r.43*bis*.1 will be considered to be a written opinion of the International Preliminary Examining Authority for the purposes of r.66.2(a) unless the International Preliminary Examining Authority has notified the International Bureau that it will not apply this procedure in respect of written opinions established under r.43*bis*.1 by one or more International Searching Authorities specified in the notification (such notification not applying where the International Searching Authority and International Preliminary Examining Authority are the same Office or organisation). Such notification will be published by the International Bureau in the Gazette.

WIPO   The EPO has filed reservations. It only considers the written opinion of the ISA to be a written opinion of the IPEA when it acted as ISA.

Comment   When the International Searching Authority notifies the International Search Report and the written opinion to the applicant, the written opinion (form PCT/ISA/237) invites the applicant to file a response to the written opinion with the International Preliminary Examining Authority where the written opinion is to be considered as the first written opinion of the IPEA within the time limit for filing a demand.

r.66.1*bis*(c)(d)   Where the written opinion of the International Searching Authority is not considered to be a written opinion of the International Preliminary Examining Authority, the International Preliminary Examining Authority will notify the applicant accordingly in writing and will nevertheless take into account the written opinion of the International Searching Authority when preparing its own written opinion under r.66.2(a).

39.9.9   Situation where amendments and arguments may be ignored

1674   r.66.4*bis*   Amendments, arguments and the rectification of obvious errors need not be taken into account by the International Preliminary Examining Authority for the purposes of a written opinion or the International Preliminary Examination Report if they are received by, authorised by or notified to that Authority, as applicable, after it has begun to draw up that opinion or report.

Guidelines   See Guidelines for Search and Examination at the EPO as PCT Authority, C-IV, 3 – in fact, a response received after the IPER has been started will be taken into account if it meets all objections raised.

39.9.10   Procedure where the International Preliminary Examining Authority needs a copy of the priority document or translation thereof

1675   r.66.7(a)(b)   If the International Preliminary Examining Authority needs a copy of the priority document, the International Bureau will furnish a copy on request. If such a priority document is not in one of the languages of that Authority and the priority document is necessary in order to formulate an opinion under Art. 33(1) (as to whether the claimed invention is novel, non-obvious and industrially applicable), it may invite the applicant to furnish a translation in one of the said languages within two months from the date of the invitation.

r.66.7(a)(b)   If the International Bureau cannot furnish the priority document because the applicant failed to comply with r.17.1 (i.e. supply a certified copy) and the priority document was neither filed with the International Preliminary Examining Authority in its capacity as a national Office nor available to it from a digital library in accordance with the Administrative Instructions or if the applicant fails to furnish a required translation within the time limit, the International Preliminary Examination Report may be established as if the relevant priority had not been claimed.

39.9.11   Procedure where unity is in dispute

1676   AdminInst   See s.206. The determination of unity by the International Preliminary Examining Authority must be made in line with the instructions in Annex B of the Administrative Instructions.

Art. 34(3)(a)	If the International Preliminary Examining Authority considers that the international application does not comply with the requirement for unity of invention as set forth in the Regulations (see r.13) it may invite the applicant, at his option, to restrict the claims so as to comply with the requirement or pay an extra fee (payable directly to that Authority, which decides the amount – r.68.3(a)(b)).
r.68.1	Where the International Preliminary Examining Authority decides not to invite the applicant to restrict the claims or pay extra fees it must proceed to examine the whole application (subject to Art. 34(4)(b) (certain claims not examined – see above) and r.66.1(e) (unsearched claims need not be examined)) but may indicate in any written opinion and in the International Preliminary Examination Report that it considers unity to be lacking and the reasons therefor.
r.68.2(i)–(v)	Where the International Preliminary Examining Authority does decide to invite the applicant to restrict the claims or pay extra fees, it must specify (1) its reasons for denying unity, (2) at least one restriction which, in its opinion, would comply with the unity requirement and (3) the amount of the additional fees. It will set a time limit for complying with the invitation of one month from the date of the invitation.
r.68.2(v)	It must also invite the applicant to pay, where applicable, a protest fee within one month from the date of the invitation and indicate the amount to be paid.
r.68.3(c)–(e)	Any applicant may pay the additional fees under protest, i.e. accompanied by a statement explaining why the claims comply with the requirement for unity or why the additional fees are excessive. The protest will be examined by a review body of the International Preliminary Examining Authority which may include, but not be limited to the person who made the decision under protest and which will order the total or partial reimbursement of the additional fees to the extent it finds the protest justified. If the applicant so requests, the text of the protest and the subsequent decision will be notified to the designated Offices as an annex to the International Preliminary Examination Report. Where an additional fee is paid under protest, the Examining Authority may require the applicant to pay a protest fee. Where the applicant has not within the one-month time limit according to r.68.2(v), paid any required protest fee, the protest will be considered not to have been made and the Examining Authority will so declare. The protest fee will be refunded if examination of the protest reveals that the protest was entirely justified.
Art. 34(3)(c)	If the applicant does not comply with the invitation under Art. 34(3)(a) within the time limit set (or if the applicant restricts his claims but not sufficiently to comply with the unity requirement – r.68.4), the International Preliminary Examining Authority will establish its international preliminary examination report on those parts of the application which relate to what appears to be the main invention, and indicate the relevant facts in that report.
r.68.5	In cases of doubt, the invention first mentioned in the claims is considered to be the main invention.

39.9.12   Lack of unity where the EPO is International Preliminary Examining Authority

EPC r.158(2)	An additional fee, equal to the international preliminary examination fee, is payable in respect of each additional invention.	1677
RRFArt. 2(1)(19)	The international preliminary examination fee is € 1840.	
EPC r.158(3)	Where an additional fee has been paid under protest, the EPO will examine the protest in accordance with r.68.3(c) to (e) PCT subject to the payment of the prescribed protest fee. Further details concerning the procedure are determined by the President of the EPO.	
OJ	See Decision of the President dated 09 June 2015 ([2015] O.J. A59). The protest is examined by a three-member review panel consisting of three examiners, one of whom will chair the panel and another of whom will be the examiner who was responsible for issuing the invitation to pay additional fees under Art. 34(3)(a) PCT.	
RRFArt. 2(1)(21)	The protest fee is € 980.	

39.9.13   Procedure where a sequence listing is absent or in the wrong format

r.13*ter*.2	The International Preliminary Examining Authority may demand the provision of a sequence listing under r.13*ter*.1 in the same way as the International Searching Authority (see section 33.4.3).	1678

| r.66.2(a)(vii) | The International Preliminary Examining Authority will use the first written opinion to inform the applicant where it considers that a sequence listing is not available in such a form that a meaningful examination can be carried out. |
| r.70.12(iv) | This information is also contained in the International Preliminary Examination Report. |

39.9.14   Top-up search

1679	r.66.1*ter*	The International Preliminary Examining Authority must conduct a search ("top-up search") to discover documents referred to in r.64 (definition of prior art for international preliminary examination) which have been published or have become available to the said Authority for search subsequent to the date on which the international search report was established, unless it considers that such a search would serve no useful purpose. If the Authority finds that any of the situations referred to in Art. 34(3) (lack of unity) or Art. 34(4) (no examination necessary or no examination possible) or r.66.1(e) (claims not searched) exists, the top-up search need only to cover those parts of the international application that are the subject of international preliminary examination.
	Comment	This provision applies to international applications for which a demand for international preliminary examination was made on or after 01 July 2014.
	AppGuide	See International Phase, paragraph 10.062A – the additional search would serve no useful purpose, for example, if the application related to subject matter for which no international preliminary examination was required.
	OJ	See [2014] OJ A57. The EPO will be implementing this new provision when acting as IPEA by performing a top-up search at the start of the Chapter II procedure, mainly looking for Art. 54(3) documents.
	Guidelines	See Guidelines for Search and Examination at the EPO as PCT Authority, C-IV, 5. The top-up search is not conducted for subject matter not searched by the ISA, subject matter excluded from international preliminary examination, claims that contain added matter and claims for which no basis has been provided.

39.9.15   Third party observations

| 1680 | Guidelines | See Guidelines for Search and Examination at the EPO as PCT Authority, C-VII, 3 – third party observations (see section 44.7) are taken into account by the IPEA in certain circumstances. |

39.10   The International Preliminary Examination Report (IPER)

39.10.1   Time limit for establishing the International Preliminary Examination Report

| 1681 | Art. 35(1), r.69.2 | The International Preliminary Examination Report must be established within whichever of the following periods expires last:
(i) 28 months from the priority date; or
(ii) six months from the time provided under r.69.1 for the start of on international preliminary examination; or
(iii) six months from the date of receipt by the International Preliminary Examining Authority of the translation of the application furnished under r.55.2. |

39.10.2   Requirements as to form

| 1682 | Art. 35(1) | The International Preliminary Examination Report must be established in the prescribed form. |
| | r.70.15(a) | Physical requirements relating to the prescribed form are laid out in the Administrative Instructions. |

39.10.3   Language of the report (and any annexes)

| 1683 | r.70.17 | The report and any annex must be in the language in which the international application was published or, if a translation under r.55.2 has been supplied for the purposes of international preliminary examination, in the language of that translation. |

39.10.4   *Documents on which the report is based*

r.70.2(a)(c)   The report must be based on any amended claims submitted by the applicant except that   1684
any amendment considered by the International Preliminary Examining Authority to go
beyond the disclosure of the international application as filed may be ignored and the
report will so state (indicating the relevant reasons).

r.70.2(c-*bis*)   Furthermore, the report does not have to be based on any amendment to the application
if amended sheets containing the amendment are not accompanied by a letter required
pursuant to r.46.5(b)(iii) (applicable by virtue of r.66.8(c) or r.66.8(a)) indicating the basis
for the amendments in the application as filed.

39.10.5   *Information on the first page*

r.70.15(b)   The report bears the title "International Preliminary Report on Patentability (Chapter II   1685
of the Patent Co-operation Treaty)" together with an indication that it is an International
Preliminary Examination Report established by the International Preliminary Examining
Authority.
The report contains the following information:

r.70.3   (1) the international application number;
r.70.3   (2) the international filing date;
r.70.5   (3) the classification, either as given in the International Search Report if the International
Preliminary Examining Authority agrees with that classification, or the classification according to the International Patent Classification which it considers correct;
r.70.3   (4) the name of the applicant;
r.70.4(i)   (5) the date on which the demand was submitted;
r.70.4(ii)   (6) the date on which the report was completed;
r.70.3   (7) the name of the International Preliminary Examining Authority; and
r.70.14   (8) the name of the Officer of the International Preliminary Examining Authority responsible for the report.

39.10.6   *Comments on amendments and the correction of mistakes*

r.70.11   The report will indicate whether any amendments have been made before the Interna-   1686
tional Preliminary Examining Authority and whether an amendment has resulted in the
cancellation of an entire sheet.

r.70.2(e)   If a rectification of an obvious mistake is taken into account under r.66.1, the report shall
so indicate. If a rectification of an obvious mistake is not taken into account pursuant
to r.66.4*bis* (received too late), the report shall, if possible, so indicate, failing which the
International Preliminary Examining Authority shall notify the International Bureau accordingly and the International Bureau shall proceed as provided for in the Administrative Instructions.

r.70.2(c)   The report will indicate if amendments have not been taken into account since they go
beyond the disclosure of the application as filed along with relevant reasoning.

r.70.2(c-*bis*)   The report will also indicate if amendments have not been taken into account since they
were not accompanied by a letter required pursuant to r.46.5(b)(iii) (applicable by virtue
of r.66.8(c) or r.66.8(a)) indicating their basis in the application as filed.

39.10.7   *Comments on priority*

r.70.2(b)   The report will indicate, in appropriate cases, that, pursuant to r.66.7(a) or (b), it has been   1687
established as if priority had not been claimed.

39.10.8   Comments on the non-establishment of an opinion

1688   Art. 35(3)(a)(b)   If the International Preliminary Examining Authority considers that the application relates to subject matter not requiring examination or, the claims so lack clarity or support that a meaningful opinion cannot be established (Art. 34(4)(a)) it will state as much in the International Preliminary Examination Report and give the reasons therefor (r.70.12(iii)). If only some of the claims are so prejudiced (Art. 34(4)(b)) then such an opinion and the reasons therefor will be stated in relation to the prejudiced claims and a statement as provided for in Art. 35(2) (as to novelty, inventive step and industrial applicability) will be provided for the remainder.

r.70.2(d)   Where a claim relates to an invention in respect of which no International Search Report has been established and has therefore not been examined, the report will so indicate.

r.70.12(iv)   The report will state, where appropriate, that a nucleotide and/or amino acid sequence listing was not available in such a form that a meaningful international preliminary examination could be carried out.

39.10.9   Comments on lack of unity

1689   r.70.13   The report will indicate, where the International Preliminary Examining Authority has found that the claims lack unity:
(i) whether the applicant has paid additional fees (Art. 34(3));
(ii) whether the application/examination report has been restricted (Art. 34(3));
(iii) if examination has been carried out on restricted claims (Art. 34(3)(a)) or on the main invention only (Art. 34(3)(c)), what parts of the application were and were not the subject of the international preliminary examination; and
(iv) whether the International Preliminary Examining Authority has chosen not to invite the applicant to restrict the claims or pay an additional fee (r.68.1).

39.10.10   Statement regarding patentability under Art. 35(2)

1690   Art. 35(2)   Rather than considering whether the claimed invention is patentable under national law, the international preliminary examination report will state, in relation to each claim, whether the claim is novel, inventive and industrially applicable as defined in Art. 33(1)–(4).

r.70.6(a)   The statement will employ the words "YES" and "NO" or their equivalents in the language of the report (or some appropriate sign indicated in the Administrative Instructions).

r.70.6(b)   The determination for a particular claim will be negative if any of the three criteria are not met but if one or two of the criteria taken separately is/are satisfied that fact will be acknowledged.

Art. 35(2)   The statement will be accompanied by a citation of the documents relied upon in coming to the conclusion reached, any necessary explanations required by the circumstances and any other observations provided by the Regulations (no observations have been specified).

r.70.7(a)   Documents relevant for supporting the Art. 35(2) statements should be cited, whether or not they are cited in the International Search Report. Documents cited in said search report but not considered relevant need not be cited.

r.70.7(b)   The provisions of r.43.5(b) (the method of identifying any document is given in the Administrative Instructions) and r.43.5(e) (if only certain passages are relevant/particularly relevant they should be specified) apply.

r.70.8   Whether or not any explanations under Art. 35(2) should be included, and their form, will be determined according to guidelines in the Administrative Instructions (s.604) based on the following principles:
(i) where the statement in relation to a claim is negative, an explanation should be given;
(ii) where the statement in relation to a claim is positive an explanation should be given unless the reason for citing any document is easy to imagine on consultation of that document; and
(iii) where the statement in relation to a claim is negative in relation to only one or two of the criteria (r.70.6(b), second sentence) an explanation should generally be given.

39.10.11 Certain documents cited

r.70.10	The report must mention any patent or published patent application relevant under r.64.3 (a co-pending application or patent) by indicating its date of publication, filing date and claimed priority date (if any). The report may also indicate the opinion of the Examining Authority as to whether the cited patent or application is entitled to its priority date.	1691
r.70.9	The report must mention any non-written disclosure relevant under r.64.2 by indicating its kind, the date on which the non-written disclosure occurred and the date of the subsequent written disclosure referring to that non-written disclosure was made available to the public.	

39.10.12 Certain defects in the application

r.70.12(i)	The report will mention any defects in the form or contents of the application under r.66.2(a)(iii) that the Examining Authority believes to be present.	1692

39.10.13 Certain observations on the application

r.70.12(ii)	The report may optionally include any comments under r.66.2(a)(v) regarding the clarity of the claims, description or drawings or whether the claims are adequately supported by the description. If included, such comments must be supported by reasons.	1693

39.10.14 Annexes to the report

r.70.16(a)	The following replacement sheets and letters shall be annexed to the report: (i) each replacement sheet under r.66.8 containing amendments under Art. 34 and each letter under r.66.8(a), r.66.8(b) and r.46.5(b) as applicable by virtue of r.66.8(c); (ii) each replacement sheet under r.46.5 containing amendments under Art. 19 and each letter under r.46.5; and (iii) each replacement sheet under r.26.4 as applicable by virtue of r.91.2 containing a rectification of an obvious mistake authorised by that Authority under r.91.1(b)(iii) and each letter under r.26.4 as applicable by virtue of r.91.2; unless any such replacement sheet has been superseded or considered reversed by a later replacement sheet or an amendment resulting in the cancellation of an entire sheet under r.66.8(b); and (iv) where the report contains an indication referred to in r.70.2(e), any sheet and letter relating to a rectification of an obvious mistake which is not taken into account pursuant to r.66.4*bis*.	1694
r.70.16(b)	Notwithstanding r.70.16(a), each superseded or reversed replacement sheet and letter relating to such a sheet referred to in that paragraph must also be annexed to the report where the International Preliminary Examining Authority considers that the relevant superseding or reversing amendment goes beyond the disclosure in the international application as filed and the report contains an indication referred to in r.70.2(c) or the relevant superseding or reversing amendment was not accompanied by a letter indicating the basis for the amendment in the application as filed and the report is established as if the amendment had not been made and contains an indication referred to in r.70.2(c-*bis*). In such a case, the superseded or reversed replacement sheets are marked as provided by the Administrative Instructions.	

39.10.15 Comment on top-up search

r.70.2(f)	The report must indicate the date on which a top-up search under r.66.1*ter* was made, or else state that no top-up search was made.	1695

39.11 Translation and communication of the International Preliminary Examination Report and its annexes

39.11.1   Transmission of International Preliminary Examination Report and other documents to the International Bureau and the applicant by the International Preliminary Examining Authority

1696   Art. 36(1), r.71.1(a)   The International Preliminary Examining Authority will transmit, on the same day, a copy of the International Preliminary Examination Report, together with its annexes, if any, to the applicant and the International Bureau.

r.71.1(b)   The International Preliminary Examining Authority shall transmit copies of other documents from the file of the international preliminary examination to the International Bureau in accordance with the Administrative Instructions.

39.11.2   Translation by the International Bureau of the International Preliminary Examination Report and its transmission to the elected Offices and the applicant

1697   Art. 36(2)(a)(b)   The International Preliminary Examination Report must be translated into the prescribed languages by or under the responsibility of the International Bureau.

r.72.1(a)(b)   Any elected State may require that an International Preliminary Examination Report which is established in a language which is not the/an official language of its national Office must be translated into English. Such a requirement must be notified to the International Bureau who will publish it in the Gazette.

Art. 36(3)(a)   A copy of the International Preliminary Examination Report, any annexes in the original language and any translation so prepared will be transmitted by the International Bureau to each elected Office.

r.73.1   All necessary copies for such transmittal under Art. 36(3)(a) will be prepared by the International Bureau.

r.73.2(a)   The transmittal will only take place, however, if such transmittal has been specifically asked for by an elected State in accordance with r.93*bis*.1. The timing of the transmittal will be specified by each elected State in the request pursuant to r.93*bis*.1, but may not take place before the expiration of 30 months from the priority date.

r.73.2(b)(i)   If, however, the applicant makes a request for early national processing under Art. 40(2), the International Bureau will, at the request of the applicant or the relevant elected Office, promptly effect the Art. 36(3)(a) communication (international preliminary examination report, annexes, translation) if it is in possession of the international preliminary examination report.

r.73.2(c)   The transmittal under r.73.2(a) will even take place to elected Offices affected by any withdrawal of the demand or withdrawal of one or more elections by the applicant so long as the International Bureau is already in receipt of the International Preliminary Examination Report.

r.72.2   The International Bureau will send a copy of any translation of the International Preliminary Examination Report it prepares under r.72.1(a) to the applicant at the same time as it communicates it to elected Offices.

r.72.3   The applicant has the right to make written observations as to the correctness of any translation of the international preliminary examination report prepared under r.72.1(a) which he must send to the International Bureau and each of the interested elected Offices.

39.11.3   Translation and transmission of the written opinion prepared under r.43bis.1 where the International Preliminary Examination Report is not available and the applicant has requested early processing in an elected Office

1698   r.73.2(b)(ii)   Where the applicant has made a request for early national processing in an elected Office, pursuant to Art. 40(2), the applicant or elected Office has requested the Art. 36(3)(a) transmission and the International Bureau is not yet in possession of the International Preliminary Examination Report, it will send a copy of the written opinion established by the International Searching Authority under r.43*bis*.1 instead.

r.72.2*bis*	In such circumstances, where it is necessary to transmit a copy of the written opinion of the International Searching Authority under r.73.2(b)(ii), the International Bureau must, at the request of any elected Office, translate the written opinion into English and transmit such a translation to the relevant elected Office within two months of the request. A copy is sent to the applicant at the same time who may make written observations as to the correctness of the translation and send copies of such observations to the interested elected Office and the International Bureau.
r.44*bis*.3	Such a translation of the written opinion of the International Searching Authority may also be required by designated Offices.

39.11.4 *Translation of the annexes of the International Preliminary Examination Report by the applicant and transmission of the translation to the elected Offices*

Art. 36(2)(a)(b)	Any annexes to the International Preliminary Examination Report must be translated into the prescribed languages by the applicant.	1699
r.74.1(a)(b)	Where a translation of the international application is required by an elected Office under Art. 39(1) on entry into the national phase, the applicant must translate any replacement sheets referred to in r.70.16 (i.e. those sheets annexed to the International Preliminary Examination Report) into the same language (unless already in that language). Where such a translation of the application is not required by an elected Office, that Office may nevertheless require a translation of the annexed sheets into the language of publication, where they are not already in that language.	
Art. 36(3)(b)	Such a prescribed translation must be transmitted by the applicant to the elected Offices within the prescribed time limit.	
r.74.1(a)	Where an elected Office requires such a translation it must be transmitted by the applicant before the end of the Art. 39 time limit (usually 30 months from the priority date).	

39.11.5 *Supply of documents cited in the International Preliminary Examination Report to the applicant and elected Offices by the International Preliminary Examining Authority*

Art. 36(4), r.71.2	At the request of an elected Office or the applicant, within seven years from the filing date of the relevant application, the International Preliminary Examining Authority will supply copies of any document cited in the International Preliminary Examination Report which was not cited in the International Search Report. A fee may be claimed by the International Preliminary Examining Authority from the Office or applicant who makes such a request covering the cost of preparing and mailing the copies, the level of which will be set in the agreement under Art. 32(2) between the International Preliminary Examining Authority and the International Bureau. Such an Authority may perform these obligations through another agency responsible to it.	1700

Chapter 40: National Phase Aspects

40.1 The effect of an international patent application having a filing date

40.1.1 Nature of the effect

1701   Art. 11(3)   Subject to Art. 64(4) (see section 40.1.3 below), an application satisfying the requirements of Art. 11(1)(i)–(iii) and accorded an international filing date has the effect of a regular national application in each designated State from that filing date, which is considered the actual filing date in each Contracting State.

       Art. 11(4)   An application satisfying the requirements of Art. 11(1)(i)–(iii) is equivalent to a regular national filing within the meaning of the Paris Convention.

40.1.2 Circumstances in which the effect is lost

1702   Art. 24(1)   The effect of the international application provided for in Art. 11(3) will cease in any designated State with the same consequences as the withdrawal of any national application in that State:

(i) if the applicant withdraws his international application or the designation of that State;

(ii) if the international application is considered withdrawn by virtue of Art. 12(3) (record copy not received by the International Bureau within the time limit), Art. 14(1)(b) (failure to correct defects in the application within the prescribed time limit), Art. 14(3)(a) (prescribed filing and designation fees not paid within the prescribed time limit) or Art. 14(4) (requirements for filing date not complied with) or if the designation of that State is considered withdrawn by virtue of Art. 14(3)(b) (one or more designation fees not paid – note that the designation fee is now part of the international fee), unless the finding is reversed under Art. 25; or

(iii) if the applicant fails to perform the acts necessary under Art. 22 (to enter the national phase) within the time limit (usually 30 months).

       Art. 24(2)   It is nevertheless the prerogative of any designated Office to maintain the effect of Art. 11(3) if it wishes, even when not obliged so to do under Art. 25(2) (review by designated Offices).

40.1.3 Exceptions to the effect – the prior art effect of an international application in a designated State

1703   Art. 64(4)(a)   If a State, by virtue of its national law, provides for prior art effect of its patents as from a date before publication but does not equate for prior art purposes the priority date claimed under the Paris Convention to the actual filing date in that State, it may declare that the filing outside that State of an international application designating that State is not equated to an actual filing in that State for prior art purposes.

       Art. 64(4)(b)(c)   Any State making such a declaration will, to that extent, not be bound by Art. (11)(3) (international applications to have the same effect as a regular national application in each designated State as of the filing date). Such a State must at the same time state in writing the date from which and the conditions under which the prior art effect of any international application designating that State become effective in that State. Such a statement may be modified at any time by notification addressed to the Director General.

       WIPO   Only the US has made such a declaration. Under the US law in force until 16 March 2013, an Art. 102(e) date applied in respect of an international application not published in English only from entry into the US national phase and in other cases only from the international filing date (unless a US priority was claimed). Under the current legislation, an international patent application designating the US is prior art in the US from the filing or priority date regardless of the language in which it is published and priority is always recognised whether the earlier application was filed in the US or not.

40.1.4 Definition of a Euro-PCT application

1704   EPC Art. 153(2)   An international application for which the EPO is a designated or elected Office and which has been accorded an international date of filing is equivalent to a regular European application (Euro-PCT application).

40.1.5   *Extension of the effect to successor states*

AppGuide   See International Phase, paragraph 11.089 – a successor state is a state whose territory   1705
was, before its independence, part of the territory of a PCT Contracting State that subsequently ceased to exist and which has deposited with the Director General of WIPO a
declaration indicating that the PCT continues to be applicable in that state.

r.32.1(a)   The effects of any international application whose international filing date falls in the
period defined in r.32.1(b) are extended to a State ("the successor State") whose territory
was, before the independence of that State, part of the territory of a Contracting State designated in the international application which subsequently ceased to exist ("the predecessor State"), provided that the successor State has become a Contracting State through the
deposit, with the Director General, of a declaration of continuation the effect of which is
that the Treaty is applied by the successor State.

r.32.1(b)   The period referred to in r.32.1(a) starts on the day following the last day of the existence
of the predecessor State and ends two months after the date on which the declaration referred to in paragraph (a) was notified by the Director General to the Governments of the
States party to the Paris Convention for the Protection of Industrial Property. However,
where the date of independence of the successor State is earlier than the date of the day
following the last day of the existence of the predecessor State, the successor State may
declare that the said period starts on the date of its independence; such a declaration must
be made together with the declaration referred to in r.32.1(a) and must specify the date of
independence.

r.32.1(c)   Information on any international application whose filing date falls within the applicable
period under r.32.1(b) and whose effect is extended to the successor State shall be published by the International Bureau in the Gazette.

r.32.2(a)   Where the effects of the international application are extended to the successor State in
accordance with r.32.1:
(i) the successor State will be considered as having been designated in the international
application, and
(ii) the applicable time limit under Art. 22 or Art. 39(1) in relation to that State shall be
extended until the expiration of at least six months from the date of the publication of the
information under r.32.1(c).

r.32.2(b)   The successor State may fix a time limit which expires later that that provided in r.32.2(a)
(ii). The International Bureau will publish information on such time limits in the Gazette.

40.2   The effect of a published international patent application

40.2.1   *Provisions of the PCT*

Art. 29(1)   Concerning the protection of any rights of the applicant in a designated State, the effects   1706
in that State of the international publication of an international application are the same
as those which the national law of the State provides for the compulsory national publication of unexamined national applications except that:

Art. 29(2)   (1) where the language of the published international application is different from the language of publication under national law in any designated State, national law may provide
that such effects will only apply when either (i) a translation into the latter language has
been published as provided for by national law or (ii) a translation into the latter language
has been made available to the public by laying open for public inspection as provided
by national law or (iii) a translation into the latter language has been transmitted by the
applicant to the actual or prospective unauthorised user of the invention claimed in the
international invention or (iv) both acts described in (i) and (iii) or both acts described in
(ii) and (iii) have taken place;

Art. 29(3)   (2) the national law of any designated State may provide that where an international application has been published before 18 months from the priority date at the request of the
applicant, such effects will only apply from the expiration of this period; and

Art. 29(4)   (3) the national law of any designated State may provide that such effects will apply only
from the date on which a copy of the international application as published under Art. 21
has been received in the national Office of or acting for that State, in which case the said
Office will publish the date of receipt in its Gazette as soon as possible.

40.2.2   Provisions of the EPC – publication of the translation

1707 EPC Art. 153(3)   International publication takes the place of European publication.
      EPC Art. 153(4)   However, where international publication is not in an EPO official language, provisional protection under Art. 67(1) and (2) EPC will only be effective from the date of publication of a translation in an EPO official language (and subject to Art. 67(3) EPC, regarding the language requirements of individual EPC States).
      Guidelines   See E-IX, 2.5.1.

40.3   Examination by national Offices

40.3.1   When national processing may begin

1708 Art. 23(1)(2)   No designated Office may process or examine the international application prior to the expiry of the applicable time limit under Art. 22 (usually 30 months from the priority date) unless the applicant has expressly requested it does so.

      Art. 40(1)(2)   When the election of a Contracting State has been effected before the end of the 19th month from the priority date, Art. 23 will not apply to such State and the national Office of or acting for that State may not examine or otherwise process the application prior to the expiry of the time limit under Art. 39 (usually 30 months from the priority date) unless the applicant has expressly requested it does so.

      Art. 64(2)(a)(ii)   Any State, though not having declared it is not bound by Chapter II under Art. 64(1), may nevertheless declare that the obligation to delay national processing under Art. 40 will not prevent publication, by or through its national Office, of the international application or a translation thereof, it being understood that it is not exempt from the limitations provided for in Art. 30 (confidential nature of international applications before international publication) and Art. 38 (confidential nature of international preliminary examination).

      Art. 64(2)(b)   States making such a declaration under Art. 64(2)(a)(ii) are bound accordingly.
      WIPO   Such States are Finland, Norway, Poland and Sweden.

40.3.2   Right to amend when entering the national phase under Chapter I

1709 Art. 28(1)   The applicant must be given the opportunity to amend the claims, description and drawings before each designated Office within a prescribed time limit. No designated Office may grant a patent or refuse the grant of a patent before this time limit has expired without the express consent of the applicant.

      r.52.1(a)   Where examination or processing starts without a special request, such amendment may be made
                           (1) within one month of fulfilling the requirements under Art. 22; or
                           (2) if the communication under r.47.1 (Art. 20 communication by the International Bureau to designated Offices) has not been effected by the expiry of the time limit under Art. 22, not later than four months after such expiry; or
                           (3) at any later time allowed by national law.

      r.52.1(b)   Where, under national law, examination only starts on special request, the time limit within which or the time at which amendment under Art. 28(1) is allowed is the same as would be provided for a regular national application provided that such a time limit may not expire before and such time may not come before the expiry of the time limit applicable under r.52.1(a).

      Art. 28(2)(3)   Any amendment must not go beyond the disclosure in the international application as filed unless the national law of the designated State allows it to and must be in accordance with the national law of the designated State in all respects not provided for in the PCT and its Regulations.

      Art. 28(4)   Where the designated Office requires a translation of the international application, any amendments must be in the language of the translation.

40.3.3   Right to amend when entering the national phase under Chapter II

1710 Art. 41(1)   The applicant must be given the opportunity to amend the claims, description and drawings before each elected Office within a prescribed time limit. No elected Office may grant a patent or refuse the grant of a patent before this time limit has expired without the express consent of the applicant.

r.78.1(a)	Such amendment may be made (1) within one month of fulfilling the requirements under Art. 39(1)(a); or (2) if the transmittal of the international preliminary examination report under Art. 36(1) has not been taken place by the expiry of the time limit under Art. 39, not later than four months after such expiry; or (3) at any later time allowed by national law.
r.78.1(b)	Where, under national law, examination only starts on special request, the time limit within which or the time at which amendment under Art. 41(1) is allowed is the same as would be provided for a regular national application provided that such a time limit may not expire before and such time may not come before the expiry of the time limit applicable under r.78.1(a).
Art. 41(2)(3)	Any amendment must not go beyond the disclosure in the international application as filed unless the national law of an elected State allows it to and must be in accordance with the national law of the elected State in all respects not provided for in the PCT and its Regulations.
Art. 41(4)	Where an elected Office requires a translation of the international application, any amendment must be in the language of the translation.

40.3.4 *Right to amend on entering the EPO regional phase*

EPC r.161	See section 38.12.12.	1711

40.3.5 *Procedure where unity has been impugned in the international phase*

Art. 17(3)(b)	Where the International Searching Authority has invited the applicant to pay extra fees in response to a finding of lack of unity and the additional fees have not been paid, the national law of a Contracting State may provide that where the national Office of that State considers the International Searching Authority justified on the question of unity, the parts of the application consequently unsearched will be considered withdrawn in that State unless a special fee is paid by the applicant to that national Office.	1712
Art. 34(3)(b)	Where the applicant has elected to restrict his claims in response to a lack of unity objection during international preliminary examination, the national law of an elected State may provide that those parts of the application which are not the subject of international preliminary examination will, as far as that State is concerned, be considered withdrawn unless a special fee is paid by the applicant to the national Office of that State.	
Art. 34(3)(c)	The national law of any elected State may provide that where its national Office finds an invitation of the International Preliminary Examining Authority to restrict the claims or pay extra fees justified, the applicant has not complied and that Authority has only examined the main invention, those parts of the application which do not relate to the main invention will, as far as that State is concerned, be considered withdrawn unless a special fee is paid to that Office by the applicant.	

40.3.6 *Consideration of unity by the EPO*

EPC r.164	See sections 38.12.8 and 38.12.20.	1713

40.3.7 *Effect on a designated Office of a decision by the receiving Office to base a filing date on documents incorporated by reference in the case where reservations have been filed or errors made*

r.20.8	Where an international filing date has been awarded by the receiving Office on the basis that all or part of the application was incorporated by reference, and the designated Office has notified incompatibility of such incorporation by reference under r.20.8(a), the designated Office (or elected Office – r.76.5) may change the filing date awarded (see section 32.1.1).	1714
r.82*ter*.1(b)	Where the international filing date has been accorded by the receiving Office under r.20.3(b)(ii), r.20.5(d) or r.20.5*bis*(d) on the basis of the incorporation by reference under r.4.18 and r.20.6 of an element or part but the designated or elected Office finds that: (i) the applicant has not complied with r.17.1(a), (b) or (b-*bis*) (obligation to submit a copy of the priority document);	

	(ii) a requirement under r.4.18, 20.6(a)(i) or 51*bis*.1(e)(ii) has not been complied with; or
	(iii) the element or part is not completely contained in the priority document concerned; the designated or elected Office may, subject to r.82*ter*.1(c), treat the international application as if the international filing date had been accorded under r.20.3(b)(i), r.20.5(b) or r.20.5*bis*(b), or corrected under r.20.5(c) or r.20.5*bis*(c), as applicable (filing date becomes the later date when all the requirements of Art. 11(1) are properly met), provided that r.17.1(c) shall apply mutatis mutandis (priority claim disregarded if the applicant does not furnish a copy of the priority document).
r.51*bis*.1(e)(ii)	A translation of the priority document may be required by national law for the purposes of determining under r.82*ter*.1(b) whether an element or part is completely contained in the priority document.
r.51*bis*.1(a)(viii)	A translation of any erroneously filed element or part removed from the international application in accordance with r.20.5*bis*(b) or (c) may also be demanded for the purposes of r.82*ter*.1.
r.82*ter*.1(c)	The designated or elected Office may not treat the international application under r.82*ter*.1(b) as if the international filing date had been accorded under r.20.3(b)(i), r.20.5(b) or r.20.5*bis*(b), or corrected under r.20.5(c) or r.20.5*bis*(c), without giving the applicant the opportunity to make observations on the intended treatment, or to make a request under r.82*ter*.1(d), within a time limit which shall be reasonable under the circumstances.
r.82*ter*.1(d)	Where the designated or elected Office, in accordance with r.82*ter*.1(c), has notified the applicant that it intends to treat the international application as if the international filing date had been corrected under r.20.5(c) or r.20.5*bis*(c) (later submission of a missing part of the description, claims or drawings), the applicant may, in a notice submitted to that Office within the time limit referred to in r.82*ter*.1(c), request that the missing part concerned, or the correct element or part concerned, be disregarded for the purposes of national processing before that Office, in which case that missing part, or that corrected element or part, shall be considered not to have been furnished and that Office shall not treat the international application as if the international filing date had been corrected.

40.3.8   *Requirements relating to form or contents additional to those in the PCT may not be imposed by national Offices*

1715	Art. 27(1)	It is forbidden for national law to require compliance with requirements relating to the form or contents of international applications different from or additional to those provided for in the PCT and its Regulations.
	Art. 27(2)	The provisions of Art. 27(1) do not affect the operation of Art. 7(2) (requirement that an applicant submit drawings that are necessary for understanding the invention).
	r.51*bis*.1(c)	Further, a national Office may nevertheless require that the application, a translation thereof or any other document relating thereto be submitted in more than one copy.
	r.51*bis*.3(a)	Where any requirement of national law that a designated Office may apply under Art. 27(1), Art. 27(2) or r.51*bis*.1(c) is not fulfilled before the time limit specified in Art. 22 the designated Office must invite the applicant to comply with that requirement within a time limit which may not be less than two months from the date of the invitation. A fee may be charged by the designated Office for complying with such a national requirement in response to the invitation.
	r.51*bis*.3(c)	Where r.51*bis*.3(a) is not compatible, in relation to the time limit, with national law on March 17, 2000, it will not apply, as regards the time limit, to any designated Office for as long as the incompatibility lasts so long as the Office informed the International Bureau of this fact by November 30, 2000. This information is published by the International Bureau in the Gazette.
	WIPO	The only Office that still has reservations in force is that of Singapore.
	r.76.5	The requirements of r.51*bis* apply equally whether national phase entry is under Chapter I or Chapter II.
	Art. 27(4)	National Offices, courts and other competent organs of or acting a designated State may apply their own national law in respect of form or contents to the processing of an international application where that law is more favourable to applicants than the requirements of the PCT and its Regulations unless the applicant objects and insists that the requirements of the PCT and its Regulations be applied.

AppGuide	See International Phase, paragraph 5.123 – unity of invention is a formal requirement according to Art. 27(1) that cannot be challenged in the national phase if the requirements of r.13 are met.

40.3.9 *Requirements relating to the submission of certain documents (e.g. as evidence) that may be imposed by national Offices*

Art. 27(2)	The provisions of Art. 27(1) do not preclude any national law from requiring, once pro-cessing of the international application has started in that Office:	1716
Art. 27(2)(i)	(1) when the applicant is a legal entity, the name of an Officer entitled to represent such legal entity;	
Art. 27(2)(ii)	(2) documents which are not part of the international application but constitute proof of allegations or statements made in the application including the signature of the applicant to confirm the application when the agent or representative signed the application as filed;	
r.51*bis*.1(a)(i)	(3) any document relating to the identity of the inventor (but see below);	
r.51*bis*.1(a)(ii)	(4) any document relating to the applicant's entitlement to apply for or be granted a patent (but see below);	
r.51*bis*.1(a)(iii)	(5) any document containing any proof of the right of the applicant to claim priority where he is different from the applicant having filed the earlier priority application or where his name has changed in the meantime (but see below);	
r.51*bis*.1(a)(iv)	(6) where the international application designates a State whose national law requires, on October 09, 2012, the furnishing of an oath or declaration of inventorship, any docu-ment containing an oath or declaration by the inventor alleging his inventorship (but see below);	
r.51*bis*.1(a)(v)	(7) evidence concerning non-prejudicial disclosures or exceptions to lack of novelty, such as disclosures resulting from abuse, disclosures at certain exhibitions and disclosures by the applicant during a certain period of time;	
r.51*bis*.1(a)(vi)	(8) the confirmation of the international application by the signature of any applicant for the State concerned that has not signed the request;	
r.51*bis*.1(a)(vii)	(9) the address, nationality and residence of any applicant, for the State concerned if miss-ing; or	
r.51*bis*.1(a)(viii)	(10) in the cases referred to in r.82*ter*.1, a translation of any erroneously filed element or part removed from the international application in accordance with r.20.5bis(b) or (c).	
r.51*bis*.2	However a designated Office may not, unless it has reasonable doubts about the veracity of the indications or declaration concerned, require any document or evidence: (i) relating to the identity of the inventor (r.51*bis*.1(a)(i)) (other than a document contain-ing an oath or declaration of inventorship (r.51*bis*.1(a)(iv)), if indications concerning the inventor in accordance with r.4.6 are contained in the request or if a declaration as to the identity of the inventor complying with r.4.17(i) is contained in the request or submitted directly to the designated Office; or (ii) relating to the applicant's entitlement, at the international filing date, to apply for or be granted a patent (r.51*bis*.1(a)(ii)), where a declaration as to that matter complying with r.4.17(ii) is contained in the request or submitted directly to the designated Office; (iii) relating to the applicant's entitlement, at the international filing date, to claim the pri-ority of an earlier application (r.51*bis*.1(a)(iii)), if a declaration as to that matter complying with r.4.17(iii) is contained in the request or submitted directly to the designated Office; or (iv) containing an oath or declaration of inventorship (r.51*bis*.1(a)(iv)), if a declaration of inventorship, in accordance with r.4.17(iv), is contained in the request or is submitted directly to the designated office.	
r.51*bis*.3(a)	Where any requirement of r.51*bis*.1(a)(i)–(iv) is not fulfilled before the time limit specified in Art. 22 the designated Office must invite the applicant to comply with that requirement within a time limit which may not be less than two months from the date of the invita-tion. A fee may be required by the designated Office for complying with such a national requirement.	
r.51*bis*.3(c)	Where r.51*bis*.3(a) is not compatible, in relation to the time limit, with national law on March 17, 2000, it will not apply, as regards the time limit, to any designated Office for as long as the incompatibility lasts so long as the Office informed the International Bureau of this fact by November 30, 2000. This information is published by the International Bureau in the Gazette.	

WIPO r.76.5	The only Office that still has reservations in force is that of Singapore. The requirements of r.51*bis* apply equally whether national phase entry is under Chapter I or Chapter II.
Art. 7(2)(ii)	If an invention can be illustrated with drawings but none were filed with the international application, any designated Office may require that such drawings be filed within a prescribed time limit.

40.3.10   *Requirements relating to the certification/verification of the Art. 22 translation that may be imposed by national Offices*

1717 r.51*bis*.1(d)	National law may, in accordance with Art. 27(2)(ii), require that the translation submitted by the applicant under Art. 22 is: (a) verified by the applicant or the translator in a statement to the effect that, to the best knowledge of that person, the translation is complete and faithful; or (b) certified by a public authority or a sworn translator (but only if the designated Office doubts the accuracy of the translation).
r.51*bis*.3(a)	Where any requirement of r.51*bis*.1(d) is not fulfilled before the time limit specified in Art. 22 the designated Office must invite the applicant to comply with that requirement within a time limit which may not be less than two months from the date of the invitation. The designated Office may charge the applicant a fee for complying with the national requirement in response to the invitation.
r.51*bis*.3(c)	Where r.51*bis*.3(a) is not compatible, in relation to the time limit, with national law on March 17, 2000, it will not apply, as regards the time limit, to any designated Office for as long as the incompatibility lasts so long as the Office informed the International Bureau of this fact by November 30, 2000. This information is published by the International Bureau in the Gazette.
WIPO r.76.5	The only Office that still has reservations in force is that of Singapore. The requirements of r.51*bis* apply equally whether national phase entry is under Chapter I or Chapter II.

40.3.11   *Consequences of submitting or not submitting a copy of the priority document in the international phase – how a designated Office obtains a copy*

1718 r.17.1(c)	If the requirements of r.17.1(a) or (b) or (b-*bis*) (supply of copy of priority document) are not met, any designated State may disregard the claim to priority as long as it has given the applicant an opportunity to furnish the priority document within a reasonable time limit (see r.163(2) EPC in section 37.12.15).
r.17.2	Where r.17.1(a), (b) or (b-*bis*) has been complied with by the applicant, the International Bureau, when requested by a designated Office, will promptly (but not before publication) furnish a copy of the priority document to that Office. The applicant may not be asked to do this himself. Where the applicant has made an Art. 23(2) request to a designated Office (for examination before publication of the application) the International Bureau will supply the relevant designated Office with a copy of the priority document, when so requested, promptly after receiving it.
Guidelines	See F-VI, 2.1 – a European patent cannot be granted until a copy of the priority document is on file.

40.3.12   *Requirement to submit a translation of the priority document*

1719 r.17.2(a)	The applicant may not be required to furnish a translation of the priority document to a designated Office before the expiry of the Art. 22 time limit (normally 30 months) or, where applicable, the Art. 39 time limit – r.76.4a.
r.51*bis*.1(e)	National law may, in accordance with Art. 27, require the applicant to submit a translation of the priority document with the proviso that such submission may only be required: (i) where the validity of the priority claim is relevant to the determination of whether the invention concerned is patentable; or

(ii) where the international filing date has been accorded by the receiving Office under r.20.3(b)(ii), 20.5(d) or 20.5*bis*(d) on the basis of the incorporation by reference under r.4.18 and r.20.6 of an element or part, for the purposes of determining under r.82*ter*.1(b), whether that element or part is completely contained in the priority document concerned, in which case the national law applicable by the designated Office may also require the applicant to furnish, in the case of part of the description, claims or drawings, an indication as to where that part is contained in the translation of the priority document.

r.51*bis*.3(a)	Where any requirement of r.51*bis*.1(e) is not fulfilled before the time limit specified in Art. 22 the designated Office must invite the applicant to comply with that requirement within a time limit which may not be less than two months from the date of the invitation. The designated Office may charge the applicant a fee for complying with national requirements in response to the invitation.
r.51*bis*.3(c)	Where r.51*bis*.3(a) is not compatible, in relation to the time limit, with national law on March 17, 2000, it will not apply, as regards the time limit, to any designated Office for as long as the incompatibility lasts so long as the Office informed the International Bureau of this fact by November 30, 2000. This information is published by the International Bureau in the Gazette.
WIPO	The only Office that still has reservations in force is that of Singapore.
r.76.5	The requirements of r.51*bis* apply equally whether national phase entry is under Chapter I or Chapter II.

40.3.13 *The effect on designated Offices of a decision by the receiving Office to restore a right of priority*

r.49*ter*.1(a)	Where the receiving Office has restored a right of priority under r.26*bis*.3 based on a finding by it that the failure to file the international application within the priority period occurred in spite of due care required by the circumstances having been taken, that restoration shall, subject to r.49*ter*.1(c), be effective in each designated State.
r.49*ter*.1(b)	Where the receiving Office has restored a right of priority under r.26*bis*.3, based on a finding by it that the failure to file the international application within the priority period was unintentional, that restoration shall, subject to r.49*ter*.1(c), be effective in any designated State whose applicable national law provides for restoration of the right of priority based on that criterion or on a criterion which, from the viewpoint of applicants, is more favourable than that criterion.
r.49*ter*.1(c)	A decision by the receiving Office to restore a right of priority under r.26*bis*.3 shall not be effective in a designated State where the designated Office, a court or any other competent organ of or acting for that designated State finds that a requirement under r.26*bis*.3(a), (b)(i) or (c) was not complied with, taking into account the reasons stated in the request submitted to the receiving Office under r.26*bis*.3(a) and any declaration or other evidence filed with the receiving Office under r.26*bis*.3(b)(iii).
r.49*ter*.1(d)	A designated Office shall not review the decision of the receiving Office unless it may reasonably doubt that a requirement referred to in r.49*ter*.1(c) was complied with, in which case the designated Office shall notify the applicant accordingly, indicating the reasons for that doubt and giving the applicant an opportunity to make observations within a reasonable time limit.
r.49*ter*.1(g)	If, on October 5, 2005, paragraphs (a) to (d) of r.49*ter*.1 are not compatible with the national law applied by the designated Office, those paragraphs shall not apply in respect of that Office for as long as they continue not to be compatible with that law, provided that the Office informs the International Bureau accordingly by April 5, 2006. The information received shall be promptly published by the International Bureau in the Gazette.
WIPO	Incompatibility with r.49*ter*.1(a)–(d) has been notified by and is still in force for the following designated Offices: Algeria, Brazil, China, Columbia, Cuba, Czech Republic, Germany, India, Indonesia, Korea, Lithuania, Mexico and Philippines.
J13/16	Restoration of the priority right by a receiving Office applying the "unintentional" criterion is not effective before the EPO – a new request under r.49*ter*.2 is necessary within the applicable time limit.

1720

Guidelines		See E-IX, 2.3.5.3. A separate request on regional phase entry is not necessary if a request for restoration of the priority claim was granted by the receiving Office based on the due care criterion. However, a separate request is necessary where no request was filed before the receiving Office, a request was refused by the receiving Office or a request was granted by the receiving Office based on the unintentional criterion.

40.3.14   *The effect on designated Offices of a decision by the receiving Office to refuse restoration of a right of priority*

1721	r.49*ter*.1(e)	No designated State shall be bound by a decision of the receiving Office refusing a request under r.26*bis*.3 for restoration of the right of priority.
	r.49*ter*.1(f)	Where the receiving Office has refused a request for the restoration of the right of priority, any designated Office may consider that request to be a request for restoration submitted to that designated Office under r.49*ter*.2(a) within the time limit under that rule.

40.3.15   *Request by the applicant for a designated Office to restore a right to priority*

1722	r.49*ter*.2(a)	Where the international application claims the priority of an earlier application and has an international filing date which is later than the date on which the priority period expired but within the period of two months from that date, the designated Office shall, on the request of the applicant in accordance with r.49*ter*.2(b), restore the right of priority if the Office finds that a criterion applied by it ("criterion for restoration") is satisfied, namely, that the failure to file the international application within the priority period: (i) occurred in spite of due care required by the circumstances having been taken; or (ii) was unintentional. Each designated Office shall apply at least one of those criteria and may apply both of them.
	OJ	The EPO applies the "due care" criterion only (see [2007] O.J. 692). See also AppGuide, National Chapter (EP).
	r.49*ter*.2(b)	A request under r.49*ter*.2(a) shall: (i) be filed with the designated Office within a time limit of one month from the applicable time limit under Art. 22 or, where the applicant makes an express request to the designated Office under Art. 23(2) (early processing), within a time limit of one month from the date of receipt of that request by the designated Office; (ii) state the reasons for the failure to file the international application within the priority period and preferably be accompanied by any declaration or other evidence required under r.49*ter*.2(c); and (iii) be accompanied by any fee for requesting restoration required under r.49*ter*.2(d).
	J14/21	Where the r.159(1) time limit for regional phase entry is not complied with but the resulting loss of rights is remedied using further processing, a request under r.49*ter*.2(a) may validly be filed along with the request for further processing even if the 1 month time limit of r.49ter.2(b)(1) has expired. See also Guidelines E-IX, 2.3.5.3(iii). This approach is based on a statement made by the PCT Assembly, expressing the intention of the legislator.
	J13/16	The time limit for filing a request for restoration of the priority right on entry to the regional phase is not subject to re-establishment under Art. 122 EPC since although Art. 48(2)(a) PCT requires a Contracting State to excuse a delay in meeting a time limit set under the PCT for reasons admitted under national law, under the EPC, it is not possible to request re-establishment of the two month period for requesting re-establishment of the priority period.
	r.49*ter*.2(c)	The designated Office may require that a declaration or other evidence in support of the statement of reasons referred to in r.49*ter*.2(b)(ii) be filed with it within a time limit which shall be reasonable under the circumstances.
	r.49*ter*.2(d)	The submission of a request under r.49*ter*.2(a) may be subjected by the designated Office to the payment to it, for its own benefit, of a fee for requesting restoration.
	RRFArt. 2(1)(13)	The fee for requesting restoration of the priority right at the EPO is € 720.
	r.49*ter*.2(e)	The designated Office shall not refuse, totally or in part, a request under r.49*ter*.2(a) without giving the applicant the opportunity to make observations on the intended refusal within a time limit which shall be reasonable under the circumstances. Such notice of intended refusal may be sent by the designated Office to the applicant together with any invitation to file a declaration or other evidence under r.49*ter*.2(c).

r.49*ter*.2(f)	Where the national law applicable by the designated Office provides, in respect of the restoration of the right of priority, for requirements which, from the viewpoint of applicants, are more favourable than the requirements provided for under r.49*ter*.2(a) and (b), the designated Office may, when determining the right of priority, apply the requirements under the applicable national law instead of the requirements under those paragraphs.
r.49*ter*.2(g)	Each designated Office shall inform the International Bureau of which of the criteria for restoration it applies, of the requirements, where applicable, of the national law applicable in accordance with r.49*ter*.2(f), and of any subsequent changes in that respect. The International Bureau shall promptly publish such information in the Gazette.
r.49*ter*.2(h)	If, on October 5, 2005, paras (a) to (g) of r.49*ter*.2 are not compatible with the national law applied by the designated Office, those paragraphs shall not apply in respect of that Office for as long as they continue not to be compatible with that law, provided that the Office informs the International Bureau accordingly by April 5, 2006. The information received shall be promptly published by the International Bureau in the Gazette.
WIPO	Incompatibility with r.49*ter*.2(a)–(g) has been notified by and continues to apply to the following designated Offices: Algeria, Brazil, Canada, China, Columbia, Cuba, Czech Republic, Germany, India, Indonesia, Korea, Mexico and Philippines.
r.76.5	The requirements of r.49*ter* apply equally whether national phase entry is under Chapter I or Chapter II.

40.3.16 *Substantive conditions of patentability that may be imposed by Contracting States*

Art. 27(5)	Nothing in the PCT and its Regulations is intended to be construed as prescribing anything that limits the freedom of each Contracting State to prescribe such substantive conditions of patentability as it desires. In particular, the definition of "prior art" under the PCT (see r.64) applies exclusively to the international procedure and any Contracting State is free to apply the criteria of its own national law in respect of prior art when determining the patentability of an invention claimed in an international application, as well as other conditions of patentability not constituting requirements as to the form and contents of applications.	1723
Art. 27(6)	Furthermore, national law may require the submission by the applicant of evidence in respect of any substantive condition of patentability prescribed by such law.	
r.51*bis*.3(b)	Where any requirement of national law that a designated Office may apply under Art. 27(6) is not fulfilled before the time limit specified in Art. 22 the applicant must have an opportunity to comply with that requirement after the expiration of that period.	
r.76.5	The requirements of r.51*bis* apply equally whether national phase entry is under Chapter I or Chapter II.	

40.3.17 *Requirement by Contracting States that the inventor(s) must be the – applicant(s) – procedure when not abided by*

Art. 27(3)	Where, in any designated State, the applicant is not qualified to apply for a national application under national law because he is not an inventor, the international application may be rejected.	1724

40.3.18 *Requirements relating to representation that may be imposed by Contracting States*

Art. 27(7)	See section 43.2.	1725

40.3.19 *Removal of reference signs in claims for publication*

r.6.2	Reference signs in claims may be removed by a designated Office for the purposes of publication by such an Office.	1726

40.3.20 *Submission of a sequence listing*

r.13*ter*.3	No designated Office may require the applicant to submit a sequence listing to it other than one which complies with the Administrative Instructions.	1727

r.76.5   r.13*ter*.3 applies whether national phase entry is under Chapter I or Chapter II.

40.3.21   Special provisions relating to utility models

1728   r.6.5   Any designated State in which the grant of a utility model is sought on the basis of an international application may substitute for r.6.1–6.4 (claims) the corresponding provisions of its national law concerning utility models once national processing of the application has begun.

r.13.5   Any designated State in which the grant of a utility model is sought on the basis of an international application may also substitute for r.13.1–13.4 (unity) the corresponding provision of its national law concerning utility models once national processing of the application has begun.

r.6.5, r.13.5   The applicant must be allowed at least two months from the expiration of the Art. 22 time limit (or the Art. 39 time limit if the election was made before the end of 19 months from the priority date – r.78.3) to adapt the application to the requirements of these provisions of national law.

40.3.22   Any requirement to supply the results of examination in other States is not allowed if an International Preliminary Examination Report has been received

1729   Art. 42   No elected Office receiving the International Preliminary Examination Report may require the applicant to provide copies of, or information regarding the content of, any papers connected with the examination of the same international application in any other elected Office.

40.4   Consequences of an incorrect translation on the scope of a patent obtained

1730   Art. 46   If, because of an incorrect translation of the international application, the scope of any patent granted on that application exceeds the scope of the international application in its original language, the competent authorities of any Contracting State concerned may accordingly and retroactively limit the scope of the patent and declare it null and void to the extent that its scope has exceeded the scope of the international application in its original language.

Chapter 41: The Calculation of Time Limits and Procedural Safeguards

41.1 Expression of dates

r.79.1   Applicants, national Offices, receiving Offices, International Searching and Preliminary   1731
Examining Authorities and the International Bureau must, for the purposes of the PCT
and its Regulations, express any date in terms of the Christian era and the Gregorian
calendar, either as the sole method of expression or in addition to their preferred method.

41.2 Time limits to be calculated from date of mailing

Art. 47(1)   The details for computing time limits referred to in the PCT are governed by the   1732
Regulations.

r.80.6   If any interested party proves that a document or letter emanating from a national Office
or intergovernmental organisation was actually mailed on a later day than the date marked
on it, then a period to be calculated from the date of that document or letter will start on
the actual date of mailing rather than the marked date.

41.3 Computation of time limits

Art. 47(1)   The details for computing time limits referred to in the PCT are governed by the   1733
Regulations.

r.80.1   When a period is expressed as one year or a certain number of years, computation shall
start on the day following the day on which the relevant event occurred, and the period
shall expire in the relevant subsequent year in the month having the same name and on the
day having the same number as the month and the day on which the said event occurred,
provided that if the relevant subsequent month has no day with the same number the period shall expire on the last day of that month.

r.80.2   When a period is expressed as one month or a certain number of months, computation
shall start on the day following the day on which the relevant event occurred, and the period shall expire in the relevant subsequent month on the day having the same number as
the day on which the said event occurred, provided that if the relevant subsequent month
has no day with the same number the period shall expire on the last day of that month.

r.80.3   When a period is expressed as a certain number of days, computation shall start on the day
following the day on which the relevant event occurred, and the period shall expire on the
day on which the last day of the count has been reached.

r.80.4(a)(b)   The applicable starting date for calculating any of the above is the date which prevails in
the locality at the time when the relevant event occurred and the applicable date on which
any period expires is the date which prevails in the locality in which the required document must be filed or the required fee must be paid.

r.80.7(a)(b)   A period expiring on a particular day expires at the moment the relevant national Office
or intergovernmental organisation with which a document must be filed or a to which a
fee must be paid closes for business on that day unless that Office or organisation allows
for a later time up to a maximum of midnight on that day.

41.4 Extension of time limits where a national Office or intergovernmental organisation is not open for business

Art. 47(1)   The details for computing time limits referred to in the PCT are governed by the   1734
Regulations.

     If a time limit relating to the supply of a document or payment of a fee to a national Office
or intergovernmental organisation expires on a day:

r.80.5(i)   (1) on which such Office or organisation is closed to the public for the transaction of
official business; or

r.80.5(iii)   (2) which, where such Office or organisation is situated in two or more localities, is an
official holiday in at least one of the localities in which such Office or organisation is located and the national law applicable to the Office or organisation provides that in respect
of national applications the time limit would be extended; or

r.80.5(iv)	(3) which, where such Office the government authority of a Contracting State entrusted with the granting of patents, is an official holiday in the part of that Contracting State and national law provides that in respect of national applications the time limit would be extended; the period will expire on the next subsequent day on which none of these circumstances exists.
OJ	See Notice from the EPO dated 18 January 2018 ([2018] O.J. A25). Where a means of electronic communication pursuant to r.89*bis* PCT is unavailable, the time limit is extended if such a means of communication is unavailable for four hours or more and the EPO has published an advance notice to this effect. In cases where a means of electronic communication is unavailable unexpectedly the safeguard also applies but the party concerned bears the burden of proof.

41.5   Extension of time limits where mail is not delivered in a relevant locality on the last day of a time limit

1735	Art. 48(1)	Where any time limit fixed in the PCT or its Regulations is not met because of interruption in the mail service or unavoidable loss or delay in the mail, the time limit will be deemed to have been met in the cases and subject to the proof and other conditions prescribed in the Regulations.
	r.80.5(ii)	If a time limit relating to the supply of a document or payment of a fee to a national Office or intergovernmental organisation expires on a day on which ordinary mail is not delivered in the locality in which such Office or organisation is situated, the period will expire on the next subsequent day when mail is delivered.

41.6   Circumstances in which a missed time limit is excused where a document is sent in good time

1736	Art. 48(1)	Where any time limit fixed in the PCT or its Regulations is not met because of interruption in the mail service or unavoidable loss or delay in the mail, the time limit will be deemed to have been met in the cases and subject to the proof and other conditions prescribed in the Regulations.
	r.82.1(a)(b)	If an interested party offers satisfactory evidence to a national Office or intergovernmental organisation showing that he mailed to that Office or organisation a document or letter five days prior to the expiration of a time limit, the mail was registered by the postal authorities (but see below) and either: (a) he mailed it by airmail; or (b) surface mail normally arrives within two days of mailing; or (c) no airmail service is available then delay in arrival will be excused or, in the case of loss, substitution with a new copy will be allowed, provided that satisfactory proof is offered that the substitution is identical with the document or letter lost.
	r.82.1(c)	Any evidence of the mailing date, a substitute document or letter and evidence concerning the identity of the replacement document/letter with the lost document/letter must be submitted within one month of the date on which the interested party noticed, or with due diligence should have noticed, the delay or loss and in any case no later than six months from the expiration of the time limit.
	r.82.1(d)(e)	Any Office or intergovernmental organisation may extend these privileges to delivery services other than postal services by informing the International Bureau, who will publish such information in the Gazette. The requirement for registered mail is replaced in these cases by a requirement that details of the mailing must be recorded by the delivery service at the time of mailing. The extension may be limited to specified delivery services or delivery services satisfying specified criteria. The Office or organisation may, in fact, apply r.82.1 even if it has not notified the International Bureau accordingly or if a non-authorised delivery service is used.
	AppGuide	See Annex B (EP). The EPO will apply r.82.1 in respect of the following delivery services: Chronopost, DHL, Federal Express, Flexpress, Skynet, TNT, Transworld and UPS.

41.7 Excuse of the delay in meeting a time limit in the case of war, revolution, civil disorder, strike, natural calamity, epidemic or unavailability of electronic communication and extension of time limits due to general disruption

r.82quater.1(a)   Any interested party may offer evidence that a time limit fixed in the Regulations for performing an action before the receiving Office, the International Searching Authority, the Authority specified for supplementary search, the International Preliminary Examining Authority or the International Bureau was not met due to war, revolution, civil disorder, strike, natural calamity, epidemic, a general unavailability of electronic communications services or other like reason in the locality where the interested party resides, has his place of business or is staying, and that the relevant action was taken as soon as reasonably possible.   1737

r.82quater.1(b)   Any such evidence shall be addressed to the Office, Authority or the International Bureau, as the case may be, not later than six months after the expiration of the time limit applicable in the given case. If such circumstances are proven to the satisfaction of the addressee, delay in meeting the time limit shall be excused.

r.82quater.1(c)   The excuse of a delay need not be taken into account by any designated or elected Office before which the applicant, at the time the decision to excuse the delay is taken, has already performed the acts referred to in Art. 22 or Art. 39.

r.82*quater*.1(d)   The need for evidence may be waived by the Office, Authority or the International Bureau under the conditions set and published by that Office, Authority or the International Bureau, as the case may be. In such case, the interested party must submit a statement that the failure to meet the time limit was due to the reason for which the Office, Authority or the International Bureau waived the requirement concerning the submission of evidence. The Office or Authority shall notify the International Bureau accordingly.

Comment   This rule was explicitly extended to cover the unavailability of electronic communications services with effect from 01 July 2016. In doing so the PCT Assembly stated that it should only apply to losses of electronic communication affecting a widespread area or many individuals and not those affecting particular buildings or users. Note that it only applies to time limits fixed in the Regulations and does not, therefore, apply to the priority period or the deadline for national/regional phase entry. It was extended to explicitly cover epidemics with effect from 01 July 2022 following the global coronavirus pandemic.

r.82*quater*.2(a)   Any national Office or intergovernmental organization may provide that, where a time limit fixed in the Regulations for performing an action before that Office or organization is not met due to the unavailability of any of the permitted electronic means of communication at that Office or organization, delay in meeting that time limit shall be excused, provided that the respective action was performed on the next working day on which the said electronic means of communication were available. The Office or organization concerned shall publish information on any such unavailability including the period of the unavailability, and notify the International Bureau accordingly.

r.82*quater*.2(b)   The excuse of a delay in meeting a time limit under r.82*quater*.2(a) need not be taken into account by any designated or elected Office before which the applicant, at the time the information referred to in r.82*quater*.2(a) is published, has already performed the acts referred to in Art. 22 or Art. 39.

Comment   New r.82*quater*.2 entered into force on 01 July 2020 and applies to any time limit to which r.82*quater*.2(a) applies that expires after that date.

OJ   See Notice from the EPO dated 22 October 2020 ([2020] O.J. A120). "Electronic means of communication" includes online filing (OLF), Web-Form Filing, New Online Filing (also known as case management system, CMS) and ePCT where the EPO is concerned. Where there is an outage (planned or otherwise) in one of these means of communication that falls under the terms of r.82*quater*.2 PCT, the EPO as an international authority will publish information concerning the outage and notify the IB who will also publish information concerning the outage in the PCT Gazette. Where a means of electronic filing is unavailable for less than four hours and the outage has been published at least two days in advance then periods will not be extended since in this case users are expected to plan accordingly. This rule (r.82*quater*.2) does not apply to the priority period which is fixed in the Paris Convention rather than the PCT Regulations but does apply to fee payments.

r.82*quater*.3(a) Any receiving Office, International Searching Authority, Authority specified for supplementary search, International Preliminary Examining Authority or the International Bureau may establish a period of extension such that time limits fixed in the Regulations within which a party has to perform an action before that Office, Authority or International Bureau may be extended when the State in which it is located is experiencing a general disruption caused by an event listed in r.82*quater*.1(a) which affects the operations at the said Office, Authority or International Bureau thereby interfering with the ability of parties to perform actions before that Office, Authority or International Bureau within the time limits fixed in the Regulations. The Office, Authority or the International Bureau shall publish the commencement and the end date of any such period of extension. The period of extension shall not be longer than two months from the date of commencement. The Office or Authority shall notify the International Bureau accordingly.

r.82*quater*.3(b) After establishing a period of extension under r.82*quater*.3(a), the Office, Authority or the International Bureau concerned may establish additional periods of extension, if necessary under the circumstances. In that case, r.28*quater*.3(a) applies *mutatis mutandis*.

r.82*quater*.3(c) The extension of a time limit under r.82*quater*.3(a) or (b) need not be taken into account by any designated or elected Office if, at the time the information referred to in r.82*quater*.3(a) or (b) is published, national processing before that Office has started.

Comment New r.82*quater*.3 entered into force on 01 July 2022 and applies to any time limit that expires on or after that date.

41.8 Extension of a time limit where a letter is received more than seven days after posting

1738 r.80.6 If the applicant offers satisfactory evidence to a national Office or intergovernmental organisation that a letter or document was received more than seven days after the date it bears, any period to be calculated from the date of the letter or document will be extended by the number of days which the document or letter was received later than seven days from the date it bears. For example, if a letter is received 9 days from the date it bears, any period will be extended by 2 days.

41.9 Chance for the applicant to escape a negative determination made in the international phase

41.9.1 Overview

1739 Comment When an application is considered withdrawn in the international phase, or does not even achieve a filing date, there is no direct means of having the decision reviewed and reversed in the international phase so that the PCT application can continue as a whole. Instead, the PCT provides the applicant with the possibility of entering the national/regional phases that he is interested in early and trying to persuade individual offices that national applications arising from the PCT application should be processed further.

Comment Under Art. 25(1), the applicant can have copies of the PCT file sent to such national/regional offices in order to demonstrate what has gone wrong. Under Art. 25(2), national/regional offices are obliged to continue prosecution of the PCT application if the relevant finding by the receiving Office or the International Bureau was the result of an error or omission (the applicant must first enter the national/regional phase and request early processing of the application) and has the discretion to continue prosecution anyway if it so wishes (Art. 24(2)). Furthermore, even if there has been no error or omission on the part of an international authority, the national/regional office is obliged to excuse any delay in meeting a time limit under the PCT if it would have excused the equivalent delay under the relevant national/regional procedure (Art. 48(2)(a), r.82*bis*) and has the discretion to excuse the delay in any event if it wishes to (Art. 48(2)(b)).

41.9.2 Duty of the International Bureau to supply documents to designated States when the International Bureau or receiving Office has made a negative determination

1740 Art. 25(1)(a)(c) Where the receiving Office has:
(1) refused to accord a filing date (Art. 11(1)); or

(2) declared that the international application is considered withdrawn (r.29.1); or or where the International Bureau has:

(3) made a finding under Art. 12(3) (record copy not received within the prescribed time limit prescribed by r.22.3);

the International Bureau will, when requested by the applicant within the prescribed time limit, promptly send copies of any documents in the file to any of the designated Offices named by the applicant.

Art. 25(1)(b)(c)   Where the receiving Office has declared that the designation of any given State is considered withdrawn (Art. 14(3) (b)/r.27.1(b)), the International Bureau will, when requested by the applicant within the prescribed time limit, promptly send copies of any documents in the file to the national office of such State.

r.51.1   The prescribed time limit under Art. 25(1) is two months computed from the date of the notification sent to the applicant under r.20.4(i) (refusal to accord a filing date), r.24.2(c) (lack of receipt by the International Bureau of the record copy) or r.29.1(a)(ii) (finding by the receiving Office that the application is considered withdrawn).

r.51.2   Where a filing date cannot be allocated (negative determination under Art. 11(1)) and the applicant requests the International Bureau to proceed as above, he must attach to his request a copy of the r.20.4(i) notice (that his application is not and will not be treated as an international application and the reasons therefor).

41.9.3   Assessment by the designated Office as to whether the applicant or the International Bureau/receiving Office is at fault according to the PCT

Art. 25(2)(a)   Each designated Office must, providing the national fee (if any) has been paid and any   1741 prescribed translation has been supplied within the prescribed time limit, decide whether the refusal, declaration or finding referred to in Art. 25(1) was justified under the PCT and its Regulations and if it finds that the refusal or declaration was the result of an error or omission on the part of the receiving Office or that the finding was the result of an error or omission on the part of the International Bureau, it will, as far as that State is concerned, treat the application as if the error or omission had not occurred.

r.51.3   The prescribed time limit is the same as the r.51.1 time limit, i.e. two months computed from the date of the notification sent to the applicant under r.20.4(i) (refusal to accord a filing date), r.24.2(c) (lack of receipt by the International Bureau of the record copy) or r.29.1(a)(ii) (finding by the receiving Office that the application is considered withdrawn).

EPC r.159(2)   The Examining Division is competent to take decisions of the EPO under Art. 25(2)(a) PCT.

Art. 25(2)(b)   However, when the record copy has reached the International Bureau after the expiry of the Art. 12(3) time limit on account of an error or omission on the part of the applicant, the provisions of Art. 25(2)(a) only apply under the circumstances referred to in Art. 48(2), i.e. where the designated Office excuses the delay in meeting the time limit under national law or for any other reason.

41.9.4   Right of any designated State to maintain the effect of an international application in that State when it does not have to

Art. 24(2)   It is the prerogative of any designated Office to maintain the effect of Art. 11(3) if it wish-   1742 es, even when not obliged so to do under Art. 25(2).

41.9.5   The duty of Contracting States to excuse missed time limits under provisions of national law

Art. 48(2)(a)(b)   Any State, as far as that State is concerned, must excuse, for reasons admitted under its   1743 national law, and may excuse for any other reason, any delay in meeting any time limit.

r.82*bis*.1   In this context, "any time limit" must be construed to include any time limit:

(a) fixed in the PCT and its Regulations;

(b) fixed by the receiving Office, the International Searching Authority, the International Preliminary Examining Authority or the International Bureau or applicable by the receiving Office under its national law; or

(c) fixed by, or in the national law applicable by, the designated or elected Office, for the performance of any act by the applicant before that Office.

r.82*bis*.2	Such provisions of national law are those which provide for reinstatement of rights, restoration, restitutio in integrum or further processing where a time limit has been missed and any other provision providing for the extension of time limits or for excusing delays in meeting time limits.
AppGuide	See National Phase, paragraph 6.022. This mechanism only operates when the national or regional phase has been entered but may then be used to excuse the missing of a time limit in the international or national/regional phase.
J19/16	In order to take advantage of the excuse procedure of Art. 48(2)(a) PCT, it is not a prerequisite that the procedure of Art. 25 PCT has been followed. The time limit for taking advantage of any national remedies under Art. 48(2)(a) is laid down by national law and the two month time limit of Art. 25 is not relevant (see point 6(c) of the reasons).

41.10 Opportunity to correct an application where allowed under national law

1744	Art. 26	No designated Office may reject an international application on the grounds that it does not comply with the PCT and Regulations without first giving the applicant the opportunity to correct the application to the extent and according to the procedure provided by national law for the same or comparable situations in respect of national applications.
	J8/01	Article 26 PCT gives a purported designated Office the authority to consider if its designation can be added or not (e.g. under r.139 EPC). However, in accordance with decisions relating to regular European patent applications, the mistake must be corrected early enough for the public to be warned on international publication.

41.11 Rectification of errors made by the receiving Office or the International -Bureau concerning filing date and priority claim

1745	r.82*ter*.1(a)	If the applicant proves to the satisfaction of any designated or elected Office that the international filing date is incorrect due to an error made by the receiving Office or that the priority claim has been erroneously considered void by the receiving Office or the International Bureau, and if the error is an error such that, had it been made by the designated or elected Office itself, that Office would rectify it under the national law or national practice, the Office will rectify the error and shall treat the international application as if it had been accorded the rectified international filing date or as if the priority claim had not been considered void.

41.12 Reinstatement of rights after failure to enter the national phase within the time limit

1746	r.49.6(a)	Where the effect of the international application provided for in Art. 11(3) ceases because the applicant fails to perform the acts referred to in Art. 22 within the applicable time limit (Art. 24(1)(iii)), the designated Office will, upon request of the applicant, reinstate the rights of the applicant with respect to that international application if it finds that any delay in meeting that time limit was unintentional or, at the option of the designated Office, that the failure to meet the time limit occurred in spite of due care required by the circumstances having been taken.
	Comment	Note that r.49.6 only applies to a failure to perform the acts referred to in Art. 22 PCT which are the furnishing of a copy of the international application and a translation thereof and the payment of the national fee. It would not therefore be applicable to any of the other acts necessary under r.159(1) EPC such as the payment of the examination fee or supplementary search fee.
	OJ	The EPO applies the "due care" criterion only (see [2007] O.J. 692).
	r.49.6(b)	Such a request must be submitted to the designated Office and the Art. 22 acts must be completed within the earlier of: (i) two months from the date of removal of the cause of the failure to meet the applicable time limit under Art. 22; and (ii) 12 months from the date of the expiration of the applicable time limit under Art. 22; provided that the applicant may submit the request at any later time if so permitted by the national law applicable by the designated Office.
	r.49.6(c)(d)	The request must state the reasons for the failure to meet the Art. 22 time limit.

r.49.6(d)(ii)	National law may provide that a declaration or other evidence be filed in support of such reasons.
r.49.6(d)(i)	Furthermore, national law may require that a fee be paid in respect of such a request.
RRFArt. 2(1)(13)	The fee for reinstatement is € 720.
r.49.6(e)	A designated Office may not refuse such a request without giving the applicant a chance to make observations on the intended refusal within a reasonable time limit.
r.49.6(f)	If, on October 1, 2002, paragraphs (a)–(e) of r.49.6 are not compatible with the national law applied by a designated Office, those paragraphs will not apply in respect of that designated Office for as long as they continue not to be compatible with that law, provided that the said Office informed the International Bureau accordingly by January 1, 2003. The information received is promptly published by the International Bureau in the Gazette.
WIPO	Such reservations remain in force in respect of Canada, China, Germany, New Zealand, the Philippines, Korea, Latvia, Mexico, India, Poland.

Chapter 42: Rectification of Mistakes

42.1 Mistakes that may be rectified

1747 r.91.1(a)

Obvious mistakes in an international application, or any other document submitted by the applicant, may be rectified in accordance with r.91 if such rectification is requested by the applicant.

r.91.1(b)

The rectification of such a mistake is, however, subject to authorisation by a competent international authority (see below).

r.91.1(c)

Rectification of a mistake will only be authorised if it is obvious to the competent authority that, as at the applicable date under r.91.1(f), something else was intended than what appears in the document concerned and that nothing else could have been intended than the proposed rectification.

r.91.1(d)

In judging whether a mistake in the description, claims or drawings or a correction or amendment thereof is obvious under r.91.1(c), the competent authority will only take into account the contents of the description, claims and drawings and, where applicable, the correction or amendment concerned.

r.91.1(e)

In judging whether a mistake in the request or a document referred to in r.91.1(b)(iv), or a correction thereof, is obvious under r.91.1(c), the competent authority will only take into account the contents of the international application itself and, where applicable, the correction concerned, or the document referred to in r.91.1(b)(iv), together with any other document submitted with the request, correction or document, as the case may be, any priority document in respect of the international application that is available to the Authority in accordance with the Administrative Instructions, and any other document contained in the Authority's international application file at the applicable date under r.91.1(f).

r.91.1(f)

The applicable date for the purposes of r.91.1(c) and (e) is:
(i) in the case of a mistake in a part of the international application as filed – the international filing date;
(ii) in the case of a mistake in a document other than the international application as filed, including a mistake in a correction or an amendment of the international application – the date on which the document was submitted.

r.20.5, r.20.6

Where the receiving Office finds that a part of the description, claims or drawing is or appears to be missing, the applicant is given an opportunity to supply the missing part and have the application re-dated (r.20.5) or to confirm that the part was incorporated by reference under r.4.18 and to retain the original filing date (r.20.6). For more information on this procedure, see section 32.1.5.

42.2 Mistakes that may not be rectified

1748 r.91.1(g)

A mistake is not be rectifiable under r.91 if:
(i) the mistake lies in the omission of one or more entire elements of the international application referred to in Art. 3(2) or one or more entire sheets of the international application;
(ii) the mistake is in the abstract;
(iii) the mistake is in an amendment under Art. 19, unless the International Preliminary Examining Authority is competent to authorise the rectification of such mistake under r.91.1(b)(iii); or
(iv) the mistake is in a priority claim or in a notice correcting or adding a priority claim under r.26*bis*.1(a), where the rectification of the mistake would cause a change in the priority date;
provided that this paragraph does not affect the operation of rr.20.4, 20.5, 26*bis* and 38.3.

42.3 Authority responsible for authorising rectification

1749 r.91.1(b)

The rectification of a mistake must be authorised by the "competent authority", that is to say:
(i) in the case of a mistake in the request part of the international application or in a correction thereof – by the receiving Office;

(ii) in the case of a mistake in the description, claims or drawings or in a correction thereof, unless the International Preliminary Examining Authority is competent under r.91.1(b) (iii) – by the International Searching Authority;

(iii) in the case of a mistake in the description, claims or drawings or in a correction thereof, or in an amendment under Art. 19 or Art. 34, where a demand for international preliminary examination has been made and has not been withdrawn and the date on which international preliminary examination starts in accordance with r.69.1 has passed – by the International Preliminary Examining Authority;

(iv) in the case of a mistake in a document not referred to in r.91.1(b)(i) to (iii) submitted to the receiving Office, the International Searching Authority, the International Preliminary Examining Authority or the International Bureau, other than a mistake in the abstract or in an amendment under Art. 19 – by that Office, Authority or Bureau, as the case may be.

42.4   Either the applicant or an international authority may initiate rectification

r.91.1(a) The applicant may request rectification.   1750
r.91.1(h) Where the receiving Office, the International Searching Authority, the International Preliminary Examining Authority or the International Bureau discovers what appears to be a rectifiable obvious mistake in the international application or another document, it may invite the applicant to request rectification under r.91.

42.5   Procedure for requesting rectification – time limit

r.91.2 A request for rectification under r.91.1 must be submitted to the competent authority   1751
within 26 months from the priority date. It must specify the mistake to be rectified and the proposed rectification, and may, at the option of the applicant, contain a brief explanation. Rule 26.4 (manner in which a correction of a formal requirement should be provided to the receiving Office) applies mutatis mutandis as to the manner in which the proposed rectification must be indicated.

42.6   Decision on the authorisation of a rectification

r.91.3(a) The competent authority must promptly decide whether to authorise or refuse to author-   1752
ise a rectification under r.91.1 and promptly notify the applicant and the International Bureau of the authorisation or refusal and, in the case of refusal, of the reasons therefor. The International Bureau will proceed as provided for in the Administrative Instructions, including, as required, notifying the receiving Office, the International Searching Authority, the International Preliminary Examining Authority and the designated and elected Offices of the authorisation or refusal.

r.91.3(b) Where the rectification of an obvious mistake has been authorised under r.91.1, the document concerned will be rectified in accordance with the Administrative Instructions.

AdminInst See s.325 (receiving Office), s.413*bis* (International Bureau), s.511 (International Searching Authority) and s.607 (International Preliminary Examining Authority). Replacement sheets are marked accordingly and transmitted to other international authorities.

r.48.2(i) Replacement pages incorporating mistakes rectified by the receiving Office, International Searching Authority or International Bureau are published as part of the international application, if received or authorised by the International Bureau in time or else separately.

r.70.16(a)(iii) Replacement pages incorporating mistakes rectified by the International Preliminary Examining Authority are annexed to the International Preliminary Examination Report.

r.91.3(c) Where the rectification of an obvious mistake has been authorised, it will be effective:
(i) in the case of a mistake in the international application as filed, from the international filing date;
(ii) in the case of a mistake in a document other than the international application as filed, including a mistake in a correction or an amendment of the international application, from the date on which that document was submitted.

r.91.3(d)

Where the competent authority refuses to authorise a rectification under r.91.1, the International Bureau will, upon request submitted to it by the applicant within two months from the date of the refusal, and subject to the payment of a special fee whose amount shall be fixed in the Administrative Instructions, publish the request for rectification, the reasons for refusal by the authority and any further brief comments that may be submitted by the applicant, if possible together with the international application. A copy of the request, reasons and comments (if any) will if possible be included in the communication under Art. 20 where the international application is not published by virtue of Art. 64(3).

AdminInst

See s.113(b) – the special fee is 50 Swiss francs and an additional 12 Swiss francs for each sheet in excess of 1.

r.91.3(e)

The rectification of an obvious mistake need not be taken into account by any designated Office in which the processing or examination of the international application has already started prior to the date on which that Office is notified under r.91.3(a) of the authorisation of the rectification by the competent authority.

r.91.3(f)

A designated Office may disregard a rectification that was authorised under r.91.1 only if it finds that it would not have authorised the rectification under r.91.1 if it had been the competent authority. However, no designated Office may disregard any rectification that was authorised under r.91.1 without giving the applicant the opportunity to make observations, within a time limit which must be reasonable under the circumstances, on the Office's intention to disregard the rectification.

42.7   Language of the correction

1753   r.12.2(b)

Any rectification under r.91.1 of an obvious mistake in the international application must be in the language in which the application is filed, provided that:
(i) where a translation of the international application is required under r.12.3(a) (for international search), r.12.4(a) (for international publication) or r.55.2(a) (for international preliminary examination), rectifications referred to in r.91.1(b)(ii) and (iii) shall be filed in both the language of the application and the language of that translation;
(ii) where a translation of the request is required under r.26.3*ter*(c), rectifications referred to in r.91.1(b)(i) need only be filed in the language of that translation.

Chapter 43: Representation

43.1 Requirements relating to representation that may be imposed by the receiving Office

Art. 27(7) Any receiving Office may apply national law in so far as it relates to any requirement that the applicant be represented by an agent having the right to represent applicants before that Office. 1754

AppGuide See Annex C (EP). Where the EPO is receiving Office, representation is required if the applicant has neither a residence nor a principle place of business within one of the EPC Contracting States.

AppGuide See Annex C (IB) – the International Bureau does not require the appointment of an agent.

43.2 Requirements relating to representation that may be imposed by Contracting States

Art. 27(7) Any designated Office, once processing of the international application has started in that Office, may apply national law as far as it relates to any requirement that: 1755
(1) the applicant be represented by an agent having the right to represent applicants before the said Office; and/or
(2) the applicant have an address in the designated State for the purposes of receiving notifications.

r.51*bis*.1(b) In accordance with Art. 27(7), national law may require that the agent representing the applicant has the right to represent applicants before the designated Office and/or has an address in the designated State for the purposes of receiving notifications and, further, that any agent is duly appointed by the applicant.

r.51*bis*.3(b) Where any requirement of national law that a designated Office may apply under Art. 27(7) is not fulfilled before the expiry of the time limit specified in Art. 22 the applicant must have an opportunity to comply with that requirement after the expiration of that period.

r.76.5 The requirements of r.51*bis* apply equally whether national phase entry was under Chapter I or Chapter II.

43.3 Right to practice before international authorities

Art. 49 Any attorney, patent agent or other person having the right to practice before the national Office with which the international application was filed is entitled to practice before the International Bureau, the competent International Searching Authority and the competent International Preliminary Examining Authority in respect of that application. 1756

r.90.1(a) A person having the right to practice before the national Office with which the international application is filed may also be appointed by the applicant to represent him before any authority specified for supplementary search.

r.83.1 The International Bureau, the competent International Searching Authority and the competent International Preliminary Examining Authority may require proof of the right to practice before a national Office referred to in Art. 49.

r.83.1*bis*(a)(b) Where the International Bureau is the receiving Office, any person who has the right to practice before the national Office of, or acting for, a Contracting State of which the applicant (or one of them if there are more than one) is a resident or national is entitled to practice in respect of the international application before the International Bureau in its capacity as receiving Office (r.19.1(a)(iii)), before the International Bureau in any other capacity and before the competent International Searching and Preliminary Examining Authorities.

r.83.2 To decide any question as to such an entitlement to practice (r.83.1*bis*), the national Office or intergovernmental organisation before which the interested person is alleged to have the right to practice will inform the International Bureau or Authority concerned, on request, whether such a person has such a right and such information is binding on the International Bureau or Authority concerned.

AppGuide See International Phase, paragraph 10.019. The International Preliminary Examining Authority may not require that the applicant be represented.

43.4   Agents and common representatives

43.4.1   Appointment of an agent

1757   r.90.1(a)   A person having the right to practice before the national office with which the international application is filed or, where the international application is filed with the International Bureau, having the right to practice in respect of the international application before the International Bureau as receiving Office may be appointed by the applicant as his agent to represent him before the receiving Office, the International Bureau, the International Searching Authority, any authority specified for supplementary search and the International Preliminary Examining Authority.

r.90.1(b)   A person having the right to practice before the national office or intergovernmental organisation which acts as the International Searching Authority may be appointed by the applicant as his agent to represent him specifically before that Authority.

r.90.1(b-*bis*)   A person having the right to practice before the national office or intergovernmental organisation which acts as the Authority specified for supplementary search may be appointed by the applicant as his agent to represent him specifically before that Authority.

r.90.1(c)   A person having the right to practice before the national office or intergovernmental organisation which acts as the International Preliminary Examining Authority may be appointed by the applicant as his agent to represent him specifically before that Authority.

r.90.1(d)   An agent appointed under r.90.1(a) may, unless otherwise indicated in the document appointing him, appoint one or more sub-agents to represent the applicant as the applicant's agent:
(i) before the receiving Office, the International Bureau, the International Searching Authority, any Authority specified for supplementary search and the International Preliminary Examining Authority, provided that any person so appointed as sub-agent has the right to practice before the national office with which the international application was filed or to practice in respect of the international application before the International Bureau as receiving Office, as the case may be;
(ii) specifically before the International Searching Authority, any Authority specified for supplementary search or the International Preliminary Examining Authority, provided that any person so appointed as sub-agent has the right to practice before the national office or intergovernmental organisation which acts as the International Searching Authority, the authority specified for supplementary search or the International Preliminary Examining Authority, as the case may be.

AppGuide   See International Phase, paragraphs 5.043–5.044 – an agent may appointed by being named in the request, if the applicant signs the request, or in a separate power of attorney (which, in any case, may be waived) if the request is signed by the agent.

AppGuide   See International Phase, paragraph 11.016 – where there are two or more applicants who have appointed one or more common agents, correspondence is sent to the agent or the first mentioned agent. Where no representative is appointed, correspondence is sent to the appointed common representative or, if none is appointed, the deemed common representative, or, if the common representative has appointed an agent, to that agent.

43.4.2   Representative where there are two or more applicants

1758   r.90.2   Where there are two or more applicants, they will be represented by:
(a) a common agent appointed by the applicants under r.90.1(a); or
(b) one of the applicants appointed by the others as common representative as long as he is entitled to file an international application under Art. 9; or, where neither (a) or (b) apply,
(c) the applicant first named on the request who is entitled to file an international application with the receiving Office under r.19.1, this applicant being considered common representative.

AppGuide	See International Phase, paragraph 11.006 – if there are two or more applicants and they do not appoint a common agent or common representative, the first-named applicant in the request that has the right to file an international application with the receiving Office is automatically considered the deemed common representative. The deemed common representative may carry out most procedural acts on behalf of the joint applicants, including signing the demand, but, importantly, may not withdraw the application or any part thereof. The deemed common representative may appoint an agent to perform any acts which he could have performed himself.
Guidelines	See Guidelines for Search and Examination at the EPO as PCT Authority, A-VIII,1.3 – if the appointed common representative or deemed common represenrive has neither a residence nor a principle place of business in an EPC contracting state then professional representation is required.

43.4.3   *Effects of acts carried out by representatives and agents*

r.90.3(a)(b)	Any act by or in relation to an agent (or, if there are two or more agents representing the same applicant or applicants, any of them) will have the effect of an act by or in relation to the applicant or applicants concerned.	1759
r.90.3(c)	Any act by or in relation to a common representative or a common representative's agent will have the effect of an act by or in relation to all the applicants, subject to r.90*bis*.5, second sentence (signatures necessary to effect withdrawal of the application, a designation, a priority claim, a supplementary search request, an election or a demand).	

43.4.4   *Manner of appointment of an agent or common representative*

r.90.4(a)	The appointment of an agent is effected by the applicant signing the request, the demand or a separate power of attorney. Where there are two or more applicants, the appointment of a common agent or common representative is effected by each applicant signing, at his choice, the request, the demand or a separate power of attorney.	1760
r.90.4(b)	Subject to r.90.5, a separate power of attorney shall be submitted to either the receiving Office or the International Bureau, provided that, where a power of attorney appoints an agent under r.90.1(b), (b-*bis*), (c) or (d)(ii), it shall be submitted to the International Searching Authority, the authority specified for supplementary search or the International Preliminary Examining Authority, as the case may be.	
r.90.4(c)	If the separate power of attorney is not signed, or if the required separate power of attorney is missing, or if the indication of the name and address of the appointed person does not comply with r.4.4, the power of attorney will be considered nonexistent unless the defect is corrected.	
r.90.4(d)	Subject to r.90.4(e), any receiving Office, any International Searching Authority, any authority competent to carry out supplementary searches, any International Preliminary Examining Authority and the International Bureau may waive the requirement under r.90.4(b) that a separate power of attorney be submitted to it, in which case r.90.4(c) does not apply.	
AppGuide, OJ	Many offices have waived the requirement for a separate power of attorney. The EPO has waived the requirement for a separate power of attorney except (a) where the agent of record changes and the new and old agents do not belong to the same office or are not employees of the applicant and (b) where there is any doubt as to the entitlement of the agent to act (see [2004] O.J. 305 and [2010] O.J. 335 and AppGuide, Annex C [EP]).	
r.90.4(e)	Where the agent or the common representative submits any notice of withdrawal referred to in any of rr.90*bis*.1 to 90*bis*.4, the requirement under r.90.4(b) for a separate power of attorney is not waived under r.90.4(d).	
r.90.5(a)	Appointment of an agent in relation to a particular international application may be effected by referring in the request, the demand or a separate notice to an existing separate power of attorney appointing that agent to represent the applicant in relation to any international application which may be filed by the applicant (i.e. a "general power of attorney"), provided that: (i) the general power of attorney has been deposited in accordance with r.90.5(b); and (ii) a copy of it is attached to the request, the demand or the separate notice, as the case may be – that copy need not be signed.	

r.90.5(b)	A general power of attorney must be deposited with the receiving Office, provided that, where it appoints an agent under r.90.1(b), (b-*bis*), (c) or (d)(ii), it must be deposited with the International Searching Authority, the authority specified for supplementary search or the International Preliminary Examining Authority, as the case may be.
r.90.5(c)	Any receiving Office, any International Searching Authority, any authority competent to carry out supplementary searches and any International Preliminary Examining Authority may waive the requirement under r.90.5(a)(ii) that a copy of the general power of attorney is attached to the request, the demand or the separate notice, as the case may be.
r.90.5(d)	Notwithstanding r.90.5(c), where the agent submits any notice of withdrawal referred to in rr.90*bis*.1 to 90*bis*.4 to the receiving Office, the authority specified for supplementary search, the International Preliminary Examining Authority or the International Bureau, as the case may be, a copy of the general power of attorney shall be submitted to that office, Authority or Bureau.
AppGuide, OJ	The EPO has waived the requirement for a copy of a general power of attorney to be submitted except (a) where the agent of record changes and the new and old agents do not belong to the same office or are not employees of the applicant and (b) where there is any doubt as to the entitlement of the agent to act (see [2004] O.J. 305 and [2010] O.J. 335). See also AppGuide, Annex C (EP).

43.4.5 *Manner of renunciation of an agent or common representative*

1761	r.90.6(a)	Any appointment of an agent or common representative may be revoked by the persons who made the appointment or by their successors in title (and a revocation of the appointment of an agent will automatically revoke the appointment under r.90.1(d) of a sub-agent working under that agent). Any appointment of a sub-agent under r.90.1(d) may also be revoked by the applicant concerned.
	r.90.6(b)(c)	The appointment of an agent under r.90.1(a) or the appointment of a common representative will, unless otherwise indicated, have the effect of revoking any earlier appointment of an agent under r.90.1(a) or a common representative, respectively.
	r.90.6(d)	An agent or common representative may renounce his appointment by filing a signed notification.
	r.90.6(e)	By application of r.90.4(b) and (c), mutatis mutandis, such a revocation or renunciation according to r.90.6 must be submitted to the receiving Office or the International Bureau, provided that where an agent was appointed specifically in respect of an International Searching, Supplementary Searching or Preliminary Examining Authority (r.90.1(b), (b-*bis*), (c) or (d)(ii)), it should be submitted to that relevant Authority. Where the revocation or renunciation is not signed, is missing or contains indications of the relevant name and address that do not comply with r.4.4, it will be considered nonexistent unless the defect is corrected.

Chapter 44: Miscellaneous Common Provisions

44.1 Relationship between the PCT and the EPC

Art. 45(1)	A regional patent treaty which gives all those persons who have the right to file an international patent application the right to file applications for a regional patent may provide that international patent applications designating or electing a state party to both the PCT and the regional patent treaty may be filed as applications for a regional patent.	1762
EPC Preamble	The European Patent Convention is a regional patent treaty within the meaning of Art. 45(1) PCT.	
EPC Art. 150(1)	The PCT is to be applied, as far as European patent applications and patents are concerned, according to the provisions of Part X of the EPC (International application under the PCT).	
EPC Art. 150(2)	In proceedings before the EPO concerning an international application filed under the PCT and its Regulations, the provisions of the PCT will be applied, supplemented by the provisions of the EPC. In the case of conflict, the provisions of the PCT will prevail.	

44.2 Rules relating to documents filed subsequently to the filing of the application

44.2.1 Need for papers to be accompanied by a signed letter

r.92.1(a)	Any paper submitted by the applicant during the international procedure provided for under the PCT and its Regulations, other than the application itself, must, if not itself a letter, be accompanied by a letter, identifying the international application to which it relates and signed by the applicant.	1763
r.92.1(b)	Where r.92.1(a) is not complied with, the applicant will be invited to remedy the omission within a time limit which is reasonable (between ten days and a month from the date of the invitation, even where the time limit so fixed expires later than the time limit for supplying the paper, or the latter time limit has already expired) and fixed in the invitation. Either the omission or the paper will be disregarded depending on whether the omission is remedied within the time limit fixed.	
r.92.1(c)	Where r.92.1(a) has not been complied with but the non-compliance is overlooked, and the paper taken into account in the international procedure, such non-compliance will be disregarded.	

44.2.2 Language of letters and documents

r.92.2(a)(b)	Any letter or document submitted by the applicant to an International Searching or Preliminary Examining Authority must be in the same language as the application to which it relates except that: (1) where a translation of the international application has been submitted under r.23.1(b) (for international search) or r.55.2 (for international preliminary examination), the language of such a translation must be used in the letter or document; (2) any letter submitted to an International Searching or Preliminary Examining Authority may be in any other language provided such an Authority authorises the use of that language; (3) the demand must be in the language specified in r.55.1; and (4) amendments and accompanying letters must be filed in the language specified by r.55.3.	1764
r.92.2(d)	Any letter from the applicant to the International Bureau must be in English, French or any other language of publication as may be permitted by the Administrative Instructions.	
AdminInst	See s.104. Such a letter should be in English (if that is the language of the application), French (if that is the language of the application) or in English or French in other cases. Any communication using ePCT can be in English, French or the language of publication.	
r.92.2(e)	Any letter or notification from the International Bureau to the applicant or to any national Office is in English or French.	
OJ	See Art. 7 and Annex D of the agreement between the EPO and the International Bureau ([2010] O.J. 304). The EPO specifies the use of English, French or German, depending on the language in which the international application is filed or into which it is translated.	

44.2.3   *Form of subsequently filed documents*

1765   r.11.14   Rules 10 (terminology and signs) and 11.1–11.13 (physical requirements) apply to any document (for example replacement sheet, amended claims, translation) submitted after the filing of the international application.

44.2.4   *The use of telegraph, teleprinter, facsimile to transmit subsequently filed documents*

1766   r.92.4(a)(h)   Notwithstanding r.11.14 (rules for documents filed later than the application) and r.92.1(a) (any paper to be accompanied by a letter), any document filed subsequent to the filing of the international application or correspondence relating to an international application may be transmitted, if feasible, by telegraph, teleprinter, facsimile or other like means of communication resulting in the filing of a printed or written document provided that no national Office or intergovernmental organisation is obliged to receive a document submitted in this way unless it has notified the International Bureau to the effect that it will and such information has been published in the Gazette.

r.92.4(c)   Where such means are used to transmit a document and part or all of the document is not received or is illegible on receipt, it will be treated as not received to the extent that it is not received or illegible. The relevant national Office or intergovernmental organisation must promptly inform the applicant accordingly.

r.92.4(d)–(g)   Where such means are used to transmit a document, any national Office or intergovernmental organisation may require:
(1) that the original and an accompanying letter identifying the earlier transmission be forwarded within 14 days of such transmission, provided that such a requirement has been notified to the International Bureau (specifying whether the requirement extends to all or only certain kinds of documents) and published in the Gazette. Where the original is not so forwarded, the relevant Office or organisation may, depending on the kind of document involved, and having regard to r.11 (physical requirements) and r.26.3 (checking of physical requirements):
(i) waive the requirement; or
(ii) invite the applicant to forward the original within a reasonable time limit fixed in the invitation; or
(iii) where the document transmitted contains defects or shows that the original contains defects warranting an invitation to correct, issue such an invitation instead or in addition to (a) or (b).
(2) even where the forwarding of an original is not required as specified under (a), but the relevant Office or organisation considers it necessary to receive the original nevertheless, that the applicant forwards the original within a reasonable time limit fixed in the invitation.

r.92.4(g)   Where the applicant fails to comply with an invitation under (1)(ii) or (2) above, then if the document is a document subsequent to an international application, that document will be considered as not having been submitted.

r.92.4(b)   A signature appearing on a document transmitted by facsimile will be recognised for the purposes of the PCT and its Regulations as a proper signature.

OJ   Subsequent documents (with the exception of authorisations and priority documents) may be filed by fax at the EPO (but not by telegraph or teleprinter). Confirmation is not routinely required (see Decision of the President dated 20.2.2019, [2019] O.J. A20). If a requested confirmation copy is not filed within the two month period set then the document is deemed not to have been received.

AppGuide   See Annex B2 (EP). Confirmation is required in the case of the withdrawal of the international application and will be requested by the EPO within a period of one month if not filed simultaneously.

44.2.5   *The use of electronic means to transmit subsequently filed documents*

1767   r.89*bis*.2   By application of r.89*bis*.1(a) mutatis mutandis, documents and correspondence relating to an international application may be filed and processed in electronic form or by electronic means (in accordance with the Administrative Instructions) but receiving Offices must also permit the filing of such documents and correspondence on paper.

r.89*bis*.2	By application of r.89*bis*.1(b)(c) mutatis mutandis, the PCT Regulations apply equally to documents and correspondence filed electronically, subject to any special provisions of the Administrative Instructions which set out the requirements for the filing and processing of documents and correspondence filed wholly or partly in electronic form including, but not limited to: (a) acknowledgement of receipt; (b) physical requirements; (c) consequences of not complying with the physical requirements; (d) signature of documents; (e) means of authentication of documents; (f) means of authentication of the identity of parties communicating with Offices and authorities; and (g) language-specific provisions.
r.89*bis*.2	By application of r.89*bis*.1(d)(e) mutatis mutandis, no national Office or intergovernmental organisation is required to receive or process documents and correspondence filed electronically unless it has notified the International Bureau that it is so prepared to do according to the provisions of the Administrative Instructions. Such notification will be published by the International Bureau in the Gazette. Having issued such notification, a receiving Office may not refuse to process documents and correspondence filed electronically which comply with the requirements of the Administrative Instructions.
r.89*bis*.3	Transmittal of notifications, communications, correspondence and other documents from one national Office or intergovernmental organisation to another may, if both sender and receiver agree, be effected in electronic form or by electronic means.
r.89*ter*	Any Office or intergovernmental organisation may provide that, where a document relating to an international application is filed on paper, a copy thereof in electronic form, in accordance with the Administrative Instructions, may be furnished by the applicant.
AdminInst	See Part 7 and Annex F.
OJ	Documents relating to PCT applications may be filed with the EPO in electronic form using EPO Online Filing (OLF), Online Filing 2.0, the webform filing service or the EPO Contingency Upload Service (see Decision of the President dated 03 May 2023, [2023] O.J. A48). The use of electronic filing does not apply to priority documents unless they have been digitally signed by the issuing authority in a manner acceptable to the EPO. Authorisations and priority documents are excluded in the case of the web-form filing service.

44.3 Withdrawal of an international application, a designation, an election, a demand or a priority claim

44.3.1 Withdrawal of an international application

r.90*bis*.1(a)	An international application may be withdrawn by the applicant at any time prior to the expiration of 30 months from the priority date.
r.90*bis*.1(b)	Such withdrawal is effected by submission of a notice addressed by the applicant to any of the International Bureau, the receiving Office or (where Art. 39(1) applies) the International Preliminary Examining Authority and is effective on receipt.
r.90*bis*.5	Such a withdrawal must be signed by the applicant, or all the applicants when there is more than one. A common representative under r.90.2(b) is not entitled to sign on behalf of another applicant
r.90.4, r.90.5	A separate power of attorney or a copy of a general power of attorney must be submitted to the relevant authority where an agent or common representative submits a notice of withdrawal under r.90*bis*.1.
AppGuide	See International Phase, paragraph 11.048 – no waiver regarding a power of attorney operates in the case of a withdrawal of an international application – it must be clear that all applicants agree.
r.90*bis*.1(c)	A withdrawal will have the effect of preventing international publication of the application if the notice of withdrawal reaches the International Bureau (from the applicant or via the receiving Office or International Preliminary Examining Authority) before the technical preparations for publication have been completed.
r.90*bis*.6(b)	International processing of the application will be discontinued.

1768

r.90*bis*.6(a)	Withdrawal of the application will have no effect in any designated or elected Office where the processing or examination of the international application has already started under Art. 23(2) or Art. 40(2) (on the express request of the applicant).

44.3.2   *Withdrawal of a designation*

1769	r.90*bis*.2(a)	The designation of any State may be withdrawn by the applicant at any time prior to the expiration of 30 months from the priority date.
	r.90*bis*.2(d)	Such withdrawal is effected by submission of a notice addressed by the applicant to any of the International Bureau, the receiving Office or (where Art. 39(1) applies) the International Preliminary Examining Authority and is effective on receipt.
	r.90*bis*.5	The requirement for the withdrawal of a designation to be signed is identical to the requirement for a withdrawal of the application to be signed (see above).
	r.90.4, r.90.5	A separate power of attorney or a copy of a general power of attorney must be submitted to the relevant authority where an agent or common representative submits a notice of withdrawal under r.90*bis*.2.
	r.90*bis*.2(a)	Withdrawal of the designation of an elected State entails withdrawal of the election of that State as well under r.90*bis*.4.
	r.90*bis*.2(c)	Withdrawal of the designation of all States is treated as withdrawal of the international application under r.90*bis*.1.
	r.90*bis*.2(b)	Withdrawal of the designation of a State which has been designated for the purpose of obtaining a national and a regional patent will be taken to mean withdrawal only of the designation for the purpose of obtaining a national patent unless otherwise indicated.
	r.90*bis*.2(e)	Where a designation is withdrawn, that designation will not be included in the international publication if the notice of withdrawal reaches the International Bureau (from the applicant or via the receiving Office or International Preliminary Examining Authority) before the technical preparations for publication have been completed.
	r.90*bis*.6(a)	Withdrawal of a designation will have no effect in any designated or elected Office where the processing or examination of the international application has already started under Art. 23(2) or Art. 40(2) (on the express request of the applicant).

44.3.3   *Withdrawal of a priority claim*

1770	r.90*bis*.3(a)	A priority claim made under Art. 8(1) may be withdrawn by the applicant at any time prior to the expiration of 30 months from the priority date.
	r.90*bis*.3(c)	Such withdrawal is effected by submission of a notice addressed by the applicant to any of the International Bureau, the receiving Office or (where Art. 39(1) applies) the International Preliminary Examining Authority and is effective on receipt.
	r.90*bis*.5	The requirement for the withdrawal of a priority claim to be signed is identical to the requirement for a withdrawal of the application to be signed (see above).
	r.90.4, r.90.5	A separate power of attorney or a copy of a general power of attorney must be submitted to the relevant authority where an agent or common representative submits a notice of withdrawal under r.90*bis*.3.
	r.90*bis*.3(b)	Where the international application contains more than one priority claim, one or more or all of them may be withdrawn.
	r.90*bis*.3(d)(e)	Where the withdrawal of a priority claim changes the priority date, time limits starting on the priority date which have not already expired will be recalculated from the new priority date with the proviso that the International Bureau may nevertheless publish the application 18 months from original priority under Art. 21(2)(a) if the withdrawal is received by the International Bureau after the technical preparations for publication are complete.
	r.90*bis*.6(a)	Withdrawal of a priority claim has no effect in any designated or elected Office where the processing or examination of the international application has already started under Art. 23(2) or Art. 40(2) (on the express request of the applicant).

44.3.4   *Withdrawal of a supplementary search request*

1771	r.90*bis*.3*bis*(a)	The applicant may withdraw a supplementary search request at any time prior to the date of transmittal to the applicant and to the International Bureau, under r.45*bis*.8(a), of the supplementary International Search Report or the declaration that no such report will be established.

r.90*bis*.3*bis*(b)	Withdrawal shall be effective on receipt, within the time limit under r.90*bis*.3*bis*(a), of a notice addressed by the applicant, at his option, to the authority specified for supplementary search or to the International Bureau, provided that, where the notice does not reach the authority specified for supplementary search in sufficient time to prevent the transmittal of the report or declaration referred to in r.90*bis*.3*bis*(a), the communication of that report or declaration under Art. 20(1), as applicable by virtue of r.45*bis*.8(b), shall nevertheless be effected.
r.90*bis*.5	The requirement for the withdrawal of a supplementary search request to be signed is identical to the requirement for a withdrawal of the application to be signed (see above).
r.90.4, r.90.5	A separate power of attorney or a copy of a general power of attorney must be submitted to the relevant authority where an agent or common representative submits a notice of withdrawal under r.90*bis*.3*bis*.
r.90*bis*.6(b-*bis*)	Where a supplementary search request is withdrawn under r.90*bis*.3*bis*, the supplementary international search by the authority concerned shall be discontinued.

44.3.5 *Withdrawal of the demand or of elections*

Art. 37(1)	The applicant may withdraw any or all elections.	1772
r.90*bis*.4(a)	The demand, or any or all elections, may be withdrawn by the applicant at any time prior to the expiry of 30 months from the priority date.	
Art. 37(3)(a)	The withdrawal of an election must be notified to the International Bureau.	
r.90*bis*.4(b)	The withdrawal of the demand or any election is effective on receipt of a notice addressed by the applicant to the International Bureau.	
r.90*bis*.4(c)	Such a withdrawal submitted to the International Preliminary Examining Authority will be date-stamped by that Authority and forwarded promptly to the International Bureau and its date of submission to the International Bureau will be considered to be the date so marked.	
r.90*bis*.5	Such a withdrawal must be signed by the applicant, or all the applicants when there is more than one. A common representative under r.90.2(b) is not entitled to sign on behalf of another applicant	
r.90.4, r.90.5	A separate power of attorney or a copy of a general power of attorney must be submitted to the relevant authority where an agent or common representative submits a notice of withdrawal under r.90*bis*.4.	
Art. 37(3)(b)	The International Bureau will notify the elected Offices concerned and the International Preliminary Examining Authority.	
Art. 37(2)	If the election of all States is withdrawn then the demand will be considered withdrawn.	
r.90*bis*.6(c)	Where the demand or all the elections are withdrawn, the processing of the application by the International Preliminary Examining Authority will be discontinued.	
Art. 37(4)(a)(b)	Withdrawal of the demand or the election of a Contracting State will, unless the national law of that State provides otherwise, be considered withdrawal of the international application, as far as that State is concerned, unless it is effected prior to the expiration of the applicable time limit under Art. 22 (usually 30 months). National law may require that the applicant supply the national Office with a copy of the international application, any prescribed translation and the national fee within the said time limit for this proviso to apply.	
r.90*bis*.7(a)(b)	Any such provision of national law must be notified by the relevant Contracting State to the International Bureau in writing and the International Bureau will publish such information in the Gazette. It has effect in respect of international applications filed more than one month after the date of such publication.	
r.90*bis*.6(a)	Withdrawal of the demand or an election will have no effect in any designated or elected Office where the processing or examination of the international application has already started under Art. 23(2) or Art. 40(2) (on the express request of the applicant).	
AppGuide	See International Phase, section 11.061 – care must be taken in respect of those countries still applying a 20 month time limit under Art. 22 since withdrawal of the demand or the election of such a state after the Art. 22 time limit will have the effect of withdrawal of the international application in that state unless national processing has already started (Art. 37(4)). Withdrawal of the demand or an election before expiry of the Art. 22 time limit will not result in withdrawal of the international application in such a state but national phase entry will not be delayed under Art. 39(1)(a).	

44.4   Recordal of changes concerning an applicant, inventor, agent or common representative by the International Bureau

1773   r.92*bis*.1(a)(b)   On the request of the receiving Office or the applicant, the International Bureau will record changes in the following indications appearing in the request or the demand:
(i) the person, name, residence, nationality or address of the applicant; and
(ii) the person, name or address of the agent, common representative or inventor;
unless it receives such a request after the expiry of 30 months from the priority date.

AppGuide   See International Phase, paragraph 11.018 – when an international application is assigned during the international phase, the change of applicant may be recorded at the IB under r.92*bis*.1(a)(i). No proof is required if the change is requested by the original applicant or his agent. If the new applicant requests the change then proof of the transfer must be provided. No fee is charged.

r.51*bis*.1(a)(ii)   Proof may be demanded in the national phase by any designated Office of the applicant's entitlement to apply for or be granted a patent.

AppGuide   See International Phase, paragraph 11.018C – if a new applicant is recorded, there is no requirement for him to be a person entitled to file a PCT application, though the right to later demand international preliminary examination may be affected.

AdminInst   See s.422 – when the International Bureau makes such a change it notifies various other international authorities and designated Offices. When the applicant changes both the old applicant and new applicant are informed unless they are using the same agent in which case only that agent is informed.

44.5   Notification by national Offices and intergovernmental organisations

1774   r.92.3   Any document or letter emanating from or transmitted by a national Office or intergovernmental organisation and constituting an event from the date of which any time limit under the PCT and its Regulations commences must be sent by airmail except that:
(1) surface mail may be used when it normally arrives within two days of mailing; and
(2) surface mail may be used where airmail is not available.

44.6   Schedule of Fees

1775   r.96.1   The amounts of the fees referred to in r.15, r.45*bis*.2 and r.57 shall be expressed in Swiss currency. They shall be specified in the Schedule of Fees which is annexed to the PCT Regulations and forms and integral part thereof.

r.96.2(a)   For the purposes of r.96.2, "Office" shall mean the receiving Office (including the International Bureau acting as receiving Office), the International Searching Authority, an Authority specified for supplementary international search, the International Preliminary Examining Authority or the International Bureau.

r.96.2(b)   Where, in accordance with these Regulations or the Administrative Instructions, a fee is collected by one Office ("collecting Office") for the benefit of another Office ("beneficiary Office"), the collecting Office shall promptly notify the receipt of each such fee in accordance with the Administrative Instructions. Upon receipt of the notification, the beneficiary Office shall proceed as if it had received the fee on the date on which the fee was received by the collecting Office.

r.96.2(c)   The collecting Office shall transfer any fees collected for the benefit of a beneficiary Office to that Office in accordance with the Administrative Instructions.

44.7   Third party observations

AdminInst

See s.801. See also AppGuide, International Phase, paragraphs 11.109 to 11.117. There   1776
is no formal mechanism under the PCT for handling third-party observations but it is
nevertheless possible to make observations on an international application via the WIPO
website between publication of the application and 28 months from the priority date.
Such observations are transmitted to relevant international authorities and designated offices and made available to the public. Observations should be restricted to matters of
novelty and inventive step and may be made anonymously. They should be in the language in which the international application was published. Only one set of comments is
allowed for each third party. The applicant is notified when third party comments are filed
and has the chance to file comments in response.

Guidelines

See Guidelines for Search and Examination at the EPO as PCT Authority, E-II. The EPO
will consider such observations if the application enters the regional phase. A request in
the observations for the EPO to issue a first office action within three months from the
expiry of the r.161 period will be honoured by the EPO, where possible, if the observations are substantiated, in an EPO language and not filed anonymously. See also [2017]
O.J. A86.

44.8   Offer to license an international application

AppGuide

See International Phase, paragraphs 11.102 to 11.108 – any applicant can indicate his in-   1777
terest in licensing his international application by filing a letter to that effect with the
International Bureau at any time until the expiration of 30 months from the priority date.
No fee is payable and any language of publication may be used. The terms that would
be acceptable may optionally be indicated. An indication that the applicant is interested
in licensing the application is included in the bibliographic data when the application is
published and the applicant's letter is also made available on the WIPO website as part of
the application file.

Chapter 45: Information Made Available by the International Authorities and Designated~Elected Offices

45.1 Confidential nature of the international application before its publication

1778	Art. 30(1)(a)(b)	The International Bureau and the International Searching Authorities may not allow access by any person or authority to the international application before its international publication, unless requested or authorised by the applicant, except in regard to any transmittal of the application to the competent International Searching Authority, any transmittal of the application to a designated Office under Art. 13 and communications to a designated Office provided for under Art. 20.
	Art. 30(2)(3)	No national Office or receiving Office may allow access to the international application by third parties (except for transmittals by the receiving Office under Art. 12(1) of the international application to the International Bureau and International Searching Authority), unless requested or authorised by the applicant, before the earlier of: (i) the date of international publication; or (ii) the date of receipt of the communication of the international application under Art. 20; or (iii) the date of receipt of a copy of the international application under Art. 22; though this does not prevent any national Office from informing third parties that it has been designated or from publishing this fact as long as the information conveyed is no more than (1) the identification of the receiving Office, (2) the name of the applicant, (3) the international filing date, (4) the international application number and (5) the title of the invention. A designated Office may also allow access by judicial authorities at an earlier date.
	Art. 30(4)	For the purposes of Art. 30, "access" covers any means by which third parties may acquire cognisance, including individual communication and general publication provided that no national Office may generally publish an international application or its translation before the international publication or, if international publication has not taken place by the expiration of 20 months from the priority date, before the expiry of 20 months from the said priority date.

45.2 Confidential nature of international preliminary examination

1779	Art. 38(1)	Neither the International Bureau nor the International Preliminary Examining Authority may, unless requested or authorised by the applicant, allow access to any file of the international preliminary examination by any person or authority at any time except by the elected Offices once the International Preliminary Examination Report has been established. For these purposes, "access" is as defined by Art. 30(4) and covers any means by which third parties may acquire cognisance, including individual communication and general publication. The proviso of Art. 30(4) also applies – no national Office may generally publish an international application or its translation before the international publication or, if international publication has not taken place by the expiration of 20 months from the priority date, before the expiry of 20 months from the said priority date.
	Art. 38(2)	Subject to Art. 38(1) (above), Art. 36(1) (International Preliminary Examination Report to be transmitted to the applicant and the International Bureau), Art. 36(3) (International Preliminary Examination Report, translation and annexes to be transmitted by the International Bureau to each elected Office) and Art. 37(3)(b) (relevant national Offices notified of the withdrawal of their election) neither the International Bureau nor the International Preliminary Examining Authority may, unless requested or authorised by the applicant, give information on the issuance or non-issuance of an International Preliminary Examination Report or on the withdrawal or non-withdrawal of the demand or of any election.

45.3   Obligation for international authorities to keep files

r.93.1–r.93.4   The following records will be kept, optionally as photographic, electronic or other repro-   1780
ductions as long as such a reproduction allows the obligations of r.93 to be met.

Organisation	Document	To be kept for
receiving Office	Records relating to each international application or purported application, including the home copy.	At least 10 years from the filing date (or, where none is accorded, the date of receipt).
International Bureau	The file relating to each international application (including the record copy).	At least 30 years from the date of receipt of the record copy.
	The basic records of the Bureau.	Indefinitely
International Searching and Preliminary Examining Authorities	The file relating to each international application it receives.	At least 10 years from the filing date.

45.4   Access allowed to files

45.4.1   *Access to the file held by the International Bureau*

r.94.1(a)   At the request of the applicant or any person authorized by the applicant, the Internation-   1781
al Bureau will furnish, subject to reimbursement of the cost of the service, copies of any
document contained in its file.

r.94.1(b)   The International Bureau will, at the request of any person but not before the international publication of the international application and subject to Art. 38 (confidential nature
of international preliminary examination) and r.94.1(d) to (g), furnish copies of any document contained in its file. The furnishing of copies may be subject to reimbursement of
the cost of the service.

r.94.1(c)   The International Bureau shall, if so requested by an elected Office, but not before the
international preliminary examination report has been established, furnish on behalf of
that Office copies under r.94.1(b) of any document transmitted to it under r.71.1(a) or (b)
by the International Preliminary Examining Authority (international preliminary examination report, annexes, other documents from the international preliminary examination
file). The International Bureau shall promptly publish details of any such request in the
Gazette.

r.94.1(d)   The International Bureau shall not provide access to any information contained in its file
which has been omitted from publication under r.48.2(l) and to any document contained
in its file relating to a request under that rule.

r.94.1(e)   Upon a reasoned request by the applicant, the International Bureau shall not provide
access to any information contained in its file and to any document contained in its file
relating to such a request, if it finds that:
(i) this information does not obviously serve the purpose of informing the public about
the international application;
(ii) public access to such information would clearly prejudice the personal or economic
interests of any person; and
(iii) there is no prevailing public interest to have access to that information.
r.26.4 (manner of making corrections before the receiving Office) applies *mutatis mutandis* as to the manner in which the applicant must present the information which is the
subject of a request made under r.94.1(e).

r.94.1(f)   Where the International Bureau has omitted information from public access in accordance
with r.94.1(d) or (e), and that information is also contained in the file of the international application held by the receiving Office, the International Searching Authority, the
Authority specified for supplementary search or the International Preliminary Examining Authority, the International Bureau must promptly notify that Office and Authority
accordingly.

r.94.1(g)	The International Bureau may not provide access to any document contained in its file which was prepared solely for internal use by the International Bureau.
AppGuide	See International Phase, paragraph 8.053 – the supplementary International Search Report is not published as part of the international publication of the application or separately but, once the international application is published, it is made available by the International Bureau on its website as part of the application file.
AppGuide	See International Phase, paragraph 7.011 – any sequence listing furnished separately to the International Searching Authority under r.13*ter*.1 does not form part of the international application but is nevertheless, once the international application is published, made available by the International Bureau on its website as part of the application file.
AppGuide	See International Phase, paragraph 7.030 – informal comments made by the applicant on the written opinion of the International Searching Authority are, once the international application is published, made available by the International Bureau on its website as part of the application file.

45.4.2 *Access to the file held by the receiving Office*

1782 Comment r.94.1*bis*(a)	This provision only applies to international applications filed on or after 01 July 2016. At the request of the applicant or any person authorized by the applicant, the receiving Office may provide access to any document contained in its file. The furnishing of copies of documents may be subject to reimbursement of the cost of the service.
r.94.1*bis*(b)	The receiving Office may, at the request of any person, but not before the international publication of the international application and subject to paragraph (c), provide access to any document contained in its file. The furnishing of copies of documents may be subject to reimbursement of the cost of the service.
r.94.1*bis*(c)	The receiving Office may not provide access under paragraph (b) to any information in respect of which it has been notified by the International Bureau that the information has been omitted from publication in accordance with r.48.2(l) or from public access in accordance with r.94.1(d) or (e).
OJ	See Decision of the President dated 20 February 2019 ([2019] O.J. A17. The EPO will open its file for public inspection, when it acts as a receiving Office, as soon as the application publishes. Excluded, however, will be any document falling within the terms of r.94.1*bis*(c) and any document that would be excluded under the EPC. The means of inspection are the same as those applying to European patent applications.

45.4.3 *Access to the file held by the International Searching Authority and supplementary International Searching Authority*

1783 Comment r.94.1*ter*(a)	This provision only applies to international applications filed on or after 01 July 2016. At the request of the applicant or any person authorized by the applicant, the International Searching Authority may provide access to any document contained in its file. The furnishing of copies of documents may be subject to reimbursement of the cost of the service.
r.94.1*ter*(b)	The International Searching Authority may, at the request of any person, but not before the international publication of the international application and subject to r.94.1*ter*(c), provide access to any document contained in its file. The furnishing of copies of documents may be subject to reimbursement of the cost of the service.
r.94.1*ter*(c)	The International Searching Authority may not provide access under r.94.1*ter*(b) to any information in respect of which it has been notified by the International Bureau that the information has been omitted from publication in accordance with r.48.2(l) or from public access in accordance with r.94.1(d) or (e).
r.94.1*ter*(d)	r.94.1*ter*(a) to (c) apply *mutatis mutandis* to the Authority specified for supplementary search.
OJ	See Decision of the President dated 20 February 2019 ([2019] O.J. A17. The EPO will open its file for public inspection, when it acts as an International Searching Authority or Authority specified for supplementary international search, as soon as the application publishes. Excluded, however, will be any document falling within the terms of r.94.1*ter*(c) and any document that would be excluded for a direct filed European patent application. The means of inspection are the same as those applying to European patent applications.

45.4.4   *Access to the file held by the International Preliminary Examining Authority*

r.94.2(a)	At the request of the applicant or any person authorized by the applicant, the International Preliminary Examining Authority will provide access to any document contained in its file. The furnishing of copies of documents may be subject to reimbursement of the cost of the service.
r.94.2(b)	At the request of any elected Office, but not before the establishment of the international preliminary examination report and subject to r.94.2(c), the International Preliminary Examining Authority will provide access to any document contained in its file. The furnishing of copies of documents may be subject to reimbursement of the cost of the service.
r.94.2(c)	The International Preliminary Examining Authority will not provide access under r.94.2(b) to any information in respect of which it has been notified by the International Bureau that the information has been omitted from publication in accordance with r.48.2(l) or from public access in accordance with r.94.1(d) or (e).

1784

45.4.5   *Access to the file held by a designated Office*

Comment r.94.2*bis*	This provision only applies to international applications filed on or after 01 July 2016. If the national law applicable by any designated Office allows access by third parties to the file of a national application, that Office may allow access to any documents relating to the international application, contained in its file, to the same extent as provided by the national law for access to the file of a national application, but not before the earliest of the dates specified in Art. 30(2)(a) (earliest of international publication date, date of receipt of Art. 20 communication and date of receipt of international application under Art. 22). The furnishing of copies of documents may be subject to reimbursement of the cost of the service.

1785

45.4.6   *Access to the file held by an elected Office*

r.94.3	If the national law applicable by any elected Office allows access by third parties to the file of a national application, that Office may allow access to any documents relating to the international application, including any document relating to the international preliminary examination, contained in its file, to the same extent as provided by the national law for access to the file of a national application, but not before the earliest of the dates specified in Article 30(2)(a) (earliest of international publication date, date of receipt of Art. 20 communication and date of receipt of international application under Art. 22). The furnishing of copies of documents may be subject to reimbursement of the cost of the service.
OJ	Where the EPO has acted as International Preliminary Examining Authority, the International Preliminary Examination Report has been established, and the EPO is an elected Office, documents relating to international preliminary examination will be made available for third-party access ([1999] O.J. 329 and [2003] O.J. 382).
Guidelines	See A-XI, 2.3(v) and Guidelines for Search and Examination at the EPO as PCT Authority, C-VII, 2.
r.94.1(c)	The International Bureau shall, if so requested by an elected Office, furnish copies of the international preliminary examination report under r.94.1(b) on behalf of that Office. The International Bureau shall promptly publish details of any such request in the Gazette.
AppGuide	See International Phase, paragraph 9.027 – the International Bureau, having been requested by several elected Offices, makes available the International Preliminary Examination Report to third parties on its website on behalf of those elected Offices.

1786

45.5   Availability of the priority document from the International Bureau

r.17.2(b)(c)	Copies of the priority document may not be made available to the public by the International Bureau prior to international publication. After publication, they may be made available to anybody, subject to a fee, unless, prior to publication, the application has been withdrawn or the relevant priority claim has been withdrawn or has been considered not to have been made under r.26*bis*.2(b) (information in the request (r.4.10) and on the priority document do not correspond).
AppGuide	See International Phase, paragraph 9.023 – priority documents are made available on the WIPO website when international publication has taken place.

1787

45.6   Availability of information concerning national phase entry and translations required by national Offices

1788   r.95.1   Any designated or elected Office shall notify the International Bureau of the following information concerning an international application within two months, or as soon as reasonably possible thereafter, of the occurrence of any of the following events:
(i) following the performance by the applicant of the acts referred to in Art. 22 or Art. 39, the date of performance of those acts and any national application number which has been assigned to the international application;
(ii) where the designated or elected Office explicitly publishes the international application under its national law or practice, the number and date of that national publication;
(iii) where a patent is granted, the date of grant of the patent and, where the designated or elected Office explicitly publishes the international application in the form in which it is granted under its national law, the number and date of that national publication.

r.95.2(a)   At the request of the International Bureau, any designated or elected Office shall provide it with a copy of the translation of the international application furnished by the applicant to that Office.

r.95.2(b)   The International Bureau may, upon request and subject to reimbursement of the cost, furnish to any person copies of the translations received under r.95.2(a).

45.7   Availability of citations in the International Search Report from the International Searching Authority

1789   Art. 20(3), r.44.3   The International Searching Authority will supply copies of documents cited in the International Search Report to any designated Office or the applicant when requested by such an Office or the applicant at any time during seven years from the international filing date of the corresponding application. A fee for preparing and mailing the copies may be requested, the amount of which will be fixed in the agreement under Art. 16(3)(b) between the International Searching Authority and the International Bureau. The Searching Authority may use an agency to perform this function if it wishes.

45.8   Availability of citations in the International Preliminary Examination Report from the International Preliminary Examining Authority

1790   Art. 36(4), r.71.2   At the request of an elected Office or the applicant, within seven years from the filing date of the relevant application, the International Preliminary Examining Authority will supply copies of any document cited in the International Preliminary Examination Report which was not cited in the International Search Report. A fee may be claimed by the International Preliminary Examining Authority to the Office or applicant who makes such a request covering the cost of preparing and mailing the copies, the level of which will be set in the agreement under Art. 32(2) between the International Preliminary Examining Authority and the International Bureau. Such an Authority may perform these obligations through another agency responsible to it.

Index

The numbers indicate the relevant paragraphs of the text.